The Way a Writer Reads

A COLLEGE READER

Elizabeth Cowan Neeld

SCOTT, FORESMAN AND COMPANY
Glenview, Illinois   London, England

An Instructor's Manual and Comprehension Quizzes on the readings are also available. Either may be obtained through your local Scott, Foresman representative or by writing English Editor, College Division, Scott, Foresman and Company, Glenview, Illinois, 60025.

Library of Congress Cataloging-in-Publication Data

The Way a Writer Reads.

1. College readers.   2. English language—Rhetoric.   I. Neeld, Elizabeth Cowan.
PE1417.W28   1987   808'.0427   86–29779
ISBN 0–673–18396–3

Cover and part opening photographs (pp. 2–3, 104–105, 450–451, 490–491, and 532–533) by André Kertész. Copyright © André Kertész/Archive.

The credit lines for copyright material appearing in this book are placed either on the first page of the section or in the acknowledgments section, which begins on page 627. These pages are to be considered an extension of the copyright page.

1 2 3 4 5 6—MVN—91 90 89 88 87 86

PREFACE

We all know the value of using a reader in a college writing class. A good collection of readings will

- broaden students' horizons
- provoke thinking
- stimulate class discussion
- provide subject matter for writing essays

An up-to-date reader will also give some insight into how and why the essays were written, making the text even more valuable for teaching.

But can a reader do more than complement and support the teaching of writing? Can a reader actually *teach* writing? The answer is **yes.** Here is the secret of a text that has all the strengths of a good reader and also *teaches* writing. This book helps students

- see the relationship between reading and writing,
- learn to read with a writer's eye, and
- learn to think about writing at the same time that they are reading.

The Way a Writer Reads is such a text. The selections will broaden students' horizons, provoke thinking, stimulate class discussion, and provide subject matter for writing essays. And this text provides more. *The Way a Writer Reads teaches* writing. It is a *teaching* reader.

WHAT IS IN THE TEXT?

The Way a Writer Reads has five parts. Part 1, Reading to Enjoy, contains selections which motivate students to want to read—and to want to write. The readings in this section illustrate the rich variety of forms by which people use words to communicate about experiences, events, interests, joys, sorrows, commitments, and concerns. From Shirley

MacLaine writing about her passion for dancing to Martin Luther King, Jr., writing about his desire for peace; from Bob Greene writing about the birth of his first child to the victims of an airplane crash in Japan writing their final words of good-bye to their families; from John Dornberg writing about Swiss Army Knives to Thomas Pew lamenting the passing of Route 66: students are inspired by their reading and recognize the importance of writing in people's everyday lives.

Reading to Learn to Write

Part 2, Reading to Learn to Write, is the teaching core of the text. In this section, students learn to read *constructively*, to read to see how the writer "built" the writing. By learning to read *constructively*—to think about how the piece was written *while* they are reading it—students begin to learn about the craft of writing. They can see how a writer has shaped, organized, and structured the piece of writing.

Part 2 teaches *constructive* reading by focusing on four characteristics of good writing:

1. *Originality*
   What makes a piece of writing fresh and engaging?
2. *Thesis*
   What is the thread weaving through a piece of writing that holds it all together?
3. *Form*, both *traditional* (definition, comparison/contrast, classification, process, and so on) and *created* (mixed and original forms)
   What is the writer's purpose and how does this determine the form the writing takes?
4. *Gusto, Vividness, and Clarity*
   What makes writing alive, stimulating, provocative, clear?

A separate section in Part 2 is devoted to each of these qualities of good writing. Sections begin with an introduction defining the quality: for instance, the section on Originality begins by discussing what makes writing original and how student writers can achieve this quality in their own work. The introduction to each section is followed by a collection of essays that eloquently illustrate that particular characteristic of good writing.

Part 2 has a feature you will not find in any other college reader: a teaching commentary following the conclusion of every essay. This teaching commentary—informal, conversational, and student-oriented—gives provocative and stimulating information that includes information about the author, the place of publication, and other facts and observations about the essay.

Most important, the *teaching commentary* points out what makes each essay worth reading:

- How does the writer's originality perk up an ordinary subject?
- What does the placement of the thesis contribute to the essay's unity?
- How is the author's purpose related to the form used in this essay?
- What is this writer's secret to producing an essay that has gusto, that is alive and clear?

The *teaching commentary* mines every essay for its salient features of good writing, while encouraging students to produce similar qualities in their own writing. This commentary is designed to teach students to read *constructively*, to learn to see how reading and writing are related.

Reading to See the Whole Picture

Part 3 contains eight essays on the same subject—and a luscious one, at that—chocolate. Each essay is completely different. One writer discusses chocolate from a health point of view; another talks about the economics of selling chocolate; a third talks about its molecular structure—and so on.

This group of essays allows students to see the whole picture: how the audience, the author's perspective, the essay's purpose, and the place of publication come together to determine which aspect of a particular subject is emphasized. Students can see that each essay, therefore, is a special and unique configuration depending on who wrote it, out of what interests, under what circumstances, for which publication, with what particular point in mind.

Part 3 teaches students a central truth: writing is not done in a vacuum. Writing is done in a specific context—one that is different every time a person sits down to write. To be effective writers, students need to learn to take into account the context in which their writing occurs. They can learn this maxim by Reading to See the Whole Picture.

The Way a Writer Reads

Part 4 includes essays for further study by E. B. White, Jorge Luis Borges, Joan Didion, Richard Rodriguez, Beryl Markham, Donald Hall, and Barry Lopez. This section allows students to pull together everything they have learned in the first three parts of the text: Reading to Enjoy, Reading to Learn to Write, and Reading to See the Whole Picture. Students can see how master writers combine all the qualities of good writing in essays that have a specific context, a personal voice, and a strong stance on the subject. This section of *The Way a Writer Reads* solidifies and reinforces all that has been learned earlier in the course.

Study Section

The last part of the text presents in-depth reading and writing questions for each essay. Questions in the *Participatory Reading* section ask students about the content of the essays and about the writer's viewpoint or perspective. *Constructive Reading* questions allow students to discover how the various writings are made, what strategies and choices the writers employed to achieve their purpose for writing. *Inquiry Reading* questions cover language, concepts, and distinctions that are central to the understanding of the essays. Finally, there are questions on *The Larger Picture*. These questions encourage students to make connections between what they have read and other areas of knowledge and/or life.

Part 5 also includes a wide variety of writing possibilities. The suggested contexts and situations allow for formal academic essays, persuasive and argumentative essays, popular essays and articles, personal essays, and private writing. The instructor and the student can choose among these writing assignments based on the progression of the course, the special needs of the student, or the opportunities needed to help students move to new levels of accomplishment.

THE VALUE OF THIS TEXT

The Way a Writer Reads teaches students to read—and, therefore, to think—like writers. Reading and writing are integrated. Students see how each operation relates to the other. Everything students have learned about writing is reinforced each time they work with *The Way a Writer Reads*; and every time students write, they use what they learned when they read *The Way a Writer Reads*.

The Way a Writer Reads teaches students about writing by the very nature of its emphasis and focus. The commentary following every essay in Part 2, Reading to Learn to Write, *teaches* also. Students learn through this commentary how the qualities of good writing lauded in this section of the text are produced; more important, they learn how *they* can use the attributes of Originality; Thesis; Form; and Gusto, Vividness, and Clarity in their own writing. By reading, they are learning about their own writing.

After studying Part 3, Reading to See the Whole Picture, students will know that writing does not occur in a vacuum. They will discover how much the author's viewpoint on life and overarching purpose determine how the subject gets discussed. They will see how the audience and place of publication affect the structure and language of the writing. And they will very likely head right out for a piece of chocolate themselves after reading these essays.

From Part 1, Reading to Enjoy, students will have experienced how enticing writing can be. They will have seen that people write because they are excited about telling something that has happened to them or because they believe their writing can bring about certain desired actions, or because they want to share the exuberance—and the disappointments—of life. From this section, too, students will see how varied are the forms writing takes in ordinary people's everyday lives. They will have evidence after completing Part 1 that writing is something people do all through their lives for reasons very public and very personal alike. Students will be able to imagine that writing will be a part of their lives forever.

ACKNOWLEDGMENTS

Without a committed team, good ideas for good books almost always remain just that—good ideas. In preparing *The Way a Writer Reads*, I was privileged to work with a team who recognized the possibilities in the ideas I presented many months ago and did everything necessary to turn those ideas into a good book. With deep appreciation I salute them: Anne Smith, Constance Rajala, Lydia Webster, Lucy Lesiak, Ann Kolpak, Mary-Jo Kovach, Meredith Hellestrae, and Elizabeth Stolarek. I am also grateful to the following reviewers for their help: Michael Raymond, Stetson University; Kate Kiefer, Colorado State University; Lucy Schultz, University of Cincinnati; Jay Balderson, Western Illinois University; and Duncan A. Carter, Boston University. I am also indebted to colleagues who have given me valuable information about the use of my texts in the classroom: Jean English, Tallahassee Junior College; Tom Waldrep, The University of South Carolina; Ovid Vickers, East Central Junior College; Avon Crismore, Indiana University-Purdue University at Indianapolis; Susan Smith and her colleagues at McLennan Community College. Finally, I would like to thank my husband, Jere, for his inspiration and for his contribution to the quality of my work, and Eliot Lippman for his professional research.

Elizabeth Cowan Neeld

OVERVIEW

CONTENTS

PART THREE
READING

Seven men went through a field, one after another,
One was a farmer, he saw only the grass;
the next was an astronomer, he saw the horizon & the stars;
the physician noticed the standing water & suspected miasma;
he was followed by a soldier, who glanced over the ground,
found it easy to hold, & saw in a moment how the troops could be disposed;
Then came the geologist, who noticed the boulders & the sandy loam;
after him the real estate broker, who bethought him how the line of the house-lots should run,
where would be the driveway, & the stables.
The poet admired the shadows cast by some trees,
and still more the music of some thrushes & a meadow lark.

RALPH WALDO EMERSON

INTRODUCTION 454

PART FOUR

THE WAY A WRITER READS:

Essays for Further Study   490

PART FIVE

STUDY SECTION   532

'Tis the good reader that makes the good book.
RALPH WALDO EMERSON

Questions for All Essays

Participatory Reading:
Content, Purpose, Viewpoint

Constructive Reading:
Choices, Strategies, Style

Inquiry Reading:
Language, Concepts, Distinctions

The Larger Picture:
Other Questions to Consider

Writing Possibilities for All Essays

Alternate Tables of

CONTENTS

Example

Right and Wrong
Mankind's Better Moments
Talking Cost

Created Form

A Secret of Successful Executives
Physicians for Nuclear Disarmament
A Christmas Sermon on Peace
Let It Rain
The Munros: Dreams of Glory
Let's Seal a Deal
Got 'Ya
R. Buckminster Fuller
You're Invited . . .
Announcing a Divorce
Eating Together
Good-Bye
A Prayer
The Education of an Engineer
The Crash of Flight 90
How to Visit a Museum
No More Blues
Hiroshima Remembered: The U.S. Was Wrong
Hiroshima Remembered: The U.S. Was Right
The Temptation of Chocolate
Bittersweet Times in the Chocolate Industry
How to Get the Women's Movement Moving Again
A Writer's Notebook from the Far East
I Still See Him Everywhere
Chatterbox: Homage to Saint Catherine of Siena
The Curse of the Little Round Cans
Miss Pilger's English Class
Avalanche!
Stepping Out from Behind the Phone and Word Processor

Poetry

i love you much
Warning
Saint Teresa's Bookmark

THEMATIC TABLE OF CONTENTS

The More Things Change . . .

Physicians for Nuclear Disarmament
The Passing of Route 66
Who Was Karl Bodmer, Anyway?
The Education of an Engineer
Political Parables for Today
Right and Wrong
I Want to Be Alone
The Language of Clothes
Mexico's Two Seas
Burning Books
How to Get the Women's Movement Moving Again
Space Law: Justice for the New Frontier

The Sporting Life and Leisure

Yaz
Thirteen Ways of Looking at the Masters
Mexico's Two Seas
How to Visit a Museum
Chocolate: The Jekyll and Hyde of Sweet Treats
The Sea and the Wind That Blows
Ping Pong: Root Cellar Fiveball
Avalanche!
Dressed to Kill

Working and Business

The Best-Selling Swiss Army Knife
American Pistachios
A Secret of Successful Executives
Dancing in the Light
Got 'Ya
The Education of an Engineer
Yaz
Who Was Karl Bodmer, Anyway?
Making Money: Taking a Risk
I Want to Be Alone
A New Definition of a Cowboy
No More Blues
A Visit to a Chocolate Factory
Talking Cost
Dressed to Kill
Stepping Out from Behind the Phone and Word Processor

PART ONE

Reading
to
Enjoy

RALPH WALDO EMERSON

When shall I be tired of reading?
When the moon is tired of waxing and waning,
when the sea is tired of ebbing & flowing,
when the grass is weary of growing,
when the planets are tired of going.

2

Introduction

While you are learning to be a writer, you can also learn to read like a writer. The first way a writer reads? Just *to enjoy.*

When writers sit down to read, they read to enjoy and appreciate the way another person has interacted with life and then written about it. Writers read to enjoy and appreciate information others have gathered. Writers read to go places they haven't been to, to learn things they don't know. Writers read with the recognition that every person who puts words on paper is risking something, and writers appreciate this courage.

Writers read to enjoy others saying:

This is how I perceive things.
This is my solution to the problem.
These are the results I produced.
This is what I learned.
This is what I saw.
This is what I think is true.
This is what I believe.
This is what I promise.
This is what I declare.

When people put words on paper, they say, "I was here. I participated in life. And now I communicate this to you. I didn't do this, think this, learn this for myself only. I write to record and communicate who I am and what I do with myself in the world. I enjoyed discovering this. I enjoyed studying this. I care about this. I know this."

When writers read, they read in partnership and collaboration with the person who put the words on the page, knowing that these words communicate the thoughts, the experience, and the knowledge of another human being.

How to Read This Section

Now is a good time to start practicing reading the way a writer reads: *To Enjoy.* (In Part 2, we'll see how writers *Read to Learn to Write;* in Part 3, how writers *Read to See the Whole Picture;* and in Part 4, how writers *read to pull everything together.*)

Read this opening section of your text uncritically and with a light touch. Revel in finding out inside information. Expand your horizons with new facts and information. Ponder the problems and concerns others have cared enough to write about. Laugh with writers who write about happy things and cry with writers who are grieving. Applaud the winners, smile at the crafty, be touched by friendship and love.

Writing *is* an act of generosity. Accept these writers' gifts. Celebrate the words on the page.

Read and enjoy.

READING
to Enjoy
Information

In these first four selections, the writers give information by revealing facts and details. In other words, they are writing to *tell* us something. The *content* of these pieces is what is important. The writer takes a back seat and does not draw attention to himself or herself. Instead, the focus is on the information. The tone is conversational—you know that human beings are speaking, not androids or talking tape recorders—but the emphasis is on what the writers have to say, not their self-expression.

John Dornberg tells you all about the Swiss Army Knife: who first made it, how and why it was made. You'll learn how the knife was used by a West German businessman to cut himself out of a flaming aircraft. You'll learn how the knife was used by climbers on Mt. Everest. And you'll learn what makes this knife so very good.

Noel Vietmeyer will tell you about the American pistachio nut. His piece reads like a mystery story. You'll discover the drama, serendipity, coincidence, and individual accomplishment that it took to get a pistachio seed to grow in America. Almost forty years after the first seed was smuggled out of Persia and brought to America, the first American pistachio crop was harvested.

Bob Young, vice-president of Lockheed Corporation, reveals a secret of powerful business management: to ask the right questions rather than to find the right answers. In this essay he shares his experience as a seasoned, successful senior executive.

Ralph Martin gives inside information on Charles and Di's wedding: What did they say at the altar? Who wanted a kiss on the palace balcony? Who said Di looked like a thatched cottage? The answers are all in this article, which is gossip at its best.

JOHN DORNBERG

The Best-Selling Swiss Army Knife

An editorial cartoon in a Swiss newspaper told the story in a nutshell. It pictured outer space full of odd-shaped satellites floating around earth. One of them was a bright-red pocketknife, its eight multipurpose blades extended like the solar cell wings of orbiters. There was no caption but the message was obvious: *Das Schweizer Soldaten und Offiziersmesser*—the "Swiss Army Knife"—had done it again.

A Work of Art

As much standard equipment for American astronauts as for Swiss army recruits, a Swiss Army Knife was the principal tool used by crew members aboard the Discovery space shuttle in April to make the "fly swatter" with which they tried to restore power to a crippled $80 million communications satellite. To be sure, the gambit failed, but the knife had proved its versatility once more.

Together with the jagged Alps, powerful banks, precision watches, cheese and chocolate, the little red-handled pocketknife embossed with the white Cross of Helvetia has become virtually synonymous with Switzerland. It is not only renowned for its practicality but, as an example of top-quality workmanship, has been enshrined in the design collection of New York's Museum of Modern Art. Moreover, since American soldiers discovered it as a souvenir after World War II, it has become one of Switzerland's top export items and a goldmine for the two Swiss companies that produce it: Victorinox and Wenger S.A.

Admirers of the Swiss Army Knife run the gamut from explorers to heads of state. It accompanied the climbers in the 1975 conquest of the southwest face of Mount Everest and the team on the 1977 British North Pole Expedition. President Lyndon Johnson handed out 4,000 of them as keepsakes, and Ronald Reagan, shortly after beginning his first term, placed an order for 2,000— embossed in gold with the Presidential seal and his own signature. Even U-2 pilot Gary Powers had a Swiss Army Knife with him when he was shot down over Russia in 1960; it was displayed by the Soviets along with such other tools of his trade as secret code capsules and the suicide needle he didn't use.

Testimonials from users who have found the knife a life-saver in emergencies also are legion. Helmut Knosp, a West German businessman, used it to cut his way out of the flaming wreck of a light aircraft in which his three companions had been killed on impact. Doug Scott of the 1975 Everest expedition used it to free fellow climber Dougal Haston's ice-blocked oxygen gear. And an Indian surgeon once performed an emergency operation aboard a plane enroute from Bombay to Bangalore with the Swiss Army Knife another passenger was carrying.

This year, nearly 6 million Swiss Army Knives will be produced by Victorinox (3.3 million) and Wenger (2.5 million). Of that, the Swiss defense ministry is expected to order only 40,000 for new army recruits. Around 80% of production will be directly exported— the U.S., Britain and Germany are the three biggest markets—and at least another 10% will be bought by foreign tourists in Switzerland.

While obviously pleased by the knife's worldwide popularity, to Carl Elsener III, the 63-year-old head of family-owned Victorinox, "It is still a bit like a dream, especially since we do relatively little advertising." Somewhat modestly, Elsener explains the reasons for the knife's popularity: "One may be quality. We're perfectionists about quality. But another may be that it's more than just a pocketknife—it's a multipurpose tool that everyone needs. Once you have one, you never want to be without it again."

A Success Story

The success story started 101 years ago, when Elsener's grandfather, also named Carl, returned to his native Schwyz canton after serving as an apprentice and journeyman cutler in France and Germany and set up a one-man, one-room factory in the tiny town of Ibach. From the beginning, Elsener made knives of all kinds. But it was developing a pocketknife that apparently concerned him most.

Elsener was troubled by the fact that his craft was held in such low esteem at home that even the Swiss army was buying knives for soldiers' kits from Solingen, Germany, then the center of Europe's cutlery industry. So he began making a pocketknife for Swiss soldiers, and in 1891 he persuaded the government to adopt it. It had a large blade, a screwdriver, an awl and a can opener— essentially the model still issued to Swiss recruits with improvements. The screwdriver blade was modified to include a bottle opener and a wire stripper, and now the can opener has a smaller screwdriver on its tip—for a total of seven functions on four basic blades.

Although the knife was ingenious and practical, Elsener kept tinkering to improve it and in 1897 patented a revolutionary spring mechanism that operated blades on either side of the handle. He called the knife using the spring *Offiziersmesser*—the "officer's knife"—and it is this red-handled model that became famous as the Swiss Army Knife. Besides being slimmer, lighter and more elegant, the basic model had two additional blades: a small knife blade and a corkscrew.

Rolls-Royce of Pocketknives

The knife became popular quickly, and having invented a way to operate so many blades from the same handle, Elsener soon began making variations with additional attachments such as a small wood saw, scissors and a curette for cleaning horses' and cows' hooves—a boon to Swiss dairy farmers. In 1909 the wooden handle, which had a tendency to split, was replaced by one of red fiber and embossed with the Helvetic Cross, Switzerland's coat of arms. Today, the handle of the regulation knife issued to recruits is made of a silvery-colored aluminum alloy; the red handle of the officer's line is made of a hard synthetic.

When Elsener's mother Victoria died in 1909, he chose her name as the company trademark. And after the discovery of stainless steel in 1921, the internationally recognized word for the alloy, "inox," was added to make the name Victorinox.

Today, Victorinox is Europe's largest cutler, employing more than 800 people. Revenues last year topped $30 million. And the company still produces more household, butchers' and specialized professional cutlery than Swiss Army Knives: 5.7 million pieces a year of 700 different types, models and sizes.

Perfect workmanship is what has made Victorinex the Rolls-Royce of cutlers. Standards are so high that, in an about-face the founder would have appreciated, the West German army has been buying Victorinox's pocketknives for its recruits since 1976.

In a special department, eight engineers and designers continually invent and build new blades and tools for the knife. And considering that they have already come up with 100 different combinations, it is a bit of a misnomer to speak of *the* Swiss Army Knife. For example, the Craftsman model, which the NASA astronauts use, has 22 tool functions. And the Champion, a mere 3.5 inches long, 1-inch thick and weighing about 5 ounces, is the world's smallest toolbox. Besides large and small knife blades, it has a can opener, bottle opener, awl, wire-stripper, corkscrew, three screwdrivers of different sizes, a Phillips screwdriver, wood saw, metal saw, metal file, nail file, scissors, an inch and metric ruler, a fish scaler and magnetic fishhook remover, a magnifying glass, reamer and small wood drill, tweezers and a toothpick. Hoffritz in New York sells the Champion for $48. A custom-made version, costing about $1,500, has 100 blades and tools.

Unlimited Guarantee

There are many imitations of the Swiss Army Knife—from Japan, Taiwan, Spain and even the U.S. "They even plagiarize the Swiss Cross, our national symbol," says Xaver Ehrler, Victorinox's export manager, gazing wistfully out at the snow-capped peaks above Ibach and the cows grazing in the meadows below. "But they cannot match our quality."

Every knife comes with an unlimited guarantee on materials and workmanship. But to make sure the pledge has to be honored as little as possible, sixty women inspectors check every knife that leaves the plant—an average of 15,000 a day. They hunt for flaws in the steel, the spacers between the blades and the handle and test each blade and tool for ease and precision of operation. Knives that fail the test go to the repair department, which services knives of customers in 100 countries, no matter how long ago they were bought. "The guarantee doesn't cover misuse or willful damage, like using the knife blade as a crowbar," says Elsener, a trim, gray-haired, bespectacled man who seems happier on the shop floor than in the carpeted offices or boardroom of his sprawling plant. "But that happens so rarely, we wink at it and repair the knife anyway."

Victorinox even designs and builds virtually all the intricate machines that are needed to manufacture its pocketknives and other cutlery. Only the purest steel, from a French supplier, is used. More than 400 processes go into the production of a knife like the Champion model. And much of the production process is still not automated. "Of course we try to automate, save costs and produce more efficiently, but not at the expense of quality," Elsener says. "Sure, we could trim corners and make a cheaper, more price-competitive product. But we have deliberately chosen not to compete on a price basis. That would be fatal."

Loyalty Cultivates Success

Elsener, who is Canton Schwyz's biggest employer, believes much of the company's success is due to teamwork and employee loyalty cultivated over a century. There is no trade union at Victorinox, yet wages are above the Swiss average. Like his father, Carl Elsener II, who died in 1950, he apprenticed in the Ibach plant; so did his son, Carl IV, who will ultimately succeed him. And many of the cutlers still on the line apprenticed with them. "We have ten employees who celebrated their fiftieth anniversary at Victorinox in the last couple of years," Elsener says, "and about a dozen, including myself, have worked here for more than forty years. It's a team and it's a tradition."

Elsener is also quick to give credit to those postwar American GIs who came to Switzerland on furlough in droves, and to the U.S. Army's PX store system with which Victorinox had a contract until

1949. Since the end of World War II, the company has more than quadrupled its payroll and increased revenues fiftyfold. "We will be forever grateful," he says.

Finally with all the imitations on the market, how can one tell a phony Swiss Army Knife from the Elsener original? Look for the words "Victorinox Switzerland Stainless Rostfrei" on the shank of the large knife blade. Without those four words, it's not the real thing.

NOEL VIETMEYER

American Pistachios

A young American plant scientist is alone and uncertain in Persia. It is 1929. He has quietly entered this feudal country seeking pistachio nuts, something he knows almost nothing about. He has been warned that the U.S. government can do little to help him if he encounters trouble. In the ancient suqs of Teheran, Isfahan, and Kerman, and in dusty village markets, he sifts through the piles of produce. One day in Rafsanjan his fingers close over a particular pistachio nut. It is big. It is round. The shell is nicely split at one end. He drops it into his collecting bag.

Although that pistachio looks much like the thousands of others he collects, it is a magic seed. It will give rise to an industry worth hundreds of millions of dollars and will make the United States the world's second-largest pistachio producer. Yet he will spend almost 50 years battling bureaucratic critics and developing pistachio horticulture before the world will recognize its promise.

In the history of each of our foods there is drama, serendipity, coincidence, and individual accomplishment. The story of the pistachio is no exception. It begins, strangely enough, with the great alfalfa panic of nearly 60 years ago.

Alfalfa Despair

In 1927 alfalfa was dying in fields throughout the Midwest and California. A wilt fungus was rotting our primary pasture legume. Farmers were in despair. The situation appeared catastrophic, and the U.S. Department of Agriculture was besieged with demands to do something. Although there seemed to be no cure, there was one ray of hope. Several years earlier Nikolai I. Vavilov, the great Russian geneticist, had gathered wild alfalfa in its native habitat in Central Asia; a few of his collected strains showed slight wilt resistance. He offered to help American agronomists collect more alfalfa from the Asian site, and the USDA staff in Washington was more than willing to send plant explorers. But they were thwarted because the U.S. had no diplomatic relations with the 10-year-old Soviet government.

"No American could get into Russia," recalls Knowles Ryerson, now 92, who was then head of the USDA plant-introduction division. "The State Department would have thrown a fit if they had known we were even talking about going there. You didn't dare mention Communists in the presence of Secretary of State [Frank B.] Kellogg."

As the nation's alfalfa field continued to blacken and die, the scientists waited helplessly. Then, in March 1928, President Hoover took office. Within days, the new secretary of agriculture informally suggested to the new secretary of state, Henry L. Stimson, that American plant explorers might try to enter the Soviet Union. Cautiously, Stimson agreed, but only as long as the trip was unofficial and the scientists knew that if anything went wrong after they crossed the frontier we couldn't raise a finger to help them.

To carry out the assignment Knowles Ryerson selected alfalfa specialist Harvey Westover. He also sent along William E. Whitehouse, a deciduous-fruit specialist. "Central Asia is the natural birthplace of a lot of our fruits, nuts, and melons," notes Ryerson, "so it seemed a good idea to send Whitehouse, too. I told him to look for melons, apricots, peaches, and English walnuts—they're not English at all, you know."

In addition, however, Ryerson gave Whitehouse special instructions to the effect that once the alfalfa seed was collected he should try, if possible, to "penetrate" another closed country—Persia. "Without getting into trouble or risking your life," Ryerson told Whitehouse, "go down and get across the Persian frontier. Try to get into the area where pistachios are growing; see what varieties they have and how they are handling them."

Hunting Seeds in Russia

In 1929 Westover and Whitehouse entered Russia. The Soviets were extremely helpful. Vavilov provided interpreters, two botanists, and the leading Soviet alfalfa expert as guides. "We didn't spend a ruble," says Ryerson. "The expenses were taken care of entirely. And we got what we went after."

The wild alfalfa seed that Westover carried back with him to the United States proved the key to overcoming the alfalfa wilt, and within a few years the disease was almost unheard of. But even more was accomplished. Whitehouse, a 36-year-old New Englander who had only the sketchiest knowledge of pistachios, was able to fulfill Ryerson's special instructions in Persia. It proved to be the adventure of the enthusiastic young botanist's life, and led to results more important than anyone had ever imagined.

Pistachio Mission Accomplished

The pistachio (*Pistacia vera*) is native to low mountains and barren, dry foothills in the elevated deserts of Afghanistan, the Soviet Union, Iran, and Turkey. It belongs to the family Anacardiaceae, the botanic family that includes poison ivy, sumac, cashews, and mangoes. Since the time of Job the pistachio's nut has been a rare delicacy. The Queen of Sheba demanded all her land's production for herself and her court.

Late in 1929 Whitehouse slipped across the border between Soviet Turkestan and Persia. He found himself alone in a country where there were no railways, practically no hotels, and few cars. Roads were stony, rough, and narrow. Persia was a stronghold of oriental customs: permits were needed to enter and leave each town; letters of introduction were vital for getting anything done. In his jodhpurs, pith helmet, and khaki shirt, Whitehouse stood out as a *farangi*—his Persian guide advised him to spill food on his shirt and dirty his clothes to blend in better.

For almost six months the lone scientist wandered in this land of sand and dust and dirt. Water was often a luxury, bathrooms were nonexistent, the food was often suspect. He toured pistachio plantations and pored through suqs and bazaars seeking seed that looked distinctive.

Eventually his botanic booty amounted to about 20 pounds of individually selected seed, and in 1930 he carried them out of Persia and back to Washington. Within a year he had germinated them and was growing them under observation at the USDA Plant Introduction Station at Chico, California. However, pistachio trees take 7 to 10 years to mature, so it was almost a decade before Whitehouse could get much idea of what he had gathered.

"With pistachio you need infinite patience," says USDA horticulturist Lloyd Joley. "When I began working with Whitehouse in 1945 we were just beginning to be able to judge the characteristics of the seed he had collected in Iran. Out of his 3,000 trees only 20 were worth keeping, only 3 were promising enough to name, and 2 of those subsequently proved unsatisfactory."

Thus, of all the seeds that Whitehouse had collected during six months of hardship, only one proved useful. He never saw the tree it came from. He had picked the seed out of a pile of drying nuts in the orchards of the Agah family, prominent pistachio growers at Rafsanjan in Iran's central plateau.

In the 1950s, when the tree was beginning to show exceptional promise, Whitehouse named it "Kerman," for the famous carpet-making city near Rafsanjan. He asked his superiors in Washington to allocate funds for developing it into a commercial crop. They balked, claiming that no money was available for pistachio. Find another project, he was told; pistachio would never become a viable crop in this country. The state of California was even less enthusiastic. As Joley remembers, "There never was much interest in our work. I myself never expected to see a pistachio industry in my lifetime."

But Whitehouse never lost his enthusiasm or dedication. Although stationed in Maryland, he traveled to California every year for three decades to spend several weeks working with Joley, sharing the tedious work of hand-pollination and grafting—doggedly plugging away at pistachio improvement.

Trials and Tribulations

Developing a new crop, especially a tree crop, is a monumental achievement, and the pair faced frequent setbacks and frustrations. Each time they planted a seed they had to wait five years before blossoms formed so they could tell even what sex their tree was. Severe disease rotted the roots of their trees, even attacking those of the "Kerman" tree. Some plants grew vigorously and looked marvelous, only to produce few nuts; some failed to ripen their seeds all at the same time; others yielded well initially, only to decline in subsequent years. "We would get good results one year and then couldn't repeat them the next," recalls Joley. "Every time something like that happened the pressures to cancel the program rose. Almost everyone said it would never amount to anything."

Nevertheless, the lone "Kerman" tree continued growing and yielding well. The beleaguered scientists had that alone to keep them going. Only its consistently strong growth, its large, good-tasting seeds, and its high proportion of split shells—desirable because they make the nuts easy to open—made the seemingly mad, decades-long ordeal worthwhile. Eventually they discovered that related pistachio species resisted root-rot fungi and made good rootstock. Soon they were taking buds from the "Kerman" tree and grafting them onto seedlings of these hardy species. By the late 1950s, some 30 years after the initial collection, a pistachio industry was becoming somewhat feasible: Whitehouse and Joley had a good female tree, and they had disease-resistant types to use as rootstock. But a third botanical ingredient was missing—a good male tree.

Missing Link Found

In the 1920s a Fresno farmer named A. B. Peters had discovered in his backyard a male pistachio, but it was not until the 1950s that scientists realized that this tree shed pollen not only prolifically but also at roughly the same time that "Kerman" was in bloom. With the "Peters" tree the technical stage was at last set for an American pistachio industry.

Soon after, in the 1960s, Joley began distributing free budwood and seedlings to anyone who wanted them. "People would drop in to the station and want to know about pistachio," he recalls. "I'd give them what I could. Several were nurserymen who soon began producing and selling budwood for "Kerman" and "Peters," as well as seedlings for rootstock. It was those nurserymen who got the commercial production started."

It had taken almost 40 years for William Whitehouse's collecting trip to begin to pay off. The real advance into commercialization, however, came from an unexpected source. The Internal Revenue Service in 1969 withdrew almonds and a number of other tree crops from its list of speculative agricultural investments. Pistachios, however, remained an allowable tax write-off. Suddenly alone, it became a hot investment. "A crop with no problems!" blurted the promotional brochures; "the new gold rush!" Investors were attracted to partnerships in pistachio plantations by offerings of 40-acre blocks. Getty Oil, Superior Oil, Tenneco West, and other corporations invested in pistachios too. For the first eight or nine years an investor could legally write off a good proportion of the expenses. Some prescient nurserymen made fortunes supplying the planting materials: a former bartender, a dentist, and a row crop farmer today are pistachio millionaires.

"It wasn't even known if pistachios would grow here economically," explains Dick Madsen, of Pistachio Producers of California. "It was an investors' crop. Farmers would have been more cautious; they couldn't wait seven years for a payoff."

Through the 1970s the businessmen watched their trees establish themselves, strengthen, and flower. Before 1970 there had been only a few hundred acres of pistachio trees in the San Joaquin Valley; by 1976, however, 4,350 acres were standing out as oases of green among sunburned fields of grass and wild sunflowers. By 1979 there were 20,880 acres. None of the owners knew whether they would ever be profitable.

The first trickle of American pistachios began in 1976, amounting to only 150,000 pounds. The next two years were better, and in 1979 the first commercially significant harvest—more than 17 million pounds—came off the trees.

Big Time Nuts

For the fledgling industry 1979 could not have been a better year. With little warning, revolution burst out in Iran, so that almost overnight the world's main pistachio supply disappeared. Prices zoomed from $1.24 a pound in 1978 to $2.05 a pound in 1980. The investors cashed in. Those overwritten promotional brochures of 10 years earlier proved true.

Although by the mid-1970s the pace of new planting had leveled off, the Iranian revolution caused it to leap up again. Today, there are some 45,000 acres of pistachio trees in California, and about 4,000 additional acres are planted every year.

The 1982 American crop of 43 million pounds of nuts was valued at more than $60 million. While Iran is still the world's top pistachio producer, the U.S. has bumped Turkey out of the number-two spot. Greece and Italy are fourth and fifth. American productivity will continue to increase at a healthy rate; the oldest of our trees are only 15 years old, so their yields will keep rising for several years yet. This advantage, together with the new plantings, indicates that by the 1990s the U.S. crop will be 70 or 80 million pounds; eventually it could top 120 million pounds.

All this is based on the one seed that William Whitehouse dropped into his collecting bag the day in 1929 that he visited the Agah family in Rafsanjan.

"The greatest service which can be rendered any country," said Thomas Jefferson in 1813 (perhaps justifying his illegal acts of 1784, when he smuggled out rice in contravention of Italian law), "is to add a useful plant to its culture."

William Whitehouse, who died in 1982 at age 89, still overflowing with enthusiasm in the fulfillment of his dreams, would have made Jefferson proud.

BOB YOUNG
Vice-President, Lockheed Corporation

A Secret of Successful Executives

Why is it we don't all see things the same?

"They don't see 'eye to eye' " is a long-standing way to speak about conflict. It's legend that several observers seeing the same event describe it differently. People seen committing a crime are described differently and what happened during the crime is described differently. The usual explanation for the discrepancies is that everything happened so fast or the observers were excited.

But why didn't they see the same thing?

I can remember the years I spent coaching baseball. There were some players who hit the ball well and some who didn't. We attempted to coach hitters in technique to improve them. Sometimes it worked; sometimes it didn't. Also, there were hitters with good form who hit poorly and hitters with poor form who hit well.

Why are there differences in ability?

BB's and Grapefruit

Suppose we were to clock a high-school pitcher's fast ball with a radar gun at 82 mph. Then let's have a major-league player, a high-school player, and a Little League player bat against this pitcher, using the radar gun to verify the speed of the ball. How might we expect the players to describe the ball in flight?

The high-school player sees it as an 82 mph fastball—something he sees all the time. The Little League player sees a smaller ball and may say it looks like a BB in flight. On the other hand, the major-leaguer sees a ball he may describe as the size of a grapefruit. (There is a famous saying in baseball about pitchers with good fastballs: "He throws BB's.") Clearly, there is some phenomenon associated with how we see things, and this phenomenon results in our not seeing the same thing in the same way.

Things "Show Up"

There are many other examples of people looking at the same thing and seeing something different. One might say that it isn't a case of what's *there* that we react to but, rather, what we *perceive* to be there. If we consider that what we see represents how things "show up" for us and that the same thing "shows up" differently for other people, we can begin to see that maybe one of the sources of conflict is the expectation that we each see the same thing when we don't.

Well, now, that's interesting. If several of us look at the same circumstances and see something similar but different and at the same time operate as if we are seeing the same thing, we have the seeds for potential conflict already planted. This difference between what is *actually present* like a physical reality and how it *shows up* for each of us may be a fertile ground to understand something about conflict and human relations.

What if we recognized that there is or may be a difference between what is present and what we say about it. What difference would that make to us? Let's see.

That would mean that I would be interested in what's really there—like how fast is the ball really traveling? I'd be interested in how it "shows up" for me. Do I see BB's or do I see a grapefruit? I'd also be interested in how people I interact with see it. Do they see BB's or do they see a grapefruit? And I'd be interested in the differences between what we see so that differences could be reconciled in our interactions.

Whoa, not so fast.

It may be fine to take note of the differences between what you see and what I see so that we end up talking about the same thing, but what about taking action? We may have reconciled how something "shows up" to each of us and are now dealing with the same "showing up" of what's actually present. In other words, we agree on what we see in common and disagree on what we don't see in common, so we are clear between us. What happens, though, when we operate consistently with what shows up for us, and we are off the mark with what's really there? If we see what we see and act on it, but that's not really what's there—what about our results?

Dodging the Ball

In baseball, I've seen Little Leaguers step back from the plate as the ball is thrown to keep from getting hit—and the ball was nowhere near them when it came over the plate. So, they were reacting to some "showing up" that wasn't reality.

How many similar instances to dodging the ball are there in life when what shows up is different from what is really there? In how many circumstances in business, in politics, in our families, in our everyday life are we dodging the ball?

This is a really interesting question. If we act consistently with what we perceive rather than what's there, our results are likely to be inconsistent. We may wonder why people act as they do. We may get angry with someone for not seeing the obvious or someone may get angry with us. We may do something which looks dumb in retrospect when we reinterpret what originally "showed up" for us.

This is disconcerting.

Approximations

If we are trying to work something out between us and we are both talking about our interpretation and neither of us has an interpretation, a "showing up" consistent with what's actually there, how in the world can we expect to be effective in anything? More than that, if this is true, how have we managed to produce all the things we have produced? Sounds as if we are living in a world of *approximations*. We see *approximately* what's there. We see *approximately* the same things, and in the end our *approximations* are near enough to produce workability.

If we were aware of this phenomenon of *approximations*, this nature of things as a "showing up" rather than as a reality, wouldn't we be a lot more effective in action? Wouldn't we be careful not to jump too quickly to conclusions in what we see? Wouldn't we look behind our interpretations of what people say to us to get some idea of how they really see things rather than take what they say at face value? Wouldn't we be careful not to confuse our interpretation with theirs so that we don't hear the wrong thing?

This whole idea is mind-boggling. How can we sort this out simply and easily?

First, what we perceive about what is physically present is probably not what is actually present, even though what we perceive might be a close approximation to what is present.

Second, you and I might not perceive the same thing when looking at the same thing. More than that, it's likely that we won't.

Third, when we take action, we are acting on our perception, not on what's actually there.

Given these three points, so what?

Well, for one thing, we could stay open to new possibilities of interpretation so that we enhance two areas of our effectiveness: (1) by being open to alternate interpretations, we are better able to understand and interact with people and (2) by being open to alternate interpretations, we are better able to operate on what's really present because we will continue to move our interpretation of reality closer to reality itself.

No Right Answers

There may even be a third and more powerful benefit to seeing this conflict between perception, how things "show up" for us, and reality. We may put more attention on what's actually present than on how we feel about it and become more effective in action. If we have our attention on the ball when we are up to bat rather than on how we feel about the possibility of getting hit by the ball, we may be a better batter. We are certainly less likely to step away from the plate when the ball is thrown and the ball's not coming anywhere near us.

Wait a minute.

If all this is so, that would mean there are no right answers where interpretation is concerned. The powerful orientation, then, is not finding the right answer but rather finding a question or questions to keep open as we get into action so that we continually enhance our relationships with people and our insights into what's actually present in reality.

A strange orientation. We propose to act without any right answers. Well, not strange at all, on second thought. It's what we already do all the time.

ACCOMPLISHMENT
IS INEVITABLY BASED
ON WORKABLE APPROXIMATIONS.

RALPH G. MARTIN

Charles & Diana Get Married

Wat was in Diana's mind on her wedding day as she rode down the Mall in her glass coach, looking like Cinderella, on her way to marry a handsome Prince?

Only a year before she was a teenager in jeans serving beer in a place called Slim Jim's—part of an apprentice program in a cooking course. Now, more than 750 million people all over the world were watching her every move on television, with millions of women wanting to know absolutely everything about her—what she wore, how she fixed her hair, why she bit her fingernails.

What was she thinking as she sat in that coach . . . .

Everybody's Watching

Despite the uncertain weather, everything looked rosy for Britain. In the two months since the engagement had been announced, the

Financial Times share index rose 100 points. Compared to the 10,000 people who watched the coronation of King George VI on television, there would now be an estimated 750 million people in 74 countries glued to their sets, the only Communist country included being Yugoslavia. It was the largest single-day event ever undertaken by the BBC, but in the United States, the coverage was even greater.

But *Boston Globe* editorial writer Otile McManus summed up the mood of millions by writing, "I don't care what anybody says. I'm going to bed early tonight. I'm going to set my alarm clock for the middle of the night. I'm going to get up in time for the royal wedding. I don't want to miss a word . . . I will toast Prince Charles with Rice Krispies and orange juice. I will wish them health, long life, and happiness. Just pass the Kleenex, please."

Peter Jennings, the ABC commentator, explained why American television was devoting more time to the Royal Wedding than it had to the space shuttle flight or the return of U.S. hostages from Iran. "It's the last of the great royal spectacles. It's got color, sweep, music, occasion, and it's a great romantic story. It captures the imagination."

"The royal scene is simply a presentation of ourselves behaving well," observed novelist Dame Rebecca West. "If anybody is being honored, it is the human race." . . .

It's a Great Day to Be British

The wedding day was declared a national holiday, and the heart of London was closed to all public traffic. If the spirit somewhat resembled a Brazilian carnival, the scheduled efficiency was split-second British. The doors of St. Paul's Cathedral opened at 9:00 A.M. sharp and all 2,500 guests were advised to be in their seats by 9:30. At 10:14 a fleet of black Rolls-Royces left Buckingham Palace with nearly all of Europe's kings and queens. At 10:22, the Queen's procession of carriages—eight state landaus and divisions of Household Cavalry—left the Palace. . . .

It was such a joyous crowd, singing, cheering, waving, applauding, loving, and waves of loving. . . . BRITAIN NEEDS CHARLIE AND DI read one sign. Another showed a huge photo of Diana with the words I HAD TO KISS A LOT OF FROGS.

Six Cambridge University students were wearing dinner jackets. They had come the night before, set up a formal table on the Mall with an elegant candlelit dinner of poached salmon and champagne. Other young people were still wet from splashing happily in the fountains at Trafalgar Square.

"It's a great day to be British," said seventy-two-year-old retired factory worker Geoffrey Tirson. His voice breaking slightly, he told how he was standing on that very same spot of grass the night Prince Charles was born, "and now, here he is, about to be married. I say God bless him and her and all of us."

Spontaneously, people started singing "Rule, Britannia" and "God Save the Queen," many obviously in tears. Thousands of cameras were clicking constantly. Parents everywhere were thrusting their children into the air to get a better look at the proceedings and transistor radios were switched on to give the crowds an added dimension of what was happening elsewhere. Along the route, Diana saw all the hanging baskets of blue, pink, and white petunias, verbena, and phlox, and everywhere flags, bunting, banners, emblems of heraldry. A small group was loudly singing a new song, "Lady Di."

Since Diana had read everything about the wedding, she surely knew that some people had paid thousands of dollars for ringside windows near St. Paul's. Thirty Houston, Texas, socialites had paid $250,000 for a super-luxury wedding week which included rooms at the St. James Club and a Cordon Bleu lunch catered by Parisian chefs.

The Glass Coach Arrives

The climactic moment for the waiting crowds at St. Paul's, and for worldwide television, was the arrival of the glass coach, with the butterfly emerging from her chrysalis. It was the world's first look at the fabled dress.

A footman wearing scarlet and gold opened the coach door. Earl Spencer . . . came out first. Then out came Diana, carefully holding the folds of her dress as she stepped onto the red carpet. Two of her bridesmaids were waiting to catch and spread out her train.

Perhaps in a petulant moment, Dame Rebecca West had said days earlier that Diana looked like a thatched cottage. At that instant on television, she might well have choked on her words. Diana looked like a dream.

In Lagos, Nigeria, a small group of British listened intently to the announcer describing the wedding dress. It was at a party given by Her Majesty's Acting High Commissioner. "They said it was taffeta," said a girl named Louise. She paused and asked, "What's taffeta?"

When they played the national anthem and the congregation stood to sing "God Save the Queen," a British diplomat at a party stood at awkward attention, a sherry glass in his hand, singing the words with shy defiance.

She climbed the twenty-four imposing granite steps to the west door of St. Paul's while the crowd roared. Women wept. There were shouts of "Good luck." A police sergeant did a bit of a jig. A dozen trumpets blared her arrival.

In an impish aside, Diana asked her bridesmaids, "Is he here yet?" Then, "Am I ready?" She asked the Emanuels, who were just inside the entrance to give the gown a final check before she made her grand entrance. They both said, "Oh, no," making frantic final adjustments to smooth the crumples.

"She was incredibly calm," said David Emanuel. "We were the ones who were nervous."

But afterward, she said, "I was so nervous I hardly knew what I was doing." . . .

The Wedding Begins

Then came the sound of the wedding processional, the sound of trumpets stationed around the Whispering Gallery playing Jeremiah Clarke's "Trumpet Voluntary," composed three centuries ago, backed up by the 7,080 pipes of the Cathedral organ . . . .

The clergy parted, and there was her waiting Prince in full uniform as a Commander of the Royal Navy, wearing his blue sash as a Knight of the Garter. He grinned and moved toward her, whispering, "You look wonderful!"

"Wonderful for you!" she said.

The two now stood side by side in front of the high altar, their right hands clasped. . . .

Suddenly, without preamble, came the voices of the choir and a congregation singing the hymn, "Christ is made the sure foundation." The Prince had predicted that all the music would be so moving, "I shall, I think, spend half the time in tears." He did not. He had other things to think about now.

The lesson of the 70-minute ceremony, read by a close friend of Prince Charles, a Welsh Methodist, came from St. Paul's passage on love in the First Letter to the Corinthians: "Love never faileth . . . Love is patient; love is kind and envies no one." Poet Laureate

Sir John Betjeman also had written a poem to celebrate the ceremony, and it began, "Let's all in love and friendship hither come
. . . " The President of Zimbabwe, the Reverend Canaan Banana,
also had written a verse which read in part, "It was worth living for
the one most loving . . . "

What was so touching to the watching millions was how often
Charles and Diana looked at each other, and held hands.

"Here is the stuff of which fairy tales are made," said the Archbishop of Canterbury in his sermon. "A marriage which really
works is one which works for others . . . May the burdens we lay on
them be matched by the love with which we support them . . . "

The service really began when the Dean of St. Paul's, the Very
Reverend Alan Webster, intoned, "Dearly beloved, we are gathered
here in the sight of God and in the face of this congregation to join
this man and this woman in Holy Matrimony . . . "

It seemed as if the whole world was listening, as if this marriage was their marriage. The Archbishop later reminded people,
"There is an ancient Christian tradition that every bride and groom
on their wedding day are regarded as a royal couple . . . "

They were both obviously nervous. The Prince unconsciously
rubbed his nose. Diana was grateful to have her face hidden by her
veil.

"Diana Frances, wilt thou have this man to be thy wedded
husband, to live together according to God's law in the holy estate
of matrimony? Wilt thou love him, comfort him, honour and keep
him, in sickness and in health; and, forsaking all others, keep thee
only unto him, so long as ye both shall live?"

"I will," she answered quietly, but firmly.

As Diana repeated the words of the ancient marriage vow, she
seemed to be swaying ever so slightly in rhythm with the phrases.
She gave the impression of being immersed in it, oblivious to all
but Charles and the Archbishop.

Prince Charles's nervousness showed when he muffed one of
his lines. Instead of saying "all my worldly good with thee I share,"
he said "all thy goods with thee I share." Watching a repeat of the
ceremony on television with other members of the Royal Family
later, Princess Anne laughed and said, "He meant it. It wasn't a
mistake at all!"

Diana's nervousness showed when she referred to her husband
as "Philip Charles Arthur George" instead of "Charles Philip Arthur
George." . . .

The Couple Rides Home

Finally it was done. "With this ring I thee wed . . . "

Then, "Those whom God hath joined together let no man put asunder . . . "

When the Archbishop of Canterbury declared, "I pronounce that they be man and wife together," the crowds outside Buckingham Palace, listening on their radios, stood up and cheered. . . .

As they left St. Paul's, the bride had a word of warning for her new husband: "Mind the steps . . ." . . .

Diana had taken off her veil now, and the newlyweds rode together in an open carriage to the roar of the crowds. People along the route threw rice, confetti, and rose petals. There was a big banner alongside a church: LOVE FROM AMERICA. Another proclaimed: LOVE IS CHARLIE AND DI. The nearby Ritz Hotel had photographs of them on its front, nearly a full floor high. The *Times* of London had dedicated its entire front page to an unprecedented full-length picture of the couple, referring to this "day of romance in a gray world." At the Strand Palace Hotel, the management released a spray of red rose petals and 1,000 doves as the royal couple passed.

From the crowd there was another song, "Lady Di, Lady Di, Lady Di" (chick-a-boom, chick-a-boom-boom . . .). The pace of the carriages now slowed so the crowd could get a longer look.

At Buckingham Palace, a butler appeared outside the fence carrying a silver salver with two glasses and a bottle of champagne. Behind him came another man carrying a jeroboam of wine followed by two yeomen of the guard in their colorful uniforms. They marched toward the gate, poured the wine, drank a toast to the people, then turned and drank a toast to the Palace. The crowd roared.

A Kiss on the Balcony

When the newlyweds returned to Buckingham Palace, the crowds broke ranks, the whole Mall becoming a swaying human mosaic of people. Once the Royal Family were all inside the Palace, the crowd kept yelling for them to come out on the balcony. And, when the Prince and Princess came out onto the balcony, many in the crowd started singing "You'll Never Walk Alone." The yelling was particularly insistent for Cinderella. "We want Di, we want Di, we want Di."

It was unmistakably the face of Charles behind the curtained window of the balcony, peering out at the people. They could see Charles reaching for Diana's hand to lead her out to the balcony. She seemed slightly shy the first time they appeared, less so the second time. "Go ahead and wave," he told her, and she did. The third time, the crowd was chanting, "Kiss her, kiss her, kiss her." He kissed her on the hand. The crowd called them back a fourth time, and now they were yelling, "Kiss her *properly*."

Hired lipreaders, looking through binoculars, reported that the Prince said to her, "I'm not going in for that caper. They want us to kiss." But, utterly relaxed and exuberant now, she smiled and said, "Why ever not?" Prince Andrew reportedly also egged him on. Most of the family was on the balcony with them now, and the Prince took a quick look at Her Majesty to see if she objected. She didn't. He then turned to his bride and kissed her lingeringly on the mouth. The crowd went wild.

READING
*to Enjoy
Persuasion and
Argument*

In the next four selec-
tions, the writers want to effect a change in their readers' thoughts
and actions. In other words, the writers want to persuade readers
to take note of a certain thing or to believe a certain thing or to do
a certain thing. They want their readers to change. These writers
are motivated by their commitments and passions, by what they
stand for. They hope that by reading their writing, people will be
convinced, persuaded, and moved to take specific action. The
action which the writer hopes for may range from something as
simple as readers becoming more aware of what the writer considers to be an untenable situation to something as profound as
readers making a lifelong commitment to work actively to bring
about change.

In the first selection, *Evgueni I. Chazov*, the controversial Soviet
M.D. who, with his American colleague Bernard Lown, received the
Nobel Peace Prize in 1985 for the work of the International Physicians

for the Prevention of Nuclear War, argues that physicians must take a stand for nuclear disarmament. He asserts that life on earth has never been in such danger as now.

Thomas W. Pew, Jr., editor of *American West* magazine, writes a beautiful tribute to the passing of Route 66, America's "Mother road," that glory-road-of-old which has been so important in the settlement of the American West. He pleads for saving the road signs for Route 66 at least and giving them a last resting place as close to the old road as possible.

Juthica Stangl, a native of India who has lived in the United States for the past twenty-three years, writes of the suicide of one of her best friends in India. Stangl suggests that her friend's death is a modern form of the ancient practice of suttee—in which a widow throws herself on the burning funeral pyre with her husband's body. She argues that the life of an Indian woman is not considered to be worth much and conveys her anger at the situation she sees.

The last selection is *Martin Luther King's* "Christmas Sermon on Peace," first preached at the Ebenezer Baptist Church in Atlanta and later broadcast on Christmas Eve, 1967. Three months later, on April 4, 1968, Dr. King was murdered on a motel balcony in Memphis.

Evgueni I. Chazov, M.D., (USSR)

Physicians for Nuclear Disarmament

Life on earth has never been in such danger as now. This danger is because of the nuclear arms race and the production of weapons whose devastating power cannot be compared to that of any earlier types of weaponry. Europeans recall with horror World War II, which snuffed out 50 million lives, leaving behind ruined cities and tragedies for millions of families. Twenty million people were killed in the USSR. Virtually every family was affected.

We know very well what war means. But what could happen to our planet in no way compares to what humanity lived through during World War II. It has been calculated that about five megatons of various kinds of explosive substances were used during the whole of that war. To get an idea of what could happen today as a result of nuclear war, we must remember that the explosive power of just one thermonuclear charge is several times greater than the total of all explosions made in the course of all wars.

A Million Hiroshimas

The radioactivity from nuclear weapons is as devastating to human life as is their destructive power. Even an hour after a one-megaton nuclear explosion, the radioactivity at the place of explosion is equal to the radioactivity of 500 million kilograms of radium. It is scores of millions of times greater than that which is included in the powerful gamma installations used in medicine for the treatment of malignant tumors. Few people in the world realize the dire consequences a nuclear war would have for each one of us, for our loved ones, for humanity. The total explosive power of the nuclear arsenals stockpiled in the world today is equal to a million bombs of the kind dropped on Hiroshima. Figuratively speaking, we are now sitting on a powder keg that holds about 5 tons of TNT for each one of us. Around this powder keg, certain people are waving the torch of a "nuclear policy strategy," which at any second, even accidentally, may cause an explosion that would be a world catastrophe.

Little by little, with the joys and sorrows of daily life, people forget the horrors of Hiroshima and Nagasaki. Some military and public functionaries and even some scientists are trying to minimize the possible consequences of nuclear war. Statements appear that a nuclear war can be won; that a limited nuclear war can be waged; that humanity and the biosphere will persist, even in conditions of total nuclear catastrophe.

These are illusions that must be dispelled. Hiroshima and Nagasaki are a reality, historical facts that show that science and technology have fostered power that can lead to global annihilation of every living thing. The bell that tolls in Hiroshima reminds people of the danger. It calls on them to be vigilant. It calls on them to do their utmost to prevent the tragedy of nuclear war.

The Cost Is Too High

Even now the nuclear arms race is very costly for humanity. Serious psychological harm stems from the fear experienced by people all over the world as a result of the threat of a nuclear war. Tremendous sums are being spent on the technology of a nuclear war at a time when millions of people go hungry, when they suffer from disease, when illiteracy is still widespread. Huge expenditures on manpower and material resources render difficult the solution of numerous world problems—health, energy, education, economics, and more.

In developing countries today, 100 million children are in danger of dying because of malnutrition and vitamin shortage, and 30 percent of the children have no possibility of going to school. Yet military expenditures worldwide are 20 to 25 times bigger than the total aid provided annually to the developing countries by the developed states. For example, in the past ten years the World Health Organization spent about $83 million on smallpox eradication—less than the cost of one modern strategic bomber. According to some World Health Organization calculations, $450 million is needed to eradicate malaria, a disease that affects more than 1000 million people in 66 countries of the world. This is less than half of what is spent in the world on arms every day.

Pugwash Meetings

Outstanding scientists and physicians have realized the threat to humanity of the nuclear arms race and understood the need to work for a ban on nuclear weapons. Twenty-seven years ago Albert Einstein, Bertrand Russell, Frédéric Joliot-Curie, Joseph Rotblat, and others issued the Russell-Einstein Manifesto, which began the Pugwash movement. They stated: "In the tragic situation which confronts humanity, we feel that scientists should assemble in conference to appraise the perils that have arisen as a result of the development of weapons of mass destruction." And they warned: "We are speaking on this occasion, not as members of this or that nation, continent, or creed, but as human beings, members of the species Man, whose continued existence is in doubt."

Since 1957 leading scientists from around the world have held regular Pugwash meetings, focusing their expertise on the dangers of nuclear weapons and urging governments to eliminate these weapons from their arsenals. Yet the world has not heeded the warnings of these great scientists.

Today, the four million physicians working all over the world must regard the struggle against the danger of a nuclear war to be not only the duty of an honest, humanitarian person, but also a professional duty. We are dealing not with political problems, but with the preservation of the health and lives of all people. No country or people will remain unaffected by a nuclear catastrophe.

Preserve Life on Earth

Raising our voice of protest against the arms race and nuclear war, we must at the same time find the most effective path for our cause. We must explain to the peoples of the world and to governments possessing nuclear weapons, on the basis of our knowledge and precise research data, the danger to life on earth from the unleashing of nuclear war. We must discuss not only the immediate consequences of a nuclear explosion, but also the global problems resulting from the radioactive contamination of the stratosphere—the disruption of the ozone layer of the earth, the changes of the climate, ecology, and more.

We must convince the peoples and the governments that under conditions of nuclear war, medicine will be unable to provide aid to the hundreds of thousands of wounded, burned, and sick, because of the deaths of doctors and the destruction of the transportation system, drugs, blood supplies, hospitals, and laboratories. Epidemic outbreaks will reach far beyond the affected centers.

As physicians, our knowledge of the tragic consequences of nuclear war enables us to make a vital contribution to the cause of preventing it. Our patients entrust themselves to us. It is in keeping with our professional honor and with the oath of Hippocrates that we have no right to hide from them the danger that now threatens us all.

We must preserve life on earth. We must struggle for the survival of our children and grandchildren. People of all political outlooks, nationalities, and religions must urge their governments to concentrate their attention not on what steps to take to attain victory in nuclear war, but on what must be done so that the flames of such a war will never burn our planet.

We face many difficulties, and the path to the achievement of our goal will be thorny and full of impediments. But we have no alternative: when we hear that "humanity is in danger," physicians must rise to the challenge. We call on all the physicians of the world, on all medical workers, to merge their efforts for the salvation of life on earth.

THOMAS W. PEW, JR.

The Passing of Route 66

Little town, black top
Narrow bridge, four-way-stop
Soft shoulder, dash stripe
Pop-a-top, hitchhike
Falling rock, race-the-clock
Neon bright, city light
Truck stop, car hop
Out of gas, overheat
Dead dog, road hog
Little camp, foot asleep
Midnight rain, race a train
Here at last, push to pass
End of trip.   66.

Highways have rhythm. Or at least the old ones did, and for as long as I can remember I've been a real sucker for the rhythm of highways. Just the crinkle of a road map, the smell of luggage hauled out of storage, and—as though the moment would never come—the turn down the driveway feel-

41

ing the gravity of thousands of undriven miles just ahead waiting to lap up the tire tread and pull me over the horizon puts clouds of rising butterflies in my middle.

And if there were a scale of rising butterflies from one to one thousand, the highway that stirs them up the most is old Route 66. Route 66: Mountain Man Bill Williams's way West beyond the Osage Trail, long before anyone dreamed of highways in the American West. Secretary of War Jefferson Davis's pathway to the Pacific, a plan delayed by the War between the States. John Steinbeck's "Mother road," "the path of a people in flight." Woody Guthrie's folkroad metronome, rhythm for a score of America's favorite hard-time travelin' ballads.

Route 66: the way West that's tatooed in colors of hardship and expectation in the hearts and dreams of millions of American pioneers. Route 66: the ultimate symbol for America's primary rhythm of settlement. Feet on a path. Wheels on a trail. Steel on a track. Tires on a road. Route 66: the way West for gold-seekers bound for Arizona in the 1860s, and the way West for dust refugees running to California, fleeing the dark clouds of foreclosure and blowing top-soil out of Oklahoma, Arkansas, and Texas in the 1930s.

Let Us Pause

Now that the old road is about to disappear forever, now that the highway department has paved over her roadbed, bypassed her little towns in three time zones and eight states, and stripped her of her familiar black and white, double-six logo, can't we who've driven her in fun, sorrow, or flight pause a moment to remember the grand old route of American emigration. It's our guess that the glory-road-of-old means a lot more to millions of Americans living today and to those long in their graves than a chute on a tilting continent, as architect Frank Lloyd Wright unkindly described it, down which "everything loose seems to be sliding into southern California."

Camels Cut the Trail

Many paths, trails, and eventually highways served the way West for Americans, but when Lieutenant Edward Fitzgerald Beale, aided by the first and only American camel corps, was ordered by Congress in 1857 to blaze a new road through to California from Fort Defiance, New Mexico, along the 35th parallel, along what

Beale correctly predicted would "inevitably become the great emigrant road to California," America found her "Mother road."

Few who have traveled the route of the double sixes know of the history of Mountain Man Bill Williams, or of Lieutenant Edward Beale. Some may remember what a big part the highway played in John Steinbeck's *Grapes of Wrath*, and there's hardly an American alive who doesn't know at least one or two of Woody Guthrie's songs of the road. But even if they don't know the history or the names of those who came before them, they do and did personally know the rhythm of highways, and in that beat is the whole rhythm of a nation of emigrants drawn, fascinated, driven with the idea of seeking something better just a little further West.

Don't Erase a Symbol

That rhythm was a thing you could hear on the old road just as plain as day if you listened as you drove and paid attention to the folks encountered along the way. It's a rhythm that's been effectively erased by the Interstate System that travels through the heartland of the little towns along the way as though folks there had the plague.

We don't think much of the new road, although it is a convenient way to miss the country as you get from Chicago to Los Angeles, avoiding all human contact in between. But when the highway department took the 66 sign and put it on some little dinky road outside Washington, D.C., they erased a symbol of our history that has marked a lot of determined miles of a lot of determined American families for generations.

We think it's a kind of official vandalism. And even if it takes an act of Congress to restore the old shields to their proper road—or as close to it as possible—we think it would be worth the effort, and maybe it would remind us just a little of how this country was settled and the path people traveled as they went a little further along toward the end of their trip on Route 66.

JUTHICA STANGL

India: A Widow's Devastating Choice

On October 26, 1981, while Delhi prepared for Deevali, the festival of lights, Anjali Banerji and her 14-year-old son Ashok each swallowed a lethal handful of sleeping pills. They had already fed a dose to the family dog, Tepi.

Anjali Banerji died four days later; Ashok and Tepi survived, thanks to police officers who pumped their stomachs after the attempt.

A November issue of India Today magazine reported the suicide. Anjali Banerji's husband, Rajib, a doctor at the Hindu Rao Hospital, had been hit by a car and, after a lengthy hospitalization, had died the previous January. In time, the widow began searching for work. She had a degree in social work and 14 years experience in West Bengal, but no job came her way. She received little sympathy from her family and from friends—only the advice to move in with relatives. After 10 frustrating months, she decided to follow her husband in death, and to take the rest of the family with her.

The reporter noted her meticulous preparations—notes written to the police and her brother, the refrigerator emptied and defrosted, kitchen stocked with food for relatives or whoever came to take care of the possessions left behind.

Two weeks after her death, friends sent the clipping to me in California.

A Special Friend

Anjali had been very special to me. We were both about 16 when we met outside a classroom on the first day of college at the University of Calcutta. I still remember it clearly. I was standing alone in an archway, watching a crow feed her little ones. Suddenly I heard footsteps and there was a tall, slender girl with two short braids, wearing a well-starched white sari. Like me, she wore no jewelry, not even the customary thin gold bracelets every middle-class girl wore like a uniform. I had not met anyone before who also rebelled against the prescribed dress code. What we were wearing would be considered a widow's garb. I felt close to her instantly.

I smiled and asked if she was also waiting for room three. She nodded with a smile and said, "Yes, and am I glad to find someone to talk to. None of my friends got into this college. I was so nervous when my father dropped me off at the gate that I didn't sleep all night."

"I can understand that, since I have no old friends here either. My name is Juthica, but everyone calls me Julie." . . .

From then on, for four years, we were inseparable. We took the same classes, joined the National Cadet Corps, helped each other learn to ride bikes, and visited each other after school. I always invited her home for Christmas dinner, and spent Hindu feasts at hers. We covered for each other, telling little white lies when doing something or going somewhere our families wouldn't approve. We comforted each other through difficult times, and teased and poked fun at each other. She was quiet and sensible, with an irresistible sense of humor. I was wild, impulsive, and boisterous—we complemented each other well.

What Could Have Happened

Now she is dead.

All those times when I felt that the world had come to an end, that my great love was over, or that I would surely flunk the final, she would patiently listen to my stories, then put her arm around me and reassure me. Even now, 30 years later, the memory of her strength pulls me through difficult times. What could have happened to her strength, her confidence, her optimism?

As I read through the clipping, I found I couldn't help blaming myself that I wasn't there when she really needed someone. I began to feel angry at her family.

Traditionally, the extended Indian family comes to the rescue in times of trouble. What had happened to them? Her father was a scholarly gentleman who taught high school. She had two older brothers, one an army doctor, the other an engineer, and an older sister, who was already married and out of the house by the time I met her. Anytime I was visiting I was always struck by how quiet and peaceful the household was. They all spoke in gentle voices. It seemed unnatural to me, being used to seven children playing, laughing, fighting, and loving in my family. When I commented once on this, she said it was true, nothing much was ever going on. Her father spent most of the time in his study, her mother kept the house. I had an image of trees in the forest, growing near, but never touching, except in a big storm, when the contact results in a broken limb.

Anjali did produce a storm when she married Rajib. She went against her family's expectations by finding her own future husband, rather than waiting for her match to be arranged. What's more, he was from a lower caste.

Rajib's family was even more resentful. Even though Anjali was higher caste, which on one level meant a social achievement, the family missed out on a potentially major dowry. Had Rajib married within his own caste, the family would have been offered clothes, jewelry, and money, and considering that he was a doctor, perhaps even a car or house. His family counted on this; it would have helped with providing Rajib's sisters' dowries. The loss was significant.

In the wake of the storm, both Anjali and Rajib ended up as limbs broken off family trees. They established themselves on their own. Except for a few sticks of furniture they had nothing, but seemed very happy. By then I was living in California; I visited her each time I was in India, sometimes really going out of my way to do so to catch up with their frequent moves. Each time I saw them I was impressed with the intimacy of their relationship. They were two people who genuinely enjoyed and respected each other, who truly shared their life in the best sense of the word. I kept up with her every way I could.

She was overjoyed when her son was born. Her family, at last, showed some interest in the new grandson. However, Rajib's family did not respond even then. She was determined, with or without the families' support, to continue providing a happy home. From everything I saw, she succeeded. But underneath it, I could tell that she was hurt by her isolation from her family, a feeling of sadness remained for not being accepted by her in-laws.

The last time I saw her was in a hotel room in Delhi. Rajib, Anjali, and Ashok lived outside of town at that point; they took a long bus drive to come to see me and my family. She brought some fried fish, my favorite kind, which she remembered from our college days. Her son by this time was about 12, very bright and friendly. I fantasized about our children developing the kind of friendship Anjali and I had, knowing full well that with the distance between us that would not be possible. The relationship I had been impressed with over the years between Anjali and Rajib obviously was still there, and now included their son. I was particularly happy to see that our children and Ashok got along well.

We parted with the promise of writing more often. We even talked about her sending Ashok to the United States for a year, when he would stay with us.

I Never Heard Again

Is it possible that the article in my hand was about the same Anjali? Suddenly I was furious with her. How could this wonderful woman, this pillar of strength, this model friend and mother, simply do away with herself? What about the promises? How could she just abandon everything, including me?

When I was still in India with my family, I got a letter from her about her husband's car accident. I left India knowing only that he was seriously injured and in the hospital. For months I had had no news, despite my many letters to Anjali. I would have called, but they could never afford a telephone. I felt helpless, but not knowing anyone in the area where they were living at the time, there was nothing I could do.

The next news came in the form of an invitation to a memorial service for Rajib. It was signed by Ashok, as is the custom. The eldest son takes matters into his hands on the father's death. At this time he was barely 14. I could not imagine my own son, three years younger—having to—or being able to do this. But knowing Anjali I knew that if Ashok was anything like his mother, he would perform his duty admirably.

All I could do was to write, offering my help and whatever support I could, long distance. I felt I had failed her completely; I was never there when I might have been able to help.

I never heard from her again. I wrote to all our common acquaintances trying to get news. No one seemed to be in touch with her.

How It Was

But the India Today reporter described the last nine months of her life in great detail. The family had had a comfortable existence, but their modest savings were used up quickly during Rajib's hospitalization after the hit-and-run accident.

In India, of course, accident insurance is uncommon. The application for his life insurance benefit was lost by the company. After months, the company had not responded to the duplicate application. The promised assistance from her husband's employer had not come through despite her repeated appeals. Within weeks she was totally without funds.

Given India's unemployment problem, there were few jobs available even to experienced and highly educated men. It is not surprising then that a woman, out of the job market as long as Anjali had been, was not seriously considered by most employers. Further, she did not have the necessary personal connections, or the know-how to pay bribes to secure a job.

The prospect of being destitute, with no source of support for herself, her son, or even the dog, must have been devastating to her. India is, of course, best known for its poverty. But perhaps just because of this, extreme poverty is even more unthinkable for someone like Anjali who had never before had to worry about it.

The article told of her difficulties with the bureaucratic maze and her resulting depression and loneliness. Her family, whom, according to the article, she had abandoned to marry the man she chose, did not come to her. Her parents had died by now, only her brothers and sisters remained. It is less surprising that her in-laws did not respond either. They considered their son dead once he had married against their wishes.

A reporter interviewed Anjali's brother after the tragedy, and he claimed the family never knew what kind of difficulty she was in. Perhaps her pride kept her from turning to them. Rejected once, she did not want to risk it again.

Anjali's whole life had revolved around her husband and son. She simply couldn't imagine leaving Ashok to other people's mercy. Once she decided to end her life she saw no other way but to take her son with her.

Suicide Is Better

I suddenly realized that, as I was reading on, the image the article conjured up was not of Anjali, but of a women's demonstration I had seen in Delhi during my last trip to India. Hundreds of angry women, mostly villagers, marched with banners, demanding the reinstatement of suttee, the ancient custom in which a widow is to throw herself onto her husband's funeral pyre. The British had outlawed suttee in 1829.

The custom is a testimony to the fact that the life of a widow is superfluous. Once the man is dead, there is no further purpose for the woman. Her role is to bear children; with her husband's death that job is done. Religious tradition holds that her sacrifice helps her husband atone for his sins and for this she becomes a saint.

Despite the established tradition, not all widows had always willingly killed themselves in this way. Village elders and family members often had to force a young wife to follow her husband into death. They would do so not just for religious or traditional reasons, but because the burden of supporting the surviving wife was usually too much for the family.

When I saw that demonstration I could hardly believe my eyes. How could women, in this day and age, especially in a country where the prime minister is a woman, actually campaign for the right to commit suicide just because their husbands had died?

The demonstration dramatized the fact that the ancient custom still has social and economic relevance today. The marching women realized that by outlawing the custom, the British had succeeded only in making it illegal, not in removing its significance.

Even today, India's society has no mechanism to help a woman in a traditional role develop her own identity and avoid becoming a burden. The women were making a statement that suicide is the easier alternative to a life of dependency on unwilling families.

Anjali was an educated and sophisticated woman, with a background and social circle totally different from that of the demonstrators. For her, living in 20th-century Delhi, suttee, in its traditional form, was unthinkable. But, in the end, didn't she find herself forced onto her husband's funeral pyre anyway?

MARTIN LUTHER KING, JR.

A Christmas Sermon on Peace

PEACE ON EARTH . . .

This Christmas season finds us a rather bewildered human race. We have neither peace within nor peace without. Everywhere paralyzing fears harrow people by day and haunt them by night. Our world is sick with war; everywhere we turn we see its ominous possibilities. And yet, my friends, the Christmas hope for peace and goodwill toward all men can no longer be dismissed as a kind of pious dream of some utopian. If we don't have goodwill toward men in this world, we will destroy ourselves by the misuse of our own instruments and our own power.

War Is Obsolete

Wisdom born of experience should tell us that war is obsolete. There may have been a time when war served as a negative good by preventing the spread and growth of an evil force, but the very destructive power of modern weapons of warfare eliminates even the possibility that war may any longer serve as a negative good.

And so, if we assume that life is worth living, if we assume that mankind has a right to survive, then we must find an alternative to war—and so let us this morning explore the conditions for peace. Let us this morning think anew on the meaning of that Christmas hope: "Peace on Earth, Good Will toward Men." And as we explore these conditions, I would like to suggest that modern man really go all out to study the meaning of nonviolence, its philosophy and its strategy.

Practice Nonviolence

We have experimented with the meaning of nonviolence in our struggle for racial justice in the United States, but now the time has come for man to experiment with nonviolence in all areas of human conflict, and that means nonviolence on an international scale.

Now let me suggest first that if we are to have peace on earth, our loyalties must become ecumenical rather than sectional. Our loyalties must transcend our race, our tribe, our class, and our nation; and this means we must develop a world perspective. No individual can live alone; no nation can live alone, and as long as we try, the more we are going to have war in this world. Now the judgment of God is upon us, and we must either learn to live together as brothers or we are all going to perish together as fools.

Yes, as nations and individuals, we are interdependent. I have spoken to you before of our visit to India some years ago. It was a marvelous experience; but I say to you this morning that there were those depressing moments. How can one avoid being depressed when one sees with one's own eyes evidences of millions of people going to bed hungry at night? How can one avoid being depressed when one sees with one's own eyes thousands of people sleeping on the sidewalks at night? More than a million people sleep on the sidewalks of Bombay every night; more than half a million sleep on the sidewalks of Calcutta every night. They have no houses to go into. They have no beds to sleep in. As I beheld these conditions, something within me cried out: "Can we in America stand idly by and not be concerned?" And an answer came: "Oh, no!" And I started thinking about the fact that right here in our country we spend millions of dollars every day to store surplus food; and I said to myself: "I know where we can store that food free of charge—in the wrinkled stomachs of the millions of God's children in Asia, Africa, Latin America, and even in our own nation, who go to bed hungry at night."

All Life Is Interrelated

It really boils down to this: that all life is interrelated. We are all caught in an inescapable network of mutuality, tied into a single garment of destiny. Whatever affects one directly, affects all indirectly. We are made to live together because of the interrelated structure of reality. Did you ever stop to think that you can't leave for your job in the morning without being dependent on most of the world? You get up in the morning and go to the bathroom and reach over for the sponge, and that's handed to you by a Pacific islander. You reach for a bar of soap, and that's given to you at the hands of a Frenchman. And then you go into the kitchen to drink your coffee for the morning, and that's poured into your cup by a South American. And maybe you want tea: that's poured into your cup by a Chinese. Or maybe you're desirous of having cocoa for breakfast, and that's poured into your cup by a West African. And then you reach over for your toast, and that's given to you at the hands of an English-speaking farmer, not to mention the baker. And before you finish eating breakfast in the morning, you've depended on more than half of the world. This is the way our universe is structured, this is its interrelated quality. We aren't going to have peace on earth until we recognize this basic fact of the interrelated structure of all reality.

Now let me say, secondly, that if we are to have peace in the world, men and nations must embrace the nonviolent affirmation that ends and means must cohere. One of the great philosophical debates of history has been over the whole question of means and ends. And there have always been those who argued that the end justifies the means, that the means really aren't important. The important thing is to get to the end, you see.

So, if you're seeking to develop a just society, they say, the important thing is to get there, and the means are really unimportant; any means will do so long as they get you there—they may be violent, they may be untruthful means; they may even be unjust means to a just end. There have been those who have argued this throughout history. But we will never have peace in the world until men everywhere recognize that ends are not cut off from means, because the means represent the ideal in the making, and the end in process, and ultimately you can't reach good ends through evil means, because the means represent the seed and the end represents the tree.

It's one of the strangest things that all the great military geniuses of the world have talked about peace. The conquerors of old who came killing in pursuit of peace, Alexander, Julius Caesar, Charlemagne, and Napoleon, were akin in seeking a peaceful world order. If you will read *Mein Kampf* closely enough, you will discover that Hitler contended that everything he did in Germany was for peace. And the leaders of the world today talk eloquently about peace. Every time we drop our bombs in North Vietnam, President Johnson talks eloquently about peace. What is the problem? They are talking about peace as a distant goal, as an end we seek, but one day we must come to see that peace is not merely a distant goal we seek, but that it is a means by which we arrive at that goal. We must pursue peaceful ends through peaceful means. All of this is saying that, in the final analysis, means and ends must cohere because the end is pre-existent in the means, and ultimately destructive means cannot bring about constructive ends.

All Life Is Sacred

Now let me say that the next thing we must be concerned about if we are to have peace on earth and goodwill toward men is the nonviolent affirmation of the sacredness of all human life. Every man is somebody because he is a child of God. And so when we say "Thou shalt not kill," we're really saying that human life is too sacred to be taken on the battlefields of the world. Man is more than a tiny vagary of whirling electrons or a wisp of smoke from a limitless smoldering. Man is a child of God, made in His image, and therefore must be respected as such. Until men see this everywhere, until nations see this everywhere, we will be fighting wars. One day somebody should remind us that, even though there may be political and ideological differences between us, the Vietnamese are our brothers, the Russians are our brothers, the Chinese are our brothers; and one day we've got to sit down together at the table of brotherhood. But in Christ there is neither Jew nor Gentile. In Christ there is neither male nor female. In Christ there is neither Communist nor capitalist. In Christ, somehow, there is neither bound nor free. We are all one in Christ Jesus. And when we truly believe in the sacredness of human personality, we won't exploit people, we won't trample over people with the iron feet of oppression, we won't kill anybody.

Three Words for Love

There are three words for "love" in the Greek New Testament; one is the word "*eros*." Eros is a sort of aesthetic, romantic love. Plato used to talk about it a great deal in his dialogues, the yearning of the soul for the realm of the divine. And there is and can always be something beautiful about *eros*, even in its expressions of romance. Some of the most beautiful love in all of the world has been expressed this way.

Then the Greek language talks about *"philos,"* which is another word for love, and *philos* is a kind of intimate love between personal friends. This is the kind of love you have for those people that you get along with well, and those whom you like on this level you love because you are loved.

Then the Greek language has another word for love, and that is the *"agape."* *Agape* is more than romantic love, it is more than friendship. *Agape* is understanding, creative, redemptive goodwill toward all men. *Agape* is an overflowing love which seeks nothing in return. Theologians would say that it is the love of God operating in the human heart. When you rise to love on this level, you love all men not because you like them, not because their ways appeal to you, but you love them because God loves them. This is what Jesus meant when He said, "Love your enemies." And I'm happy that He didn't say, "Like your enemies," because there are some people that I find it pretty difficult to like. Liking is an affectionate emotion, and I can't like anybody who would bomb my home. I can't like anybody who would exploit me. I can't like anybody who would trample over me with injustices. I can't like them. I can't like anybody who threatens to kill me day in and day out. But Jesus reminds us that love is greater than liking. Love is understanding, creative, redemptive goodwill toward all men. And I think this is where we are, as a people, in our struggle for racial justice. We can't ever give up. We must work passionately and unrelentingly for first-class citizenship. We must never let up in our determination to remove every vestige of segregation and discrimination from our nation, but we shall not in the process relinquish our privilege to love.

Too Much Hate

I've seen too much hate to want to hate, myself, and I've seen hate on the faces of too many sheriffs, too many white citizens' councilors, and too many Klansmen of the South to want to hate, myself; and every time I see it, I say to myself, hate is too great a burden to bear. Somehow we must be able to stand up before our most bitter opponents and say: "We shall match your capacity to inflict suffering by our capacity to endure suffering. We will meet your physical force with soul force. Do to us what you will and we will still love you. We cannot in all good conscience obey your unjust laws and abide by the unjust system, because noncooperation with evil is as much a moral obligation as is cooperation with good, and so throw us in jail and we will still love you. Bomb our homes and threaten our children, and, as difficult as it is, we will still love you. Send your hooded perpetrators of violence into our communities at the midnight hour and drag us out on some wayside road and leave us half-dead as you beat us, and we will still love you. Send your propaganda agents around the country, and make it appear that we are not fit, culturally and otherwise, for integration, and we'll still love you. But be assured that we'll wear you down by our capacity to suffer, and one day we will win our freedom. We will not only win freedom for ourselves; we will so appeal to your heart and conscience that we will win you in the process, and our victory will be a double victory."

The Morality of the Universe

If there is to be peace on earth and goodwill toward men, we must finally believe in the ultimate morality of the universe, and believe that all reality hinges on moral foundations. Something must remind us of this as we once again stand in the Christmas season and think of the Easter season simultaneously, for the two somehow go together. Christ came to show us the way. Men love darkness rather than the light, and they crucified Him, and there on Good Friday on the Cross it was still dark, but then Easter came, and Easter is an eternal reminder of the fact that the truth-crushed earth will rise again. Easter justifies Carlyle in saying, "No lie can live for ever." And so this is our faith, as we continue to hope for peace on earth and goodwill toward men: let us know that in the process we have cosmic companionship.

I Have a Dream

In 1963, on a sweltering August afternoon, we stood in Washington, D.C., and talked to the nation about many things. Toward the end of that afternoon, I tried to talk to the nation about a dream that I had had, and I must confess to you today that not long after talking about that dream I started seeing it turn into a nightmare. I remember the first time I saw that dream turn into a nightmare, just a few weeks after I had talked about it. It was when four beautiful, unoffending, innocent Negro girls were murdered in a church in Birmingham, Alabama. I watched that dream turn into a nightmare as I moved through the ghettos of the nation and saw my black brothers and sisters perishing on a lonely island of poverty in the midst of a vast ocean of material prosperity, and saw the nation doing nothing to grapple with the Negroes' problem of poverty. I saw that dream turn into a nightmare as I watched my black brothers and sisters in the midst of anger and understandable outrage, in the midst of their hurt, in the midst of their disappointment, turn to misguided riots to try to solve that problem. I saw that dream turn into a nightmare as I watched the war in Vietnam escalating, and as I saw so-called military advisers, 16,000 strong, turn into fighting soldiers until today over 500,000 American boys are fighting on Asian soil. Yes, I am personally the victim of deferred dreams, of blasted hopes, but in spite of that I close today by saying I still have a dream, because, you know, you can't give up in life. If you lose hope, somehow you lose that vitality that keeps life moving, you lose that courage to be, that quality that helps you to go on in spite of all. And so today I still have a dream.

I have a dream that one day men will rise up and come to see that they are made to live together as brothers. I still have a dream this morning that one day every Negro in this country, every colored person in the world, will be judged on the basis of the content of his character rather than the color of his skin, and every man will respect the dignity and worth of human personality. I still have a dream today that one day the idle industries of Appalachia will be revitalized, and the empty stomachs of Mississippi will be filled, and brotherhood will be more than a few words at the end of a prayer, but rather the first order of business on every legislative agenda. I still have a dream today that one day justice will roll down like water, and righteousness like a mighty stream. I still have a dream today that in all of our state houses and city halls men will be elected to go there who will do justly and love mercy and walk humbly with their God. I still have a dream today that one day war will come to an end, that men will beat their swords into plowshares and their spears into pruning hooks, that nations will no longer rise up against nations, neither will they study war any more. I still have a dream today that one day the lamb and the lion will lie down together and every man will sit under his own vine and fig tree and none shall be afraid. I still have a dream today that one day every valley shall be exalted and every mountain and hill will be made low, and rough places will be made smooth and the crooked places straight, and the glory of the Lord shall be revealed, and all flesh shall see it together. I still have a dream that with this faith we will be able to adjourn the councils of despair and bring new light into the dark chambers of pessimism. With this faith we will be able to speed up the day when there will be peace on earth and goodwill toward men. It will be a glorious day, the morning stars will sing together, and the sons of God will shout for joy.

READING
to Enjoy
a Personal Voice

This section of Part 1 is a collection of writings that allows readers to know the authors directly. The emphasis of these selections is on the writer's personal feelings, experiences, imagination, and sensitivities.

In other words, the writers are writing to express themselves. Since the writing is the *expression* of the person writing it, the forms are as individual as the person writing. There are personal reminiscences, familiar essays, poems, business memos and contracts, announcements and invitations, letters, prayers and meditations, and even an obituary.

You will not be interested in this section for any obviously utilitarian reason, although, in the long run, such pieces of authentic personal expression are often some of the most useful we ever read. They are useful because we find *ourselves* in the writing, too— our own lives, dreams, thoughts, and experiences. Other people telling their stories and speaking in their voices awaken us to our stories and our voices. We identify with them and are enlarged by their expressing what we, too, have thought, felt, or experienced.

In the first selection in this section, *Rosalynn Carter* writes about the day her husband became president of the United States of America—her pride, her sense of responsibility, and her joy.

Then, *Shirley MacLaine* tells us what it is really like to be a dancer—the practice, the performance, the pain and the passion. What it is like to dance with God.

Andy Rooney writes about how much he enjoys the rain, and you are reminded of your own love for the sound of the rain beating down on a tin roof.

Israel Shenker gives us a humorous tongue-in-cheek account of his dream of climbing all 276 Munros. (A Munro is any Scottish hill at least 3,000 feet high.) Reading Shenker we remember all those athletic feats *we* planned to accomplish but soon discarded.

Twenty-one immigrant factory workers wrote a contract for the New York Lotto Game in which they each won $650,793. The halting English with which they wrote this contract does not hinder in any way the clear intent of these men's plans or the partnership of their dreams.

Roger Enrico, president of Pepsi-Cola, wrote a memo on April 23, 1985, as a result of what may go down in marketing history as one of the biggest coups of all time: Coca-Cola was withdrawing its product from the marketplace to reformulate Coke to be "more like Pepsi." Enrico's memo informed all Pepsi-Cola employees that everybody could take the day off Friday. Victory was sweet!

Columnist Bob Greene's journal entry tells of his little daughter's first year of life, while a fellow architect pays tribute to Buckminster Fuller upon the completion of that grand old man's last year of life.

There are personal expressions of the cycle of love in relationships: falling in love, marriage, divorce, friendship. There are letters that say good-bye, and a poem that says hello—to life! And, in conclusion, there's a prayer from *Saint Francis of Assisi* and a gentle meditation from *Saint Teresa of Avila*.

Read and enjoy.

ROSALYNN CARTER

The Day We Moved into the White House

I t is early, too early, when we wake up on January 20, 1977, in Blair House the morning Jimmy is to be sworn in as the thirty-ninth President of the United States. It's dark outside and bone-chilling cold, so cold that the outdoor concert on the Mall last night had to be canceled for fear the mouthpieces of the instruments would stick to the musicians' mouths. In Union Station, the doors on a train filled with people coming to the inauguration froze shut and couldn't be thawed open for several hours.

Now, at 5:30 A.M., Jimmy and I can see the White House dimly across the street, a few lights twinkling in the morning dawn. Already two hundred soldiers are at work along Pennsylvania Avenue, using jackhammers to break up the ice on the sidewalks in preparation for the inaugural parade.

I look at Jimmy, the President-elect, the man for whom the Kennedy Center was filled just last night with some of America's greatest artists performing for him, the one person who would command all the world's attention today. He is still the same person who spent yesterday morning with me, mopping up the garage in Plains after the hot water pipes burst from the cold, the same son who had called Miss Lillian later to admit the motorcade had forgotten to pick her up on the way to the airport. "Stay right there," he told her. "We'll send someone for you."

This morning we are all safely in Washington somewhere, even Misty Malarky Ying Yang, Amy's cat, who had crawled all over the plane on the flight from Plains. Jimmy, Amy, and I have an early breakfast in our bathrobes in the Blair House bedroom. While Jimmy works on his inaugural address, listening to it for the last time on his tape recorder, I fuss over my hair. I had a haircut and a permanent just before we came to Washington, and my hair feels strange . . . and much too short and curly. In a futile attempt to make it look longer, I roll it on big curlers, but it still comes out just as short. It seems incredible that the day my husband is to be sworn in as President, what worries me most is my hair!

And the cold. Jimmy asked me a few days ago what I thought about walking instead of riding from the Capitol to the White House after the inauguration. The Secret Service, he told me, had cleared it if there was no publicity and absolutely no one knew about it ahead of time. Thomas Jefferson had walked to the Capitol for his inauguration, and I thought it was a wonderful idea, a symbol of the open and accessible atmosphere Jimmy hoped to return to the presidency. Now, suddenly, I'm not so sure. Will Amy, at age nine, be able to make it all the way in the cold? Will I have to get in the car and let Jimmy walk without me? And what about Chip's wife, Caron, who is eight months pregnant? But it's too late for second thoughts. It's time to dress, and warmly. For good luck, I put three small crosses on the gold chain around my neck, one each for Amy, our grandson, Jason, and the new grandbaby yet to be born. For warmth, I put on my boots and my knee-length knit underwear. It doesn't seem like the most stylish way to dress for your husband's inauguration, and I laugh at myself a little as I bundle up, but I'm determined to enjoy this day, which may be the most important one in my life, without my teeth chattering.

Live Wisely Under This Roof

As the day begins to unfold, I soon forget completely about my hair and almost about the cold. The significance of the events becomes far more important and humbling. Chip, who had been working with the inaugural committee in Washington since the election, had been to several churches in the city and had picked the First Baptist Church as the one he thought we would like to join. Now we assemble there with our family, the Mondales, and several of the Cabinet and staff members for a private prayer service. The Reverend Nelson Price, a special friend from Georgia, invokes the words of President John Adams, words that are inscribed on a White House mantel: "I pray Heaven to bestow the best of blessings on this house and on all that shall hereafter inhabit it. May none but honest and wise men ever rule under this roof." The thoughts Nelson borrowed from Thomas Jefferson are just as pertinent to what Jimmy hopes to bring to his presidency: "Our generation needs persons with hearts like unto that of James Monroe, who was so honest that if you turned his soul inside out, there would not be a spot on it."

It's now Jimmy's turn to live "wisely" under the White House roof, to try to keep his soul as spotless as James Monroe's, to become one of the leaders children will read about in history books. How I wish his father could have been here to see him take the oath of office—my father as well. All these thoughts and more are milling around in my head as I ride in the limousine from the White House, where we all gathered briefly, to the Capitol. Jimmy rides with President Ford and I follow with Mrs. Ford. I'm sure her thoughts are as deep and varied as mine, but like most people, we do not express them. Instead we chat, mostly about Camp David, where the Fords had just spent their last weekend. The food is so delicious there, Mrs. Ford tells me, that she is going to have to go on a diet.

I Have Never Felt So Proud

We are met at the Capitol and taken to a small waiting room, where I talk with Happy Rockefeller, Betty Ford, and Joan Mondale. I feel numb. All that Jimmy and I have worked for so hard is about to become a reality. Then it is time, and Joan Mondale and I walk down the aisle between the dignitaries and our families to take our positions on the presidential platform. Dimly I hear applause from the crowd. This is the moment I have anticipated so long, but all I can do is go through the motions. Then it is President Ford's turn to make his way down the aisle, and I tremble slightly as the Marine Band strikes up "Ruffles and Flourishes" and "Hail to the Chief." The next time they play it, it will be for Jimmy.

As the sound of the brass, the vastness of the crowd, and the American flags snapping in the cold wind contribute to the overwhelming sense of pageantry, Amy slips over onto my lap. She is used to big crowds and had been to Jimmy's inauguration as governor of Georgia, but she seems awed by the scene. She is old enough to know what is going on, though, and I am thankful for her presence. She comforts me at this moment as much as I comfort her.

The band plays the Navy Hymn, one of Jimmy's favorites from his days at the Naval Academy, and more memories stir . . . of our Navy days and my sentimental visits with Jimmy to the chapel at Annapolis, when I was young and filled with the anticipation of an exciting and unknown future. The hymn also reminds me of John Kennedy, not only of the excitement and promise he brought to our country, but of his funeral as well, when that excitement was extinguished too soon. I look out at the sea of faces on all sides, as far as the eye can see, and feel the air of expectancy and hope and promise in the crowd. I also feel an awesome responsibility now that Jimmy is about to be President. All these people. And we are responsible to them, and for them.

Jimmy appears, and a sudden hush falls over the crowd before an explosion of applause and cheers. "We love you, Jimmy," someone yells. Then another: "God be with you, Jimmy." I stand to join him at the front of the platform and hold the Bible his mother gave him a few years ago while he takes the oath of office. It is a moment I will never forget. I look right at him, the same person I've looked at so long, and smile, thinking what a wonderful thing this is for our country, what a good, honest, and capable man we are getting for our President, a man who is going to work hard and wisely for all the people of the country, not just the elite few. I have never felt so proud.

Even the words of his inaugural address, one of the shortest in American history, sound fresh and new to me, though I have heard and read them many times before. We studied all the inaugural addresses of past presidents in our den in Plains, and I read the drafts over and over as Jimmy was writing them, surrounded by bits and scraps of paper. I even made a small contribution, suggesting that he add the strengthening of the American family as one of his goals for the presidency. Now these words, so familiar and yet so new, bring tears not only to my eyes, but to the eyes of many around us as well. And the applause of the crowd takes the frost out of the air as he finishes.

Jimmy Carter has been inaugurated, and the celebration begins. . . .

We Take a Tour

On our first afternoon in the White House, the photographs I had taken home from my first visit were becoming a reality. Our family roamed from one end to the other of the second-floor hall, which runs the entire length of the house, with beautiful semicircular windows at each end. It is an art gallery, with masterpieces on the walls, comfortable sitting areas, and many bookshelves. We had read about the secret stairway that connects the presidential living quarters on the second floor to the third floor, and the children quickly found it, pushing a portion of the wall that opens to reveal the stairway. We were surrounded by history, evoking both recent and past memories of American presidencies. We explored the Lincoln Bedroom and the Queen's Bedroom, on the east end of the hall, and found Nixon's favorite room, the Lincoln Sitting Room, which adjoins the Lincoln Bedroom. It's a small, cozy room with a corner fireplace, and Julie Nixon Eisenhower once said that her father liked a fire so much that he would build one here even in warm weather and turn on the air conditioning. Tucked away behind a stairway was a little room that Pat Nixon had made into a beauty parlor.

Originally, when the White House was built, the President's offices were also on the second floor, and Jimmy's favorite room became the Treaty Room, which had been the Cabinet room for ten administrations. It looked solid and masculine and was decorated in deep green and maroon; when I saw it I thought a man would feel comfortable smoking a cigar in this room. Most of its furniture was bought by Ulysses S. Grant, including a walnut table on which the peace treaty ending the Spanish-American War was signed. Later, we took this same table out onto the front lawn for the signing of another historic peace treaty, that between Egypt and Israel.

Our excitement mounted that first evening as we explored the third floor and found other rooms that would become very important to our family life in the White House. There were two guest bedrooms, a billiard room, laundry and ironing rooms, and the Solarium with a magnificent view of the Washington Monument. The Solarium had served as a kindergarten for the Kennedy children and as a courting place for the Johnson girls. The Johnsons had put in a soda fountain for the young people. It became the favorite hangout for our children and their friends, the lovely setting for my Spanish lessons with Gay Vance, and a favorite spot to watch Saturday afternoon football games on television with the children.

We even went out on the rooftop that first night, something we would do often during the next four years. One can walk almost all around the house just behind the façade that is part of the familiar picture of the White House, and the view of the heavens is wondrous. Jeffrey, who is a keen amateur astronomer, used his own telescope on the roof to view the stars and planets and occasionally would borrow a larger one from the Naval Observatory. Jeffrey and Amy used to call the Dial-a-Phenomenon recording at the Smithsonian to learn what was happening in the sky, and on special nights we would all go out and view the phenomena. There was also a nice wide open space on the roof just outside the Solarium, where we could put the playpen for Chip and Caron's new baby as well as sunbathe in privacy.

No Shakespeare in the House

Back inside the long hall, we took a quick look at the extensive library. Bookshelves lined the hall on the third floor as well as on the second floor, and the variety of books looked wonderful to this family of avid readers. Amy could do her homework from the sets of encyclopedias, collections of U.S. histories, and books on the presidency as well as American novels, nonfiction, and picture books. These volumes were almost exclusively written by or about people in the United States. One night Jimmy was looking for a quotation from *Macbeth* and, amazingly, we could find no Shakespeare in the White House. There were plenty of other books to choose from. Many authors send personalized copies of their works to the President, and the American Booksellers Association gives every President two hundred and fifty new volumes at the beginning of his term. It's a wonderful gift, and we asked for a portion of them each year, instead of getting them all in one batch, so we would always have a supply of current issues; for the first time the ABA added selections of children's stories as well for Amy. But even with all these books and bookshelves, we needed space for Jimmy's personal volumes, so we had the carpenters make a bookcase to cover most of one wall in Jimmy's second-floor study. A beautiful piece, it was made of mahogany, with doors at the bottom that locked for the notebooks that contained his daily diary notes. The day the carpenters installed the bookcase, I overheard one say to the other: "We haven't had a President who read this much in a long time."

The living arrangements we had chosen were perfect for our family. Amy was on the second floor with us; Jeff and Chip and their wives, on the third floor, with a nursery all ready for the new baby. Jeff was going to attend George Washington University, and Chip would be working for the Democratic National Committee in Washington. We would miss Judy and Jack, but Jack was practicing law with his father-in-law in Calhoun, Georgia, and they could only come to Washington for visits. We delighted in the children and enjoyed their comings and goings and their friends. The third floor had not been completed until the Truman renovation, and I wondered how Benjamin Harrison had fitted his large family—which included his wife, her ninety-year-old father, her sister and niece; their son Russell and his wife and daughter; and their daughter Mary McKee and two infants—into five rooms on the second floor. No wonder Mrs. Harrison began the campaign for enlarging the White House.

Jimmy Behind the President's Desk

We hadn't finished the tour that first afternoon before we lost Jimmy. He had been anxious not only to visit the Oval Office for the first time as President, but to keep an appointment with Max Cleland, a Vietnam veteran and triple amputee whom he was going to ask to become head of the Veterans' Administration. After a while, the children and I walked over to the West Wing ourselves, laughing happily and talking about the excitement of the day. All of a sudden, as we entered the Oval Office, no one was saying anything. We were just standing there, looking at the room and at Jimmy, sitting behind the President's desk, framed by the President's flag and the flag of the United States. It was an unforgettable moment.

I had to catch my breath to believe I was really there, to absorb the reality that my husband was actually President of the United States and that I was First Lady. The Oval Office is filled with the history of our country. It is where presidents have struggled with decisions that affected the whole world. Jimmy grinned, and I smiled back at him. He looked just right sitting there.

Dancing in the Light

I remember the choreography contest. We were allowed complete freedom to choreograph what we wanted. I wasn't interested in "steps" or matching movements. I wanted to express what I was feeling. As I was discussing it with Mother, she revealingly said, "Why don't you choreograph movement that expresses a person willing to die for her art?" At first, that sounded melodramatic to me, but her *feeling* was so intense, I realized it was "acceptable" because that was just where she lived.

I chose some Russian symphonic music. I designed my body movements to express the anguish of the Russian soul in its suffering. I dragged myself across the floor as though being held down by an invisible force and finally convulsed into an outburst of triumph in the last movement.

When I performed my choreography, Mary Day had me do it twice. The second time, I spontaneously altered the final position.

She gave me second prize because she felt I had been more involved with performing than with choreographing. I felt spontaneity was essential to choreography.

Thus began my personal conflict with the classical forms of dancing and consequently the dilemma of whether I wanted to be a dancer or a star. When I graduated from high school I went straight to New York and into the chorus of a Broadway show. I was finally a professional dancer.

An Art That Impresses the Soul

Dancers, or gypsies, as we refer to each other, are soldiers with talent, artists who are not allowed freedom, exponents of the living body who are in constant pain.

No one who hasn't done it can possibly understand what the inherent contradictions mean. It is an art that imprints on the soul. It is with you every moment, even after you give it up. It is with you every moment of your day and night. It is an art that expresses itself in how you walk, how you eat, how you make love, and how you do nothing. It is the art of the body, and as long as a dancer possesses a body, he or she feels the call of expression in dancer's terms. Dancers are always aware of how they look physically. Such is the name of the game. I, as a dancer, may move awkwardly, but I am always aware of it. I may profess to be relaxing, but my body speaks to me when the time is up. I may revel in what strength I have, but I always know I could use more. And I always know when I look beautiful, when the line of a crossed leg is exquisitely angled, when my posture denotes certitude, and when a proud bearing commands respect. I, as a dancer, also know that when depression sets in, I cave in in the middle, become slovenly in my movements, and find it very difficult to look in the mirror.

I, as a dancer, may run with graceful strides to catch a cab, but I am intrinsically involved with every crevice of the street because I don't want to become injured. I may adore a certain dress, but I will never wear it if it doesn't enhance the body line. I choose clothes not for style or color or fashion, but for line . . . a dancer's obsession.

Each Slice of Chocolate Cake

When you have observed the progress of your body year after year in the dancing-class mirror, you are aware of each centimeter and bulge. You are aware of how beads of sweat look when they fall glistening from the end of a strand of your hair because you have worked hard.

You know that each slice of chocolate cake you indulge in the night before will have to be lifted in an arabesque the following day.

You learn how to apply your dancer's knowledge to small everyday tasks, how to warm a pot of milk and set a table at the same time. How to talk on the phone and stretch your hamstrings on a tabletop in order to save time. You can deftly change your entire wardrobe in an airplane seat without being noticed because your body is your domain of manipulation and you know you can do anything with it.

Your relationship to pain becomes complex. There is good pain and bad pain. Good pain becomes a sensation you miss. Bad pain becomes a sensation of danger. With age you learn to pace yourself. You learn that breathing is as important to the movement as the physical technique itself. You learn to never breathe *in*. You understand that nature involuntarily takes care of that, as it does when you sleep. You learn to only breathe *out*. By doing that, you release the toxins in the body. Whenever you engage in a high kick, you breathe out toward the kick. With that, you know you can go on kicking indefinitely.

An Art of Honesty

And the personality of a gypsy is volatile. With a solo artist, eruptions of temperament are expected; with gypsies they are misunderstood.

Gypsies and soloists have put in the same amount of time in class, have slogged through their own self-doubt, and have endeavored to touch the soul of their being in similarly confrontational terms. To dance at all is to confront oneself. It is the art of honesty. You are completely exposed when you dance. Your physical health is exposed. Your self-image is exposed. Your psychological health is exposed, and your senses of humor and balance are exposed, to say nothing of how you relate to time, space, and the observer. It is impossible to dance out of the side of your mouth. You tell the truth when you dance. If you lie, you hurt yourself. If you "mark" it and don't go full out, if you don't commit your body totally, you hurt yourself. And if you don't show up for work, it is relatively impossible to live with the guilt. That is why dancers give the impression of being masochistic. Masochism is not a dancer's gimmick. Dancers fear being hurt. They do, however, enjoy the challenge of overcoming. That is, after all, what the art of dancing is all about. Overcoming the limitations of the body.

Big Black Giant

Dancers know that the mind, body, and spirit are inextricably intertwined.

You know it the first time you face an audience. There is "the big black giant" (as Oscar Hammerstein put it) out there and your task is to make them feel something through your body. You know you have to mean it. You know you have to have faith in your balance, your flexibility, and your strength. You know also that they will readily identify with your physical feats because they all have bodies too. You know that if you trip and fall, you humiliate *them* because that is what they are afraid of in themselves. You know that the easier you make it seem, the more hope you give them for themselves. You know they are rooting for you, otherwise their attendance would be called into question. You represent what they would like to be able to do themselves, because each and every one of them have their own problems with their bodies.

And so you continue day after day to keep yourself in shape, driving each muscle one last mile in order to become a role model for what can be done with the body. . . .

You Begin to Soar

The mirror is your conscience. You've rehearsed with its definitive image in front of you for weeks. Then the choreographer turns you around, away from the mirror. You are on your own. You're not sure where you are. Your image is no longer there to ratify your existence. Your orientation to space is altered. You become aware of the meaning of movement and your need to communicate to the audience because you can no longer communicate with your own image. The music sounds different. Your spacing is off. You are unable to check out your line, not only in relation to yourself, but also in relation to whomever else you may be dancing with.

Then you begin to soar, you begin to become what you mean. You find a hidden subtext in your movement. You bend and flow and jump to the music when you allow it to carry you aloft. You begin to fill every space with body language; no move is gratuitous. You learn to think ahead, knowing which combination of moves requires the most anticipation. You learn which movements are the most fulfilling and which are defiantly dangerous. You employ shortcuts and pain-saving devices. You know how much breath you'll need to pace yourself.

Your shoes become your support system. If the size varies one centimeter, it throws your balance askew. If there is a clump of harmless dust on the floor, you eye it at every available moment until you dance out of its range because the slightest inconsistency under your moving weight can cause you to lose your footing.

You test the speed of the floor under the rubber soles of your shoes. You know that if the speed is slow, you'll have to exert that much more effort in turns. Yet if it's too fast, you'll lose your control.

Then you begin to need the lights, the costumes, the scenery, and the audience.

You leave everything you learned in the classroom and the rehearsal hall behind you. All of it was only the preparation, the bare bones of expression.

You mold the choreography with additional magic. Your costume feels foreign to you until you learn to work with it, use it, enhance it, make it part of the movement. You complain at first that it inhibits the movement, but you know from experience that it always feels that way at first. You rustle the skirt and toss a scarf, rendering new meaning to the original movement.

Then you have a dress rehearsal with costumes, lights, and a full complement of musicians. Up to that time you have danced to a work light and a piano. Now you feel the complete musical poetry of the composer and orchestrator. There are levels of subtlety to the music that you never dreamed would be there. It is full, rich, awe-inspiring. It confuses you at first because you had been used to dancing only to the melody of one piano. Now there are forty musicians who are as integral a part of the overall illusion as you, the performer, are. You familiarize yourself with the totality of the sound and find that the music kicks your movement to another level and makes you certain you can do anything.

Then come the lights, lovingly painted from the front of the theater. You realize that every nuance of your face and body will be visible. The pink jells leave your skin with a silky glow. The spotlight following you burns through your eyes. The bumper lights stage right and left add dimensional color to your arms and legs. You can see absolutely no one in the audience. It is alienatingly black. Then you realize it is all up to you. You are a performer. You forget everything you ever learned. You forget the intricate processes of technique. You forget your anxieties and your pain. You even forget who you are. You become one with the music, the lights, and the collective spirit of the audience. You know you are there to help uplift them. They want to feel better about themselves and each other.

Then they react. Their generously communal applause means they like you—love you even. They send you energy and you send it back. You participate with each other. And the cycle continues. You leap, soar, turn, extend, and bend. They clap, yell, whistle, stomp, and laugh. You acknowledge their appreciation for what they see and give them more. And so it goes.

Dancing with God

The long years were worth it. The miraculous magic of expression overrides everything. It becomes everything. Once again, you realize you are everything you are aware of. You are part of the audience. They are a part of you. You and they are one expressing talent. The talent of giving and receiving, of resonating to a greater spirit by means of the body; the talent of souls appreciating one another, of together creating life on a larger scale. The talent of understanding the shadow awareness that makes us all one, part of a divine perfection which is the essence of sharing. You are dancing with God. You are dancing with yourself. You are dancing in the light.

ANDY ROONEY

Let It Rain

It is raining as I write. I'm snug and comfortable here in this room. I'm surrounded by familiar things and tools like this typewriter that I know how to use. The rain can't get at me. I'm dry. Being warm and dry inside when it's cold and wet outside is one of the few victories man scores over Nature. We ought to enjoy it. This isn't a wet cave I've crept into in order to avoid the worst of the storm. This a comfortable home where I can forget all about the rain if I choose to.

I've never understood why Longfellow wrote that famous line of his or why it's famous. You remember:

> Into each life some rain must fall,
> Some days must be dark and dreary.

It's clear that Longfellow associated rain with all the bad things that happen to us. I don't associate rain with that at all. Maybe it was raining when I was born. Rain is as important to people as it is to plants. I've lived in climates where they don't have much rain and hated it. I'm not the cactus type. The human brain needs a good, hard rain at least once every two weeks . . . snow if it's cold. You can't keep going out in the bright sun every day without having it get on your nerves and dry you up. Maybe smog is nature's way of protecting Los Angelenos from all that sun they used to get.

One of the few lines I remember from what little Chaucer I read is better than Longfellow's. I never really understood Chaucer's olde English spelling but even that adds flavor to the lines he wrote about rain:

> Lord, this is an huge rayn!
> This were a weder for to slepen inne.

That has a wonderful feel to it and it evokes memories of all the good Saturday mornings I've decided to turn over and sleep for another hour under the lulling rhythm of the rayn on the roof.

People are always knocking rain but I don't think they mean it. It's just pass-the-time-of-day weather talk. We're all expected to make negative comments about a rainy day. "It's raining cats and dogs," someone will say. I've never understood what that means or where the phrase came from. No rain ever reminds me of cats and dogs coming down from the clouds and I don't know why we keep saying it.

I went to a football game in the rain earlier this year and had the time of my life. I had rubber shoes, a sailor's rubber, foul-weather suit and a wide-brimmed rain hat that kept the water from going down my neck. In addition, I had a four-foot-square rubber sheet that I brought along to keep on my lap. Under that I kept my program, my lunch and a thermos bottle filled with hot chicken broth. There I sat in a dry little island, surrounded by a sea of rain trying unsuccessfully to get at me. I was happily isolated from every outside distraction except the good game on the lighted playing field below me.

The players on the field were as happy as I was although it would be hard to explain that to anyone who has never played football. Football players don't mind rain at all unless they're quarterbacks or pass catchers. Once a player gets sloppy and wet all over, it's fun slopping around in the mud. It's John Madden's kind of football weather.

Nothing is perfect, of course, and there are one or two little things that keep me from being totally enthusiastic about rain. First there's that persistent leak in the back corner of the basement by my woodworking shop. It isn't much but a small puddle always forms on the cellar floor after a hard rain and I can't seem to find a way to stop it.

The only other thing I don't like about rain is that eight or ten inches of pants between the tops of my shoes and the bottom of my raincoat that always get soaked when I go out in a downpour.

Other than those two minor inconveniences, I say, let it rain!

ISRAEL SHENKER

The Munros: Dreams of Glory

People climb Everest because it's there. But the heights of Scotland are here, and I haven't stirred myself.

From the windows of my home in Perthshire I can see mountains all about, and I dream of turning to the Scottish Mountaineering Club Journal and finding myself listed as the latest Munroist.

Climb All 276 Munros

A Munroist is anyone who has climbed all 276 Munros—Scottish hills of at least 3,000 feet. They are named for Sir Hugh Munro, who compiled Munro's Tables of 3,000-footers. He was a pioneer mountaineer who never flinched, even when—as at Diranean—they had to scrape him down with a knife to remove the frozen snow. In 1919, when he died, he had only two Munros to go—Carn Cloichmhuilinn and the Inaccessible Pinnacle.

The first Munroist was the Rev. Archibald Eneas Robertson, who conquered his 276th Munro in 1901 and celebrated by kissing the summit cairn and his wife, in that order. It was another 22 years before a second Munroist triumphed, and the third added the "Furth of Scotland"—all the hills above 3,000 feet in England, Wales and Ireland. ("Furth" means "outside.")

In 1974, Hamish Brown logged all the Munros in a single traverse: 1,639 miles, 449,000 feet of ascent, 42 food parcels. He endured freezing cold (tent pegs stuck to his fingers, his tent folded like cardboard), burning heat (the sun fried his ears), boggy ground, rain, snow, ice, loneliness, depression, wind that knocked him down, nocturnal mice in his boots, French girls who shared his hut and snored, a detached boot sole and a misplaced spoon (he ate Rice Krispies with a knife). He was determined to finish the Munros before the stalking began in August, since mountaineers can be dead ringers for deer. Mr. Brown has now done the Munros seven times, the Furth five. The most recent list of Munroists totals 322. Alister Sword (No. 321) climbed his first Munro in 1936, his last in 1984.

William Wallace, the 52-year-old honorary secretary of the Scottish Mountaineering Club, has been climbing for 35 years. "I don't suffer from Munrosis," he insisted, but he has done 215, including the Inaccessible Pinnacle.

You Have to Be Lean

When I told him I dreamed of becoming a Munroist, he swallowed hard. "It's best to have a good power-height ratio," he said, "which means you have to be lean, and be able to pull yourself up with one hand."

"One of the principal hazards is the very rapid changes in weather," Mr. Wallace said. "You can have a balmy day and within two hours a raging arctic storm." (Notes a Scottish Mountaineering Club "Guide": "We must remember that it may be winter *any day in the year* on the higher hills of Scotland.")

In the Cairngorm Mountains conditions are arctic indeed, with gale-force winds blowing more than 200 days a year. On Ben Nevis, in Scotland, Britain's highest mountain (4,410 feet), a relative humidity of 6 percent has been registered—and the snow can often be seen and heard evaporating. The average annual rainfall on Ben Nevis is 134 inches. Showers, mist and fog are everywhere present, sleet and hail common. Avalanches can be triggered by low-flying planes or helicopters as well as by sudden thaws. "Almost every winter there's a thaw followed by a very rapid freeze, and then the hills are encased in armor plate," said Mr. Wallace, "and when there's thunder and lightning your hair can start sizzling and burning."

He spoke feelingly of midges, the miniature flies that bite with unadulterated malice. "Last August we were just about demented by the midges," he said. "I come out in red spots, others come out in bumps." Mr. Wallace has encountered only two live adders. "You may not die from their bite," he said, "but it's wise to be careful." In the rutting season, stags have been known to attack and kill.

I'll Climb the Stairs

The very notion of Munros is in peril from metrication, which converts them into hills of 914 meters or more. "It's silly at 914 meters," said Mr. Wallace, "but it's magic at 3,000 feet."

He told me that the application to join the Scottish Mountaineering Club is six pages long, that applicants must have rock-climbing experience of "Very Difficult" standard and must have bagged 50 Munros, a third of them in snow and ice. My face fell. "Start on the easy hills," he advised. "Gradually work up until you can do more and more."

I am starting at the beginning, with the stairs at home. From level zero to the next floor the height is 8 feet 8 inches, which means that 346 ascents equal one Munro. On reaching the second floor I am breathing heavily. What's the rush? A 75-year-old man has just been accepted by the Scottish Mountaineering Club, so I have years to go—or stay.

Let's Seal a Deal

Winner of New York Lotto Game '41M
8/21/1985

We are joint together purchase this Lotto ticket on August 21st 1985 Wendesday. All the 21 people are the shareowner of this ticket and will get the prize. As a group we will share the money equaly & fairly to each other and make the payment to 21 shares to everyone of the shareownes.

Sign of shareowner =

1.	8.	15.
2.	9.	16.
3.	10.	17.
4.	11.	18.
5.	12.	19.
6.	13.	20.
7.	14.	21.

Around 3 P.M. on Wednesday, August 21, 1985, Celso Manuel Garcete, Philbert Benjamin, Frank Sukchai, Walter Sobolak, Peter Lee, Chit Wah Tse, Jaroslaw Siwy, Luis Ramos, Lajos Kato, Kidong Yeung, Mariano Martinez, Joseph Smith, and nine other members of a work group that assembles printing press components at Hantscho Inc. in Mount Vernon, New York, decided to form a lottery pool. Each man contributed a dollar to the pool, and Peter Lee went around the corner to buy the tickets. By Thursday night, these immigrant workers from China, the Dominican Republic, Poland, Trinidad, Thailand, Yugoslavia, Paraguay, and Hungary had each won $650,793. Their dreams had come true!

Got 'Ya

To all Pepsi Bottlers and
Pepsi-Cola Company personnel:

It gives me great pleasure to offer each of you my heartiest congratulations.

After 87 years of going at it eyeball to eyeball, the other guy just blinked.

Coca-Cola is withdrawing their product from the marketplace, and is reformulating brand Coke to be "more like Pepsi." Too bad Ripley's not around . . . he could have had a field day with this one.

There is no question the long-term market success of Pepsi has forced this move.

Everyone knows when something is right it doesn't need changing.

Maybe they finally realized what most of us have known for years . . . Pepsi tastes better than Coke.

Well, people in trouble tend to do desperate things . . . and we'll have to keep our eye on them.

But for now, I say victory is sweet, and we have earned a celebration. We're going to declare a holiday on Friday.

Enjoy!

Best Regards,

Roger Enrico

Roger Enrico
President, Chief Executive Officer
Pepsi-Cola U.S.A.

Good Morning, Merry Sunshine

July 19—Mornings are the time. I have always been in a rush in the morning; I am up and in the shower and out the door as fast as I can manage; I can't wait to get to work and get started on the day's column.

Until now.

Mornings are the time that I almost can't believe how lucky we are to have Amanda here. I'll wake up—Susan will be asleep from having fed her just before dawn—and I'll go into Amanda's room, and she will just be stirring awake. Good morning, merry sunshine.

I'll pick her up, and she will blink and look around; she will just be coming out of sleep, too, and she won't know quite where she is. So she will make her noises and stare up at the ceiling, and finally she will fix her eyes on me and start to smile.

I'll take her in the bedroom and put her on the bed, right between Susan and me. I'll pull the covers up so that she's like a real person in a real bed; I'm not sure she knows what this means yet, but she seems to like it.

For ten or fifteen minutes I'll talk softly to her; even if she's hungry again and ready to cry, she'll hold off at least this long. I'll talk to her and tell her stories, and although she has no idea what I'm saying, apparently she likes the sound of the words—she looks at me as if to encourage me. I'll stick my first finger out and touch her hand, and she will grasp it tightly and grin with the exertion.

When Susan wakes up she will roll over; we're past the point now where it's really shocking when we realize Amanda is with us, so Susan will just say, "Well, who do we have *here*," and now Amanda will turn toward her and give her the smile.

I'm sure this is no different from the way things have been in a hundred million households over the centuries. But it's new for us, and I can't compare it to anything I've experienced before. Things change daily for Amanda; every day something different comes into her life, and because of that it's as if every day is her birthday. And morning is the time we feel it; morning, in that hour before the world begins, as in the quiet of the new day she lies between us, is when my good fortune shakes me so hard I almost feel weak.

JOHN PASTIER

R. Buckminster Fuller
1896–1983

I live on earth at present, and I *don't know what I am. I know that I am not a category. I am not a thing—a noun. I seem to be a verb, an evolutionary process—an integral function of the universe.*

On July 1, the verb changed its tense from present to past, when R. Buckminster Fuller died at 87 in Los Angeles. Ah, but I have already fallen into one of those obsolescent thought patterns that Bucky Fuller was so fond of identifying and correcting. Past and present tenses seem to be illusory: "Time is not linear but probably consists of wave propagations in all directions simultaneously. Allatonceness." This thought was neither new nor original with Fuller. An Irish priest proposed something similar in a religion class I attended in the Bronx, when he attributed the ability to see all time in one instant to God. Fuller's concerns were often religious, although he took pains to couch them in the language of either the material universe or the processes of human thought.

But the best way to convey his concerns, as well as his distinctive way of communication, is by quoting a statement he called "What I am trying to do":

As a conscious means of hopefully competent participation by humanity in its own evolutionary trending while employing only the unique advantages inhering exclusively to the individual who takes and maintains the economic initiative in the face of the formidable physical capital and credit advantages of the massive corporations and political states I seek through comprehensively anticipatory design science and its reduction to physical practice to reform the environment instead of trying to reform man also intend thereby to accomplish prototyped capabilities of doing more with less whereby in turn the wealth-regenerating prospects of such design-science augmentations will induce their spontaneous and economically successful production by world-around industrialization's managers all of which chain-provoking event will both permit and induce all humanity to realize full lasting economic and physical success plus enjoyment of all the Earth without one individual interfering with or being advantaged at the expense of another.

There, in a single-sentence, unpunctuated, 153-word nutshell is Bucky Fuller: optimistic, skeptical of established institutions, convolutedly precise, concerned with human consequences as well as physical results. He wrote those words in the 1920s, after considering suicide but resolving instead to pursue the complicated challenge described above. The task was more than enough for a million people, let alone a single human verb, but he retained his immense optimism throughout the six added decades of life that he decided to give himself and us. Buckminster Fuller was inarguably one of a kind, yet he was also one of the most characteristic embodiments of the 20th century, whether verb or noun, and past, present, future or *allatonce*.

E. E. CUMMINGS

i love you much

i love you much (most beautiful darling)

more than anyone on the earth and i
like you better than everything in the sky

—sunlight and singing welcome your coming

although winter may be everywhere
with such a silence and such a darkness
noone can quite begin to guess

(except my life) the true time of year—

and if what calls itself a world should have
the luck to hear such singing(or glimpse such
sunlight as will leap higher than high
through gayer than gayest someone's heart at your each

nearerness)everyone certainly would(my
most beautiful darling)believe in nothing but love

FRANCIS RAYMOND LINE
HELEN E. LINE

You're Invited . . .

An invitation to accompany us on our 60th wedding anniversary hike down to Phantom Ranch and back, in the Grand Canyon, on May 1, 1988—overnight in dorm, with dinner and breakfast.

The Fred Harvey Reservations Department on the South Rim of Grand Canyon has just phoned us, giving us permission to make reservations this far in advance, for the friends and relatives we will be inviting to share our 60th anniversary hike down to Phantom Ranch on the Colorado River, Sunday May 1, 1988, and back out next day. YOU ARE INVITED! as our guest.

This will include overnight at Phantom Ranch, in separate dorms for men and women, and also dinner upon arrival, and breakfast next morning. Of necessity this will not include lodging or meals on the South Rim but we can help you with reservations there if you let us know very soon. Everyone should plan to stay on the Rim the night before the hike.

Helen and I expect to be hale and hearty at that time but it will still be a bit of an effort for two octogenarians, so these rigid rules will need to apply:

1. We cannot be responsible for seeing that others make it down, and especially back up; that they can stand the heat (sometimes over 100 degrees, or the cold (sometimes snow and hail) or the mud and rain. We have experienced all of these on various May 1st hikes.
2. Anyone accepting this invitation must start getting in shape, well ahead of time, for a strenuous (but highly enjoyable) hike. The best plan is to make a hike several miles long, at least three times a week, over terrain which includes *very steep up hills* and also *very steep down hills*. It is often harder on the feet to hike down very steep grades than it is up them. The training schedule should also include occasional hikes of 10 or 12 miles in length. We'll be going down the *very steep* Kaibab Trail, seven miles long, and coming back out on the 10 mile long Bright Angel Trail. A 10 mile hike, with many steep switchbacks, can be a real test, especially if the weather should be hot.
3. The elevation at Phantom Ranch is approximately 2500 feet, and it is one mile higher on the South Rim, about 7000 feet. We don't happen to be affected by altitude but if you are, then you should try to get training for this as well.
4. Ample supply of water must be carried; there is none on the Kaibab Trail. Two water sources are available on the Bright Angel Trail, but much water is needed between these. Also dried fruit and other lightweight foods should be carried for lunches. As well as rain gear, lotions for sun, and many similar needs. Please read our *Grand Canyon Love Story* for details in this regard. If you accept this invitation we'll be sending further suggestions for making the hike enjoyable.

5. In going both down and up, we will have to set our own pace. You can go faster or slower, as you desire, and we will not expect to follow your pace, whatever it may be. We like to get down to Phantom Ranch in time for a shower and a nap before dinner. We will probably all go *very early* by taxi-bus to the head of the Kaibab Trail for our hike down. At Phantom, breakfast, for the hikers, is at 5:30 a.m. (unless they change the time) and we try to get started up by 6 a.m.

Please give us a tentative answer, within a month if possible, if you think you might go. (Only 50 spaces available.) Then, as soon as you are certain, be sure to let us know definitely. The whole experience should make for a wonderful adventure. We hope that you can be with us!!

September 24, 1985.

CLARICE and
TREY LARKSTON

Announcing a Divorce

Dear Friends,

  The purpose of this letter is to let you know that we will be changing the form of our relationship after the first of the year. We will not be living together and we expect to complete the legal formalities required for a divorce sometime in 1987.

  In our experience, friends are often uncertain how they should feel about a divorce. We thought it might help to let you know how we feel.

  We have been close virtually since the time we were born and we continue to be the best of friends. We love and respect each other very much. But in the fifth decade of our lives, we find that we have grown in different ways. We have different values and priorities. We have different visions of the future.

  For the past twenty-four years, we have been committed to supporting each other and providing opportunities for Joe and Tad to develop and mature. Our goal has been for each one of us to be an independent, centered and strong human being. Now, we feel that we have done as much as can be done to achieve that goal within the framework of our marriage. We have reached a point when it is time to embark in new directions.

  For all of us, this is a time of completion and of new beginnings. It is a time of mourning and of anticipation. As we begin the new year, we ask your love and support, even as we shall continue to love and support each other.

  CLARICE   TREY

LILLIAN HELLMAN
PETER S. FEIBLEMAN

Eating Together

Her Way: Lillian Hellman

All writers are lonely people and all writers are nervous people, particularly as they come to the end of a work. But Peter Feibleman takes the gold ring. I have lived around writers all my life and have never seen anything to match Peter's frantic nervousness as he finishes a book.

This was the case with *The Columbus Tree*, a good novel about Spain, that he finished in New Orleans in 1972.

I was so depressed and worried by the long-distance phone calls I was getting from him that I flew down to New Orleans to see what I could do. There was, of course, very little I could do, except to listen, and to listen was a horror: What, for example, should happen if the publishers (who had always published him) decided not to publish him? What, for example, would happen if the manuscript got lost going to the publisher? What, for example, would happen if he were shot the next day? (Although who besides myself would have done the shooting, I do not know.)

At the end of two or three days, I began to cry. This evidently touched Peter, who invited me to go to Brennan's for dinner. I was in such a state of nerves by this time from answering his numbskull questions, that three vodkas and half a bottle of wine went to my head. I was off to the ladies' room and on my way out afterward, I fell on a stone step, cut my knee very badly and was knocked unconscious for a minute or two.

People flew to get Peter, who came into the ladies' room, only to be told, by a lady dressed in a man's outfit, that he was in the wrong room.

He stopped bathing my wound long enough to say, "No madam, but perhaps you are."

In any case, the book was eagerly accepted by the publishers, who sold it almost immediately to the Book-of-the-Month Club. Peter made some money. The book got good reviews. And so on. This story has a happy ending. But before it had a happy ending, it was decided to give him a publication party.

Now, publication parties are strange affairs. They can consist of your own friends, if you like, or they can consist of the influential part of the press, leaving out the rest, or they can be large enough for the entire press. The publishers and I decided on a small party of friends.

I cannot remember the guest list at this party, but I had it in my apartment and it was a Sunday lunch party. I always enjoy talking over a menu with someone I'm fond of—in this case, I telephoned my friend Hannah Weinstein, who happened to be in London producing a movie. When I told her that I couldn't decide on the right dessert, she didn't hesitate. "Chocolate cake," she said, "and use my recipe." So that was it, and I did, and it was wonderful.

Here are the recipes for the special occasion lunch to celebrate a publication.

FRESH SALMON MOUSSE

Serves 6

2 pounds fresh salmon
3 teaspoons salt
1 teaspoon white pepper
2 egg whites
1 cup sour cream
1 cup heavy cream, whipped to stiff peaks
green mayonnaise (recipe below)

Preheat oven to 350 degrees. Cut salmon into 1-inch pieces. Place salmon, salt, white pepper, egg whites and sour cream in the bowl of a food processor or blender. Blend until mixture is smooth and remove to a large bowl. Use a rubber

spatula to gently fold in the whipped cream. Grease a tube pan mold generously with butter and fill with mousse mixture. Place mold in a baking pan and pour in boiling water to reach half the height of the mold. Bake at 350 degrees for 1½ hours or until the internal temperature of the mousse is 120 degrees.
Allow to cool, unmold, and serve with green mayonnaise.

GREEN MAYONNAISE
Yields about 1½ cups

1 cup spinach leaves, stems removed
10 leaves of fresh basil
1 clove of garlic
1 teaspoon salt
½ teaspoon pepper
pinch of cayenne pepper
3 egg yolks
2 tablespoons lemon juice
1½ cups olive oil
1 green onion, chopped

Boil spinach and basil leaves in plenty of water for 3 minutes. Drain and cool completely under cold water. Press leaves in a towel to dry, and set aside. Place garlic, egg yolks, salt and pepper in bowl of food processor or blender. Blend until egg yolks thicken slightly and begin to pale in color. Add lemon juice. Continue to blend and add oil in a slow, steady stream. When mixture has the consistency of a thick mayonnaise, add the spinach leaves, basil leaves and green onion. Blend until mixture is very green. Adjust seasoning with additional salt and a dash of cayenne pepper. Add hot water to achieve desired consistency.

HANNAH WEINSTEIN'S CHOCOLATE CAKE
Yields 1 cake

¼ pound sweet butter, softened
½ cup granulated sugar
3 eggs, separated
12 ounces semisweet chocolate bits
3 tablespoons bourbon
1 teaspoon espresso coffee
⅓ cup almonds, ground
¼ teaspoon almond extract
¾ cup flour
pinch of salt

Preheat oven to 350 degrees. Cream the butter and sugar. In a separate bowl, beat egg yolks until thick and combine well with butter and sugar. In a small saucepan, melt chocolate, bourbon and espresso, and cool. Combine chocolate mixture with butter and sugar. Mix in almonds and almond extract. In a separate bowl, beat egg whites to stiff peaks. Alternate folding in flour and beaten egg whites until both are incorporated. Put batter in a greased and floured 8-inch cake pan and bake for 25 minutes. The center should be soft and the edges of the cake should be firm.

His Way: Peter Feibleman

Food in America is often dismissed as the least important part of what Americans call "entertaining," a term that seems to mean feeding people. "Do you entertain a lot?" is genteel jargon for "Do you ask people to eat with you?," but too much attention is paid to who's asked and not enough to what's eaten. Perhaps in response to this mistake, Lilly tends to the opposite extreme.

One Monday morning on the Vineyard I came down to find her making a guest list for a dinner she was planning the following Saturday. This did not bode well. It left six days during which she was apt to change the menu maybe fifty times, settling on it only at the very last minute, so that around five P.M. on the Saturday in question she could begin to resent the people she had invited, because they had accepted her invitation and had to be fed.

Martha's Vineyard was a curious place for a dinner party: a guest list sounded like an exercise in name-dropping. As a general rule, nobody is as impressed by celebrities as other celebrities, and the covey of famous people on the island drifted from house to house, week to week, depending largely on who had the best weekend guest to be honored. Lillian was expecting Mike and Annabel Nichols, which was considered top of the line even in that rarified atmosphere. She was an expert at seating people, but most of her friends had heard each other's stories years before. By the end of July, Vineyard gossip was hard to come by, and by mid August a certain frantic quality began to set in.

"I think," Lillian said as I reached for the coffee, "I'll ask the Herseys, Anne and Art Buchwald, Kay Graham, Bob Brustein, Jules Feiffer, Bill and Rose Styron. Tony Lewis, Walter Cronkite, Lally Weymouth, Norman Mailer—he's staying with somebody for the weekend—and Teddy Kennedy, if he's with the Styrons. What do you think?"

I said I thought that would be fine.

"Okay," she said, "about the menu. Maybe I'll cook a simple pasta dish, and just have some salad and lemon sherbert. How does that sound?"

A few seconds went by.

"Please don't stare at me that way, Peter," she said. "There's lots of fresh basil in the garden. We could begin with spaghetti and diced tomatoes and basil. Okay?"

I said okay.

Lillian wrote it down, and then lifted the pencil and looked at it. "The trouble," she said thoughtfully, "is that I ordered fresh mussels last week from a fisherman I met. He said he'd deliver them Saturday morning, he's charging me almost nothing. We *can't* have mussels *and* spaghetti with basil. That's two first courses."

"So have the mussels," I said.

"Don't answer before you think," Lillian said. "If we have mussels, what am I going to do with all the basil in the garden?—What about *that*?"

I swallowed another half cup of coffee and said she could have them both if she put them together.

"You see?" Lilly said, brightening, "if you'd just try thinking once in a while your whole life would be different. Basil and mussel sauce." She wrote it down. "Do you think we should have it as a first course . . . or as a main course?" she added, setting herself up for an impossible choice.

"A main course," I said.

"That means we don't have any first course," Lillian said.

"Skip the first course," I said.

"What's the matter with you?" Lillian said, "you're too young to cave in like that. Why am I having such a problem with it?"

"You want the problem," I said, "you don't want the solution."

"Let's not have any Woolworth Freud," Lillian said, "let's stick to the menu."

I said nothing.

"So what's the first course?" Lillian said.

An hour and three menus later, she was struggling over a choice between mussels and bluefish.

When Saturday came she sat down in the same chair at five o'clock, dressed for the party, and said: "I don't see why all those people are coming to my house expecting me to feed them. It's your fault," she said to Mike, who was coming downstairs with Annabel. "I'm only doing this for you."

"I didn't want a party," Mike said gently; "I came to rest."

That's no excuse and you know it," Lillian said, "getting this meal ready in time has taken ten years off my life. Nobody else on the island cares about food—they'll probably hate it."

I made some inane remark about nobody hating a good meal, and Mike said he was sure Lillian's guests would like whatever she served them.

"They should all be honored you invited them," Annabel said loyally . . .

The social mores of the artist-intellectual set on the Vineyard are the flip side of Easthampton, which is to say that a man who wears a tie is gauche, elegance is outré, discomfort a virtue, modesty a must, casual living reigns and nobody who has air conditioning in a bedroom admits to it. Wealth is seldom displayed except in real estate, and frayed cuffs are chic. In all countries the rules of rebellion are more strict than what is being rebelled against (nobody is as judgmental as a bohemian) and the casual life on this part of the Vineyard is more rigidly mannered than its black-tie opposite. A hostess giving a formal Easthampton buffet might go the whole hog and have an ice-sculpture swan; but Lillian had to keep things looking like just folks. In an effort to keep it plain, she had stayed in the kitchen all day and I had made an ordinary chopped vegetable salad with one lone leftover radish stuck on top.

Just as the doorbell rang, Lillian took the radish off and buried it in the salad.

"You don't want people to think you're decorating food around here," she said "Some of them would never speak to you again."

PASTA WITH BASIL AND TOMATOES
Serves 6

1 cup olive oil
2 cloves garlic, minced
12 tomatoes, peeled, seeded and chopped
1 bunch fresh basil leaves, minced
salt and pepper
2 pounds pasta (angel hair or vermicelli)
grated Parmesan cheese

Heat olive oil in a large skillet. Add garlic and cook until it begins to turn golden. Add tomatoes and basil and continue cooking over medium heat until warmed. Season with salt and pepper to taste. Cook 2 pounds thin pasta. Drain, toss with sauce, adding up to 1 additional cup of olive oil to coat. Spinkle with grated Parmesan cheese and serve.

JENNY JOSEPH

Warning

When I am an old woman I shall wear purple
With a red hat which doesn't go, and doesn't suit me,
And I shall spend my pension on brandy and summer gloves
And satin sandals, and say we've no money for butter.
I shall sit down on the pavement when I'm tired
And gobble up samples in shops, and press alarm bells
And run my stick along the public railings
And make up for the sobriety of youth.
I shall go out in my slippers in the rain
And pick the flowers in other people's gardens
And learn to spit.

You can wear terrible shirts, and grow more fat
And eat three pounds of sausages at a go
Or only bread and pickle for a week
And hoard pens and pencils and beermats and things in boxes.

But now we must have clothes that keep us dry
And pay the rent and not swear in the street
And set a good example for the children.
We must have friends to dinner and read the papers.

But maybe I ought to practice a little now?
So people who know me are not too shocked and surprised
When suddenly I am old and start to wear purple.

Good-bye

On August 13, 1985, a Japanese airliner crashed in a mountain with 524 people on board. Four people survived. Among the wreckage were found letters that the crash victims had written during the thirty minutes or so that the plane flew out of control before it crashed.

On the back of an airsick bag:

Osaka
Mino

Machiko, please take care of my children.

Masakazu Taniguchi
6:30

On the back of an architectural firm document:

I want you to be strong.

Kazuo Yoshimura

On the pages of an appointment calendar:

Be good to each other and work hard.
Help your mother.
I'm very sad, but I'm sure I won't make it.
I don't know the reason.
I don't want to take any more planes.
Please, Lord, help me.
To think that our dinner last night was the last time.

There was smoke that seemed to come
from an explosion in the cabin,
and we began making a descent.
What will happen from here?

Tsuyoshi, I'm counting on you.

Mother, to think something like this would happen.
It's too bad, Goodbye.
Please take care of the children.

It's 6:30 now.
The plane is rolling and descending rapidly.

I am grateful for the truly happy life I have enjoyed until now.

Hirotsugu Kawaguchi

A Prayer

Lord, make us instruments of your peace.
Where there is hatred, let us sow love;
where there is injury, pardon;
where there is discord, union;
where there is doubt, faith;
where there is despair, hope;
where there is darkness, light;
where there is sadness, joy.
Grant that we may not so much seek to be consoled
    as to console;
to be understood as to understand;
to be loved as to love.
For it is in giving that we receive;
it is in pardoning that we are pardoned;
and it is in dying that we are born to eternal life. *Amen.*

St. Teresa's Bookmark

Let nothing trouble thee,	Nada te turbe,
Let nothing affright thee,	Nada te espante,
All things are passing,	Todo se pasa.
God never changes;	Dios no se muda.
Patience obtains everything,	La paciencia todo lo alcanza,
Nothing is wanting to him who	Quien a Dios tiene nada
possesses God,	le falta.
God alone suffices.	Solo Dios basta.

PART TWO

Reading to Learn to Write

RALPH WALDO EMERSON

If an author gives us just distinctions, inspiring lessons, or imaginative [writing], it is not so important whose they are. If we are fired and guided by these, we know them as a benefactor, and shall return to them as long as they serve us so well.

Introduction

We've already seen in Part I that one way writers read is to enjoy the work of others. They read to amuse themselves, to have fun, to satisfy their curiosity, to share in others' experiences, to feel delight. But writers read for other purposes also. Writers also read to teach themselves more about their craft.

Writers always have an eye out for something new they can learn. Perhaps it's a way to organize an essay. A lot of writers learned how to write essays in a fresh way after they read Tom Wolfe's "The Kandy-Kolored Tangerine-Flake Streamline Baby" in 1963. Perhaps it's a way to frame several individual stories naturally and organically inside a larger story. Willa Cather's *Death Comes to the Archbishop* taught a lot of writers how to accomplish this technique. Perhaps it's an original way to use words. In the '20s, '30s, and '40s, Gertrude Stein taught writers new ways to use words. Or perhaps it's a way to depict images and scenes on the page that make the writing so real you think you're there. Garrison Keillor's *Lake Wobegon Days* is many writers' teacher here.

When writers study other people's writing to improve their own craft, they read differently than when they read only to enjoy what someone else has written. When you *read to learn to write*, you read *constructively*. The writing you are reading has been *constructed*. It has been *composed*. The writer has, by putting first this word and then that word and then the next word, *built* something.

Andy Rooney described this *building* that happens when authors *construct* their writing after he finished building a small structure on his farm to have a place in which to write. When he sat down to write an essay, he realized how much alike the building and the writing were, how much they were both acts of *construction*:

> Standing back and looking at my odd-shaped building, I've been impressed with how much like my writing it is. . . . My satisfaction in making it springs from the same well, too. For a man or a woman to take any raw material like lumber or words and shape these formless materials into a pattern that bears the stamp of his or her brain or hand, is the most satisfying thing to do in the whole world.

When writers read to add to their knowledge of how to write, they are keenly aware that the authors of the works they are reading have *built* something. And in order to learn from these authors, writers study how the writing is *constructed*.

It's best when you are going to *read to learn to write* that you first go over the essay, as you would if you were simply *reading to enjoy*. This first reading will give you the "global" view, the overall view, before you begin your study. Then you read the essay again. You *read to learn to write*. You read *constructively* by asking yourself questions at all times. What is the writer doing here? What makes this work so well? Why do I like this passage so much? Why don't I like that? What was the writer's aim? How did she achieve it? How did the writer connect the parts of the essay together? How did the writer get from point to point?

When you read to learn to write, you monitor your reading. And you relate your reading to your writing: If this author connects his points this way, could I do that, too, in the piece I'm writing? I see that this writer makes a scene come alive by using short sentences and vivid verbs. Can I do that in my own writing? Ah, now I see how that writer includes points in an essay that wouldn't, on first glance, seem to fit. Why don't I do that for the piece I'm working on right now?

In reading to learn to write you're doing two things at once. You are paying close attention to how a writer has *constructed* the piece of writing. And you're talking to yourself all along as you read. You're comprehending the *text structure* of the piece of writing, and you're commenting on it to yourself at the same time. You are studying the writing and, in effect, teaching yourself as you go. Those who study the kind of reading that includes internal dialogue refer to it as the *metacognitive* aspect of reading. This means that you not only understand the text you are reading but you also recognize the *strategies* the author used in writing the piece. Reading to learn to write requires metacognitive reading, because you read first to notice *how* the writer has constructed or composed the piece of writing and then to generate a hypothesis that enables you to adapt the author's construction and way of composing to your own writing.

Of course, the possibilities are limitless for what you can look for in someone else's writing when you are reading to learn to write. This section highlights four of these possibilities. These four characteristics are at the heart of good writing, and each of them is one you can study and incorporate into your own writing immediately.

As you read the essays that follow, you'll have an opportunity to study how writers achieve these important qualities in their work:

Originality
Thesis
Form
Gusto, Vividness, and Clarity

Each of these characteristics of good writing will be illustrated by a group of essays. In the essays illustrating *Originality*, for instance, you'll have an opportunity to see how writers manage to write in an original way on even commonplace subjects. You will be able to see the "foundation" on which they constructed their writing that makes originality possible. And by studying these pieces as you read, by reading to learn to write, you will be able to see what these writers' strategies and approaches were; if you are willing to practice, you can use them in your own work.

In another section—*Form*—you will see how writers use both traditional and created forms to organize and shape their writing. All of the selections in Form will interest you and catch your attention, even if you are going to do nothing more than read to enjoy— which you should do first to understand what the piece is about. But they are also excellent examples of a wide variety of forms and organizational methods and approaches that you can use as models for your own writing. When you read them to learn to write, you will see how you can become a better writer.

In fact, that's the promise to you of Part 2. When you read these essays *constructively* and practice using the strategies and approaches of these writers in your own work, you will become a better writer. You will see possibilities you had not seen before. You will be amazed that by *reading* you can *learn to write*.

READING

to Learn to Write: Originality

RALPH WALDO EMERSON

And what is originality? It is being, being somebody, being yourself, and reporting accurately what you see and are.

One of the things we learn by reading other people's writing is that good writing is always *original*. But what does this mean?

It's hard to come up with something to say that doesn't rely in some way on conversations we've heard, information someone else has given us, books we've read. What we have in our heads is a collection we've picked up along the way. So, how can we be original, when practically everything we know we learned from someone else?

We can be original by thinking *for ourselves* about those things we've learned from others. We can make our own connections. We can test out what we hear against our own experience. We can engage *who* we are with the subject at hand. And it can be *any* subject. All you have to do is be certain that you're awake when you start to think about something. You should be committed to *engaging* with your subject, rather than just bumping into it. If you are awake, you won't sound like a parrot, just repeating what you've heard. Being awake and engaged will keep you from being a tape recorder merely playing back somebody else's message. You won't be guilty of "automatic bumbling."

Ralph Waldo Emerson told the secret about being original a long time ago: "If only you can be the fanatic of your subject, and find a fibre reaching from it to the core of your heart, so that all your affection and all your thought can freely play." Emerson also said that the poorest experience is rich enough for all the purposes of expressing thought—you just have to look at this experience with newness, with fresh eyes.

We can all write with originality. We can engage with any subject to see what connections we can make, what our experience matched with the subject will produce, what insights we bring to the topic. The question is, however, "*Will* we write with originality?" Because it takes courage. You have to be willing to do something risky. When you write with originality, you are willing to be yourself and to report what you have thought or seen. It's an act of self-confidence. It's an act of authenticity. It's the act that is the heart of good writing.

The selections that follow have been written by people with the courage and integrity to be original. They have taken a subject—in each case a subject anybody could talk about—and they have engaged with that subject, bringing with them interest, curiosity, and life. The result is a piece of writing that only this person could have done—a piece of writing that is fresh, new, unusual, interesting, and authentic. The writers have achieved originality.

As you read these pieces, you probably won't be able to point to a specific sentence or a particular paragraph and say, "Ah, there she's being original." Originality doesn't show up directly on the page in constructions you can pinpoint. (Personal style in writing does easily show itself and, though style is related to originality, the two are not the same.)

Originality is present in a piece of writing because of something that happened *before* the writer prepared the final draft. The source of originality is in the thinking/looking/observing/noticing stage of the writing process. For many people the original connection between themselves and the subject occurs in their early drafts; for others, engaging with the subject starts long before they sit down to write. The point to remember is that originality comes from who you are and how you think about a subject, not from something you can arrange on the page.

When we discuss the essays which follow, therefore, we won't be looking for specific, pinpointed evidence of originality. We'll instead look at how a particular person has looked at a certain subject and found something to say that only that person could have said. We'll see how writers are their authentic selves when they write, whether discussing science or geography or engineering or accidents. How exciting to realize that any subject can be written about with originality if only the authors are willing to be themselves. It will be a bit like trying to catch a sunbeam; but the brightness will be undeniable to us as we read, even if we can't ''catch'' it.

ARTHUR E. GROSSER

The Culinary Alchemy of Eggs

How often do American scientists prove of value putting together a dinner? Are we just substitutes for a food processor—cutting, peeling, slicing, shredding, chopping, grating—all with our gray matter on standby? Not too pleasant a way to spend time. And what about following recipes? They are just a series of imperative statements, orders without justifications, treating us like Marine recruits. It would be more fun to be able to use our heads while we cook.

But can it be done? I did not know until I tried to figure out why I kept on doing what my mother had told me all those years ago when I was six: to put salt in the water when hard-cooking an egg. (Because the water should not be boiling while the egg cooks, "hard-cooking" is a more accurate term than "hard-boiling.") I went to a good cookbook and checked out the recipe. It looked something like this:

HARD- OR SOFT-COOKED EGGS
(one serving)

2 eggs at room temperature
1 quart cold water
2 tablespoons salt

Make a hole in the large end of each egg. The hole should be $\frac{1}{16}$ inch in diameter. Put the eggs in a pot with the water and salt. Add more water (and salt) if necessary, to cover the eggs. Heat the pot until the water boils, then reduce the heat so that the water simmers.

Cook 2 to 3 minutes for soft-cooked, and 10 to 12 minutes for hard-cooked. Immediately remove the pot from the heat, put it in the sink, and let cold water run into it until the eggs are cool enough to handle. Shell them and serve.

My mind started to boggle. Not only was the salt really in the recipe (for no apparent reason), but so were some other unexplained requirements. Why did the eggs have to be at room temperature, and why did the cooking water have to start off cold when I was going to heat it up right away? Why a hole in the egg, and why simmered rather than conveniently boiled? And finally, did the cold-water rinse do any more than make the shelling job less painful on my tender hands? The choice was obvious: either accept the orders and forget the whys, or dig into the reasons. And the most satisfying and generally useful reasons would be molecular.

If a recipe for hard-cooked eggs is any good at all, it will try to keep each egg in one piece and prevent the shell from cracking. Eggs crack because they are built to do so. They carry around a little heat-sensitive detonator. If you want to verify this, here's an experiment to try:

Heat an egg is a pot of cold water and watch the large end. You will see a stream of air bubbles coming through the shell from a pocket of air held captive between the membranes in the egg. Now make a pinhole in the large end of the egg and put the egg back into the pot of (what should be lukewarm) water, continuing to heat it. This time you will see, instead of little bubbles, a jet of air expelled from the hole.

As the egg heats up, the air inside expands and tries to find a way out of the shell. Cleverly foreseeing this eventuality, the egg has provided itself with an escape hatch: pores in the large end of the shell. The air bubbles you saw in the first part of the experiment had forced their way through these tiny pores. Now a race begins between the buildup of pressure within the egg and its release as the air oozes out. If the air pocket is heated faster than the air can escape through the shell, there is terrific internal pressure, and the shell cracks.

But not every egg, like not every person, will crack under stress. Some eggshells have bigger pores than others, which means they let the air out more readily and are relatively uncrackable. Still other eggs have a fairly small air pocket. Unfortunately, there is no way of knowing which type of egg we have before cooking it, so to make sure the air can get out through the shell before the pressure becomes too great, the recipe has us poke a hole in the large end of the shell.

Not content with attending to the thermodynamics of gases, the recipe is also sensitive to the kinetics of crack-prevention. By starting the eggs in cold water, it ensures that the temperature rises gradually and allows more time for the air to seep out. Reducing the heat to simmering lessens the chance of cracking as well and prevents overcooking, which toughens the white before the yolk has cooked.

There is an aesthetic bonus hidden here. Egg white cooks very quickly, and if it sets into shape before the air gets out, the shelled egg has a flat end like a boxer's nose. The egg with a pinhole in the shell, on the other hand, mirrors the beautiful ovoid shape of the shell, because the white flows into the space vacated by the escaping air. Of course, a flat bottom may be useful if eggs sitting at attention is what you are after.

Pin-holing is especially important when you are dealing with old eggs. As an egg ages, more air gets into it, and the air pocket enlarges, sometimes enough to make the egg float in water. These floaters are best used for scrambled eggs.

Sometimes it is terribly inconvenient to start eggs in cold water. If the pot is too small to cook them all in one batch, it seems silly to throw out the hot water and start all over again. But an egg started in hot water can bring another cracking mechanism into play—thermal shock.

When an egg straight out of the refrigerator is tossed into boiling water, the different regions of the shell, which are of different thicknesses, cannot expand in unison, and the shell cracks. So, if you must put the eggs in hot water, use the pinhole trick, and then run some warm tap water over them to lessen the shock when they are put in the pot. And then put in some salt! Unreasonable? Illogical?

At first glance it does seem ridiculous. Although air can get in and out of the eggshell, salt cannot, so what effect can it have on the egg snug inside? Salt does raise the temperature of the boiling water a bit, but not enough to be important. And it does not prevent cracking, which can happen to even the best-laid and most apprehensively watched eggs. So why add salt?

Egg Chemistry

Egg white is almost all water (88%) and protein (11%). In its natural state the white is semifluid, and when cooked it becomes firm but resilient. This change mirrors on a visible level the fate of the molecules when we turn up the heat.

An egg protein is a shy molecule, and when left alone it will curl up into itself, coiling into a ball. Held in this shape by very weak chemical bonds inside the ball, it is content to examine its navel and to float serenely around in the 88% sea, without any interest in the other protein balls. This leisured, snobbish existence is destroyed if the temperature is raised.

Then, hordes of water molecules carom off each other and the proteins in frenzied and chaotic collisions. As the temperature increases, the action becomes more energetic until a molecular demolition derby is under way. The weak internal bonds of the egg protein can no longer hold the ball together, and it opens out into a floppy streamer.

Only now do we find the real reason for the protein's solitary behavior. It coiled itself up not from narcissism, but as a defensive maneuver, for when it opens out into a streamer, it exposes a soft underbelly of richly seductive targets for chemical attack and bonding. As these protein streamers bump into each other, they immediately bond and form strong links; others latch on randomly as well, until finally there is a three-dimensional protein network, semirigid and immobile—to our touch, firm and resilient. The difference between the semifluid raw egg and the semirigid cooked one is just the difference between the natural sea state of the protein balls and the network that heating has driven them into.

Not only will high temperature and the consequent molecular massage pummel the solitary protein molecules, opening them up and allowing them to form a network, but so will salt or food acids. Chemical bonds are electrical, and the charged particles from dissolved salt or acid can change the electrical environment of the solitary proteins so much that their weak internal bonds break spontaneously. The proteins then uncoil and enter the dance that leads to the interlocking molecular network. In other words, the protein cooks a lot faster.

This is the reason the dissolved salt or acid in the cooking water helps keep a cracked egg neat—there are no ugly streamers of white floating about. Adding salt makes the cooking water much more efficient and faster at its job. If the egg cracks, the white is cooked at the crack and seals it right away, an instantaneous self-repair job. Salting the water is a sort of first aid for a ruptured egg.

Finally, what about that cold-water rinse after boiling an egg? Couldn't it just be the cookbook writer's sissifying excess, easily eliminated while you get your macho kicks, toughing out the pain as you scrabble off the hot shell? Perhaps so, were there not another pitfall to avoid when hard-cooking eggs—the dreaded green yolk. Indeed, how does a beautiful white and yellow egg get such a bilious coating on its innermost parts?

The egg does it to itself, really, but we help it along with overcooking. As the egg is warmed, a small portion of the protein in the white decomposes, and its sulfur and hydrogen unite to form hydrogen sulfide gas, which has a deservedly bad name as "the smell of rotten eggs." The egg is not rotting, however, just cooking.

This gas generated in the white collects in the coolest part of the egg, which during cooking is in the center, where the yolk is. Yolks contain iron, which has a terrific attraction for sulfur. The iron kicks out the hydrogen and forms solid iron sulfide. This union is so swift and tempestuous that it happens at the first opportunity—when the gas reaches the surface of the yolk and forms the dark iron-sulfide deposit.

You can prevent this unnatural liaison by using the cold-water rinse. This not only prevents overcooking, which gives the reaction more time for dirty work, but also quenches it altogether. After the cooking period, the egg is heated through; by chilling the shell in cold water, we force the hydrogen sulfide gas to collect there, pulling it away from the iron-laden yolk.

Egg Physics

When you have produced the perfect hard-cooked eggs and stored them (unshelled) in the refrigerator, it will inevitably happen that you forget which of your eggs are cooked, especially if there is no telltale pinhole. Fortunately, physics can rescue you from this dilemma. Just twirl the eggs on a table. Pretty soon you will come across some that spin faster than the others; these will be the hard-cooked ones, as any student of the physics of figure skating can tell you. The yolk of the hard-cooked egg is spinning quite close to the vertical axis of rotation. But when you spin a raw egg, the yolk, much denser than the white, moves toward the shell, away from the rotation axis, increasing the moment of inertia. The kinetic energy, fixed by the initial impulse, is directly related to the moment of inertia, I, and the angular velocity, ω:

$$\text{constant kinetic energy} = \tfrac{1}{2}I\omega^2$$

Since the moment of inertia may be crudely approximated as $\overline{mr^2}$, where m is the major mass and r its distance from the rotation axis, $I \ \alpha \ mr^2 \ \alpha \ 1/\omega^2$. And as the mass moves away from the axis of rotation, increasing the average radius, the rotational frequency must get smaller. A figure skater will often act like these eggs in reverse, starting a "scratch spin" with arms and even a leg extended out from the body, then wrapping them tightly around the body to increase the spin rate.

After all is said and done, there is one big advantage—in addition to educating and impressing your friends, and figuring out how to ad-lib around recipes—that is gained by explaining all these things in the kitchen: your listeners may not notice that you are not doing your share of the work.

Elizabeth Neeld Comments:

✦ *Can you imagine a serious chemist writing about boiling eggs? On top of that, the writer is a university professor who specializes in studying molecular beam kinetics! But that's an example of what originality is made of: a serious person willing to connect with a seemingly trivial subject that has come to his attention, in order to discover what's unusual, fresh, appealing, and interesting about it. And that's exactly what Dr. Arthur Grosser, Associate Professor* of Chemistry at McGill University, did. He even went so far as to write an entire book called The Cookbook Decoder or Culinary Alchemy Explained. Grosser wants the public to understand science, and he wants scientists to see how their specialties relate to everyday life. What better way to do this than to juxtapose instructions in a simple, ordinary recipe for boiling eggs with the scientific explanation for why those instructions are necessary and why they work. This is a most original way to illustrate science's relevance to daily living. ✦ This essay was printed in American Scientist, the journal of Sigma Xi, the Scientific Research Society, which since 1886 has been the honor society of scientists. It has a circulation of 123,000 scientists around the world in over five hundred chapters on university campuses and in government and industrial laboratories. Although it is likely that Grosser wrote the essay for the general public since it is part of his book on cooking and science, it is interesting that the editors of a prestigious scientists' magazine would print this essay for their readers. Hint: they, too, must have found something original in Grosser's treatment of the subject. ✦ What does Grosser do that makes this essay a piece of good writing? What makes it fresh and interesting? What makes it original? Well, the first thing you notice is that he acknowledges his audience, fellow scientists who read American Scientist. He begins by addressing them directly: What are we good for in the kitchen, he asks. Just to cut up vegetables? And why do we doggedly follow recipes without asking what we are doing? He begins by getting his readers' attention. ✦ The next thing to notice is that right away Grosser is willing to be present as a human being, not an anonymous chemist giving some dry information. He relates enough of his personal life to allow you to see him as a person who was in the kitchen with his mother when he was six, when she taught him how to boil an egg. ✦ Then Grosser tells us why we should prick a hole in the end of the egg, why we should add salt to the water, and why we should rinse the cooked egg in cold water when finished. And he gives this information with a generous spirit. He writes so clearly that anyone, not just a scientist, can understand what he is saying. ✦ Notice the continued presence of Grosser: "My mind started to boggle," "on my tender hands." He ends with humor: keep busy explaining this kind of thing in the kitchen and nobody will notice that you're not doing your share of the work. ✦ What else does this writer do that works? He uses words and phrases that are alive, that paint a picture, that work as an analogy we can understand: "eggs crack because they carry around a little heat-sensitive detonator," "hordes of water molecules carom off each other," "treating us like Marine recruits." He asks a lot of questions, engaging the reader: "Why did the eggs have to be at room temperature, and why did the cooking water have to start off cold when I was going to heat it up right away?" He personifies the subject, eggs: "now a race begins," "if eggs sitting at attention is what you are after." Look at his use of action words like "carom," "frenzied," "chaotic collisions." Look at his use of metaphor and simile: "A molecular demolition derby is underway." "A figure skater will often act like these eggs in reverse, starting a 'scratch spin,' with arms and even a leg extended out from the body, then wrapping them tightly around the body to increase the spin rate." This is something almost any reader could understand, although unable to comprehend the "constant kinetic energy" physics Grosser has just been describing. ✦ So, here's a generous writer who has care and concern for his readers. He wants us to understand. He wants his information to be clear. He is willing to sound like a human being as he writes. He lets us get to know a bit about him, while he still keeps the focus on this subject. He must have cooked in the kitchen with his mother when he was a little boy. He must at least watch demolition derbies on television, if he doesn't go to them, and figure skaters, although I'd bet he's one of those himself. He is extremely creative: imagine realizing that information which can attract, interest, and educate a wide range of readers lurks in a subject like the recipe for boiling eggs! That's what originality means: Engaging with the subject. Seeing the possibilities. Writing about what you're interested in. Seeing something in the subject that only you, with your interests, experience, and way of responding to life, can see. Being yourself, and reporting accurately on what you see and are. Originality—it works every time, for you and for the reader. ✦

LEWIS THOMAS

The Lie Detector

Every once in a while the reasons for discouragement about the human prospect pile up so high that it becomes difficult to see the way ahead, and it is then a great blessing to have one conspicuous and irrefutable good thing to think about ourselves, something solid enough to step onto and look beyond the pile.

Language is often useful for this, and music. A particular painting, if you have the right receptors, can lift the spirits and hold them high enough to see a whole future for the race. The sound of laughter in the distance in the dark can be a marvelous encouragement. But these are chancy stimuli, ready to work only if you happen to be ready to receive them, which takes a bit of luck.

I have been reading magazine stories about the technology of lie detection lately, and it occurs to me that this may be the thing I've been looking for, an encouragement propped up by genuine, hard scientific data. It is promising enough that I've decided to take as given what the articles say, uncritically, and to look no further. For a while, anyway.

Lying Is a Strain

As I understand it, a human being cannot tell a lie, even a small one, without setting off a kind of smoke alarm somewhere deep in a dark lobule of the brain, resulting in the sudden discharge of nerve impulses, or the sudden outpouring of neurohormones of some sort, or both. The outcome, recorded by the lie-detector gadgetry, is a highly reproducible cascade of changes in the electrical conductivity of the skin, the heart rate, and the manner of breathing, similar to the responses to various kinds of stress.

Lying, then, is stressful, even when we do it for protection, or relief, or escape, or profit, or just for the pure pleasure of lying and getting away with it. It is a strain, distressing enough to cause the emission of signals to and from the central nervous system warning that something has gone wrong. It is, in a pure physiological sense, an unnatural act.

Now I regard this as a piece of extraordinarily good news, meaning, unless I have it all balled up, that we are a moral species by compulsion, at least in the limited sense that we are biologically designed to be truthful to each other. Lying doesn't hurt, mind you, and perhaps you could tell lies all day and night for years on end without being damaged, but maybe not—maybe the lie detector informs us that repeated, inveterate untruthfulness will gradually undermine the peripheral vascular system, the sweat glands, the adrenals, and who knows what else. Perhaps we should be looking into the possibility of lying as an etiologic agent for some of the common human ailments still beyond explaining, recurrent head colds, for instance, or that most human of all unaccountable disorders, a sudden pain in the lower mid-back.

Truth: Genetically Required?

It makes a sort of shrewd biological sense, and might therefore represent a biological trait built into our genes, a feature of humanity as characteristic for us as feathers for birds or scales for fish, enabling us to live, at our best, the kinds of lives we are designed to live. This is, I suppose, the "sociobiological" view to take, with the obvious alternative being that we are brought up this way as children in response to the rules of our culture. But if the latter is the case, you would expect to encounter, every once in a while, societies in which the rule does not hold, and I have never heard of a culture in which lying was done by everyone as a matter of course, all life through, nor can I imagine such a group functioning successfully. Biologically speaking, there is good reason for us to restrain ourselves from lying outright to each other whenever possible. We are indeed a social species, more interdependent than the celebrated social insects; we can no more live a solitary life than can a bee; we are obliged, as a species, to rely on each other. Trust is a fundamental requirement for our kind of existence, and without it all our linkages would begin to snap loose.

The restraint is a mild one, so gentle as to be almost imperceptible. But it is there; we know about it from what we call guilt, and now we have a neat machine to record it as well.

It seems a trivial thing to have this information, but perhaps it tells us to look again, and look deeper. If we had better instruments, designed for profounder probes, we might see needles flipping, lines on charts recording quantitative degrees of meanness of spirit, or a lack of love. I do not wish for such instruments, I hope they will never be constructed; they would somehow belittle the issues involved. It is enough, quite enough, to know that we cannot even tell a plain untruth, betray a trust, without scaring some part of our own brains. I'd rather guess at the rest.

What Happens When We Lie?

There is, of course, one problem that will have to be straightened out sooner or later by medicine, duty-bound. It concerns placebos. The sugar pill is sometimes indispensable in therapy, powerfully reassuring, but it is essentially a little white lie. If you wired up the average good internist in the act of writing a prescription, would the needles go flying?

Let others go to work on the scientific side issues, of which there are probably many. Is there a skin secretion, a pheromone, secreted in the process? Can a trained tracking hound smell the altered skin of a liar? Is the total absence of this secretion the odor of sanctity? I can think of any number of satisfying experiments that someone ought to be doing, but I confess to a serious misgiving about the possible misuses of the sort of knowledge I have in mind. Supposing it were found that there is indeed a special pentapeptide released into the blood on the telling of a lie, or some queer glycolipid in the sweat of one's palms, or, worst of all, something chemically detectable in balloons of exhaled breath. The next thing to happen would surely be new industries in Texas and Japan for the manufacture of electronic sensing devices to be carried in one's pocket, or perhaps worn conspicuously on one's sleeve depending on the consumer's particular need. Governments would become involved, sooner or later, and the lawyers and ethicists would have one field day after another. Before long we would stop speaking to each other, television would be abolished as a habitual felon, politicians would be confined by house arrest, and civilization would come to a standstill.

Come to think of it, you might not have to do any of the research on human beings after all, which I find a relaxing thought. Animals, even plants, lie to each other all the time, and we could restrict the research to them, putting off the real truth about ourselves for the several centuries we need to catch our breath. What is it that enables certain flowers to resemble nubile insects, or opossums to play dead, or female fireflies to change the code of their flashes in order to attract, and then eat, males of a different species? What about those animals that make their livings by deception—the biological mimics, the pretenders, the fish dangling bits of their flesh as bait in front of their jaws, the malingering birds limping along to lie about the location of their nests, the peacock, who is surely not conceivably all that he claims to be? It is a rich field indeed, open to generations of graduate students in the years ahead, risk-free. All we need is to keep telling ourselves that this is not a human problem, to understand that we have evolved beyond mendacity except under extraordinary conditions, and to stay clear of the instruments.

It would be safe enough for the scientists themselves, of course, because good science depends on truth-telling, and we should be willing to wear detectors on the lapels of our white coats all day long. I have only one small reservation about this. Scientists do have a tendency to vanity—some of the best ones are vanity-prone—and there is probably a mechanism at work here with a fundamental connection to lying. Perhaps this is one kind of human experimentation that ought to be done early on, if it can pass review by the local ethics review board: catch hold of an eminent researcher at the moment when he is involved in a press conference, looking and sounding for all the world like the greatest thing since the invention of the nucleated cell, and hook him up to the machine, or stick a sensor on his necktie. Then we could learn how to control the work for background noise, and move on to the insects.

I don't want to go over this again. I didn't write any of the above.

Elizabeth Neeld Comments:

✦ *Lewis Thomas is a physician whose medical speciality is pathology, the study of diseases and things abnormal. His position is chancellor of the Memorial Sloan-Kettering Cancer Center; his avocation, however, is the observation of the natural world. Lewis Thomas looks at everything from the structure of a single cell to snails to how we smell to Bach to what we have in our "attic of the brain." Calling himself a Biology Watcher, he began writing about these subjects back in 1971 for the* New England Journal of Medicine *in a column called "Notes of a Biology Watcher." (In 1974 these columns were published in book form as* The Lives of a Cell: Notes of a Biology Watcher. *The book won a National Book Award in that same year.)* ✦ *What makes Lewis Thomas' writing original? His vision, for one thing. Thomas believes the world is symbiotic: all organisms, he asserts, are related to each other in a beneficial and reciprocal manner. He writes, "There is a tendency for living things to join up, establish linkages, live inside each other, return to earlier arrangements, get along whenever possible. This is the way of the world." ✦ Thomas views the earth as a single cell in its membrane of atmosphere. He believes, too, that our minds are constructed from birth with the ability to make meaning. Thomas has a vision that is bold, encouraging, and optimistic. He is willing to see possibility where others see only gloom and doom. His essays end on the upbeat. He believes there is an "underlying force" that drives creatures together into union. This force he sometimes calls "luck . . . our fantastic luck." ✦ In this essay, Thomas' vision, in which all forms of life on earth are interdependent and harmonious, is at the heart of what he has to say. In being himself, being somebody, and reporting accurately what he sees and what he is, (Emerson's definition of originality), Thomas asks us: Were we made to be moral? Is that why our bodily functions change when we tell a lie? Perhaps, then, we are a moral species by compulsion. Perhaps we're made to tell the truth to each other. If so, he says, it would be one conspicuous and irrefutably good thing to think about ourselves. "Lying doesn't hurt, mind you, and perhaps you could tell lies all day and night for years on end without being damaged, but maybe not—maybe the lie detector informs us that repeated, inveterate untruthfulness will gradually undermine the peripheral vascular system, the sweat glands, the adrenals, and who knows what else." If that is true, perhaps we are a better human race than some of our daily newspaper accounts show us up to be.* ✦ *This essay illustrates originality in discussing something that is part of society, yet little talked about except in a technical or professional fashion. Thomas looks at this object, the lie detector machine, and he engages with it. He brings who he is and what his vision of the world is to bear on that subject. And something original and fresh, provocative, and potentially encouraging comes out of it. Thomas, given who he is in the world, could have said or written nothing less. He is authentic, a writer who is willing to be himself in his writing.* ✦ *A thing or two to notice about how Thomas writes: You can read his essays on two levels; in fact, to get the full value of his writing you must read his essays on two levels. You read on one level for the scientific information the essay contains. And there is always a lot to learn. You also read Thomas on another level: to discover what is the human truth "too mysterious for old-fashioned common sense" contained in the essays. Read the following example first to glean the scientific information contained and then to understand, the human truth of the passage: "Any word you speak this afternoon will radiate out in all directions, around town before tomorrow, out and around the world before Tuesday, accelerating to the speed of light, modulating as it goes, shaping new and unexpected messages, emerging at the end as an enormously funny Hungarian joke, a fluctuation in the money market, a poem, or simply a long pause in someone's conversation in Brazil. . . . Maybe the thoughts we generate today and flick around from mind to mind, like the jokes that turn up simultaneously at dinner parties in Hong Kong and Boston . . . are the primitive precursors of more complicated, polymerized structures that will come later, analogous to the prokaryotic cells that drifted through shallow pools in the early days of biological evolution. Later, when the time is right, there may be fusion and symbiosis among the bits."* ✦ One last thing to note about originality. Did you notice in the opening paragraphs of "The Lie Detector" that Thomas says, "I have been reading magazine stories about the technology of lie detection lately, and it occurs to me . . ." Here is a secret to being original when you write (or when you live, for that matter!). Thomas is a cancer specialist and a hospital administrator, so what is he doing reading about lie detector machines? These are certainly not part of his daily activities. He doesn't need to know about lie detectors in order to do his job well. Reading outside your field and your specialty, however, stimulates thinking. It gets you out of the rut you may have fallen into in your daily life. Wide-ranging reading enables you to see connections or relationships between things in worlds outside your own that enrich you—and when you write you enrich others. Lewis Thomas was reading outside his field and his speciality when he began to get the ideas he is writing about in this essay, an excellent way to be original. ✦

CALVIN TOMKINS

Who Was Karl Bodmer, Anyway?

Karl Bodmer's America" is one of those pleasant, out-of-the-way exhibitions that turn up only in the summer. At least, that is what I thought when I went to see it at the Metropolitan Museum the other day.

. . . About a third of the way through the exhibition, though, while looking at a watercolor called "Junction of the Yellowstone and the Missouri," I began to notice how good Bodmer really is. A sense of vast, almost limitless space inhabits this small picture. Dry, eroded hills lead from the foreground to the river's meandering curve, to its disappearance behind more distant hills and its eventual meeting with the other river, behind which more open, flat space merges with a yellow sky. The coloring is all in earth tones—brown and ochre and shades of green. Three hovering, ragged-looking vultures—the only sign of life—heighten the effect of impersonal nature, untouched by and unaware of man.

Some watercolors of Sioux, Hidatsa, Assiniboin, and Blackfoot warriors next commandeered my attention. Bodmer drew individuals, not ethnic types. His meticulous emphasis on the details of costume and the exact rendering of symbolic ornament did not prevent him from painting real men and women. Sometimes the facial expression is masklike, the deep-set eyes fixed on a distant horizon; but this is not always so, and no face is like another. The Blackfoot known as Iron Shirt is shown with his handsome face ceremonially blackened, the mouth slightly parted, the red-rimmed eyes fixed coolly on the viewer. The Yankton Sioux chief whom the traders called Big Soldier, about sixty years old and more than six feet tall, has a relaxed dignity that accords with his years and his victories. Tátsicki-Stomíck, a Piegan Blackfoot shown in three-quarter profile, has an expression of intelligent skepticism. No matter how exotic they looked in their ceremonial robes, paint, and feathers, Bodmer did not romanticize Indians. He had been hired by his wealthy German patron, Prince Maximilian of Wied-Neuwied, to provide accurate visual data for what was essentially a scientific expedition, and that is what he did. But Bodmer went further than that.

He Never Did It Again

During his time in America, he made many drawings that stand up as first-rate works of art. He had never done this before, and once he left the New World and returned to Europe he never did it again, and that, it seems to me, raises some interesting questions.

Who was Karl Bodmer, anyway?

. . . He was born in Zurich in 1809, and . . . before he set out for America, at the age of twenty-three, he had made his living as a journeyman illustrator. He specialized in travel pictures— paintings of romantic vistas along the Moselle and the Rhine, following the well-established pictorial conventions of that prephotographic era. His meeting with the Prince changed his life. Maximilian, a landed German from an old and aristocratic family, had found his vocation as an explorer and a naturalist. He had spent the years 1815 to 1817 exploring and naturalizing in the jungles of Brazil, inspired by the example of his great countryman Alexander von Humboldt, and when Bodmer met him, in 1832, he was preparing to embark on a similar expedition into the North American wilderness west and north of St. Louis. Maximilian wanted a professional artist to go along, and after looking at samples of Bodmer's work he wrote to a friend that the young Swiss "will be able to draw what is put before him." Their contract was simple and straightforward. Bodmer was to be paid a regular salary, and his original drawings would belong to the Prince. (He was allowed to make copies for himself, if he chose.) Bodmer was a technician, in other words, hired to perform a specific service.

Painting the Badlands

Once they reached St. Louis, in the spring of 1833, and boarded an American Fur Company steamboat headed up the Missouri, Maximilian's letters show increasing respect for Bodmer. The artist sketched tirelessly, in all weathers, and his skill seemed to increase day by day. He painted the prairies and grasslands, the herds of elk and other game, the twisting, snag-infested course of the turbulent river, and, later on, the fantastic, water-and-wind-carved rock formations of the Mauvaises Terres, the badlands of the upper Missouri. He responded to the challenge of depicting these landscapes, which resembled nothing he had seen in Europe, largely by abandoning the formal conventions of European landscape painting.

. . . His technique is dazzling—subtle color laid down in delicate washes, every topographical detail brought off with clarity and finesse. He was reinventing the art of landscape painting, and doing so under difficult, sometimes dangerous conditions—driving himself to do what had not been done before.

The travellers spent more than a month at Fort McKenzie, the westernmost outpost of the American Fur Company, not far from present-day Great Falls, Montana. The tiny fort was surrounded by an encampment of ferocious Blackfeet, who had only recently started trading with the Americans. A few of them were reluctant to pose for Bodmer, but his persistence usually won them over. They marvelled at the accuracy of his likenesses. An elderly Piegan insisted that the strong magic of Bodmer's portrait of him had saved his life during a bloody early-morning raid by a detachment of Cree and Assiniboin.

Prophetic Paintings

Bodmer clearly admired these magnificent-looking people, and on the return trip both he and Maximilian developed warm friendships with the more settled Mandan, near whose village they spent that winter. The Mandan village was above what is now Bismarck,

North Dakota, close to the Canadian border, and the visitors' makeshift accommodations there offered little protection from the below-zero weather. Bodmer's paints often froze, but he thawed them out and painted every day, with the diligence and intensity of a man possessed. There is something about his Indian portraits— an impenetrable sadness in the eyes—that I am tempted to call prophetic. In the same way that some of the Missouri landscapes carry a weight of desolation and emptiness, the portraits suggest (to me, at least) the historical doom that was about to descend on those people. Four years after Bodmer painted the upper-Missouri tribes, smallpox struck them, wiping out about half the Blackfeet and virtually the entire Mandan culture. The pattern of white conquest and betrayal was already accelerating. I can't argue that Bodmer was alert to these historical currents. But in his best work he cut so close to the truth of appearances that I think he broke through it into something more profound: the extreme stillness at the moment of great change.

He Never Returned

For Bodmer, that moment ended even more suddenly than it did for the tribes. He sailed back to Europe in 1834 and never returned. For some years, he worked on aquatint etchings of his American drawings, for an illustrated volume to go with Prince Maximilian's two-volume narrative of their trip. When the work came out, in 1841, after many delays, it was a financial failure. Having found no takers for his original watercolors, which the Prince had allowed him to exhibit in Paris, Bodmer eventually turned to oil, canvas, and tradition. He became a salon artist whose subjects were life-size paintings of animals and sentimental forest scenes. Apparently, he never again attempted to draw a human face.

After some years in Paris, he moved out to the suburban village of Barbizon, near Fontainebleau, where his friend Jean-François Millet and other artists of the Barbizon school were living. For two decades, he was moderately successful, winning prizes at the salon, selling work, and earning a supplementary income as an illustrator of books and magazines, but fame eluded him. Sometimes he blamed this on his North American adventure. The years he spent on the publication of his American drawings, he wrote to Maximilian in 1853, "did great damage to my career which I will never again be able to recoup or recover." Eventually, his animals and forest scenes went out of fashion. He moved back to Paris, where he lived out his last years in increasing poverty. He died, blind and forgotten, in 1893. Nobody would have heard of him today if the original watercolors and drawings of the expedition had not been discovered, after the Second World War, in a store-room of Prince Maximilian's estate on the Rhine, near Koblenz. The Prince's descendants put them on exhibition, and eventually sold them to M. Knoedler & Company. In 1962, Knoedler sold them to the Northern Natural Gas Company of Omaha (now called Inter-North, Inc.), which put them on permanent loan at the Joslyn Art Museum.

Bodmer: What Happened?

What are we to make of this story? A mediocre artist (artisan, really) is presented with an immense challenge and for a brief period produces great art, or something close to great art; then he subsides into mediocrity for the remainder of his life, presumably unaware of what he achieved at his finest moment. Was he simply unwilling to keep on paying the enormous price for work of that quality? Bodmer appears to have become a fairly unpleasant chap after his return to Europe, complaining constantly about his pub-lishing arrangements with the Prince (who, by contrast, was unfail-ingly generous and forbearing toward him), regularly demanding more money, and feeling generally put upon by life. But the fact remains that for more than a year on that trip up the Missouri he worked like a demon, rarely complaining, always pushing his talent to surpass itself. It has been said that during a great period in art, such as the Italian Renaissance, it is possible sometimes for a minor artist to paint a great picture—the work going on around him can actually pull him up to a higher level. For Bodmer, how-ever, alone in an alien wilderness, the pictorial conventions of his time were no help at all.

It could be argued that Bodmer was responding also to the stimulation of his employer's mind. Prince Maximilian was no mere dilettante. A serious naturalist, he was, in addition, a product of those currents in nineteenth-century German thought which demanded a merging of the real and the ideal, of pragmatic obser-vation and grand philosophical truth. It was Alexander von Hum-boldt, Darwin's mentor, who urged Maximilian to take an artist on his North American trip. Humboldt, who was interested in practi-cally everything, saw a need for new forms of landscape art. In his monumental work "Cosmos," he wrote, "Landscape painting will flourish with a new and hitherto unknown brilliancy when artists of merit shall more frequently pass the narrow limits of the Mediterranean, and when they shall be enabled, far in the interior of continents . . . to seize, with the genuine freshness of a pure and youthful spirit, on the true image of the varied forms of nature." Maximilian may very well have communicated such ideas to Bodmer, for the two men became close friends during their long trip together . . . .

Bodmer's . . . Indians are not noble savages; his landscapes are never sublime. Quite often, in fact, these small-scale watercolors of treeless plains and hills have an inhospitable look that seems very close to what we can see today in certain parts of the country. The beauty of our Western landscape (what's left of it) is a harsh beauty, and impressive for that reason. Bodmer caught the harshness as well as the beauty, and in his Indian portraits he caught something else—the authentic look of people whose way of life had endured for a long time, knowing nothing of Europe. He got it all down accurately and truthfully, seized it with Humboldt's "genuine freshness," and then he went home to paint noble stags and sylvan glades.

It could never happen to a contemporary artist; and even if it could, how would we know? . . . He had a disappointing life, and felt he had wasted his time in America. What a joy it must have been, though, to work at that high level, in that high country, in 1833. Among the Mandan, he was called Kawakapuska, "the one who makes pictures." Years later, Bodmer is reported to have spoken nostalgically and a bit sentimentally about those vanished people: "In Europe I have acquaintances," he said, "but over there I had friends."

Elizabeth Neeld Comments:

✦ *Between 1830 and 1835 America's population ranged from approximately twelve million to fifteen million. There were twenty-four states, none further west than Missouri. The national debt ranged from four to forty-eight thousand dollars. Andrew Jackson was president. America was still young.* ✦ *Many Indian tribes were ceding land to the United States. The Choctaw Indians ceded almost eight million acres of their land east of the Mississippi in exchange for what is now Oklahoma. The Sioux, Sauk, and Fox Indians ceded land that is now Iowa, parts of Missouri,* and Minnesota. The Cherokee nation lost their battle to be considered a foreign nation. The Seminole Indians signed a treaty in Florida in exchange for lands in the west. A lot of attention was on the Indians who were moving across the country and the Indians who already lived out west. ✦ This interest was particularly high in Europe where people were fascinated with the American wilderness and its native inhabitants. On April 10, 1833, Prince Maximilian, who was a wealthy German adventurer, brought his valet David Dreidoppel and one other traveler with him to America to explore the Western lands. This other person was an artist named Karl Bodmer, hired especially for this trip to paint pictures of the lands and peoples the travelers met on their journey. Maximilian was particularly interested in the study of natural history and ethnology. He was concerned with the climates and natural habitats where other human groups lived, with close scientific observation of facts and the collecting of specimens. Maximilian had already spent two years studying people and their environment in Brazil. ✦ Bodmer, on the other hand, had no special interest in America or its inhabitants. He was an illustrator who specialized in watercolor studies of leaping stags, brooding forests, and towering mountains. Bodmer was along on this trip because someone had shown a travel book he had illustrated to Prince Maximilian; the Prince hired Bodmer to accompany him and collect specimens from the West and study the "aboriginal nations of America." The men sailed for America on May 17, 1832; they returned home to Germany in July of 1834. ✦ In the two years the men traveled in America, Bodmer painted pictures that have never been equaled. The Indians of the Great Plains had a very striking physical appearance, wore colorful costumes, and were known for their warriors, horsemen, big game hunters, dances, and religious ceremonies. Artists loved to paint them, and Bodmer was no exception. He painted these Indians as individual people. Every detail is accurate—the features of an Indian's face, the pattern of a face painting or a body tattoo, the size and shape of a hair, ear, or neck ornament, the furnishings of an Indian earth lodge. As a portrayer of the Indians of the upper Missouri and their customs,

Bodmer ranks as the realist who was never surpassed. (Bodmer never had trouble getting people to pose for him: news got out that being painted by Bodmer made you invincible should a bullet hit you. The Indians came asking to have their portraits done!) Much of what we know about these Indians—many of whom were to be completely wiped out by smallpox and other calamities within a very few years—we know because of Bodmer's pictures. ✦ *But here's the startling thing. After achieving this phenomenal artistic success, after painting scenes and people that the world would never forget, Bodmer went back home to Germany and to obscurity. He never painted a masterpiece again. He declined to go on an expedition to Egypt and finally retired to an artists' colony in France where he painted forests and animals and became in one critic's words "as silly as he had once been honest." His last years were spent alone, melancholy, sick, and out of artistic favor, although he and Maximilian continued to correspond.* ✦ *This essay, "Who Was Karl Bodmer, Anyway?" was written by Calvin Tomkins, and it illustrates originality in writing about art. Tomkins is a staff writer for the* New Yorker *magazine, and he is also a highly respected author of novels, short stories, and biographies. His books and articles on art were once described this way: "His quiet, meticulously detailed prose is the voice of reason calmly explaining the work of madmen." He is known for making material enjoyable and for being able to explain clearly what is often puzzling to others.* ✦ *Calvin Tomkins went to the Metropolitan Museum to see an art exhibit that he thought would be a way to while away some time. He did not expect what he found. As he says in the essay, about a third of the way through the exhibit, he got hooked. He realized how good Bodmer was, and Calvin Tomkins, the writer, became engaged. Instead of just moving along the walls of the exhibit hall glancing at the paintings as he walked by, he began to look and he began to think, (marks of the potential for being an original writer.) He started wondering, "How did this obscure German illustrator do this magnificent work?" He became interested in finding out what he could about the artist. And in so doing, he could not get away from the gripping question: Why did this man never paint anything worthwhile again? Why did he never paint again with power and force and authenticity? Those questions are at the heart of this essay, an essay which illustrates originality at its best. A writer hooked on his subject. Engaged with thinking about: Why? What? When? How? A writer reporting what he sees and is.* ✦

ANNIE DILLARD

In the Jungle

Like any out-of-the-way place, the Napo River in the Ecuadorian jungle seems real enough when you are there, even central. Out of the way of *what*? I was sitting on a stump at the edge of a bankside palm-thatch village, in the middle of the night, on the headwaters of the Amazon. Out of the way of human life, tenderness, or the glance of heaven?

A nightjar in deep-leaved shadow called three long notes, and hushed. The men with me talked softly in clumps: three North Americans, four Ecuadorians who were showing us the jungle. We were holding cool drinks and idly watching a hand-sized tarantula seize moths that came to the lone bulb on the generator shed beside us.

It was February, the middle of summer. Green fireflies spattered lights across the air and illumined for seconds, now here, now there, the pale trunks of enormous, solitary trees. Beneath us the brown Napo River was rising in all silence; it coiled up the sandy bank and tangled its foam in vines that trailed from the forest and roots that looped the shore.

Each breath of night smelled sweet, more moistened and sweet than any kitchen, or garden, or cradle. Each star in Orion seemed to tremble and stir with my breath. All at once, in the thatch house across the clearing behind us, one of the village's Jesuit priests began playing an alto recorder, playing a wordless song, lyric, in a minor key, that twined over the village clearing, that caught in the big trees' canopies, muted our talk on the bankside, and wandered over the river, dissolving downstream.

This will do, I thought. This will do, for a weekend, or a season, or a home.

Why Am I Going Back?

Later that night I loosed my hair from its braids and combed it smooth—not for myself, but so the village girls could play with it in the morning.

We had disembarked at the village that afternoon, and I had slumped on some shaded steps, wishing I knew some Spanish or some Quechua so I could speak with the ring of little girls who were alternately staring at me and smiling at their toes. I spoke anyway, and fooled with my hair, which they were obviously dying to get their hands on, and laughed, and soon they were all braiding my hair, all five of them, all fifty fingers, all my hair, even my bangs. And then they took it apart and did it again, laughing, and teaching me Spanish nouns, and meeting my eyes and each other's with open delight, while their small brothers in blue jeans climbed down from the trees and began kicking a volleyball around with one of the North American men.

Now, as I combed my hair in the little tent, another of the men, a free-lance writer from Manhattan, was talking quietly. He was telling us the tale of his life, describing his work in Hollywood, his apartment in Manhattan, his house in Paris. . . . "It makes me wonder," he said, "what I'm doing in a tent under a tree in the village of Pompeya, on the Napo River, in the jungle of Ecuador." After a pause he added, "It makes me wonder why I'm going *back*."

We're Here Only Once

The point of going somewhere like the Napo River in Ecuador is not to see the most spectacular anything. It is simply to see what is there. We are here on the planet only once, and might as well get a feel for the place. We might as well get a feel for the fringes and hollows in which life is lived, for the Amazon basin, which covers half a continent, and for the life that—there, like anywhere else—is always and necessarily lived in detail: on the tributaries, in the riverside villages, sucking this particular white-fleshed guava in this particular pattern of shade.

What is there is interesting. The Napo River itself is wide (I mean wider than the Mississippi at Davenport) and brown, opaque, and smeared with floating foam and logs and branches from the jungle. White egrets hunch on shoreline deadfalls and parrots in flocks dart in and out of the light. Under the water in the river, unseen, are anacondas—which are reputed to take a few village toddlers every year—and water boas, stingrays, crocodiles, manatees, and sweet-meated fish.

Low water bares gray strips of sandbar on which the natives build tiny palm-thatch shelters, arched, the size of pup tents, for overnight fishing trips. You see these extraordinarily clean people (who bathe twice a day in the river, and whose straight black hair is always freshly washed) paddling down the river in dugout canoes, hugging the banks.

Some of the Indians of this region, earlier in the century, used to sleep naked in hammocks. The nights are cold. Gordon Mac-Creach, an American explorer in these Amazon tributaries, reported that he was startled to hear the Indians get up at three in the morning. He was even more startled, night after night, to hear them walk down the river slowly, half asleep, and bathe in the water. Only later did he learn what they were doing: they were getting warm.The cold woke them; they warmed their skins in the river, which was always ninety degrees; then they returned to their hammocks and slept through the rest of the night.

The riverbanks are low, and from the river you see an unbroken wall of dark forest in every direction, from the Andes to the Atlantic. You get a taste for looking at trees: trees hung with the swinging nests of yellow troupials, trees from which ant nests the size of grain sacks hang like black goiters, trees from which seven-colored tanagers flutter, coral trees, teak, balsa and breadfruit, enormous emergent silk-cotton trees, and the pale-barked *samona* palms.

Jaguars, Armadillos, and Texaco Derricks

When you are inside the jungle, away from the river, the trees vault out of sight. It is hard to remember to look up the long trunks and see the fans, strips, fronds, and sprays of glossy leaves. Inside the jungle you are more likely to notice the snarl of climbers and creepers round the trees' boles, the flowering bromeliads and epiphytes in every bough's crook, and the fantastic silk-cotton tree trunks thirty or forty feet across, trunks buttressed in flanges of wood whose curves can make three high walls of a room—a shady, loamy-aired room where you would gladly live, or die. Butterflies, iridescent blue, striped, or clear-winged, thread the jungle paths at eye level. And at your feet is a swath of ants bearing triangular bits of green leaf. The ants with their leaves look like a wide fleet of sailing dinghies—but they don't quit. In either direction they wobble over the jungle floor as far as the eye can see. I followed them off the path as far as I dared, and never saw an end to ants or to those luffing chips of green they bore.

Unseen in the jungle, but present, are tapirs, jaguars, many species of snake and lizard, ocelots, armadillos, marmosets, howler monkeys, toucans and macaws and a hundred other birds, deer, bats, peccaries, capybaras, agoutis, and sloths. Also present in this jungle, but variously distant, are Texaco derricks and pipelines, and some of the wildest Indians in the world, blowgun-using Indians, who killed missionaries in 1956 and ate them.

Long lakes shine in the jungle. We traveled one of these in dugout canoes, canoes with two inches of freeboard, canoes paddled with machete-hewn oars chopped from buttresses of silk-cotton trees, or poled in the shallows with peeled cane or bamboo. Our part-Indian guide had cleared the path to the lake the day before; when we walked the path we saw where he had impaled the lopped head of a boa, open-mouthed, on a pointed stick by the canoes, for decoration.

This lake was wonderful. Herons, egrets, and ibises plodded the sawgrass shores, kingfishers and cuckoos clattered from sunlight to shade, great turkeylike birds fussed in dead branches, and hawks lolled overhead. There was all the time in the world. A turtle slid into the water. They boy in the bow of my canoe slapped stones at birds with a simple sling, a rubber thong and leather pad. He aimed brilliantly at moving targets, always, and always missed; the birds were out of range. He stuffed his sling back in his shirt. I looked around.

The lake and river waters are as opaque as rain-forest leaves; they are veils, blinds, painted screens. You see things only by their effects. I saw the shoreline water roil and the sawgrass heave above a thrashing *paichi*, an enormous black fish of these waters; one had been caught the previous week weighing 430 pounds. Piranha fish live in the lakes, and electric eels. I dangled my fingers in the water, figuring it would be worth it.

In or Out of the Way?

We would eat chicken that night in the village, and rice, yucca, onions, beets, and heaps of fruit. The sun would ring down, pulling darkness after it like a curtain. Twilight is short, and the unseen birds of twilight wistful, uncanny, catching the heart. The two nuns in their dazzling white habits—the beautiful-boned young nun and the warm-faced old—would glide to the open cane-and-thatch schoolroom in darkness, and start the children singing. The children would sing in piping Spanish, high-pitched and pure; they would sing "Nearer My God to Thee" in Quechua, very fast. (To reciprocate, we sang for them "Old MacDonald Had a Farm"; I thought they might recognize the animal sounds. Of course they thought we were out of our minds.) As the children became excited by their own singing, they left their log benches and swarmed around the nuns, hopping, smiling at us, everyone smiling, the nuns' faces bursting in their cowls, and the clear-voiced children still singing, and the palm-leafed roofing stirred.

The Napo River: it is not out of the way. It is *in* the way, catching sunlight the way a cup catches poured water; it is a bowl of sweet air, a basin of greenness, and of grace, and, it would seem, of peace.

Elizabeth Neeld Comments:

✦ *Once I was marooned for several days in the middle of July in a small, sleepy, dusty Wyoming town, waiting for the Greyhound bus to bring a part for my broken-down car. Being in this town was a waste of time; I was on my way to somewhere else—a big important place. After spending an evening being bored, then a morning being bored, with nothing to look forward to but an afternoon to be bored, I decided to pay attention to the place I was in and see what I could make out of my stay. The end result was that I enjoyed being in this little out-of-the-way town, got invited by the local librarian to a barbeque in her backyard, learned something about fence mending, and found in the feed store a canvas bag made to carry rope which I still use as a piece of luggage when I travel.* ✦ *What I did out of necessity—or boredom—that summer in Wyoming, Annie Dillard does every day of her life: she pays attention to wherever she is and looks at whatever is in front of her. The result is that she is able to see a place, a person, an event for itself, not as a figment of any preconceived ideas or opinions. What richness results. What originality.* ✦ *Let's take this essay as an example. Dillard is on a trip in South America. She's deep in a jungle in Ecuador, at night, camped beside the Napo River in a tiny village called Pompeya. This village is what just about anybody would call an out-of-the-way place. But Dillard asks, "Out of the way of what?" (Questioning presumed opinions and commonly agreed upon ideas is absolutely essential if you're going to think with originality.) Dillard wonders about the village— surely this place can't be out of the way of "human life, tenderness, or the glance of heaven."* ✦ *Then for much of the rest of the essay she contrasts the strangeness which might make the location "out-of-the-way" with those things that make the village, the Napo River, and the jungle very much "in the way." While she and the other visitors are holding cool drinks, there are hand-sized tarantulas seizing the moths that hover around the lightbulb on the generator. There are green fireflys, pale trunks of solitary trees, a brown river rising—and in the thatched-roof house across the clearing a Jesuit priest is playing a musical instrument. There are little girls that loved to plait hair and little boys that wear blue jeans and kick volleyballs. There are also Indians who get up at three o'clock in the morning to take a bath so they can warm their skins. The solitary trees have ant nests the size of grain sacks. There are lakes and dugout canoes—and there are anacondas that eat toddlers. There are moths, but there are also jaguars, ocelots, armadillos, tapirs—and a Texaco oil derrick. There are children singing "Nearer My God to Thee" in Quechua and Annie and her friends singing "Old MacDonald Had a Farm" in English. About all this mixture of ordinariness and strangeness Dillard says, "The point of going some-*

where . . . is not to see the most spectacular anything. It is simply to see what is there. We are here on the planet only once, and might as well get a feel for the fringes and hollows in which life is lived." ✦ Annie Dillard started this commitment to observing and engaging with whatever she comes into contact with when she was just a little girl. In Pittsburgh one day, when she was ten years old, she checked out "a small blue-bound book," The Field Book of Ponds and Streams, which she reread every year, giving her an awareness of the great variety of life to be found in ponds and streams. A couple of years later she started studying insects and larvae under a child's microscope. She also always wanted to be an artist and draws "obsessively" all down the margins of her manuscripts. All this contributes to her being able to see. ✦ Dillard, in her way of engaging with whatever she sees, has been described as a person without conventional prejudices, who starts from zero to make sense of what she sees. At the heart of her originality is this ability to look at something unencumbered by preconceived ideas. She scrutinizes real phenomena, such as the village in Ecuador, and then she reflects on this reality. Dillard sees her task as a writer is to be fully alert, to be a conscious receptacle of all impressions. She offers new insight into human existence. We all have available to us the ability to learn to see and to reflect on what we see. We, too, can be original. ✦

SAMUEL C. FLORMAN

The Education of an Engineer

I became an engineer."

Thus begins John Hersey's novel A *Single Pebble*, in which the protagonist travels to pre-revolutionary China seeking a site for a dam along the Yangtze River. As he encounters a civilization little changed since the Middle Ages, the young man finds his faith in technology giving way to awe and self-doubt. I, too, became an engineer and have spent a number of years thinking about, as well as practicing, this much-misunderstood profession, albeit in less dramatic settings than the chasms of the Yangtze, and with less discouraging conclusions than Mr. Hersey's.

How does one decide to become an engineer? Studies made a generation ago indicate that it used to be the quest for "interesting work." According to what I hear today, employment opportunities are what count. Doubtless both motives pertain, with the less lofty one having recently come to the fore.

How I Decided to Become an Engineer

I made the decision in 1942 during my senior year at the Fieldston School, a sylvan campus in the Riverdale section of the Bronx, forty-five minutes by subway from where I lived in Manhattan. The ideal had occurred to me earlier—especially during several visits to the 1939 World's Fair—but I was far from the stereotypical engineer. I did not, for example, build radios, assemble models, or fiddle with car engines. Like my fellow students at Fieldston, I read a lot of books and wrote a lot of papers. My favorite subject by far was English, particularly a senior seminar in which we reviewed great Western literature from Aeschylus to Joyce. Nevertheless, I did my best work in mathematics and was gently urged by several teachers to consider a career in science.

There were no two cultures in those days. I can recall no division between students of different sorts of talents, but rather a mutual respect and a shared appreciation of achievement. If this sounds idyllic, well, it was. Which is not to say that we lived in a state of constant elation—we were teenagers, after all—but, academically, the place was heaven. We knew that we would follow many different career paths; the world seemed wonderfully open and full of possibilities—in the arts, the sciences, and the professions. Business, however, we regarded with a scorn compounded of intellectual elitism and post-1930s radicalism. Ironically, the fathers who paid our not inconsiderable tuition were mostly hard-working small businessmen. Of the acceptable careers, science, medicine, and engineering were considered more or less on a par with law, journalism, and the arts. Excellence is what counted; our class had an abundance of it, and our expectations were high. We were not surprised in later years when Roger Lazarus, the most accomplished student, studied physics at Harvard, got his doctorate there, and ended up at Los Alamos, any more than we were when Joe Kraft, president of the student council, became a nationally syndicated newspaper columnist, often called a pundit. We were a class full of potential pundits.

Although I wanted my life's work to be creative and stimulating, I was not totally oblivious to money. A part of my depression-bred consciousness was concerned about someday being able to support a family. For all the appeal of mathematics and physics, it wasn't clear to me how one made a living in those fields. This was even more true of writing and the arts. Business, as I have said, was out of the question, and as for medicine, needles made me queasy.

So I chose engineering. Engineers, from the little I knew, studied science and used their brains. They also got jobs and earned salaries—and, after a fashion, they were cultural heroes. The newsreels that I saw every weekend, between two movies at Loew's 83rd Street, often featured the dedication of a new TVA dam or some other impressive public work. There was much cutting of ribbons and drinking of toasts, each event celebrating a counter-attack against rural dust bowls or urban slums. When the movies themselves depicted engineers—usually in the B films, to be sure—they were stalwart men in high-laced boots engaged in heroic endeavors, such as building railroads or prospecting for oil. Intellectually challenging, financially sensible, and withal a touch of romance and adventure—engineering seemed an ideal calling.

An Exploitable Sub-Class

I had never heard it suggested that engineers were lower-middle-class, eccentric, or uncultivated (today I believe the epithet is "nerd"), and it did not occur to me that anybody held such opinions. The only sour note was sounded by an uncle who observed that instead of wanting to *be* an engineer I should aim to be someone who *hires* engineers, thus implying that I was about to join an exploitable sub-class. The remark enraged my father, who had no clear idea of what engineers do but was proud to have a son about to enter a profession.

When it came time to select a college, I naturally thought about M.I.T. Two of my engineering-bound classmates, including my best friend, went to that distinguished institution and never regretted their choice. But something about the huge labyrinth of laboratories made my heart sink, and still does in spite of all the good things I know about the place. Instead, I chose Dartmouth College, whose beautiful New Hampshire campus captured my fancy. I was also concerned about something called "college spirit" and impressed by the mystique of the Ivy League. Quaint and embarrassing as this seems in retrospect, I confess that traces of these feelings remain with me today.

I had only the vaguest idea of how one went about getting an engineering education. According to the Dartmouth catalog, I would "go to college," earn a bachelor of arts degree while majoring in the sciences, then pursue an engineering degree in graduate school.

General Sylvanus Thayer

This is how General Sylvanus Thayer thought it ought to be when in 1867 he gave Dartmouth forty thousand dollars for the purpose of establishing the Thayer School of Engineering. As superintendent of the U.S. Military Academy from 1817 to 1833, the general had overseen the development of that institution into a distinguished school of applied science, and in his later years he decided to endow a graduate school of engineering at a liberal arts college. He believed that before embarking upon professional training one ought to become "a gentleman." The Thayer School's two-year program originally was designed to follow after a full four-year undergraduate education, although in 1893 a five-year program was devised that combines the senior year of college with the first year of engineering school. That five-year program endures to this day.

In most of the nation, however, engineering education evolved along different lines. The technical institutes, and later the land-grant colleges, developed four-year programs that carried students directly from high school into engineering studies. This effectively did away with the concept of a liberally educated engineer, although the accrediting arm of the profession eventually required that an engineering curriculum have a minimum 12.5 percent liberal component.

Of all this I was blissfully unaware as I arrived in Hanover, New Hampshire, in July of 1942. (A year-round program had been instituted because of the war.) I embarked on a typical course of study: English literature and French, sociology and economics, psychology and political science. As a pre-engineering student, I also took mathematics, physics, and chemistry, and two other subjects— then required but long since discarded—graphics and surveying. I will not argue that these courses deserved to maintain their place in higher education, but I recall vividly the delights of T-square, triangle, and India ink, and the thrill of carrying a transit through the autumn woods. These sorties into the tangible world, combined with the abstract fancies of mathematics and the sciences, reinforced my conviction that I was headed toward the best of all possible careers.

A Vocational Revolution

I was barely into my sophomore year when, almost imperceptibly, I began to undergo a metamorphosis. As if under a spell, I became increasingly absorbed in my technical, pre-professional studies.

Looking back, I find it difficult to explain what happened, although, since the experience is undergone each year by many of the more than one hundred thousand Americans who enter engineering, how extraordinary can it be? What I do know is that the liberal arts began to pale and seem trivial, even annoying. Mathematical formulas took on the quality of fun-filled games, and the physical world became an enchanted kingdom whose every secret seemed worth exploring. I began to think exclusively of how courses would help me become a better engineer, more thoroughly grounded in the sciences, more perceptive and quick-witted, and—let us face facts—more desirable to some future employer. Despite the educational advantages I had enjoyed in high school, and notwithstanding the proclaimed policy of the liberal arts college I was attending, I came down with a bad case of vocationalism. I lost interest in becoming an educated person—the "gentleman" envisioned by Sylvanus Thayer. I wanted to become an engineer.

Could an inspiring humanities professor have prevented this from happening? I like to think so. Surely the situation was not helped by a freshman English course devoted to the painstaking dissection of *Lord Jim*, or by the introductory social science courses, which were informative but deadly dull. More exciting teachers and better planned classes might have made the difference, but it is common knowledge that when one is embarked on an affair of the heart, the most prudent counsel, even skillfully presented, often falls on deaf ears. And there can be no doubt but that my feeling about engineering was not altogether different from falling in love.

As it happened, my most exciting professors were mathematicians. I recall winning a prize in a mathematics competition—second prize, to be exact—and being invited along with the other winners to dinner at the home of the department head. After dining, we sat in the living room sipping brandy and listening to recordings of Mozart sonatas. Although at the time my musical taste ran more to Glenn Miller and Artie Shaw, I found the experience extremely agreeable. I associated my euphoria with the delights of mathematics, not giving adequate credit, I now believe, to Mozart and the winning of prizes, to say nothing of brandy.

Along with my commitment to mathematics and science, I developed a taste for free-time activities that I can only characterize as anti-intellectual. My pre-engineering fellows and I spent our leisure hours attending movies and sporting events. Occasionally we hitchhiked to Smith College and looked for girls. When lectures, concerts, and plays were offered on campus, it seemed natural that they be attended by other students, those strange young men who had decided to major in history, philosophy, or literature. One of my dormitory mates was enrolled in a special course with Robert Frost, who was at the time poet in residence at Dartmouth. Several times my friend invited me to join him for an evening of readings and discussion with the noted poet, but I was always too busy writing up my laboratory experiments or else committed to a party at some local tavern. Today I cannot believe—*simply cannot believe*—that I never even saw Robert Frost, much less spent an evening with him when I had the chance.

A Civil Engineer

Shortly after entering college, I had enlisted in the Navy V-12 program on campus. At the end of each term, a period of uncertainty set in while we recruits waited to hear what the government had planned for us. After a year, we were called to active duty, but this merely meant putting on a uniform and learning how to march in formation. Those of us who were heading for engineering were encouraged to continue with our studies. After twenty-four months of non-stop schooling, I had accumulated the equivalent of three years of credits and was ready to enter the professional phase of my education.

I had by this time resolved to become a "civil" engineer. The term was coined in mid-eighteenth-century England by John Smeaton, builder of the Eddystone lighthouse. He used the term *civil* to demonstrate that his work had no military implication, which is ironic in that most military engineers subsequently have been trained in civil engineering. Civil engineers design and construct buildings, dams, bridges, towers, docks, tunnels—structures of all sorts. Civil engineering also encompasses highways, railroads, and airports, along with water supply and sewage disposal. In short, civil engineering is basic and of the earth—historically, along with mining, the root of all engineering. In the eighteenth century the development of the steam engine led to a new specialty called mechanical engineering, and each major technological advance has brought with it a fresh division of the profession: electrical, chemical, aeronautical, petroleum, computer, and so forth. I make this digression into the self-evident only because so many otherwise well-informed people keep asking me what it is that engineers *do*. Every technological product has to be designed and its manufacture overseen, and that is what engineers do. They occupy the vast middle spectrum between theoretical scientists and sub-professional technicians.

Buildings are usually planned by architects, but engineers design the structural and mechanical components within them, and civil engineers often oversee the actual construction process. These overseers are sometimes called construction engineers, and this is what I have become—more of a business manager, I suppose, than a creative spirit, more of a master builder than a man of science, yet still a member of the engineering family.

I have long forgotten most of the theorems that I learned in engineering school, but I recall vividly the nature, the "feel" of that learning. Like all engineers, I took basic courses in electricity, fluid mechanics, metallurgy, and thermodynamics (the study of heat and energy, particularly the workings of internal combustion engines, air conditioners, and the like). As a civil engineer, I took a series of courses in "structures," learning how to design beams, walls, slabs, and trusses. Then there were the more specialized studies: highways, water supply, and sanitation. In all of this there was a good amount of hands-on work. We poured concrete, cured it, and tested it to failure, analyzed the behavior of water in pipes and weirs, and experimented with a variety of motors and generators. Occasionally we ventured out into the field, visiting construction jobs and sewage treatment plants, or—a great favorite— measuring the flow of a river while perched above it in a tiny hand-operated cable car. The theoretical work was difficult—some of it exceedingly so—but the physical *doing* made it seem worthwhile.

Nowadays engineering education is much more scientific than it used to be. In addition to the subjects that were taught in the 1940s, a contemporary curriculum will include computing and information processing, probability and statistics, systems, optimization, and control theory, even system dynamics (policy design and analysis based on feedback principles and computer simulation). Much of the so-called shop work has fallen by the wayside, relegated to students who take two-year technician courses or four-year technology programs. The change came about in the 1950s, particularly in the aftershock of Sputnik when the quality of American science and engineering was called into question. Also, the growth of new disciplines means that there is simply more material to learn and so less time for knocking about in overalls and muddy boots. This has been inevitable, appropriate, and a darned shame.

An Island Education

In the spring of 1945, the Navy decided to call in my debt, so to speak, and I was ordered to officers' training school. After a few weeks of shooting guns, large and small, and studying semaphore code and naval etiquette, I was commissioned an ensign in the Civil Engineer Corps and sent to serve with the Seabees. I arrived in the Philippines just as the war was ending and went with the Twenty-ninth Construction Battalion to occupy Truk, an atoll in the Caroline Islands that had been bypassed during the westward move across the Pacific.

It was a pleasant enough life for a young would-be engineer. During the day we worked on construction projects, repaving the airstrip with fresh coral dredged from the sea, erecting Quonset huts, and building roads and a water supply system. In the evenings we drank beer, played cards, and talked—mostly about our work, baseball, and girls. Also—and I could not remember this happening since early childhood—I found myself with long periods of spare time. As the tropical sun sank into the sea behind implausible palm trees, it was impossible not to become introspective.

Among myths of self-discovery and inner change, life on a desert island has an honored place. It helps, of course, if the island has a supply of books. Our battalion had a library of sorts, stocked with those chunky, squarish paperbacks printed especially for the armed forces. To pass the time, I started to read again. At first my reading was purely recreational: the mysteries of Erle Stanley Gardner, the historical novels of Thomas Costain and Samuel Shellabarger, the best-sellers of Lloyd Douglas and Irving Stone, and the outlandish burlesques of Max Shulman and H. Allen Smith. I had forgotten how much fun books could be, even ordinary unprepossessing ones. Besides contemporary reprints, our island library held a number of Modern Library classics, and to these I turned next. One evening I started to read *Crime and Punishment*. It was as if I had stepped through a looking glass and found myself back in my high-school English seminar. Here once again were supercharged words and ideas and people and passions and questions of justice and the meaning of life.

It was like high school again and yet different because, though I was only four years older, I felt forty years more mature. According to a remark one hears time and again at engineering conferences, during their first ten years out of college, engineers wish that they had taken more technical courses; for the next decade they wish they had studied more business and economics; thereafter they regret that they had not delved more deeply into literature, history, and philosophy. On a Pacific island, thousands of miles from what we call civilization, the decades condense and the urge for meaning wells up in a young engineer as if he were at the peak of his career. At least this is what happened to me as I read *Crime and Punishment*, then *Madame Bovary*, *The Scarlett Letter*, *Pride and Prejudice*, *Fathers and Sons*, *Tess of the D'Urbervilles*, and other works I cannot now recall.

Boring Engineers

I did not discuss with my fellow officers the books that I read and the thoughts that these books engendered. During the day, as the bulldozers roared and dust clouds rose, I immersed myself in the work as if nothing had changed, and in the evenings I idly chatted and joked like one of the guys. But I began to wonder why we engineers, as a group, seemed to live in a world so far removed, intellectually and emotionally, from the ferment I was rediscovering in literature.

The only officer in the battalion who was not an engineer was the chaplain. One night he joined several of us in a game of cards. Between hands the conversation droned on in the usual way, which, as I have said, meant anecdotes about our work, the current baseball season, and girls. The chaplain tried to interject some thoughts about the United Nations and prospects for international order. We did not respond. He then tried other topics: the morality of nuclear weapons, the ethical responsibility of war criminals, the role of religion in the post-war world, and so forth, but each time we returned to our trivia. Finally the chaplain slammed his cards down on the table, looked upward, and said in a loud voice, "Dear Lord, I know that I am unworthy, I confess that I have sinned, but why did you have to abandon me on this island with nobody for company but these boring engineers?"

I cannot say that from that moment on my life was totally changed, but it was an epiphany of sorts, a moment that I have never forgotten. I do not, needless to say, advocate wars or even universal military service, but there is much to be said for a forced interruption in a professional career. Every young engineer (or doctor or physicist or lawyer) would, I am convinced, benefit from a year on a desert island. The island should be well stocked with books and, ideally, should include among its inhabitants at least one outspoken chaplain.

Feeding the Hunger for Books

When I returned to New York in the summer of 1946, I intended to look for a job. I had, after all, received a degree from Dartmouth and was entitled to call myself an engineer. (It was not until a few years later that I took the examinations necessary to acquire a state professional engineer's license, but that document is not a prerequisite for practice except in special circumstances, and less than half of American engineers ever bother to get one.) Many of my friends, however, were returning to school to resume educations that had been interrupted by the war, and this tended to make me feel that I was still properly a student. Besides, I was only twenty-one years old, the G.I. Bill of Rights enticingly offered free tuition, and the hunger for books that had been aroused during my stay in the Pacific was far from satisfied. I thought things over for a few weeks, then impetuously one September morning I took a bus uptown to Columbia University and signed up for a master's program in English literature. My parents reacted to this as if I were manifesting some form of battle fatigue—without having been in a battle. They were only partly placated by my assurances that I still planned to earn my livelihood as an engineer. The people at Columbia were likewise bemused. With only two semesters of English to my credit (and freshman English at that), I was surely the least qualified candidate ever to knock at their door. But my intentions appeared honorable, and the mood of the day favored giving veterans a break.

I enrolled in four courses: American Literature Since 1870, taught by Lionel Trilling; Modern Drama, taught by Joseph Wood Krutch; the History of the English Novel, taught by a professor whose name I do not recall; and the Romantic Movement, taught by a professor whose name I do recall but will not record since he read his lectures in a monotone and almost managed to make Wordsworth, Shelley, and Keats seem lifeless. Aside from this one bad choice—for which I compensated by monitoring an undergraduate course in the Age of Reason—I found the classes altogether absorbing. I remember with delight not only the lectures and the books we read, but also the arguments and small storms that were constantly erupting. When Trilling announced in class one day that Henry James was a far greater novelist than John Steinbeck, and that anybody who didn't think so ought to reconsider his plans to teach English for a livelihood (most of my classmates were budding academics), the booing was loud and raucous. On the other hand, when Trilling entered the classroom after having testified in court on behalf of Edmund Wilson's *Memoirs of Hecate County*—which, strange as it may seem today, was almost proscribed for being pornographic—he was greeted with a standing ovation. When Krutch argued on behalf of trusting one's own judgement instead of kowtowing to so-called literary authorities, he was challenged by a student who said individual taste was suspect since "even monkeys know what they like"; to which Krutch replied, after a moment's thought, "I guess I prefer an honest monkey to a dishonest student." On another occasion, Krutch pointed to a political demonstration taking place on campus within view of the classroom window. "Who here," he asked, "believes that there is a radical solution to the discontents of mankind?" There then ensued a political debate, followed by a discussion of the tragic view of life. This was totally different from anything I had ever experienced in an engineering classroom.

Galloping Intellectualism

The entire campus seethed with excitement, and I hardly knew where to look first. When Jacques Barzun was scheduled to lecture to the freshman Contemporary Civilization class, I wangled my way into the hall. A friend of mine recommended the music appreciation classes of the noted composer Douglas Moore, so when I was in the mood—which was often—I dropped in. It was a small class where I could hardly pass unnoticed, but Mr. Moore was a gentle man who said I was welcome. To this day, I remember how he analyzed with us the final movement of Mozart's Forty-first Symphony, the four themes intertwining in heavenly combinations. Paul Henry Lang, a well-known musicologist and critic, was also on the faculty, and for a while I added one of his classes to my schedule. One day Lange confessed that he had begun to write a book on the aesthetic theory of opera only to give it up in dismay. Opera was beautiful and soul-stirring, he said, but its formal rules were undefinable. It simply is what it is. This is the way I felt about my experiences at Columbia. I was no closer to Truth than I had ever been, but the overall experience was as thrilling as a Verdi duet.

In the evenings, after I had finished the required reading in Dickens, Ibsen, and Faulkner, I turned hungrily to the classics of earlier times, Homer, Shakespeare, Dante, and then, for a nightcap, I read the *Partisan Review*, where I expected to learn what the heavy thinkers of the day were up to. On social outings, I started frequenting Carnegie Hall instead of the Fifty-second Street jazz joints that had previously been my haunts. About the only habit not affected by my galloping intellectualism was the way I approached the *New York Times* on Sunday: I still started with the sports section—as I do to this day.

Ending a Literary Excursion

In order to qualify for a master's degree, I was required to write a thesis. I resolved to pick a topic that was all-embracing, no hidden facet of some obscure author, but something "hot" that would reveal to me the essence of the contemporary cultural scene. With some trepidation, but determined to seek advice from the highest possible source, I took the problem to Lionel Trilling. He was not enchanted by my idea, saying that it lacked subtlety, but then, on second thought, the question seemed to amuse him. After a moment's reflection, he suggested Franz Kafka. Kafka was culturally hot, he said, and getting hotter. This idea presented two problems: first, I had never read Kafka and had scarcely heard of him; second, and more serious, my selected area of interest—to which my thesis had to relate—was American literature. Well, said Trilling, why not American criticism of Franz Kafka? Why not, indeed? It was an inspired choice, for not only did I immerse myself in the anguished fantasies of this quintessential twentieth-century writer, but in tracking down his reviewers I came face to face with Marxism, Freudianism, existentialism, and all the other *-isms* of the day. This excursion into the world of literary criticism showed me that intellectuals can be as petty, inconsistent, and plain foolish as anybody else, a fact that an awestruck student of literature—and that is what I was—tends to overlook.

I had anticipated that the thesis would be a chore, but it turned out to be hard work, which is different and better. I enjoyed the research, delighted in the reading, and much to my surprise, relished the writing. I don't suppose that anybody has read that thesis, or ever will, other than the kindly assistant professor whose job it was to do so, but a more rewarding task I have never undertaken. At times I found myself beginning to envy the men and women whose life's work is reading, researching, writing, and teaching, who traffic in words and ideas instead of goods.

Yet, when the academic year ended, I said farewell to the campus on Morningside Heights in much the same way one leaves an enchanting foreign land to return home. It never occurred to me that I might stay, become a scholar, and change the direction of my life. For one thing, it was high time to start earning money. I was committed to engineering; I was trained, and deep down I believed that I was better suited to building than to reading and writing. In fact, deep down I had concluded that the main business of humankind was to build, to be technologically creative. Literature, I felt in my bourgeois heart of hearts, is commentary upon life, while engineering is the very stuff of life itself. What was the meaning of all those great novels except to explore the ways in which people work, trade, farm, war, earn, spend, cooperate, and compete? (Also love and hate and create art, to be sure, but only within the framework of an economically workable society.) What was the bitter joke with which Kafka wrestled during his short, sad life except that the state of grace that ever eludes the artist is found in the daily round of ordinary affairs? The protagonist of *The Castle*, after all, seeks confirmation of his appointment as land surveyor. And does not Goethe's Faust in the end find salvation in a land-reclamation project?

Much as I was enchanted with literature and the life of the mind, I had come to resent the condescending attitude that some intellectuals had toward so-called "materialism" and the technological impulse. It was all very well for Plato to say that thinking is better than doing, but this seems ironic when one considers that the glory of Athens rested upon the marvels of Greek mining, farming, seamanship, and weaponry—that is, upon Greek technology. My affection lay with Homer, whose world was rich with the feel of metals, woods, and fabrics, and whose robust characters took delight in buildings and ships, in objects designed, manufactured, used, given, admired, and savored.

The Rewards

Shortly after leaving Columbia, I began my first honest-to-goodness job as aide and lackey to a house builder on Long Island. I could not consider the work exalted, professionally speaking, but when I started to measure and calculate, set up my transit and wave directions to the backhoe operator, I knew that I was in a place where I belonged. Eventually my career took me into an office, and today I visit construction sites less often than I would like. But, when the cranes lift steel beams to dizzying heights, or when the wet concrete flows into huge wooden forms as the laborers yell and bang their shovels against the chutes, I say to myself, as Robert Louis Stevenson did when he came upon a scene of railroad construction on the western American plains, "If it be romance, if it be contrast, if it be heroism we require, what was Troy to this?"

I have had no reason to regret the choice of career I made, somewhat cavalierly, in high school. If life has not been one grand adventure interspersed with ribbon-cutting ceremonies, as shown on the screen in Loew's Eighty-third Street, well, life isn't the movies. Engineering provides its own rewards. I have a special affection for civil engineering, although I recognize the appeal of the other branches of the profession and vicariously enjoy the work of my more "scientific" fellows—for example, those along the frontiers of electronics.

Yet, for all the satisfactions inherent in my work, I thank the fates that I had time with the humanities and that I do not, like so many engineers in mid-career, lament lost opportunities. Mark Van Doren overstated the case, but not by much, when he wrote of the happiness that comes to the student of the liberal arts:

> That happiness consists in the possession of his own powers, and in the sense that he has done all he could to avoid the bewilderment of one who suspects he has missed the main thing. There is no happiness like this.

No one person can be all things at once. It is unrealistic to expect engineers to be artists or poets or literary scholars, and vice versa. Civilization flourishes because specialists rely upon one another to perform particular tasks. By nature and inclination, engineers are different from poets and artists. Having said that, I still think it regrettable that Sylvanus Thayer's ideal of a liberally educated engineering profession is so far from being realized.

A Withered Heritage

The Thayer School at Dartmouth is today the only American institution that requires engineers to invest at least five years in their education and to qualify for a bachelor of arts degree to boot. A number of other schools, Columbia among them, used to make the same demands but have succumbed to the economic competition. The five-year program is still widely available as an option, but little used. The average young person is reluctant to do in five years what can be achieved in four. The "progressive" schools require a 20 percent liberal component in an engineering education, and the "traditional" schools go along with the minimum 12.5 percent required for accreditation. Because most large universities fall into the latter category, the average engineering student takes only six nontechnical courses during his four years of college; and, since most of these courses are liable to be selected in the "useful" social sciences, an engineer can enter professional life having taken only one or two college courses in the humanities. In other words, the typical American engineer is a high-school graduate with four years of mostly technical training. (About a quarter of these students go on for graduate courses in their specialty.) While Sylvanus Thayer's dream has thus turned to ashes, other Americans have been going to college in ever-increasing numbers. This means that engineers, compared to their fellow citizens, are less educated—less cultured, if you will—than ever before. This is so in spite of the fact that engineering students are smarter than their fellows, as measured by S.A.T. scores, verbal as well as mathematical.

The historical origins of engineering lie in simple craftsmanship. When engineering is looked at in this light, any college education at all can be considered an improvement. But there is another engineering tradition that verges on patrician. John Augustus Roebling, designer of the Brooklyn Bridge and student of Hegel, wrote in his spare time a work entitled "The Harmonies of Creation."Charles Steinmetz, a genius from the early days of electrical engineering and an ardent socialist, was a strong advocate of liberal education for engineers. Herbert Hoover, a mining engineer who became the thirty-first president, was a scholar who not only wrote several books but also translated Agricola from the Latin.

This noble heritage of engineering has withered and is all but moribund. According to historian David F. Noble, author of *America by Design*, the decline started after World War I when engineering educators "sold out" to American industry and agreed to furnish sub-professional graduates to fill specific job slots. I see no reason to characterize what happened in terms of malice or capitulation. The nation needed technically trained personnel, and there were thousands of young people in whom the technological impulse swelled up like a passion. I have related how I myself was overcome by the feeling—or, let us say, the infatuation. Educators were caught in the middle. Today, with the nation fearful of the Soviets, intimidated by the Japanese, and mesmerized by computers, the pressures toward vocationalism are increasingly intense.

Yet I cannot believe that the current situation benefits either engineering students or the nation. Everyone agrees that most engineers are unable to write decent prose. Since communication is essential to successful engineering (a recent study found that a group of Exxon research and development engineers spend one-third of their time writing reports), it is clear that engineering students should be studying college-level English. As for working together with people, which engineers must do to be effective, literature and history could surely provide much-needed knowledge and understanding. I say this out of the depths of my own experience.

Engineers Should Study Liberal Arts

It is also widely agreed that American technological products would be "better" if engineers were more "sensitive"—aesthetically, morally, and socially. People who voice this opinion often have confused ideas about how technology is shaped and directed; they give engineers too much credit (and blame) and society as a whole not nearly enough. Nevertheless, a cadre of truly civilized engineers could not help but contribute to a more satisfactory technology.

It is also likely, though difficult to prove, that immersion in the humanities can invigorate the imaginative faculties and make an engineer more able and creative. Nikola Tesla, for example, said that his invention of the polyphase system and the a.c. induction motor came in a flash of insight as he was walking with a friend and reciting Goethe: "Oh, that spiritual wings soaring so easily / Had companions to lift me bodily from earth." "In an instant I saw it all," relates Tesla. What he saw was a motor without brushes and commutator, turned by a rotating magnetic field. In physics, Niels Bohr said that he arrived at the concept of complementarity by speculating on the ancient theological dilemma of the impossibility of reconciling perfect love with perfect justice. Lewis Mumford has pointed out that people flew in dreams and communicated instantaneously in myths and fairy tales long before they achieved the technical apparatus for doing so.

For all these reasons, and many more, engineers should be studying the liberal arts. This is no luminous insight of my own, but only what is generally conceded when, every few years, committees are formed to study engineering education. Yet the economic realities prevail. Within the confines of a four-year program, it is argued, there is simply not enough time. Add to this the inertia of university administrations and the uninterest, verging on hostility, of students, and the possibility of improvement seems remote. In political terms, there simply is no constituency for change. Many people agree that the four-year program should be lengthened to five, but it appears that is is now too late to make that change—or too early. For the moment, at least, the chill at the heart of engineering education is deepening. The situation brings to mind the oft-quoted statement by Franz Kafka: "A book must be the axe for the frozen sea inside us."

Kafka reportedly was much impressed by an anecdote about Gustave Flaubert, who once spent a day in the country visiting a jolly, robust family wholly without intellectual pretentions. On his way home, the great novelist, who had sacrificed his life to his art, kept thinking of these simple folk with their simple pleasures, and he muttered over and over, "*Ils sont dans le vrai!*" To be in the right, or to follow the true way, is the aim of each of us, and the tragic fact is that by choosing one path we relinquish the opportunity to travel others that are of great interest and charm. But different sorts of paths can cross or run side by side for a while; this is one of life's most pleasant surprises.

An Alternate Education

Ah, well, nobody is more tiresome than a reformed sinner, and that, I suppose, is what I have become. Occasionally I try to sell my brand of salvation to young engineers, but I do not delude myself about the extent of my success. If I try to speak of my own experience, some smart whippersnapper will tell me what I know only too well, that my education was something of a fluke. Not every engineer can go to a fine private high school and a liberal arts college, then spend a year on an island in the Pacific, followed by another year studying the humanities at government expense.

Yet, who can predict the future? When the current frenzy over computers and technical training has run its course, the inevitable counter-reaction will set in. Engineers, being bright, curious, and pragmatic, may well conceive new patterns for their education and careers. Perhaps women, who are just beginning to enter engineering in large numbers, will show the way. I read recently that, in the Soviet Union, female engineers devote three times as much of their leisure time to "humanitarian and artistic activities" as do their male colleagues.

Enough of speculation. There are buildings to be built and things I should be doing at the office. Samuel Johnson—whom I learned to love at Columbia in 1947 and who, in truth, was more an engineer's kind of man than Franz Kafka—once said in a letter to Boswell: "Life is not long, and too much of it must not pass in idle deliberation how it shall be spent."

Elizabeth Neeld Comments:

✦ *One of the characteristics of originality is a writer's willingness to say, "This is what I think is so. This is how I see things." And this willingness extends to saying it even if others do not agree with you. Samuel Florman is such a writer. He has the courage to take risks when he writes. An essay such as this one rings with an authentic voice and a committed stand, both hallmarks of originality.* ✦ *Samuel Florman is a practicing engineer. He is vicepresident of Kreisler Borg Florman Construction Company of Scarsdale, New York. He is also a prolific writer on the subject of engineers and engineering. One of his central messages, in books like* Blaming Technology: The Irrational Search for Scapegoats *and* The Existential Pleasures of Engineering, *is that engineers make a unique contribution: the engineer is "the somebody in our society [who] has to design, create, fabricate, build—to do. A world full of coordinators, critics, and manipulators would have nothing in it but words. It would be a barren desert, devoid of things." Samuel Florman also argues that we are in trouble when we look down on or don't give appropriate power to the people who make things work.* ✦ *Florman celebrates the satisfactions and pleasures of engineering. In his essay "The Existential Engineer," he says: "The engineer today, for all his knowledge and accomplishment, can still look out on seas scarce charted and on coasts still dark. Each new achievement discloses new problems and new possibilities. The allure of these endless vistas bewitches the* engineer of every era." Florman believes engineering is a joyful occupation because it springs from the most basic impulse of humanity—the desire to change the world we see before us. ✦ In this essay Florman suggests that the training engineers are getting now is so specialized and so narrow that it is easy to miss the larger satisfactions that should accompany engineering. The stand he takes opposes virtually his entire profession—certainly its practices, if not its theories. He says that engineers should study literature, music, art—the liberal arts—as well as engineering. And he says why. He tells how he became an engineer and how the liberal arts education he got along with his engineering degree made all the difference in his work and in his life. He gives the history of engineering education, a history that shows how engineering changed from a professional training program you did after you completed a full four-year undergraduate education to a five-year program that is not based on a liberal arts background. In the "old days"—the 1800s—you were expected to become "a gentleman" before you became an engineer. Now engineers are inundated with courses in electricity, fluid mechanics, metallurgy, thermodynamics, structures, probability and statistics, systems. Florman laments the over-specialization and the lack of a liberal arts foundation in today's engineers. (He tells an amusing incident of being stationed on the island Truk while he was serving in the Navy. Every member of his battalion was an engineer except one: the chaplain. One night, after the chaplain could generate no conversation at all with the engineers, he raised his voice and said, "Dear Lord, I know that I am unworthy, I confess that I have sinned, but why did you have to abandon me on this island with nobody for company but these boring engineers?" Florman said from that moment on his life was changed. He decided that he would be an engineer, but he would not be a dull one. This essay is an attempt to convince others of the same thing. To say what no one else is willing to say but what you really believe is one way you write with originality. Samuel Florman does it at its best. ✦

ROBERT TRIVERS and
HUEY P. NEWTON

The Crash of Flight 90

Science Digest Editor's note:

The following article is unsettling. The editors believe that its disturbing thesis may help us understand why some disasters occur and enable us to place what is sometimes labeled negligence in a larger context. While some of the language of the story may seem brutally frank, the editors believe the story has a constructive purpose, and they feel only sympathy and respect for the aircrew and the others who perished.

Seven months after a Tampa-bound Air Florida 737, Flight 90, slammed into a bridge and plunged into the Potomac River, killing 78 people, the National Transportation Safety Board reached its verdict. It attributed the crash to several factors. First, the crew failed to activate the anti-ice system of the plane's engines before and during takeoff. This in turn caused an engine-pressure-ratio (EPR) sensor to give false readings that registered more thrust than in fact was there. Also implicated were the pilot's decision to take off with snow and/or ice on the plane's wings and his failure to abort takeoff after being informed by the copilot (who was at the plane's controls) that the EPR readings were inconsistent with other instrument readings. The board also concluded that the pilot could have averted the crash by applying full thrust seconds after lift-off.

Air Florida has disputed these findings, charging that the crash was caused by a flaw in the design of the 737 that makes it pitch sharply and by "undetected and undetectable" ice that formed on the leading edge of Flight 90's wing.

Drs. Robert Trivers and Huey P. Newton, biologists at the University of California, Santa Cruz, have drawn a more startling conclusion after reviewing the available evidence. The roots of the disaster, they say, lie in evolutionary biology. The adaptive mechanism of self-deception, they say, doomed Flight 90. Their article offers a unique interpretation of a tragic event.

The benefit of self-deception is the more fluid deception of others. The cost is an impaired ability to deal with reality. Ultimately we measure the cost of self-deception by its negative effects on reproductive success and survival, but we are often far from able to make this final connection. One approach is to begin with a disaster and work backward, looking for evidence of a pattern of self-deception leading up to the event.

Reality Evasion

Consider, for example, the crash of Flight 90 immediately after takeoff on January 13, 1982, during a heavy snowstorm. The transcript of the final 30 minutes of conversation between the pilot and copilot suggests a pattern of self-deception and reality evasion on the part of the pilot that contributed directly to the tragedy. By contrast, the copilot comes across as reality oriented, but insufficiently strong in the face of his captain's self-deception. These are relatively crude characterizations, but useful to bear in mind as we try to capture the complex way in which patterns of self-deception may generate a human disaster.

Let us begin as the airplane is cleared for takeoff and its engines are fired up to head down the runway. It will roar down the runway for 47 seconds before reaching the speed at which a final decision must be made about whether to go or not. At any moment during this time the pilot can abort the flight safely. Ten seconds after starting down the runway the copilot responds to instrument readings that are inconsistent.

Copilot: *God, look at that thing.*

Then, four seconds later:

Copilot: *That don't seem right, does it?*

Three seconds later:

Copilot: *Ah, that's not right.*

Two seconds later:

Copilot: *Well . . .*

Two seconds later:

Pilot: *Yes it is, there's 80.*

It takes 11 seconds for the pilot to respond to the copilot. Apparently referring to an air speed of 80 knots, he seeks to explain away the instrument readings that are troubling the copilot. This fails to satisfy the copilot, and one second later:

Copilot: *Naw, I don't think that's right.*

Nine seconds later, having received no support from the pilot, the copilot wavers:

   Copilot: Ah, maybe it is.
Two seconds later, the pilot states the speed at which they are traveling:
   Pilot: 120.
Two seconds later:
   Copilot: I don't know.

Caught between his own doubts and the pilot's certainty, the copilot finally lapses into uncertainty. Eight seconds later the pilot says, "V–1." This is the go/no go decision speed. After this point, the flight can no longer be aborted safely because it would run out of runway. Now we note a striking reversal in the roles of pilot and copilot. So far the copilot has done all the talking, the pilot only giving routine information. Now that they have passed the speed at which they are committed to their course, the copilot no longer speaks, and the pilot speaks repeatedly. Two seconds after V–1, the pilot says "Easy." Four seconds later he says, "V–2." This is the speed that you must maintain to clear the end of the runway if an engine fails. Two seconds later the sound of the stickshaker, a device that signals an impending stall, is heard in the cockpit. Six seconds later:
   Pilot: Forward, forward.
Two seconds later:
   Speaker undetermined: Easy.
One second later:
   Pilot: We only want 500.
Two seconds later:
   Pilot: Come on, forward.
Three seconds later:
   Pilot: Forward.
Two seconds later:
   Pilot: Just barely climb.

Fantasy or Truth?

The pilot is apparently urging the copilot to reduce the rate of climb to avert the stall. Before the pair were committed to the fatal flight, the pilot had little or nothing to say. Now that they have made their mistake, he comes out into the open and tries to reason. Four seconds later:
   Speaker undetermined: Stalling, we're falling.
One second later:
   Copilot: Larry, we're going down, Larry.

One second later:

Pilot: *I know it.*

Almost simultaneously, the recorder picks up "sounds of impact."

The copilot did all his talking while it still mattered. At the end, he is only heard from telling his pilot what the pilot has been so reluctant to see: "Larry, we're going down, Larry." And the pilot finally says, "I know it."

The dichotomy between self-deceiver and reality-seeker was evident in earlier exchanges between pilot and copilot as they sat in the cockpit together prior to departure and in extremely cold weather and a driving snowstorm. A half hour before takeoff the following exchange took place:

Copilot: *We're too heavy for the ice.*

Copilot: *They get a tractor with chains on it? They got one right over here.*

He is referring to the unsuccessful efforts of a tractor to push the plane from the deicing and anti-icing position back to its runway position. The tractor has failed because of icy ground.

Copilot: *I'm surprised we couldn't power it out of here.*

Pilot: *Well, we could of if he wanted me to pull some reverse.*

The copilot is suggesting using the plane's own power to get back into position. The pilot replies that it could be done with reverse thrust. They try, but the attempt fails and in the end a tractor with chains on does the job.

Just before takeoff, the condition of the wings is considered. Given the seating arrangements in the cockpit, each man checks the wing on his own side.

Pilot: *Get your wing now.*

Copilot: *D'they get yours? Can you see your wing tip?*

Pilot: *I got a little on mine.*

Copilot: *This one's got about a quarter to half an inch on it all the way.*

We see that the self-deceiver gives an imprecise and diminutive answer concerning a danger, while the copilot gives a precise description of the extent of the danger. The copilot also curses the snow, saying it is "probably the [expletive deleted] snow I've seen."

Seven minutes before takeoff:

Copilot: *Boy, this is a losing battle here on trying to deice those things, it gives you a false feeling of security, that's all that does.*

Pilot: *That, ah, satisfies the Feds.*

Copilot: *Yeah—As good and crisp as the air is and no heavier than we are I'd . . .*

Pilot: Right there is where the icing truck, they oughta have two of them, you pull right.

The pilot and copilot now explore a fantasy together on how the plane should be deiced just before takeoff on the runway. Note that the copilot begins this exchange with an accurate description of their situation; they have a false sense of security. The pilot notes that the arrangement satisfies the higher-ups, but then switches the discussion to the way the system *should* work. This is not without its value and may, indeed, lead to an improved system in the future, but in their immediate situation concentration on the general issue rather diverted attention from the difficulties at hand.

Just before takeoff the copilot asks the pilot for advice on their situation:

Copilot: Slushy runway, do you want me to do anything special for this or just go for it?

Pilot: Unless you got anything special you'd like to do.

Copilot: Unless just takeoff the nose wheel early like a soft field takeoff or something.

The pilot, to whose greater experience the copilot appears repeatedly to defer, has no help to offer on how to take off in these particular circumstances. This makes their final conversation all the more vivid. The copilot is at the controls of the plane. Having failed to give his copilot any advice and having failed to plan in the slightest for difficulty in takeoff, the pilot's only responsibility is to read the instruments and warn the copilot of any problem. Yet it is the copilot who first calls attention to the strange instrument readings. It is the copilot who refers to them three times before the pilot responds to him.

It Could Have Been Averted

The transcript suggests how easily the disaster could have been averted. Imagine that earlier conversations about the snow on the wings, the heavy weight of the airplane and the slushy conditions underfoot had induced a spirit of caution in both pilots. How easy it would have been for the pilot to say, "Well, this is a somewhat tricky situation. I think we should take off with full speed but watch our instruments carefully, and if we fail to develop sufficient power, I think I should abort the takeoff." Yet the conversation never had a chance to turn in this direction, for every time the copilot approached the subject, the pilot chose either not to respond or to divert attention from the problem they faced. Mechanisms of self-deception, having deprived him of even the most rudimentary advance planning, offer him a quick fix for the disturbing instrument readings and, after the fateful decision is made, a 10-second illusion that he may be able to get the plane into the air safely.

A Disturbed Feeling

Dr. Aaron Waters, a noted geologist and professor emeritus at the University of California, Santa Cruz, who has been a member of mountain rescue groups, responded to our account as follows (in a letter dated 2/23/82):

> Your example of the Flight 90 crash, however, left a disturbed feeling about the way you wrote it up. You correctly blame the pilot for the crash, but maybe you do not bring out clearly enough that it was the pilot's complete insensitivity to the copilot's doubts, and to his veiled and timid pleas for help, that was at the root of all this trouble. The pilot, with much more experience, just sat there completely unaware and without any realization that the copilot was desperately asking for friendly advice and professional help. Even if he [the pilot] had gruffly grunted, "If you can't handle it, turn it over to me," such a response would have probably shot enough adrenaline into the co-pilot so that he would either have flown the mission successfully or aborted it without accident.
>
> From limited experience in mountain rescue work, and considerable experience with dangerous work in abandoned mines, I've found that the people who lead others into trouble are the hale and hearty insensitive jocks trying to show off. They cannot perceive that a companion is so terrified that he is about to "freeze" to the side of a cliff—and for very good reason. And once this has happened the one that led him into it becomes an even worse basket case, and the most difficult one to rescue. I think the copilot "froze" and immediately the pilot "froze" even worse and began talking to the airplane. However, the copilot is also at fault; left to himself he would have called the tower and not flown the mission, but in the presence of his companion he was guilty of self-deception.

The media have concentrated on the icing of the wings, but the master geologist sees a human parallel to the freezing weather. Each man, in turn, "freezes" in fright and the disaster is complete. The most recent evidence on the faulty instrument readings bears out Dr. Waters's interpretation. It is now known that the airplane was getting 25 percent *less* thrust than its instrument readings showed! The takeoff consumed almost 17 seconds more time (and a greater length of the runway) than it should have. Had the pilot, in fact, aborted at the go/no go speed, he would have run out of runway.

If the copilot was cold prior to takeoff, the pilot was positively "cool." Nothing fazed him. The situation in which he found himself was nothing new to his industry nor to his company. In the previous September, for example, Air Florida's chief 737 pilot attached a 737 winter-flight note to the monthly Air Florida crew newsletter. He specifically warned of the dangers of winter flying at the more northerly airports. "Nobody can be *too* prepared for La Guardia, O'Hare, White Plains or Washington National." He told crews to look for snow and ice buildup and to arrange for as late an airframe deicing as practical: "*If heavy freezing precipitation exists, it may be necessary to get deiced again if significant ground delays occur*" (emphasis added). Nine airliners taking off before Flight 90 were deiced between 9 and 44 minutes before takeoff, but Flight 90 went 49 minutes between its last deicing and anti-icing and takeoff.

We now see the final deicing discussion between pilot and copilot in a new light. Both pilot and copilot know that their plane needs a second deicing, but instead of seeking it, the pilot leads them into a fantasy world in which they get their second deicing without losing their place in line waiting to take off.

The American Airlines maintenance chief whose men serviced the Air Florida plane said he twice told the pilot that he should wait until just before takeoff for deicing; otherwise, the deicing fluid could cause wet snow to collect, which is precisely what happened. A picture taken of the plane just after deicing shows snow already covering the upper fuselage.

Moving the Aircraft

The problem of snow and ice on the wings may have been compounded by the decision to use the plane's own power to try to move the aircraft back from the gate. This kind of casual incaution is exactly what one would expect from an "airplane jock." Certain types of adventurous men are especially prone to this form of self-deception. (Both pilot [age 34] and copilot [age 31] had been military pilots before turning to commercial work.)

The use of the reverse thrust could have pushed the slush to the leading edge of the wings. This is precisely where ice and snow do the greatest damage. Indeed, in a 1980 bulletin, Boeing, the plane's manufacturer, had already warned against using 737 reversers during snowfalls. If reverse thrust *is* used, Boeing advised, the wings' edges should be cleared of any ice or snow. It can cause the plane's nose to "pitch up" too far at takeoff and roll to the side, threatening a stall. This is what seems to have happened to Flight 90.

A second consequence of using reverse thrust is that it may have caused snow to swirl up and block the sensors that caused the false readings on the amount of the engine thrust and speed of forward movement.

Superimposed on all the detailed information stands one obvious fact. On the mission in question the copilot was flying the plane. That is, he was playing the role of pilot and the pilot, meanwhile, was playing the role of copilot. This is intended to be educational for the copilot, since he thereby learns how to become a pilot, but the pilot is still in charge. In effect, he is to do two things at once: discharge the duties of copilot while remaining responsible for the flight itself.

Did this confusion of roles contribute to the disaster? We believe it did. Had the pilot been flying the plane that day, we believe the chances for survival would have been better. The copilot shows himself to be a careful man. In this flight, he even discharges some of his customary duties, such as reading the instruments. By contrast, the pilot handles the airplane the way one might handle a horse, by seat-of-the-pants control. The pilot himself might have ignored the instrument readings, heading down the runway at full speed as judged by his own body. In his split role he neither discharges the copilot's role nor assumes full responsibility for the flight. Indeed, he repeatedly seeks to convey to the copilot the message that this is a routine flight, requiring nothing more than the usual self-confidence.

Elizabeth Neeld Comments:

✦ *Robert Trivers and Huey P. Newton are biologists. Trivers is a professor in the applied biology department at the University of California at Santa Cruz, and he has written extensively about the relationship between biology and social evolution. In 1985 he published a major work,* Social Evolution, *which discusses self-deception in ani-*

mals as well as human beings. Authors Trivers and Newton exhibit originality by relating their speciality, their expertise, to an event or situation that on the surface seems completely unrelated. They applied their theories of deception in animal behavior to behavior in human beings, and used this model to come up with a very unusual theory explaining what caused a specific airplane crash. ✦ In order to understand self-deception as a biological trait, first look at deception in the animal world. Communication is very important to animals. Communication for animals is an "enabling device." It enables the communicator to increase its likelihood of success in survival and reproduction. It lets an animal manipulate its environment. Often, this manipulation involves deception. For instance, if two animals are hunting for food and there is only enough food for one, one of the animals may lead the other astray, pretending to look for food far away from where he has already spotted it. Then, when the second animal is gone, the first can go back and get the food. ✦ A fish might develop an "eyespot" on its tail while concealing its own eye with a stripe: an animal seeking to head it off moves in one direction while the fish moves in another. A harmless king snake may make red, yellow, and black stripes on its body like a dangerous coral snake to keep predators away. An orchid emits a scent like that of a female wasp; the male wasp then pollinates the orchid. The killdeer bird will feign injury in a "broken wing display," drawing predators away from its nesting area. A lot of communication among animals involves deceiving each other. For animals, deception is a way to survive. ✦ Trivers and Newton's point in this essay is that human beings also use deception to survive, in this case self-deception. Biologists maintain that deceit is built into our systems, that we human beings deceive ourselves, making some facts and motives unconscious so that we won't betray, by subtle signs of self-awareness, the deception we are perpetuating. If individuals are unaware of their intent, they will be more convincing, the theory goes, in their arguments and will thus have a greater likelihood of achieving their ends. Biologists say that natural selection in the evolution of human beings may have favored tendencies for humans to be unaware of what they are really *doing and why they are doing it. Self-deception is an un-conscious function that enables the ego to justify con-sciously its existence and maintain self-control.* ✦ *This kind of self-deception that allows the ego of a human being to justify its existence and maintain self-control may have been the cause of the crash of Flight 90. Trivers and Newton analyze the conversation between the pilot and copilot and hear, from their biology background, evidence that the pilot was deceiving himself. The authors maintain that this trait has evolved in human beings as one of our ways to survive. The irony here is that death—not survival—was the result.* ✦ *Being alert to the possibility that some-thing in which you have expertise or personal experience may be related to something that seems completely differ-ent is a way to promote originality in your thinking. Whether or not we agree with Trivers' and Newton's hy-pothesis, we learn from them. And we should emulate their commitment to connecting what they know to many other things. They have a wide vision, not a tunnel view; original-ity is the result.* ✦

DAVID WETMORE

Yaz

In 1967 the Boston Red Sox won the American League pennant and went to the World Series. I, who grew up in Boston, was just turning seven years old, which was exactly the right age to be marked for life as a Red Sox fan. That same year a lean Boston Red Sox outfielder named Carl Yastrzemski won the batting Triple Crown, leading all other American League hitters in batting average, home runs, and runs batted in. Hooked, you might say, and double hooked: I had a team and I had a hero. I have been a Red Sox fan all my life; I expect to go to my grave a Red Sox fan; and through all these years, the Red Sox have seemed to me best represented by the spirit and quality of Carl Yastrzemski, or Yaz, as he is known in the press and to all Red Sox diehards like me. This spring, for the first time in twenty-four years, Carl Yastrzemski is not in a Red Sox uniform, and the feeling of his not being a member of the team is strange, even a little eerie.

To let you know at the outset the quality of fanatic you are dealing with here, I made it a point last year to travel from my present home in Minnesota to Boston to see Carl Yastrzemski play his last two games in Fenway Park. The first of these games, played on Saturday, October 1, 1983, dawned rainy and cold, soaking the crowd that waited hopefully in the street outside Fenway Park for the last thousand standing-room-only tickets to go on sale. The rain fell all weekend, but baseball was played both days, and the party for Yaz went off as scheduled. Because fans and sportswriters in Boston took the retirement of Carl Yastrzemski seriously, there was the not unfamiliar ceremony accompanying the retirement of a great athlete who has played out his career in a single city— ceremonies that have been accorded players from Lou Gehrig to Willie Stargell—with praise, applause, and gifts strewn around the infield. In Yaz's case all this was done, too, but the rain gave an oddly funereal cast to the proceedings, making one realize that the retirement of a great athlete represents a service for his death in miniature. Certainly the ceremony in honor of Carl Yastrzemski was a sad, even difficult one for Boston's fans and a no less difficult one for Yaz himself. Sitting in the stands, I felt a sense of loss.

The Spiritual Sports Fan

Following certain teams brings with it an accompanying spiritual condition. To be a Chicago Cub fan is to live with a permanent condition of hopelessness, one that has been almost unrelieved for nearly four decades, as that team—as its fans bitterly joke— now enters the thirty-ninth year of its rebuilding program. To be a New York Yankee fan is to expect victory, and to turn instantly against one's team when it doesn't arrive. To be a Red Sox fan, though, is to live with constant hope. Growing up in Boston, I knew that I could not expect our team to win every summer. But some summers, when the Red Sox won, have been perfect. In 1967, when I first began following the team in earnest, we won a pennant, a Cy Young Award for pitching, and Yaz's Triple Crown. Another pennant in 1975 brought the best World Series—against the Cincinnati Reds—played in recent memory, a seven-game contest that a good many fans in Boston still refuse to admit we lost. In 1978 the Sox blew a big midseason lead, then battled back to tie the Yankees, the hated Yankees, on the last day of the season. Our loss in the play-off game never happened for some of us. The last pop fly never came down. The dream of winning again has continued over the years. Each spring the Red Sox slip off to training camp in Florida, and each March the word comes north: Maybe this year.

For myself, I keep the fan's faith, settling into the bleachers when I can and tuning in the televised games. By and large, it has been immensely rewarding. Like the Red Sox manager said back in 1967, "We'll win more than we lose." He was right then, and he remains right. For sixteen consecutive years the Red Sox played better than .500 ball. Throughout all those years Carl Yastrzemski was on the Red Sox. Last year the streak ended, and Yastrzemski retired. This year, as spring training got under way, Yaz wasn't there.

Every year I find myself falling under the spell of spring training, with all the hope that it promises for the year ahead. I wake up to reports from the Red Sox training camp in Winter Haven; these have always included Yaz's name in the box scores of Grapefruit League games. Each year I would follow his progress as he rounded into shape, noting the first home run he hit off veteran pitching. As Yaz went, so went the team, whose leader he has for so long been. Yaz and the Red Sox—that's how I have always thought about spring, for as long as I can remember.

An Era Ends

I especially looked forward to last year, knowing it was to be Yaz's final season, though I did not know it at the outset. I learned it from a friend, who brought me an article by the sportswriter Leigh Montville from the March 22, 1983, *Boston Globe*, under the headline, "Yaz Has Gone Deep." A closeup photograph of the profile that Boston baseball fans have come to know so well carried the following caption from Montville's story: "This isn't some disposable hero. This is the perpetual Boston hero. The old-line hero. A landmark. Let these other cities buy and trade and deal for heroes. . . . That's right, Yaz." But in the story itself I first learned that Yaz had finally decided to call it quits. Somehow I had dreamily assumed he would go on forever, endlessly, year after year batting .280-plus, blasting fifteen or twenty home runs, knocking in eighty or so RBIs. But now he had announced that he would go through one more season and then retire. Knowing that 1983 would be Yaz's final year in baseball, I used it to look back as much as forward, reading old Red Sox yearbooks and rehashing Red Sox statistics, trying to recall as much about Carl Yastrzemski's career as I could and, while I was at it, looking into the career of that other Boston baseball legend, the one who came before Yaz.

Two Legends, Two Tales

Ted Williams is reported to have been the greatest natural hitter ever to have played baseball, a perennial all-star. Today he is a certified baseball legend. I never saw him play, but over the years I have been told stories about Ted Williams that have at least partially revealed to me the wonders that I missed. That Williams was a great player is plain; that he received an undeservedly bad press in Boston is also plain. I still do not know why the ill feeling that the reporters had for him carried over to affect the way his fans viewed him. One thing is clear: Williams never claimed the devotion of Red Sox fans. He surely never was allowed to feel the emotion that was bestowed upon Yaz, the man who replaced him in left field. For Williams's final game in Boston only ten thousand fans showed up. He responded to this rather sad turnout by creating his own fitting tribute and crashing a home run to center field his final time at bat. Circling the bases he ran quickly, unsmiling, displaying that stern pride and self-confidence that, resented though it was by Boston's sportswriters, was a hallmark of his magnificent career.

By contrast, when Yaz left the field for the last time on October 2, 1983, it was to tumultuous ovations from a full house. Before the game he stood in front of the Red Sox dugout to say good-bye for the last time. It was not the spectacle of the day before, when the gifts to him of new cars and a new fishing boat stood parked along the first-base line, but when the cheering subsided enough for him to be heard over the stadium's public address system, he made a short yet impressive speech. "As I look around the ball park today," he said, "I see signs that say, 'Say it ain't so, Yaz.' I wish it wasn't." The cheers roared once more as he stepped away from the microphone to join his teammates, who had assembled on the field. Then he stepped back to the microphone, said a few more words, and trotted his home-run trot around the field, shaking hands with those fans who had bunched themselves along the railings of the stands. People who had eaten a loaf or two of Yaz Bread in their day, or had shopped for cars at Yaz Ford, filled the stands. Many of them brought their children, who were just discovering baseball and would have to learn about Yaz when they grew older. But they were here today and would in future be glad of it.

At the 1983 All-Star game, Joe Cronin, one of the Red Sox great managers, for reasons known only to himself, told the press that Carl Yastrzemski was a better all-round ballplayer than Ted Williams, and that stirred up a great many older fans who thought otherwise. Yet comparisons between the two players are meaningless; each was of his time, and both were extraordinary. Yaz made no one forget Williams, but neither is his own record diminished by the Williams legend. For me, of course, for reasons of my age, Yaz will always be the man—my ideal of the heroic in sports.

My Past and His

Until the magical year 1967, I had been concerned with baseball solely through the games the kids in my neighborhood played in the schoolyard. I had had no sense of the institution known as the major leagues. I don't recall questioning why other people's names were written in the "autograph model" baseball gloves we kids used. But 1967 was a wonderful year for a kid from Boston to become interested in big-league baseball—better than 1975, when we knew from the start that we had a winning team; and certainly better than 1978, when it was a crime that, with such a solid team, we lost.

Still, in some ways it was a shame that 1967 was the start of my interest in baseball. It has provided me with a terrific high from which I have never quite come down. Nineteen sixty-seven was the year we won a pennant that was not decided until the last game of our season, the year we had Jim Lonborg (a twenty-game-winning pitcher), and the year Yaz brought off the miracle of the Triple Crown. In 1967 I was still too young to appreciate the statistical side of baseball, but I was nonetheless swept up in the general excitement of the season. I cheered wildly when number eight, Yaz, hit home runs, and I knew that I had nothing much to worry about when Lonborg was pitching. It was fun and it was beautiful, even to a kid of six.

In the years since 1967 Yaz had his share of rough spots. Memories of seasons that ended with his average hovering around .260 or when he had to struggle to drive in sixty runs are nearly as prominent in my mind as the memories of his good seasons. Some years, boos and catcalls rained down on him from the stands. There were not enough homers, his average was too low, he was accused of not hustling. The Red Sox played well, but they were unable to put together a string of championships, as the Boston Celtics had done in basketball. The feeling was that Yaz was letting us down; he wasn't giving us 1967 again. He gave us instead four dismal seasons between his last great year, 1970—when he hit forty home runs, 102 RBIs, and had a batting average of .329—and the year the Red Sox won the pennant again in 1975. Yaz's ninety-five RBIs and .295 average in 1973, followed by a .301 average in 1974, were impressive, but we Sox fans wanted more. We wanted 1967 again.

Yaz: Bad, Good, Great

Fans are famously fickle—and cruel. With the introduction of the Red Sox starting lineup, Yaz's name usually brought cheers, but on a bad day, his appearance on the field and at the plate brought catcalls, epithets, moans. An out could cause him to be called a bum; a hit and he was a hero again. When Yaz came through I felt relief. Each time he stepped to the plate I felt a faint fear—the fear that some crucial failure on his part could make me turn against the hero of my childhood and stop following the Red Sox.

The 1975 Boston Red Sox gave us a very good year. It was a team led by our great rookie outfielders, Jim Rice and Fred Lynn. Yaz, it must be said, was not special in 1975. By then he had become the older ballplayer, the veteran who had a sense of where the team was headed, someone whom other players may have looked to on the bench and in the clubhouse, but who, on the field, played below his standard. It began to look as if it were time for him to pass the baton on to another, younger generation of players.

Then, at the close of the season, Jim Rice suffered a broken wrist as a result of being hit by a pitch. The three-time World-Series-winning Oakland A's came to Boston to begin a series that would decide the American League pennant. Without Jim Rice, things looked bleak. Yaz went from first base back to his old spot in left field for the series opener in Fenway Park. Suddenly, it was almost as if 1967 were being replayed; Yaz did everything. He made sparkling defensive plays (of a kind that the rookie Rice, at that time, could not have made), and he hit as he had not hit all season. His batting average in the Red Sox surprising three-game sweep of the A's was .455. He had four assists from left field, made no errors, and in one unforgettable play he dove across the outfield grass to grab a Reggie Jackson line drive that was headed for the wall and extra bases. Yaz held Jackson to a single, keeping the tying run at first base in the eighth inning of what was to be the final game of the series. Yaz's play ended Oakland's threat; the next hitter bounced into a double play, and Boston had another pennant. Yaz's performance against Oakland made the championship perfect; the team seemed a fine union of younger and older players. Best of all, Yaz proved that he still had it.

In his twenty-three-year career with the Boston Red Sox, Carl Yastrzemski compiled superior statistics in less than half his seasons. In 1977, his seventeenth year in the big leagues, Yaz finished his last successful season with twenty-eight home runs, 102 RBIs, a .296 batting average, and the last of his seven Golden Glove awards for fielding. He could still play the game, no question about it, but often he seemed to be working with something held in reserve. He called on that little bit extra in important games and he must have called on it, too, to play while wrapped in yards of tape used to bind his endless, nagging injuries: the weak wrist, the sore ankles, the strained back. His seasonal averages might have been even more impressive if he had been able to play at full tilt every day, but he probably owed the longevity of his career to his ability to pace himself. I'll take the longevity. Throughout his long career Yaz was very good; at times he was great; and he never really faded.

Media On/Media Off

The Boston sports press, which some say is the toughest in the country, has been up and down on Yaz. In his early years, it pictured him coming of age as an acknowledged leader in the clubhouse, helping younger players without criticizing them, keeping the Sox together as a team: it is the picture of the completely selfless athlete, Frank Merriwell at Fenway Park. With later years, however, the negative stories started to flow: Yaz doesn't hustle, Yaz no longer cares, Yaz is aloof, Yaz is concerned only about number eight. Yet somehow, perhaps through sheer endurance, Yaz rose above all these stories and played his way through twenty-three years to become the forty-four-year-old athlete standing beside his manager in the Red Sox dugout, respected by everyone who cares about the game of baseball.

The *New Yorker* writer Roger Angell, himself a Boston Red Sox fan, has written that "there is more involved in baseball than the accomplishments of a few athletes and teams." There is, for one thing, the game itself. There is a structure to baseball different from the structure of all other games; it is a structure—if you will forgive that vague word—that never quite follows the laws of the universe as they pertain to everyday life. The game of baseball enacts fantasy, drama, and tragedy on a wide stage, in a spectacle that lasts for more than six months every year, with ups and downs reversing and repeating themselves in daily episodes.

When I read the box scores every day with my morning coffee, noting the hits, runs, and errors, it strikes me that following a baseball team offers me not only an escape from the daily grind of my life, but something of a parallel to it in the way that it encompasses both the easy and the difficult portions of life. Baseball is a game most American men have played in their youth, and as such, it is a game that, in odd ways, recaptures our youth. The simplicity of its fundamental confrontations—throwing and hitting, catching and running—is part of its charm. It is a game with a long tradition behind it. It is also a game of skill and violence and control, a game of waiting and of unleashed energy quickly checked. It is, above all, a game of individuals meeting tests; it's not a team game at all, really. Each act of pitching, swinging, running, or fielding is an isolated moment frozen and apart from the rest of the game—acts that each player must perform alone. The play is made: hit or error, safe or out. And then the game repeats itself, the same hitters and pitchers and fielders facing one another again and again over nine innings, day after day, throughout the long season. The repeated chances for success or failure over 162 games make baseball a game of survivors as much as of winners.

The Great Survivor

Carl Yastrzemski has been one of baseball's great survivors. As has become increasingly rare in modern-day baseball, he played out his entire career with one team. He is wholly and solely identified with Fenway Park, one of the oldest ball parks left in baseball, with the goofy angles and corners in its outfield, its stands jutting out into the field, and its famous left-field wall (known as the Green Monster), in front of which he stood for the better part of his career. Yastrzemski standing in the outfield—the features of his face worn smooth and rounded by the weather, creased by lines of concentration, his hair gray at the temples—perfectly fit my image of baseball as something storybook yet real, as something grand and symbolic and lasting. Even in defeat he managed to maintain dignity. The memories of the great years of Yaz end with him at the plate at Fenway Park, flying out to end the World Series against the

Reds in 1975 and popping up for the final out of the 1978 play-off game against the Yankees, a game that began with his hitting a home run. His career ended at Fenway Park, too, when, after singling to left and walking in his earlier appearances at the plate, Yaz hit a towering pop fly in his last time at bat, and the ball landed in the second-baseman's glove.

For that final game Yaz was back in left field. Early in the game, with a runner on second base, he charged a ground-ball single and came up throwing, looking as he had in my earliest memory of him. But taking the ball off the wet outfield grass, he made a terrible throw; the ball bounced at shortstop and rolled weakly through the infield to the plate. He turned and walked back to his position, looking toward the center fielder as though unable to explain what had happened. Then, later in the game, Toby Harrah, batting for Cleveland, hit a line drive halfway up the wall in left-center field. Yaz was waiting for the ball as it came off the wall, and he fielded it cleanly. Then he turned and threw in one motion. It wasn't a spectacular play—he had done it hundreds of times before—but it was nice. His throw was a perfect strike to second base, holding Harrah at first with a long Fenway Park single. The applause was appreciative—a small sign of what was to come.

Yaz went out to left field to start the eighth inning after having popped out in the bottom of the seventh, but when he reached his position, a replacement came onto the field. Yaz trotted back in, shaking hands with his teammates and waving to the crowd. He stood in front of the dugout, the stadium lights shining down on him as he turned and saluted the crowd in each corner of the ball park. He looked once more around the field and reached to his uniform shirt. Unbuttoning it, he walked to the dugout and removed his Red Sox jersey number eight, showing it to the fans before he tossed it into the dugout and made his departure. The ovation and game continued, the overcast sky lightened, the clouds broke up. It was an early October baseball afternoon again when Yaz stepped to the top of the dugout steps and satisfied his fans with one final wave. From my seat in the stands, I felt, along with much else, gratitude and a sense of privilege in having grown up watching this man play ball.

Elizabeth Neeld Comments:

✦ *On October 2, 1983, Carl Yastrzemski, at the age of forty-four, played his last baseball game. For more than twenty years, Carl had played left field for the Boston Red Sox. He had played 3,309 games, made 3,419 hits and 452 home runs. In 1967 he won the batting Triple Crown, leading all other American League hitters in batting average, home runs, and runs batted in. Yastrzemski, known by his fans as Yaz, never played for another team except the Boston Red Sox; for thousands of fans in Boston he was one of their own.* ✦ *Emerson said that you can write powerfully about anything if "only you can be the fanatic of your subject and find a fibre reaching from it to the core of your heart." David Wetmore is a fanatic about baseball—and Carl Yastrzemski in particular—and the subject does cut deeply into his heart. He writes with originality about the last games Yastrzemski played for the Boston Red Sox. Because "the fibre" reaches "the core of his heart," Wetmore also writes about the importance of baseball in his life from the time he was six years old, about heroes, about beginnings and endings. He raises deep philosophical questions almost unintentionally—just by exploring what it means to watch a hero play his last games.* ✦ *Wetmore is a twenty-five-year-old graduate of Northwestern University, who formerly lived in Boston. What adds depth to his treatment of Yastrzemski's last games? What makes the discussion more than a newspaper account? For one thing, Wetmore combines his own love for baseball—talk of his own feelings, experiences, and thoughts—with information about the game and about Yaz. We learn how long Yaz has been playing, which his best seasons were, what made him a special player, how his teammates felt about him, when he decided to quit, what the last day was like. All this is very real. "He stood in front of the dugout, the stadium lights shining down on him as he turned back and saluted the crowd in each corner of the ball park. He looked once more around the field and reached to his uniform shirt. Unbuttoning it, he walked to the dugout and removed his Red Sox jersey number eight, showing it to the fans before he tossed it into the dugout and made his departure. The* ovation and game continued, the overcast sky lightened, the clouds broke up." We know that David Wetmore lives and breathes baseball, reading the box scores as he has his coffee every morning. He follows spring training, keeps statistics, remembers forever single moments of special games. And Yaz was the epitome of baseball for Wetmore. "Yastrzemski . . . perfectly fit my image of baseball as something storybook but real, as something grand and symbolic and lasting. . . . I felt, along with much else, gratitude and a sense of privilege in having grown up watching this man play ball." ✦ After retirement Carl Yastrzemski became a part-time sportscaster for WNEV–TV in Boston, a marketing officer for Kahn's meats, and a minor-league hitting instructor for the Sox. When one reporter asked him why he quit playing ball in 1983, Yaz said he hadn't been planning to quit but when the team dropped out of the pennant race, "something dropped out of me." The years caught up with him. Yaz told how much harder he had to work as he got older—by the end, he said, he was working out eleven and a half months a year: ten miles of cycling a day; weightlifting and Nautilus, hours swinging the lead bat. He kept the pressure on himself. Up to the last game, he kept a note on his locker door that said, "Wait on the ball." When he was a player, he focused on only one thing— what do I have to do to get ready for the season? Finally, at age forty-four with the team out of the running, he didn't have enough incentive to go on another year. When he retired he received a car, a boat, a pickup truck, a rocking chair, a captain's chair, a Notre Dame jacket (he went there one year on a baseball scholarship), and several checks, which he gave to his alma mater Merrimack College. His teammates gave him a rod and a reel. Yaz's remarks on his last day to play, "I have no regrets, none whatsoever. I never thought I'd get through the first two and a half months of my career, but I lasted twenty-three years and loved every minute of it." ✦

READING

to Learn to Write: Thesis

RALPH WALDO EMERSON

Every composition . . . should contain in itself the reason of its appearance. Thousands of volumes have been written and mould in libraries of which this reason is yet to seek—does not appear.

Quoting his college writing teacher, William Strunk, Jr., E. B. White said that readers are in serious trouble most of the time—trying to follow and understand what they are reading—and that it is the duty of anyone attempting to write English "to drain this swamp quickly" and get the readers "up on dry ground, or at least throw [them] a rope." That's what a *thesis* is in a piece of writing: it is the rope the readers can hold onto to find their way through the essay.

A *thesis* is defined as *a setting down, putting something forward to be discussed, proved, or maintained*. The thesis reveals to the reader your *focus* on the subject, your *angle* of discussion, your *point*. In the thesis you let the reader know what you are up to, what will be discussed. You take some position on your subject, determine an attitude or stance about your subject, highlight some part of your subject, state an opinion about your subject, or pinpoint some aspect of your subject. This *thesis* reminds the readers what the piece is about. The thesis *is* a rope the readers can hold onto.

What makes a thesis a *good* thesis? Well, several things. First, the writer makes as pointed a statement about the subject as possible. The focus of the subject is sharp, not vague. You know exactly what aspect of the subject the writer promises to discuss.

Second, a good thesis shows that the writer is an insider on the subject, has some special qualifications to make the assertion she or he is making. Perhaps the writer has done research or has had a personal experience that relates to the subject. Perhaps the writer has spent a lot of time thinking about the subject. There is some evidence in a piece of writing with a good thesis that the author is an expert on what he or she is writing about.

Third, a good thesis has something in it for the reader—there is some special value the reader is going to get and the thesis and its development make this clear. It might be entertainment. Or perhaps the reader will be educated or warned or provoked or stimulated or encouraged or informed. After they have read the writing, the readers will feel that the writer's work was an act of generosity. The writer gave something of *value* to the reader.

Finally, a good thesis is always developed. This means that the writer sticks to the thesis and doesn't go off on a tangent to another topic altogether. The writer isn't seduced into discussing another part of the subject. The writer doesn't forget what was promised. The writer delivers the promise.

In addition to sticking to the specified subject, a writer who is developing a thesis also gives adequate proof or evidence or examples or facts that back up the thesis. The information used to develop a thesis must be in abundant supply. To develop means to "unwrap," so in developing a thesis the writer is unwrapping the subject for the reader.

One of the most common problems a new writer faces is that she or he forgets how much it will take for the readers to *understand* what is being said, how plentiful the information needs to be to make sure the writer's points are clear. At the heart of developing a thesis is extravagance in the use of proof.

If the thesis is the *promise* a writer makes to readers, the rest of the essay is the *delivery* of that promise. The fact that the thesis is a promise makes it not only an important part of the *structure* of the writing but also an essential part of the *integrity* of the writing. To fail to ensure that the reader can see a clear thesis—a focus, a reason for the writing, a direction in which the writing is going to go—is to act arrogantly and selfishly. The purpose of all writing is to communicate, and a writer is obligated to do everything possible to make sure that communication happens. That's why a thesis is an important means for achieving integrity or wholeness in the writing as well as a means for providing order, structure, and focus for what is being said.

In the essays that follow you will be able to see the writer's thesis clearly. But you will also discover the variety of ways a thesis can appear. Sometimes it is a pointed statement. Sometimes two or three sentences are used to state the thesis. At times the thesis may simply be "understood," which means it is not stated in so many words, but the writer has, nevertheless, made the direction of the essay and the focus of the subject very clear.

You will also notice in the essays that follow the variety of ways writers *deliver* the promise of their thesis. Different kinds of development have been used. One writer may use anecdotes as evidence to prove his thesis. Another writer may use empirical data to back up his assertion. Someone else may tell a story to illustrate the point the thesis makes. Some writers develop their thesis quite formally: point one, point two, point three. Others deliver the promise of their thesis more dramatically or even flamboyantly.

You will learn a lot about the importance of having a good thesis in your own writing when you read the following essays *constructively.* (Be sure to read first just to enjoy the piece, however, so that you have a sense of the whole before you begin reading the second time.) By reading to see how these writers *built* the thesis for their essays, you can learn how to build your own theses better. You will be *reading to learn to write.*

ROBERT B. REICH

Political Parables for Today

The 1986 campaign season is almost upon us, a prelude to the 1988 Presidential race. In short order, we will be treated to a new round of speeches, debates and interviews concerning America's most pressing problems. Some of the proposals will be original, a few of the perspectives novel. But underlying the rhetoric will be stories we have heard many times before. They are the same stories we tell and retell one another about our lives together in America; some are based in fact, some in fiction, but most lie in between. They are our national parables.

These parables are rooted in the central experiences of American history: the flight from an older culture, the rejection of central authority and aristocratic privileges, the lure of the unspoiled frontier, the struggles for social equality. One can distill four central themes:

The Rot at the Top

This parable is about the malevolence of powerful elites, be they wealthy aristocrats, rapacious business leaders or imperious government officials. It is the story of corruption in high places, of conspiracy against the public. At the turn of the century, muckrakers like Upton Sinclair and Ida Tarbell uncovered sordid tales of corporate malfeasance; their modern heirs are called investigative reporters. The theme arises from the American detective story whose hero—such as Sam Spade, Serpico or Jack Nicholson in "Chinatown"—traces the rot directly to the most powerful members in the community. The political moral is clear: Americans must not allow any privileged group to amass too much power.

The Triumphant Individual

This is the story of the little person who works hard, submits to self-discipline, takes risks, has faith in himself, and is eventually rewarded with wealth, fame and honor. Consider Benjamin Franklin's "Autobiography," the first of a long line of American manuals on how to become rich through self-denial and diligence. The theme recurs in the tale of Abraham Lincoln, log-splitter from Illinois who goes to the White House; in the hundred or so novellas of Horatio Alger, whose heroes all rise promptly and predictably from rags to riches, and in modern success stories, such as "Rocky" and "Iacocca." Regardless of the precise form, the moral is the same: Anyone can "make it" in America through hard work and perseverance.

The Benign Community

The third parable is about the American community. It is the story of neighbors and friends rolling up their sleeves and pitching in to help one another, of self-sacrifice, community pride and patriotism. The story is rooted in America's religious traditions, and its earliest formulations are found in sermons like John Winthrop's "A Model of Christian Charity," delivered on board ship in Salem Harbor just before the Pilgrims landed in 1630. He envisioned a "city set upon a hill" whose members would "delight in each other" and be "of the same body." Three hundred years later, these sentiments echoed in Robert Sherwood's plays, John Steinbeck's novels, Aaron Copland's music and Frank Capra's films. The last scene in "It's a Wonderful Life" conveys the lesson: Jimmy Stewart learns that he can count on his neighbors' generosity and goodness, just as they had counted on him. They are bound together in a spirit of dependence and compassion. The principle: We must nurture and preserve genuine community.

The Mob at the Gates

The fourth parable is about social disintegration that lurks just below the surface of democracy. It is the tale of mob rule, violence, crime and indulgence—of society coming apart from an excess of democratic permissiveness. It gives voice to the fear that outsiders will exploit the freedom and openness of America. The story shows up in Federalist writings about the instabilities of democracy, in Whig histories of the United States and in the anti-immigration harangues of the late 19th and early 20th centuries. Its most dramatic appearance in recent years has come in fictionalized accounts of vigilante heroes who wreak havoc on muggers—like Clint Eastwood's Dirty Harry or Charles Bronson in "Death Wish"—and in Rambo's messy eradication of platoons of Communist fighters. The lesson: We must impose social discipline, lest the rabble overrun us.

The Art of Political Rhetoric

These four parables are completely familiar to most of us. They shape are political discourse. They confirm our ideologies. Every American retells and listens repeatedly to all four stories; every politician and social commentator borrows, embellishes and seeks legitimacy from them.

But the parables can be linked together in different ways, each arrangement suggesting a distinct political message. At any given time in our nation's history one particular configuration has been dominant, eventually to be replaced by another. The art of political rhetoric has been to reconfigure these stories in a manner that affirms and amplifies the changes already occurring in the way Americans tell the tales.

In the early part of the century, for example, leaders of the Progressive era emphasized the link between the parables of Rot at the Top and the Triumphant Individual. Big business—the trusts— blocked worthy citizens from their rightful places in society; corruption at the top was thwarting personal initiative. Woodrow Wilson put the matter succinctly in a speech during the 1912 Presidential campaign, promising to wage "a crusade against the powers that have governed us . . . that have limited our development . . . that have determined our lives . . . that have set us in a straitjacket to do as they please." In his view, the struggle against the trusts would be nothing less than "a second struggle for emancipation."

By the 1930's, the parables had shifted. Now the key conceptual link was between Rot at the Top and the Benign Community. The liberties of common people were under attack by leaders of big business and finance. In the 1936 Presidential campaign, Franklin D. Roosevelt warned against the "economic royalists" who had impressed the whole of society into "royal service."

"The hours men and women worked, the wages they received, the conditions of their labor . . . these had passed beyond the control of the people, and were imposed by this new industrial dictatorship," he warned in one speech. "The royalists of the economic order have conceded that political freedom was the business of the Government, but they have maintained that economic slavery was nobody's business." What was at stake, he concluded, was the "survival of democracy."

The shift from the Progressives' emphasis on the Triumphant Individual to the New Deal's Benign Community was more than an oratorical device. It represented a change in Americans' understanding of social life. The Great Depression had provided a national lesson in social solidarity; nearly every American family felt the effects of poverty. The Benign Community became intimately relevant as relatives and neighbors sought to help one another, as Government became the insurer of last resort, and then as Americans turned together to winning the "good war" against fascism. The Benign Community embraced the entire nation.

One Parable's Descendant

In the decades following World War II, however, the Benign Community became a less convincing parable. Much of the country's middle class began to enjoy a scattered suburban affluence, far removed from the experiences of mutual dependence that had characterized American life a generation before. The prewar images of the common people and the forgotten man were less compelling now that most Americans felt prosperous and not at all forgotten; the story of Rot at the Top was less convincing now that life at the top was within plain sight.

The descendant of the Benign Community was a feeble impulse toward social altruism. Lyndon Johnson's War on Poverty was sold to the American public as being relatively costless. The idea was that proper Keynesian management of the economy required substantial public expenditures, which might as well be for the benefit of the poor. The economy was buoyant enough that America could afford to enlarge its welfare state; the "fiscal dividend" could be spent on the less fortunate. And in any event, "we" were only giving "them" an "equal opportunity," simply allowing the Triumphant Individuals among them to come forth and find their true potential. Under the banner of civil rights and social justice, Triumphant Individuals joined the nation's Benign Community.

Once again, the configuration of stories Americans told one another began to shift. As the economy slowed in the 1970's, a public tired of belt tightening became less tolerant of social altruism.

As the Parable Turns

Enter Ronald W. Reagan, master storyteller. His parables draw upon the same four American tales, but substantially recast. This time the Rot at the Top refers to career bureaucrats in government and liberal intellectuals. The Triumphant Individuals are America's business entrepreneurs. The Benign Community comprises small, traditional neighborhoods in which people voluntarily help one another, free from government interference. And the Mob at the Gates is filled with criminals, pornographers, welfare cheats, illegal immigrants, third-world debtors and revolutionaries, ornery trading partners and Communist aggressors—all of them encouraged by liberal acquiescence. The Reagan Revolution will discipline "them," to liberate the Triumphant Individuals in "us." Political choices in this story are cast as how "hard" or "soft" we should be on "them." Hard always emerges as the only decent American response.

Inevitably, the configuration of stories Americans tell one another will change yet again. The "us" and "them" recountings of the present era eventually may be superseded by a new version that reflects a more complex, interdependent world. Perhaps, in the next version, the parable of the Benign Community will be expanded to include more of the earth's peoples, and that of the Triumphant Individual will embrace our collective aspirations for freedom and dignity. Indeed, it is just possible that Americans already are telling one another these sorts of stories, and are only waiting for a new set of political leaders to give them voice.

Elizabeth Neeld Comments:

✦ *Robert Reich teaches political economy and management at Harvard's John F. Kennedy School of Government. He is a watcher of American's reaction to and relationship with our politicians, business leaders, and economic events. For instance, one of his recent books is on the revival of the automobile company Chrysler and what that reveals about the American system of doing business.* ✦ *In this essay Reich talks about the stories our politicians use in their speeches and how we listeners respond to them. He states his thesis very clearly, making this assertion: the stories underlying America's political rhetoric are the stories we tell and retell one another about our lives together in America; and some are based on fact, some on fiction, but most lie somewhere in between. Reich's commitment—his promise to us, his readers—is to tell us what these stories are and how we Americans live with them.* ✦ *Before Reich gives us the four parables that our politicians tell us, he makes a very important point: these parables are rooted in experiences from American history. (A parable is a simple story illustrating a lesson.) For example, the fact that the country was settled by people who left an older culture to come to this country, and the fact that these people, for the most part, rejected central authority and aristocratic privileges are experiences that helped shape America. However, these experiences are so much a part of our culture that we don't question the assumptions we hold as a result of them. Reich also says that politicians use the stories they do because of two other American experiences that are part of our heritage— the lure for Americans of the unspoiled frontier and our struggles for social equality. With these shared experiences, we respond to stories that embody them or reflect them. And politicians use the stories because we respond to them.* ✦ *To deliver on his thesis, Robert Reich, then, gives us the four stories: "Rot at the Top"—a parable that* shows corruption can be traced to the most powerful members of the community; "The Triumphant Individual"—the Benjamin Franklin and Horatio Alger type stories in which the poor become rich and successful through hard work and dedication; "The Benign Community" parable—a story of neighbors rolling up their sleeves and pitching in to help one another; and "The Mob at the Gates"—which warns that social disintegration lurks just below the surface of democracy, a tale of mob rule tearing society apart at the seams. ✦ Reich contends that these parables are familiar to all of us. They shape our political discussions. Every American retells and listens repeatedly to all four stories, and politicians use them in every campaign. Reich also shows that these stories can be linked together in different ways. In the early years of this century, politicians linked Rot at the Top and the Triumphant Individual. The powers that had governed had limited Americans' development. By the 1930s, Rot at the Top was being linked with the Benign Community—the liberties of common people were under attack by leaders of big business and finance. He gives other examples of the changes in the ways the stories are linked together. Today, he says, we use Rot at the Top to talk about career bureaucrats and liberal intellectuals. We use the Triumphant Individual to describe America's business entrepreneurs. The Benign Community refers now to small, traditional neighborhoods in which people help each other, and the Mob at the Gates are the pornographers, welfare cheats, illegal immigrants, criminals, and so on. The author's final point is that inevitably the configuration of the stories we tell ourselves and that our politicians tell us will change yet again. But the stories will remain the same. ✦ Robert Reich did not waver from his thesis. He focused on the four stories and how these stories show up in American life over the years. People used to say that the best way to give a speech was to tell the people what you were going to tell them, tell them, and then tell them what you told them. Robert Reich delivered on his promise in this essay in much the same way. ✦

KEVIN STREHLO

Talk to the Animals

Almost all of us are intrigued by the idea of intelligent life forms outside the human race. We search the stars, send out satellites, dream of the meeting between equal minds from different worlds. We look "out there" for our answers. But some researchers and scientists think we should keep our eyes earthbound—or rather, ocean-bound—in the quest for intelligent companionship.

These seekers have set their sights on the ocean's most perplexing, precocious, and bewitching of mammals—cetaceans, specifically dolphins.

We apparently share many traits of intelligence with our bottle-nosed brethren, and there is good evidence to suggest that one of those traits is speech. Other characteristics of intelligence are not shared—toolmaking, for instance. The creation and application of tools is, to all appearances, a cornerstone of human intellectual ability and sets us clearly apart from our planetmates.

Dolphins don't seem to make tools—whether from a lack of intellectual ability or a lack of hands is open to question. But, somewhat paradoxically, it is our toolmaking ability that may enable us to narrow the gulf between the species. Through the use of our Ultimate Tool (so far)—the computer—we may soon share with the dolphins our respective gifts of speech.

The Human/Dolphin Foundation, led by Dr. John C. Lilly, famed for his dolphin research in the 1960s, is attempting to make communication between humans and dolphins a reality. By means of a powerful signal-processing system, which includes several Apple microcomputers, Lilly and his group hope to demonstrate dolphins' true capacity for language and to establish the basis for an interspecies exchange of information.

If they are successful, the day may come when a dolphin swims to the seaside facility of the Human/Dolphin Foundation to deliver the oral history of the dolphin—a 30-million-year history that dwarfs our own tenure on earth.

Popular skepticism concerning human/dolphin communication prevails—the field has yet to produce the kind of breakthrough that makes front-page headlines. But John Lilly and John Kert are confident of eventual success.

Dolphins Smart Enough to Talk?

Kert, the associate director of research for Lilly's Human/Dolphin Foundation, has a background in real-time computer analysis of satellite-data transmissions. He has immersed himself in the work Lilly did with dolphins back in the sixties, and in the cognitive development and human-potential theories that guide Lilly's efforts today, in order to develop a computer system called JANUS. JANUS consists of two Apple microcomputers performing input and output functions for a Digital Equipment Corporation PDP–11 configured for signal processing; tone and waveform generators and a frequency analyzer complete the setup. The purpose of JANUS: to translate human communication into underwater sound waves a dolphin can understand, and vice versa.

"I think the JANUS project will lead to communication about the things we share together," Kert says of his work with Joe and Rosalie, two dolphins at Marineworld/Africa USA in Redwood City, California. "As for our rate of progress, I use the development of a human child as a minimum time scale. With a child, it takes at least two years to begin an interchange of ideas. There's no reason to think communication with another species will come sooner."

Time may not be the only barrier. As Lilly once said, "A non-human language may use a logic that is totally strange, an apparent external form that may be bizarre to humans, and a way of looking at information that may be totally unfamiliar."

Lilly believes dolphins are more intelligent than any man or woman. His interest was first aroused in the 1960s by his discovery that the bottlenose dolphin (*Tursiops truncatus*) had 40 percent more cognitive brain capacity than man. It is this cognitive brain capacity, housed in the silent associational cortex of the brain, that allows abstract mental functions and separates man from the apes and—or so we once thought—the rest of the animal kingdom.

The dolphins seemed willing, even eager, to cooperate once Lilly and his colleagues began to indicate an interest in communication. Long known to carry on underwater exchanges of high-pitched whistles and clicks among themselves, the dolphins tried talking to the scientists in the same manner. They soon discovered, however, that their underwater utterances went unheard. So the dolphins learned to rise out of the water on their powerful tails and vocalize in the air; they were encouraged by the loud, and, to them, low-pitched chatter returned by the scientists.

Dolphin Says 1-2-3

John Lilly first set up a computer to sift the normal conversational intercourse of dolphins for meaningful patterns in 1961, but he learned very little (his biggest discovery was that their wolf-whistle sound was a distress call). It was the dolphins, working only with their own magnificent biocomputer, who made the first real breakthrough.

One day, listening to a playback of a tape he had made with a dolphin named Elvar, Lilly thought he heard something remarkable. Playing it back at half-speed, it was really there, if only in a squeaky, Donald Duck voice: one of the dolphins had unmistakably repeated, after Lilly, the numbers "one, two, three."

The scientists began trying to teach the dolphins English. Lilly set up an affectionate, long-term interchange with the dolphins to prevent their normal, adverse reaction to treatment as ordinary lab animals in an experiment. The dolphins responded by lowering the pitch of their noises and making what seemed to the scientists to be a serious effort to imitate the vocalizations of men. Lacking the lips, tongue, and vocal chords necessary for human speech, the dolphins had little success with correct pronunciation, but succeeded in picking up such verbal nuances as the southern drawl of one of Lilly's associates. Another dolphin mimicked Lilly's voice so well his wife laughed aloud: the dolphin promptly mimicked her laugh.

Meanwhile, the human scientists came up with proof that dolphins did indeed transmit complex information via rapid underwater clicks and whistles when a dolphin in one tank taught a dolphin in an adjacent tank a sizable part of a newly learned routine. The dolphins couldn't see each other—their only contact was an acoustic link between the tanks. Thus, the knowledge had to have been passed in "conversation."

The increasing evidence of the dolphin's intellectual capacity delighted Lilly, but it also bothered him: what right did he have to confine a creature that was the intellectual equal of man? Dolphins in captivity exhibit listless, repetitive swimming patterns similar to the pacing of human prisoners in solitary confinement, and have been known to commit suicide. In 1962, John Lilly made up his mind; he left the study of dolphins to others.

JANUS: *Face on Both Sides*

In 1978, after a 16-year absence from dolphin research, Lilly returned to the field. He had been following the work of others and he simply wasn't satisfied with their efforts, so, along with his wife Toni and actor Burgess Meredith, Lilly formed the Human/Dolphin Foundation. Its goal: to create an interspecies laboratory to which both humans and dolphins could freely come and go to study one another.

At the heart of the new effort is JANUS.

JANUS stands for "Joint-Analog-Numerical-Understanding System." More to the point, the acronym formed by the phrase captures the spirit of Lilly's studies. "Janus" is the name of the ancient god of entrances and exits, symbolized by a mask with a face on both sides. The computerized JANUS has a dolphin face and a human face; Lilly hopes it will be the historic doorway through which the alien intelligences of man and dolphin can first meet and speak.

"In 1962," Lilly says, "we used a ponderous computer, a tube type. Everything we had then on two six-foot racks, both two feet wide, now fits one single microchip."

The new system, built around a Digital Equipment Corporation

PDP 11/04 minicomputer, has an operating speed over 80 times faster than the transistorized LINC III Lilly was using in the 1960s. The new speed, coupled with eight times the memory of the older machines, makes Lilly believe he can accomplish nearly instantaneous translation between English and a language the dolphins can understand.

Several approaches have been contemplated. One approach would use the computer as a vocoder. That is, the computer would transform human speech to a higher pitch and the dolphin's vocalizations to a lower pitch, so that each species would hear the other in their optimal hearing range and medium (air or water).

Translation would be up to the two species, however, and this presents a problem. Dolphin speech proceeds at what to humans seems an incredibly rapid pace: a typical dolphin vocalization contains about ten times as much information per second as human speech. To complicate matters, dolphins have two sound-emitting mechanisms in their blowhole cavity and are capable of producing a series of rapid whistles with one, while simultaneously clicking with the other. It seems unlikely that humans will be able to cope unaided with the complexity of dolphin vocalization.

The large portion of the dolphin brain devoted to audio is matched in the human brain by the size of the area devoted to processing visual information. Indeed, hearing is to dolphins what vision is to humans. It has long been known that dolphins have an extraordinary ability to recognize objects underwater by sending out high-pitched sounds and listening to the echoes. Through this sounding process, similar to but much more sophisticated than the sonar used by submarines, the dolphins can tell each other apart, identify objects, and even differentiate human friends from human strangers. In effect, the dolphin "sees" as clearly with his ears as a human does with his eyes.

Dolphins Listen Pictures

Lilly has theorized that "Delphinese"—his term for the dolphin language—is partially derived from this ability to form clear images from incoming sound. When the dolphin wishes to name an object, or a particular dolphin, he might do it by vocalizing an abstract version of the characteristic echo associated with that object or dolphin. It is as if humans could communicate by transmitting visual images directly.

One of Lilly's eventual goals is to develop a process whereby the computer transforms what the dolphin "sees" with his sonar into a video picture for humans, and vice versa. This would allow a human to see the image that Lilly theorizes is contained in some dolphin vocalizations.

This audio/visual transformation, however, requires more processing power than JANUS presently possesses. According to John Kert, cost estimates for a sufficiently powerful computer system and underwater microphone array exceed a million dollars.

Presently Kert is pursuing a more basic approach at Marineworld's Redwood City facility. The JANUS project will first develop unique code elements usable by man and dolphin; then, through a teaching program, assign mutually understood meanings to strings of these elements. To this end, Kert is attempting to teach Joe and Rosalie how to communicate by whistling tones that stand for letters of the English alphabet. The computer system translates the whistle spelling into an English printout, and keyboard entered English words into whistle spelling.

"In principle," says John Kert, "dolphins can spell a word as fast as we can say it. . . . "

The fundamentals of communication established by JANUS should provide the basis for a more intimate and longstanding partnership between human and dolphin.

"We'll go as far as we can with this approach," Kert says, "but I don't think we'll share things about life in the ocean. That may come in the next phase."

A Human/Dolphin Community

Ultimately, the Human/Dolphin Foundation plans to set up a laboratory in a house on the ocean. The house will be flooded with 18 inches of water: enough for dolphins to swim, not too much for humans to walk. The people and the dolphins involved will live together continuously in the kind of affectionate interspecies domesticity Lilly feels is important for further progress. The house will be connected by a channel to the surrounding warm-water sea so that participating dolphins can come and go at will. . . .

But what is to come from all this? What's in it for us if man succeeds in breaking the interspecies barrier and communicates with the dolphin, a creature who has lived peacefully in the sea for many times longer than man has been on earth? The American humorist James Thurber, in a serious moment, perhaps anticipated what our hopes might be.

"I observed a school of dolphins," Thurber said, "and something told me that here was a creature, all gaiety, charm, and intelligence, that might one day come out of the boundless deep and show us how a world can be run by creatures dedicated not to the destruction of their species, but to its preservation."

Elizabeth Neeld Comments:

✦ *Kevin Strehlo writes often about breakthrough technology, particularly computers. In this essay, which appeared in* Popular Computing *magazine, he discusses the use of computers in dolphin and human communication. He makes a mild and gentle assertion as his thesis: through the use of the computer we may soon share with the dolphins our respective gifts of speech. In his introduction Strehlo states that all of us are intrigued by the thought of intelligent life forms other than the human race. He says that there is good evidence that dolphins are one of these intelligent life forms, and that one of the traits dolphins and humans share is speech. But, he says, dolphins don't have the ability to make tools; by providing computers we may be able to demonstrate that dolphins do have a true capacity for language, and we may be able to establish the basis for exchanging information with them. Strehlo devotes the rest of his essay to developing (or unwrapping) this thesis for the reader. Note that Strehlo uses words like "good evidence," "may soon share," and "hope to demonstrate." This sort of wording relieves him from having to prove his assertion. In his thesis he suggests that these things might be so. To deliver on the promise of the thesis, then, he needs only to refer to the evidence and give information that shows what might be so in the future. Consequently he can talk about something that isn't yet provable but which is far enough along to provide hints at least of what may happen in the future. ✦ To develop his thesis, Kevin Strehlo explains how a computer system is being used to communicate with dolphins. Two Apple microcomputers translate human communication into underwater sound waves which a dolphin can understand. To make his discussion of this computer system meaningful, he briefly describes the history of research in dolphin language and then returns to describe the new computer system. In ef-*

fect, the way Strehlo delivers his thesis is to report on the activities of this computer project. He told us at the beginning that he couldn't prove what he was going to say, but he could give us information that pointed toward what may be possible in the future. By letting us know, then, what is happening in the JANUS project, how the computers work, and what the scientists are finding out about dolphins' speech and communication, Strehlo is able to deliver what he promised. And he gives us clues to his position on this matter—by pointing out that dolphins have a thirty-million-year history on earth, that they have lived peacefully in the sea for many times longer than man has been on earth, and by hinting (in the quote from Thurber) that dolphins might show us how a world can be run by creatures dedicated not to the destruction of their species, but to its preservation. Strehlo, then, delivers his thesis through reporting. We are left to do with it what we will. ✦ This essay appeared first in 1982. Since that time much research has been done on dolphins' ability to communicate. For instance, one recent research article reports that dolphins can understand grammatical features of sentences—a whistle or gesture stands for an object, an action, or a modifier—and they can understand the grammatical rules that allow these "words" to be combined in many ways to form sentences. They can also, according to this research, respond correctly to sentences with novel word combinations and can comprehend references to objects they cannot see. It looks as if the observations offered in the development of Strehlo's thesis will be proven right. ✦

AKIO MORITA
Chairman, Sony Corporation

How to Be Creative in Modern Industry

The ability to think of something that has not been known before is creativity. This is an ability that is unique to man. No matter how much a computer may be developed to accumulate knowledge, and no matter how great its capacity may be for processing the information, it cannot have the ability to be creative. The leap, which is necessary in creative thinking or invention, might be described as giving birth to a new concept beyond a system of theory already known, or discovering a concept that breaks through the walls surrounding the existing theory. This is true creation.

Cooperation Leads to Innovation

We live in a different age from the Renaissance when a creative genius like Leonardo da Vinci appeared, in which one man's creativity elevated the entire level of science and scholarship, or produced innovative changes in the structure of society, or generated a major new industry.

Today, however, it has become possible to stimulate many persons to be creative by providing them with a goal in a broad sense. Although it has become very unlikely that one person will create a scholastic discipline or revolutionize an industry, it has now become possible to obtain collaboration from all corners of the globe, which neither Newton nor Edison could ever have obtained. Present-day society with its complex network of information channels provides cooperation among many disciplines. This leads to innovation that coordinates many specialized fields of knowledge in a way that no single genius could ever have covered in preceding eras. These days major breakthroughs in industry are done by many in teamwork.

Creativity Generators

We are living in an age of innovation. We constantly see improvements and changes in every aspect of our lives. These may be said to have been brought about by the exercising of man's creativity in its broadest sense. The question is, "How can such creative energy by generated?" Two factors suggest themselves as generators of creativity. These two factors are (1) the clear establishment of goals (2) the provision of outside stimulation.

Although great inventions or discoveries of a high level are likely to appear suddenly, without incentives supplied from the outside, it is often possible to motivate technologists to become creative by providing such outside influences as a specific goal or stimulation. The great goal of sending men to the moon was established and as analyses were conducted to determine what needed to be accomplished, many specific objectives became clear. As each one of the specific objectives was further analyzed, the potential for new creativity was revealed. It may be said that in most cases in modern industry this is the process by which the creative quality of man is brought out.

In the case of outside stimulation we can see many examples. One form of this is learning of other creative results which happens very often in an industry that operates under the principles of free competition; very often the knowledge that a competitor has come out with a new product is enough to stimulate a different idea and produce a new product that serves the same purpose better.

Creativity into Reality

An invention or discovery, no matter how good, will not become an industry until it is made into a product of excellent feasibility. A newly developed item produced through creativity will not lead to a new industry unless excellent manufacturing technology accompanies the effort. This is extremely important to industry and may be considered the difference between industry and academic science. Creativity in industry, to be brought to fruition, requires the development of the necessary technology in the production process.

And yet a good product that is successfully produced might still disappear. The newer and more innovative a product is, the more likely it is that the public might not appreciate it at the beginning. In 1950 our company marketed a tape recorder. Despite the fact that it was a great achievement and a technological innovation for us at the time it looked like a toy to the general public. Nobody thought about recording speeches or using a tape recorder to learn languages. I believe in the case of an entirely new product a market must be created not surveyed. Another way to say this is that a new product is the creator of a market and a new product cannot survive without the creation of a new market.

Good collaboration and communication are needed over a very wide range of countless numbers of persons. Perhaps it can be said that the most important matter in modern industry is to get such countless numbers of persons working together in one direction without wasted effort. To bring into collaboration many persons in this way is the function and responsibility of management.

In modern industry a strong management force is necessary that follows through with consistent philosophy from the stage of scientific research to the stage of production and marketing. Among the enterprises around the world the ones with this capacity are the ones that bring to maximum fruition the ability of man to create. They are the ones that continue to grow.

Thus we see that in this age of collaboration, modern industry can draw from man's creativity far greater fruits for his well-being than ever before in history. This transcends barriers of nation, race or creed. In its best form this flowering of creativity is mankind's greatest hope.

Elizabeth Neeld Comments:

✦ *Akio Morita co-founded Sony Corporation in 1946 and has been chief executive officer since 1976. Even though he was expected to take over his family's sake (rice wine) company in Japan, he became an engineer. He was fascinated with sound reproduction, particularly in music. With five hundred dollars in working capital, he and his partner founded Tokyo Telecommunications Engineering Corporation, which was later renamed Sony. Morita's company is responsible for numerous advances in technology—the transistor radio (which made Morita a laughing stock when he first suggested it), black-and-white and color television, portable cassettes, and videotape recorders. Sony produced the "tummy television" set, advanced the Trinitron color picture tube for TV, and made significant improvements in tape recorders and clock radios. Among its most recent innovations, Sony has created the compact disc and player, a system for hearing music that does not use a needle and mechanical vibration but instead uses recordings made digitally and reproduced with lasers, allowing perfect sound reproduction.* ✦ *Without a doubt, Akio Morita knows how to stimulate creativity and invention among his employees. What is the secret, he's been asked again and again. An interviewer once queried Morita: "As you develop new products, do you rely on market research?" And Morita answered: "Not very much. In new technology, consumers do not know what can be offered. So it's not a good idea to ask, 'What do you need in the future?' It is up to management to be creative and decide on a target. For example, Sony's honorary chairman, Masaru Ibuka, once came back from the U.S. with a paperback book. He gave it to our development people and said, "That's the size of videocassette we should sell.' It was a clear target, and from that came Betamax."* ✦ *In the essay we have here, "How to be Creative in Modern Industry," Morita elaborates on the secret for assisting people to be inventive and original in their work. His thesis is that two factors generate creativity: (1) setting goals, and (2) providing outside stimulation. Before he gets to the point where he states his thesis, Morita talks about today's possibilities for international collaboration. He maintains that although in this age one person can no longer create a discipline or revolutionize an industry, we can now coordinate specialized fields of knowledge, and therefore innovation can occur that no single genius could ever produce. This leads Morita to say that today major breakthroughs in industry are done in teamwork. Then he states his thesis.* ✦ *How does the author develop the thesis and deliver what he promised? First, he discusses this point: you help people in industry be creative by providing them with a goal. The example of the paperback book and the Betamax illustrates this point. Workers at Sony were asked to produce something that did not exist. And because this goal was given to them, they created something new. Morita uses in his essay the example of men going to the moon. When that goal was set, everything that had to be discovered, worked out, and accomplished surfaced; and people had to be creative to meet the challenge.* ✦ *Morita then discusses the second part of his thesis: people in industry are creative when stimulated from the outside. Morita has often said that when a new idea comes along, it creates competition. And competition forces everyone to work harder on development of a new product. In this essay he makes a similar point. Often merely the fact that "a competitor has come out with a new product is enough to stimulate a different idea and produce a new product that serves the same purpose better."* ✦ *Finally, Morita says that to bring creativity in industry to fruition requires the development of necessary technology and good collaboration and communication. This development, collaboration, and communication, he says, is the job of management. A good manager is one who inspires human beings to create. And this flowering of creativity, Morita says, is humankind's "greatest hope."* ✦ *This essay illustrates a very straightforward promise and delivery system. Without much elaboration of his points, Morita says what he came to say: There are two things that produce creativity in modern industry. Here they are. And, he adds, this is why they are important. Clear. Clean. Even spartan, perhaps. But the point is made. His assertion stands.* ✦

K. C. COLE

Right and Wrong

Several years ago, I was invited to speak to a group of "gifted" junior high school students in our community on the subject of Science and Creativity. Thinking that nothing could be quite as creative as Einstein's theory of relativity (what could be more creative than refashioning our fundamental notions of matter, space, and time?), I decided to try them out on that. All went well until the end, when a girl sitting way in the back asked: "But what if Einstein was wrong?"

What indeed? It was a fair question, to be sure. Science seems littered with the mostly forgotten remnants of "wrong" ideas, much as old love affairs are littered with false promises. Heat is not a fluid; the earth is not flat nor does it reside at the center of the universe; the planets do not revolve in perfect circles on fixed celestial spheres; Mars is not covered with canals; no luminiferous ether pervades our space, undulating invisibly as a carrier of light. On the other hand, empty space is now described as incredibly curved, and even vacuums are said to come in several exotic varieties. It seems as if the outrageous ideas of yesterday are the scientific facts of today—and vice versa. So why shouldn't Einstein be wrong?

Einstein Will Be Proven Wrong

Einstein will almost certainly be proved wrong in the long run. Or, at least wrong in the sense that he himself proved Newton wrong. But "wrong" is obviously the wrong word for it. The girl's question reminded me of a conversation I once had with M.I.T.'s Philip Morrison about whether some current views of the universe were "right" or "wrong." Finally, Morrison said to me: "When I say that the theory is not right, I don't mean that it's wrong. I mean something between right and wrong."

Unfortunately, the territory *between* right and wrong is uncomfortably unfamiliar to most of us—especially when it comes to sciences. "It's a scientific fact" is virtually synonymous with "It's absolutely true." Smearing social theories with shades of gray is one thing, but everyone knows that scientific knowledge is black and white. Or so goes the popular misconception: "In the conventional model of scientific 'progress,' we begin in superstitious ignorance and move toward final truth by successive accumulation of facts," writes Stephen Jay Gould in *Ever Since Darwin*:

> In this smug perspective, the history of science contains little more than anecdotal interest—for it can only chronicle past errors and credit the bricklayers for discerning glimpses of the final truth. It is as transparent as an old-fashioned melodrama: truth (as we perceive it today) is the only arbiter and the world of past scientists is divided into good guys who were right and bad guys who were wrong.

Anyone who has ever taken a science course knows how important knowing right from wrong is; the questions on quizzes allow only "right" or "wrong" answers, so no wonder we so often think that the point of science is getting it "right." There are only right and wrong answers to such engineering questions as How much weight can be carried by such-and-such a bridge? But it turns out that very little in science is actually wrong—and nothing in science is ever completely right.

Take Isaac Newton, for example. There is no argument about the fact that Einstein proved Newton wrong. Newton said that time and space were absolute, and Einstein proved they were not. Newton never conceived of gravity as an unseen curvature of space. Newton didn't realize that mass was a form of energy, or that inertia would become infinite as you approached the speed of light.

Yet Newton's "wrong" ideas still chart the paths of space shuttles and place artificial satellites into nearly perfect orbits. Apples still fall and the moon still orbits according to Newton's formulas. For that matter, Newton's theories work well for everything in our daily experience. They break down only at extreme velocities (approaching the speed of light), where relativity comes into play, or at extremely small dimensions, where quantum theory takes over, or in the presence of extremely massive objects such as black holes. "Einstein's correction of Newton's formula of gravity is so small," writes Arthur Koestler, "that for the time being it only concerns the specialist." Einstein's equations even give the same answers as Newton's equations for the things that Newton was dealing with.

Einstein proved Newton wrong only in the sense that he stood on Newton's shoulders and saw things that Newton could not see— like what happens to time and space under extraordinary (to us) conditions. Mostly, Einstein proved Newton *right*, since his theories were built on Newton's foundations. Einstein took Newton's ideas and stretched them to previously unimagined limits, brought them into a new dimension, made them broader, bolder, more sophisticated. Einstein added to Newton just as today's physicists are adding to Einstein. Einstein climbed the tower of Newton's scaffolding and saw things from a better perspective. If the scaffolding hadn't been strong, he would have fallen flat on his face.

Right and wrong turn out to be surprisingly *unscientific* ways of describing ideas—especially scientific ideas. Rarely do revolutionary concepts overthrow old ways of thinking in unexpected coups. Physicist Hendrik Casimir goes so far as to argue that no sound theory is *ever* completely refuted: "There is no 'stage of refutation,' but there is all along a process of demarcation and limitation," he writes in his book *Haphazard Reality*. "A theory, once it has reached the technical stage, is not refuted, but the limits of its domain of validity are established. Outside these limits new theories have to be created."

Or as British physicist David Bohm put it: "The notion of absolute truth is shown to be in poor correspondence with the actual development of science. . . . Scientific truths are better regarded as relationships holding in some limited domain."

Sins of Omission

New ideas expand, generalize, refine, hone, and modify old ideas— but rarely do they throw them out the window. Some "wrong" ideas are misconceived, or wrong only in that they are awkwardly formulated. Some turn out to be not so much wrong as unnecessary or irrelevant. Like the luminiferous ether, or James Clerk Maxwell's "wheels and idlers in space," or the notion that heat is a fluid, new theories render these constructs superfluous. But the misconceptions at the root of most "wrong" ideas in the history of science are sins of omission: they were wrong because they failed to take something into account, to see some part of nature that was keeping itself invisible, to notice connections among things that seem on the surface totally unconnected. "Wrong" more nearly means "limited."

For centuries, people argued over whether the wave theory of light or the particle theory of light was correct. But light turned out to be both: part wave and part particle. Both theories were right, but restricted. A correct theory requires aspects of both.

Even the idea that the earth is flat was largely the result of a limited outlook at our large, spherical planet. The earth certainly *seems* flat enough as you walk around town. But the view from home is always somewhat parochial, and the earth doesn't begin to look round until you get far enough away from it. Today, most people have seen the spherical earth in its true shape and colors in images brought back from orbiting satellites. Yet hundreds and even thousands of years ago people like Columbus and Eratosthenes were able to see much the same view with the aid only of their imaginations. Physically or intellectually, the difference between a round earth and a flat one is primarily one of perspective—a broad versus a narrow point of view. Space-time itself only begins to look curved when your measurements cover a large enough territory. And quantum mechanics and relativity are merely ways of offering larger perspectives on classical ways of viewing things.

It's Like Climbing a Hill

As Einstein described it, constructing a new theory is not like tearing down old buildings to erect new skyscrapers. It is rather like climbing a hill from which you can get a better view. If you look back, you can still see your old theory—the place you started from. It has not disappeared, but it seems small and no longer as important as it used to be.

Yet how easy it is to gloat over the wrong ideas of other people! Many years ago, I was asked to write an article about an amateur inventor who thought he had invented a "reactionless" space drive—that is, a rocket that pushed off into space without pushing off anything. This would certainly be a marvelous invention, for it would mean that rockets wouldn't have to carry the huge amounts of heavy fuel they need to "push back" on space so that the reaction can propel them forward. It would also be in clear violation of Newton's Third Law: that every action produces an equal and opposite reaction. The idea was silly enough; but what really struck me was the way the inventor was reveling in the belief that he had proved Newton wrong! (This was no big deal, of course, since Einstein had already proved Newton wrong—but the pleasure this fellow was getting out of it seemed totally out of proportion.)

It reminded me of the time my son came home from school and announced that his friend was stupid because he believed that the earth was flat. Even adults tend to equate "flat earth" with (at the very least) backwardness. And it does seem silly to think of the earth as a large pancake of a platform floating in the center of space. But isn't it even sillier to suppose that we live on a great spinning ball, and that people in China are hanging upside down by their feet in thin air?

Laughing over other people's wrongs comes largely from taking what we know for granted. Once, in a science class for first-graders, I heard a teacher casually mention that feathers and rocks would fall at the same rate in a vacuum—as if it were the most obvious thing in the world. Not a hint that it had taken humanity thousands of years to even notice it (much less to explain it).

The following week, another teacher explained to the children how sand and soil came from crushed rocks, and life came from the soil. I later mentioned to the teacher that the children might misunderstand the notion that "life comes from soil." And she said: "Oh, they know what I meant." But the truth is that if you go and look at the soil or the sand with a magnifying glass and see that it's teeming with life, you naturally come to the conclusion that life springs from soil. To say that every bit of life has to come from another bit of life—not to mention that the instructions for this life are encoded in submicroscopic spiral strands of DNA—sounds utterly fantastic.

Today, we know all about falling rocks and round planets and DNA. The previous ideas that people held were clearly wrong—just as it was wrong to think of heat as a fluid instead of a form of energy, or to imagine that planets and stars needed a constant push to keep them going. But this is hardly something to gloat about.

People do not call Ernest Rutherford a dummy, even though after he discovered the atomic nucleus he went on to insist that anyone who saw something practical in its application was "talking moonshine." If you call Rutherford wrong, then you have to say that anyone who cannot see clearly into the future is wrong, because "right" becomes synonymous with "clairvoyant." So to gloat (or even worry) over the finding that Newton (or Einstein) might be wrong seems somewhat silly. Of *course* they were wrong. Neither Einstein nor Newton could resolve every unanswered riddle, or foresee every possible consequence of every conclusion. They did not (could not) claim to be all-seeing or all-knowing. People who do claim to possess this kind of knowledge are not in the business of science—because right and wrong in that sense are not questions of science. They are only matters of dogma.

Nothing Is Ever Completely Right

In fact, science never proves anything completely right because there is so much left to be learned. "Each piece, or part, of the whole of nature is always merely an *approximation* to the complete truth," writes Richard Feynman, with his own italics. "In fact, everything we know is only some kind of approximation, because *we know that we do not know all the laws yet*. Therefore, things must be learned only to be unlearned again, or, more likely corrected."

Or as Sir James Jeans put it: "In real science, a hypothesis can never be proved true. If it is negatived by future observations we shall know it is wrong, but if future observations confirm it we shall never be able to say it is right, since it will always be at the mercy of still further observations." (Students who take physics courses often are asked to prove things—like "Prove Ohm's Law"—as if one could really prove such a thing in the course of a three-hour experiment!)

To be sure, scientists are people, and as such enjoy an aura of "rightness" as much as anyone. But from Aristotle to Einstein, the tenets of the greatest thinkers were often held much more tentatively than popular histories have acknowledged. Newton, for example, never regarded his theory of gravity as "right." As Einstein remarked on the two-hundredth anniversary of Newton's death: "I must emphasize that Newton himself was better aware of the weaknesses inherent in his intellectual edifice than the generations of learned scientists which followed him. This fact has always aroused my deep admiration."

Politicians and journalists and social scientists are not so apt to "admire" others for admitting their mistakes; on the contrary, the admission that even part of a policy or theory is wrong is frequently touted as proof that it was (and is) completely without merit. When it comes to metaphysics at least, fixing the blame for wrong and the credit for right become almost obsessions. People say that everything from welfare to national defense, from sex education to pornography, is clearly either right (or at least okay), or wrong (or not okay) because some aspect has been misconstrued or gone awry or been vaguely associated with something useful.

In fact, the rightness or wrongness of scientific ideas tends to become tinged with dogma precisely when those ideas enter the realm of philosophy. And no wonder: categorizing ideas as cleanly right or wrong may not be scientifically useful, but *philosophically* it is immensely appealing. No one likes being left in an intellectual purgatory. And so the slow evolution of scientific theories is rewritten as a series of revolutionary coups:

"Scientific revolutions are not *made* by scientists," writes Casimir.

> They are *declared* post factum, often by philosophers and historians of science. . . . The gradual evolution of new theories will be regarded as revolutions by those who, believing in the unrestricted validity of a physical theory, make it the backbone of a whole philosophy. . . . Physics may even feel flattered by this homage, but it should not be held responsible for the unavoidable disappointments.

Some Ideas Are Righter Than Others

Even in science, of course, some ideas are righter than others. But how do you tell which is which? Right ideas seem to be those that lead to further investigation, to whole new categories of questions, to an even more passionate quest for knowledge. Right tends to open our eyes, wrong tends to close them. In this sense, Newton was right, but someone like Aristotle was wrong, because (as George Gamow puts it): "His ideas concerning the motion of terrestrial objects and celestial bodies did probably more harm than service to the progress of science." Galileo, among others, spent a lifetime trying to right Aristotle's wrong ideas about the immutable heavens, the geocentric universe, and so on.

But even this interpretation can be open to question. One of the things Aristotle was most "wrong" about was his assertion that all bodies naturally stop moving if they are no longer being pushed by a force. But in a passage I was surprised to find in a physics textbook, author Douglas Giancoli states:

> The difference between Galileo's and Aristotle's views of motion is not really one of right and wrong. . . . Aristotle might have argued that because friction is always present, at least to some degree, it is a natural part of the environment. It is therefore natural that bodies should come to rest when they are no longer being pushed. . . . Perhaps the real difference between Aristotle and Galileo lies in the fact that Aristotle's view was almost a final statement; one could go no further. But the view established by Galileo could be extended to explain many more phenomena.

Right ideas are seeds that flower into righter ideas, whereas wrong ideas are often sterile and do not bear fruit. Right ideas have deep roots that often reveal surprising connections among seemingly unconnected things, and have an uncanny knack for sprouting the unexpected. Once Newton got the right idea about gravity, he explained a great deal more than falling apples, or even the orbit of the moon. He tied together the universe with one cosmic force in a way that allowed later astronomers to understand the motions and masses of all the stars and planets.

It is in this sense that right ideas allow scientists to "predict" novel phenomena: this kind of prediction doesn't imply looking into the future, but it does tell people where to look in the present to find, for example, radio waves. Once Maxwell got the right idea that visible light was an electromagnetic vibration, then it was not so farfetched to think that there might be other identical but "invisible" vibrations with higher or lower frequencies. The lower frequencies are microwaves and radio waves. The higher frequencies were later recognized as X rays.

Many scientists say that these *connections* are as good a guide to rightness as anything—especially when it comes to drawing lines between science and the so-called pseudosciences such as astrology. The idea that the positions of the planets may influence your day-to-day life simply doesn't fit in with anything else people know about gravity or other aspects of nature. Any idea that seems completely unconnected with the rest of knowledge is usually greeted with suspicion.

This interpretation of "right," of course, is a lot more loose-ended than the kinds of right answers most people are used to—especially from science. Right turns out to be a risky business. As Morrison says of his own work:

> The whole business contains a certain amount of danger and a high tolerance for ambiguity. You get one piece of the puzzle and you try to make it fit, or re-form the puzzle around it. But this is always with the assumption that the whole construct may be wrong, that there is no right answer, that these are all ways of looking at things which are useful to different extents, and that allow you to go to the next step.

You Don't Have to Be 100% Accurate

Right ideas are stepping-stones. They do not require—or even imply—100 percent accuracy. Therefore Newton (or Darwin or Freud) can still be considered essentially "right" even though his theories have undergone substantial modification, Freud was probably wrong in that he overemphasized the importance of early sexual experiences, but his far greater contribution was his essentially right and quite revolutionary recognition that *any kind of early experience* could influence adult emotions and attitudes. The creationists who argue that Darwin's supporters can't be "right" because, after all, they even argue among themselves are missing the point. Updating a theory in light of new knowledge doesn't destroy its credibility—quite the contrary. The better an idea holds up to the rigors of conflict and change, the more likely it is to prove "right" in the end. (There's probably no better example of this than the idea of democracy, a political system that incorporates mechanisms for airing conflicts and producing changes as part of its very structure.)

Realizing that there's a *better* way to be "right," in other words, does not necessarily mean that everything previous is wrong. And this is an area where science has produced an especially sweet "sentimental fruit," as my friend the physicist would say. Evolution is often a sounder foundation for progress than revolution. Just because something needs to be modified or retooled doesn't mean that all its premises are mistaken. Yet this is precisely what we usually assume when it comes to social ideas. If an overbloated bureaucracy badly administers an inoculation program for young children, wasting money in the process, the answer is to throw the program out—throwing out the babies with the bureaucracy. If a feminist leader like Betty Friedan revises her ideas in light of changing social and economic realities, people cite it as "proof" that feminism was a bad idea in the first place (and some feminists cry "Foul play!"). Newspapers are full of pronouncements about who was right and who was wrong—as if predicting the future was the point of things. Far more useful is the resiliency to adjust when ideas turn out to be somewhat wrong or in need of modification—as they almost always do. If social and political science has anything to learn from physical science, it is undoubtedly that the way to build new ideas and institutions is *on top of old knowledge*—not in its ashes.

"When we find out something new about the natural world this does not supersede what we knew before," said J. Robert Oppenheimer.

> It transcends it, and the transcendence takes place because we are in a new domain of experience, often made accessible only by the full use of prior knowledge. . . . Thus what has been learned and invented in science becomes an addition to the scientist, a new mode of perception. . . . A perpetual doubting and a perpetual questioning of the truth of what we have learned is not the temper of science. . . . The old knowledge, as the very means for coming upon the new, must in its old realm be left intact; only when we have left that realm can it be transcended.

You Have to Lie a Little to Tell the Truth

A society or a science can accumulate a righter and righter (or more and more useful) perspective on things by building on a foundation of partially wrong half-truths. So can an individual. And when it comes to learning science, the process is almost inevitably one of replacing one "wrong" idea with another. But these ideas aren't any wronger in their context than Newton's ideas of gravity were wrong in his context. In fact, when it comes to explaining the essence of scientific ideas in everyday language, Victor Weisskopf likes to say that "you always have to lie a little to tell the truth." Some science writers get their feathers ruffled at this thought, but in my experience it's true.

For example, Weisskopf often talks about how amazing it is that the difference of a single electron can make such a big difference in the nature of an element. Neon, with ten electrons, is a chemically inactive gas. Sodium, with eleven electrons, is one of the most chemically active metals. Why is this so? The reason is basically that neon's ten electrons form a completely closed shell around its nucleus and leave the atom so self-contained that it has no inclination whatsoever to interact with anything else (which is why it and others sharing its place on the periodic table of elements are called "noble gases"). Sodium, on the other hand, has one extra electron buzzing around just itching to interact with practically anything that comes along. This extra electron is common to metals—and it is these free electrons that so freely conduct electricity.

I know a very bright young science writer, however, who insists that Weisskopf is "wrong" and his example should not be used. Weisskopf is wrong, says the science writer, because the only difference between sodium and neon is *not* one electron; sodium also has an extra proton in the nucleus. And of course, he is technically right. But he is also missing the point. Nuclear particles have almost nothing to do with chemical reactions, which are determined solely by the configuration of an atom's outer electrons. If we followed the young writer's vision of truth, we would never be able to say much about nature at all, because *everything* one says about science (about anything, for that matter) is always partially false—especially if you judge something false for the crime of being incomplete.

People often shy away from science precisely because they are afraid of being wrong. Somewhere along the line they have been led to believe that all scientific questions have clear, unambiguous answers. They have been taught that science is all work and no play, all knowledge and no wonder, all logic and no guesswork. Unfortunately, this attitude excludes them not only from the point but also from the fun of the game.

Wrong Ideas Are Valuable

In the end, the importance of being wrong is greater than one might think—because a well-thought-out wrong idea serves as a basis of comparison, a springing-off point, for right ideas. Even the ubiquitous bald billiard ball is invaluable as a model precisely because of its obvious wrongness: "We know from the outset that it is wrong in the strict sense that it cannot possibly be true," says B. K. Ridley, "and so an assessment of how wrong it is in the particular case can begin straightaway."

Weisskopf tells a story about the impatient German tourist who asks why the Austrians even bother to publish railroad schedules, when the Austrian trains are never on time. The Austrian conductor answers: "If we didn't have timetables, we wouldn't be able to tell how late we are." Many scientific models, says Weisskopf, are like Austrian timetables. (Weisskopf can tell this story because he was born in Vienna, and is still an Austrian citizen.) Some of them are partly wrong and some of them are very wrong. "But what's interesting is to see *how* and *why* they are wrong," he says. "You always need the timetables."

Elizabeth Neeld Comments:

✦ *K. C. Cole writes about science, particularly physics. She is widely acclaimed for having a "glowingly warm analytical mind," not the "cold analytical mind" so often associated with a discussion of science. Her focus on the human side of physics, and her ability to help readers visualize scientific concepts, make mysteries easier to understand. Her enthusiasm for the great theories of modern physics and their relevance to daily life shows up in everything she writes. She writes for The New York Times, Newsday, The Washington Post, and Discover magazine, and many other publications. The book from which this essay is taken is called Sympathetic Vibrations: Reflections on Physics as a Way of Life. The book has been praised widely by critics: "A truly original and inspired book," "a quantum leap in understanding."* ✦ *In "Right and Wrong" Cole asserts her thesis: " 'Wrong' is obviously the wrong word for it." What she is talking about here is the difficulty in calling "wrong" a scientific theory that led to a later scientific theory which we now call "right"—at least until later, when some scientist finds out our theory is "wrong" and another new one is "right." Her thesis focuses on that "uncomfortably unfamiliar" territory between right and wrong* in science. ✦ Cole develops her thesis through several means: She uses anecdotes from personal experience—in fact, she opens the essay with an account of a visit she made to a junior high school. She uses excerpts from other writers—such as the paragraph she quotes from Stephen Jay Gould. She uses examples—"Take Isaac Newton, for example," she says. She gives facts, explanations, and references. ✦ The heart of the development of her thesis is in the middle of her essay: "New ideas expand, general-ize, refine, hone, and modify old ideas—but rarely do they throw them out the window." Up to that point she has been compiling her "evidence" to support that central de-velopment statement. Following the statement she contin-ues to give proof and explanation of the point. The state-ment is clearly the apex of her argument. ✦ One of the things that makes Cole's thesis so clear to the reader is the abundance of information she provides to "unwrap" her point. She does not give just one example from science: She gives not only Newton, but Einstein. And not only Ein-stein, but Ernest Rutherford. And not only Ernest Ruther-ford, but . . . and the list of scientific examples could go on. There is not just one expert quoted to back up her claims, but there are many. Gould is joined by Sir James Jeans who is joined by Arthur Koestler who is joined by Hendrik Casi-mir who is joined by David Bohm who is joined by Douglas Giancoli who is joined by . . . and that list of experts could go on, too. It is worth noticing that Cole gives many, many instances, examples, illustrations, and other pieces of evi-dence to develop her thesis. ✦ It is also worth noticing that Cole keeps in mind at all times that she is writing to human beings, not computers or robots. She herself sounds like a person, not a scientific explanation. And she treats us, her readers, like people. She tells us about things she's done, places she's been, a conversation she had with her son. She talks about teachers and things she has heard visiting classes in school. This real-life context probably helps her develop her thesis as much as anything else she has done—because it helps keep us interested. If we aren't interested, if her writing doesn't keep us engaged, she could develop her thesis forever, and it would make no difference to us. We'd be off playing tennis while she con-

tinued to write. ✦ *But this woman is a smart writer. She cares that we stay engaged and that we understand what she says. And because she cares she assumes the responsibility of treating us well, of being considerate of our likes and dislikes as readers, (she knows, for instance, that we don't like to read an essay that sounds like a physics textbook). She locates her thesis in real life, in everyday life, so that it can matter to us. Without our concern, any formal methods for developing and proving her thesis would be unnecessary. We wouldn't be awake to read them.* ✦

MAX GUNTHER

Making Money: Taking a Risk

Axiom: Worry is not a sickness but a sign of health. If you are not worried, you are not risking enough.

Two young women friends graduated from college many years ago and decided to seek their fortunes together. They went to Wall Street and worked at a succession of jobs. Eventually both ended as employees of E. F. Hutton, one of the bigger stock brokerages. That was how they met Gerald M. Loeb.

Loeb, who died a few years ago, was one of the most respected investment counselors on the Street. This bald, genial man was a veteran of the hellish bear markets of the 1930s and the astounding bull markets that followed the Second World War. He kept his cool through all of it. He was born poor but died rich.

His book *The Battle for Investment Survival* may have been the most popular market-strategy handbook of all time. It was certainly among the most readable, for Loeb was a born storyteller.

He told this story about the young women one night at a restaurant near the American Stock Exchange, where he had met Frank Henry and me for dinner. The story made a point he felt needed to be made about risk.

Sober Sylvia; Mad Mary

The young women both shyly approached him for investment advice. They approached him at separate times, but he knew of their close friendship and was certain they compared notes. Their financial situations in the beginning were identical. They had launched promising careers and were moving up modestly in pay and status. Their salary checks were beginning to do more than cover the bare essentials of existence. They had something left over after settling with the Internal Revenue Service each year. The amount was not large, but it was enough to be concerned about, and there was the promise of more in the future. Their question to Gerald Loeb: What should they do with it?

Over toast and tea at his favorite snack shop, the fatherly Loeb tried to sort out the trade-offs for them. But it quickly became apparent to him that each of them already had her mind made up. All they wanted from him was confirmation.

In telling the story, Loeb mischievously dubbed one of the women Sober Sylvia and the other Mad Mary. Sylvia's ambition for her money was to find a haven of perfect safety. She wanted to put the money into an interest-bearing bank account or some other savings-like deposit with an all-but-guaranteed return and all-but-guaranteed preservation of capital. Mary, on the other hand, wanted to take some risks in the hope of making her little handful of capital grow more meaningfully.

They carried out their respective strategies. A year later Sylvia had intact capital, an increment of interest, and a cozy feeling of security. Mary had a bloody nose. She had taken a beating in a stormy market. The value of her stocks had declined about 25 percent since she had bought them.

Sylvia was generous enough not to crow. Instead, she seemed horrified. "That's terrible!" she said when she learned the extent of her friend's misfortune. "Why, you've lost a quarter of your money. How awful!"

The three of them were having lunch together, as they occasionally did. Loeb watched Mary intently. He winced as he waited for her reaction to Sylvia's outburst of sympathy. He was afraid Mary's early loss would discourage her and drive her out of the game, as happens to many a neophyte speculator. ("They all expect to be big winners instantly," he would say mournfully. "When they don't triple their money the very first year they go off pouting like spoiled kids.")

But Mary had what it takes. She smiled, unperturbed. "Yes," she said, "it's true I've got a loss. But look what else I've got." She leaned across the table toward her friend. "Sylvia," she said, "*I'm having an adventure.*"

Have an Adventure

Most people grasp at security as though it were the most important thing in the world. Security does seem to have a lot going for it. It gives you that cozy immersed feeling, like being in a warm bed on a winter night. It engenders a sense of tranquillity.

Most psychiatrists and psychologists these days would consider that a good thing. It is the central assumption of modern psychology that mental health means, above all, being calm. This unexplored assumption has dominated shrinkish thought for decades. *How to Stop Worrying and Start Living* was one of the earlier books dealing with this dogma, and *The Relaxation Response* was one of the later ones. Worry is harmful, the shrinks assure us. They offer no trustworthy evidence that the statement is true. It has become accepted as true through sheer relentless assertion.

Devotees of mystical and meditational disciplines, particularly the eastern varieties, go still further. They value tranquillity so much that in many cases they are willing to endure poverty for its sake. Some Buddhist sects, for example, hold that one shouldn't strive for possessions and should even give away what one has. The theory is that the less you own, the less you will have to worry about.

The philosophy behind the Zurich Axioms is, of course, the exact opposite. Perhaps freedom from worry is nice in some ways. But any good Swiss speculator will tell you that if your main goal in life is to escape worry, you are going to stay poor.

You are also going to be bored silly.

Life ought to be an adventure, not a vegetation. An adventure may be defined as an episode in which you face some kind of jeopardy and try to overcome it. While facing the jeopardy, your natural and healthy response is going to be a state of worry.

Worry is an integral part of life's grandest enjoyments. Love affairs, for instance. If you are afraid to commit yourself and take personal risks, you will never fall in love. Your life may then be as calm as a tidal pool, but who wants it? Another example: sports. An athletic event is an episode in which athletes, and vicariously spectators, deliberately expose themselves to jeopardy—and do a powerful lot of worrying about it. It is a minor adventure for most of the spectators and a major one for the athletes. It is a situation of carefully created risk. We wouldn't attend sports events and other contests if we didn't get some basic satisfaction out of them. We need adventure.

Perhaps we need tranquillity at times too. But we get plenty of that at night when we sleep—plus, on most days, another couple of hours at odd times while we are awake. Eight or ten hours out of twenty-four ought to be enough. . . .

Expose Yourself

Adventure is what makes life worth living. And the way to have an adventure is to expose yourself to risk.

Gerald Loeb knew this. That was why he could not applaud Sober Sylvia's decision to put her money into a bank account.

Even when interest rates are relatively high, what is the payoff? At the beginning of the year you give a banker $100. At the end of the year he hands you back $109. Big deal. And what a dull business.

True, the safety of your $100 capital is just about guaranteed, at least in any reputable bank in the industrialized western world. Barring a major economic calamity, you aren't going to lose anything. The banker may lower the interest rate during the course of the year, but at least he won't hand you back any *less* than your original $100. But where is the fun? The fire? The passion? Where are the big brass bands?

And where is any hope of getting rich?

That $9 of interest is taxable as income. What's left after taxes will keep you even with inflation, perhaps. You won't make any appreciable change in your financial status that way.

Nor are you ever going to get rich on salary or wage income. It is impossible. The economic structure of the world is rigged against you. If you depend on job income as your main pillar of support, the best you can hope for is that you will get through life without having to beg for food. Not even that is guaranteed.

Oddly, the vast majority of men and women do depend principally on job income, with savings as a backup. It used to annoy Frank Henry that middle-class people in America are pushed in this direction inexorably by their education and social conditioning. "A kid can't escape it," he would grumble. "Teachers, parents, guidance counselors, and everybody else, they all keep hammering at the kid: 'Do your homework or you won't get a good job.' Getting a good job—that's supposed to be the high point of anybody's ambitions. But what about a good speculation? Why don't they talk to kids about that?"

I was one kid who got talked to about it plenty. Frank Henry's rule of thumb was that only half of one's financial energies should be devoted to job income. The other half ought to go into investment and speculation.

For here is the cold truth. Unless you have a wealthy relative, the only way you are ever going to lift yourself above the great unrich—*absolutely the only hope you have*—is to take a risk.

Yes, of course, it is a two-way street. Risk-taking implies the possibility of loss instead of gain. If you speculate with your money, you stand to lose it. Instead of ending rich, you can end poor.

But look at it this way. As an ordinary tax-hounded, inflation-raddled American income-earner, carrying much of the rest of the world on your back, you are in a pretty sorry financial state anyhow. What real difference is it going to make if you get a bit poorer while trying to get richer?

You aren't likely to get much poorer, not with the Zurich Axioms as part of your equipment. But you *can* get very much richer. There is farther to go upward than downward—and no matter what happens, you will have an adventure. With the potential gain so much bigger than the potential loss, the game is rigged in your favor.

Payoff and Cost

Gerald Loeb's two friends, Sylvia and Mary, illustrate what can happen. When I last had any news of them they were in their middle fifties. Both had been married and divorced, and both had continued to manage their financial affairs in the ways they had discussed with Loeb when they were starting out.

Sylvia had put all her spare cash into savings accounts, long-term certificates of deposit, tax-free municipal bonds, and other "safe" havens. The municipals were not as safe as she had been promised, for they all lost big percentages of their capital value during the wild and unexpected rise of general interest rates in the 1970s. Her bank accounts and CDs kept the rest of her capital intact, but the equally unexpected two-digit inflation of the 1970s eroded her money's spending power disastrously.

Her best move had been to buy a house when she was married. She and her husband were on the books as co-owners. When they divorced, they agreed to sell the house and split the equity fifty-fifty. The house had appreciated pleasantly in value during their years of ownership, so they walked away with considerably more money than they had put into it.

Still, Sylvia was not rich or anywhere near rich. She went back to work in a brokerage after her divorce and must continue to work until she becomes eligible for a pension in her sixties. The pension will not be much, but she cannot afford to abandon it, for her net wealth isn't big enough to carry her through her old age. She has designed her life so that job income is her main pillar of support. She probably will not starve, but she will always have to think hard before buying a new pair of shoes. She and her pet cats will live out their lives in a one-bedroom flat that never gets quite warm enough in the winter.

As for Mary, she got rich.

She was always concerned about safety of capital, as any sane person is, but she didn't let that one concern overwhelm all else in her financial philosophy. She took risks. After a painful start, she began to see some of the risks paying off. She did well in the buoyant stock market of the 1960s, but her most magnificent speculation was in gold.

The yellow metal first became available to American citizens as an investment medium in 1971, when President Nixon severed the official link between gold and the dollar. Until then the price had been pegged immovably at $35 per Troy ounce. After the President's action, the price jumped. But Mary was quick. Against the advice of a lot of conservative counselors, she bought holdings in the metal at various prices in the range of $40 to $50.

Before the end of the decade, it hit $875. She sold most of her holdings at around $600. She had been comfortably well off before, but now she was rich.

She owns a house, a condominium, and a piece of a Caribbean island. She spends much of her time traveling—and she travels first-class, of course. She quit her job long ago. As she explained to Gerald Loeb, job income had become a minor element in her financial picture. Her yearly take in stock dividends alone was more than her salary. It seemed disproportionate, therefore, to spend five of every seven days earning that salary.

It is true that Mary's financial affairs have given her a good deal of worry over the years, probably much more worry than Sylvia has ever known. Perhaps this will be some consolation to Sylvia in her unrich old age. Sylvia has never had to go to bed wondering if she would wake up rich or poor. She has always been able to make some kind of calculation about her financial condition next year or ten years hence. The calculation has not always been accurate, especially during the years when her municipals were melting like ice in the sun, but at least she could arrive at an approximation. That must have been comforting.

Mary, by contrast, was never able to do more than make wild guesses about her future during the years when she was acquiring her wealth. There were undoubtedly nights when she slept poorly or not at all. There were times when she was frightened.

But look what she got in return. . . .

Specifically, what does the axiom advise you to do with your money?

It says put your money at risk. Don't be afraid of getting hurt a little. The degree of risk you will usually be dealing with is not hair-raisingly high. By being willing to face it, you give yourself the only realistic chance you have of rising above the great unrich.

The price you pay for this glorious chance is a state of worry. But this worry . . . is not the sickness modern psychology believes it to be. It is the hot and tart sauce of life. Once you get used to it, you enjoy it.

Elizabeth Neeld Comments:

✦ *Max Gunther had a famous father. His name was Franz Heinrich Gunther when he was born and grew up in Switzerland. After he came to America, Franz Heinrich became known as Frank Henry Gunther. Frank Henry was a banker by profession, heading up the New York branch of the huge Swiss Bank Corporation. But his hobby was speculation.*

He loved to play the market with his cronies, other men from Switzerland who also moved to America. Over the years these men came up with a group of rules or principles which they used in making their investments. These rules broke almost every piece of investment advice on the books. They would tell you quickly that if conventional investing wisdom really worked, everybody would be rich. So, they made up their own rules which flew in the face of what almost everybody else said. ✦ *Before Frank Henry died, he taught his son, Max, what by now were called The Zurich Axioms. In 1985 Max put these axioms in a book called* The Zurich Axioms: Investment Secrets of the Swiss Bankers. *This essay comes from that book. (Max is a longtime investor himself and the author of more than twenty books on that subject and others.)* ✦ *The thesis of this essay is that to make money you have to take risks. Gunther then delivers his thesis by giving examples of people who did and did not take risks and advice about what kind of risks to take. Unlike the essay on political parables or the one on being creative in modern industry, this essay does not deliver its points in a 1-2-3 fashion. Instead, Gunther "talks" his thesis into delivery. He delivers on what he promised— to discuss making money by taking risks—but he does not do this in a straightforward, to-the-point way. Let's see exactly what he does.* ✦ *The first step Gunther takes to deliver on his promise is to give the example of two women, one of whom was willing to take a risk and one who was not. Sober Sylvia was too scared, so she never made any money. Mad Mary was willing to take a risk. She often lost money, but in the end she was way ahead of the game.* ✦ *Then Gunther moves to make a point that this example has led him to: have an adventure. Consider worry an enjoyment. This is the only way you have any hope of getting rich. Returning to Sylvia and Mary, Gunther shows the payoff and the cost for each of them.* ✦ *The final words—don't be afraid to get hurt a little. The kind of worry you do when you risk to make money is the "hot and tart sauce of life." Once you get used to it, Gunther says, you'll enjoy it.* ✦ *Gunther proves his thesis by examples and personal anecdotes. He uses stories of people in real life to convince us that his thesis is sound. And the reader* leaves either convinced to not convinced (or somewhere in between), depending on how convincing the examples have been and how many "yea but's" have been answered. If the examples and anecdotes "ring true" for the reader, bring an "aha" or an insight of agreement, then the thesis will be accepted. If, on the other hand, the examples ring hollow and the anecdotes superficial, the reader will leave the essay unconvinced. Either way, however, Gunther has delivered his promise in the essay: to discuss how you cannot make money unless you risk. The thesis was stated and developed. How the reader responds to the information can never be guaranteed, no matter how well the promise and delivery of the thesis is done. ✦

LAWRENCE WRIGHT

I *Want to Be Alone*

This fall my wife, Roberta, decided to go back to work. She's a public school teacher, but for most of the last nine years she has been home raising our children. Her family relies on her—and on the cleaning, chauffeuring, cooking, nursing, and general maintenance a full-time mother is expected to provide. These days, however, having a mother on the household staff is a wild luxury, and for some time I had been encouraging Roberta to return to work, without fully realizing the consequences. As soon as she was hired I began to feel like Hercules holding up the vault of heaven; it was a job I would like to hand back to Atlas.

Who was going to take Gordon to the dentist? Who was going to make Caroline's lunch? What if they were sick—who would stay home? Since I *am* home (I work here), recalling Roberta from work was hard to justify. Before school even started I watched the condition of the house deteriorate as Roberta spent weeks fixing up her classroom and going to orientation meetings. Scraps of construction paper—the dandruff of the kindergarten teacher—began to litter the floor around our dining table. Gordon opened the refrigerator, and there was nothing inside. "Hey! It looks like poor people live here," he complained. At night our quiet time together became even quieter, as Roberta would fall asleep with her glasses still on her nose and her lesson plans scattered across the bed.

"How are you going to get the kids to school?" Roberta asked. It was a question I had been putting aside because the answer wasn't clear. Last year both children went to the west side of town, and we had a neighborhood car pool, so Roberta took them three times a week. This year Gordon would be going east, Caroline west, Roberta south, and our car pool had dissolved. I was facing 45 minutes of driving every morning. Roberta would pick the children up in the afternoons.

Now that the question had been posed, I got angry. By itself, driving every morning wasn't such an impossible imposition on my time, but when it joined with all the other demands that Roberta's new job placed upon me, I began to feel crowded and compromised. The walls of my day had been breached and child care and housework were rushing in. What frightened me most, I suppose, was the notion that Roberta and I had traded places, that she would be going out in the world, earning a steady wage, while I was at home making do.

As usual when I get angry, I went for a run. Part of my anger was the guilt I felt about my ambition and the resentment I had toward my family for holding me back. I knew marriage requires balance. I wanted Roberta to achieve, to find herself in her work as happily as I did in mine, but as that process was actually happening I felt myself seesawing down into the drudgery of laundry and lunch boxes. I needed to puzzle out the relative values of love and success; you have to trade a little of one for a little of the other.

The history of our marriage has been a series of concessions on my part to fairness. We began married life in 1970, before the women's movement got its steam up. I look upon those days the way Englishmen must remember the British Empire. There was a time when all my meals were prepared for me, my dishes washed, my clothes cleaned—even though Roberta was holding down a job of her own because my own labor wouldn't pay the rent. Roberta never marched in the streets, but she waged her own lonely battle at home. She won her first campaign in 1971; since then she's cooked the dinner and I've done the dishes. That's fair enough, but in terms of the Empire it was like losing India. From that point on, it has been a slow slide toward equality.

On my wall I have a Steig cartoon of a man stuffed in a cannon; his bold nose is directed toward the clouds, and one of his hands is lighting the fuse; it's titled "Ambition." It helps me keep perspective on my own ambition, which can be fearful at times. I don't like to talk about it, even to Roberta. People who display their ambition seem pathetic to me, like men who wear elevator shoes. I want so much to succeed, yet often in the middle of work I find myself adjudicating quarrels or sitting through a PTA dinner or worrying about my children's teeth or performing any of the million unrewarding tasks parents must do. I want to say, "No, leave me alone." Instead, I usually do what's required, then resent my wife and children for imposing on my time. I feel that by taking on more of Roberta's load I am losing ground in my career; it's like swimming with rocks in my pockets.

As I ran along the jogging trail, past the picnickers and fishermen and then over the dam, my mind entered that state of free association that comes from being bounced around under the noon sun. Suddenly, Pete Rose steps to the plate. It's the thirteenth inning, the Reds against the Dodgers, the game is tied with a man on third and two men out. When Rose comes to bat, he is 23 hits from breaking Ty Cobb's record of 4191 base hits. Rose may be the greatest player in the game; certainly he's the most driven, the most ambitious, and, in this particular game, the most surprising. He lays down a bunt.

In the world of baseball fans it is the most electric news of the week. Rose wins the game with his two-out bunt. His teammates are laughing in astonishment, the Dodgers leave the field humiliated; all the next day phones are ringing—"Did you hear about Rose's bunt in the thirteenth?"—and sportscasters are shaking their heads with the awe that comes so easily to them. Pete Rose lives for this. He's always advertising his dedication to the game and his relentless pursuit of base hits. And yet, as I was running, I began to wonder what his excellence has cost his family.

Pete Rose is divorced from his first family and now lives with his second. That's a normal arrangement in a country where half of all marriages fail. The question I ask myself is whether Pete Rose would have had a happier family life if he had allowed himself fewer base hits. I can't possibly know the answer, but the question is important to me because I'm constantly trying to find a balance between my aspirations and the demands of my wife and children.

William Faulkner's daughter recalled that she once asked her father not to drink on her birthday. He refused, saying, "You know, no one remembers Shakespeare's child." Since I heard that I have had trouble appreciating Faulkner's work, although I suppose one should not look too closely at the cost of greatness in any man, whether he is Shakespeare or Pete Rose. When I hold my daughter or brush out her hair or tell her stories, I am frightened by the side of me that wants to push ahead at her expense.

Sometimes when my wife and children are away, I've imagined their dying in a car wreck or suffering some convenient catastrophe that would leave me free. Then I quickly put the cap on such thoughts, chilled that any part of me could want such things. Losing my family is the greatest fear in my life, but there is a part of me, the devil ambition, that wants to buck loose. Because I have a superstitious fear of letting unconscious wishes out of the bottle even momentarily, I feel that I have already committed several small acts of murder.

I can easily picture myself alone, living a fashionable and pleasingly self-indulgent existence in a loft in Manhattan or perhaps in a cabin in Montana, devoting myself entirely to my own pursuits. I know writers in both places, and I have imagined how much more successful I could be if I weren't so encumbered and how pleasant life could be if my income were spent on my small needs, rather than being drowned in the mortgage and dental bills. "He that hath wife and children hath given hostages to fortune, for they are impediments to great enterprises, either of virtue or mischief," saith Francis Bacon. I console myself with the belief that the compromises of family life bring dividends of wisdom, love, and peace. However, at that moment I was confused, angry, and resentful.

My immediate concern was 45 minutes of my morning. It was more than I wanted to give up, and I loathed myself for admitting it. Roberta couldn't help; she had to be at school at the screech of dawn. I began to think about my children and whether I could steal my time back from them.

For the last two years we had been sending Gordon to what we believed was a better school than the one in our neighborhood. We are ambitious for our children just as we are for ourselves. We want them to have the best education, and before Roberta went to work the driving had not seemed to be such a tremendous chore. Now I wondered just how important Gordon's schooling was. How much better an education, really, would he be getting? How could I weigh that against my 45 minutes?

Caroline is in a Montessori nursery school. It used to be close by, but our friend who ran the school bought a larger facility across town. Caroline feels comfortable there, and because of our ambivalence about sending her to day care, her comfort was important to us. But how important? Twenty minutes of my morning, not counting the time it would take to walk her into her classroom, put up her jacket and her lunch, and kiss her goodbye? Could she be as happy at a school closer to home?

I began to compare my children's needs. It's a damn cold business. I was willing, I decided, to ferry one of the children to school but not both. Roberta and I made an exploratory trip to the neighborhood school Gordon would go to, and she spent two hours watching Caroline in her class. I had not meant for Roberta's new job to affect our children's lives, except to make them better. And yet every change in a family requires a new balance and compromises all around.

Caroline was used to being picked up at two-thirty, right after her nap, but with our new schedule Roberta would not be able to pick her up until nearly five. That's a long day for a three-year-old. We had occasionally let her stay late, and when I picked her up I noticed that most of the other children were gone and that she was occupied with one of those queer interior games children fall into when no one is paying attention. I saw her on the playground when it was ninety degrees, and she walked over to a bowl of damp washcloths to wipe her red face. The stoicism of that gesture made me approach her respectfully. Naturally I want her to grow into independence, but I realized when I force her onto her resources by keeping her in school all day long, I am pushing her away from the vital carefreeness of childhood. To take her out of the school she knows and place her elsewhere is not acceptable to me, at least not now.

I called Gordon in Mobile, where he was visiting Roberta's mother during the last few days of summer. I proposed that when he came back he would be going to the neighborhood school, and he heard me out quietly. I added that if he went to his old school he would have to spend extra hours after school at Extend-A-Care, which is a sort of study hall for children whose parents both work. "I don't want to go to Extend-A-Care," he said. He said he would rather go to the school nearby, so he could ride his bike home and turn on cartoons. For him, it didn't seem like much of a compromise, but for his father it was an admission that I could accept less than the best for him. I had always thought that I held Gordon's education above everything, but it turned out that it wasn't worth my time, at least not twenty or so minutes every day. That was a rueful discovery to make about myself.

The other day we went to register. Roberta was busy enrolling children at her own school, so I took Gordon. I looked around defensively at the other children and parents, the teachers, and the facilities; I was more apprehensive than Gordon. Of course, it went all right. I was there to be pleased and relieved, to place part of my load in the hands of the teachers who are paid to receive it. I pictured Roberta at the other school and knew how well she would put her parents at ease, how they would come home confident that their child would be cared for and educated, and I thought again about the costs we all have to bear for love.

Elizabeth Neeld Comments:

> ✦ *This personal-reflection essay by Lawrence Wright has a topsy-turvy thesis. The way the piece is written is an exception to the rule. The thesis does not appear early in the essay; in fact, we really don't know the point of it all until we get to the end. We know the subject he is writing on, and we know very early in the essay what bothers him. But we don't know until he's finished writing what he really thinks about it all. ✦ Here's the situation: Lawrence Wright is married and has two children. For a long time he has been urging his wife to go back to work. But he had not realized the consequences until she got a job teaching school. Then the problems compounded. Wright first tells us some of the consequences of Roberta's going back to work. The refrigerator is empty. A new method has to be devised for getting the kids to school. Very soon he feels guilty about his career ambitions because he resents his family for interfering with that ambition. He realizes he has*

to puzzle out the relative values of love and success. ✦ *The movement of the essay includes us, the readers, in this puzzling out. This means the thesis—the point he wants to make—can't come until the end because he's in the process, as he writes the essay, of discovering what that point is. The resentment increases; he feels that by taking on more of Roberta's load he is losing ground in his own career. He thinks about Pete Rose and wonders what his commitment to excellence cost him and his family. (Wright notes that Pete Rose has been married twice.) He wonders if Pete Rose would have had a happier family life if he had let himself make fewer base hits. He doesn't know the answer, but the question is important because he is constantly trying to find a balance between his aspirations and the demands of his wife and children. He imagines how successful he could be if he didn't have a family, yet losing them is his greatest fear. He consoles himself with the belief that the compromises of family life bring dividends of wisdom, love, and peace. Finally, by the end of the essay, Wright has worked out a compromise about taking the kids to school (not one he is really proud of) and has reached the only conclusion he is able to reach. He then states his thesis. "I thought again about the costs we all have to bear for love."* ✦ *In this kind of essay we follow the thoughts of the writer to some kind of resolution or conclusion. If the thesis in this piece had come early most of the interest would have disappeared. What carried us along (since we don't know this man) was either an interest in his predicament coupled with curiosity about how he was going to work it out or an interest in his predicament because we had been in a similar one. In a way, he is writing a problem/solution essay. Except there is no solid solution. There is just an attempt to tell the truth as he sees it now. The thesis is not something he can prove. It is only something he can arrive at by relating and reflecting on his situation. We read this kind of essay for the story and the resolution of the plot, not for proof or explanation. The thesis here sums up rather than launches or introduces.* ✦

READING
to Learn to Write: Form

RALPH WALDO EMERSON

The laws of composition are as strict as those of sculpture and architecture. There is always one line that ought to be drawn or one proportion that should be kept.

RALPH WALDO EMERSON

Why not write as variously as we think and dress?

These two quotations seem contradictory. If the laws of composition are not to be deviated from, how can we even think about writing as variously as we think and dress?

The answer lies in being true to one's purpose.

All good writing has *form*. It is form that holds the thoughts together and shows the reader how to follow what the writer is saying. Form is the structure that allows you to have order instead of chaos when you are communicating your thoughts on the page. Form shows how your points are connected, how this thought relates to another. Form is what produces writing that "makes sense" to readers. It is what shapes your thoughts so others can understand them.

What determines the form is the writer's purpose. Because of the wide range of purposes, the form varies. The form of the essay may be based predominately on one recognizable thought pattern—say, comparison—a thought pattern inherent in how the human mind operates. Let's call this *traditional form*. (*Traditional form* follows what Emerson called "laws of composition.")

But what happens when a writer's purpose cannot be served by the use of one predominate thought pattern? When the writer needs to do much more than compare, for instance? When there is not going to be one predominate way of talking about the subject? Then the writer invents a form for that essay, one that very likely combines many of the traditional forms but goes beyond them, one that is unique to the subject and the purpose at hand. Let's call this *created form*. (*Created form* is as original as the writer and does not follow a set of rules or "laws of composition.")

Let's say that your purpose when you sit down to write is to send a friend a new recipe for Mississippi Mud Cake (traditional form: analyze a process) or a recommendation for which motorcycle to buy (traditional form: comparison/contrast). In both these cases, the laws are strict. If you are going to do your job as a writer, you must organize or *form* your writing to accomplish your purpose. For instance, with the cake recipe, you will be obliged to keep the steps in exact order. Details and precise, clear instructions will have to be emphasized. You won't have much, if any, leeway to be "creative" in giving the basic steps of the recipe; there won't be anything you can substitute for an instruction such as "fold egg whites into sugar mixture." The "laws" of how things are cooked dictate the way you write about how things are cooked.

Laws of composition also apply to the recommendation for which motorcycle to buy. Let's say your friend is undecided between a Honda and a Yamaha. Since your purpose is to let your friend know which motorcycle you think is better, you will have to decide which features you are going to comment on; you will also have to discuss these same features for both bikes. While you will be able to choose whether you want to talk about the Honda first and then the Yamaha or whether you want to talk about a feature and relate it to both bikes at the same time, you will be obliged to follow the laws of comparison/contrast when you write.

Let's look now at what the case would be if you have a different kind of purpose when you sit down to write. You aren't going to send a recipe or a motorcycle recommendation to a friend. Instead,

your purpose this time is to write about whales. Your zoology professor requires an essay based on current research, and you've
chosen whales. Here there are no basic laws of composition. Your
purpose is not the same kind of purpose as writing a recipe or a
recommendation. You're going to give information, but it could be
organized according to any design you wish. In fact, until you do
your research, you won't even know what angle you want to take on
the subject. And once you complete the research and decide that
your essay is going to concentrate on experiments exploring
whales' ability to hear, you still have all the freedom in the world
to decide how to organize your essay. You have to create the form;
your purpose for writing this time does not have a traditional form
inherent in it. You will just have to make it up. The form you use
will *include* several of the traditional forms, most likely, but it will
not follow *one* of the traditional forms exclusively. In this case, you
will be able to write, as Emerson suggests, as variously as you
think and dress.

What this discussion comes down to is this: for some writing
you do your purpose will demand that you use a predominate
traditional form. This form will have rules and conventions which
define it, and you will write according to these rules. (Good writers
even then find a way to write creatively and individually, even while
they abide by the laws of the form.) The writing will have *traditional
form.*

For other writing that you do, however, your purpose will not
dictate a predominate form. Instead, you will be required to decide
for yourself how you want to organize the writing. You will have
many options. Your purpose will allow a multiplicity of ways to
organize what you have to say. It's your choice. Then your writing
will have *created form.* And you will be the creator.

In the essays that follow, we'll first study traditional form.
These pieces are organized as they are because the purpose and
intention of the writer corresponded to one of the predominate
forms of thought inherent in the human mind. The subject was
treated by looking at it basically just one way, from just one perspective: to define, to classify, to compare, and so on.

In the next set of essays we'll study created form. These pieces
illustrate organization and form determined by the writer's personal preferences, whims, penchants, individual ways of thinking,
personality. These essays have a subject, or the writer has a purpose, that does not correspond to one predominate way of think-

ing. The pattern of organization for these essays will be as individual as each writer. The form will have suggested itself to the writer after she or he mulled over the subject, explored its possibilities, and decided on the focus the essay was going to have. In other words, a single thought pattern is not inherent in the subject or the essay's purpose itself. The writer invents the organizational pattern. It is *created form*.

READING

to Learn to Write: Form

Traditional Form

At least as long ago as Aristotle's time, we have had discussions about patterns of thinking that are used as organizing forms in writing. The human mind has a constant tendency to think about subjects in certain ways—to compare, to classify, to analyze, for instance. Naturally, therefore, if you use these patterns to think with you are likely to use them to write with. These predictable ways of looking at the world are inherent in the way the human mind works.

Recognizing this fact and being determined to make this tendency of the human mind useful, Aristotle suggested that we think of our minds as a land or country. This land or country, he said, had several regions or "haunts" in it. (We refer to Aristotle's regions or "haunts" in the mind as *topoi*.)

Just as each part of the country—desert or mountains—has a climate of its own, so each area of the mind has its characteristic way of thinking, Aristotle suggested. He named one area *definition* and said if you go to that part of your mind, you see your subject in a certain way. You ask certain kinds of questions about your subject. Does this subject need to be defined? What group of things does this subject seem to belong to? When is the meaning of this subject misunderstood? Aristotle's point is that if you locate yourself in a particular place in the "land of your mind," you will think a particular way about your subject.

Sometimes when people write, their purpose and their subject correspond to a specific way that the mind works. For instance, if you are going to write to explain what started the Civil War, you will probably use the predominate thought pattern *cause and effect*. That form is organic to your subject and your purpose. You won't have to make up a way to approach your subject. Your purpose contains within itself the way you are going to organize your thinking.

Take a moment and look at the essay that follows on how to bake on a boat. The writer *must* follow the predominate form by giving the steps that describe the *process*. That form is inherent in the author's purpose, and there is no way she could talk about her subject without using the thought pattern known as process. She is using traditional form.

When the writer of the essay about the two seas of Mexico promised that he would discuss the merits of the two oceans as vacation spots, he was obliged to use the thought pattern of *comparison/contrast* in order to accomplish his purpose. He is using traditional form.

The eight essays that follow illustrate some of the patterns of organization that correspond to thinking patterns in the human mind. They illustrate traditional form: narration/description, classification, process, definition, cause and effect, analogy, example, and comparison/contrast. These will be familiar to you because they are patterns we think in every day. But there are two things to note about traditional form. Although an essay will be organized by a predominate pattern or form (for instance, definition is the overall thought pattern informing the essay about a cowboy), no essay will have *only* that form present. There will be some narration in the definition essay, for example. There will be description in the cause-and-effect essay. One form always dominates and serves as the organizing principle for the essay written in traditional form, but never to the exclusion of other forms.

The second thing to note is that not a single one of the writers of the essays that follow said, "I'm going to sit down today and write a comparison/contrast essay." Good writers don't write into a form; they use a form to accomplish their purpose. Purpose is the greatest influence on form; this point will become clear to you as you read the following essays. In each, the writer's purpose carried with it the form the writing would take.

THE NEW YORKER
Talk of the Town

A Snake in the Studio

A young woman who lives in New Mexico writes:

This afternoon, about three o'clock, there was a snake in the studio where I work. He—it?—entered through the crack below the door, which was closed because of the wasps, who are dreamy and vicious in the heat and seem to be cruising, lately, for places to build. The snake came so rapidly, threading through the crack, that I looked up from the typewriter disbelieving, and the snake curved along the wall by the door with a movement like pouring— only a horizontal pouring, an asymmetrical, rapt progress, not quite silent, because it sounded like a very deliberate, faint sand-papering of the floor. The snake moved in alternating arcs, one arc in muscular contraction while the others were suspended—not slack but held in an easy suspension, alert to the arc that was, for the moment, doing the moving; it happened very fast, yet each arc was elegantly positioned for the fraction of an instant that it lasted, almost as if it had been drawn by the snake, or as if the snake were drawing with its body and erasing as it went. There was something electric and delicate in the way the head advanced, parallel to the floor and a few inches above it, with a minnowlike imprecision consisting of many infinitely fine readjustments of aim, reversals, and slantwise investigations, and certain pauses in which for the space of a breath (mine) the head was held frozen in place while the body worked in quick windings and contractions, and seemed to feel itself out—as a cat does, stretching—down to the least vertebra, which was drawn across the floor in an abbreviated frisson that seemed to imply, *All is intact, the length of me is unhurt and alive.* In those pauses, the eye stared out at me from the flat profile, the mouth as tightly sealed as the crevice in an almond shell and turned down at the corner, the face—eye; tiny, dainty nostril; line of mouth and jaw—a single facet. This stare was quite free of personality or intent: it was a pure stare, simple and functional, in itself neither benign nor threatening. The snake appeared to stare at me because I had backed away, screaming. I've always been vain of how I've acted around snakes—calm and collected, in the belief that they won't hurt you unless you directly threaten them, that they are, in their way, shy and judicious, with nothing to gain by doing harm to you. I've never screamed at one before, and don't, in fact, like to think of myself as a screamer at all. It's odd to say this, because I did scream at it, but I don't think I was frightened of the snake—not at first. I think what scared me was being visually disoriented—having to look up from the typewriter and deal with a fairly large snake unreeling from the crack below the door. This has also been my (small) experience in earthquakes—that a glass sliding across the table or a mirror cracking by itself simply *looks* wrong.

But the snake was long—perhaps two and a half or three feet—its swiftly tapering tail disappearing around the corner of my bookcase (the bookcase, near the wall, is not quite flush with the wall, because the wall, adobe, slants to the floor instead of being perfectly vertical; there is a shadowed gap of several inches), but apparently it did not feel that it had found a safe place, for its head

immediately reappeared, and, with most of its length still hidden
behind the books (the lowest shelf holds the glossy, wide spines of
Virginia Woolf's diary, each volume showing, like a cameo, an oval
photograph of her most noble and horsey profile), it began searching the wall for an opening. This was the most beautiful part to
watch, for the snake soon paused, its head poised opposite an
opening that has been carved out for a pair of electrical sockets
that haven't been put in yet, so there is a little rectangular cave,
with crisp metal edges, and bristling with red and white electrical
cord, in the wall. This cave the snake examined with the utmost
precision, moving its head in a neat rectangle that matched the
rectangular opening, swiftly covering each of the corners. Yet its
attention was directed (I *felt*) mainly and furiously at me; and when
(this is really shameful) I screamed again, and again backed away,
the snake turned on me and lashed a few feet across the floor
toward my desk. This was a warning, I think, and meant, very economically, *Be still.* It retreated back to the wall, lowered its head a
few inches from the socket, and began systematically searching the
surface of the adobe for a hole. It knew there was a way out; it had
clearly got over its original fright and deduced that it *could* get out,
because it had got *in.* But while it conducted its inch-by-inch, nerv-
ously sustained quizzing of the wall it did not allow me to forget its
hostility, and it accomplished this by projecting a quality of the
most vigorous, alert menace. Snakes could teach something to
actors, I think, because menace was in the *air.*

Yet at that moment, too, the snake began to seem not ordinary,
exactly, but no longer quite so surrealistically regal. It was perhaps
even explicable, for yesterday we had a backhoe come in to shore
up the foundations of the house—which is on the slope above the
studio—with tons of river rock and gravel, and it was possible that,
as so much earth got turned up and shifted around, the snake's
habitat had been destroyed, and it was still disoriented—that its
old, snug routes beneath clumps of chamiso and among familiar
stones had vanished, and been replaced by a sort of moonscape
with tire tracks. The snake had muddy khaki-brown stripes or
smudges along its back, and a tan belly with coral along the sides,
a very distinct, rouge-like rose I've never seen on a snake before;
and as I watched it thinking—or what I assumed was thinking—it
narrowed down the possibilities to the one last, necessary possibility, and with great finesse its head arrowed neatly through the
crack below the door, and its body quirked back and forth in those
brief, balanced arcs, and there was again the very pleasant, work-

manlike sound of sandpaper on wood, and the snake flowed steadily across the old wooden sill and out into the light and the shocking heat.

Elizabeth Neeld Comments:

◆ *Something happened to this writer. (That's her subject.) She wanted to tell somebody else about this event. (That's her purpose.) There is one predominate thought pattern in the human mind that will allow her to do what she wants to do. (That's her organizational form—narration/description.) So she tells her story from start to finish.* ◆ *A snake comes into her studio. That's how it begins. Through the narrative line of the essay we can follow what happened first, then after that, and following that . . . until the end. The narrative is organized chronologically—according to events in time.* ◆ *The narrative is also organized spatially. The snake enters here, moves there, goes yonder, exits here. We watch the snake move around the room. We see the snake explore the electrical outlet socket. We see the snake slither behind the bookcase. The snake moves the narrator, the narrative—and us—around the room.* ◆ *The narrative is also organized experientially. The writer is startled; the writer screams (more than once); the writer is frightened by the hostile advance of the snake toward her; the writer notices specific movements; the writer figures things out; the writer is relieved. We go through the experience the writer had as we read the narrative.* ◆ *The power of this narrative lies not only in its subject matter but also in the writer's ability to describe the scene and events that the narrative relates. We know that even while she was screaming she was observing the snake. Perhaps fright increases the keenness of the eyes! Whatever the explanation for her ability to observe the snake so astutely as it moved around her studio, we are the winners. Through her description, we live the event with her.* ◆ *First of all, the writer gives us the ambience. It's hot. The door to the studio is closed. Dreamy and vicious wasps are looking for a place to build. The writer is at her typewriter working. Enter the snake!* ◆ *Our senses are heightened because the writer stimulates them with her words: "the snake* curved with a movement like pouring," "sounded like sand-papering of the floor," "as if the snake were drawing with its body and erasing as it went," "body worked in quick windings and contractions," "the eye stared out at me," "snake was long—two and a half or three feet," "glossy, wide spines of Virginia Woolf's diary, each volume showing, like a cameo, an oval photograph of her most noble and horsey profile," "crisp, metal edges," "red and white electrical cord," "while it conducted its inch-by-inch quizzing of the wall," "its old, snug routes beneath clumps of chamiso," "a sort of moonscape with tire tracks," "The snake had muddy khaki-brown stripes," "a tan belly with coral along the sides, a very distinct, rouge-like rose," "its body quirked back and forth in those brief, balanced arcs," "the snake flowed steadily across the old wooden sill and out into the light and the shocking heat." Sight, sound, touch—our senses are aroused. ✦ The writer allows us to see what she saw by using phrases like "with a minnowlike imprecision," by juxtapositions like "for the space of a breath (mine)," by a simile like "as a cat does, stretching." We are able to understand more clearly the writer's state of mind when she tells us that seeing the snake visually disoriented her the way an earthquake does: a glass sliding across the table or a mirror cracking by itself simply looks wrong. Between such explanations and the account of the repetition of the writer's screams, we are as relieved as she is when the snake leaves, its head arrowing neatly through the crack below the door. ✦ The writer of this essay did not have to search for a form. She did not have to invent an organizational pattern. The story happened the way it did. She then told us the story. To tell it vividly and accurately, she described. To describe was inherent in her purpose. ✦ The writer did have to make some decisions inside the predominate form of narrative/description. She had to decide, for instance, when to insert into the narrative her explanation for where the snake came from and why it was out of its usual home. That was not part of the story as it happened in the studio. She had to decide how much descriptive information to include about the snake. These decisions were made inside the predominate form of narrative/description which provided the shape for the whole. ✦

JOHN UPDIKE

Thirteen Ways of Looking at the Masters

1. As an Event in Augusta, Georgia

In the middle of downtown Broad Street a tall white monument—like an immensely heightened wedding cake save that in place of the bride and groom stands a dignified Confederate officer—proffers the thought that

> No nation rose so white and fair;
> None fell so pure of crime.

Within a few steps of the monument, a movie theater, during Masters Week in 1979, was showing H*air*, full of cheerful miscegenation and anti-military song and dance.

This is the Deep/Old/New South, with its sure-enough levees, railroad tracks, unpainted dwellings out of illustrations to Joel Chandler Harris, and stately homes ornamented by grillework and verandas. As far up the Savannah River as boats could go, Augusta has been a trading post since 1717 and was named in 1735 by James Oglethorpe for the mother of George III. It changed hands several times during the Revolutionary War, thrived on tobacco and cotton, imported textile machinery from Philadelphia in 1828, and during the Civil War housed the South's largest powder works. Sherman passed through here, and didn't leave much in the way of historical sites.

The Augusta National Golf Club is away from the business end of town, in a region of big brick houses embowered in magnolia and dogwood. A lot of people retire to Augusta, and one of the reasons that Bobby Jones wanted to build a golf course here, instead of near his native Atlanta, was the distinctly milder climate. The course, built in 1931–32 on the site of the Fruitlands Nursery property, after designs by Dr. Alister Mackenzie (architect of Cypress Point) and Jones himself, has the venerable Augusta Country Club at its back, and at its front, across Route 28, an extensive shopping-center outlay. At this point the New South becomes indistinguishable from New Jersey.

2. As an Event Not in Augusta, Georgia

How many Augusta citizens are members of the Augusta National Golf Club? The question, clearly in bad taste, brought raised eyebrows and a muttered "Very few" or, more spaciously, "Thirty-eight or forty." The initial membership fee is rumored to be $50,000, there is a waiting list five years long, and most of the members seem to be national Beautiful People, Golfing Subspecies, who jet in for an occasional round during the six months the course is open. When Ike, whose cottage was near the clubhouse, used to show up and play a twosome with Arnold Palmer, the course would be cleared by the Secret Service. Cliff Roberts, chairman of the tournament from its inception in 1934 until his death in 1977, was a Wall Street investment banker; his chosen successor, William H. Lane, is a business executive from faraway Houston.

A lot of Augusta's citizens get out of town during Masters Week, renting their houses. The lady in the drugstore near the house my wife and I were staying in told me she had once gone walking on the course. *Once:* the experience seemed unrepeatable. The course had looked deserted to her, but then a voice shouted "Fore" and a ball struck near her. The ghost of Lloyd Mangrum, perhaps. The only Augustans conspicuous during the tournament are the black caddies, who know the greens so well they can call a putt's break to the inch while standing on the fringe.

3. As a Study in Green

Green grass, green grandstands, green concession stalls, green paper cups, green folding chairs and visors for sale, green-and-white ropes, green-topped Georgia pines, a prevalence of green in the slacks and jerseys of the gallery, like the prevalence of red in the crowd in Moscow on May Day. The caddies' bright green caps and Sam Snead's bright green trousers. If justice were poetic, Hubert Green would win it every year.

4. As a Rite of Spring

"It's become a rite of spring," a man told me with a growl, "like the Derby." Like Fort Lauderdale. Like Opening Day at a dozen ballparks. Spring it was, especially for us Northerners who had left our gray skies, brown lawns, salt-strewn highways, and plucky little croci for this efflorescence of azaleas and barefoot *jeunes filles en fleurs*. Most of the gallery, like most of the golfers, had Southern accents. This Yankee felt a little as if he were coming in late on a round of equinoctial parties that had stretched from Virginia to Florida. A lot of young men were lying on the grass betranced by the memories of last night's libations, and a lot of matronly voices continued discussing Aunt Earlene's unfortunate second marriage, while the golf balls floated overhead. For many in attendance, the Masters is a ritual observance; some of the old-timers wore sun hats festooned with over twenty years' worth of admission badges.

Will success as a festival spoil the Masters as a sporting event? It hasn't yet, but the strain on the tournament's famous and exemplary organization can be felt. Ticket sales are limited, but the throng at the main scoreboard is hard to squeeze by. The acreage devoted to parking would make a golf course in itself. An army of over two thousand policemen, marshals, walkway guards, salespersons, trash-gleaners, and other attendants is needed to maintain order and facilitate the pursuit of happiness. To secure a place by any green it is necessary to arrive at least an hour before there is anything to watch.

When, on the last two days, the television equipment arrives, the crowd itself is watched. Dutifully, it takes its part as a mammoth unpaid extra in a national television spectacular. As part of it, patting out courteous applause at a good shot or groaning in chorus at a missed putt, one felt, slightly, *canned*.

5. As a Fashion Show

Female fashions, my wife pointed out, came in three strata. First, young women decked out as if going to a garden party—makeup, flowing dresses, sandals. Next, the trim, leathery generation of the mothers, dressed as if they themselves were playing golf—short skirts, sun visors, cleated two-tone shoes. Last, the generation of the grandmothers, in immaculately blued hair and amply filled pants suits in shades we might call electric pastel or Day-Glo azalea.

6. As a Display Case for Sam Snead and Arnold Palmer

Though they no longer are likely to win, you wouldn't know it from their charismas. Snead, with his rakishly tilted panama and slightly pushed-in face—a face that has known both battle and merriment—swaggers around the practice tee like the Sheriff of Golf Country, testing a locked door here, hanging a parking ticket there. On the course, he remains a golfer one has to call beautiful, from the cushioned roll of his shoulders as he strokes the ball to the padding, panther-like tread with which he follows it down the center of the fairway, his chin tucked down while he thinks apparently rueful thoughts. He is one of the great inward golfers, those who wrap the dazzling difficulty of the game in an impassive, effortless flow of movement. When, on the green, he stands beside his ball, faces the hole, and performs the curious obeisance of his "side-winder" putting stroke, no one laughs.

And Palmer, he of the unsound swing, a hurried slash that ends as though he is snatching back something hot from a fire, remains the monumental outward golfer, who invites us into the game to share with him its heady turmoil, its call for constant courage. Every inch an agonist, Palmer still hitches his pants as he mounts the green, still strides between the wings of his army like Hector on his way to yet more problematical heroism. Age has thickened him, made him look almost muscle-bound, and has grizzled his thin, untidy hair; but his deportment more than ever expresses vitality, a love of life and of the game that rebounds to him, from the multitudes, as fervent gratitude. Like us golfing commoners, he risks looking bad for the sake of some fun.

Of the younger players, only Lanny Wadkins communicates Palmer's reckless determination, and only Fuzzy Zoeller has the captivating blitheness of a Jimmy Demaret or a Lee Trevino. The Masters, with its clubby lifetime qualification for previous winners, serves as an annual exhibit of Old Masters, wherein one can see the difference between the reigning, college-bred pros, with their even teeth, on-camera poise, and abstemious air, and the older crowd, who came up from caddie sheds, drove themselves in cars along the dusty miles of the Tour, and hustled bets with the rich to make ends meet. Golf expresses the man, as every weekend foursome knows; amid the mannerly lads who dominate the money list, Palmer and Snead loom as men.

7. As an Exercise in Spectatorship

In no other sport must the spectator move. The builders and improvers of Augusta National built mounds and bleachers for the crowds to gain vantage from, and a gracefully written pamphlet by the founder, Robert Jones, is handed out as instruction in the art of "letting the Tournament come to us instead of chasing after it." Nevertheless, as the field narrows and the interest of the hordes focuses, the best way to see anything is to hang back in the woods and use binoculars. Seen from within the galleries, the players become tiny walking dolls, glimpsable, like stars on a night of scudding clouds, in the gaps between heads.

Examples of Southern courtesy in the galleries: (1) When my wife stood to watch an approach to the green, the man behind her mildly observed, "Ma'am, it was awful nice when you were sittin' down." (2) A gentleman standing next to me, not liking the smell of a cigar I was smoking, offered to buy it from me for a dollar.

Extraordinary event in the galleries: on the fourth hole a ball set in flight by Dow Finsterwald solidly struck the head of a young man sitting beside the green. The sound of a golf ball on a skull is remarkably like that of two blocks of wood knocked together. *Glock.* Flesh hurts; bone makes music.

Single instance of successful spectatorship by this reporter: I happened to be in the pines left of the seventh fairway on the first day of play, wondering whether to go for another of the refreshment committee's standardized but economical ham sandwiches, when Art Wall, Jr., hooked a ball near where I was standing. Only a dozen or so gathered to watch his recovery; for a moment, then, we could breathe with a player and experience with him—as he waggled, peered at obtruding branches, switched clubs, and peered at the branches again—that quintessential golfing sensation, the loneliness of the bad-ball hitter.

Sad truth, never before revealed: by sticking to a spot in the stands or next to the green, one can view the field coming through, hitting variants of the same shots and putts, and by listening to the massed cheers and grunts from the other greens, one can guess at dramas unseen; but the unified field, as Einstein discovered in a more general connection, is unapprehendable, and the best way to witness a golf tournament is at the receiving end of a television signal. Many a fine golf reporter, it was whispered to me, never leaves the set in the press tent.

The other sad truth about golf spectatorship is that for today's pros it all comes down to the putting, and that the difference between a putt that drops and one that rims the cup, though teleologically enormous, is intellectually negligible.

8. As a Study in Turf-Building

A suburban lawn-owner can hardly look up from admiring the weedless immensity of the Augusta National turf. One's impression, when first admitted to this natural Oz, is that a giant putting surface has been dropped over acres of rolling terrain, with a few apertures for ponds and trees to poke through. A philosophy of golf is expressed in Jones's pamphlet: "The Augusta National has much more fairway and green area than the average course. There is little punishing rough and very few bunkers. The course is not intended so much to punish severely the wayward shot as to reward adequately the stroke played with skill—and judgment."

It is an intentional paradox, then, that this championship course is rather kind to duffers. The ball sits up on Augusta's emerald carpet looking big as a baseball. It was not always such; in 1972, an invasion of *Poa annua*, a white-spiked vagabond grass, rendered conditions notoriously bumpy; in remedy a fescue called Pennlawn and a rye called Pennfine were implanted on the fairways and greens respectively and have flourished. Experimentation continues; to make the greens even harder and slicker, they are thinking of rebuilding them on a sand base—and have already done so on the adjacent par-three course.

From May to October, when the course is closed to play, everything goes to seed and becomes a hayfield, and entire fairways are plowed up: a harrowing thought. The caddies, I was solemnly assured, never replace a divot; they just sprinkle grass seed from a pouch they carry. Well, this is a myth, for I repeatedly saw caddies replace divots in the course of the tournament, with the care of tile-setters.

9. As Demography

One doesn't have to want to give the country back to the Indians to feel a nostalgic pang while looking at old photos of the pre-World War II tournaments, with their hatted, necktied galleries strolling up the fairways in the wake of the baggy-trousered players, and lining the tees and greens only one man deep.

The scores have grown crowded, too. The best then would be among the best now—Lloyd Mangrum's single-round 64 in 1940 has not been bettered, though for the last two years it has been equalled. But the population of the second-best has increased, producing virtually a new winner each week of the Tour, and stifling the emergence of stable constellations of superstars like Nelson-Hogan-Snead and Palmer-Player-Nicklaus. In the 1936 and 1938 Masters, only seven players made the thirty-six-hole score of 145 that cut the 1979 field to forty-five players. Not until 1939 did the winner break 280 and not again until 1948. The last total over 280 to win it came in 1973. In 1936, Craig Wood had a first-day round of 88 and finished in the top two dozen. In 1952, Sam Snead won the Masters in spite of a third-round 77. That margin for intermittent error has been squeezed from tournament golf. Johnny Miller chops down a few trees, develops the wrong muscles, and drops like a stone on the lists. Arnold Palmer, relatively young and still strong and keen, can no longer ram the putts in from twenty feet, and becomes a father figure. A cruel world, top-flight golf, that eats its young.

10. As Race Relations

A Martian skimming overhead in his saucer would have to conclude that white Earthlings hit the ball and black Earthlings fetch it, that white men swing the sticks and black men carry them. The black caddies of Augusta, in their white coveralls, are a tradition that needs a symbolic breaking, the converse of Lee Elder's playing in the tournament.

To be fair, these caddies are specialists of a high order, who take a cheerful pride in their expertise and who are, especially during Masters Week, well paid for it. Gary Player's caddie for his spectacular come-from-nowhere victory of 1978 was tipped $10,000—a sum that, this caddie assured an impudent interrogator, was still safe in the bank. In the New South, blacks work side by side with whites in the concession stands and at the fairway ropes, though I didn't see any in a green marshal's coat. I was unofficially informed that, at the very time when civil rightists were agitating for a black player to be invited to play even if one did not earn qualification—as Elder did in 1975—blacks were not being admitted to the tournament *as spectators.* I wonder about this. On pages 26–27 of the green souvenir album with a text by Cliff Roberts, one can see a photograph of Henry Picard hitting out of a bunker; behind him in the scattering of spectators are a number of ebony gentlemen not dressed as caddies. At any rate, though golf remains a white man's game, it presents in the Masters player and caddie an active white-black partnership in which the white man is taking the advice and doing the manual work. Caddies think of the partnership as "we," as in "We hit a drive down the center and a four-iron stiff to the pin, but then *he* missed the putt."

11. As Class Relations

Though the Augusta National aspires to be the American St. Andrews, there is a significant economic difference between a Scottish golf links thriftily pinked out on a wasteland—the sandy seaside hills that are "links"—and the American courses elaborately, expensively carved from farmland and woods. Though golf has plebeian Scottish roots, in this country its province is patrician. A course requires capital and flaunts that ancient aristocratic prerogative, land. In much of the world, this humbling game is an automatic symbol of capitalist-imperialist oppression; a progressive African novelist, to establish a character as a villain, has only to show him coming off a golf course. And in our own nation, for all the roadside driving ranges and four o'clock factory leagues, golf remains for millions something that happens at the end of a long driveway, beyond the MEMBERS ONLY sign.

Yet competitive golf in the United States came of age when, at The Country Club, in Brookline, Massachusetts, a twenty-year-old ex-caddie and workingman's son, Francis Ouimet, beat the British legends Vardon and Ray in a playoff for the U.S. Open. And ever since, the great competitors have tended to come from the blue-collar level of golf, the caddies and the offspring of club pros. Rare is the Bobby Jones who emerges from the gentry with the per-fectionistic drive and killer instinct that make a champion in this game which permits no let-up or loss of concentration, yet which penalizes tightness also. Hagen acted like a swell and was called Sir Walter, but he came up from a caddie's roost in Rochester. The lords of golf have been by and large gentlemen made and not born, while the clubs and the management of the Tour remain in the hands of the country-club crowd. When genteel Ed Sneed and Tom Watson fell into a three-way playoff for the 1979 Masters title, you knew in your bones it was going to be the third player, a barbarian called Fuzzy with a loopy all-out swing, who would stroll through the gates and carry off the loot.

12. As a Parade of Lovely Golfers, No Two Alike

Charles Coody, big-beaked bird. Billy Casper, once the king of touch, now sporting the bushy white sideburns of a turn-of-the-century railroad conductor, still able to pop them up from a sandtrap and sink the putt. Trevino, so broad across he looks like a reflection in a funhouse mirror, a model of delicacy around the greens and a model of affable temperament everywhere. Player, varying his normal black outfit with white slacks, his bearing so full of fight and muscle he seems to be restraining himself from break-ing into a run. Nicklaus, Athlete of the Decade, still golden but almost gaunt and faintly grim, as he feels a crown evaporating from his head. Gay Brewer, heavy in the face and above the belt, nevertheless uncorking a string-straight mid-iron to within nine inches of the long seventh hole in the par-three tournament. Miller Barber, Truman Capote's double, punching and putting his way to last year's best round, a storm-split 64 in two installments. Bobby Clampett, looking too young and thin to be out there. Andy Bean, looking too big to be out there, and with his perennially puzzled expression seeming to be searching for a game more his size. Hu-bert Green, with a hunched flicky swing that would make a high-school golf coach scream. Tom Weiskopf, the handsome embodi-ment of pained near-perfection. Hale Irwin, the picture-book golfer with the face of a Ph.D. candidate. Johnny Miller, looking heavier than we remember him, patiently knocking them out on the prac-tice tee, wondering where the lightning went. Ben Crenshaw, the smiling Huck Finn, and Tom Watson, the more pensive Tom Saw-yer, who, while the other boys were whitewashing fences, has be-come, politely but firmly, the best golfer in the world.

And many other redoubtable young men. Seeing them up close, in the dining room or on the clubhouse veranda, one is struck by how young and in many cases how slight they seem, with their pert and telegenic little wives—boys, really, anxious to be polite and to please even the bores and boors that collect in the interstices of all well-publicized events. Only when one sees them at a distance, as they walk alone or chatting in twos down the great green emptiness of the fairway, does one sense that each youth is the pinnacle of a buried pyramid of effort and investment, of prior competition from pre-teen level up, of immense and it must be at times burdensome accumulated hopes of parents, teachers, backers. And with none of the group hypnosis and exhilaration of team play to relieve them. And with the difference between success and failure so feather-fine.

13. As a Religious Experience

The four days of 1979's Masters fell on Maundy Thursday, Good Friday, Holy Saturday, and Easter Sunday. On Good Friday, fittingly, the skies darkened, tornadoes were predicted, and thousands of sinners ran for cover. My good wife, who had gone to divine services, was prevented from returning to the course by the flood of departing cars, and the clear moral is one propounded from many a pulpit: golf and churchgoing do not mix. Easter Sunday also happened to be the anniversary of the assassination of Abraham Lincoln and the sinking of the *Titanic*, and it wasn't such a good day for Ed Sneed either.

About ninety-nine percent of the gallery, my poll of local vibes indicated, was rooting for Sneed to hold off disaster and finish what he had begun. He had played splendidly for three days, and it didn't seem likely he'd come this close soon again. When he birdied the fifteenth and enlarged his once huge cushion back to three strokes, it seemed he would do it. But then, through no flagrant fault of his own, he began "leaking." We all knew how it felt, the slippery struggle to nurse a good round back to the clubhouse. On the seventeenth green, where I was standing, his approach looked no worse than his playing partner's; it just hit a foot too long, skipped onto the sloping back part of the green, and slithered into the fringe. His putt back caught the cup but twirled away. And his putt to save par, which looked to me like a gimme, lipped out, the same way my two-footers do when I lift my head to watch them drop, my sigh of relief all prepared. Zoeller, ten minutes before, had gently rolled in a birdie from much farther away. Sneed's fate seemed sealed then: the eighteenth hole, a famous bogey-maker, waited for him as ineluctably as Romeo's missed appointment with Juliet.

He hadn't hit bad shots, and he hadn't panicked; he just was screwed a half-turn too tight to get a par. The gallery of forty thousand felt for him, right to the pits of our golf-weary stomachs, when his last hope of winning it clean hung on the lip of the seventy-second hole. It so easily might have been otherwise. But then that's life, and that's golf.

Elizabeth Neeld Comments:

✦ *Every day when John Updike gets through writing and has had his 1:30 p.m. lunch, he tries to get in a game of golf. He writes at home in a room that used to be an antique store, and he gives himself a quota of three pages to complete for each day. (He publishes a book about every year.) When he finishes each day, playing golf is a way he likes to relax. (Although he sometimes breaks eighty, Updike says he plays a mediocre game.)* ✦ *Knowing that Updike often plays golf himself, you're not surprised to discover that this author of such best-selling novels as* Rabbit, Run; Centaur; Couples; *and* Rabbit Is Rich *went to the Masters Golf Tournament in Augusta and wrote an article for* Golf *magazine about the event. This essay is the result.* ✦ *Updike uses the traditional form* classification *to organize his essay. This is a clever organizing principle because it allows Updike to discuss the tournament from thirteen different perspectives, without having to relate any one of these perspectives to another. You can go from "hole to hole" in his essay, knowing you are playing the same course, but each hole is different. He talks about fashion; he talks about race; he talks about spectatorship. In fact, the use of* classification *as the organizing principle adds zest and interest. Even people who might not want to read an extended article about the Masters Golf Tournament could get interested in seeing what direction Updike was going next as he moved through his thirteen ways of looking at the tournament. And it is a unique form for an article reporting on a sports event. Updike has used a tradi-*

tional form in an original way. ✦   Each vignette in this essay is complete, not dependent on what came before or what comes afterward to make sense. Part of what makes each "way of looking at the Masters" work is Updike's commitment to exact detail. He said once, "I cannot do justice to the bliss that attends getting . . . even the name of a weed right. Naming our weeds, in fact, seems to be exactly where it's at." Then he related that he goes into the scruffy meadow outside his window to try to identify the wildflowers along the fringes, using a book as his guide. "It's remarkably difficult to match reality and diagram," Updike said. This is the same kind of concentration Updike brings to writing about the Masters. The attention to detail makes the golf tournament seem real to us as we read. ✦   Updike talks about what it is like to write: "Oh, Lordy. The terror of launching yourself into the blank page. Nelson [a character in his new novel] . . . hang-glides, and now I see why: a writer hang-glides all the time, out over that terrible whiteness." In "Thirteen Ways of Looking at the Masters" Updike catches the wind, and there's a smooth ride all the way down to the ground. ✦

SUE LUCKSTED

How to Bake on a Boat

Sailing over the horizon, away from the supermarket and the electric four-burner stove with an oven, is certainly stimulating for creative cooking. . . . By far, the most challenging aspect is baking without an oven. There have been several methods which I have used with varying degrees of success. Baking yeast bread has always been a favorite, so I started the "dutch oven experiment." Use a large heavy dutch oven; set three metal rings (canning jar lids) on the bottom of it, and place your baking dish on top of them. Place two flame tamers on the burner (these can be purchased, but I went to my local junk man and bought aluminum disks, 6–8" in diameter and about ¼–½" thick). These and the rings in the oven spread the heat and prevent burning; in addition the flame tamers can be arranged to control

Homemade aluminum "flame tamers."

Dutch oven with 3 metal rings on the bottom of the inside.

the heat. Be certain to preheat the empty oven at least 10 minutes prior to cooking. Baking in the dutch oven takes about 15–20 minutes longer than the recipes call for, and you cannot regulate the temperature exactly. Also, watch that the contact between the dutch oven and the flame tamers is good and that the lid is tight, or you will waste a lot of heat and greatly lengthen the cooking time. Caution: don't try any fussy French breads, try basic ones. When I put the first yeast bread I tried in the oven, all was well until the galley became perfumed with a faint burnt incense. Alas, I had filled the pan too full; the dough rose right up out of the pan, sticking to the top of the lid. So, watch your recipe and pan size. Later I successfully used 4 coffee cans to bake in; 2 cans equal 1 loaf pan. These are great for storage and slicing; just cool and cover.

Pressure cooker, without pressure valve.

The second method proved more heat efficient and quicker. Use a heavy 4-quart pressure cooker, grease the bottom and sides and coat heavily with cornmeal. It acts as an insulator and burns instead of the bread. Preheat and bake as before, using flame tamers. Do not use the pressure valve or the gasket on the cooker.

POOR MAN'S YEAST BREAD

½ tsp. salt
2 cup whole wheat flour
½ cup dry milk
1½–2 cup warm water
2 T. (2 pkg.) yeast

1 tsp. honey
Optional:
½ cup sprouts
½ cup nuts/raisins

The flour that we use is 100% whole wheat. We grind our own fresh flour in a simple hand mill, sometimes mixing it with store-ground.

Dissolve yeast and honey in ½ cup warm water; cover; let rise 5 minutes. Put dry ingredients in a bowl; stir in 1 cup warm water and yeast mixture. Add enough of the remaining water to make dough thick, sticky, and stirable. Put mixture directly into the pressure cooker that has been previously prepared. Let rise 45 minutes, until double in bulk. The best way to do this is to cover with a dark towel and set in the sun, out of the wind. Cook as stated; when 25 minutes have passed, loosen from sides of the cooker and turn over for the remaining 15 minutes; this helps both sides brown, but is optional.

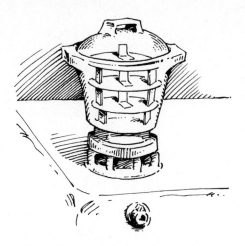

Dutch oven fitted with 3 tiered aluminum cookie "sheets."

Crunchy food is very appealing at sea and so the third type of oven is especially adapted for baking cookies. Use the same dutch oven and flame tamers which we will rig for the cookies. First, go back to your junk man and purchase 3 round flat pieces of aluminum (the weight of a pie pan) making certain they fit in the oven; ideally they should be graded, each smaller, though equal sizes will work. Next, bend 12 pieces of aluminum, ½ by 3", drill and screw one to the center top of each circle and three on the bottom for legs. Now you are ready to stack your favorite recipe onto the greased tins.

AGGRESSION COOKIES

1 cup brown sugar	½ tsp. soda
1 cup whole wheat flour	½ tsp. baking powder
1 cup uncooked rolled oats	½ tsp. salt

Mix thoroughly in a bowl; make a well in the center and add: ½ cup Crisco (use very soft; don't use butter as it causes runny cookies), 1 egg and ½ tsp. vanilla. The easiest way is to dig in with your hands and mix away all those aggressions.

Add: ¾ cup chocolate chips, ½ cup raisins, ½ cup nuts and bake 10 minutes.

I have found that you can use the baking times as specified in the given cookie recipes. After the time has elapsed, lift out the

Reading to Learn to Write: Traditional Form

bottom layer; refill; place it on the top; repeat until the batch is done. The bottom layer always finishes first.

Modern ovens certainly are marvelous devices, but despair not, "O fair galley slave," for you can bake almost anything in those ovens and be a true galley gourmet. With patience, time, experimentation, and inventiveness your 'one burner' will reap bushels of praise from your fit and happy crew.

Elizabeth Neeld Comments:

✦ *Something seems inconsistent, doesn't it, about being on a boat and* baking? *We usually associate baking with a warm kitchen on a cold, rainy day—not a busy, unpredictable sailing vessel. People go on boats to relax, sun, tussle with the breezes, and feel the wind and the rain in their hair. They don't often go on a boat in order to stand at a stove and cook.* ✦ *Yet in spite of the seeming inconsistency, there is something that being on a boat and baking on a boat have in common: both require a sense of adventure. Both demand that you adapt to the elements and the circumstances in which you find yourself. Both sailing and baking require you to be ingenious in solving problems caused by the limitations of the boat. In order to guide a boat or bake on a boat, you have to keep a sense of humor. You have to be willing to roll with the waves.* ✦ *Sue Lucksted, the author of this essay, has clearly spent a lot of time on a boat. And she probably likes to cook. But I'm guessing that Lucksted learned how to bake on a boat as much because of the challenge involved in figuring out how to do it as she did because she wanted the bread or the cookies. The voice she uses in this essay makes you think she is that kind of person. And we are interested in reading about how to accomplish this unlikely feat, whether we have spent time on a boat or not—because we, too, are interested in the challenge, in the unusual solution to a fascinating problem. We revel as much in her success in figuring out how to bake on a boat as we benefit from her instructions on how to. Whether or not we ever plan to use the information she has given us, we enjoy reading about how the baking could be done—simply be-*

cause it's such an unlikely thing to be able to pull off. ✦ The instructions Lucksted gives in this essay require the would-be baker to have some ability with metal. I suppose she assumes that if you can be on a boat long enough to need to cook, then you must be the kind of person who can get 3 "round flat pieces of aluminum" and "bend 12 pieces of aluminum, ½ by 3", drill and screw one to the center top of each circle and three on the bottom for legs." If you're going to be plucky enough to try to bake on a boat, you're likely to be plucky enough to be willing to figure out how to "build" the necessary equipment. The two tasks would probably appeal to the same kind of person. ✦ Lucksted also assumes that you already know how to bake bread in conventional ovens. For instance, she doesn't tell you how to know if the dough has doubled in bulk. (The way you can tell if this has happened: make a dent in the dough with one finger; if the dent fills back up, the dough has not risen double; if the dent stays dented, the dough has doubled in bulk. This is something only a breadbaker would know.) She doesn't tell you what the baking time is for the "given cookie recipes." She doesn't tell you how she substituted the coffee cans for the loaf pans when you bake in the dutch oven. It's as if she is talking to someone like herself—someone inventive, willing to experiment, and patient. She doesn't talk to her readers as if they needed to be led step by step. (This essay first appeared in Multihulls magazine, a monthly boating magazine, so the author knew that her readers were probably of the adventurous sort who had a lot of common sense and willingness to learn in the doing.) If the readers were complete novices at baking, they would probably do well to bake bread and cookies first in their home oven before attempting to follow the instructions for the process of baking on a boat. ✦ There is something unspoken in the words in this essay but clearly present in spirit: the author's willingness to try and try again. She first used the dutch oven with loaf pans; then she used the dutch oven with coffee cans. She used the pressure cooker—but without the gauge and the rubber gasket. (Wonder how she figured out she couldn't use the gasket?) She filled the pan too full and learned the hard way what result that produced. She knows that the three round flat pieces of aluminum needed to bake cookies ideally should be graded, each smaller than the other; but she also knows that three pieces of equal size will work. She's learned that the bottom batch of cookies always finishes baking first. She recommends a "dark towel" over the dough that you set in the sun. As readers of her essay, we are the recipients of all the experimentation and trial and error she has gone through.

✦ This essay is an example of a piece of writing that delineates a process for an alternative way to do a basic task. To benefit most from the how-to instructions in the essay, you need to know something about the basic process itself—in this case, baking bread. The writer assumes that you wouldn't be interested in baking on a boat if you never baked on land. But if you do have some previous experience in baking on land, you can follow her instructions step by step and accomplish the impossible—having fresh homemade bread and cookies right out of the "oven" as you sail the high seas! ✦

GRETEL EHRLICH

A New Definition
of a Cowboy

When I'm in New York but feeling lonely for Wyoming I look for the Marlboro ads in the subway. What I'm aching to see is horseflesh, the glint of a spur, a line of distant mountains, brimming creeks, a reminder of the ranchers and cowboys I've ridden with for the last eight years. But the men I see in those posters, with their stern, humorless looks, remind me of no one I know there. In our hellbent earnestness to romanticize the cowboy we've disesteemed his true character. If he's "strong and silent" it's because there's probably no one to talk to. If he "rides off into the sunset" it's because he's been on horseback since four in the morning moving cattle and he's trying, fifteen hours later, to get home to his family. If he's a "rugged individualist" he's also part of a team: ranch work is teamwork, and even the glorified open-range cowboys of the 1880s rode up and down the Chisholm Trail in the company of twenty or thirty other riders. Instead of the macho, trigger-happy man our culture has perversely wanted him to be, the cowboy is more apt to be convivial, quirky, and softhearted. To be "tough" on a ranch has nothing to do with conquests and displays of power. More often than not, circumstances—like the colt he's riding or an unexpected blizzard—overpower him. It's not toughness but "toughing it out" that counts. In other words, this macho cultural artifact the cowboy has become is simply a man who possesses resilience, patience, and an instinct for survival. "Cowboys are just like a pile of rocks—everything happens to them. They get climbed on, kicked, rained and snowed on, scuffed up by wind. Their job is 'just to take it,'" one old-timer told me.

Ain't This Little Rat Good-lookin'

A cowboy is someone who loves his work. Since the hours are long—ten to fifteen hours a day—and the pay is thirty dollars, he has to. What's required of him is an odd mixture of physical vigor and maternalism. His part in the beef-raising industry is to birth and nurture calves and take care of their mothers. For the most part his work is done on horseback, and in a lifetime he sees and comes to know more animals than people. The iconic myth surrounding him is built on the American notion of heroism: that a man's value is measured in physical courage. Such an idea has perverted manliness into a self-absorbed race for cheap thrills. In a rancher's world, courage has less to do with facing danger than with acting spontaneously—usually on behalf of an animal or another rider. If a cow is stuck in a boghole, the rancher throws a loop around her neck, takes his dally (a half hitch around the saddle horn), and pulls her out with horsepower. If a calf is born sick, he may take her home, warm her in front of the kitchen fire, and massage her legs until dawn. One friend, whose favorite horse was trying to swim a lake with hobbles on, dove underwater and cut her legs loose with a knife, then swam her to shore, his arm around her neck lifeguard-style. Because these incidents are usually linked to someone or something outside himself, the Westerner's courage is selfless, a form of compassion.

If a rancher or cowboy is thought of as a "man's man"—laconic, hard-drinking, inscrutable—there's almost no place in which the balancing act between male and female, manliness and femininity, can be more natural. If he's gruff, handsome, and physically fit, he's androgynous at the core. Ranchers are midwives, hunters, nurturers, providers, and conservationists, all at once. What we've interpreted as toughness—weathered skin, callused hands, a squint in the eye, and a growl in the voice—only masks the tenderness inside. "Now don't go telling me these lambs are cute," one rancher warned me the first day I walked into the football-field-sized lambing sheds. The next thing I knew he was holding a black lamb. "Ain't this little rat good-lookin'?"

Southern Chivalry and Western Traits

So many of the men who came to the West were Southerners—men looking for work and a new life after the Civil War—that chivalrousness and strict codes of honor were soon thought of as Western traits. There were very few women in Wyoming during territorial days, so when they did arrive (some as mail-order brides from places like Philadelphia), there was a standoffishness between the sexes and a formality. These persist: ranchers still tip their hats and say, "Howdy, ma'am," instead of shaking hands with me.

Even young cowboys are often evasive with women. It's not that they're Jekyll and Hyde creatures—gentle with animals and rough on women—but rather that they don't know how to bring their tenderness into the house and lack the vocabulary to express the complexity of what they feel.

The geographical vastness and social isolation of the West make emotional evolution seem impossible. Those contradictions of the heart between respectability, logic, and convention, on the one hand, and impulse, passion, and intuition, on the other, played out wordlessly against the paradisiacal beauty of the West, give cowboys a wide-eyed but drawn look. Their lips pucker up, not with kisses but with immutability. They may want to break out, to stay up all night just talking with a lover, but they don't know how and can't imagine what the consequences will be. Those rare occasions when they do bare themselves result in confusion. "I feel as if I'd sprained my heart," one friend told me a month after such a conversation.

Their Strength Is a Softness

My friend Ted Hoagland wrote, "No one is as fragile as a woman but no one is as fragile as a man." For all the women here who use "fragileness" to avoid work or as a sexual ploy, there are men who try to hide theirs, all the while clinging to an adolescent dependency on women to cook their meals, wash their clothes, and keep the ranch house warm in winter. But there is true vulnerability in evidence here. Because these men work with animals, not machines or numbers, because they live outside in landscapes of torrential beauty, because they are confined to a place and a routine embellished with awesome variables, because calves die in the arms that pulled others into life, because they go to the mountains as if on a pilgrimage to find out what makes a herd of elk tick, their strength is also a softness, their toughness, a rare delicacy.

Elizabeth Neeld Comments:

◆ *Gretel Ehrlich's purpose in this essay is to give a new definition of cowboy. Most people think of cowboys as macho, tough, rough, rowdy, and maybe even a little uncouth. Gretel Ehrlich sets out to put that traditional definition in perspective and to give her own definition which comes out of years of living in Wyoming and working with cowboys on the ranch.* ◆ *If you know a little about Ehrlich's background, you will have a clue that you can use in your own writing, a clue about what it takes to come up with a fresh definition of a common term. The author was a filmmaker and writer who lived in New York City. About ten years ago she went to Wyoming on assignment, to shoot a film of sheepherders in the Bighorn Mountains. While she was there, the man she loved, who lived back east, died. She was devastated. After roaming around for a while, Ehrlich decided to return to Wyoming, where she learned to ride, rope, and punch cattle; to help deliver calves and lambs; and to live in thirty-below-zero weather. She herded sheep alone in the mountains, and she became friends with dozens of Wyoming ranchers and cowboys.* ◆ *Because she came to Wyoming with fresh eyes, Ehrlich was able to see past the stereotypical definition of a cowboy and say for herself what a cowboy was. The characteristics she ascribes to cowboys come out of her own experience birthing calves with them, riding the range with them, drinking in bars with them. This means that the definition is new. It's not more of the same. She says cowboys are strong and silent because they have no one to talk to. If he rides off into the sunset it's because* he's been on horseback since four in the morning moving cattle and he's trying, fifteen hours later, to get home to his family. Because Ehrlich has been with cowboys while calves were birthing, she knows that they are tender as well as tough. "If a calf is born sick, he may take her home, warm her in front of the kitchen fire, and massage her legs until dawn." Quoting an old-timer, she says, "Cowboys are just like a pile of rocks—everything happens to them. They get climbed on, kicked, rained and snowed on, scuffed up by wind. Their job is 'just to take it.'" This new definition of a cowboy breaks up the old stereotypes. The definition comes out of direct experience and thinking about that experience. The author takes several of the characteristics that have been accepted as true and shows how they are myths. ✦ Because the author's purpose was to alter misconceptions about what a cowboy is, she was obliged to use definition as her main organizing principle for the essay. At the same time she tells stories: "Now don't go telling me these lambs are cute," one rancher warned me . . . the next thing I knew he was holding a black lamb, 'Ain't this little rat good-lookin'?'" She compares: "So many of the men who came to the West were Southerners . . . that chivalrousness and strict codes of honor were soon thought of as Western traits." She analyzes a process: "If a cow is stuck in a boghole, the rancher throws a loop around her neck, takes his dally (a half hitch around the saddle horn), and pulls her out with horsepower." The overall organizing principle is definition, but the essay contains many other patterns of thought, as well. ✦ Gretel Ehrlich met a rancher in Wyoming and married him. They live in Shell, Wyoming, where they both work on the ranch. ✦

ALEXANDER D. LANGMUIR, M.D.
THOMAS D. WORTHEN, PH.D.
JON SOLOMON, PH.D.
C. GEORGE RAY, M.D.
ESKILD PETERSEN, M.D.

The Thucydides Syndrome: A New Hypothesis for the Cause of the Plague of Athens

The plague of Athens, 430 to 427 B.C., was perhaps the most disastrous and fateful epidemic of recorded ancient history. It fell upon a city that had in just two generations created or nurtured such basic pursuits of Western culture as philosophy, history, tragedy, comedy, and of course, democracy. Her empire spanned the Aegean Sea and generated enough taxes to finance the magnificent Parthenon. But within three decades Athens had been defeated in the Peloponnesian War against Sparta and would never again reveal that incredible energy and creative spark. The beginning of her downfall can be directly connected to the outbreak of the epidemic, which killed tens of thousands of her 300,000 inhabitants and thereby created numerous military disadvantages, chief among which was the death of the great Athenian leader, Pericles.

Ironically, another general, Thucydides, who was destined to be better known as the first analytical historian, also acquired the disease but lived to record its outbreak in such detail that classicists and medical historians have for centuries been using his information to attempt a diagnosis of this renowned disease. But the symptomatologies of the many proposed diseases do not match Thucydides' description. The most recent discussions by Poole and Holladay and by Longrigg therefore dismiss such previously proposed diseases as smallpox, bubonic plague, scarlet fever, measles, typhus, typhoid fever, and ergotism, as well as Kobert's suggestions (in 1899) of cerebrospinal fever and influenza. Poole and Holladay also reject the possibility, supported by Kobert and Longrigg, of a simultaneous outbreak of two or more diseases and focus instead on the processes of bacterial and viral mutation and selection. They then conclude that "the Plague is now extinct" or has so "changed in its clinical manifestations during the past 24 centuries that the modern descendant cannot be recognized in Thucydides' account." In the light of newly discovered knowledge, we now believe that all the clinical and epidemiologic findings described by Thucydides can be attributed to infection with influenza virus complicated by a toxin-producing strain of noninvasive staphylococcus.

The Thucydidean Text

We offer here our own selected translations made with an aim toward literal interpretation and scientific accuracy.

> At the beginning of the summer the Peloponnesians and their allies invaded Attica. They had not been many days in Attica before the plague first broke out among the Athenians. As to the question of how it could first have come about or what causes can be found adequate to explain its powerful effect on nature I must leave that to be considered by other writers, with or without medical experience. I myself shall merely describe what it was like, and set down the symptoms, knowledge of which will enable it to be recognized, if it should ever break out again. I had the disease myself and saw others suffering from it.

Insofar as other maladies go, by all accounts this year was the most free. Indeed, if anyone did have a prior illness, it always eventuated in this disease. Those having no prior complaint were seized suddenly in the midst of good health without premonitory symptoms.

First, overwhelming fever in the head and redness and inflammation of the eyes came over them; internally, right away, the throat and tongue became blood red. The breath became foul with an unprecedented smell. From these beginnings there ensued sneezing and hoarseness, and in short order the distress settled in the chest with a violent cough. When the malady progressed to the stomach [literally, "heart"], it upset it, and there followed the emesis of every kind of bile for which physicians have a name. The vomiting was very stressful; the majority were afflicted with empty retching which led to violent spasms alleviated in some after [the vomiting ceased] but persistent in others for some time [or: which came on in some after (the vomiting) abated but in others only after some time].

Externally, the skin was not especially hot, nor was it pale. It was flushed, livid, and broken out with small blisters and open sores. Internally, the patient burned with fever so extreme that he could not tolerate being covered with the lightest linen garment, choosing rather to go naked. Their desire was to cast themselves into cold water, and many of those who were unsupervised did throw themselves into public cisterns, consumed as they were by unceasing thirst. But no matter how much or how little they got to drink, the outcome was similar.

There was continuous agitation and sleeplessness throughout the illness. For however long the disease was in force, the body did not waste away but, despite the suffering, held out to a surprising degree. The result: most perished of the fever on the ninth or the seventh day while still having some strength. If they survived this stage, the disease settled in the bowels, eventuating in severe ulceration and watery diarrhea. Later, most of these perished from the associated prostration.

The latter fact confirms the general course of the disease through the body, beginning at the top, with the head as focus. Even if one escaped the disease's worst symptoms, its attack upon the extremities left its mark. Here it afflicted the genitals, fingers, and toes. Having lost these parts, many survived; some even lost their eyes. Loss of memory was also a sequel, coming on some immediately after regaining their feet. The amnesia was almost total; they did not know themselves or their relatives.

Symptoms of the Plague

This clinical description clearly indicates the involvement of specific organ systems. Anatomical diagnoses are quite possible. There is an obvious inflammatory condition of the eyes and the respiratory tract from the nose to the trachea and bronchi. Similarly, there is severe involvement of the gastrointestinal tract. The initiation with vomiting followed by empty retching and later by "watery diarrhea"—a clear distinction from the well-known mucous and bloody stools of dysentery—strongly suggests a gastroenteropathy mediated by the central nervous system rather than a local inflammatory process. The word "spasms" to describe the condition accompanying the vomiting and retching may well be simply descriptive of the violence of the symptoms. The spasms that were "persistent for some time" may well have reflected an alkalosis caused by the excessive vomiting.

The description of the skin lesions as "small blisters and open sores" is woefully inadequate. It would be helpful to know the stage of disease when they appeared and their evolution. The "skin not especially hot, nor pale," but "flushed and livid" again is inadequate. We are unable to conclude whether there was a sunburn or a scarlatiniform rash. What evidence we have at least suggests bullous impetigo in a patient with high fever.

From the descriptions of the patients' behavior over the duration of the illness, we can form several important negative conclusions. Stupor, coma, and early profound shock could not have been prominent symptoms. These are inconsistent with "continuous agitation and sleeplessness" and rising to jump into cisterns. We interpret the statement that "most perished of the fever on the ninth or seventh day still having some strength" as a vivid description of hyperthermic death. The later deaths from "diarrhea" and "associated prostration" suggest a combination of slowly developing hypovolemic and toxic shock. On recovery, the gangrene of genitals, fingers, and toes, and the blindness and amnesia attest to the severity of a peripheral circulatory disturbance late during the course of the disease.

We omit a long list of presumptive negative findings that include vivid symptoms generally known to physicians at the time of Thucydides. In view of the clarity of his description of the positive findings, it seems reasonable to suppose that he would have observed and recorded rigors, dyspnea, pleurisy, icterus, desquamation, copious pus in any form, gross lymphadenopathy, or hemorrhagic diathesis.

The use of the word "ulceration" of the bowels is unclear, but we do not believe that this warrants the conclusion that there were bloody or mucous stools, since the word "dysentery" appears commonly in the Hippocratic writings as a symptom quite distinct from diarrhea.

From this review of the clinical descriptions of the disease we feel confident in making the following anatomical diagnoses:

Acute respiratory infection, severe and probably necrotizing.
Acute toxic gastroenteropathy, centrally mediated.
Bullous impetigo.

This constellation of symptoms, findings, and clinical course is so vivid that we propose it be termed the Thucydides syndrome.

Even Birds of Prey Disappeared

In the interest of economy of space, we condense, paraphrase, and add interpretive comments on the most meaningful epidemiologic features of Thucydides' account.

The plague originated in Ethiopia or upper Egypt and spread throughout Egypt, Libya, Persia, and Lemnos. This was a substantial part of the world then known to Thucydides, or at least from which he would have been likely to receive reports.

It broke out so suddenly among the population of the Athenian port city of Piraeus that they believed the Peloponnesians had poisoned the reservoirs. But it spread rapidly to the upper city. Whole households were left empty. Mortality among doctors, as among other attendants of the sick, was especially high. They "died like the sheep."

Because of the Spartan invasion, country dwellers moved into the city. Living as they did during the hot season in badly ventilated huts, they died like flies. No one caught the disease twice, or if someone did, the second attack was never fatal. Its full force was felt at Athens, and after Athens, in the most densely populated of the other towns. It never seriously affected the Peloponnesians despite deserters' going over.

Though there were many dead bodies lying about unburied, there was a complete disappearance of birds of prey and apparently of dogs.

In the same summer, Hagnon took the fleet and sailed to Potidaea. The plague traveled there, too, and made dreadful havoc among the Athenian troops. Even those who had been there previously and had been in good health caught the infection from the forces under Hagnon. And so Hagnon lost 1050 men out of 4000 in about 40 days—an epidemic attack rate of 262.5 per 1000.

In Athens the first outbreak occurred in 430 B.C., immediately after the Spartan siege of the city began early that summer. A peak case rate was reached during the Spartan siege, which lasted 40 days, after which the crowded refugees dispersed. The disease remained residual through 429 (when Pericles died of it) and returned in force in the summer of 428, again at the time of a Spartan siege. From the winter of 428 until the summer of 427, the disease was quiescent or even absent, but broke out again in the autumn or early winter of 427. This epidemic lasted no less than a year, but there is no further mention of the disease after this.

The total number of Athenians who died is not recorded. Over the three-year period, of 13,000 enrolled hoplites (soldiers), 4400 died—a mortality rate of 33 per cent.

Thus, our subject of inquiry has the epidemiologic characteristics of a specific infectious disease spreading progressively along common routes of travel and trade encompassing a large part of the Mediterranean and Middle East. The infectious process was communicable from person to person, with a relatively short incubation period (days rather than weeks); it recurred in three waves in Attica from the summer of 430 to 427, apparently in association with military sieges and consequent overcrowding in the cities. Partial immunity followed recovery. Birds of prey disappeared; dogs and possibly sheep were involved in some manner not clearly specified.

Was It the Flu?

In seeking a specific pathogenesis for the Thucydides syndrome, we maintain that the clinical characteristics of the acute respiratory symptoms are completely compatible with infection with influenza virus. . . .

The epidemiologic characteristics also closely resemble those of pandemic influenza. Classically, pandemics arise in a single focus or area. Spread occurs along common routes of trade or travel to most but not necessarily all parts of the known world.

Pandemics may appear at any season. The 1918 pandemic developed in the summer and fall, first among military personnel. It devastated Australia during its summer of 1919. Recurrent waves over a period of three or more years occurred after the 1918 pandemic, and also in the period 1889 to 1892.

The importance of crowding in relation to the severity and intensity of influenza epidemics is universally recognized. In this regard the absence of recorded "plague" in Sparta is often used as an argument against the influenza hypothesis; however, it should be emphasized that Athens, and not Sparta, was under siege and severely overcrowded.

To accept the influenza hypothesis for the plague of Athens we must account for several notable differences from other pandemics: the apparent absence of pneumonia in any form, the extreme mortality, and the severe gastrointestinal symptoms.

Pneumonia may, in fact, have occurred. Thucydides was a general observer of the whole community; no hospital or general clinic existed in which the most severe cases would have congregated. In most epidemics of influenza the incidence of pneumonia is markedly increased, but even during the 1918 pandemic, pneumonia constituted only a small fraction of total cases. It was the severity, the predilection for young adults 20 to 40 years of age, and the fulminating course of the pneumonias, with the heliotrope cyanosis before death, that characterized the influenza of the 1918 pandemic. In view, however, of Thucydides' acuity of clinical observation, we reject the idea that he failed to observe the symptoms and signs of pneumonia among the fatal cases in Athens. Although pneumonia may have been present, we doubt that it was prominent.

The extremely high mortality in Athens is out of proportion to that of all the known influenza epidemics. Mortality rates of 3 to 5 per cent were the highest recorded in other than primitive, remote, isolated areas in 1918. We suggest that the answer is to be found in that notorious enemy of humanity, the versatile staphylococcus. Many pandemics as well as interpandemic epidemics have been associated with severe, fulminating staphylococcal infections.

The extremely severe and characteristic gastrointestinal symptoms described by Thucydides are quite similar to those of staphylococcal enterotoxic food poisoning, except that the onset of these appeared to follow rather than be concurrent with the initial respiratory symptoms, and their duration extended a matter of days or even more than one week. Our hypothesis, therefore, entails a slow and progressive absorption of the toxin from staphylococcal growth in the damaged respiratory mucosa or from impetiginous skin lesions. The strain or strains of staphylococcus must have been relatively noninvasive.

Such a hypothesis would have been dismissed as fanciful speculation even as recently as a decade ago. The discovery of the toxic shock syndrome by Todd et al. in 1978 and many subsequent reports of that syndrome have shown that relatively slight, almost trivial-appearing, superficial lesions can lead to sudden, severe, sometimes fatal disease. Todd described one case of gangrene of the extremities. Nan Robertson's personal account of her bout with toxic shock syndrome described deep shock and gangrene of her fingers. She also reported a case of convalescent amnesia.

Toxic Shock Syndrome

We do not maintain that the Thucydides syndrome was identical to the modern toxic shock syndrome. However, we believe that the same basic pathogenetic mechanisms were involved, in that there was infection in predisposed hosts by a possibly noninvasive staphylococcus that was capable of producing an exotoxin similar to the toxic shock syndrome's toxin-1. This toxin may have differed from that of toxic shock syndrome in that it produced predominantly enterotoxic effects and less profound circulatory collapse, and had only moderate or no erythrogenic potential.

The disappearance of birds of prey and the apparent involvement of domestic dogs make an exotic record. The literal translation regarding the effect of the disease on those who attended patients is "dying like the sheep"; this raises the possibility that even sheep succumbed during the epidemic. Few historical records throw light on these observations, but recent discoveries relating to the influenza viruses may be relevant.

The host range of the influenza viruses both in naturally occurring and in experimental infections is steadily expanding. Among animals, swine were proved infected before human beings. A wide variety of mammals have been shown to be naturally infected by influenza viruses that infect human beings; however, the infections in animals are usually inapparent. Conversely, mammalian and avian strains of influenza viruses can wreak havoc in their natural hosts, without apparent crossover to human beings. It is now known that there are at least 13 major hemagglutinin and 9 neuraminidase subtypes of influenza A virus in nature, and that recombination as well as frequent mutations occur. Although only three hemagglutinin and two neuraminidase subtypes are currently considered to be important in human influenza infections, it is possible that mutants of these or other combinations may have existed in the past and been capable of causing disease simultaneously in various species. Furthermore, the potential for a future reemergence of such strains should be considered.

Finally, we wish to suggest the possibility that the Thucydides syndrome may not be extinct. It may have occurred in the past and may be present now at such a low frequency that no one has yet identified a sufficient number of cases to make a convincing series worthy of publication. The criteria for a "confirmed" diagnosis of toxic shock syndrome are quite rigid. A search among the cases that have not met these criteria might reveal some cases with severe respiratory symptoms, bullous impetigo, exquisitely sensitive skin, and violent gastroenteropathy. Only a few such cases, if characteristically consistent and possibly occurring during periods of influenza prevalence, would be sufficient to establish the syndrome.

The well-known capacity of both the influenza virus and the staphylococcus to mutate, transfer, adapt, survive, and "plague" the human race raises the possibility that the Thucydides syndrome may reappear as a minor or even major manifestation of some future epidemic or pandemic of influenza.

Regardless of what the future may have in store for us, both the medical and epidemiologic professions should rediscover Thucydides as one of the most brilliant observers of all time and place him in the pantheon with the greatest of epidemiologists. The romance he did not perceive in his history is now apparent.

Elizabeth Neeld Comments:

✦ *Thucydides was a well-born Greek who enjoyed inherited riches from his family's gold mines. He was also a writer. When the Peloponnesian War between Athens and Sparta broke out in 431 B.C., Thucydides began writing about the war. He completed eight books of this history* before he died. His writing is known for its exactness: Thucydides was a keen, analytical observer. Many critics have said that no other ancient historian achieved the same clearness of writing as did Thucydides. ✦ Between 430 and 427 B.C. a terrible plague broke out in Athens. Thucydides caught this plague. He gave a detailed account of the effects of the plague on his body and of the demoralizing impact it had on Athens. He wrote, "As a rule . . . there was no visible cause; but people in good health were all of a sudden attacked by violent heats in the head, and redness and inflammation in the eyes, the inward parts, such as the throat or tongue, becoming bloody and emitting an unnatural and fetid breath. These symptoms were followed by sneezing and hoarseness, after which . . . " And the vivid description continues for several pages. ✦ The art of medicine was in its infancy, and physicians were unable to treat the unknown disease that defied every remedy and was aggravated by the overcrowding in the heat of the summer. The dead lay unburied, the temples full of corpses. ✦ Thucydides' account of this plague was so clinical and vivid that doctors have been using his writing for hundreds of years to attempt to determine the cause of the plague. The doctors who wrote this essay, using Thucydides' information, suggest a cause for the plague. Up to now, physicians have not been able to agree on a diagnosis of the cause. The cause of the plague, as suggested in this cause-and-effect essay, has a very modern name: toxic shock syndrome, the same illness associated with females' use of tampons. Only time will tell whether the medical community accepts these doctors' explanation of the cause of the plague. Until then, however, the discussion makes for fascinating reading. ✦ Little needs to be said about the rationale for the writers' choosing the form they did for this essay. Clearly, their purpose is to discuss the cause of the plague. Therefore, they are obliged to use the "composition laws" of the cause-and-effect essay: either discuss the effect first and then suggest a cause, or give the cause first and then discuss the effects. In this essay the writers begin with the effects and proceed to the cause. They focus mainly on support of their assertions, building their case for the cause they believe is the answer to the question, what caused the plague? They marshall their evidence and explain their line of reasoning. Clearly, their purpose dictates the form of their essay, and their evidence dictates the order in which they present their explanation to the reader. The overall structure of the essay and the internal order of the discussion of the cause of the plague are determined by the writers' intentions and purpose. ✦

ALISON LURIE

The Language
of Clothes

For thousands of years human beings have communicated with one another first in the language of dress. Long before I am near enough to talk to you on the street, in a meeting, or at a party, you announce your sex, age and class to me through what you are wearing—and very possibly give me important information (or misinformation) as to your occupation, origin, personality, opinions, tastes, sexual desires and current mood. I may not be able to put what I observe into words, but I register the information unconsciously; and you simultaneously do the same for me. By the time we meet and converse we have already spoken to each other in an older and more universal tongue.

The statement that clothing is a language, though occasionally made with the air of a man finding a flying saucer in his backyard, is not new. Balzac, in *Daughter of Eve* (1839), observed that for a woman dress is "a continual manifestation of intimate thoughts, a language, a symbol." Today, as semiotics becomes fashionable, sociologists tell us that fashion too is a language of signs, a non-verbal system of communication. The French structuralist Roland Barthes, for instance, in "The Diseases of Costume," speaks of the-atrical dress as a kind of writing, of which the basic element is the sign.

None of these theorists, however, have gone on to remark what seems obvious: that if clothing is a language, it must have a vocab-ulary and a grammar like other languages. Of course, as with human speech, there is not a single language of dress, but many: some (like Dutch and German) closely related and others (like Basque) almost unique. And within every language of clothes there are many different dialects and accents, some almost unintelligi-ble to members of the mainstream culture. Moreover, as with speech, each individual has his own stock of words and employs personal variations of tone and meaning.

The Vocabulary of Fashion

The vocabulary of dress includes not only items of clothing, but also hair styles, accessories, jewelry, make-up and body decora-tion. Theoretically at least this vocabulary is as large as or larger than that of any spoken tongue, since it includes every garment, hair style, and type of body decoration ever invented. In practice, of course, the sartorial resources of an individual may be very re-stricted. Those of a sharecropper, for instance, may be limited to five or ten "words" from which it is possible to create only a few "sentences" almost bare of decoration and expressing only the most basic concepts. A so-called fashion leader, on the other hand, may have several hundred "words" at his or her disposal, and thus be able to form thousands of different "sentences" that will express a wide range of meanings. Just as the average English-speaking person knows many more words than he or she will ever use in conversation, so all of us are able to understand the mean-ing of styles we will never wear.

To choose clothes, either in a store or at home, is to define and describe ourselves. Occasionally, of course, practical considera-tions enter into these choices: considerations of comfort, durabil-ity, availability and price. Especially in the case of persons of lim-ited wardrobe, an article may be worn because it is warm or rainproof or handy to cover up a wet bathing suit—in the same way that persons of limited vocabulary use the phrase "you know" or adjectives such as "great" or "fantastic." Yet, just as with spoken language, such choices usually give us some information, even if it is only equivalent to the statement "I don't give a damn what I look like today." And there are limits even here. In this culture, like many others, certain garments are taboo for certain persons. Most men, however cold or wet they might be, would not put on a woman's dress, just as they would not use words and phrases such as "simply marvelous," which in this culture are considered specifically feminine.

When Is Old Beautiful?

Besides containing "words" that are taboo, the language of clothes, like speech, also includes modern and ancient words, words of native and foreign origin, dialect words, colloquialisms, slang and vulgarities. Genuine articles of clothing from the past (or skillful imitations) are used in the same way a writer or speaker might use archaisms: to give an air of culture, erudition or wit. Just as in educated discourse, such "words" are usually employed sparingly, most often one at a time—a single Victorian cameo or a pair of 1940s platform shoes or an Edwardian velvet waistcoat, never a complete costume. A whole outfit composed of archaic items from a single period, rather than projecting elegance and sophistication, will imply that one is on one's way to a masquerade, acting in a play or film or putting oneself on display for advertising purposes. Mixing garments from several different periods of the past, on the other hand, suggests a confused but intriguingly "original" theatrical personality. It is therefore often fashionable in those sections of the art and entertainment industry in which instant celebrities are manufactured and sold.

When using archaic words, it is essential to choose ones that are decently old. The sight of a white plastic Courrèges minirain-coat and boots (in 1963 the height of fashion) at a gallery opening or theater today would produce the same shiver of ridicule and revulsion as the use of words such as "groovy," "Negro," or "self-actualizing."

In *Taste and Fashion*, one of the best books ever written on costume, the late James Laver proposed a timetable to explain such reactions; this has come to be known as Laver's Law. According to him, the same costume will be

Indecent	10 years before its time
Shameless	5 years before its time
Daring	1 year before its time
Smart	
Dowdy	1 year after its time
Hideous	10 years after its time
Ridiculous	20 years after its time
Amusing	30 years after its time
Quaint	50 years after its time
Charming	70 years after its time
Romantic	100 years after its time
Beautiful	150 years after its time

Laver possibly overemphasizes the shock value of incoming fashion, which today may be seen merely as weird or ugly. And of course he is speaking of the complete outfit, or "sentence." The speed with which a single "word" passes in and out of fashion can vary, just as in spoken and written languages.

A Head Full of Half-Baked Western Ideas

The appearance of foreign garments in an otherwise indigenous costume is similar in function to the use of foreign words or phrases in standard English speech. This phenomenon, which is common in certain circles, may have several different meanings.

First, of course, it can be a deliberate sign of national origin in someone who otherwise, sartorially or linguistically speaking, has no accent. Often this message is expressed through headgear. The Japanese-American lady in Western dress but with an elaborate Oriental hairdo, or the Oxford-educated Arab who tops his Savile Row suit with a turban, are telling us graphically that they have not been psychologically assimilated; that their ideas and opinions remain those of an Asian. As a result we tend to see the non-European in Western dress with native headgear or hairdo as dignified, even formidable; while the reverse outfit—the Oriental lady in a kimono and a plastic rain hat, or the sheik in native robes and a black bowler—appears comic. Such costumes seem to announce that their wearers, though not physically at ease in our country, have their heads full of half-baked Western ideas. It would perhaps be well for Anglo-American tourists to keep this principle in mind when traveling to exotic places. Very possibly the members of a package tour in Mexican sombreros or Russian bearskin hats look equally ridiculous and weak-minded to the natives of the countries they are visiting.

More often the wearing of a single foreign garment, like the dropping of a foreign word or phrase in conversation, is meant not to advertise foreign origin or allegiance but to indicate sophistication. It can also be a means of advertising wealth. When we see a fancy Swiss watch, we know that its owner either bought it at home for three times the price of a good English or American watch, or else he or she spent even more money traveling to Switzerland.

Slang and Vulgar Words

Casual dress, like casual speech, tends to be loose, relaxed and colorful. It often contains what might be called "slang words": blue jeans, sneakers, baseball caps, aprons, flowered cotton housedresses and the like. These garments could not be worn on a formal occasion without causing disapproval, but in ordinary circumstances they pass without remark. "Vulgar words" in dress, on the other hand, give emphasis and get immediate attention in almost any circumstances, just as they do in speech. Only the skillful can employ them without some loss of face, and even then they must be used in the right way. A torn, unbuttoned shirt, or wildy uncombed hair, can signify strong emotions: passion, grief, rage, despair. They are most effective if people already think of you as being neatly dressed, just as the curses of well-spoken persons count for more than those of the customarily foul-mouthed.

Items of dress that are the sartorial equivalent of forbidden words have more impact when they appear seldom and as if by accident. The Edwardian lady, lifting her heavy floor-length skirt to board a tram, appeared unaware that she was revealing a froth of lacy petticoats and embroidered black stockings. Similarly, today's braless executive woman, leaning over her desk at a conference, may affect not to know that her nipples show through her silk blouse. Perhaps she does not know it consciously; we are here in the ambiguous region of intention vs. interpretation which has given so much trouble to linguists.

In speech, slang terms and vulgarities may eventually become respectable dictionary words; the same thing is true of colloquial and vulgar fashions. Garments or styles that enter the fashionable vocabulary from a colloquial source usually have a longer life span than those that begin as vulgarities. Thigh-high patent leather boots, first worn by the most obvious variety of rentable female as a sign that she was willing to help act out certain male fantasies, shot with relative speed into and out of high fashion; while blue jeans made their way upward much more gradually from work clothes to casual to business and formal wear, and are still engaged in a slow descent.

Adjectives and Adverbs: The Decorated Style of Dress

Though the idea is attractive, it does not seem possible to equate different articles of clothing with the different parts of speech. A case can be made, however, for considering trimmings and accessories as adjectives or adverbs—modifiers in the sentence that is the total outfit—but it must be remembered that one era's trimmings and accessories are another's essential parts of the costume. At one time shoes were actually fastened with buckles, and the buttons on the sleeves of a suit jacket were used to secure turned-up cuffs. Today such buttons, or the linked brass rods on a pair of Gucci shoes, are purely vestigial and have no useful function. If they are missing, however, the jacket or the shoes are felt to be damaged and unfit for wear.

Accessories, too, may be considered essential to an outfit. In the 1940s and 1950s, for instance, a woman was not properly dressed unless she wore gloves. Emily Post, among many others, made this clear:

> Always wear gloves, of course, in church, and also on the street. A really smart woman wears them outdoors always, even in the country. Always wear gloves in a restaurant, in a theatre, when you go to lunch, or to a formal dinner, or to a dance. . . . A lady never takes off her gloves to shake hands, no matter when or where. . . . On formal occasions she should *put gloves on* to shake hands with a hostess or with her own guests.

If we consider only those accessories and trimmings that are currently optional, however, we may reasonably speak of them as modifiers. It then becomes possible to distinguish an elaborately decorated style of dress from a simple and plain one, whatever the period. As in speech, it is harder to communicate well in a highly decorated style, though when this is done successfully the result may be very impressive. A costume loaded with accessories and trimmings can easily appear cluttered, pretentious or confusing. Very rarely the whole becomes greater than its many parts, and the total effect is luxurious, elegant and often highly sensual.

The Changing Vocabulary of Fashion

As writers on costume have often pointed out, the average individual above the poverty line has many more clothes than he needs to cover his body, even allowing for washing and changes of weather. Moreover, we often discard garments that show little or no wear and purchase new ones. What is the reason for this? Some have claimed that it is all the result of brainwashing by commercial interests. But the conspiracy theory of fashion change—the idea that the adoption of new styles is simply the result of a plot by greedy designers and manufacturers and fashion editors—has, I think, less foundation than is generally believed. Certainly the fashion industry might like us to throw away all our clothes each year and buy a whole new wardrobe, but it has never been able to achieve this goal. For one thing, it is not true that the public will wear anything suggested to it, nor has it ever been true. Ever since fashion became big business, designers have proposed a bewildering array of styles every season. A few of these have been selected or adapted by manufacturers for mass production, but only a certain proportion of them have caught on.

As James Laver has remarked, modes are but the reflection of the manners of the time; they are the mirror, not the original. Within the limits imposed by economics, clothes are acquired, used and discarded just as words are, because they meet our needs and express our ideas and emotions. All the exhortations of experts on language cannot save outmoded terms of speech or persuade people to use new ones "correctly." In the same way, those garments that reflect what we are or want to be at the moment will be purchased and worn, and those that do not will not, however frantically they may be ballyhooed.

In the past, gifted artists of fashion from Worth to Mary Quant have been able to make inspired guesses about what people will want their clothes to say each year. Today a few designers seem to have retained this ability, but many others have proved to be as hopelessly out of touch as designers in the American auto industry. The classic case is that of the maxiskirt, a style which made women look older and heavier and impeded their movements at a time (1969) when youth, slimness and energy were at the height of their vogue. The maxiskirt was introduced with tremendous fanfare and not a little deception. Magazines and newspapers printed (sometimes perhaps unknowingly) photos of New York and London street scenes populated with hired models in long skirts disguised as passers-by, to give readers in Podunk and Lesser Puddleton the impression that the capitals had capitulated. But these strenuous efforts were in vain: the maxiskirt failed miserably, producing well-deserved financial disaster for its backers.

The fashion industry is no more able to preserve a style that men and women have decided to abandon than to introduce one they do not choose to accept. In America, for instance, huge advertising budgets and the wholehearted cooperation of magazines such as *Vogue* and *Esquire* have not been able to save the hat, which for centuries was an essential part of everyone's outdoor (and often of their indoor) costume. It survives now mainly as a utilitarian protection against weather, as part of ritual dress (at formal weddings, for example) or as a sign of age or individual eccentricity.

Elizabeth Neeld Comments:

✦ *There is a wonderful little book called* Comparisons: An Ingenious Visual Guide to the Relative Speed, Size, Strength, Area, Height, Depth, Length, Quantity, Shape, Mass, Hardness, Temperature, Noisiness . . . of Man, Woman, Animals, Birds, Fish, Insects, Dinosaurs, Cars, Trains, Oceans, Planets, Galaxies Plus Comparisons of Systems of Numbers, Design, Geometry, Calendars . . . *and the title goes on. The authors, known collectively as the Diagram Group, set out to make the universe intelligible by taking things the readers are likely to know to explain things they probably don't know. In other words, the authors use comparisons of two things—one familiar and one unfamiliar—to make a point. For instance, what will help someone comprehend the size of Central Park in New York City? The authors say, "If Central Park . . . were transformed into a vast parking lot, there would be space for over 300,000 cars." Want to know something about the twenty-five-foot long dinosaur, the stegosaurus? It had a brain the size of a walnut. Interested in the solar system? "If we suppose that the sun's diameter is equal to the height of an average man, then Jupiter, the largest planet,* would be slightly smaller than the man's head, while Earth would be slightly bigger than the iris of his eye." Curious about the fruit bat from Indonesia? The kalong has a wing span of up to five feet, seven inches—or roughly one and a half times the length of a baseball bat, which is three feet, six inches. ✦ A comparison extended long enough becomes an analogy. If you take one thing which is familiar to readers and compare it on a point-by-point basis to something that isn't so familiar, you are using an analogy to help explain what is unfamiliar. The difference between a simple comparison (often called a metaphor) and an analogy is that the comparison is extended; the writer continues the analogy throughout the discussion to help make a point. Writers often use analogy as a way to cause readers to think about a common subject in a new way. In this case, for instance, we think of clothes all the time. But we may not be inclined to think of clothes in the way Alison Lurie wants us to think about them now. So she uses an analogy to break up the ordinary way we might think about the subject. ✦ The more unusual or more surprising the analogy, the more effective it will be. In this excerpt from her book on clothes, Lurie uses the analogy of language to make a point about how we wear clothes. Do you have a friend who insists on shopping at antique stores to get her clothes? She is "using archaic words." Remember the Miami Vice fashion of a tee shirt with an expensive jacket? Don Johnson was "speaking slang." ✦ By using the analogy of language, Alison Lurie helps us understand why we dress the way we do. She shows us how we communicate with one another through what we choose to wear. By using something she knows we can understand—words and other facets of language—the author educates us about something less familiar to us: why we do what we do when we get dressed. ✦

BARBARA W. TUCHMAN

Mankind's Better Moments

For a change from prevailing pessimism, I should like to recall some of the positive and even admirable capacities of the human race. We hear very little of them lately. Ours is not a time of self-esteem or self-confidence—as was, for instance, the nineteenth century, when self-esteem may be seen oozing from its portraits. Victorians, especially the men, pictured themselves as erect, noble, and splendidly handsome. Our self-image looks more like Woody Allen or a character from Samuel Beckett. Amid a mass of worldwide troubles and a poor record for the twentieth century, we see our species—with cause—as functioning very badly, as blunderers when not knaves, as violent, ignoble, corrupt, inept, incapable of mastering the forces that threaten us, weakly subject to our worst instincts; in short, decadent.

The catalogue is familiar and valid, but it is growing tiresome. A study of history reminds one that mankind has its ups and downs and during the ups has accomplished many brave and beautiful things, exerted stupendous endeavors, explored and conquered oceans and wilderness, achieved marvels of beauty in the creative arts and marvels of science and social progress; has loved liberty with a passion that throughout history has led men to fight and die for it over and over again; has pursued knowledge, exercised reason, enjoyed laughter and pleasures, played games with zest, shown courage, heroism, altruism, honor, and decency; experienced love; known comfort, contentment, and occasionally happiness. All these qualities have been part of human experience, and if they have not had as important notice as the negatives nor exerted as wide and persistent an influence as the evils we do, they nevertheless deserve attention, for they are currently all but forgotten.

The Making of the Zuider Zee

Among the great endeavors, we have in our own time carried men to the moon and brought them back safely—surely one of the most remarkable achievements in history. Some may disapprove of the effort as unproductive, too costly, and a wrong choice of priorities in relation to greater needs, all of which may be true but does not, as I see it, diminish the achievement. If you look carefully, all positives have a negative underside—sometimes more, sometimes less—and not all admirable endeavors have admirable motives. Some have sad consequences. Although most signs presently point from bad to worse, human capacities are probably what they have always been. If primitive man could discover how to transform grain into bread, and reeds growing by the riverbank into baskets; if his successors could invent the wheel, harness the insubstantial air to turn a millstone, transform sheep's wool, flax, and worms' cocoons into fabric—we, I imagine, will find a way to manage the energy problem.

Consider how the Dutch accomplished the miracle of making land out of sea. By progressive enclosure of the Zuider Zee over the last sixty years, they have added half a million acres to their country, enlarging its area by eight percent and providing homes, farms, and towns for close to a quarter of a million people. The will to do the impossible, the spirit of can-do that overtakes our species now and then, was never more manifest than in this earth-altering act by the smallest of the major European nations.

A low-lying, windswept, waterlogged land, partly below sea level, pitted with marshes, rivers, lakes, and inlets, sliding all along its outer edge into the stormy North Sea with only fragile sand dunes as nature's barrier against the waves, Holland, in spite of physical disadvantages, has made itself into one of the most densely populated, orderly, prosperous, and, at one stage of its history, dominant nations of the West. For centuries, ever since the first inhabitants, fleeing enemy tribes, settled in the bogs where no one cared to bother them, the Dutch struggled against water and learned how to live with it: building on mounds, constructing and reconstructing seawalls of clay mixed with straw, carrying mud in an endless train of baskets, laying willow mattresses weighted with stones, repairing each spring the winter's damage, draining marshes, channeling streams, building ramps to their attics to save the cattle in times of flood, gaining dike-enclosed land from the waves in one place and losing as much to the revengeful ocean somewhere else, progressively developing methods to cope with their eternal antagonist.

The Zuider Zee was a tidal gulf penetrating eighty miles into the land over an area ten to thirty miles wide. The plan to close off the sea by a dam across the entire mouth of the gulf had long been contemplated but never adopted, for fear of the cost, until a massive flood in 1916, which left saltwater standing on all the farmlands north of Amsterdam, forced the issue. The act for enclosure was passed unanimously by both houses of Parliament in 1918. As large in ambition as the country was small, the plan called for a twenty-mile dike from shore to shore, rising twenty feet above sea level, wide enough at the top to carry an auto road and housing for the hydraulic works, and as much as six hundred feet wide on the sea bottom. The first cartload of gravel was dumped in 1920.

The dike was but part of the task. The inland sea it formed had to be drained of its saltwater and transformed from salt to fresh by the inflow from lower branches of the Rhine. Four polders, or areas rising from the shallows, would be lifted by the draining process from under water into the open air. Secondary dikes, pumping stations, sluices, drainage ditches to control the inflow, as well as locks and inland ports for navigation, had to be built, the polder lands restored to fertility, trees planted, roads, bridges, and rural and urban housing constructed, the whole scheduled for completion in sixty years.

The best-laid plans of engineers met errors and hazards. During construction, gravel that had been painstakingly dumped within sunken frameworks would be washed away in a night by heavy currents or a capricious storm. Means proved vulnerable, methods sometimes unworkable. Yet slowly the dike advanced from each shore toward the center. As the gap narrowed, the pressure of the tidal current rushing through increased daily in force, carrying away material at the base, undermining the structure, and threatening to prevent a final closing. In the last days a herd of floating derricks, dredges, barges, and every piece of available equipment was mustered at the spot, and fill was desperately poured in before the next return of the tide, due in twelve hours. At this point, gale winds were reported moving in. The check dam to protect the last gap showed signs of giving way; operations were hurriedly moved thirty yards inward. Suspense was now extreme. Roaring and foaming with sand, the tide threw itself upon the narrowing passage; the machines closed in, filled the last space in the dike, and it held. Men stood that day in 1932 where the North Sea's waves had held dominion for seven hundred years.

As the dry land appeared, the first comers to take possession were the birds. Gradually, decade by decade, crops, homes, and civilization followed, and unhappily, too, man's destructive intervention. In World War II the retreating Germans blew up a section of the dike, completely flooding the western polder, but by the end of the year the Dutch had pumped it dry, resowed the fields in the spring, and over the next seven years restored the polder's farms and villages. Weather, however, is never conquered. The disastrous floods of 1953 laid most of coastal Holland under water. The Dutch dried themselves out and, while the work at Zuider Zee continued, applied its lessons elsewhere and lent their hydraulic skills to other countries. Today the *Afsluitdijk*, or Zuider Zee road, is a normal thoroughfare. To drive across it between the sullen ocean on one side and new land on the other is for that moment to feel optimism for the human race.

Gothic Cathedrals: One of History's High Tides

Great endeavor requires vision and some kind of compelling impulse, not necessarily practical as in the case of the Dutch, but sometimes less definable, more exalted, as in the case of the Gothic cathedrals of the Middle Ages. The architectural explosion that produced this multitude of soaring vaults—arched, ribbed, pierced with jeweled light, studded with thousands of figures of the stone-carvers' art—represents in size, splendor, and numbers one of the great, permanent artistic achievements of human hands. What accounts for it? Not religious fervor alone but the zeal of a dynamic age, a desire to outdo, an ambition for the biggest and the best. Only the general will, shared by nobles, merchants, guilds, artisans, and commoners, could command the resources and labor to sustain so great an undertaking. Each group contributed donations, especially the magnates of commerce, who felt relieved thereby from the guilt of money-making. Voluntary work programs involved all classes. "Who has ever seen or heard tell in times past," wrote an observer, "that powerful princes of the world, that men brought up in honors and wealth, that nobles—men and women—have bent their haughty necks to the harness of carts and, like beasts of burden, have dragged to the abode of Christ these wagons loaded with wines, grains, oil, stones, timber and all that is necessary for the construction of the church?"

Abbot Suger, whose renovation of St.-Denis is considered the start of Gothic architecture, embodied the spirit of the builders. Determined to create the most splendid basilica in Christendom, he supervised every aspect of the work from fund-raising to decoration, and caused his name to be inscribed for immortality on keystones and capitals. He lay awake worrying, as he tells us, where to find trees large enough for the beams, and went personally with his carpenters to the forest to question the woodcutters under oath. When they swore that nothing of the kind he wanted could be found in the area, he insisted on searching for them himself and, after nine hours of scrambling through thorns and thickets, succeeded in locating and marking twelve trees of the necessary size.

Mainly the compelling impulse lay in the towns, where, in those years, economic and political strengths and wealth were accumulating. Amiens, the thriving capital of Picardy, decided to build the largest church in France, "higher than all the saints, higher than all the kings." For the necessary space, the hospital and bishop's palace had to be relocated and the city walls moved back. At the same time Beauvais, a neighbor town, raised a vault over the crossing of transept and nave to an unprecedented height of 158 feet, the apogee of architects' daring in its day. It proved too daring, for the height of the columns and spread of the supports caused the vault to collapse after twelve years. Repaired with undaunted purpose, it was defiantly topped by a spire rising 492 feet above ground, the tallest in France. Beauvais, having used up its resources, never built the nave, leaving a structure foreshortened but glorious. The interior is a fantasy of soaring space; to enter is to stand dazed in wonder, breathless in admiration.

The higher and lighter grew the buildings and the slenderer the columns, the more new expedients and techniques had to be devised to hold them up. Buttresses flew like angels' wings against the exteriors. This was a period of innovation and audacity, and a limitless spirit of excelsior. In a single century, from 1170 to 1270, six hundred cathedrals and major churches were built in France alone. In England in that period, the cathedral of Salisbury, with the tallest spire in the country, was completed in thirty-eight years. The spire of Freiburg in Germany was constructed entirely of filigree in stone as if spun by some supernatural spider. In the St.-Chapelle in Paris the fifteen miraculous windows swallow the walls; they have become the whole.

Embellishment was integral to the construction. Reims is populated by five thousand statues of saints, prophets, kings and cardinals, bishops, knights, ladies, craftsmen and commoners, devils, animals and birds. Every type of leaf known in northern France is said to appear in the decoration. In carving, stained glass, and sculpture the cathedrals displayed the art of medieval hands, and the marvel of these buildings is permanent even when they no longer play a central role in everyday life. Rodin said he could feel the beauty and presence of Reims even at night when he could not see it. "Its power," he wrote, "transcends the senses so that the eye sees what it sees not."

Explanations for the extraordinary burst that produced the cathedrals are several. Art historians will tell you that it was the invention of the ribbed vault. Religious historians will say it was the product of an age of faith which believed that with God's favor anything was possible; in fact it was not a period of untroubled faith, but of heresies and Inquisition. Rather, one can only say that conditions were right. Social order under monarchy and the towns was replacing the anarchy of the barons, so that existence was no longer merely a struggle to stay alive but allowed a surplus of goods and energies and greater opportunity for mutual effort. Banking and commerce were producing capital, roads were making possible wheeled transport, universities nourishing ideas and communication. It was one of history's high tides, an age of vigor, confidence, and forces converging to quicken the blood.

Explorers: What Engine Drove Them?

Even when the historical tide is low, a particular group of doers may emerge in exploits that inspire awe. Shrouded in the mists of the eighth century, long before the cathedrals, Viking seamanship was a wonder of daring, stamina, and skill. Pushing relentlessly outward in open boats, the Vikings sailed south, around Spain to North Africa and Arabia, north to the top of the world, west across uncharted seas to American coasts. They hauled their boats overland from the Baltic to make their way down Russian rivers to the Black Sea. Why? We do not know what engine drove them, only that it was part of the human endowment.

What of the founding of our own country, America? We take the *Mayflower* for granted—yet think of the boldness, the enterprise, the determined independence, the sheer grit it took to leave the known and set out across the sea for the unknown where no houses or food, no stores, no cleared land, no crops or livestock, none of the equipment or settlement of organized living awaited.

Equally bold was the enterprise of the French in the northern forests of the American continent, who throughout the seventeenth century explored and opened the land from the St. Lawrence to the Mississippi, from the Great Lakes to the Gulf of Mexico. They came not for liberty like the Pilgrims, but for gain and dominion, whether in spiritual empire for the Jesuits or in land, glory, and riches for the agents of the King; and rarely in history have men willingly embraced such hardship, such daunting adventure, and persisted with such tenacity and endurance. They met hunger, exhaustion, frostbite, capture and torture by Indians, wounds and disease, dangerous rapids, swarms of insects, long portages, bitter weather, and hardly ever did those who suffered the experience fail to return, re-enter the menacing but bountiful forest, and pit themselves once more against danger, pain, and death.

Above all others, the perseverance of La Salle in his search for the mouth of the Mississippi was unsurpassed. While preparing in Quebec, he mastered eight Indian languages. From then on he suffered accidents, betrayals, desertions, losses of men and provisions, fever and snow blindness, the hostility and intrigues of rivals who incited the Indians against him and plotted to ambush or poison him. He was truly pursued, as Francis Parkman wrote, by "a demon of havoc." Paddling through heavy waves in a storm over

Lake Ontario, he waded through freezing surf to beach the canoes each night, and lost guns and baggage when a canoe was swamped and sank. To lay the foundations of a fort above Niagara, frozen ground had to be thawed by boiling water. When the fort was at last built, La Salle christened it Crèvecoeur—that is, Heartbreak. It earned the name when in his absence it was plundered and deserted by its half-starved mutinous garrison. Farther on, a friendly Indian village, intended as a destination, was found laid waste by the Iroquois with only charred stakes stuck with skulls standing among the ashes, while wolves and buzzards prowled through the remains.

When at last, after four months' hazardous journey down the Great River, La Salle reached the sea, he formally took possession in the name of Louis XIV of all the country from the river's mouth to its source and of its tributaries—that is, of the vast basin of the Mississippi from the Rockies to the Appalachians—and named it Louisiana. The validity of the claim, which seems so hollow to us (though successful in its own time), is not the point. What counts is the conquest of fearful adversity by one man's extraordinary exertions and inflexible will.

Man Loves Pleasure, Too

Happily, man has a capacity for pleasure too, and in contriving ways to entertain and amuse himself has created brilliance and delight. Pageants, carnivals, festivals, fireworks, music, dancing and drama, parties and picnics, sports and games, the comic spirit and its gift of laughter—all the range of enjoyment from grand ceremonial to the quiet solitude of a day's fishing has helped to balance the world's infelicity.

The original Olympic Games held every fourth year in honor of Zeus was the most celebrated festival of classic times, of such significance to the Greeks that they dated their history from the first games in 776 B.C. as we date ours from the birth of Christ. The crown of olive awarded to the winner in each contest was considered the crown of happiness. While the Romans took this to be a sign of the essential frivolity of the Greek character, the ancient games endured for twelve centuries, a longer span than the supremacy of Rome.

Homo ludens, man at play, is surely as significant a figure as man at war or at work. In human activity the invention of the ball may be said to rank with the invention of the wheel. Imagine America without baseball, Europe without soccer, England without cricket, the Italians without bocci, China without Ping-Pong, and tennis for no one. Even stern John Calvin, the examplar of Puritan self-denial, was once discovered playing bowls on Sunday, and in 1611 an English supply ship arriving at Jamestown found the starving colonists suppressing their misery in the same game. Cornhuskings, logrollings, barn-raisings, horseraces, and wrestling and boxing matches have engaged America as, somewhat more passively, the armchair watching of football and basketball does today.

Play was invented for diversion, exertion, and escape from routine cares. In colonial New York, sleighing parties preceded by fiddlers on horseback drove out to country inns, where, according to a participant, "we danced, sang, romped, ate and drank and kicked away care from morning to night." John Audubon, present at a barbecue and dance on the Kentucky frontier, wrote, "Every countenance beamed with joy, every heart leaped with gladness . . . care and sorrow were flung to the winds."

Play has its underside, too, in the gladiatorial games, in cockfights and prizefights, which arouse one of the least agreeable of human characteristics, pleasure in blood and brutality, but in relation to play as a whole, this is minor.

Much of our pleasure derives from eating and sex, two components which have received an excess of attention in our time— allowing me to leave them aside as understood, except to note how closely they are allied. All those recipes, cuisines, exotic foods, and utensils of kitchen chic seem to proliferate in proportion to pornography, sex therapy, blue movies, and instructive tales for children on pederasty and incest. Whether this twin increase signifies decadence or liberation is disputable. Let us move on to other ground.

To the carnival, for instance. Mardi Gras in all its forms is an excuse for letting go; for uninhibited fun before the abstinence of Lent; for dressing up, play-acting, cavorting in costumes and masks, constructing imaginative floats; for noise, pranks, jokes, battles of flowers and confetti, balls and banquets, singing and dancing, and fireworks. In the Belgian carnival of Gilles-Binche, originating in the sixteenth century in honor of Charles V's conquest of Peru, the dancers are spectacular in superlatively tall feather headdresses representing the Incas, and brilliant costumes trimmed with gold lace and tinkling bells. They wear wooden shoes to stamp out the rhythm of their dance and carry baskets of oranges symbolizing the treasures of Peru with which they pelt the onlookers. In the celebrated Palio of Siena at harvest time, a horse and rider from each neighborhood race madly around a sloping cobblestoned course in the public square, while the citizens shriek in passionate rivalry. Walpurgis Night on the eve of May Day is an excuse for bacchanalia in the guise of witches' revels; winter's festival at Christmas is celebrated by gift-giving. Humanity has invented infinite ways to enjoy itself.

No people have invented more ways than have the Chinese, perhaps to balance floods, famine, warlords, and other ills of fate. The clang of gongs, clashing of cymbals, and beating of drums sound through their long history. No month is without fairs and theatricals when streets are hung with fantasies of painted lanterns and crowded with "carriages that flow like water, horses like roaming dragons." Night skies are illuminated by firecrackers—a Chinese invention—bursting in the form of peonies, flowerpots, fiery devils. The ways of pleasure are myriad. Music plays in the air through bamboo whistles of different pitch tied to the wings of circling pigeons. To skim a frozen lake in an ice sleigh with a group of friends on a day when the sun is warm is rapture, like "moving in a cup of jade." What more delightful than the ancient festival called "Half an Immortal," when everyone from palace officials to the common man took a ride on a swing? When high in the air, one felt like an Immortal; when back to earth once again, human—no more than to be for an instant a god.

In Europe's age of grandeur, princes devised pageants of dazzling splendor to express their magnificence, none more spectacular than the extravaganza of 1660 celebrating the marriage of Leopold I of Austria to the Infanta of Spain. As the climax to festivities lasting three months, an equestrian contest of the Four Elements was performed in the grand plaza, each element represented by a company of a thousand, gorgeously costumed. Water's company were dressed in blue and silver covered with fish scales and shells; Air's in gold brocade shaded in the colors of the rainbow; Earth's decorated with flowers; Fire's with curling flames. Neptune, surrounded by marine monsters and winds, rode in a car drawn by a huge whale spouting water. Earth's car contained a garden with Pan and shepherds, drawn by elephants with castles on their backs; Air rode a dragon escorted by thirty griffins; Fire was accompanied by Vulcan, thirty Cyclopes, and a flame-spouting salamander. A rather irrelevant ship carrying the Argonauts to the Golden

Fleece was added for extras. The contest was resolved when a star-studded globe, arched by an artificial rainbow representing Peace, rolled across the plaza and opened to display a Temple of Immortality from which emerged riders impersonating the fifteen previous Hapsburg emperors, ending with Leopold in person. Dressed as Glory, in silver lace and diamonds, and wearing his crown, he rode in a silver seashell drawn by eight white horses and carrying seven singers in jeweled robes, who serenaded the Infanta. Then followed the climactic equestrian ballet performed by four groups of eight cavaliers each, whose elaborate movements were marked by trumpet flourishes, kettledrums, and cannon salutes. In a grand finale a thousand rockets blazed from two artificial mountains named Parnassus and Aetna, and the sky was lit in triumph by the Hapsburg acrostic AEIOU standing for *Austria Est Imperare Onme Universo*, meaning, approximately, "Austria rules the world."

The motive may have been self-aggrandizement, but the results were sumptuous and exciting; viewers were enthralled, performers proud, and the designer of the pageant was made a baron. It was a case of men and women engaged in the art of enjoyment, a function common to all times, although one would hardly know it from today's image of ourselves as wretched creatures forever agonizing over petty squalors of sex and drink as if we had no other recourse of destiny. . . .

Think of Him When We Grumble

. . . Happiness, too, is an individual matter. It springs up here or there, haphazard, random, without origin or explanation. It resists study, laughs at sociology, flourishes, vanishes, reappears somewhere else. Take Izaak Walton, author of *The Compleat Angler*, that guide to contentment as well as fishing, of which Charles Lamb said, "It would sweeten any man's temper at any time to read it." Though Walton lived in distracted times of revolution and regicide, though he adhered to the losing side in the English Civil War, though he lost in their infancy all seven children by his first wife and the eldest son of his second marriage, though he was twice a widower, his misfortunes could not sour an essentially buoyant nature. "He passed through turmoil," in the words of a biographer, "ever accompanied by content."

Walton's secret was friendship. Born to a yeoman family and apprenticed in youth as an ironmonger, he managed to gain an education and, through sweetness of disposition and a cheerful religious faith, became a friend on equal terms of various learned clergymen and poets whose lives he wrote and works he prefaced— among them John Donne, George Herbert, and Michael Drayton. Another companion, Charles Cotton, wrote of Izaak, "In him I have the happiness to know the worthiest man, and to enjoy the best and truest friend any man ever had."

The Compleat Angler, published when the author was sixty, glows in the sunshine of his character. In it are humor and piety, grave advice on the idiosyncrasies of fish and the niceties of landing them, delight in nature and in music. Walton saw five editions reprinted in his lifetime, while unnumerable later editions secured him immortality. The surviving son by his second wife became a clergyman; the surviving daughter married one and gave her father a home among grandchildren. He wrote his last work at eighty-five and died at ninety after being celebrated in verse by one of his circle as a "happy old man" whose life "showed how to compass true felicity." Let us think of him when we grumble.

Is anything to be learned from my survey? I raise the question only because most people want history to teach them lessons, which I believe it can do, although I am less sure we can use them when needed. I gathered these examples not to teach but merely to remind people in a despondent era that the good in mankind operates even if the bad secures more attention. I am aware that selecting out the better moments does not result in a realistic picture. Turn them over and there is likely to be a darker side, as when Project Apollo, our journey to the moon, was authorized because its glamour could obtain subsidies for rocket and missile development that otherwise might not have been forthcoming. That is the way things are.

Whole philosophies have evolved over the question whether the human species is predominately good or evil. I only know that it is mixed, that you cannot separate good from bad, that wisdom, courage, and benevolence exist alongside knavery, greed, and stupidity; heroism and fortitude alongside vainglory, cruelty, and corruption.

It is a paradox of our time in the West that never have so many people been so relatively well off and never has society been more troubled. Yet I suspect that humanity's virtues have not vanished, although the experiences of our century seem to suggest that they are in abeyance. A century that took shape in the disillusion which followed the enormous effort and hopes of World War I, that saw revolution in Russia congeal into the same tyranny it overthrew, saw a supposedly civilized nation revert under the Nazis into organized and unparalleled savagery, saw the craven appeasement by the democracies, is understandably marked by suspicion of human nature. A literary historian, Van Wyck Brooks, discussing the 1920s and '30s, spoke of "an eschatological despair of the world." Whereas Whitman and Emerson, he wrote, "had been impressed by the worth and good sense of the people, writers of the new time" were struck by their lusts, cupidity, and violence, and had come to dislike their fellow men. The same theme reappeared in a recent play in which a mother struggled against her two "pitilessly contemptuous" children. Her problem was that she wanted them to be happy and they did not want to be. They preferred to watch horrors on television. In essence this is our epoch. It insists upon the flaws and corruptions, without belief in valor or virtue or the possibility of happiness. It keeps turning to look back on Sodom and Gomorrah; it has no view of the Delectable Mountains.

We must keep a balance, and I know of no better prescription than a phrase from Condorcet's eulogy on the death of Benjamin Franklin: "He pardoned the present for the sake of the future."

Elizabeth Neeld Comments:

◆ *The "bones" of this essay are easy to see. Barbara Tuchman states her thesis clearly: "I should like to recall some of the positive and even admirable capacities of the human race." The rest of her essay consists of examples to prove her point. The examples are unrelated except that each of them is evidence to support the author's contention that the good things we human beings have done deserve attention in a time when they are almost forgotten.* ◆ *Each example is a separate illustration of Tuchman's point: that human beings have done positive things. She talks about the accomplishment of the Dutch in building the Zuider Zee, and she praises the building of Gothic cathedrals, the courage of explorers, and the Olympic games and other frivolities we human beings have devised to illustrate our positive side. An individual's commitment to friendship is her final example of what is possible in positive human behavior.* ◆ *Tuchman did not begin writing about history until she was in her mid-forties and had raised three daughters. She has since become America's foremost popular historian and is the winner of two Pulitzer Prizes. She writes history, she says, as a story. "There should be a beginning, a middle, and an end, plus an element of suspense to keep a reader turning the pages." She has been praised for her ability to organize her material coherently and to trace bright narrative threads without sacrificing complexities.* ✦ *This essay appeared in the* American Scholar, *a magazine which intends "to fill the gap between the learned journals and the good magazines for a popular audience." The magazine editors say, "We are interested not so much in the definitive analysis as in the lucid and creative exploration of what is going on in the fields of science, art, religion, politics, and national and foreign affairs." The magazine has thirty-two thousand subscribers.* ✦ *Barbara Tuchman's theme in this essay pervades all of her work. In an interview after her book* The March of Folly *was published, she said, "Our situation today is quite dangerous, since so many people spend so much time creating adversary situations. Everybody seems to be searching for the worst in everybody else. . . . All this is drastically dangerous for democracy. I have always believed that good will prevail. . . . It is not a matter of optimism, it's a matter of hope. I cannot live without hope."* ✦

CARLOS FUENTES

Mexico's Two Seas

When we were children back in the 1940's, vacation time in Mexico came in the winter. Between December and March, liberated schoolchildren flocked to the traditional family beaches, Veracruz and Mazatlán. The more adventurous wandered into a small fishing village with few hotels and no pollution: Acapulco.

School vacations were changed to summertime only in the 60's, and so Mexican children adapted to a general custom in the Northern Hemisphere. But our previous eccentricity had a reason: The winter months are the best holiday season in the Mexican tropics, especially on the coasts. Days are balmy, nights breezy and soft. Summer in Mexico is a much more dramatic affair, but no less attractive for that reason.

Indeed, this is a country of two seasons, rainy and dry, the former between May and October, the latter the rest of year. It is also a country of two seas: the Gulf and the Caribbean on the east, the Pacific on the west. So I must choose constantly between the two seas and the two seasons. I always go to Veracruz on the Gulf and Ixtapa-Zihuatanejo on the Pacific, as if I could only understand Mexico in the classical image of Janus, facing two ways, backward and forward.

Melting Pot of Mexico

Veracruz is the land of my father. He was born in that port city and told me of his childhood there in the big town house my grand-father occupied as manager of the National Bank of Mexico. A house full of patios and potted palms and a giant gym where my father dramatized "The Three Musketeers" in the tropics. Every first Monday of the month, the mails would arrive from Europe and my father, then a child, would stand on the dock with his elder brother, my uncle Carlos, who died of typhoid fever at 20, both holding the hands of my grandfather Rafael, a stocky man with a big nose and Mephistophelean eyebrows, always dressed in a three-piece suit, a straw boater being his only concession to the climate. They were waiting for the monthly arrival of back issues of *La Vie Parisienne* and *The London Illustrated News*, the latest novels by Jules Verne and Thomas Hardy. Veracruz was their lifeline to the world.

The Veracruz of the turn of the century no longer exists; the old town house is no longer there; no mail boats from Europe conde-scend to visit. Yet what my father felt there as a child is still true to me: Veracruz is the final beach of the Mediterranean. It is as if a long, generous wave from Tyre and Sidon, Syracuse and Cádiz were constantly coming to rest on the far reaches of the Mediterranean of the soul. This is a city laden with history and lore, the first municipality on the North American mainland, founded by the conquistador Hernán Cortés himself in 1519, guarded by a Spanish fortress, San Juan de Ulúa, which later, in the 19th century, served as an infamous political prison. Yet the charm of Veracruz is not in its history. It is not in its beaches, dark and muddy and shallow— and containing too many reminders, in the form of wire-net fences strung in the sea, that this is a playground for the Mexican breth-ren of the great white shark of "Jaws."

The charm is elsewhere, and it is enormous. This is not a town for international tourism. It is for Veracruzanos (who call themselves Jarochos) first, for Mexicans second and thirdly for open-minded foreigners who do not thrive on fast-food chains. On summer evenings, entire families set up their straw and wooden chairs on the long dock, circles form and magical tales are told. The municipal bands play, and children run around freely. Days are long and slow there, and adventure not far way. The islands of Sacrificios and Enmedio are as virgin as the day Cortés arrived, the fish and other marine life is abundant and colorful, and one can wade for miles in the clear Gulf waters, watching its rainbow passage.

But the real life of Veracruz is centered in its wonderful old square. There is certainly no place in all Mexico where gaiety and hospitality are so spontaneous, so inherent to the nature of the people. The portales, the great arches around the square, are Veracruz's living room. The extraordinary local bands, based on the harp and the guitar, beat a lovely, sensuous rhythm throughout the night; the best mint juleps in the world are served in the portal of the ancient Diligencias Hotel; the grand traditional New Orleans and Havana-style restaurants of the plaza present red snapper in the Veracruz manner, smothered in olives and tomatoes, giant shrimp and shark fillets. The aroma is of coffee and tobacco and vanilla, and vendors carry around their monkeys and parakeets, which add their screeches to this Mexican Babel whose summer-time culminates on the night of Sept. 15, the eve of Independence.

The plaza and the portales are then everyone's province; there is no boundary set on comradeship, drinking together, singing together, swapping tales, talking in verse and answering good-natured taunts from a neighboring table. The melancholy Mexico of the highlands is absent. Veracruz is the smiling Mexico that few non-Mexicans can or dare penetrate.

It is just as difficult, but necessary, to understand ritual in Veracruz's great cafe, La Parroquia, now declared a national landmark. There, in the glare of white tiles, and under the slow, elegant flight of the old-fashioned ceiling fans, an army of waiters takes orders from afar, much like brokers at the New York Stock Exchange. Old men occupy the tables that have been theirs for 40 years and give orders to waiters who have been there as long and who will take orders from no one else, and the varieties of egg dishes, the French bread toasted with beans and melted cheese, the brittle sweet breads and the giant tin urns, from which the coffee tinted with hot milk is continuously served, add up to a declaration of traditional values, permanence and provincial identity that I, for one, greatly appreciate in a Mexico in which the illusions of the modern are crumbling before everyone's eyes. La Parroquia just goes on, to the click of domino chips.

Paradise

A paradise, both old and new, is the tale of the other sea. Zihuatanejo is an old fishing village, very much like Acapulco during my childhood. The beaches are splendid on this bay. Limpid waters meet white sand ringed with small hotels and restaurants, the most delightful being Villa del Sol, a hostel created and kept alive by a German engineer, Helmut Leins, who gave up winters in Munich for year-round freedom on Playa la Ropa—the Beach of Clothes, where women of the village once came to do the washing, or where a shipwrecked galleon once let loose a fanciful flight of Spanish linen, who knows?

Ixtapa, the neighboring development on the ocean, is a recent creation, and high-rises are the word there. But the Camino Real Hotel is astonishing in the way it blends into the landscape. Seen from the air, the Camino Real looks like an overbaked typewriter left too long in the sun. At closer range, one recognizes the way in which the architect, Ricardo Legorreta (a favorite disciple of the dean of Mexican architecture, Luis Barragán), refused to build in opposition to the slope of the mountain, but rather adapted the building to the decline from sierra to sea. I am told that Mr. Legorreta examined a fistful of the red earth of Ixtapa and decided the hotel should be the color of the land. At one time, this must have looked like the land of the pharaohs: 2,000 workers were busy building here. But the Camino Real is no strobe-lighted Luxor. It is intimate, partly because everything public is also private: palm trees and bougainvillea, dramatic organ cactus, hibiscus and Monet-looking lagoons, laden with lilies. Andrés Rosetto runs this stranded leviathan as if it were his own garden.

Summer is not monsoon time around here. As in Veracruz, rain happens at night, if at all. But in Veracruz a norther is never far away. In Ixtapa-Zihuatanejo, a furious tropical downpour might last for a couple of hours. Then the world changes, and lush greens transform the dry winter's austerity. The dominant colors of the place—emerald and blue—become vastly purer in the summer, but they are tempered by the misty silver of daybreak and then by the red bonfires the people here love at night. I have yet to see, in my travels, a night sky as limpid as this. The charts of the heavens are right there, near your fingertips, for the naked eye to see: the Dipper, Orion, the Bear—visual realities in the nights of Ixtapa-Zihuatanejo. They no longer need be explained or illustrated.

But Mexican paradises last only a short while. That is precisely why they are paradises and why one must rush to them. The defacing of Ixtapa-Zihuatanejo can be observed in the ugly replica of the Parthenon at Athens built by the infinitely corrupt chief of police in Mexico City during the López Portillo regime. On a salary of something like $800 a month, Gen. Arturo Durazo Moreno, known as El Negro, erected this offense to good taste and public morality, facing the sun. He had, then, to cover it up with coarse peasant blankets against the glare. It was like the skin of Mexico's poverty covering the warts of Mexico's wealth. General Durazo has now fled the country, leaving behind golden faucets and marble columns. But his palace stands as a monument to Mexico's disenchantment with easy money, extreme inequity and offensive arrogance as the social products of our illusions of industrial modernity.

Sweet Veracruz

That is why I like to go back, finally, to the other, humble sea of Veracruz, sit around the plaza, read and write endlessly in a cafe. I remember that Mexico has a history and an imagination from which to arise, and I think of my grandfather, my father and my uncle waiting on the docks for the mails to arrive and then sitting at La Parroquia to ponder the news of the world while meeting old friends, tasting splendid foods and drinks, smelling the sweetness of the tropics and having time to be themselves.

Elizabeth Neeld Comments:

✦ *Carlos Fuentes is one of the most well-known Latin American writers. He is interviewed often, and when he is asked what interests he has other then writing, he always includes* swimming *among the list of life's pleasures. In fact, he said once, "God did not make us to scribble little things on paper. He made us to hunt and swim and swing from trees." It's not surprising, then, that Fuentes would* write an essay for Sophisticated Traveler on the two oceans that bound his home country, Mexico. ✦ It's easy to see that Fuentes' purpose—to compare the two oceans as vacation spots—results naturally in the use of the thought pattern and form, comparison/contrast. The creativity allowed by this traditional form lies in arranging the information about the things being compared. For instance, will he talk about one ocean and then the other? Or will he talk about a feature of oceans—say, kinds of waves—and relate that feature to both oceans before going on to the next feature he wants to discuss? ✦ In this essay Fuentes chooses the A/B pattern: he talks first about Veracruz as a vacation spot on the Gulf of Mexico and then he talks about Ixtapa and Zihuatanejo on the Pacific. He uses points he has already made about Veracruz to discuss the vacation spots on the Pacific. The Veracruz discussion is his reference point when he talks about the other sea. (For instance, when he's talking about the weather in Ixtapa, he'll say, "Summer is not monsoon time around here. As in Veracruz, rain happens at night, if at all. But in Veracruz a norther is never far away. In Ixtapa-Zihuatanejo, a furious tropical downpour might last for a couple of hours." When he completes the comparison of the two seas, Fuentes comes back to his favorite, Veracruz. His final remark is, "That is why I like to go back, finally, to the other, humble sea of Veracruz." He gives us a clue much earlier that the comparison will favor Veracruz—by placing Veracruz first in the essay, discussing it more fully, and using this discussion as the basis or reference point for the second section, the discussion of Ixtapa on the western coast. Fuentes' willingness to choose between the two coasts adds interest to the essay. A more timid travel writer might try to be "objective" and give both equal coverage. This, however, is what makes much classroom writing of comparison/contrast a mere exercise. There is no person present who is willing to take a stand on the matter. Fuentes as a person is present in the comparisons he makes in this essay. ✦ A final point to note is how personal Fuentes makes this essay, even though it is an informative essay printed in a travel magazine. He centers his comparison in his own life—specifically, his childhood—and in the lives of his family

members. Just as he does not shy away from choosing between the two seas, he also does not attempt to write a
factual piece about the two oceans that reveals nothing
about the person who is doing the writing. This personaliz-
ing of the comparison/contrast essay adds zest and interest. Without the presence of the writer in the essay, you
would have little more than a sterile, uninspiring, robot-
like piece of prose. ✦

READING

to Learn to Write:
Form

Created Form

Most essays and articles do not have a single predominate organizing form, such as those shown in the section on *traditional form*. Writers use traditional form when their approach to a subject corresponds to one of the recognized ways the human mind tends to think. If you are writing about a new product in order to show that it is better than the competition, the predominate organizing principle you are going to use is comparison. Your purpose and that predominate thought pattern make a perfect match.

Most of the time, however, writers' purposes cannot be accomplished by using some kind of predominate form as an organizing principle. Instead, to say what they want to say and to achieve their intention, writers are required to use many thought patterns in a kind of mix-and-match arrangement which they, in response to their purpose, design themselves. The writers *create form*.

315

This *created form* will be as varied as the writers themselves. The forms will not be recognizable as a predominate pattern of thought. In fact, the form may be difficult to label. It's as if the writers take traditional dance steps—the dip of the tango, the one-two-three of the waltz, the kicks of the schottische—and make up their own dances. Created form may have some narration here, some classification there, some definition there, some examples in another place. Or writers may use deductive or inductive reasoning or problem/solution essay form yet *create* an original arrangement of them in their essays. Mixed in with these bits and pieces of traditional form or ways of thinking may be other features: a one-sentence paragraph designed for drama and surprise, a theme of emotion around which the facts of the essay are woven, a structure of sentences and paragraphs that in rhythm corresponds to what is being said. (John McPhee once wrote an essay, for instance, about the basketball player Bill Bradley, and critics pointed out that the sentence and paragraph structure of the essay had the rhythm and movement of someone dribbling a basketball up and down a court. That really is *creating form*.)

There is a lot of choice in created form. There are a lot of options. There is a lot of room for the writer's personal style. The writing is free to follow the author's thoughts and make its own form, rather than the author's thoughts having to be molded and shaped to fit a traditional organizing form.

This means that there can be no standard set of instructions about how to write with created form. Each essay using created form is individual, unique to that writer and that piece of writing. The writer's purpose may dictate, for instance, that the essay not even be written in paragraphs. Look at Maxine Hong Kingston's essay that appeared in *Ms.* magazine. The organizing form for this essay is a list, which is certainly not a customary way of writing an essay at all. Kingston *created* her own form. It served the purpose she had for the essay. And the essay found a publisher.

Look at the essay called "I Still See Him Everywhere." It shows another unusual way to organize an essay, a form that does not follow the standard rules. The authors alternate two voices, one carrying one thread of thought and one another thread of thought. Yet the essay is coherent. The authors *created* their own form. This form allowed them to include information that would not have fit if they had organized their essay in a traditional way.

When you read the essays in this section, you will notice that the writers have taken a lot of liberties. Their work does not fall into a structure or a quickly recognized pattern of thought. Many people are surprised to discover the variety of forms of writing that are written, published, and read! The evidence shows that there is no standard way to organize and form a piece of writing and that almost any organizational pattern will work, so long as it is integral to the message and purpose of writing. Far more than we may think, the writer calls the game. The writer can write as she or he wishes, as long as the message is clear. The writer can *create form*. It's an exhilarating and liberating discovery. Knowing that you can create your own form is at the heart of being a satisfied and happy writer!

DAVID FINN

How to Visit a Museum

There is no right or wrong way to visit a museum. The most important rule you should keep in mind as you go through the front door is to follow your own instincts. Be prepared to find what excites you, to enjoy what delights your heart and mind, perhaps to have esthetic experiences you will never forget. You have a feast in store for you and you should make the most of it. Stay as long or as short a time as you will, but do your best at all times to let the work of art speak directly to you with a minimum of interference or distraction.

You'll Be Stunned

The first moment you walk into a museum is filled with excitement and expectation. You may be so anxious to get started that you overlook the map posted at the entranceway or printed in a folder available at the front desk. However, taking a minute or two to get an overview of what is in the museum could save you the frustration of missing a part of the collection you would particularly enjoy—like the extraordinary "black paintings" by Goya, which many visitors to the Prado in Madrid do not realize are hung in the basement galleries. If you want to prepare yourself more thoroughly, spend some time before you start through the galleries studying the official museum guidebook or a general one such as the Blue Guide, which offers a room-by-room description of the works on display. When I have taken the time to do so, underlining the works I want to be sure to see, it has been rewarding. Not that I always hunt for those particular works when I get to the museum—that could be too distracting. But just knowing what kinds of works to expect somehow helps put me in the right frame of mind for the visit.

No matter how much or little preparation you have done, however, you cannot help being stunned when the first major gallery turns out to be an enormous room filled with extraordinary works of art. Take, for example, the Egyptian Gallery at the British Museum, which must include a hundred large and small objects. Where and how to begin? The giant roaring Assyrian lion at the entranceway seems almost part of the architecture, so you may ignore it unless you look carefully at its fantastic head and mouth and sense its enormous strength. Nearby is the famous Rosetta Stone, its label explaining that it was this fragment of black basalt that enabled archaeologists to unravel the mystery of hieroglyphics. There is a thrill in standing before an object that played such an important role in deciphering the past.

But what about the rest of the Egyptian Gallery? Do you look at one object after another, noting how large some of the monumental figures are, how curious the animal forms seem to be, how remarkable it is that the figures were so realistic thousands of years ago? Should you make a point of examining them all? How much time should you spend in the little side rooms off the main gallery where some especially important objects may be on display? What should you *think about* as you look at the objects? How beautiful they are? How historically significant? How being near them brings you closer to an ancient civilization?

Any one of these or a thousand other thoughts may go through your mind. You may wonder about the identity of the royal personage portrayed in a monumental head mounted on a tall pedestal, and be impressed by the giant arm mounted below, which appears to be another fragment of the same sculpture. If you look at both casually, you will probably see only a curious remnant from another civilization, where people wore strange headdresses and created enormous monuments. But if you look at the features of the face more closely you will find a wonderfully sensitive portrait of a handsome young man who may even remind you of someone you know. And if you walk around the clenched fist, you will discover a symphony of form that is a sculptural tour de force in its own right.

What was there about that era and the attitude people had toward their godlike rulers, you may ask yourself, that produced these overpowering images? And what should our attitude be toward them today? Once I visited the Egyptian Gallery with a renowned theologian and asked why these figures, which seem like such great sculptures to our eyes, were condemned in the Old Testament as idols. "It's one thing to appreciate the figures as art," he replied, "but quite another to worship them." I tried vainly to look at the images as the ancient Egyptians or Israelites must have seen them and had an eerie sense of the changes wrought over millenniums, bridged in a remarkable way by the universality of artistic expression that dazzled my eyes.

Bleary Eye Inevitable

Most of the problems you are likely to find in walking through a museum come from within yourself. You may worry about paying too little attention to the most important paintings and sculptures in the collection. When you recognize the name of a well-known artist, you may be excited by what you see but wonder if it is his reputation or his work that impresses you. You also may worry because you are ignoring works by artists you do not happen to know. You are anxious not to miss anything as you wander through the galleries, but at the same time you know you cannot do justice to *everything* in the museum.

It is natural to want to look at least once at everything on your initial visit to any museum. This is certainly true if the museum is in a distant city and you do not know when you will have a chance to visit it again. It is hard to curb this tendency, and most often you just have to give in to it, hoping that some vivid memory of greatness will stand out from the blur. Too often one thinks that going to a museum is like reading a book; if one does not read every page all the way through to the end, one is not doing right by the author. It takes some courage to stop reading a book in the middle, and one only does so if the author totally fails to excite one's interest. A museum is just the opposite. The problem is how not to become surfeited.

There is a distinct, almost measurable response curve in visiting a museum, with those objects you see at the outset making a greater impact than those you see later on. The rate of diminishing response varies from individual to individual and may also vary from museum to museum. The climax of your visit could come at any point along the way, but the bleary-eyed phenomenon is inevitable, and you definitely will be able to absorb less of what you see as time goes on. There is nothing you can do about this, so do not worry about it. If you want to be sure at least to *see* everything even though you no longer *feel* anything, walk through the rest of the museum quickly. It will give you an overview of what is there. But you may prefer to quit when your capacity to react has worn out, for it can be a great trial to walk through gallery after gallery after you have become numb to what you are seeing.

Remember you are not going to take a quiz at the end of your visit, so you do not have to account for all the objects in the museum. If you can leave the museum with a sense of having seen some magnificent works and with a few images indelibly imprinted in your brain, even if you cannot remember where they came from or even who the artists were, your visit will have been a success.

Some people give themselves an arbitrary one-hour limit for any museum visit. Some can go two hours without running into trouble, but others tire after a half-hour. I find that the length of time I can spend in a museum varies, depending on where I am, what I am seeing, what my mood is, and probably many other unidentifiable influences. But I know there is always *some* limit to my endurance.

Often it is possible to take a break and relax for a few minutes on a couch in one of the galleries. Seating areas are designed for your convenience, and if you feel your feet wearing out or your mind filling up with too many images, a change of pace can do a lot of good. This is particularly rewarding if you sit in front of a work of art that you would enjoy looking at in some detail.

An even longer break for a cup of coffee or lunch in the cafeteria can be especially useful if you are in a large museum and want to visit a new section or special exhibition with a fresh mind. . . .

Nips of Information

As you move around the gallery you may wonder how much time it takes to absorb the qualities of a major work of art. The answer has to be that the depth of appreciation is not a function of time. It is possible to look at an object for five seconds and be overcome by its beauty. Or one may spend many minutes discovering details in an object that are not apparent at first sight.

Kenneth Clark once wrote that initially he could enjoy an esthetic sensation in front of a work of art for about as long as he could enjoy the smell of an orange—which in his case was less than two minutes. The only way he could stay longer was to look attentively at different aspects of the painting or sculpture and "fortify himself with nips of information" about both the artist and the work until finally he became "saturated" with it. To emphasize the importance of looking carefully at each section of a painting to discover its deeper qualities, he published two volumes of his favorite details from paintings in the National Gallery in London.

You probably will not have a chance to become *saturated* with an individual work of art on your first visit to a great museum. Even in two or three hours you will probably not find it possible to do more than glance at each of the works on display. But if one or two strike you as really exciting, stay a little longer and enjoy the experience of discovering beautiful forms in the details.

A scientist I know developed his own approach to absorbing the qualities of a work of art. He took a six-month leave of absence to travel around the world and broaden his cultural horizons, and spent hours in museums trying to absorb the richness of individual works of art. He told me that he would sit in front of a painting studying all its parts until he thought he knew it thoroughly; then he would close his eyes and try to reconstruct in his mind's eye what was there. Usually he found that he could not remember certain sections of the painting, so he would open his eyes and examine those parts more carefully. He would repeat the exercise until he satisfied himself that he knew the whole painting.

The main advantage of this unusual idea is that it makes one *look* carefully at what is there, and if one *looks* hard there is a good chance one will learn to *see*. It is not the memorizing itself that is important, but the deep response within oneself to what the artist created. If one looks at a detail of a painting and is moved by some quality one finds there—the masterly rendition of an object, or the exquisite combination of colors, or the fascinating interplay of forms, or the portrayal of a human experience, or the ingenious creation of a mood, or the presentation of a brilliant idea—or something one cannot put one's finger on but finds somehow extraordinarily exciting—then one is *seeing* rather than just *looking*. Any technique that can help rivet one's eyes on a work of art for more than a few seconds increases the chance of having such an experience. And it is that experience which makes art something of great value in human life.

Elizabeth Neeld Comments:

✦ *David Finn is the co-founder of a public relations firm, Ruder & Finn, Inc., in New York City. This firm has developed new techniques and concepts in public relations and publicity and has clients not only in the United States, but also in Japan, Israel, Mexico, New Zealand, and Malaysia. Their offices are spread all over the world.* ✦ *David Finn is also a specialist in photographing sculpture and has published over a dozen books that he says are "aimed at revealing the inner qualities of three-dimensional works of art." His books have been translated into Spanish, Japanese, Chinese, and Arabic. In addition, he is an artist (a painter and a sculptor) and has had a one-man show at the New School for Social Research in New York City. His paintings have also been exhibited at schools and museums, including the National Academy and the Boston Museum of Art.* ✦ How to Visit a Museum *is Finn's latest book. It is an informal and rather personal text in which Finn gives his own feelings about museum-going. He has visited literally hundreds of museums around the world both as a tourist and as a photographer. When he began to work on the book, Finn realized, in talking with his friends, that almost everybody wanted to know how to get more out of going to a museum. He reported, "It seems that the uncertainty of what to do when one has passed through the portals of a museum is almost universal." In* How to Visit a Museum *Finn's goal was to present some thoughts that might help people feel more confident about themselves and more open to rewarding experiences during future museum visits.* ✦ *Because the nature of* How to Visit a Museum *is personal, though informative and useful, the* form in which David Finn presents his thoughts is one he must create for himself as he writes. He is not presenting a one-two-three book: do this, do this, do this. He is not giving rules or instructions. Therefore, the steps of "first you do this and then you do that" seen in many how-to pieces of writing don't apply here. How, then, is he to organize what he has to say? ✦ He organizes the writing by giving it the form of conversation. He offers friendly guidance and advice, based on his observations, but there is no "logical explanation" for why he talks about this first and then moves to talk about that next. Perhaps he is following the progression of someone's thoughts upon entering a museum. Perhaps he is able, based on his extensive experience, to know what someone visiting a museum is likely to experience as obstacles to enjoying the museum, and perhaps he even knows the order in which those are likely to occur. Whatever the source of his decision to discuss this point first and that point next, it is internal. The information and discussion he wants to impart do not contain within themselves a clear and definite order. He must create his own form. ✦ In this excerpt David Finn begins by offering reassurance: there is no right or wrong way to visit a museum. Then he talks about the overwhelming feeling one is likely to experience upon entering a museum. Where do you begin? His first piece of advice is to urge visitors to a museum to take a minute to get their bearings. Then Finn imagines the confusion most people feel: You are standing in the huge Egyptian gallery. What do you do? What do you think? Finn offers some types of questions you might ask yourself, some avenues of thought that he has found useful as he stood in front of a piece of art. He gives personal examples of conversations he has had with others and what these conversations made him think of as he looked at a sculpture. ✦ Next Finn moves to what is probably his most important point in this selection—most people's problems are from within—they worry too much, want to see everything, are afraid they'll never get back to that museum. Finn offers suggestions for combating these problems: Recognize there is only so much you can absorb on one museum visit. Stop your visit before you get bleary-eyed and overcharged. Lighten up;

relax; recognize there is some limit to your endurance. Finn then concludes this selection by reassuring the reader that appreciation of a piece of art is not connected with how much time you spend in front of it. Appreciation comes from looking hard at a piece of art and creating a deep response within oneself to what the artist has created. Appreciation comes from seeing, not looking. This can be done in a moment's time. ✦ *The created form of this piece of writing has a psychological order and an intentional order, determined solely by the writer. The psychological order is arranged according to what Finn thought would be the first questions and concerns a museum visitor would have. He addresses these in the order he is guessing or imagining they occur. The intentional order of the writing is determined by what David Finn wants to tell the reader, the advice and guidance he wishes to impart. He has certain principles or observations that his experience tells him make a difference in visiting a museum. He intends to make these points as he converses with the reader. So his intention-based-on-experience determines what points he includes. It is likely that the psychological order of the essay—imagining what thoughts occur in the museum-goer's mind and in what order—determined when David Finn related this principle or observation and when he related that one.* ✦

PHYL GARLAND

No More Blues

Back in the early sixties, when Diana Ross was working as a secretary at Motown, she used to pick up an extra $2.50 a session doing background singing behind Marvin Gaye and other artists at the Detroit record firm. The money came in handy, since she was earning only $20 a week. That was in the days when few people other than Motown's owner, Berry Gordy, thought she had any talent as a singer. Her voice was too sharp-edged and nasal for most tastes.

Taking Care of Business

Today this 41-year-old woman, who grew up in the projects of Detroit, controls her own multimillion-dollar corporation, Diana Ross Enterprises, while still managing to stay on the charts with her recordings—a remarkable feat of professional longevity. But superstardom in itself has not been enough. This determined singer-actress has become as shrewd with a balance sheet as she is with a music sheet—presiding over a network of recording, film and entertainment companies.

Diana Ross Productions oversees all her recording activities (including the albums she produces for release on the RCA label). Two music-publishing companies control the material she writes, and another handles her appearances. Anaid Film Productions develops movies, television specials and videos for her. (The firm is currently working on a film about the legendary Josephine Baker, which Ross will star in as well as produce.) Still another company is devoted to research on prospective cosmetics and fashion lines.

This lady is about taking care of business. And, as such, she has become the prototype for a new breed of Black women in the music business—a brutally tough field where fame can be both elusive and fleeting for those who do not seek to control their own affairs.

Ironically, it was Ross's portrayal of Billie Holiday that lifted her status from star to superstar and earned her an Oscar nomination for best actress. Ironic because Ross's professional life has been in such stark contrast to that of Holiday's and others of her musical predecessors who shaped the roots of Black music through generations of struggle, frustration and humiliation. They established the foundation on which the Diana Rosses have been able to build.

Ma Rainey's Blues

It was during the classic-blues period of the twenties that Black women first recorded their songs for wide distribution. The blues—song-stories about everything from wrongdoing womanizers and monumental hangovers to good sex, bad feet and every conceivable personal disaster—evolved from the chants, field hollers and work songs of slavery. In part it was the success of the first blues record, by Mamie Smith in 1920, that led early white record companies to scour the North and South, looking for women who could sing them. This led to the discovery of Gertrude Pridgett "Ma" Rainey, the first great female singer of the blues, who had been singing them in tent shows throughout the South since 1902.

The coming together of a great folk art and the commercial music industry usually benefited the industry more than the artist.

This was dramatized in a scene from August Wilson's current Broadway play, *Ma Rainey's Black Bottom*, in which Rainey, after a fracas with the police, arrives an hour late for a recording session, then petulantly insists that the producer fetch her some Coca-Cola before she'll sing one note. While the errand is being run, Ma tells one of her musicians that the whites—who record her songs for their own profit—treat her like little more than a whore and, once they have her voice on record, have no further regard for her as a human being. So prior to recording, she says: "They're gonna treat me the way I want no matter *how* much it hurt 'em."

The blues had begun to fade in popularity by 1928, and Rainey, who had recorded 92 records, returned to the southern tent-show circuit. Until her death in 1939, at the age of 53, she supported herself by operating two movie theaters that she owned in Rome, Georgia. This scenario summarizes the relationship the earlier Black female musician had with the producers, promoters and assorted hustlers on whom she had to depend. Shut out of all levels of control and exploited, she was a creature whose image was shaped by a history of hard times, raw deals and short change.

Victims of the Times

During the twenties the recordings of Bessie Smith sold so many copies that she was an important factor in saving the early Columbia Record Company from bankruptcy. Yet the Empress of the Blues did not have a royalty agreement and was paid only a flat fee for each session. In his research for the biography *Bessie*, Chris Albertson discovered old bookkeepers' records that showed Bessie Smith was paid a total of only $28,575 for the 160 recordings she made for Columbia, or little more than some contemporary artists receive for a single performance. And when the blues no longer sold so well, Columbia simply did not renew her contract. But like Ma Rainey, Smith was resourceful, making most of her money in traveling shows she often produced herself. At her peak she could command up to $2,000 a week, a considerable amount for those days, and she spent most of it supporting an unemployed, unfaithful husband and a host of ungrateful relatives.

The lore of Black music is spattered with such stories of illustrious victims. Smith, the most popular blues singer of all time, was pronounced dead at 42 in a Black hospital in Clarksdale, Mississippi, after a highway automobile accident that raised questions about whether her race had prevented her from getting prompt and proper medical treatment. Billie Holiday, the beautiful woman with the tear at the edge of her voice who influenced a generation of singers, was silenced at the age of 44 after being arrested on her death bed in a New York hospital for narcotics addiction. Dinah Washington, who was known as the Queen of the Blues but was actually the mother of modern rhythm and blues, died at the age of 39 after mixing too much booze with too many pills. And most recently, Esther Phillips, an R & B success since childhood, died last August in a California hospital at 48, her body ravaged by years of drug and alcohol abuse.

In his obituary on Phillips, Leonard Feather, the jazz chronicler, noted the dangers she faced in the music business. She had told him in a 1970 interview that she could identify with Judy Garland because she too had endured a childhood of "being underpaid and used by people. With her [Garland] it was a movie company; with me, it was record companies that sold millions of copies and just literally took your money," Phillips said.

Paving the Way

It is hard to think of any of these women as winners in anybody's game. Yet they were, in a strange kind of way. By the sheer force of their creative powers, they defied the constraints imposed on them to influence American musical tastes and to create a rich musical heritage. The legacy of Ma Rainey was carried on by her friend Bessie Smith, who was a major influence on Billie Holiday. In turn, Holiday's style is reflected in the work of Nina Simone and Abbey Lincoln (Aminata Moseka), major song stylists.

The blues continuum was most heavily felt in rhythm and blues. It resounded in Dinah Washington's work during the fifties and early sixties. She passed it on to Esther Phillips, who credited Washington with being her idol and friend—the person who showed her how to fix her hair and gave her her first designer gown to wear on-stage. And it was Washington who passed the mantle on to a young Aretha Franklin, the most important popular singer to emerge in the past 25 years. In 1968, when Aretha was riding the wave of phenomenal popular success as Lady Soul, I told her she was the new Queen of the Blues. She replied, in her usual understated drawl: "The Queen of the Blues was and still is Dinah Washington."

The pattern of pioneers paving the way for others also holds true for classical music. In 1939, the contralto Marian Anderson, said to have "a voice heard but once a century," was denied an opportunity to sing at Washington's Constitution Hall. Although a crowd of 75,000 came to hear her sing instead at the Lincoln Memorial, segregation limited her career. She was past her prime in 1955, when she became the first Black to sing at the Metropolitan Opera. But she opened the door for Leontyne Price, who reigned as the first Black prima donna of opera. Today, Price is one of the most honored women in the world, numbering among her trophies 19 Grammies and two Emmy awards.

Strategies for Longevity

But the lessons that the present generation of singers are learning aren't only musical ones. For them, the key to success lies in mapping personal strategies for not just short-term survival but longevity. For Patti LaBelle, longevity has meant diversification. She has undergone many transformations since the sixties, when she made her first hits with a Philadelphia "girl group" called The Bluebells, later renamed LaBelle. They wore long gowns and huge wigs, following the style set by Ross and the Supremes in a period that saw the first big breakthrough of Black rhythm and blues groups into the white crossover market. After LaBelle disbanded in 1976, Patti LaBelle concentrated on developing a broader-based career as a mature solo artist. Since then she has appeared on Broadway and on television as both a singer and an actress while continuing to make hit records. Last year she made her film debut in A *Soldier's Story*.

Valerie Simpson fits in snugly behind the scenes because that's where she began her career, more than 20 years ago, as a pianist and songwriter, collaborating with Nick Ashford, who later became her husband. They quickly established their reputation by writing "Let's Go Get Stoned" for Ray Charles and, as house writers at Motown, went on to conceive a host of R & B classics, including "Your Precious Love," "Ain't Nothing Like the Real Thing" and "Ain't No Mountain High Enough" for Marvin Gaye, Tammi Terrell and others.

It wasn't until 1971 that Simpson began to record on her own, producing two superb solo albums that remain collector's items. In 1973 the team of Ashford and Simpson finally established the extraordinary act that enables them to sell out the nation's largest entertainment emporiums whenever they perform. But Simpson, along with Ashford, has remained just as active behind the scenes, writing and producing for such artists as Quincy Jones, Gladys Knight & the Pips and Chaka Khan. Furthermore, they have maintained a separate career as creators of music for television commercials, a highly lucrative field in itself.

Chaka Khan, the woman who sings like she has seven lungs, initially attracted attention in 1974, when she was the voluptuous lead singer with the intergrated rock group Rufus. Since 1978 she steadily has built her reputation as a solo artist in the popular domain while experimenting with jazz, her first love. One of the few singers of her generation to tackle the demanding rhythmic and harmonic intricacies of jazz singing, she has recorded with such major artists as Dizzy Gillespie, Freddie Hubbard and Chick Corea. "If you ask Chaka what she'd like to do, she'd say she wants to sing jazz, which she does very well," says Bob Gibson, her publicist, "but the dollars aren't there. Any artist today wants to make it in the popular mainstream, even as compared with being in rhythm and blues."

A Number-Driven Industry

These strides toward popular acceptance are based on simple economics—there are far more whites than Blacks who buy records. To have a million-selling platinum record, an artist must cross over into that larger market; and more than anything, the record industry, a $4-billion-a-year enterprise, responds to numbers. The industry is a performer's lifeline, providing widespread exposure that will generate interest and guarantee choice bookings at top prices. International in nature and dominated by a few large firms that exercise a control that girdles the globe, the record industry has been able to provide mass acceptance of an artist all over the world instantaneously.

The success many Black female artists currently enjoy indicates that they're moving into a period of greater influence and acceptance in the music business, diversifying their activities and broadening their stylistic base to reach a larger share of the overall audience. Says Gibson, whose West Coast firm also handles The Pointer Sisters and Natalie Cole: "It's been a good year for women in music, and for Black women, it's been particularly good. Tina Turner, The Pointer Sisters and Chaka Khan all have had platinum records, meaning that they have attracted huge crossover followings."

At 46, the irrepressible Tina Turner exudes a sensuality and raw energy that might by the envy of her juniors. Back in the sixties and seventies, when she formed half the soul team of Ike and Tina Turner, she intoxicated British rockers as well as Black music lovers, belting out blues-flavored hits such as "Proud Mary" in an engagingly husky voice. Though others might have shared the stage, it was impossible to watch anyone but Tina Turner as she pranced about, thrashing her thighs, executing complex dance steps with the Ikettes at breakneck tempo in killer high heels and hip-high skirts.

After leaving Ike in 1976, Tina went into a state of semieclipse but burst back onto the record charts last year with the Grammy award-winning single "What's Love Got to Do With It," a spin-off from her best-selling, critically acclaimed album *Private Dancer*. Phoenixlike, she has risen from the ashes of her old career to be cast in a new setting, this time produced by British rockers favoring synthesized high-tech effects and an acid-edged sound. The result has been renewed interest on the part of her old fans while teens of all races, from Memphis to Melbourne, Australia, embrace her as a new discovery.

Produce Your Own

Massive exposure can make a performer into a star overnight, but there is a price to be paid. The desire to produce hits or to duplicate a currently "hot" sound can crush one's individualism, destroying that special distinctiveness that attracted the public in the first place. One way artists attempt to protect themselves is to move toward producing their own records, so they'll have the right to determine the material to be recorded and how it will sound.

This is what motivated Deniece Williams, a former nursing student and gospel singer who started out as a backup singer with Stevie Wonder's group Wonderlove back in 1971. A successful solo artist since 1976, she has coproduced two gold albums and produced several hits on the CBS label in recent years. "I got into the production side," she says, "because I wanted to ensure my longevity in the industry by retaining uniqueness in my sound and presentation."

Over the past two years Williams has also served as her own manager. To prepare herself, she enrolled in courses in accounting and business management at UCLA "to help me count my own money." She says it's not easy to manage yourself, "especially if you're a woman," because promoters and agencies have a difficult time dealing directly with you. In recent months she has acquired a manager to free up more of her time for her new Christian Production Company, which will produce gospel records.

Meanwhile, Williams will continue to record secular material for CBS and has negotiated a new contract that will grant her the freedom to record religious music on her own. But her management experience has been valuable. "It has given me insight into what a manager should be doing for the artist," she observes. She urges other musicians to learn more about backstage business. "They need to know not only how to make money but how to make that money make *more* money for them," she says.

Still, even the most successful artists are dependent in some way on the record industry—even Diana Ross. Is there not some way to get around this formidable establishment? At least one Black woman has found a way to do so while functioning at the very highest creative level. She might well be the most independent woman in the music business.

Freedom Is Power

Betty Carter, 54, is part of a pantheon of jazz singers that includes Ella Fitzgerald, Sarah Vaughan and Carmen McRae, among living artists. This year she will be celebrating 35 years in the business. But jazz, like its individual creators, has been a victim of commercial tides in the music industry. "I had the foresight to realize that record companies were not going to get behind jazz artists to promote them or record them except for a few they thought might make them some money real fast," she says.

Since 1969 Betty Carter has released four albums on her own BetCar Records label, handling the whole process herself. This way she maintains absolute control. She has offices in Chicago, San Francisco and New York and distributes overseas as well. She says she can sell 20,000 copies of an album in a year, which compares favorably with the sales of jazz records by name artists on major labels. Both her last two albums, The Audience With Betty Carter and Whatever Happened to Love?, were nominated for Grammies, which made her the first independent jazz producer so honored. When Carter performs, she usually produces her own shows, and her level of public recognition and critical acclaim are at peak.

About the different presidents of the major record companies, Carter says, "If they come to you, then you are in a position to tell them what you want them to do, but if you go to them, they can tell *you* what they want you to do. I wasn't *about* to have anyone tell me what to do, so it was a standoff, in a sense. And they don't want no woman telling them what to do, especially a Black woman."

Stressing the need to be independent, she said her inspiration was Gladys Hampton, the late wife of vibraphonist Lionel Hampton, whom she met at the beginning of her career when she sang with his band and was known as Betty Bebop. "I wanted to be with Dizzy Gillespie then," she recalls, "because his was the hippest band, but Lionel Hampton's was the better-run band. It was controlled and organized by Gladys Hampton. She was my role model. I looked at her and watched her manage the band and keep a bunch of musicians working. It was wonderful for me to see a Black woman doing this way back in the mid-forties. And look at Hamp now. He's not hurting for anything. It's because of the wise moves Gladys made at an early age."

Carter, asked if she thinks she has attained any sort of power in the music business, ponders the matter for a moment then says, "*Power*—that's a mean word!" She defines it her own way: "My power comes in when I'm dealing with these young kids. I have a trio with three young musicians in their early twenties, and they're not much older than my two sons. I'll take the chances, so this means these young musicians have to take the chances too. And I have freedom. It's really wonderful to have this kind of freedom, because people feel it when they see you and they can feel free too."

And maybe that's what power is all about.

Elizabeth Neeld *Comments:*

> ✦ *Phyl Garland has been writing about Black music for more than twenty years and is the author of* The Sound of Soul. *She is an associate professor at the Columbia University Graduate School of Journalism and is a frequent contributor to several magazines. In this essay, published in 1985, Phyl Garland compares the status and success of today's black women singers with the status and success of yesterday's. She does not, however, merely use the traditional form of comparison/contrast to structure the essay. Instead, she creates her own form.* ✦ *The created form of*

this essay begins with an anecdote about Diana Ross, something the author could be fairly certain would engage the reader's attention. This anecdote does in miniature what the essay as a whole accomplishes: it compares and contrasts Diana Ross's past, when she was singing background for Marvin Gaye, with her present, in which she controls her own multimillion-dollar operation. This change of affairs, represented by Diana Ross, is the thesis Garland will give evidence for in the rest of the essay.
✦ *Following the Diana Ross example that sets up the whole essay, the author then begins her discussion of Black women singers of the twenties, thirties, forties, and fifties—Mamie Smith, Ma Rainey, Bessie Smith, Billie Holiday, Dinah Washington, and Marian Anderson. Garland relates stories of the hard times of these Black women singers "who shaped the roots of Black music through generations of struggle, frustration, and humiliation."* ✦ *Following the paragraphs that describe the history of Black women singers, the author deftly moves into the modern era. She shows how Dinah Washington's mantle fell on Aretha Franklin and how Marian Anderson set the stage for Leontyne Price. Following this transition from past to present singers, Garland begins to make clear the main point of her essay: that the key to success for modern Black women singers is to map personal strategies for longevity, rather than short-term survival. The author uses Patti LaBelle as her first example, followed by a discussion of several other Black women singers now thriving in the music industry. She says that the success of many Black female artists gives them greater influence and acceptance in the music business; Tina Turner is her example here. After discussing other singers, Garland concludes that Black women have more freedom now, and suggests that perhaps this is what power is all about.* ✦ *What is interesting to note is that Garland creates an assertion inside a comparison/contrast format. She does not settle for just comparing Black women singers of earlier times with Black women singers today. This kind of A/B or A + B traditional form would have been a boring approach for this essay and would not have allowed the author to make the point she wanted to make. She was not interested merely in showing how to-*

day's Black women singers are different. She also wanted to make a point about that difference; she wanted to discuss the implications of that difference. And this makes for much more interesting reading. This created form required Garland to put more on the line, as a writer, of course; she couldn't just gather her facts and organize them into two categories: "classic Black women singers were like this" and "modern Black women singers are like that." Instead, she chose to comment on the differences she saw. And this leaves us with much more to think about. ✦ There is personality in this created form. There's spark. The writer has taken traditional thought patterns—comparison/contrast and examples—and to these has added her own presence in the essay. This gives us an original piece of work. ✦

WOODRUFF T. SULLIVAN III

Our Endangered Night Skies

Viewed by day from hundreds of miles in space, our planet shows no clear signs of intelligent life. But at night the scene changes as lights from cities and campfires alike trace the the activities of billions of people across the globe.

For the astronomer, all of this human activity has created a grave situation. Even the slightest contamination from city lights can be disastrous when observing faint astronomical objects. With the amount of "light pollution" ever growing, observatories face severe limitations on the types of projects they can undertake. Only by fighting to stem the polluting tide through regulation—local, federal, and international—can we hope to continue observing the universe from the surface of our planet.

Nightwatch From Space

Nighttime views are obtained by the Air Force's Defense Meteorological Satellite Program. The DMSP craft were designed to provide global weather coverage on a daily basis. These spacecraft travel in nearly polar orbits 800 kilometers up, scrutinizing the terrain at visual and infrared wavelengths. Every 0.4 second each satellite scans a 3,000-by-3-km swath on the ground using a 5-inch telescope. Successive scans are built up to produce an image.

A DMSP telescope can detect about the same amount of light that a ground-based observer sees on a dark night from all the sky's sources combined (primarily the Milky Way and zodiacal light, but excluding moonlight). Consequently, the lights of Earth fall within easy reach of the satellites. (For those interested in specifics, the DMSP telescope can detect about four 10-millionths of a watt per square meter per steradian over its bandwidth from 4500 to 7500 angstroms.)

What do the DMSP images reveal of the Earth at night? As expected, a large fraction of the light leakage to space corresponds to heavily urbanized regions. Metallic-vapor lamps used in streetlights emit a large fraction of their energy at visible wavelengths, and only 50 watts of energy need escape upward from a streetlamp for it to register in DMSP data.

A closer look reveals many other sources apart from cities. The most prominent of these are auroras, and geophysicists have made extensive use of satellite imagery in their studies of this phenomenon. Thomas Croft, of Technology for Communications International, has analyzed DMSP images in great detail for natural light sources. He finds that contributions also arise from high-altitude airglow, reflected moonlight, lightening, forest fires, and even erupting volcanoes.

Human activity gives rise to a number of light sources. Surprisingly, many controlled fires in the tropics show up (the results of cooking and heating fires, slash-and-burn agriculture, and widespread clearing of forests). While the exact number of these at any given location depends on the season, the yearly average is high. In the images shown here, they are prominent throughout Southeast Asia, southern India, and to a lesser extent just south of the Sahara desert in the African savanna.

In many of the world's oil fields, the burn-off of unwanted natural gas, which comes up with the oil in a frothy mixture, is another light source. Look for flares in Indonesia, the Persian Gulf states, the Tashkent region of the Soviet Union, Libya, Algeria, northeastern South America, and in the Canadian province of Alberta.

Japanese and Korean squid fishermen regularly use hundreds of megawatts of lights, strung along the decks of their boats, to lure squid to the surface. When the fleets are out squidding, the Sea of Japan appears as bright as Japan itself!

Of all these nighttime beacons, the ones of most concern to the astronomer are electric lights. Their extent corresponds strikingly to the high-income population centers of the world. For example, lighting has severely handicapped professional astronomy in almost all of the eastern United States, western Europe, and Japan. Not only city skies are affected. Even away from urban areas, observers are suffering.

The Radio Earth

While optical astronomers battle the onslaught of light pollution, their radio counterparts curse interference from the world's transmitters. Most troublesome are those used for communications and radar, since their beams often stray into the reception patterns of radio telescope antennas. Fortunately, the radio spectrum is carefully managed by international and national agencies. This has allowed astronomers to gain exclusive rights to certain bands of frequencies so that, in principle, they can use these bands with little interference. In reality, however, the situation is not so rosy.

For example, a satellite transmitting to its ground station need only emit one-millionth of its power at a frequency reserved for astronomy to render a modest-sized telescope useless. It would be similar to an optical observer working at midnight suddenly seeing the sky brighten to the level of twilight! Besides satellites, other common causes of radio-frequency interference are aviation, weather and military radars, radio and television broadcasts, industrial activities (such as welding), and even automobile engines. Unlike the optical case, there are no natural radio emissions in competition with artificial noise.

Our civilization's radio noise, aside from the hardships it brings to astronomers, announces our presence in the universe to whatever instruments might be listening. Imagine yourself on a planet circulating another star, tens or hundreds of light-years from the Sun. At such distances the Sun would appear as just another star and would overwhelm the feeble light from Earth. But in certain narrow bands of radio frequency the Earth far outshines the Sun and can be detected at great distances with equipment at our level of technology.

If on your hypothetical planet you had access to a 1,000-foot radio antenna like that at Arecibo, the strongest military radars— those of our Ballistic Missile Early Warning System (BMEWS)— would be within range at a distance of about 25 light-years. If you had an array of 1,000 100-meter-diameter dishes, on the other hand, you could eavesdrop on Earth as far away as 250 light-years. On this basis a million stars are within the "sphere of detectability" of the radio Earth, though the strongest signals, which first left our planet some 25 years ago, have only begun to fill that sphere.

Television transmitters are second on the list of radio leaks to space (with about one-hundredth the power of the military radars). A map of the world's television transmitters resembles somewhat the view of nighttime Earth—activity is strongly concentrated in heavily populated, high-income regions. With most of its radio emissions clumped into narrow ranges of longitude, the spinning Earth sweeps over the heavens like an interstellar radio lighthouse.

What We Have Lost

Electromagnetic pollution is clearly a serious problem for the modern astronomer. Its menace is increasing every day. Observatories must now be located not only where natural conditions are ideal, but where people are absent as well. If anything like the present rate of growth continues, it seems certain that astronomy will eventually be forced into space, where the expense for comparable capabilities may be a hundred times greater. Future astronomy will face tremendous difficulties.

Light pollution's greatest damage to our global culture, however, has already arrived. It is sad to note that hundreds of millions of people, perhaps even a majority of the inhabitants of North America and Europe, are now regularly denied the nighttime universe. Meteors shooting across the sky and the resplendent band of the Milky Way are among the wonders they have lost. At a time when our species desperately needs a continual nightly vision, we have instead wrapped the Earth in an electromagnetic fog.

Elizabeth Neeld Comments:

✦ *Woodruff Sullivan, a professor at the University of Washington, is an astronomer who is writing about a serious but unusual problem: light and noise pollution that hinders scientists in their study of the heavens. The created form of this essay is problem/solution, and the emphasis here is on the problem. The organization of the essay, therefore, follows Sullivan's presentation of the problem of light and noise pollution. The way he decided to lay out the problem determines the form of the essay; the form, then, is inherent in the author's intention and purpose, not in his subject matter.* ✦ *Sullivan begins by letting the readers know what his subject is—pollution of the skies. Then he gives information on how light pollution is noticed and measured, explaining how scientists know that light pollution is increasing. Sullivan is able to establish his own credibility by giving information early in the essay that shows how he knows what he is talking about. Later, his credibility will strengthen our confidence in his delineation of the problem.* ✦ *The author next discusses what causes the problem of light pollution—streetlights, auroras, reflected moonlight, lightning, forest fires, and even erupting volcanoes. These non-human sources of light pollution are followed by a discussion of human sources—cooking and heating fires, slash-and-burn agriculture, clearing of forests, burn-off from oil fields, flares, fishing lights, and electric lights. In determining the order he would put these sources of light pollution in, Sullivan made a personal choice. There was nothing inherent in the information that said he should talk about non-human sources of light pollution first and then human sources. As the writer, he just made a choice. This—and all other choices made throughout the essay—determine the created form the essay takes, a form determined by Sullivan as he wrote.* ✦ *A new subject—radio interference— begins next. Since the title of the essay is "Our Endangered Skies," the writer is able to include more than one thing that constitutes the problem of sky pollution. He talks in this section of the essay about noise pollution— interference from transmitters, satellites, weather radar,* television broadcasts, welding, and even automobile engines, among others. He then talks about the problem this noise causes for astronomers and speculates on how this noise "announces our presence in the universe" to whoever or whatever might be listening. ✦ Sullivan concludes his essay with a short discussion of the implications of this serious problem of light and noise pollution in the skies. He says that if things continue as they are going, astronomers will be forced to go into space to do their study, where the expense will be hundreds of times greater. Already, Sullivan says, all of us have lost something very precious—the ability to see our nighttime universe. We have wrapped ourselves in an electromagnetic fog. ✦ This problem/solution created form, here concentrating on a problem, illustrates the way a writer's intention and purpose rather than the content of the information itself shape the essay. The information Sullivan had could have been put in any number of configurations, shapes, order, and form. His purpose determined what he included and his execution of personal options and choices created the form of what he wrote. ✦

GAR ALPEROVITZ

Hiroshima Remembered: The U.S. Was Wrong

Though it has not yet received broad public attention, there exists overwhelming historical evidence that President Harry S. Truman knew he could almost certainly end World War II without using the atomic bomb: The United States had cracked the Japanese code, and a stream of documents released over the last 40 years show that Mr. Truman had two other options.

The first option was to clarify America's surrender terms to assure the Japanese we would not remove their Emperor. The second was simply to await the expected Soviet declaration of war—which, United States intelligence advised, appeared likely to end the conflict on its own.

Instead, Hiroshima was bombed Aug. 6, 1945, and Nagasaki on Aug. 9. The planned date for the Soviet Union's entry into the war against Japan was Aug. 8.

Turning Point

The big turning point was the Emperor's continuing June-July decision to open surrender negotiations through Moscow. Top American officials—and, most critically, the President—understood the move was extraordinary: Mr. Truman's secret diaries, lost until 1978, call the key intercepted message "the telegram from Jap Emperor asking for peace."

Other documents—among them newly discovered secret memorandums from William J. Donovan, director of the Office of Strategic Services—show that Mr. Truman was personally advised of Japanese peace initiatives through Swiss and Portuguese channels as early as three months before Hiroshima. Moreover, Mr. Truman told several officials he had no objection in principle to Japan's keeping the Emperor, which seemed the only sticking point.

American leaders were sure that if he so chose "the Mikado could stop the war with a royal word"—as one top Presidential aide put it. Having decided to use the bomb, however, Mr. Truman was urged by Secretary of State James F. Byrnes not to give assurances to the Emperor before the weapon had been demonstrated.

Additional official records, including minutes of top-level White House planning meetings, show the President was clearly advised of the importance of a Soviet declaration of war: It would pull the rug out from under Japanese military leaders who were desperately hoping the powerful Red Army would stay neutral.

Gen. George C. Marshall in mid-June told Mr. Truman that "the impact of Russian entry on the already hopeless Japanese may well be the decisive action levering them into capitulation at that time or shortly thereafter if we land."

A month later, the American-British Combined Intelligence Staffs advised their chiefs of the critical importance of a Red Army attack. As the top British general, Sir Hastings Ismay, summarized the conclusions for Prime Minister Winston Churchill: "If and when Russia came into the war against Japan, the Japanese would probably wish to get out on almost any terms short of the dethronement of the Emperor."

Mr. Truman's private diaries also record his understanding of the significance of this option. On July 17, 1945, when Stalin confirmed that the Red Army would march, Mr. Truman privately noted: "Fini Japs when that comes about."

Eisenhower Appalled, Leahy Shocked

There was plenty of time: The American invasion of Japan was not scheduled until the spring of 1946. Even a preliminary landing on the island Kyushu was still three months in the future.

Gen. Dwight D. Eisenhower, appalled that the bomb would be used in these circumstances, urged Mr. Truman and Secretary of War Henry L. Stimson not to drop it. In his memoirs, he observed that weeks before Hiroshima, Japan had been seeking a way to surrender. "It wasn't necessary," he said in a later interview, "to hit them with that awful thing."

The man who presided over the Joint Chiefs of Staff, Adm. William D. Leahy, was equally shocked: "The use of this barbarous weapon at Hiroshima and Nagasaki was of no material assistance in our war against Japan. The Japanese were already defeated and ready to surrender."

A Bomb to Manage Russia

Why, then, was the bomb used?

American leaders rejected the most obvious option—simply waiting for the Red Army attack—out of political, not military, concerns.

As the diary of one official put it, they wanted to end the war before Moscow got "in so much on the kill." Secretary of the Navy James V. Forrestal's diaries record that Mr. Byrnes "was most anxious to get the Japanese affair over with before the Russians got in."

United States leaders had also begun to think of the atomic bomb as what Secretary Stimson termed the "master card" of diplomacy. President Truman postponed his Potsdam meeting with Stalin until July 17, 1945—one day after the first successful nuclear test—to be sure the atomic bomb would strengthen his hand before confronting the Soviet leader on the shape of a postwar settlement.

To this day, we do not know with absolute certainty Mr. Truman's personal attitudes on several key issues. Yet we do know that his most important adviser, Secretary of State Byrnes, was convinced that dropping the bomb would serve crucial long-range diplomatic purposes.

As one atomic scientist, Leo Szilard, observed: "Mr. Byrnes did not argue that it was necessary to use the bomb against the cities of Japan in order to win the war. Mr. Byrnes' . . . view [was] that our possessing and demonstrating the bomb would make Russia more manageable."

JOHN CONNOR

Hiroshima Remembered: The U.S. Was Right

Forty years ago this week in Hiroshima: the dreadful flash, the wrist watches fused forever at 8:16 A.M. The question still persists: Should we have dropped the atomic bomb?

History seldom gives decisive answers, but recently declassified documents point to a clear judgment: Yes, it was necessary to drop the bomb. It was needed to end the war. It saved countless American and Japanese lives.

Surrender: Worse Than Death

In the early summer of 1945, Japan, under tight control of the militarists, was an implacable, relentless adversary. The Japanese defended territory with a philosophy we had seldom encountered: Soldiers were taught that surrender was worse than death. There was savage resistance to the end in battle after battle.

Of the 5,000-man Japanese force at Tarawa in November 1943, only 17 remained alive when the island was taken. When Kwajalein was invaded in February 1944, Japanese officers slashed at American tanks with samurai swords; their men held grenades against the sides of tanks in an effort to disable them.

On Saipan, less than 1,000 of the 32,000 defending Japanese troops survived. Casualties among the Japanese-ruled civilians on the island numbered 10,000. Parents bashed their babies' brains out on rocky cliff sides, then leaped to their deaths. Others cut each other's throats; children threw grenades at each other. America suffered 17,000 casualties.

Just 660 miles southeast of Tokyo, Iwo Jima's garrison was told to defend the island as if it were Tokyo itself. They did. In the first day of fighting, there were more American casualties than during "D-Day" in Normandy. At Okinawa—only 350 miles south of Kyushu—more than 110,000 Japanese soldiers and 100,000 civilians were killed. Kamikaze attacks cost the Navy alone some 10,000 casualties. The Army and Marines lost more than 50,000 men.

Desire for Peace Irrelevant

In the early summer of 1945, the invasion of Japan was imminent and everyone in the Pacific was apprehensive. The apprehension was justified, because our intelligence was good: With a system code-named "Magic," it had penetrated Japanese codes even before Pearl Harbor. "Magic" would play a crucial role in the closing days of the war.

Many have maintained that the bomb was unnecessary because in the closing days of the war intercepted Japanese diplomatic messages disclosed a passionate desire for peace. While that is true, it is irrelevant. The Japanese Government remained in the hands of the militarists: *Their* messages indicated a willingness to fight to the death.

Japanese planes, gasoline and ammunition had been hoarded for the coming invasion. More than 5,000 aircraft had been hidden everywhere to be used as suicide weapons, with only enough gas in their tanks for a one-way trip to the invasion beaches. More than two million men were moving into positions to defend the home islands.

The object was to inflict such appalling losses that the Americans would agree to a treaty more favorable than unconditional surrender. The Army Chief of Staff, Gen. George C. Marshall, estimated potential American casualties as high as a million.

The willingness of the Japanese to die was more than empty bravado. Several of my colleagues at Kyushu University told me that as boys of 14 or 15, they were being trained to meet the Americans on the beaches with little more than sharpened bamboo spears. They had no illusions about their chances for survival.

Shadow Casting

The Potsdam declaration calling for unconditional surrender was beamed to Japan on July 27. On July 30, the Americans were informed that Japan would officially ignore the ultimatum. A week later, the bomb was dropped.

Could we not have warned the Japanese in advance, critics asked, and dropped a demonstration bomb? That alternative was vetoed on the grounds the bomb might not work, or that the plane carrying it might be shot down. Moreover, it is questionable how effective a demonstration bomb might have been. The militarists could have imposed a news blackout as complete as the one imposed after the disastrous battle of Midway and continued on their suicidal course. That is exactly what happened at Hiroshima. Within hours, the Japanese Government sent in a team of scientists to investigate the damage. Their report was immediately suppressed and was not made public until many years after the war.

After midnight on Aug. 10, a protracted debate took place in an air-raid shelter deep inside the Imperial Palace. The military insisted that Japan should hold out for terms far better than unconditional surrender. The peace faction favored accepting the Potsdam declaration, providing that the Emperor would be retained. The two factions remained at an impasse. At 2 A.M., Prime Minister Kantaro Suzuki asked the Emperor to decide. In a soft, deliberate voice, the Emperor expressed his great longing for peace. The war had ended.

It was impossible, in August 1945, to predict the awesome shadow the bomb would cast on humanity. The decision to drop it seemed both simple and obvious. Without it, the militarists might have prevailed, an invasion ordered. And the loss of both American and Japanese lives would have been awesome.

The atomic bomb accomplished what it had been designed to do. It ended the war.

Elizabeth Neeld Comments:

✦ *On August 6, 1945, the United States of America dropped an atomic bomb on the city of Hiroshima in Japan. On August 4, 1985, the* New York Times *published these two essays: Gar Alperovitz asserting the United States was wrong to drop the bomb and John Connor asserting the United States was right. Each of these writers uses a created form to organize and present his argument.* ✦ *Let's look at the form of Alperovitz's essay first. The main claim of the argument appears in the opening paragraph: there is historical evidence that President Truman knew he could end the war without using the bomb and that he had two options that would allow him to accomplish this. This claim is one of fact. Claims of fact use statistics, examples, testimony, or other empirical evidence to prove the case. To be convincing, the data must be applicable to the argument and there must be enough of it to convince the reader. Also, any authorities referred to must be reputable and creditable to the reader.* ✦ *Alperovitz sets out to prove his claim of fact by providing concrete evidence. He quotes President Truman's secret diaries, which had been lost until 1978. He refers to other documents, including newly discovered secret memorandums from William J. Donovan, director of the Office of Strategic Services. He refers to conversations Truman had with several officials in government and to official records, including minutes of top-level White House planning meetings. He quotes Eisenhower and William Leahy, who presided over the Joint Chiefs of Staff.* ✦ *After offering this evidence that Truman did have other options and did not have to drop the bomb to end the war, Alperovitz suggests why Truman went ahead and ordered the bomb dropped. Again, he quotes an official's secret diary and the diary of Secretary of the Navy James Forrestal to provide evidence that the bomb was dropped for diplomatic purposes, not to end the war.* ✦ *Alperovitz is using what are referred to as* warrants of authority *in presenting the kinds of evidence he does. He believes that the reader will accept diary entries by chief participants in the decision, minutes and records of meetings, and other historical documents. If readers are not willing to accept these as warrants of authority, Alperovitz, of course, has already lost his claim.* ✦ *The explanation of why Truman did drop the bomb is more speculative than the argument that Truman had two options other than dropping the bomb. Here Alperovitz must interpret rather than amass evidence. He "puts two plus two together," as he sees the situation, and offers an explanation for why Truman went ahead and dropped the bomb. The reader must also decide in this case how much to credit the warrants of authority that Alperovitz provides and how much credibility to give to Alperovitz himself, who is a historian and political economist and the author of* Atomic Diplomacy: Hiroshima and Potsdam. ✦ *Let's look now at the opposing essay. John Connor is a professor of anthropology at California State University in Sacramento. He was attached to General Douglas MacArthur's headquarters in Tokyo in 1949 and 1950. He argues in his essay that the United States was right to drop the bomb. And he uses other kinds of warrants to support his claim. Connor asserts that by dropping the bomb Truman saved countless American and Japanese lives. Then he supplies the warrants to support his claim. The first warrant Connor provides is a kind of warrant called a* sign. *In using a sign as a warrant, a writer gives facts that he or she argues indicated a particular condition. The facts Connor provides are that the Japanese were "an implacable, relentless adversary." He cites a previous battle where only seventeen Japanese soldiers out of five thousand remained alive, illustrating the "savage resistance" the Japanese would put forth in battle. He quotes other statistics of battles when Japanese casualties were enormously high, showing that to the Japanese, surrender was worse than death. Connor's use of this data is as a "sign." If the Japanese had done this in the past, they certainly were going to do it again. The past was an indicator, for Connor, of a condition that would be true again.* ✦ *Connor also uses a particular kind of language to make his point. "Parents bashed their babies' brains out on the rocky cliff sides . . . . Others cut each other's throats; children threw grenades at each other." This vivid and emotive language is used to support Connor's claim.* ✦ *Connor's conclusion is an induction. If these facts are true, if the Japanese have done these atrocities in the past, if the government remained in the hands of the militarists regardless of what the Emperor and other politicians were saying about wanting peace, then Truman had to drop the bomb. Connor uses statistics to show how ready the Japanese were to fight: five thousand aircraft had been hidden all over to be used for suicide flights, two million men were moving into place to defend the home islands, young boys had been trained to fight on the beaches with only sharpened bamboo spears.* ✦ *Connor makes his final point of induction (a generalized conclusion based on observation of particular circumstances) at the end of the essay. He says that without the bomb, "the militarists might have prevailed, an invasion ordered. And the loss of both American and Japanese lives would have been awesome." The word* might *must carry the full weight of John Connor's argument.* ✦

BETTY FRIEDAN

How to Get the Women's Movement Moving Again

This is addressed to any woman who has ever said "we" about the women's movement, including those who say, "I'm not a feminist, but. . . ." And it's addressed to quite a few men.

It's a personal message, not at all objective, and it's in response to those who think our modern women's movement is over—either because it is defeated and a failure, or because it has triumphed, its work done, its mission accomplished. After all, any daughter can now dream of being an astronaut, after Sally Ride, or running for President, after Geraldine Ferraro.

I do not think that the job of the modern women's movement is done. And I do not believe the movement has failed. . . .

I do believe, though, that the movement is in trouble. I was too passionately involved in its conception, its birth, its growing pains, its youthful flowering, to acquiesce quietly to its going gently so soon into the night. But, like a lot of other mothers, I have been denying the symptoms of what I now feel forced to confront as a profound paralysis of the women's movement in America. And this, in turn, has forced me to think about how we can get the women's movement moving again—a new round of conscious-ness-raising, for instance, or utilizing the networks of professional women, or ceasing the obsession with the matter of pornography.

I see as symptoms of the paralysis the impotence in the face of fundamentalist backlash; the wasting of energy in internal power struggles when no real issues are at stake; the nostalgic harking back to old rhetoric, old ideas, old modes of action instead of confronting new threats and new problems with new thinking; the failure to mobilize the young generation who take for granted the rights we won and who do not defend those rights as they are being taken away in front of our eyes, and the preoccupation with pornography and other sexual diversions that do not affect most women's lives. I sense an unwillingness to deal with the complex realities of female survival in male-modeled careers, with the new illusions of having it all in marriage and equality in divorce, and with the basic causes of the grim feminization of poverty. The po-tential of women's political power is slipping away between the poles of self-serving feminist illusion and male and female oppor-tunism. The promise of that empowerment of women that enabled so many of us to change our own lives is being betrayed by our failure to mobilize the next generation to move beyond us. . . .

In Nairobi

Aware of these symptoms, and yet denying my own sense that the American women's movement was over, not ready to admit defeat but wanting to move on to other things myself, I went to Kenya last summer out of a sheer sense of historic duty. . . .

Most card-carrying American feminists were not even bother-ing with the meeting in Nairobi. NOW had scheduled its own con-vention in New Orleans at the same time as the United Nations World Conference of Women.

Ten years earlier, when the modern women's movement was spreading from America to the world, I had joined women wanting to organize in their countries in appealing to the U.N. to call a world assembly of women. At the first two world women's meetings, in Mexico in 1975 and Copenhagen in 1980, I had seen the beginnings of international networking among women broken up by organized disrupters led by armed gunmen shouting slogans against "imperialism" and "Zionism." I had been appalled at the way the official male delegates from Arab countries and other third-world and Communist nations that control the U.N. showed contempt for women's rights, using those conferences mainly to launch a new doctrine of religious and ethnic hate, equating Zionism and racism. And I had been repelled by the way the delegates from Western countries, mostly male officials or their wives and female flunkies, let them thereby rob those conferences of the moral and political weight they might have given to the advance of women worldwide. This year, the United States delegation had instructions from President Reagan to walk out if the question of Zionism was included in the conclusions reached at Nairobi.

To my amazement, the women's movement emerged in Nairobi with sufficient strength worldwide to impose its own agenda of women's concerns over the male political agenda that had divided it before. Despite, or because of, the backlash and other problems they face at home, nearly 17,000 women from 159 nations assembled, some 14,000 having paid their own way or been sent by volunteer, church or women's groups to the unofficial forum that is part of every such U.N. conference. Some traveled by plane three and four days, or by bus from African villages.

There was a bypassing, or bridging, of the old, abstract ideological conflicts that had seemed to divide women before—a moving beyond the old rhetoric of career versus family, equality versus development, feminism versus socialism, religion versus feminism, or feminism as an imperialist capitalist arrogance irrelevant to poor third-world women. What took the place of all this was a discussion of concrete strategies for women to acquire more control of their lives. Third-world revolutionaries, Arab and Israeli women, as well as Japanese, Greeks and Latins, gathered under a baobab tree where, every day at noon, like some African tribal elder, I led a discussion on "Future Directions of Feminism."

We shared common concerns about how to move ahead and earn a living in man's world—as women, even in African villages, now have to do—without losing, even using, one's best values and strengths as women. We talked about how to keep forging ahead as women when other questions—like the Israeli-Arab conflict or the superpowers' nuclear-arms race—are preoccupying our nations and using up their resources. We shared ideas on how to keep advancing, even underground, when fundamentalist groups try to take away a woman's right to control her own body or to move independently in the world, as they are doing in Egypt and the Unites States and have done in Iran.

When the black-veiled Iranian women, in their chadors and with their armed male guards, occupied my tree one day, we moved to another, and when they occupied both trees, we carried on our dialogue in the sun. "That's the way women have to move now everywhere in the world," I said. "We go forward, we get pushed back, we regroup. It's not a win-lose battle, to be finished in any year." "And we don't waste energy on nonessentials," said an African teacher. . . .

I and other Americans—as many black as white among the 2,000 of us at Nairobi—went home strengthened, resolved not to accept backward-nation status for American women. For though we had gone to Nairobi subdued by our own setbacks and sophisticated enough not to offer Western feminism as the answer to the problems of women of the third world, it was truly humiliating to discover that we are no longer the cutting edge of modern feminism or world progress toward equality. Even Kenya has an equal rights clause in its Constitution!

Jump-Starting the Movement

How can we let the women's movement die out here in America when what we began is taking hold now all over the world? I would like to suggest 10 things that might be done to break the blocks that seem to have stymied the women's movement in America:

1. *Begin a new round of consciousness-raising for the new generation.* These women, each thinking she is alone with her personal guilt and pressures, trying to "have it all," having second thoughts about her professional career, desperately trying to have a baby before it is too late, with or without husband, and maybe secretly blaming the movement for getting her into this mess, are almost as isolated, and as powerless in their isolation, as those suburban housewives afflicted by "the problem that had no name" whom I interviewed for "The Feminine Mystique" over 20 years ago. Those women put a name to their problem; they got together with other women in the new feminist groups and began to work for political solutions and began to change their lives.

That has to happen again to free a new generation of women from its new double burden of guilt and isolation. . . .

Putting new names to their problems, they might stop feeling guilty for not being able to conduct their professional lives just like men, might give each other support in new patterns of professional advance and parenting, might together demand new political solutions of parental leave and child care from company or profession or community, or even, once again, from government. They might, then, find new energy to save the rights they now take for granted or even secretly resent, because they are so hard to live with.

2. *Mobilize the new professional networks and the old established volunteer organizations to save women's rights.* We can't fight fundamentalist backlash with backward-looking feminist fundamentalism. Second-stage feminism is itself pluralistic, and has to use new pluralist strengths and strategies. The women who have been 30 and 40 percent of the graduating class from law school or business school and 47 percent of the journalism school classes, the ones who've taken women's studies, the women who grew up playing Little League baseball and cheered on those new champion women athletes, the new professional networks of women in every field, every woman who has been looking to those networks only to get ahead in her own field, must now use her professional skills to save the laws and executive orders against sex discrimination in education and employment. They must restore the enforcement machinery and the class-action suits that opened up all these opportunities to her in the first place.

The volunteer organizations, it became clear in Nairobi, have been given new goals and gumption and professional expertise by the women's movement. Let NOW heal its internal wounds and join with these other groups, as it did in the E.R.A. struggle, to face the current emergency, rather than indulge in wishful thinking about refighting the E.R.A. battle.

3. *Get off the pornography kick and face the real obscenity of poverty.* No matter how repulsive we may find pornography, laws banning books or movies for sexually explicit content could be far more dangerous to women. The pornography issue is dividing the women's movement and giving the impression on college campuses that to be a feminist is to be against sex. More important, it is diverting energies that need to be spent saving the basic rights now being destroyed.

But I think the secret this obsession with pornography may mask for women alone, for aging women, and for women still more economically dependent on men that they would like, is fear of poverty, which is the ultimate obscenity for Americans. . . .

Perhaps an unspoken reason so many women are protesting sexually explicit materials is that their own sexuality is denied by society. But I suspect that as long as sex is distorted by women's economic dependence, or fear of it, it can't be truly, freely enjoyed. The obscenity that not even many feminists want to confront in personal terms is the sheer degradation of being poor in opulent, upwardly mobile America. Of course, the women's movement in America, like all such revolutions everywhere, has been mainly a middle-class movement, but the shameful secret it has never really dealt with is the fact that more and more middle-class women are sinking into poverty.

4. *Confront the illusion of equality in divorce.* Economists and feminists have been talking a lot lately about "the feminization of poverty" in theoretical terms, but the American women's movement has not developed concrete strategies that get at its root cause. It's not just a question of women earning less than men—though as long as women do not get equal pay for work of comparable value, or earn Social Security or pensions for taking care of children and home, they are both economically dependent on marriage and motherhood and pay a big economic price for it. And this is as true for divorced aging yuppies as for welfare mothers.

Feminist Law

A startling new book by the sociologist Lenore J. Weitzman, "The Divorce Revolution: The Unexpected Social and Economic Consequences for Women and Children in America," reveals that in the 1970's, when 48 states adopted "no-fault" divorce laws treating men and women "equally" in divorce settlements—laws feminists originally supported—divorced women and their children suffered an immediate 73 percent drop in their standard of living, while their ex-husbands enjoyed a 42 percent rise in theirs.

In dividing "marital property," Lenore Weitzman reports, judges have systematically overlooked the major assets of many marriages—the husband's career assets that the wife helped make possible, his professional education that she may have helped support, the career on which he was able to concentrate because she ran the home, and his salary, pension, health insurance and earning power that resulted. They have also ignored the wife's years of unpaid housework and child care (not totally insured by Social Security in the event of divorce) and her drastically diminished job prospects after divorce. And, for most, the "equal" division of property means the forced sale of the family home—which used to be awarded to the wife and children. Child support, which has often been inadequate, unpaid and uncollectable, usually ends when the child is 18, just as college expenses begin. Thus the vicious cycle whereby an ever-increasing majority of the truly poor in America are families headed by women.

A new generation of feminist lawyers and judges has now drafted, and must get urgent grass-roots political support for, the kind of law needed, a law that treats marriage as a true economic partnership—and includes fairer standards of property division, maintenance and child support. It should be a law that does not penalize women who have chosen family over, or even together with, professional career.

Having Children

5. *Return the issue of abortion to the matter of women's own responsible choice.* I think feminists have been so traumatized by the fundamentalist crusade against abortion and all the talk of fetuses and when life begins that they are in danger of forgetting the values that made abortion a feminist issue in the first place. Underneath the hysteria, poll after poll shows that the great majority of women in this nation, and most men, still want to decide when and whether to have a child in accordance with their own conscience. This includes women of faith, including the majority of Catholic women. Attacks on the Pope and picketing the churches, as some desperate or deranged male and female abortion champions have lately proposed, would play right into the hands of our "right to life" enemies, who love to paint feminists as satanic opponents of God and family. We must not surrender family values and religious principles to the far right. Let the new women theologians and feminist women of faith in every church take on the fundamentalist preachers.

I think women who are young, and those not so young, today must be able to choose when to have a child, given the necessities of their jobs. They will, indeed join their mothers, who remember the humiliations and dangers of back-street butcher abortions, in a march of millions to save the right of legal abortion. I certainly support a march for women's choice of birth control and legal abortion. NOW has called for one in the spring of 1986.

6. *Affirm the differences between men and women.* New feminist thinking is required if American women are to continue advancing in man's world, as they must, to earn their way, and yet "not become like men." This fear is heard with more and more frequency today from young women, including many who have succeeded, and some who have failed or opted out of male-defined careers. More books like Carol Gilligan's "In a Different Voice" and consciousness-raising sessions are needed. First-stage feminism denied real differences between women and men except for the sexual organs themselves. Some feminists still do not understand that true equality is not possible unless those differences between men and women are affirmed and until values based on female sensitivities to life begin to be voiced in every discipline and profession, from architecture to economics, where, until recently, all concepts and standards were defined by men. This is not a matter of abstract theory alone but involves the restructuring of hours of work and patterns of professional training so that they take into account the fact that women are the people who give birth to children. It must lead to concrete changes in medical practice, church worship, the writing of history, standards of ethics, even the design of homes and appliances.

7. *Breakthrough for older women.* The women's movement has never put serious energy into the job that must be done to get women adequately covered by Social Security and pensions, especially those women now reaching 65 who spent many years as housewives and are ending up alone. The need for more independent and shared housing for older women now living alone in suburban houses they can't afford to sell, or lonely furnished rooms—and the need for services and jobs or volunteer options that will enable them to keep on living independent, productive lives—has never been a part of the women's movement agenda. But that first generation of feminist mothers, women now in their 60's, is a powerful political resource for the movement as these women retire from late or early professional or volunteer careers. Women in their 50's and 60's are shown by the polls to be more firmly committed than their daughters to the feminist goals of equality. Let the women's

movement lead the rest of society in breaking the spell of the youth cult and drawing on the still enormous energies and the wisdom that may come to some of us in age.

Men and Women Too

8. *Bring in the men.* It's passé, surely, for feminists now to see men only as the enemy, or to contemplate separatist models for emotional or economic survival. Feminist theorists like Barbara Ehreneich cite dismal evidence of the "new men" opting out of family responsibilities altogether. But in my own life I seem to see more and more young men, and older ones—even former male chauvinist pigs—admitting their vulnerability and learning to express their tenderness, sharing the care of the kids, even though most of them may never share it equally with their wives.

And as men let down their masks of machismo, and admit their dependence on the women in their lives, women may admit a new need to depend on men, without fear of sinking back into the old abject subservience. After all, even women who insist they are not, and never will be, feminists have learned to defend themselves against real male brutality. Look at Charlotte Donahue Fedders, the wife of that Security and Exchange commissioner, who testified in divorce court about his repeated abuse—his repeated beatings caused black eyes and a broken eardrum. At one time, a woman in her situation would have kept that shame a secret. The Reagan Administration had to ask him to resign, because wife-beating is no longer politically acceptable, even in conservative America in 1985.

I don't think women can, or should try to, take the responsibility for liberating men from the remnants of machismo. But there has to be a new way of asking what do men really want, to echo Freud, a new kind of dialogue that breaks through or gets behind both our masks. Women cannot restructure jobs or homes just by talking to themselves.

9. *Continue to fight for real political power.* Although feminists do not now, and never really did, support a woman just because she is a woman, there is no substitute for having women in political offices that matter. But more women are discovering that they have to fight, as men do, in primaries where victory is not certain, and not just wait for an "open seat." After the E.R.A.'s defeat, feminists and their supporters raised money nationally to run women candidates

in virtually every district in Illinois, Florida and North Carolina where legislators voted against the amendment. And in that single election they increased sizably women's representation in those state legislatures.

10. *Move beyond single-issue thinking.* Even today, I do not think women's rights are the most urgent business for American women. The important thing is somehow getting together with men who also put the values of life first to break through the paralysis that fundamentalist backlash has imposed on all our movements. It is not only feminism that is becoming a dirty word in America, but also liberalism, humanism, pluralism, environmentalism and civil liberties. The very freedom of political dissent that enabled the women's movement to start here has been made to seem unsafe for today's young men as well as young women. I think the yuppies are afraid to be political.

Women may have to think beyond "women's issues" to join their energies with men to redeem our democratic tradition and turn our nation's power to the interests of life instead of the nuclear arms race that is paralyzing it. I've never, for instance, seen the need for a separate women's peace movement. I'm not really sure that women, by nature, are more peace-loving than men. They were simply not brought up to express aggression the way men do (they took it out covertly, on themselves and on their men and children, psychologists would say). But the human race may not survive much longer unless women move beyond the nurture of their own babies and careers to political decisions of war and peace, and unless men who share the nurture of their children take responsibility for ending the arms race before it destroys all life. In that sense, I think the women's movement is only a particular moment in human evolution, and once its job is *really* done, then it can and should be allowed to fade away, honorably discharged.

Elizabeth Neeld Comments:

✦ *Betty Friedan is an author and a social reformer. While she was a housewife and mother living in the suburbs of New York and doing free-lance magazine work, she circulated a questionnaire among her classmates with whom she had attended Smith College many years earlier. The answers she got on this questionnare suggested to her that many of these women were deeply dissatisfied with their lives. She did more studies on this topic and published, in 1963, the findings and her own experience in a book called* The Feminine Mystique. ✦ *Friedan's central thesis was that women were victims of a system of delusions and false values under which they were expected to achieve personal satisfaction. Friedan said women were expected to cheerfully devote their lives to their husbands and children and that this expectation resulted in a general malaise and an absence of genuine and creative work. In 1966 Friedan founded NOW, the National Organization for Women.* ✦ *Friedan has continued to work over the years for the betterment of the lives of women; but, as in this essay, she has done so in the larger context of the problems of men and women and the problems of the world. She had said earlier, "I would be bored to write only about women's liberation. Women are as involved with the life-and-death questions of war and peace, the crisis of the planet and our cities, the unknowns of technology and art and space, as they are with food and children and home. I believe the women's liberation movement cannot remain isolated from everything else that's happening . . . today."* ✦ *The form of this* essay *is* created *by the message Betty Friedan wants to deliver. This how-to essay does not describe a process (such as baking on a boat), so there is no sequential arrangement of steps that the author must follow. Instead, the essay gives Friedan's opinions and her recommendations. These she can put into any form she wishes. Since the message of the essay does not carry with it a clear, inherent form, she creates her own form.* ✦ *What Friedan creates, then, is this: She begins by summarizing what she sees as the state of affairs in the women's movement today. Then she discusses her trip to Nairobi to the World Conference of Women and relates the insights and realizations she had while attending this conference. Then she comes to the heart of her essay. She lists ten things that can be done to get the women's movement moving again. This list is placed in the larger context of Friedan's general discussion of the women's movement and of her recent trip to Africa. The problem is stated first (current state of affairs for women's movement in America); a time* of insight related to solving the problem comes next (Africa events); and then ten possible solutions to the problem are given (the list). Friedan has used many traditional thought patterns such as cause and effect, analysis, and comparison/contrast to show readers what can be done to revitalize the women's movement in this country, but she has not attempted to fit her message into one predominate thought pattern. Instead, she has used the thought patterns to fit her purpose, to assist in making her points. She has created her own form. ✦

RICHARD MORSILLI,
with JO COUDERT

I *Still See Him* *Everywhere*

On February 22, 1983, young Todd Morsilli of Warwick, R.I., was struck and killed by a drunk driver. He was one of 19,500 Americans who lost their lives that year in accidents caused by intoxicated drivers. A few months later, Todd's father was asked to speak to students at Riverdale Country School, just north of Manhattan, about teen-age drunk driving.

As he looked around the assembly hall, Richard Morsilli wondered what he could say to persuade the students to listen. They seemed bored, restless. He felt he couldn't lecture. All he really wanted to do was to tell them how much he missed Todd. Which, more or less, is what he did.

His talk, interspersed with his thoughts as he addressed the teenagers, follows.

Good Morning. My name is Richard Morsilli. Eight months ago my son Todd was struck and killed by a 17-year-old drunk driver. Todd was 13. He was a wonderful boy.

Why did I say he was wonderful? Every father thinks his kid is special. But Todd really was. He had a knack of making people feel good about themselves. The day before he was killed, I heard him say to Carole, "Hey, Mom, my friends think you're pretty."

Todd was a tennis player. He was ranked No. 3 in his age group in New England in singles, No. 1 in doubles. He was also a baseball player, and when he was younger that's all he cared about, even after we got a tennis court. Then one day his older brother had no one to play with and persuaded Todd to pick up a racket. In six months Todd was winning tournaments.

That's what made us so close, my driving him to tournaments, and having all that time in the car together. That fellow in the third row with the sun-bleached hair has the same thoughtful look Todd would get when we'd discuss things.

It sounds like Todd was really competitive, but he wasn't. I'd say, "Todd, how will you play this guy? I hear he's got a terrific cross-court return." And he'd say, "Gee, Dad, I don't know. I haven't thought about it." He liked to win, but he didn't much like to beat people. His coach urged him to play older kids to sharpen his skills, but he hated to do it because he knew it upset them to get beaten by a youngster.

I was the one who had visions of Wimbledon. All Todd ever said was, "That's a long way off, Dad. A lot can happen." Did he sense what was coming, like the garden that blooms like crazy just before frost?

Last February 22, Todd was walking along the street with his cousin Jeff. The two boys were only five weeks apart in age, and inseparable. Jeff had been watching Todd play tennis that morning, and they were on their way to rent skis for a Catholic Youth Organization weekend. First they stopped at our house to get money for ice-cream cones. "You know, Mom," Todd said after she had given him what change she had in her pocketbook, "what we'd really like are milkshakes." His mother laughed and went upstairs for more money.

That girl in the third row with the sweet face just caught her breath. She's thinking what Carole can't help but think—that if she'd said no, the boys would have left the house earlier; they'd have turned the corner before the car came.

An elderly neighbor told us afterward that he was out shoveling his driveway when the boys went by. It was a holiday, Washington's Birthday, and the sun sparkling on the snow made the world seem paved with diamonds. The boys offered to finish the job for him, but he said he was glad to be outside, and they went on. The neighbor saw the car coming. Jeff saw it too. The car was weaving. They both shouted and Jeff jumped into a snowbank, but Todd . . . Todd . . . couldn't get out of the way.

Oh, God, help me get through this without crying. I've got to keep going.

The car . . . struck Todd. He was . . . thrown 90 feet . . . The car didn't stop. . . .

It's been eight months. Will I ever be able to talk about it without breaking down?

I'm sorry. Forgive me. You just can't imagine how . . . overwhelming it is. I got a call at my office. It was someone at the hospital. The voice said a boy's been hurt. We think it's your son. Can you come right away? All I remember is saying, over and over: Just let there be a chance. He'll make it, if he has a chance, because he doesn't give up.

He didn't get his chance. At the hospital a priest met me and took me into a little room . . . Todd's mother and I didn't even have time to hope. By the time we knew about it at all, he was gone.

He's gone, and I still see him everywhere. I see him as I glance around this hall. In the clean line of your chin, there on the aisle. And there, first row middle, in your slim, strong frame. And in you, too, young lady, in the way he bit his lip to keep the tears from coming.

The next thing you know you're preparing for a funeral. You're saying things like: His grave's got to be under a tree. You're making telephone calls. You're answering the doorbell. His friends. . . .

Little girls asking if they could have one of Todd's tennis shirts. Little boys intending just to shake hands, but then moving into my arms as though, if we hugged hard enough, we could blot out the emptiness.

Nine hundred people jammed the church for his funeral. "It was like he was everyone's best friend," a 15-year-old who spoke at the service said. "You were just glad he was your friend too."

We buried Todd in his warm-up suit and his cap. Everyone knew that beige-felt cap. It was like the one worn by Frew McMillan, the South African tennis player. Todd admired him because he was always a gentleman on court.

Afterward, we got letters from all over the country—hundreds of letters—from people who'd met Todd at tournaments. They pretty much said the same thing: We knew your son. He was a terrific tennis player. But, even more, he was such a nice boy.

I called one father to ask if his son Andrew, a black friend of Todd's, would be a pallbearer. "Andrew would really like that," his father said. "He thought the world of your boy, ever since the first time they played a match against each other. Andrew had forgotten his water bottle, and Todd leaned over and said, 'Share mine.'"

A black boy, a Chinese boy and two Jewish boys, his tennis rivals and friends, helped carry Todd to his grave. They followed everyone else up to the altar for communion.

Then the funeral was over. You've buried your son, and you go back to work. The world goes on. But things don't mean the same. I'm no different from your fathers. I wanted to provide a bright future for my family. All I can tell you now is I'd give up all I have in a minute if I could just have Todd back.

Shall I tell them about the fox? No, probably not. I don't want them to turn me off.

Because of Todd's tennis playing, there was a lot in the newspapers about the tragedy. They called it a hit-and-run accident, which it was, except that the girl ran into a tree a mile down the road so the police caught her right away. She'd spent the holiday drinking beer at a friend's house, starting at ten in the morning, and later they switched to vodka.

She goes to school. I see her at the supermarket. Is her life going on as usual? Did Todd's death make any difference?

People wanted to do something. They started a Todd Morsilli Memorial Fund. Somebody suggested renaming the tennis courts at Roger Williams Park in Providence in honor of Todd. In June the first annual Todd Morsilli Memorial Tournament was held there.

Sometimes I tell myself: He was just a 13-year-old boy. How could he have touched so many lives? Sometimes I think: It was just another tragedy. How could so many lives be so terribly changed by it? But it's true.

I worry about Todd's brother David. He looks so much like Todd that people expect him to *be* Todd. I worry about Todd's sister Lisa, because she and Todd were closest. I worry about Todd's kid sister Kristin. She was visiting a friend before the accident and hadn't seen Todd in two days. She's recently become very enthusiastic about tennis. Is she genuinely interested? Or is she trying to make up to us for Todd? And I worry about Jeff, Todd's cousin, because he lost his father four months before Todd was killed.

I pray every day he'll make it. I pray every day that all of us make it.

They say grief brings people closer together. It's not true. Grief is isolating. It locks you up in your own heart. If Carole and I hadn't had such a good marriage, I think we'd have come apart. I was out of the house all day, but Carole was home, and everywhere she looked there was something to remind her of Todd. And I think the strain began to tell.

What saved us was the squirrel. If Kristin hadn't told Carole about the car in front of us hitting a squirrel and my getting out, pointlessly, to move the poor broken body to the side of the road and then sitting down on the curb sobbing, the silence might have won out over us. But that squirrel saved Carole and me. We talked to each other then. We realized we had to get help, and Carole took a part-time job to get out of the house.

I'm not on a crusade. As you know by now, I'm no speaker. And I didn't come to tell you not to drink. I only came to say that when you do drink, please, *please,* don't drive. If you're with someone who's drinking, please, *please,* call your parents to come get you. Because if something happens to you, it won't be just another tragedy; it'll be their beloved child. And if you kill someone else's child, it'll be someone like my son Todd. It doesn't have to happen. Don't let it happen.

I guess that's all I have to say. Thank you for listening.

Did I say enough? Did I say too much? Why, they're applauding. They're all standing up. That fellow is coming up on the platform. He's holding out his hand. They're lining up. Are they all going to shake my hand?

Thank you. I'm glad I came too. No, she didn't go to jail. Her three-year sentence was suspended. Her probation terms included regular psychological counseling, work at a halfway house and no drinking. And, her driver's license was suspended for five years.

Thank you. Take care of yourselves. All of you, please, *please,* take care of yourselves.

What nice kids they are. I think if I'd told them about the fox, they'd have understood. They'd have appreciated how astonishing it was, when we'd never seen a fox before, to have one come and stand on the patio two days after Todd's death—just come and stand there staring at the kitchen window before it turned and slowly moved away.

Carole's pregnant sister came to be with her that afternoon. "I've been looking at a book of baby names," she said. "Did you know when you named Todd that it meant 'fox'?"

Was Todd trying to tell us he's all right? I think these kids would understand how much we want to believe that.

Elizabeth Neeld Comments:

✦ *In July of 1984,* Reader's Digest *printed this essay describing a father's account of the loss of his thirteen-year-old son, killed by a drunk driver. The essay was the top-rated article of the year, by* Reader's Digest's *fifty million readers. According to* Reader's Digest, *no magazine article in 1984 was more widely read; no magazine article in 1984 was more deeply felt. And, perhaps, no magazine article in 1984 will have such a lasting impact.* ✦ *Naturally, the subject of the essay—a young thirteen-year-old boy walking down the road and getting killed by a car driven by a seventeen-year-old girl who had been drinking beer and then vodka at a friend's house since ten in the morning— stands to make an impact in its own right. There is much increased consciousness in our country about the cost to the life, well-being, and property of individuals who drive while they are drunk.* ✦ *Added to the impact of the subject itself, however, is the form that Jo Coudert and Richard Morsilli created for this essay, a form described by rhetoricians as* Grammar B form. *Grammar B form is an alternative way of putting material together that uses devices we see in films (such as Woody Allen in "Play It Again Sam" talking to the ghost of Humphrey Bogart at the same time he talks to Diane Keaton in the present) or in art (for example, a collage of scenes patched together to make another picture) or in music video (which jumps from one image to another with no logic provided by the director to join them). Grammar B, as it was named by Winston Weathers, professor of English at the University of Tulsa, has been around for at least two hundred years. This style of writing, which allows for more originality, has achieved a new popularity, however, in the last twenty years. (Although two hundred years old, Grammar B style is not tra-ditional form. It does not correspond to one predominate thought pattern or tendency of the mind.)* ✦ *Tom Wolfe reintroduced Grammar B form when he was trying to write an article for* Esquire *in 1963. He could not complete the article, and he got so aggravated that he just typed up all his notes in a rush and sent them off to the editor at Es-*

quire. *He expected that someone at the magazine would take his notes and write the story. What happened, though, was that the magazine printed the notes just as he had sent them in—and a created form called* new journalism *was born. (The notes were given the title "The Kandy-Kolored Tangerine-Flake Streamline Baby."* ✦ *One of the characteristics of the created form known as Grammar B (of which Tom Wolfe's type of writing is an example) is synchronicity. This means that several things are happening in the writing at once, and as the reader you are aware of all of them. One of the ways synchronicity is achieved is through the use of the double voice. There is the voice of the narrator, perhaps speaking directly to the reader, and then there is another voice of the same narrator, perhaps speaking to herself or himself. These two voices, double voices, play off each other throughout the writing. Usually they are printed in two styles of type to distinguish one from the other. Because you read both in an alternating fashion, you get more layers of meaning than if there were only a traditional form and one voice.* ✦ *This essay is a superb example of Grammar B created form, with a slight twist. The author had some assistance in writing the essay; notice the byline: Richard Morsilli, with Jo Coudert. The twist in the created form is that the first voice you hear is Jo Coudert's. She tells us, the readers, that on such and such a day Todd Morsilli was killed and that Todd's father is about to address the students at Riverdale Country School. Then, in the next paragraph, we are inside Richard Morsilli's mind. We are discovering what he is thinking as he looks out at the students to whom he is about to speak. Coudert tells us in the third paragraph that Morsilli's talk is about to begin and that what we are about to read is what Morsilli said that day. These three paragraphs provide the preamble for what is to follow.* ✦ *In paragraph four, we hear the objective voice of Morsilli. He is speaking to the students. "Good morning. My name is . . . Eight months ago my son Todd was struck and killed . . . " Then in italics there is the second voice, Mr. Morsilli's subjective voice. He is thinking to himself. "Why did I say he was wonderful? . . . The day before he was killed, I heard him say to Carole,*

'Hey, Mom, my friends think you're pretty.' " The double voice of synchronicity has been established. ✦ For the rest of the essay we hear these two voices. Because there are double voices, we learn much, much more than we could have if the essay had been written to give us only Morsilli's speech. Through the subjective second voice we learn about the father's private grief, something he doesn't want to make public in this talk to the students. We know when he is about to cry, and this makes us privy to more than the students listening to him are privy to. Unless Morsilli's demeanor betrays him and unless the students are keen observers, they cannot know what we, the readers, know through the second voice. We learn intimate details of the funeral, which the audience is not told. We find out that Morsilli sometimes sees the girl who was driving the death car when he goes to the grocery store. We learn, because of the double voice, that the relationship of Morsilli and his wife was very tense and near the breaking point after their son died—until she learned about his sitting on the curb and crying after he saw the dead squirrel in the road. ✦ It is through the double-voice technique that we learn the private facts as well as the public facts. It is the second voice that tells us at the end about the appearance of the fox, which stood at the patio door two days after Todd had died. And it is the second voice that tells us that the meaning of the name Todd is "fox." ✦ This created form, Grammar B, allows the writers to tell us much more than they could have using traditional form. Had Morsilli related the deep, private facts to us in a singular voice, he would have sounded maudlin, sentimental, and inappropriate. By using the double-voice created form, Morsilli can keep his private thoughts private, all the while that we, the readers, know what they are. This technique provides an intimacy with the author that would have been hard to accomplish in any other form. ✦

MAXINE HONG KINGSTON

A Writer's Notebook from the East

I just went on a tour of Japan, Australia, Indonesia, Malaysia, and Hong Kong, sponsored by the United States International Communications Agency and the Adelaide Arts Festival.

—In Kuala Lumpur at a newspaper's auditorium:

Me: "The reason Asian American literature has flourished is even from the start we aggressively exercised our right to a free press."

My translator (in English): " 'Free press'?"

Me: "Yes, 'free press.' "

My translator: " 'Free press'?" Then he said something to the audience which made them laugh.

An audience member later: "He knew the words for 'free press.' He didn't want them in his mouth."

—In Kuala Lumpur: "I hope that girl who told you about the suppression of Chinese identity wasn't reported by a deputy tonight."

"College professors who are reported lose their jobs. Some people go to jail."

—In Kuala Lumpur: "When the censors cut 'The White Shadow,' they left in the part where the father beat up the son, and cut where the son hit the father. In 'Superman,' they cut out Lois Lane coming back to life."

—In Kuala Lumpur: "Can you tell us how to write political messages disguised subtly as fiction?" Given my background and education, I found that I could not. On the other hand, these writers face a censorship that I have never encountered. I will have to put my mind to answering that question before I go there again. (In the old days, Chinese poets had a code system of flower metaphors.)

—In Hong Kong: "Your writing is un-Confucian." "Chinese women don't act or talk like that."

—In Penang, Malaysia: " 'Hamlet' is anti-Islamic." The government prohibited its showing on television.

—In Hong Kong at a discussion about my book, *The Woman Warrior*, in which Moon Orchid comes to America and does not survive the culture shock: "The reason that Moon went crazy is that she did not have any sons."

—In Penang:
Me: "That gas station sent four children to college."

Audience member: "About that gas station that sent four sons to college . . . "

—In the *Thung Pau*, a Malaysian Chinese language newspaper after an interview about swordswomen and Amazons: "*The Woman Warrior* is about how the introverted, chaste, and conservative Chinese women patiently and silently overcome all odds in a challenging new world."

—In Jakarta:
Women: "Read again the part about Amazons capturing the man and binding his feet."

—In Medan, Indonesia: "There are people who say that after Russia and America destroy each other, Indonesia can rule the world."

—In Hong Kong: "How can there be Asian Americans? How can a Chinese and a Japanese get together?"

—In Surabaya, Indonesia: "There are Chinese women who have converted to Islam. What are they up to?"

—In Tokyo: "The way the junior faculty, who are women, get out of pouring tea for the senior faculty, who are all men, is to be very clumsy at pouring tea. This is not good politics. I personally don't pour tea because I am clumsy. The custom doesn't change."

"The custom of women pouring tea for men in the faculty lounge is not going to change in a hundred years."

—In Sapporo: "People in Tokyo have a surface sophistication. At our university, all the work is divided evenly among all faculty members regardless of pay or rank."

—In Adelaide, there is a big statue of the Angel of Sacrifice with a man, a woman, and a child in pleading positions at its feet. It commemorates the wars of Gallipoli, Israel, and Africa.

—In Jakarta, there is a giant statue of Kartini, a feminist martyr who died at the age of 25. She refused to be sent to Holland to be educated and fought for Indonesian independence from the Dutch. There is a magazine named *Kartini*, whose writers believe that men and women have a tradition of helping one another.

—In Adelaide at a book launching, a Cuban myth: "All God's children are beautiful, but Truth and Falsehood were fighting one day. Truth knocked Falsehood's head off. It was shaped like a pig's. Truth picked up the head and put it on, and couldn't take it off. And that is why truth must always speak in the guise of fiction."

There were riots in Jakarta, and we saw tanks and soldiers with bayonets. In Medan we saw soldiers tear down a squatter house and drag the women out. The women were raging, weeping, throwing rocks. Jakarta was the first place where I saw a censored newspaper. There is a kind of black tar over the censored article, and a page from an old *Reader's Digest* on top of the tar. The authorities in Jakarta paint over Chinese words that are on shop signs and other advertising on the street. There are still Chinese words here and there, but people say they are Japanese words. In Medan, the teenagers had me autograph their T-shirts with my Chinese name.

Many, many of God's children are beautiful. An Indian artist was painting squatters being evicted. The squatters are grandmothers, mothers, and children. A Malaysian dramatist is videotaping 70- and 80-year-old storytellers and dancers. The Adelaide Arts Festival voted to protest a "reading tax" on books. Young writers have pledged themselves to write about "Hong Kong poverty." Hong Kong is turning the farms in the New Territories into more public housing, which I once saw as dungeons and now understand as heroic—Hong Kong, city of refuge. A choreographer in Sapporo is taking her troupe to dance a nuclear bomb dance in Moscow.

Our planet is as rich and complex as a Balinese painting, which is covered every inch with life. To stop the bombs, to free ourselves—we are nations of hostages—we continue dancing, painting, telling stories, writing whether or not there is a free press.

Elizabeth Neeld Comments:

✦ *Maxine Hong Kingston is a Chinese American whose first book* The Woman Warrior *won the National Book Critics Circle Award and whose second book* China Men *won the American Book Award. Both these books were on the best-seller list at the same time. Kingston is a storyteller who writes about her Chinese heritage, particularly about her own and other Chinese families in America. She explores the relationship between her people's history, original culture, past experiences and the life they live now.* ✦ *In this piece, she writes about conversations she had and events that occurred when she was traveling in the Far East, visiting Japan, Australia, Indonesia, Malyasia, and Hong Kong. Everywhere she went she talked with people: about writing, about literature, about stories. She also listened. She listened to others talk about culture, freedom of speech and freedom of the press, censorship, about books and writing books, about what they liked in her writing. During this trip Kingston also paid attention to her surroundings: she noticed; she saw.* ✦ *Among the things she heard were the blind cultural prejudices of many people with whom she talked. She also saw signs and symbols of courageous acts which had been carried out in the past under extremely unfavorable circumstances. She realized from many of the questions that her listeners had no experience in their lives corresponding to a concept like "free press." Equality for women was not expected, as evidenced by several remarks made by people with whom she talked. She divined wisdom in many remarks; writers, for instance,* knew they could hide truth in fiction, and thereby say what they believed, even in an oppressive climate. ✦ Kingston's notes, overall, give a mixed picture. There is prejudice, cultural blindness, and resignation, but there is also hope, action, and commitment. The author's overall reaction was one of optimism after returning from this trip. In spite of everything, she reports, "we continue dancing, painting, telling stories, writing, whether or not there is a free press." This is a powerful and an encouraging message. ✦ The form of this article, which appeared in Ms. magazine, is a series of notes from Kingston's notebooks that she kept on the trip. These notes are drawn together by the author with a short concluding statement. "So, what is the form?" you might ask. (That someone can take her notes, list them in the order she wishes, write a short conclusion, and produce in this way a publishable article of value should change the mind of anyone who thinks that writing must always be organized in traditional forms, carefully developed, and explained.) The form is a created one, made by Kingston's choice and selection from her notes of certain bits of conversation, parts of dialogue, questions, and sights that reflect the insights she gained on the trip. From these snippets you get something whole— a sense of the concerns of writers and readers around the world. Even though the notes are not connected in any formal way, they are connected in what they reveal, in what they let us see. ✦ This created form allows Kingston to make some very strong and moving points without being heavy-handed and moralistic. She doesn't have to explain. She doesn't have to preach. She lets other people and events speak her message, through the excerpts from her notes. In the form's simplicity lie its enormous possibilities, its authenticity, and its power. ✦

RICHARD SELZER

Chatterbox:
Homage to Saint
Catherine of Siena

It is not always the doctor who heals. Sometimes it is another patient.

The following is taken verbatim from the diary of a woman who was a patient of mine some years ago. It is in the form of a letter to her brother Raymond. The diary was mailed to me by her brother some months after her death.

Catherine Goodhouse had been what in high-school yearbooks is called a "chatterbox," and in textbooks of psychiatry is called a "compulsive talker." Catherine was a talker the way other people are writers or actors. Talking vouchsafed her life. "Do you hear me?" she seemed to be saying. "Then I am alive." It satisfied her as sucking satisfies the baby who likes the feel of his lips and tongue working.

Talking was an affliction of which life had made her painfully aware. One day, her husband Joe had stood up in the middle of Sunday dinner and walked out of the house. She never saw him again. When he was sixteen, her son Warren had said to her, "Why the hell don't you shut up?" Then he was gone—enlisted in the Navy. For four years Catherine lived alone, talking to whoever would hold still long enough, or to herself. She couldn't help it.

When I first went into practice, I used to work part-time at Golden Gardens to make ends meet. The Nursing Home was far enough outside town to enable the owners to describe it in the brochure as "rustic" and "rural." What the people in Golden Gardens needed was not so much country air as someone to talk to. Company. All day long they sat encased in silence, unable to find a way out of it.

"You ought to sign up at Golden Gardens," I told Catherine. "Go out once or twice a week to visit with the patients. They're lonesome, and you have what it takes." The next day Catherine called to say she could go every Tuesday and Friday from two to three in the afternoon.

Catherine Goodhouse was one of those petite, doll-like women given to lavender sachets and dresses made of organdy or dotted swiss. Every time she came to Golden Gardens she looked and smelled like spring itself. The patients adored her. She was assigned five of them, the same five each time, so that they would come to look upon her as family. There were four women and a man. Two of the women were in wheelchairs. When she arrived at five minutes to two, they would already have been assembled in the "parlor," and had been drawn up into a little semicircle in front of which Catherine would stand babbling on about what she was wearing, where she learned to bake, what she was going to plant in her garden. The weather. It was only fair, she told an attendant at the home, to start with what she was wearing because Mr. Freitas and Mrs. Celli were blind. As far as anyone knew, none of the five was ever heard to utter a word in reply. It didn't matter. They just sat there for the hour, rapt and adoring, as though she were the most beautiful, most charming, the freshest thing in the world. As time went on, it was plain to see that the five old people were stronger and more alert than they had been before. They certainly looked better. Their faces were pink, their lips moist. Pretty soon, Catherine was going to the home five days a week.

"Well now," she would say at the close of each of her visits, "we've had a lovely time, haven't we?" And she would walk slowly toward the door. All five, including the two blind ones, would turn to follow her right up to the last second. About a year later, I stopped working at the home, and lost touch with Catherine. Three years later I heard that she had died. And then there was this diary.

My dear brother Raymond,

For some time I have been going out to a convalescent home to talk with the patients. They don't have much company, you know. I cannot believe now that when I first saw them I was horrified. That first day and for a while afterwards, they seemed not only grotesque but dangerous. Were they contagious? I wondered. Or violent? And with all their bodily functions—salivation, excretion—unpredictable, sort of wild. If one of them touches me, I thought, I'll die. There was Mrs. Greenwald, with her wet chin and that cackle that just welled up out of her every little while. And Mr. Freitas, with those boiled swollen hands that looked like blutwurst. His fist on the handle of his cane was like a just-born infant's face, engorged, angry. His hands seemed always to be hot. He would reach for things to cool them on, like the armrest of his chair or the knob of his cane.

But right from the beginning there was something about them that drew me. It was their pathetic confidence that they were human. I saw bravery in their very act of coming to listen to me. And they never missed a visit. I knew that they needed me as much as I needed them.

One day there were only four of them. Mrs. Greenwald was missing. "Where is Mrs. Greenwald?" I asked. Of course, they didn't answer.

"A massive hemorrhage from the stomach," one of the nurses explained. "She was dead in an hour." A hemorrhage, I thought. As though the old woman's blood somehow knew it was dwelling in a doomed body, and had hurried to escape it. I swear it seemed that the other four were embarrassed that I should have to find out and be upset by something that one of them had done. All at once I felt bereft, deprived of something, like an old coat that, without knowing it, I had been wearing to keep myself warm; and now that it was gone I was chilled to the bone. From that moment I never had any doubt that I would be going to Golden Gardens for the rest of my life.

And now, Raymond, I want to tell you as well as I can what happened. On the day of the event, I bathed and dressed carefully. I had bought a new white dress, and I was wearing it for the first time. White is so virginal, the clerk in the dress shop had said, and she had smiled knowingly. And she was right. It did make me feel . . . well . . . cleansed to put it on. I don't know why I am telling you about that except that now it does seem important to me somehow. It was such a good visit. I told them so many things. You should have seen how they were nourished by my talking. I like to think that they would have been dead long ago if I didn't talk to them like that. I had been told to limit my visits to one hour so as not to tire them, but on this day about which I am writing, they didn't seem a bit tired at the end of an hour, and truthfully, I hadn't had enough either. I just went right on for another hour, while the four old people sat there and listened.

At the end of the second hour, I stood up. "Well," I said as usual, "we've had another lovely visit." First I brought the two women in wheelchairs out to their rooms. The third woman followed on her own. When I returned to our meeting place, I saw that Mr. Freitas had stood up but had made no move to leave. "So, Mr. Freitas," I said, "it's time for me to go home." Still, the old man made no move to leave. Instead he took one step closer to me so that he could almost have reached out and touched me. Another step brought him still closer. We were standing facing each other. All at once I was aware of a strange, warm sensation. As though my body were darkening, and even my dress were pink. I could have heated the building with my presence. Thus we stood for a long moment. I studied the old man. Every bit of his clothing took on an immense importance, just as my dress had seemed to me important before—his stained vest, the yellowed armpits of his shirt, the crumpled stovepipe trousers. It seemed to me special raiment. Even the angle of inclination of his head had meaning.

Then slowly the old man raised his arms and held them out. If I were a clock, he would have been pointing to ten minutes before and ten minutes after the hour of twelve, which was my throat. My gaze was lashed to the dance of the calcified artery at his wrist, which beat at the same rhythm as the pulse clapping in my ear. As though our blood had hurled itself across the distance between us, receding from me to flow into him, then back again. Even so, I had the most ordinary thoughts. I wondered, for instance, what direction I faced. Was it north? No, impossible. It was east. Yes, I was facing east. I remembered something that had happened a long time ago when I was a young girl. A boy at school had approached me. His hand had been made into a cage. Through the aperture formed by the curled index finger and the web of him thumb, I could see the head of a little bird. A purple finch, it was. The bird lay still in the firm grasp of the boy. Beneath the row of fingers which dipped into his palm, I caught sight of three tiny talons and a tiny foot.

"Would you like to hold it?" he asked me. I felt desire and revulsion at one and the same time. I *wanted* to hold that bird more than anything else in the world. And I did *not* want to hold it with exactly the same intensity.

"Here," said the boy, "take it." I held out my two hands, covering his fist with both of mine, and I received the little bird. In the quick movement of departure of the boy's hand from mine, I felt the fluttering of the bird's wings. All of a sudden, I became terrified, and I screamed.

"Take it back. Please take it back!" He did, relieving me of it as gently as possible.

Now I stood in front of the old man, feeling the same confusion of desire and dread. My blood was tumbling. I felt that I must leave at once, or die.

"I must go," I managed to say. But I made no move to leave. He was like the stub of a white candle melted, run over, but with the flame undiminished. With each intake of my breath, that flame bowed toward me, designating me, electing me. I could feel its heat up on my cheek.

Suddenly, I was afraid. Perhaps he meant to throttle me. Do it! I thought. Do it! Whatever it is you are going to do, for God's sake, do it! Slowly his hands enfolded my neck, closing upon it with a perfect balance of lightness and firmness, as though it were a small bird. And when, at last, his fingers reached me (they were so long in coming), I slipped into them, was caught, lay still, quieted, the way a bird, once caught, ceases its frantic efforts to escape and embraces captivity, understanding at last that captivity was what it had wanted all along.

His opaque blue eyes, all scarred and milky, were fixed upon me. They took in no sight, I knew, but seemed now to give forth a light of their own, as though far behind them they kept an everlasting source of it which needed no ignition from the outside. And just as a sailor *confides* in a lighthouse, so did I confide in this light, certain that long after he left me, his eyes would glow on. His eyes contained the world. They conjured me. I existed in those eyes.

What a feeling of utter renunciation I had! I would not have held anything back from him, would have surrendered blood, breath and whatever else he would have. I remained still, listening to the singing fingers about my neck, and my heart dwelt in a snug cottage. For his touch was hushing, the way a finger to the lips is hushing. With just such infinite gentleness the old man bade me be quiet. And I was quiet, silenced, healed.

For a long moment the old man held me between his palms. At last his grasp lightened and he withdrew. The shuffling of his feet and the tapping of his cane told me that he had gone. I did not dare to turn and look. Alone, I had the feeling that something had at long last been set right, as though a room full of awkward, ungainly furniture had been rearranged by someone with style and good taste. Long after the old man had left me, I stood honoring the event, letting comfort fill me up, expand in me the way dough expands into bread or sleep swells a lover's face into softness. Had he really touched me? I wondered. Had it really been his flesh upon mine? Or merely a close proximity, something that had come careening from a great distance to swipe within a hair of me, then dash away? But I knew that he had.

I still go to Golden Gardens to visit. But it is different now. Sometimes, I don't talk at all. Sometimes I just sit with them. I bring flowers and arrange them, or cookies that I have made. These things they receive with the same pleasure as my talking. Now and then, one of them will smile happily at me the way a mother does whose child has been ill and has recovered.

Elizabeth Neeld Comments:

✦ *Richard Selzer is a physician, but it is hard to call him just that. He is also a poet, a teacher, and a philosopher. He writes books that relate medicine, suffering, and healing to the human condition. Books with titles like* Mortal Lessons: Notes on the Art of Surgery; Confessions of a Knife, *and* Rituals of Surgery; *and* Letters to a Young Doctor, *from which "Chatterbox: Homage to Saint Catherine of Siena" is taken. (Saint Catherine [1347–1380] lived in Siena, Italy and was a mystic who spent her time serving God and doing good.) The theme that ties the essays together in* Letters to a Young Doctor *is the theme of self-knowledge, that quality that arises through humility, and the theme of our shared mortality—we must all learn that we share the same foibles and the same fate.* ✦ *Selzer begins "Chatterbox" with these lines: "It is not always the doctor who heals. Sometimes it is another patient." Then he tells the story. And he does so in a very free and created form. He gives background information to set the context: He purports to have received a diary from one of his patients. The diary was in the form of a letter to her brother. When the patient died, Selzer said her brother mailed him the diary. Selzer gives information about who the patient was: Her name was Catherine Goodhouse. She was what is known as a compulsive talker. Selzer, her doctor, urged her to go out and talk to people who were living in the Golden Gardens Nursing Home. She did go and was assigned five patients to talk to. She talked a full hour with each one, and nobody was ever known to utter a reply. But she enjoyed herself, and always ended her talking visits with the patients by saying, "Well now, we've had a lovely time, haven't we?"* ✦ *Selzer lets the diary entry reveal how Catherine Goodhouse had been cured of her obsessive talking by one of the patients in the nursing home. He inserts a diary entry into the essay.* ✦ *What we have here is a created form that resembles those Chinese boxes that fit inside each other. Selzer starts an essay. He makes the point of the essay at the very beginning: it is not always the doctor who heals. Then he gives background information so that the readers of his essay will have a context for understanding the diary form he is going to use. Then he gives the diary entry and that entry makes up most of his essay. Who would ever think of writing an essay that pre-sumably consists—for the most part—of a long quote? But Selzer had something to say that he thought could best be said this way.* ✦ *So we have Selzer's story about his patient. Then we have the diary which has another story inside it—the story of how this patient was cured of her obsessive talking. And with her story, the essay ends.* ✦ Created form. *Form that allows a writer to do what he wants to do. Form that provides the opportunity to put together parts that may not seem to go together in an ordinary organizational pattern. The writer takes the liberty to write his essay in the form that will let him do what he wants to do—in this case, put a diary entry inside an essay because he thinks it's the best way to make his point. Sel-zer did not worry whether or not people would think this was an acceptable form for his essay.* ✦ *Even though the essay includes a diary entry, Selzer authored the entire piece. He had something he wanted to say, something he wanted to share, and this was the form that would get the job done. So it is the form he* created *and the form that he* used. *Bravo to him.* ✦

READING

to Learn to Write: Gusto, Vividness, and Clarity

RALPH WALDO EMERSON

Life, authentic life, you must have or you can teach nothing.

RALPH WALDO EMERSON

Cut these words and they would bleed; they are vascular and alive; they walk and run . . . a shower of bullets . . . salt & fire in [them].

RALPH WALDO EMERSON

The writer must live & die by his writing.

Gusto, *vividness,* and *clarity*: qualities that bring writing alive. *Gusto* means "hearty and keen enjoyment; to have an individual taste or liking for." When a person writes with *gusto* you can tell that he or she *enjoyed* talking about this subject. It is clear that the subject is a favorite of the writer. There is a spirit, an exuberance, an enthusiasm that you can feel as you read.

Vividness shows up as strikingly bright or intense images, as descriptions that are full of life, as fresh analogies and examples, as strong and distinct statements. When a writer's work is vivid, you have no trouble "seeing" what is meant. Vivid writing is likely to stimulate all your senses—seeing, hearing, smelling, touching, and tasting. Concrete pictures make general or abstract facts or statements real for you when you read.

Nobody has talked about *clarity* better than the rhetorician Quintilian who lived back in the first century A.D. Discussing inattentive readers, he said:

> Many things will distract his thoughts unless what we say is so clear that our words will strike into his mind, like sun in the eyes, even though he is inattentive. Hence, our care must be, not that he will be able to understand us, but that it be impossible for him to misunderstand.

That is what a writer strives for who is committed to clarity.

How do writers achieve these sterling qualities of Gusto, Vividness, and Clarity?

Gusto

Writers achieve *gusto* by writing only about subjects they can genuinely care about, be interested in, and enjoy. And doing so shouldn't be all that hard. There are millions and millions and millions of subjects about which one can write. Especially when a writing opportunity is self-generated, writers can choose subjects they can enjoy, appreciate, and like. And it is ridiculous to do otherwise.

If the writing task is imposed by someone or something else other than one's own decisions and inclination—e.g., a report at work, a brochure for the marketplace, an assigned topic for an essay—then it is important that a writer explore the *possibilities* of the subject before beginning to write the piece itself. If writers don't *explore* and *discover* something in the subject or task that they can get excited about or interested in, then the writing will only be difficult and inauthentic.

People who have been writing for some time and who write both outside-imposed and self-generated pieces will tell you that there is no such thing as a boring subject. There is only a subject about which the writer has not yet discovered the excitement and interest the subject contains.

Vividness

Vividness is a pleasure to produce on the page. We all like to tell stories, and stories always have distinct scenes, specific incidences, and bright descriptions. We enjoy reporting on our five senses:

My skin crawled as she told about that night.
I could smell the bacon frying as I jogged down the street.
Every time I closed my eyes, I saw her as she was waving from the
    steps of the plane.
I could taste that pepperoni pizza even before I put it in my mouth.
The reggae beat droned on all night as we lay under the stars.

The five senses are what make vivid writing possible. When you write, using your senses, you produce colors, scenes, images, sounds, pictures in the reader's mind. If you do so, you know that the reader will not forget what you wrote.

Clarity

Clarity results from two things: writers being clear in their own minds about what needs to be communicated and writers caring— and caring deeply—that the message is also clear to the reader. Clarity means being free from ambiguity, being translucent, having lucid understanding. When something is *clear*, it is free from darkness and cloudiness. It is easily seen and sharply defined, evident and easily understood.

One of the ways to achieve clarity in your writing is to read an early draft to a collaborator and ask, "What questions are you left with?" The collaborator's answers will direct you to what you need to revise to make your writing more clear. Another way you can achieve clarity is to outline the essay *after* it is written. By seeing the skeleton of the essay—the bones of its structure—you can see if this part connects to that, if this point leads to that. You can also increase the clarity in your writing by cutting as many words out of your final draft as you possibly can. Excess words make writing muddy. And so do abstractions and generalizations which are not supported by specifics. Here is where vividness overlaps with clarity. The more *vivid* your writing, the clearer it will be.

It is gusto, vividness, and clarity that separate the pro from the amateur, the well-paid from the poverty-striken, the often-read from the never-read writer. If your writing has these qualities, it is almost impossible for you not to be read, These qualities are infectious. They draw readers to your writing the way a sunny day draws people to the beach.

In the essays that follow you will find a mixture of gusto, vividness, and clarity in each piece. These qualities reinforce each other. They play off each other in such a way that while one of the qualities may be emphasized more than the other two in any particular essay, it is not possible to isolate one of them individually. Every one of these pieces reflects the author's vigorous enjoyment of the subject; exhibits bright, distinct images and words; and presents lucid, easy-to-understand information. Each essay is *spirited*. You can almost feel the authors' enthusiasm, excitement, and commitment as you read each essay. The commentaries that accompany each essay will point to specific things the authors did to produce the qualities of gusto, vividness, and clarity at their best. And you will see how to do this in your own writing. You can then put into practice what these writers have done.

PENNY WARD MOSER

The Curse of the Little Round Cans

I was in my tiny city kitchen when I realized it had all gone wrong. It was a night like any other. I was feeding my cats something better than I was feeding my husband. We were having plain chicken with rice. The cats, however, would be having Savory Stew, a meat and vegetable dish in a wonderful caramel-colored gravy. Our dinner would run 79 cents a pound, the cats' $1.18. What's more, if my husband didn't like his dinner, he'd still love me. But if the cats found something unsavory in their stew, they'd yowl, break things, and maybe pee in my shoe.

This didn't seem right. I never planned to have cats in the city. But one day when the back door was left open, a cat walked in. He looked hungry. (Cats always look hungry.) I fed him and set off to find his owner. That was in 1977. My second cat was given to me to care for until his family could relocate and send for him. That was in '79.

Now, whether I like it or not, these two giant street-tough feline bums are a permanent part of my home. . . .

Hind Legs Dancing on the Floor

It's because of them that I've fallen under what I consider to be "the curse of the little round cans." You know, the cans that take up more shelf space in America's groceries with each passing year, the cans that add 30 per cent to the amount of time it takes to check out and about that much to the bill.

That night in the kitchen I took a hard look at the little round can of Savory Stew in my hand. Morris the Cat looked back at me from the label, which exclaimed NOW BETTER TASTING. Morris isn't only an American institution; he has also come to personify the new relationship of cats to people in the U.S. He's a curmudgeonly, spoiled creature who intimidates adult human beings into picking only the best from the cat food aisle so that his conniving heart will leap for joy at every meal.

Both my cats, cued by my reach for the can opener, struck their preprandial frenzy pose, hind legs dancing on the floor, front feet clawing at the cabinet doors. Undaunted by this display, I took the time to read the ingredients on the label. They included carrots, bell peppers, peas, potatoes, and a host of strange things like thiamin mononitrate, ethylene-diamine dihydriodide, pyrodixone hydrochloride, and biotin, which all turn out to be vitamins or minerals. What's more, the label assured me, the little round can contained a complete and nutritionally balanced diet as recommended by the NRC. I pondered what role the Nuclear Regulatory Commission played in cat food. As I fed the cats, I resolved that the time had come to get to the bottom of what has swept over the cat food industry.

This first thing I learned was that I've been caught up in a national trend. According to polls that examine such things, the cat is "the pet of the Eighties." Some time in the '70s, probably as a result of smaller families, urbanization, or a nationwide madness, people started keeping more and more cats. This sudden infatuation is hard to explain, since it has always seemed to me that cats only occupy space and think about three things: food, sex, and nothing. If they're neutered, that leaves food.

Forty-eight Million Cats

Be that as it may, there are now some 48 million cats living in more than 27 million American households. This is ten million more cats and eight million more households than just five years ago. Tinier households, combined with convenience foods, mean fewer scraps. The cat food industry, which was a rather humble presence on the grocer's shelf, is off and running. And we're no longer talking about little factories grinding up fish eyeballs and chicken feet and sticking them into cans. We're talking about a big, complicated, and—wary of industrial espionage—security-conscious business.

Today in this country serious scientific research into the mysteries of feline taste preferences is hot stuff. Every morning dozens of scientists, technicians, and computer operators commence another exciting day of tests in the field of feline nutrition. At locations in California, Missouri, Kansas, Illinois, and Washington, some 2,700 test-kitchen cats warm up their taste buds for another round of determining what their brethren will eat tomorrow.

Two Billion Spent on Cat Food

Nearly $2 billion worth of cat food will be sold in the U.S. this year, and with that kind of market to be divvied up, it isn't surprising that there's been a boom in an area of science that most of us don't even know exists—the study of feline palatability. Not what cats taste like, but what tastes good to cats. These scientists and their gourmand cats have conspired to make the hands of cat owners pass over the cheaper, less tasty brands and land as if by magnetism on the more expensive little round cans.

The Big Four cat food makers, like the Big Four auto makers, are corporate giants, each with its own feline research department. Of the Big Four, only the folks at Ralston Purina are who they appear to be—the old animal chow company at Checkerboard Square in St. Louis. More cats crunch their dry food than any other brand. But 9-Lives, the canned food king, is owned by Star-Kist—making Morris the Cat and Charlie the Tuna distant cousins. Star-Kist is in turn owned by Heinz, the catsup company. Carnation, the maker of Friskies, is owned by Nestle's, the chocolate people. This makes perfect sense when you realize that Mars, the candy company, makes Kal Kan, the other major brand of cat food.

The cat food canners bank on the fact that cats, because of their keen sense of smell, preference for certain flavors, and general pain-in-the-neck attitude will often consider their food at length before eating—and maybe decide not to eat at all, at least while we're looking. We cat owners, most of us descendants of starving immigrants, can't stand to see something go hungry.

Cats' Keen Sense of Smell

Cats have such a highly developed sense of smell it's hard to sneak anything past them. They notice even minute changes in their food. But the industry, which must contend with the availability and prices of farm and marine commodities, sometimes has to make recipe substitutions. Say a mackerel boat comes in with a load of fluke, or the bottom has fallen out of the pork belly market and a million tons of pork lungs are for sale cheap. "We have to be ready to deal with limitations and substitutions," Ed Kane, a nutritionist at Carnation, says.

During a market emergency, Carnation chefs in Van Nuys, California can whip up a trial batch of cat food and air-express it to Kane. An emergency panel of cats—sometimes awakened from naps—is assembled to begin tasting pronto. Down the coast, an entire cat food factory may be on hold, awaiting the cats' final word. . . .

Only in America

Only in America is so much fuss made about cat food. Kane says that not long ago he gave a tour of the cattery to some visiting bureaucrats from the Soviet Union. He explained the whole palatability concept to them as they stared at him. "They were very polite," Kane says, "and in the end, they had only one question. They asked me what we did with the pelts."

Beyond worrying about how the food tastes, the scientists fuss over how it smells and feels. 9-Lives scientists look at something they call the relish factor—how a cat responds to the sound and smell of the can being opened. Ralston Purina researches "mouth feel," which is supposed to determine whether cats prefer their food round, square, oval, or star-shaped. Carnation is proud of the way their Fancy Feast product plops out of its pull-tab can without anyone having to dirty a spoon. This makes it the consummate yuppie cat food for the busy one-cat household.

The plop factor is only one of the concessions to human attitudes and sensibilities that cat food researchers must make. It's no good for business if the food makes the consumer cringe when he opens the can. "After all, people are the ones taking if off the shelf," says Norm Riggs, 9-Lives general manager for product development and quality assurance.

This explains why my cats' food frequently looks better than my own. The 9-Lives people have come up with a meat and cream gravy line that's so good that more than one consumer has wondered if there's a secret ingredient—like catnip—in the gravy that makes it addictive. There isn't. According to 9-Lives, the reason cats freak out over the cream gravy is that it contains real cream. What's more, Riggs explains, "they tend to lick it off first because they don't like to get the gravy stuck on their noses when they eat the meat."

This is a lot of information to get out of a cat food company. While a company must list a can's ingredients on the label in order of their preponderance, the exact formulas are kept as secret as the combination to the vault at Fort Knox. . . .

There is, however, one magic sauce used throughout the industry—a substance called "digest." Digest is liquefied, predigested meat, added to the yummy gravies on canned foods and baked into the dry chow. In the manufacture of digest, meat is enzymatically broken down—in a tank, not in a cat's stomach—until it reaches the desired consistency. Then it's covered with phosphoric acid to halt the process, after which it's added to the food and cooked with it. Cats just love its tangy taste.

Cats Are Spoiled

One might well wonder where all this commotion has gotten the cat. Well, it's gotten him spoiled. Veterinarians will tell you that for your average healthy feline, you can just serve a well known brand of inexpensive cat food, and he'll be fine. He simply won't know any better. (However, most vets warn against generic brands, some of which have attained notoriety for making kitty's hair fall out.) At the other end of the scale, some vets are afraid that the super-gourmet foods in little cans, with their high fat content, are giving cats too many calories, and maybe even more protein than they need. Actually, the better known low-priced, nutritionally complete brand names in larger cans, which use a higher percentage of cereals, are just as good for the cat, perhaps better. "Most of the research done at major cat food companies is on palatability," says veterinarian Lon Lewis of Topeka, Kansas, a leading small-animal clinical nutritionist. "People judge pet food by how much their animals like it. They have no way of knowing whether it's best for the specific animal. But palatability is a terrible way to judge a food. . . ."

The question remains, of course: Why did our old barn cats, eating Jell-O and Cheerios, live to be 20 years old, reproducing successfully, in fact *very* successfully, their whole lives? The answer is mice—mice and their nutritionally comparable rodent cousins.

According to Kane, because a mouse's tiny body provides all the necessary amino and fatty acids and its little bones all the right vitamins and minerals, it's "the perfect food for a cat." But, Lewis counters, "only if it's cooked," pointing out that mice can harbor bacteria and parasites.

So why doesn't some enterprising company cook some mice, grind the little suckers up, and put 'em in a can? Well, for one thing, the human consumer probably wouldn't go for it. And the cat might not be nuts about it, either. A friend of mine has a persnickety young female cat that he found in a steam tunnel under the Smithsonian Institution in Washington, D.C. For a year the cat presumably had lived on nothing but mice and water. My friend rescued her and treated her to a pricy brand of food. Today, he says, "a mouse could do a handstand on her head without disturbing her nap."

A Canadian study some years back showed that when given a choice, cats prefer canned cat food—even the cheaper, less tasty, brands—to rats. (They also preferred cold rats to warm rats, and salmon to anything else.) For reasons we don't know, cats prefer cooked foods to raw.

This could lead us to conclude logically, if not scientifically, that cats eat rodents because that's what they can get. If cats were bigger and handier, they'd knock off a cow or a salmon and throw it in the microwave.

None of this explains why America's cats last year packed away some 880 million pounds of hard, crunchy nuggets known as dry cat food. My own little darlings have something called Special Dinners Farm Style [hah!] Dinner for breakfast. The label lists 42 different ingredients, which come in beige triangles with a dairy-based coating. The cats, which love it, are obviously harking back to an ancestral time when triangular, beige, milk-covered mice roamed the earth.

In fact, my cats are on to something, and they aren't the only ones. During one of my research trips, something happened that I knew would occur somewhere along the line. A man, an old cat food hand, reached into a bag of 9-Lives Crunchy Meals, picked out a few pieces, and popped them in his mouth. "They're really not bad," he said. Others followed suit. Finally, I reached in, selected a golden nugget, chewed it up, and swallowed it. Nothing to it. It tasted just like a Cheerio. With a little milk and sugar you'd never know.

If You Ever Get Stranded

I was reminded of a story told me by a Kansas veterinarian. He said he was a pilot and often flew to remote regions of Canada and Mexico. "Before I take off I always make sure I've got a ten-pound bag of dry pet food in the plane," he said. "If I ever got stranded, I'd have with me the most nutritious food, ounce per ounce, that money can buy."

I'm wondering now if by any chance the next time the cat's dinner looks better than ours, maybe if I served it with rice and a nice salad . . .

Elizabeth Neeld Comments:

✦ *Even though this article was written for a science magazine,* Discovery, *Penny Ward Moser writes with* spirit. *You can tell that she enjoyed divulging to her readers the almost unbelievable information she discovered when she researched cat food in America. She clearly was surprised— maybe even shocked—at what she found. And it's clear that she expects her readers to feel the same way.* ✦ *One of the first things that reveals Penny Moser's gusto for her subject is her revelation of how she got hooked on this subject. "I was in my tiny kitchen when I realized it had all gone wrong. . . . Our dinner would run 79 cents a pound, the cats' $1.18. . . . I resolved that the time had come to get to the bottom of what has swept over the cat food industry." We have been made part of someone's personal story. The subject—cat food—has been connected to a live human being—Penny Moser—in a real situation—one* evening in her kitchen. She's engaged in the topic, and we are, too. (Remember, being engaged with what you are writing about is at the heart of writing with gusto) ◆ Penny Moser's exuberance and spirit show up in the snappy language she uses: "I've fallen under what I consider to be 'the curse of the little round cans' "; "And we're no longer talking about little factories grinding up fish eyeballs and chicken feet and sticking them into cans"; "Today in this country serious scientific research into the mysteries of feline taste preferences is hot stuff"; "We cat owners, most of us descendants of starving immigrants, can't stand to see something go hungry"; "Down the coast, an entire cat food factory may be on hold, awaiting the cats' final word"; "This makes it the consummate yuppie cat food for the busy one-cat household"; "One might well wonder what all this commotion has gotten the cat. Well, it's gotten him spoiled"; "Why did the old barn cats, eating Jell-O and Cheerios, live to be 20 years old"; "So why doesn't some enterprising company cook some mice, grind the little suckers up, and put 'em in a can?"; "If cats were bigger and handier, they'd knock off a cow or a salmon and throw it in the microwave"; "I'm wondering now if by any chance the next time the cat's dinner looks better than ours, maybe if I served it with rice and a nice salad . . ."◆ There's verve and energy and interest and excitement flashing around every paragraph Moser writes, all communicated to us, the readers, by the vividness of the words and the conversational tone and rhythm of the sentences.◆ The wealth of information Moser has gathered also assures the presence of gusto, vividness, and clarity. She has interesting facts to tell us: there are forty-eight million cats in America; we spend two billion dollars on cat food each year; twenty-seven hundred test kitchens research what cats like to eat. The facts are startling, surprising, perhaps even amazing. We are hooked by these facts. The information itself stimulates our interest. She can hardly believe what she discovered, and we can't either. The research findings themselves contribute to Moser's gusto on the page.◆ The sterling qualities of this writing can be reproduced in your writing, also, if your are committed to (1) becoming engaged in *your subject; (2) finding hopping-alive words and phrases to describe your subject; and (3) gathering surprising, interesting information about your subject. You will then be able to write with increased gusto, vividness, and clarity. And you'll have as much fun as Penny Ward Moser did, in the process.* ✦

MILTON KAPLAN

Adult Education

When my daughter presented her baby son to me for the first time, I was, of course, curious to see what he looked like. I had to admit that he looked like the helpless creature he was, his eyes unfocused and his head wobbling on the thin stem of his neck. My daughter, however, was ecstatic. After all, this was her baby, who had grown inside of her as she nurtured him month after month. The father was also transfixed with joy. It was his baby, too, his son. As for me, I held the baby carefully in my arms. I wanted to feel my kinship with him, but somehow I couldn't experience the surge of joy that is supposed to engulf grandfathers; yet I will acknowledge that my wife dissolved when she first beheld her grandson.

The Blob Began to Develop

No, there was curiosity, but the infant was hardly a person one could love. Little by little, I must report, the blob of humanity began to develop more definite features and to focus his attention. He even learned to smile, and I smiled back and spoke to him, although I was sure he couldn't understand a word I said. I didn't see him every day—my daughter lives too far away for anything like that—but every time she visited, the baby revealed some new sign of progress.

There was the time, for example, long before he was a year old, when he was given a piece of bread, which he munched with considerable but toothless enjoyment. Finding the room a bit cool, his mother slipped his left arm through the sleeve of a sweater. "Now put your bread in your other hand," she said. The baby complied at once, and his right arm went into the sleeve, I was thunderstruck. This tiny tot understood language! He could think!

On their visits to us, I was entrusted with the privilege of wheeling the infant in his stroller. I found that I liked to job because I could show the child the wonders of the world, wonders that were completely new to him. Sitting in the stroller, his eyes round with amazement, he reacted to the miracles around him. I wheeled him slowly down the street, stopping every now and then to allow him to fasten his eyes on a new wonder.

On the corner, for instance, was the fire hydrant, so familiar a sight that it had become invisible to me until the baby's eyes lingered on the topknot set in the mushroom head and then traveled down to meet the flare of two enormous nostrils. The apparition suddenly loomed so hideous that I began to back off. A squawk of protest halted me in my tracks, and I remained rooted while the youngster completed his inventory. Then we moved on.

A cat darted across the road, too quick for the baby's scan, but I managed to snare a squirrel in our gaze, and it stood up and stared at us. The little boy stared back. I broke the spell. "Squirrel," I explained, "Squirrel."

Continuing our journey of exploration, we rolled on. I stopped under the overhanging branches of a tree and we looked up into the dark mystery of an oak. Our pace became increasingly aware of what a strange new world I was offering. An acorn in the road won our rapt concentration briefly. I picked it up and handed it to the child. His fingers closed around the treasure in a tight grip. A dog

appeared on the lawn, barking a friendly greeting. Our eyes out-
lined his form from head to tail. "Dog," I said. "This is a dog." The
baby blinked in acknowledgment. I picked up a red autumnal leaf.
"Leaf. Leaf." The baby accepted the gift and held it in his other
hand.

A Strange Kind of Joy

By the time we got back, he was very tired, and his eyelids began to
droop. I was surprised to discover that I was tired, too, and I knew
why. I was back to the days when my daughter was an infant, and,
seeing the world once again through a baby's eyes, I found the
everyday details of my existence suddenly charged with a significance that was overwhelming.

I began to take the little explorer on similar expeditions. A
shopping mall, on one occasion, became a kaleidoscope of images
as we joined the procession of shoppers, stopping to survey a
store window and inspect a display of stuffed bears. In the pet
shop, we watched a puppy roll over and over in a bed of sawdust.
Wide-eyed, we followed the movement of an escalator rising with
its load of passengers. There were shoes to be examined, one by
one, and the sparkle of red, green and yellow in the florist's shop. It
was soon time to turn back, but we paid a last visit to the pet store
to look at the puppy once more. The baby started forward to greet
his friend. His eyes never wavered. As the puppy tumbled acrobati-
cally to entertain his audience, the boy raised his hand and
pointed at the animal. "Dog," he said. "Dog."

I was filled with a strange kind of joy. Here was an infant not
even a year old, seemingly helpless and dependent, and yet he was
beginning to use language, to identify elements in his environment and to find a place in his world. Although he was a mere
baby, he was a definite and distinct person. I felt a warm rush of
respect and affection for the little fellow. He was my grandson.

Elizabeth Neeld Comments:

✦ *Milton Kaplan is a writer and a poet who lives in New
Jersey. He is also a grandfather. In this personal essay,
which he wrote for* The New York Times *magazine, Milton
Kaplan talks about his evolving relationship with his new
grandson.* ✦ *What makes this essay so vivid? What ex-*

plains our ability—no matter what our age or experience—
to know "just exactly what he is talking about?" What did
he do that made his experience so clear to us? ✦
Probably one of Kaplan's first achievements was how he
described the new baby. Each of us has likely viewed a
newborn and thought, "How strange this creature looks."
Kaplan, even though talking about his grandson, saw a
"helpless creature . . . eyes unfocused and his head wobbling on the thin stem of his neck." This description helps
us to identify with the subject. Someone has told a truth
that we have recognized for ourselves. (Finding something
about your subject that the reader can identify as a shared
truth establishes a context in which your other points will
seem very sensible and clear.) ✦ Milton Kaplan then engages us in an unfolding drama. (Unfolding the plot of a
drama is another way for making your writing vivid for the
reader.) The baby—this "blob of humanity"—began to
develop. He smiled, He demonstrated one day that he understood language: he moved a piece of bread from one
hand to the other at the request of his mother. The grandfather saw some possibility there that wasn't there
before. ✦ The next step in the unfolding of the drama is
the grandfather taking the baby out in his stroller. Here
Kaplan is a master of vivid language: The fire hydrant with
the "topknot set in the mushroom head" and the "flare of
two enormous nostrils. The apparition loomed so hideous." There were the "dark mysteries of an oak . . . an
acorn. His fingers closed around the treasure in a tight
grip." A dog appeared, and the grandfather spoke to the
baby: "Dog . . . . This is a dog." There was a red autumnal
leaf. "Leaf. Leaf," the grandfather taught the child. ✦
Then we come to the heart of the essay: the trip to the
shopping mall. The drama which has engaged us continues
to unfold. Kaplan lets us see every detail: The store window
with stuffed bears; the pet shop where the puppy rolls over
and over in the sawdust; the escalator; shoes to examine;
colors of red, green, and yellow in a florist's shop. Then one
last trip back to the pet shop. The baby raises his hand and
points to the animal: "Dog," he said. "Dog." The grandfather "was filled with a strange kind of joy." ✦ Then Kaplan gives us the climax of the story: "Here was an infant not

even a year old, . . . and yet he was beginning to use language. . . . Although he was a mere baby, he was a definite and distinct person. I felt a warm rush of respect and affection for the little fellow. He was my grandson." ◆ *If we, the readers, have not had the same experience watching a baby explore a new world, we do remember what it was like when we were children discovering the wonders of life around us. Kaplan retells his experience so vividly and so clearly that we identify with it and make it our own. We know what he is talking about. We also marvel at the wonder a little human being is. We leave the essay a little in awe. We have had, as the title of the essay says, an "Adult Education."* ◆

Miss Pilger's English Class

The subject is spinach pie. "Spanish pie?" Tony Rosa asks eagerly, thinking he has heard the teacher say a familiar word.

"No," says Jean Pilger, the teacher. "Spinach pie."

"Ah-h-h," Tony says, a smile of understanding lighting his handsome young face. Most of the other students in this ESL (English as a second language) class are still puzzling over the topic of tonight's lesson. But Tony, a 26-year-old from Honduras who arrived in New York five months ago, knows all about the leafy green vegetable that makes you strong. To improve his English, he has been watching Popeye cartoons on television.

"Guess who uses spinach?" he prints in his black-and-white notebook, his question mark a proud flourish.

They come, some after long, hot days in factories, sweatshops and restaurant kitchens, others after caring for their families all day and making sure dinner is on the table.

Every Monday and Wednesday night from 6 to 9 P.M. in a classroom of Public School 126 in Chinatown, there is a Babel of accents, with syntax flying, tenses colliding, articles and pronouns mysteriously appearing and disappearing. Over this grammatical game of bumper cars, Jean Pilger calmly presides.

The students call her "teacher" or "Miss Pilger," although she has suggested they all be on a first-name basis. An abstract artist in her spare time, Miss Pilger draws pictures on the board to help illuminate the mysteries of "chop" versus "shop," "great" versus "grate," "okra" versus "turnips," "beating eggs" versus "beating the clock."

The students are tired when they straggle in, but as class begins, their mood becomes "jazzed up," as Miss Pilger puts it. It is her students' longing to learn that draws the teacher . . .

A Teacher's Work

The New York City Board of Education teaches English as a second language to more than 18,000 adults in 300 classes all over the city—the highest enrollment ever. Twenty years ago, when the courses first began, the students were mostly Puerto Rican; now there are many Central Americans and Asians enrolled, as well as a sprinkling of nationalities from other areas of the world . . .

Many other instructors would not be interested in teaching this demanding course. And, with a bachelor's degree from Stanford University and master's degrees in library science from Columbia University and in fine arts from the University of the Americas in Mexico City, the 63-year-old teacher concedes she is "overeducated for this job."

But she tried teaching high school and quit after a year. "It was mostly babysitting," says Jean Pilger, a rumpled, plain-spoken woman who rides a bicycle about town and wears corduroy pants and Puma sneakers.

"I spent a lot of time making sure the kids didn't smoke in the cafeteria," she adds drily, looking over the black glasses worn low on the bridge of her nose.

"I do this because I love working with foreigners," she says. "They don't come to study for fun. They are scrounging and really hustling to survive all day, and then they come here at night to learn enough English to better themselves. What these people want is a better life. That's what everyone wants. They associate that with the United States. Economically and politically, it's a big step up for them. They want to learn as much as they can, everything and anything." . . .

Even outside class, Miss Pilger enunciates each syllable, a habit developed over her 18 years of teaching English as a second language for the city's Adult Education Program. Her straightforward, somewhat gruff manner masks a gentle concern and respect for her students. Along with words and pronunciation, Miss Pilger tries to teach them more subtle lessons about pride and social mixing in the big city.

"They can't hide in their ethnic neighborhoods," she says. "There's a lot of competition for jobs out there, and they have to be willing to ask other people to help them." Her lessons, such as the one about Mrs. Tsui, an efficient saleswoman, or about Mr. Jenkins, a conscientious mailman, are geared toward economic survival in New York.

Her work is complicated by the fact that the educational backgrounds of her students vary widely. Some are well-educated professionals; others have had little formal schooling. There are cultural variables to deal with as well. The Asians, with their proper bits of British grammar, tend to be reserved, and she must encourage them to show more initiative in class and not be drowned out by the more exuberant Latins.

She tries not to correct the students too often, preferring to let them work at the blackboard or in pairs and correct one another. She reckons they face enough embarrassment over their English during the day.

"I feel sympathetic about that—it's disheartening for them," she says. "Americans are not too tolerant of foreign accents. We don't have time to treat people nicely here. When they are not understood, they get put down. "What did you say, dummy?' 'Why can't you get it right?' 'What do you mean?' "

Wanting to shield her students from such ridicule, she concentrates on questions and answers, trying to build their dialogue skills. "Foreigners get insulted when they are asked questions that they can't understand," she says. "Take the Asian women in the sweatshops, for instance. The boss picks up a pair of pants off the floor and says, 'Why-didn't-you-finish-this-before?' All they understand is the 'why' and the 'before.' So they stand there with their dumb faces hanging out and the boss thinks they're ignorant and treats them as ignorant."

Very Nice

The students gather in a circle, trying to hold a conversation about what they did over the weekend. Miss Pilger is sitting at her desk peeling an orange, listening but not interrupting.

Outside, the sounds of Catherine Street cascade: rock music blaring from box radios, firecrackers exploding, teen-agers shouting and drunks carousing. Inside, things are ominously quiet.

"I have nothing to say," announces Rosa Diaz, who always has something to say.

Rosa, 47, is a small, chubby woman with a warm personality who emits a staccato stream of fractured English. She came from Puerto Rico 29 years ago, got married and settled in New York, surviving outside her Hispanic circle with a smattering of English. Now she wants to learn to speak properly, and in class she is fearless, shouting out answers for nearly everything. She is thrilled when she is right and nearly as happy when she is wrong.

"You have nothing to say?" ask Shu Yi Yu, a delicate 29-year-old Chinese woman who works in a garment factory in the neighborhood.

"No," says Rosa, energetically shaking her head. "On weekend, I sick. I stay home, have head cold. You know, cough, cough. I no went anywhere."

"I didn't go anywhere," corrects Shu Yi.

"Me, too, I stay home," agrees Rosa good-naturedly."

Shu Yi tries another gambit. Turning her bright smile on Lydia Perez, a 37-year-old housewife from the Dominican Republic, she asks: "Are you a housewife?"

Not understanding the question, but assuming it has something to do with her weekend, Lydia answers that she went to Passaic, N.J., to visit a cousin and bought the turquoise chiffon blouse she is wearing.

Her smile starting to falter a bit, Shu Yi tries once more, this time asking the older woman next to her, Catarina Arqueta, a nurse from El Salvador who has a kind face and short coppery hair, if she has any houseplants that she tends on weekends.

But Catarina is not sure what she means. "Blintzes?" she asks. "Plans?"

"Plants," says Shu Yi. "I have pepper, tomato. I put some water on them. They open."

"Oh, *plants*," says Catarina. "In my house? No."

Conversation dies. The silence stretches for several long moments. Finally, Sigifredo Valladares, a 30-year-old factory worker from Peru who has been consulting the Spanish-English dictionary in his lap, plunges in. "Yesterday," he tells the group pleasantly, "I was fishing in Sheepshead Bay. It was very nice."

Everyone nods and smiles in relief. "Very nice," they agree.

I Feel Good in America

Alexandra Bobeczko, a willowy 26-year-old blonde from Poland, leans against the window ledge in the hall during dinner break.

"Circles," she says, pointing to the smudges under her eyes. "Terrible. All the time, tired, tired. But I'd like to stay in America, and if I stay, it's very important for me, I have to learn English."

Alexandra was nearly finished with a law course when she left her home to come to New York and stay with a Polish girlfriend 10 months ago. "I thinking about freedom," say says. "I thinking about a lot of different people, everyone making what they want of themselves."

Now she works, along with her girlfriend, as a waitress at a Ukrainian restaurant in the East Village, some days working an early shift that starts at 7 A.M. and other days a late shift that ends at 2 A.M. "All the time, speaking with customers about chicken cutlet, pea soup, lentil and nothing more," she says, rolling her eyes. "And when I come home, I have no time for reading."

Sometimes she is too tired to come to school, and sometimes she chafes at the slow pace of the class and her drop in status. "My mother says all the time, 'Come back to the Poland.' I was rich in the Poland. I had free car and apartment. It's very crazy, working in America so hard."

The people are not always friendly, she says. "And the Village is crazy! All those punks and strange people."

"But I like America," she adds with a shrug. "I feel good in America."

Their Yellow Brick Road

They all have goals, some small, some grandiose, and English is their yellow brick road.

Shu Yi Yu lives with her family in Brooklyn and sews pants in a Chinatown factory. "I no like," she says, her constant smile in place. "Hard work. Many dust." She leaves class early one night with a headache, explaining that her boss won't install an air conditioner in the hot factory. She wants to learn enough English to work as a saleswoman in a department store. Her friend, Kenna Yu, a 25-year-old from Hong Kong, confides as she munches on dinner—a sesame roll that she holds in a wax paper bag—that she, too, dreams of escaping from the sweatshop and becoming a secretary.

José Antonio (Tony) Rosa and Sigifredo Valladares were both engineering students, Tony in Honduras and Sigifredo in Peru. Tony left because he did not want to get drafted into the Honduran Army. Now he lives with his aunt and uncle near the school and stirs the dye in a Brooklyn factory that stamps slogans on T-shirts. "You know, things like 'I Love New York' or 'I Unhappy,' " he explains, as he accepts half a ham-and-cheese sandwich from Rosa during the break. A friendly, easygoing young man who rides his bike from the factory, Tony says he loves New York because of "the music, the clubs and the beautiful women."

Sigifredo is more serious and always carries his Spanish-English dictionary. He left Peru when the sol's value plunged and the jobs "were only going to ministers' sons and people with pull." Now he works in a factory downtown, repairing the numbers and dials on watches. He says the job is not demanding and lets him concentrate on English. Both young men hope to resume their engineering careers.

Francisco Lopez, 25, a delivery boy at the fashionable Water Club restaurant, has a hard time with the lessons, Miss Pilger says. But he studies doggedly, brimming with determination to make a better life for his wife and 4-year-old daughter. He hopes to move up in the restaurant if his English improves, first to stockman, then to grander things. "I like to be a waiter, a cook," says the young immigrant from the Dominican Republic, smiling sweetly as he shows off a tattered business card from the Water Club that he keeps in his wallet. . . .

Several of the Hispanic women in class have been in this country for more than 20 years, but, cloistered in ethnic neighborhoods and busy raising families, they got along with "street" English. Now, as their children draw away from their ethnic roots, these women want to learn how to read and write and speak correctly, seeing this as an important link to their youngsters' lives and futures.

Luz Gonzalez, 38, from Puerto Rico, began coming to class after her daughter Josephine, a student in the fifth grade here at P.S.

126, refused to speak to her in Spanish anymore. "She say, 'No, you have to learn,' " Luz recalls. The oldest of her five children, Mary Lou, is at City College, and Luz's pride in having a daughter at an American college is as deep as her frustration at not having enough English to say what her major is. In Spanish, she explains that Mary Lou is studying vocational work in the health field.

Luz was shy about her reading and writing skills at first, afraid to join in. So Miss Pilger suggested that she take charge of serving coffee during the breaks. Her confidence grew with her new task and now she is always one of the students chosen to work at the blackboard.

"I want to learn English to help my kids," she says, as she sets up her coffee pot in the back of the classroom. "I go to doctors with them and I need an interpreter. I can't help with their homework." Josephine, 11, and Mildred, 6, sometimes come to pick Luz up after school.

She always comes to class, even when she is tired. "It's a pleasure," she says, her eyes downcast, her smile gentle. "Every day I learn one word or two."

Her friend Rosa, who lives near Luz in a city housing project on South Street, arrived here from Puerto Rico in 1956. As the students look at pictures of fruit in class, she chatters to her seatmates about her days as a migrant worker in Florida and Michigan, picking oranges and cherries and strawberries. In New York, she worked in a clothing factory in Brooklyn, cutting material for sweaters, before she married Ramon Diaz. Her husband has a job with the city's Human Resources Administration "filling in some paper, I don't know," according to Rosa.

"I marry, I have seven kids, one died, every year a new one," she says, when asked why she waited so long to learn English. "And, you know, I don't have time for school. Cleaning house all the time. Now I have the time."

A grandmother of two, she fixes a hearty dinner for her husband and the three children still at home before she leaves for class at night.

Lydia Perez lives in a different housing project on South Street with her husband and four children. She also wants to learn English for the sake of her children, and for the time when she will go back to work. Her husband, who hurt his back in an accident at the restaurant where he worked and had to have a plastic disk implanted, is on disability. And her 9-year-old daughter has scoliosis, a curvature of the spine. "Every two weeks I go to the clinic with my daughter but I no understand too much English," she says. Miss Pilger admiringly calls her "a gutsy woman."

Sung Thach, a short, stocky man who was a lawyer, army colonel and congressman in South Vietnam, seems to be the most grimly determined student. He had the hardest time getting here and he has set the most ambitious goal for himself.

He was in prison in Vietnam for six years before escaping to Thailand in 1982. He arrived in New York nearly a year ago and now lives on welfare, spending all his time in different free English classes offered throughout the city and studying every night until past midnight in the Bronx apartment he shares with a Cambodian doctor.

"I don't have time to play," he says in his clipped English. "I want to learn. You know, I'm 51 years old. I don't have time. Very old."

He travels an hour and 15 minutes each way on the subway to get to the Chinatown class, believing that if he can become fluent in English, he can get a job as an interpreter and send for his wife and five children, who are still in Vietnam. He also hopes to give lectures in America and explain "the true situation in Vietnam" under Communist rule, both to the public and to government officials. He has written President Reagan twice but received no response, and he blames his poor communication skills.

"If I could speak I would have a better chance to tell them," he says, throwing up his hands. "It is very bad there."

Give Them More

Miss Pilger is at the blackboard, going over the lesson on spinach pie.

"Some people like to cook, but everyone likes to eat," she reads, adding, "Eating is fun."

"No," calls out Rosa, clutching her round stomach. "Fat, fat, fat!"

Suppressing a smile, Miss Pilger continues the recipe: "Beat until the mixture is smooth."

"Smooth" is a rough one, both to pronounce and to understand. Sigifredo asks if it is the same as gentle, and Miss Pilger, with the aid of a few Spanish words, explains the difference.

"'Smooth' is no lumps," chimes in Rosa helpfully. "Beat it! Beat it good!"

The recipe calls for greasing the bottom and sides of a baking dish, and Miss Pilger asks if anyone knows the difference between oil and grease.

"Oil comes from the corn," says Rosa. "Grease comes from the animal—from the pig, the lard."

When Miss Pilger gets to the section on cheddar cheese, the students have problems with "grater." So she draws the utensil on the board.

"Yes, like that," calls Rosa, admiring the art work. "I'm using it at home."

When Miss Pilger reads the end of the recipe, suggesting that the pie will serve four people, Rosa shakes her head. In her view of hospitality, surely this paltry pie, a staple of restaurants on the Upper West Side, will only be enough for two. "If somebody comes to my house," she says, "I give them more." . . .

Occasionally, the seating problems can reflect international tensions, with Thais and Cambodians feeling uncomfortable around Vietnamese students, or Vietnamese feeling uncomfortable around Chinese. But Miss Pilger tries to smooth over such political divisions.

A feminist, she tries to avoid sexual bias in her classes. In the lesson on spinach pie, she shows pictures of men cooking, and she quizzes the men, not the women, about their culinary skills.

She also fights racial bias. She recalls intervening one night when Carmen Pequero, a 40-year-old student from the Dominican Republic, winced at a remark by one of the Asian women that blacks were lazy. "Why are black people lazy?" she asked. "I'm lazy. You might feel lazy today." She hoped the woman would think more carefully about her value judgments in the future. "I hate generalizations," Miss Pilger snaps.

The students begin responding to Miss Pilger's respect and gentle prodding by trusting her with their broken English—and more.

Shu Yi asks her how to get the forms to apply for citizenship. And after Kenna Yu tells Miss Pilger about the $300 fee she paid a lawyer to help her get citizenship, the teacher intercedes with the local legal aid office in an effort to get her student's money back.

Miss Pilger frets that many of her students are being exploited, working very hard for little pay because they cannot speak English well, and her teaching reflects her determination to give them the fluency they need to make their way fairly in New York.

She measures her progress in more than vocabulary learned. "The Board of Education comes around sometimes and says the reading levels are not high enough, we should show more progress," she says, in her typically blunt fashion. "And I feel like saying, 'Where are all the jobs for these people?' We should combine English lessons with vocational training."

You've Done Well Tonight

Several students are working at the blackboard, writing out sentences from the spinach pie recipe.

"Cottage cheese" is problematic. Sung Thach writes "cottage of cheese" and Luz Gonzalez writes "cotter cheese." She also misspells "spinach."

"No *e* on 'spinach,'" whispers Francisco conspiratorially from his seat in the front row.

And, despite the helpful efforts of Shu Yi, her neighbor at the blackboard, Rosa is having a devil of a time with "tablespoons." It is coming out with extra *p*s, extra *o*s, and odd *m*s and *b*s.

Aside from these minor troubles, however, the students are feeling more comfortable with the lesson and are filling up the blackboard, and their notebooks, with reasonable facsimiles of the recipe.

Seeing her students fading after their long day, Miss Pilger decides to let them leave 10 minutes early. Brusquely, she tells them they have done especially well tonight.

Rosa, white with chalk, flushed with pride, puts on her sweater. "Now I go home," she says. "I wash the dishes. I clean my, my, my, uh . . ." She pauses, stymied, and then breaks into a grin. "My kitchen!" she calls out triumphantly, sailing out the door.

Elizabeth Neeld Comments:

✦ *Bilingual education, ESL (English as a Second Language), illegal aliens, immigration quotas, assimilation into society: all these are hotly debated and extremely complex issues in education, politics, and government. Maureen Dowd writes in this essay about these issues in such a way that we recognize with our minds the seriousness and complexity of the issues at the same time that our hearts are engaged with the personalities and actions of the individuals she writes about. "Miss Pilger's English Class" has, without a doubt, gusto, vividness, and clarity. Let's see how Maureen Dowd achieves this. ✦ The first thing we notice is that the writer begins with a specific example. A humorous specific example. The twenty-six-year-old Honduran student confuses spinach and Spanish and then is able to get it all straightened out because he has been watching Popeye cartoons on television. Maureen Dowd does not begin the essay by discussing the abstractions of the problems in teaching foreign students English; she does not make general statements about the issues. She paints a scene for us in words, a picture we can see easily. This scene, as interesting and engaging as it is, also serves another purpose: it implicitly relates several aspects of the thorny situation that arises when non-English-speaking adults attempt to learn English. We are hooked intellectually and emotionally at the very start. ✦ The next thing we notice about how Dowd achieves gusto, vividness, and clarity in her writing is the language she uses—action-packed words: "there is a Babel of accents, with syntax flying, tenses colliding, articles and pronouns mysteriously appearing and disappearing. Over this grammatical game of bumper cars . . . " A classic example of vivid, exactly-on-the-mark use of language! The teacher uses "pictures on the board to help illuminate the mysteries of 'chop' versus 'shop,' 'great' versus 'grate,' 'okra' versus 'turnip,' 'beating eggs' versus 'beating the clock.' " We learn that the "students are tired when they straggle in, but as class begins, their mood becomes 'jazzed up.' " Sharp, alive words are a secret of vivid and clear writing. ✦ Only at this point does Dowd give us background facts—eighteen thousand adults in New York City study English as a second language; there are three hundred classes over the city; here is a teacher "overeducated" for the job but committed to more than the students' language skills. By this time we are ready to be interested in these facts. We know enough to begin to care. ✦ Dowd uses humor again, describing a scene in which the students attempt to have a conversation about what they did this weekend. Rosa Diaz just cannot understand. We laugh gently with the students as we read about*

Shu Yi's attempt to lead the group into a conversation in which they communicate. ✦ *As we read on, we notice strong words like* doggedly *and* brimming with determination, *and we can again see how Dowd achieves what she does when she writes.* ✦ *The article ends with humor and triumph. Even though the students are still writing* cottage of cheese *and* spinache *and* tablespoons *with extra* ps *and* os *and odd* ms *and* bs, *we watch Rosa Diaz leave the class:* "I wash the dishes. I clean my, my, my, uh . . . . My kitchen!" *And she "triumphantly" sails out the door. The conclusion of this essay illustrates yet another feature of writing that has gusto, vividness, and clarity: the writer's humaneness, her genuine caring for the people about whom she writes. It's more than* engagement, *although it is certainly that. It is the expression of the writer's humanity. Such a commitment when we write can go a long way to compensate any lack of sophisticated writing skills we might not think we have.* ✦

TOM RICHMAN

Talking Cost

Maybe your company is different, but at most companies I know, controlling costs is a subject guaranteed to cure insomnia among employees and middle managers. It's not that they don't care about profit margins and such. They do. They just have a lot of other things on their minds, such as their jobs. Profits, revenues, costs—those are the big numbers that chief executive officers are supposed to worry about. And if the numbers get out of whack, well, that's the CEO's problem, isn't it?

This attitude is, of course, a source of considerable frustration for CEOs, who can't really do much about the big numbers without a good deal of cooperation from below. But how can they elicit the cooperation? What's the trick? There must be some technique, they figure, some clever device for getting employees charged up about controlling costs.

There isn't. When you come right down to it, cost control is almost entirely a matter of attitude—yours, as well as your employees'. You can't make them care about controlling costs unless you show them what the problem is, and how they can help solve it. That involves giving them information, often sensitive information, but more important, giving it to them in a form that they understand.

Speak English

All this came to mind recently as I was listening to Bob Popaditch, who owns Thrifty Scot Warehouse Food Inc., a chain of discount grocery stores in Orlando. It was a warm Friday afternoon, and we had just finished lunch with a half dozen or so of his store managers. Popaditch was saying a few words on the subject of cost control and profit margins. He has a pretty firm grasp of such matters. He has to: his business does not leave much room for error. Nevertheless, his managers were less than enthralled.

"Let's talk about the last 36 weeks," he began. "You could say that things look pretty good. Sales were just 2.09% off budget. Not bad. Payroll was over budget a bit, but only by 0.24%. Pretty close.

"And look at this." He flipped his hand-drawn chart. "Gross [profit] margin was off only 0.1%. It was supposed to be 15.8%, and we came in at 15.7%."

CEOs find such numbers fascinating, as do competitors. Indeed, many companies would not dream of sharing them with employees. But they held little magic for Popaditch's managers, who were clearly getting bored. They had stores to run, merchandise to move, people to supervise, and problems piling up while the CEO stood there talking about his problems. Not their problems—*his*. They slumped in their metal folding chairs.

But Popaditch knew what he was doing. "The 2% shortfall in sales comes to $244,000 for 36 weeks," he went on, apparently but quite deliberately unmindful. "You'll notice that that's just $6,000 short of being a quarter of a million dollars. If we had made those sales and converted them at our 15.7% gross margin, we'd have $38,308 that we now don't have to help us pay bills. If you assume we've paid our bills, what would have happened to that $38,308? It would have gone, swish, right to the bottom line."

There are no notes being taken. I imagine that the managers are thinking, "It's his bottom line, not mine."

"What about payroll?" Popaditch asked. "Just 0.24% over. Well, 0.24% times $11.5 million in sales over 36 weeks is $27,496.

"Year-to-date summary of missed earnings?" He had to answer his own question. "The $38,308 in gross margin plus $27,496 in over-budget payroll . . ."—he produced a long sigh—"is $65,804."

"That's the bad news."

Popaditch paused.

"But you know the joke about "How do you eat an elephant? . . . One bite at a time.' Let's break our sales down."

And here, just when he'd almost lost his listeners for good, Popaditch turned the session around.

"Sales," he said, flipping the chart again, "were short by $244,000. If you divide that by 36 weeks, it's only $6,778 a week. Divide that by three stores and you get $2,259 per week per store. That's all the more each of you had to do."

The audience perked up. Here was a number that meant something.

Talk Straight

"Let's divide the amount per week per store by the hours we're open," said Popaditch. "It comes down to $26.85 an hour. If the average customer spends about $18, that's the same thing as one and a half customers. We just need one and a half new customers per hour per store."

Now everyone was attentive. This was getting interesting. The boss was finally talking about things a store manager could visualize. After all, you can't do much with a big number like $244,000, but one and a half customers per hour—that's something store managers understand. Very clever, I thought.

"Let's look at it another way," Popaditch went on. "How much is it per customer?" Several pencils went to work. "What's $26.85 per hour divided by 87 customers per hour?"

"Thirty-one cents."

"What's 31¢ per customer? Well, what's her average ring? It's $1.09. The customer goes into the store and fills her buggy with 10 items, and it's going to cost her roughly $11. What we're talking about here is adding one-third of the average item, 31¢, to every shopper's cart. Or add one item to one person's cart, and you don't have to do it for two others. That's all we need: 31¢ per customer . . ."

A number everyone could absorb.

" . . . times 22,000 customers a week comes to nearly $7,000, which is all we'd need to come out on target."

Popaditch had engaged his managers' minds by taking his problem down to their level. The man on the sales floor can't do anything about a quarter-million-dollar revenue shortfall, but he may be able to put one extra item in every third shopper's cart. That's what he's supposed to be good at. That's a problem he can work on.

"Let's look at payroll the same way," Popaditch said to a crew that was now giving him its full attention. "We were over by $27,490; per store, that's $9,163; per week, that's $254; and per hour, it's $3.02. Our average hourly rate is $4.85. So what we're talking about is 62% of one wage, roughly half a person per hour. Could you have done without that?

"Look at it this way. We need to cut $254 per week per store. That's about 52 hours of labor. Each store has about 50 employees, so we're talking about one hour per employee per week—60 minutes.

"That's the way we gotta look at our problem: 30¢ per customer, 60 minutes per employee."

Speak Their Language

End of speech. It had lasted only 20 minutes or so, but Thrifty Scot's store managers had not only gotten a thorough briefing on the company's financial performance, they also knew exactly what their goals had to be to bring it up to expectation. Popaditch had kept them awake, and it had been real easy: he just talked their language.

Popaditch reminds me of my father. Mom *tried* to explain things. "Honey," she'd begin her little speech, "we think that until you are a little older it would be better if . . . "

Dad, on the other hand, always came right to the point. "In by one," he'd say, "or you're grounded."

"But, Dad . . . "

"Twelve-thirty."

"Oh, come on, Dad."

"Midnight. You want to try for 11?"

He may have been short on style, but there was no mistaking his message. Grounded—that I understood: no car, no date. Dad was talking my language. Executives with a message to deliver, not just a speech to make, might consider the point.

Elizabeth Neeld Comments:

◆ *This essay "Talking Costs" taken from* INC *magazine, a periodical for entrepreneurs and small-business owners, reminds me of Chinese boxes—a small box is inside a larger box which is inside a larger box, and so on. This article—written very clearly and vividly itself—is about being clear and vivid when you talk to your employees. The author, Tom Richman, writes the way he describes Bob Popaditch talking to his employees. Here's the complete story.* ◆ *Bob Popaditch owns Thrifty Scot Warehouse Food Inc. in Orlando, Florida. Bob wanted to talk to his employees about cost control and profit margins, but he knew that they weren't interested in hearing it. (Just as Richman, writing this article, tells us—the readers—that he's sure most people don't want to hear about subjects such as these. Richman counteracts this problem by using the specific story of Bob Popaditch.) Bob Popaditch counteracted his employees' lack of interest by breaking down the problem in such a clear and comprehensible way that they were engaged before they even realized it.* ◆ *Here is how Bob Popaditch did it: he broke the sales shortage down per store. What was $244,000 becomes $6,778 a week, or $2,259 per week per store. For the employees, this was now becoming personal! Popaditch went on: it comes down to $26.85 an hour. And if an average customer spends $18, that's the same as one and half customers. Then comes the bottom line.* We just need one and a half new customers per hour per store. ◆ *Richman, the author of the article, tells us that by now the employees were attentive. And we—the readers—are, too.* ◆ *Speaking to his employees, Popaditch continued. Looking at the sales shortage another way, how much is it per customer? Thirty-one cents! How can the employees get an additional 31¢ per customer? Popaditch (and the author of the essay, Richman) explains: the customer fills her buggy with ten items, costing roughly $11.* "What we're talking about here is adding one third of the average item, 31¢, to every shopper's cart. Or add one item to one person's cart, and you don't have to do it for two others. That's all we need: 31¢ per customer . . . " *How* clear *can you be?* ◆ *Popaditch* gives one more example of an action that would solve the sales shortage—cut sixty minutes per employee from the payroll. As Richman says, "End of speech." The point has been made. The message is clear. ✦ Richman is able to write so vividly and clearly not only because he is relating a conversation that was vivid and clear, but also because he takes pains to make this story interesting and engaging to the reader. He opens the essay by delineating the problem owners have in getting their employees to care about profit margins, cost reductions, etc. The rest of the essay, then, is a recounting of one successful solution to this problem. ✦ Richman also keeps himself present as he writes the essay. Not only does he speak directly to us—the readers—but he is also present when Bob Popaditch is speaking to his employees. We're hearing something the writer learned firsthand, and we are placed in the actual experience through Richman's narrative. Finally, at the conclusion of the essay, the author speaks to us personally again. He relates a story from his high-school days when what his father said was very clear. He said what he meant, and he meant what he said. Richman uses this story to emphasize the point of the entire essay. Through his writing expertise and commitment, we get the point! ✦

JONATHAN D. BEARD

Avalanche!

Tad DeFelice was indoors when the avalanche hit. It was March 1982, and DeFelice was working at California's Alpine Meadows Ski Area: "The power in the building started going off and on. Then the building started to shake, shake tremendously. Then a blast of wind and snow came through. I was pinned under the rubble and snow from the waist down. Randy was right behind me."

Randy Buck, a maintenance worker at the resort, takes up the story: "I vaguely recall seeing a piece of plywood about six feet long flying by me. I dropped to the floor and curled up into a ball, covering my head with my hands. It felt like I was caught in surf and being tumbled by a wave. Everything was happening too quickly for me to think about death."

But seven people at Alpine Meadows did lose their lives, making the avalanche one of the most deadly in recent American history. The worst occurred on March 1, 1910, near Stevens Pass in northern Washington. Two passenger trains had been stuck in the mountains by a blizzard when the snow above them suddenly gave way. Both trains were swept off the tracks and into the canyon below. Ninety-six people died.

Risk Rises

American experience with avalanches has been mild compared with that of the Europeans. In the especially severe winter of 1720, avalanches wiped out dozens of villages in Switzerland and claimed hundreds of victims. During World War I, when Austrian troops faced the Italian Army in the Alps, avalanches killed 40,000 soldiers, and some estimates double that figure.

In 1984, barring unusual snow conditions, 13 or 14 Americans will die in avalanches. "Back in the 1950s," says Betsy Armstrong of the Colorado Avalanche Information Center in Denver, "fewer than four died in an average year. By the 1970s, the toll climbed to the present levels."

As the boom in winter sports brings thousands more to the mountains each year, the number of those at risk rises. Accordingly, efforts to study and control avalanches are on the upswing. Physicists and meteorologists have begun profiling mountains, monitoring weather patterns and relying on sophisticated computer models to probe the mysteries of avalanche anatomy. High-tech hardware is being developed to help hikers and skiers maximize the likelihood of rescue should an avalanche hit.

Lab for Snow Research

It is only recently that the science has come into its own. In the United States, the principal lab for snow research is the U.S. Forest Service's Rocky Mountain Forest and Range Experiment Station in Fort Collins, Colorado. This is the only government-sponsored work in this country, but there are other labs around the world, including one at Sapporo, Japan, another at Davos, Switzerland, and a third in Grenoble, France. At all of these facilities, scientists focus on the rather specialized discipline of snow physics. What happens to snow when it leaves the atmosphere and undergoes changes within the snowpack, and—most important—how can we predict when an avalanche will take place?

Some answers are easy. Roughly 80 percent of all avalanches will occur within 24 hours of a storm because the new snow will not have had a chance to settle and adhere. They are also likely to occur on cloudless days in spring, when unobstructed sunshine helps destabilize snowpacks. Paradoxically, winter sunshine discourages avalanches by helping to compact and solidify snow.

Hits, Misses, Hunches

But apart from such givens, much snow research is still a case of hits, misses and hunches. The first step in trying to forecast avalanches is to determine their "return period." For some steep slopes exposed to high winds, there may be an avalanche after every snowfall. Other paths may avalanche once a winter. Skiers and resort managers are alert to such obvious hazards, but 10-year, 30-year and 100-year return periods are a much greater problem. In such cases, a slope may go for decades without a serious avalanche and then suddenly fracture and slide. In areas that have been densely populated for years, like the Alps, people recognize these avalanche paths even if there has been no occurrence for generations. But in places like the American Rockies, which have been populated for only about a century, avalanche history is very much a guessing game.

Sue Ferguson, physicist and publisher of *The Avalanche Review* in Seattle, says that most experts will look at slope vegetation to determine return periods. "If nothing growing on a slope is more than a year old, it probably avalanches every winter. For avalanches with longer return periods, I look at the timber in the brand-new debris at the end of the path. If, by counting tree rings, I find that it knocked down trees more than fifty years old, I know that it has been that long since an avalanche came this far into a valley."

But the timing of a slide is by no means the only variable that concerns researchers. Just as important is the avalanche's type. The destruction of Alpine Meadows was caused by what is known as a slab avalanche. Within this category are three subgroups: soft slab, hard slab and wet slab. In the first, a snow layer fractures, falls away and, almost instantaneously, breaks into huge, dusty clouds of powder. These billows of snow are free of friction with the ground and often reach tremendous speeds; 100 miles per hour is not uncommon for powder avalanches, and some researchers claim to have witnessed speeds of over 200.

Hard-slab avalanches are a different breed altogether. These, says Ferguson, "often involve old snow compacted by the wind, and they do not break up at once. Large blocks are often still intact at the base of the avalanche runout." Such slabs move at about 30 to 50 miles per hour.

Wet-slab avalanches occur when there is liquid water—from rain or spring thawing—mixed with the snow. They are unusual in that they *flow* down the mountain, following every feature of the terrain. The slides move remarkably slowly, often creeping along at only 10 miles per hour.

When snow is fresh, and neither aging, wind, water nor freezing has consolidated it into a slab, there may be "point releases," or loose avalanches. Explains Ferguson: "These are initiated by a few grains of snow losing their angle of repose." Point releases seldom result in large or dangerous avalanches.

Most avalanches last only a few minutes from the time of release until the last snow and debris have settled at the end of the runout zone. Ferguson's rule of thumb is that "if you are on a slope when it avalanches, you usually don't have time to get away, but if you are watching from nearby, you probably do have time to get out your camera." She tells of one very wet avalanche that took over a week to move down a granite slope and across a valley.

The spectacle you will be photographing is the end result of a remarkably intricate process. As soon as a snowflake lands, it begins to change its shape and size. A variety of factors, including evaporation and refreezing, cause water molecules to migrate from the ends of crystalline branches of the flakes toward the larger, more rounded centers. If the temperature throughout the snowpack is about the same as that of the air above it and the ground below it, all of the flakes will change in this fashion, creating a strong layer of dense snow not likely to trigger an avalanche.

It is only when air temperature drops below freezing that trouble looms. At Fort Collins, geophysicist Dick Sommerfield is studying a phenomenon known as "temperature gradient metamorphism." Snow, as the makers of igloos know, is a good insulator, keeping the ground beneath it at a constant 32 degrees Fahrenheit. At this temperature, crystals in the layer of snow closest to the ground are teetering between freezing and melting, and their water vapor rises. When it is far enough from the ground, it freezes into what is ominously known as the "ball-bearing layer." Snow above this icy layer is in approximately the position a man would be when trying to cross a hockey rink in street shoes. Just as any jolt from a passing skater could cause the man to tumble, any jolt from an errant skier, or even a sudden noise, could cause the slope to avalanche.

Art Judson, another Forest Service scientist, is also studying the phenomenon. But instead of conducting his experiments in the field, Judson is working on a computer model that he hopes will be able to predict the probability of avalanches in a given area. The computer is provided with data on the existing snow cover and the characteristics of various slopes; then it simulates changes occurring in the snowpack.

One man with a different perspective on avalanches is Art Mears, America's only full-time avalanche-control engineer. Mears travels the West as a consultant, advising utilities on where it's safe to put in a new line and where it's not, designing a shed for highways to protect motorists and counseling homeowners on how to strengthen their houses. Some of his recent undertakings, however, have combined engineering and politics.

"Avalanche zoning" is an idea whose time is coming in the West. Once, it was assumed that people who built houses in avalanche paths were taking a risk that was theirs to take. Today, however, towns and cities near ski areas find that real estate speculation has dramatically raised the value of land in the runout zone of avalanche paths, and local governments have begun to worry. Vail, one of the most fashionable resorts in Colorado, annexed land in 1975 that included several major avalanche paths. Officials then commissioned Mears and others to study maps and photos of the area's slopes and its recent avalanche history and to hike into the mountains for on-site inspections. At the end of this lengthy process, the investigators were able to divide Vail into Red Zones, in which powerful avalanches or avalanches occurring more than once every 25 years could be expected, and Blue Zones, for which weaker, less frequent avalanches were predicted. No residential construction is permitted in Red Zones, and anyone building in a Blue Zone must hire an engineer who will certify that the building is able to resist specified forces.

Plan Ahead

While scientists try to understand how and why avalanches happen and zoning boards try to keep buildings out of avalanche paths, an army of thousands of resort employees, National

Weather Service personnel, highway crews and assorted volunteers provide information on avalanche hazards.

The first line of defense is the forecast program. The Colorado Avalanche Information Center, modeled after the Swiss system, is now 11 years old. Every winter day, its 30 observers—most of them sheriff's deputies, highway workers, park rangers and ski patrol personnel—call a central switchboard and report on weather, snow cover and avalanche activity around the state. The center then collates the information and sends it out to newspapers, radio and TV stations and phone-in lines. In the winter of 1983, 25,000 Coloradans called the phone-ins. Similar networks are now in operation in Utah, Washington and Alaska.

At major ski resorts, the snow managers don't wait for the morning avalanche report before taking action. If there has been snow, rain or heavy wind overnight, they are out at dawn to "shoot the slopes"—using explosives to trigger small, controlled avalanches before turning the skiers loose. Typically, their arsenal is made up of one- and two-pound TNT hand charges that can be manually placed and then detonated by remote control. For hard-to-reach areas, little bombs may be dropped from lift cars or helicopters, or war-surplus artillery may be fired from adjoining slopes. As ammunition costs rise, many resort directors are turning to the Avalauncher, a compressed-nitrogen cannon that throws a two-pound charge up to 2,000 yards.

On smaller slopes, avalanches may also be triggered by the simple—and decidedly more daredevil—practice of "ski checking." With the rest of the group standing by to lend assistance, one member of a survey party will venture out on a questionable-looking slope, then ski back and forth, bouncing up and down. If the snow is unstable, this will be enough to release a modest avalanche.

To protect permanent structures that must be in the mountains, villages, resorts and railroads also use "passive control" devices: In Switzerland, elaborate rows of barriers are built to either trap snow in the starting zones or deflect it away from inhabited areas.

But avalanches sometimes frustrate all efforts at prevention and prediction, and it is against these circumstances that experts and vacationers are mastering techniques for both rescue and survival. Skiers and hikers are cautioned always to plan an escape path before crossing a hazardous slope. If an avalanche begins and

escape is impossible, the first and simplest rule is to grab anything—a tree, a boulder—that is securely anchored in the ground.

If this fails, experts suggest dumping all encumbering baggage—packs, skis, poles—and "swimming," flailing with arms and
legs, for as long as the snow is moving. "This maximizes the time
you are near the surface of the snow," says William Hotchkiss of
National Ski Patrol Systems, Inc., of Denver. "And it makes it more
likely that an arm or leg will protrude when the avalanche stops."

Just a few minutes after the snow settled at Alpine Meadows,
survivors had already set up a probe line, the oldest rescue technique known. A well-organized probe line consists of 20 to 30 people in a row, each with a 12-foot pole, marching one or two feet
apart up the slope and probing the snow for victims.

Finding a Buried Skier

People buried more than 30 minutes have only a 50-percent
chance of survival, and those buried with snow packed tightly
around the nose and mouth can die in 15 minutes or less. Technology is coming to the rescue with transceivers. These devices, which
look like a small cassette player, are worn in an inside pocket next
to the body so they cannot be swept away by the crashing snow. At
the beginning of a day of skiing, the wearer simply sets the device
on Transmit, creating a magnetic field that can be detected up to
100 feet away by another transceiver. Should an avalanche strike,
other members of the group turn their units to Receive and criss-
cross the slope until they pick up the victim's signal.

In Europe, another system is trying radar to find buried skiers
and hikers. Each skier wears a diode with a foil antenna attached
between the inner and outer layer of his boot. He can be located
from perhaps 100 feet away by means of a small radar unit either
mounted in a helicopter or carried in a backpack.

Avalanche experts are proud of their new hardware and
prouder still of their increasing understanding of what causes
snowslides in the first place. But even the starriest of researchers
do not pretend that avalanches can ever be tamed; rather, efforts
are likely to continue to focus on predicting when they'll occur and
how to get out of their way when they do. These alone can be
monumental tasks. In February 1983, a sudden avalanche struck
the Williwaw Camp 'round in Alaska. Before it was finished, the
slide had covered an area the size of 22 football fields with the
equivalent of 74,000 loads from 10-yard dump trucks full of snow—

or about a quarter of a million tons. What weighs that much? One thousand four hundred twenty-six DC-10s. The time it took for this devastation to be wrought? Around 45 seconds.

Elizabeth Neeld Comments:

♦ *Jonathan D. Beard writes about science, articles such as "Glaciers on the Run," "Wiring the World with Fiber Optics," and this essay, "Avalanche!" The subject of avalanches can be extremely complicated; but in writing this article for* Science Digest, *a magazine that intends to make science intelligible to the nonscientist, Beard must make the subject extremely clear. And he does.* ♦ *We first experience the impact of an avalanche. Beard tells us a true story about an avalanche landing on a ski resort in California. Seven people were killed. Then he gives us a short history of avalanches that have been tragic in their results—ninety-six people killed here, forty thousand killed there. We read the prediction that in 1984, the year this essay was published, thirteen or fourteen Americans would die in avalanches.* ♦ *After we experience the human element of avalanches, Beard turns our attention to the scientific aspects of his subject. We learn there is a physics of snow. We find out how well avalanches can be predicted . . . within twenty-four hours of a storm or on cloudless days in the spring . . . except when they occur at other times! We are introduced to the technical concept of avalanche "return periods." To make this concept clear to us, Beard gives us some background information and then he interviews Sue Ferguson, a physicist and publisher of The* Avalanche Review. *Through his conversation with Ferguson, Beard helps his readers understand what "return period" really means.* ♦ *We learn that there are three types of avalanches: soft slab, hard slab, and wet slab. We learn the characteristics of each. To make these definitions vivid and clear to us Beard uses terms like "billows of snow," "breaks into huge, dusty clouds of powder," "different breed altogether," "old snow compacted by the wind," "they flow down the mountain," "following every feature of the terrain."* ♦ *To make a transition from kinds of avalanches to a discussion of the process of what makes an avalanche,*

Beard again uses conversation from his interview with Fer-guson. She talks about photographing avalanches—to il-lustrate how much time you do and do not have if you see one coming—and then Beard moves into a discussion of what makes an avalanche. This discussion, although de-scribing a complex process, is very clear. Beard starts with a single snowflake. From this single snowflake he takes us to "temperature gradient metamorphism" in a snowpack. We find out about the "ball-bearing layer" in a snowpack. We learn how computers are being used to simulate changes occurring in snowpacks. ✦ *Beard then turns the essay toward the engineering and political implications of avalanches. "Avalanche zoning," which determines where people can and cannot build houses, is a controversial topic. Implications for such ski areas as Vail are discussed.* ✦ *Then Beard turns our attention to what people do to avoid the hazards of avalanches. There are forecast programs—which include using explosives to trig-ger small, controlled avalanches—to determine if condi-tions permit skiers on the slopes; there are elaborate rows of barriers to trap snow or deflect it. If you're caught in an avalanche, Beard says the best thing to do is grab a tree. If you can't do that, dump everything and try to "swim" as long as the snow is moving. Beard then tells us the ways people buried in avalanches can be found and how long they are likely to stay alive.* ✦ *Finally, at the conclusion of the essay, Beard describes another avalanche. In February 1983 there was a sudden avalanche in Alaska; the slide covered an area the size of twenty-two football fields. The snow weighed the equivalent of 1,426 DC-10 airplanes. How long did it take the avalanche to occur? About forty-five seconds. The danger and devastation of an avalanche have become very vivid and very clear.* ✦

DENNIS ESKOW

Dressed to Kill

The half-ton machine rolls down the open field, tearing up the turf beneath it and pushing aside virtually anything that stands in its way. To football fans, it's the New York Sack Exchange, a well-oiled squad of defensive football players famous for getting quarterbacks to sit down—the hard way—right in the middle of a game. The New York Jets' defensive line, like its counterparts at 27 other National Football League franchises, specializes in body contact at the most intense and destructive levels. A Stanford University study estimates that when any two professional football players collide at top speed, they release enough energy to move a 33-ton object 1 inch.

"It could be worse," quips Joe Klecko, the 6-foot-3-inch, 269-pound Jet defensive end. "It could be 15 years ago." That was before the advent of synthetic materials like Plexon, closed-cell rubber and polyester-covered cushion foam. Back then, a football player carried up to 25 pounds of equipment. Today he wears about 12 pounds of protection. And the current gear does a far better job of keeping football heroes out of hospitals. In the old days, players would collapse at half-time, suffocating from the heat and sweat beneath their armor. Nylon, urethane, vinyl and other lightweight materials have brought that to an end.

"We have a lot more to work with than we ever had before," says Jet trainer Bob Reese. In the Jet locker room he can point to several pieces of equipment developed out of special material for specific players. Sometimes the special pieces catch on and become standard gear. Sometimes they're destined to remain the hallmarks of a single player.

The best known specialized armor to catch on like wildfire was the flak jacket, first worn by Houston quarterback Dan Pastorini in 1978 to protect his broken ribs. The inflatable polyester and plastic vest invented by Byron Donzis was slipped on and laced up the front. Then it was inflated to fit snugly around the quarterback's ribs. Since Pastorini, most professional quarterbacks have worn a Donzis flak jacket at least once to protect bruised or broken ribs. Despite a price tag of $310, the jacket is even worn by college and high school players.

Perhaps a bit more esoteric are the special shoes made by Pro Keds for Klecko. The shoes have a steel plate in the front of the sole to protect the hard-running defensive end's feet. The Klecko shoe is also a high-top instead of the more popular low-cut type to provide added support to his ankles, which have been injured in past seasons.

Putting on Armor

Conrad Dobler, listed in the 1982 official Datsun Football Guidebook as "Mr. Violence," has been quoted as calling the pregame suiting-up "dressing to kill." Dobler, a former St. Louis Cardinal offensive lineman, is a veteran of the era when a uniform was part of a player's ammunition.

Up until 1979, defensive players often speared opponents, lunging into them helmet-first. The practice was banned in college ball in 1970 and has been outlawed by the pros since 1979, the year after Oakland defenseman Jack Tatum helmeted New England receiver Darryl Stingley, leaving Stingley permanently paralyzed.

Suiting up for a football game is one of the most time-consuming things a player has to do. "You give yourself a good two hours,"

Klecko says. "You want everything to go on just right. This stuff is protecting your butt."

The dressing ceremony has been compared to the preparations made by a bullfighter. The player puts on his jockstrap, and he may also want to insert a cup to protect the genitals. Then a heavy elastic support for the back and abdomen is put on.

With the help of an assistant trainer, a plastic undercoat is sprayed on the skin and on goes the tape. The undercoat prevents itching and painful over-sticking. Up to 10 yards of tape are used to protect a player's ankles and wrists. For many players, the knees also have to be taped. The knee is the most often injured joint in pro football. Sports Medicine Associates of New York reports over 100 football players undergo some form of knee surgery each season. In 1980, the Detroit Lions took on a dubious distinction when a record 21 players underwent knee surgery.

Many receivers and defensive backs also tape their forearms. It gives them a bit of stickiness to aid in catching or intercepting a pass. Players are not allowed to spray on any added stickum. Other players—guards and tackles in particular—tape their arms to make them somewhat rigid.

Layer After Layer

The taping exercise can take up to an hour, especially if the player wears elastic wraps or hand pads. Now the athlete is ready for the padding. Most players wear a set of knee-length nylon pants with snap-in thigh guards and knee insert pockets for the knee pads. The knee pads have been around for a long time, but many sprinting players of the past went without the protection rather than having the cumbersome pads flop around as they ran at top speed. Today's knee pads make it much easier. Made of half-inch-thick cushion foam with polyester backing, the new pads contract from body heat and form-fit the knee. Similar features are available in specialized shin guards.

Once the pants are cinched up, the player can put on his flak jacket and shoulder pads. The shoulder pads are the heaviest protective devices—up to 5½ pounds. They have to be cinched in tightly, and the banana flaps covering the shoulders must be pounded by the trainer or another player to make sure the pads are set perfectly in place. "That's the place where you get grabbed and shoved the most," Klecko notes. "You don't want the shoulder pads to slip at all."

Near the end of the dressing ritual, many players insert a leather neck-protector between the top of their shoulder pads and the skin of their neck. It makes the fit a bit uncomfortable, but any player who's been thrown down in the heat of combat will agree that the neck protection is vital.

In addition to the basics worn under his jersey, a player may have as many as 20 other local protective devices. There's the knee-cartilage shock absorber, which is a spring and hook device that fits onto the knee brace on the outside and helps lessen the shock to the knee from a sudden stop, as in a blind-side tackle. Soccer-type shin guards molded from the ankle to the base of the knee have become popular in the training rooms of the Jets and their New Jersey rivals, the Giants. The shin protectors were developed by Joe Rosenstein, former trainer of the New York Cosmos soccer team.

Elbow braces, biceps pads, wrist protectors and other protection may also be added before the final stage of dressing. The next step is a two-man job: pulling the jersey over the shoulder pads. Today's nylon jerseys are of fishnet fabric for better ventilation. Most have tearaway stitching. Down below, the player slips into his uniform trousers and again gets help when putting on his shoes.

Personal Foot Flair

"The shoes are part of your personality," Joe Namath once said. The retired Jets super quarterback is the one who introduced pantyhose and "funky spats" into the game back in the '60s. The pantyhose kept Namath warm in the icy end-run of the long football season. Everyone laughed, but pantyhose are now standard equipment in a pro football locker room. The spats were special low-cut white shoes. After Namath introduced the personal foot flair, Baltimore Colts player Alvin Haymond followed suit, and within two seasons half the quarterbacks in the NFL were wearing special-order shoes to enhance their personal image.

Of course, football shoe design is a far more serious business. In the old days, players dragged their feet in hightops with metal spikes. The heavy leather shoe made feet sweat and never provided as much traction as a player needed. But in the past 10 years, football shoes have undergone a revolution, even as football fields underwent revolutionary changes.

Grass shoes are lightweight running shoes with seven rubberized cleats on each sole. They're made for the basic natural-turf field. Artificial-turf shoes have 75 to 100 cleats and special composite tongues and soles to reduce heat buildup in the shoes. Artificial turf can retain heat so well that an early autumn game in the South might be played in field-level temperatures near 100° F.

Canadian broomball shoes have about 15 suction cups on the soles and have become popular where natural grass has been planted in place of artificial turf. (The Orange Bowl in Miami switched in 1976.)

Protector of Vanity

The football armor *piece de resistance* is the helmet, the second weightiest item in the player's wardrobe. The average pro football helmet weighs 3 pounds. The outer shell is a layer of shiny polycarbonate followed by a layer of aluminum lined with vinyl foam, styrene plastic and a thin sheath of leather. The inside of the helmet is lined with foam squares and plastic pods filled with an antifreeze or pure alcohol. The pods absorb shocks and carry heat to the vinyl foam layer.

One of the most popular helmets on the market today—the Bike Air Power—uses an inflated inside liner to absorb shocks. After the player puts on his helmet, a bicycle pump tube is inserted in the helmet's ear hole and into an intake valve. The liner is then pumped up.

"Believe it or not, you really want the helmet to fit as tightly as possible without breaking your skull," Klecko says. "A loose helmet can do you a lot of harm by moving around when you get hit." The air-filled model gives the tightest possible fit. The helmet itself is just the base of operations for a whole range of defensive devices for the player's head. A nose bumper of vinyl or other soft material sits at the center of the helmet above the bridge of the player's nose. A chinstrap keeps the helmet from moving sideways. Face guards and cages of various shapes and sizes complete the set of above-the-shoulder protection.

Paul Brown forced his Cleveland Brown players to be the first to wear face guards back in the 1950s. Players took to the devices grudgingly, complaining that face guards made them anonymous to the fans. By the 1960s, most teams issued face guards to all players. Many variations have come onto the scene since then. There's the single or double bar that covers the lower nose, mouth and jaw. The elongated double bar covers the upper nose down to the chin and has become popular with defensive players.

With the advent of composite materials, helmet manufacturers have been able to make elaborate cages, such as the bird-cage or the cowcatcher types, which place a grid of protective material over the entire face while leaving wide slits so the player can see who he's up against.

The boxing world has contributed mouth guards to the supposedly more docile sport of football. The trainer takes a wax impression of a player's mouth and sends it to the mouth-guard manufacturer for a device that fits the individual perfectly, protecting his teeth. In an age of toothpaste ads and other commercials emphasizing good looks, no player wants to risk a broken tooth.

Spage-Age Plastics

Space-age plastics have transformed the pro football player from a heavily laden behemoth to the modern mean-and-lean image. And the equipment promises to keep getting leaner. The players are getting bigger and faster with each passing decade. In the 1950s, the average NFL player weighed 210 pounds. Today's average player, according to figures published in *Pro Football* magazine, is over 230 pounds. The speeds at which they move are dazzling. Linemen who weigh 270 pounds have been timed in the 40-yard dash at 4.9 seconds. The greater bulk and higher collision speeds call for improvements in the armor, and football insiders say they're coming.

The biggest breakthrough will probably be in attachment of face protectors to helmets. Some experimental helmets being tried on the field this year come with face cages that break off with some ease but can be reattached right on the field.

"I've seen players tear off an opponent's face mask," Klecko says. Such violence often results in neck and shoulder injuries. The easy-off, easy-on cages will reduce those injuries.

The one thing science hasn't been able to provide football players with is a sure way to go through a whole season without a major injury. Klecko, who sat out most of 1982 after knee surgery, says "I'd give the Nobel Prize to the guy who came up with that."

Elizabeth Neeld Comments:

✦ *This essay on football uniforms, written by Dennis Eskow, appeared in* Popular Mechanics. Popular Mechanics' *principal subjects are automotive (new cars, car main-*

tenance) and how-to (woodworking, metalworking, home improvement and home maintenance.) The magazine also publishes features on new technology, sports, electronics, photography and hi-fi. The editors say they are looking for "exciting male interest articles with strong science, exploration and adventure emphasis" and for "reporting on new and unusual developments." This essay combines new technology, sports, and adventure and goes beyond being merely an exciting male-interest article. Everybody is fascinated by the item-by-item inventory of a professional football player's uniform described in this article. After reading this essay, one will always see a football uniform much more clearly than ever before. ✦ One of the tacks Eskow takes in writing this essay is to contrast current uniform parts with their prescientific-breakthrough counterparts. For instance before the invention of new fabrics, plastics, foams, etc., a football player carried up to twenty-five pounds of equipment. Today he wears about twelve pounds. The new equipment made possible by science also protects the player better. We are shown new developments in the uniform. There's the flak jacket, an inflatable polyester and plastic vest which protects bruised or broken ribs. There are the special shoes that provide extra support for the player's feet or extra lustre to his image. ✦ The writer uses the images of a soldier with ammunition and of a bullfighter to set the stage for describing the two-hour suiting-up ritual that takes place in the locker room. There are the jockstrap and cup, the plastic undercoat so the tape won't stick so hard on arms and legs (it takes ten yards of tape to protect a player's wrists and ankles), the nylon pants with snap-in thigh guards and knee-insert pockets for knee pads, the flak jacket and shoulder pads (shoulder pads weigh five and a half pounds and have to be pounded by the trainer or another player to be made to fit snugly), the leather neck-protector, and the twenty or more other optional pieces of equipment such as the knee-cartilage shock absorbers, shin guards, elbow braces, and bicep pads. ✦ Eskow then describes the last pieces of the uniform: the tear-away jersey, the shoes, and the helmet. After reading about the changes in these items, we see clearly the truth of the author's point that space-age plastics and other scientific inventions have transformed the pro foot-ball player's uniform and equipment. The vivid descriptions of the parts of a football player's uniform makes many things far more clear to us than they were before. We will look at a professional football player's uniform in a different way as a result of reading the article. We will understand things about injuries and adjustments to injuries that we did not understand before. We will appreciate Jet defensive end Joe Klecko's quip about finding a way to go through a whole season without a major injury: "I'd give the Nobel Prize to the guy who came up with that." But we may still leave the article not understanding one thing: why do they do it? Perhaps all the gusto, vividness, and clarity in the world would not provide an answer to that one! ✦

JANE E. TIFFANY

Stepping Out From Behind the Phone and Word Processor

Dear Boss,

In honor of National Secretaries Week, I ask you to forgo the usual floral arrangement in exchange for hearing me out. "Just one voice can make a difference," goes the saying, and I want to be heard and make a difference. I do not belong to any women's liberation movements or organizations. But as a secretary, I'm fed up with what goes on in offices all over the country, and it's about time you tried to understand.

When I began my career 20 years ago, I had great expectations that my salary and responsibilities would adequately reflect my experience. However, that clearly has not been the case. This company, as do most, wants highly qualified professional women working as secretaries. But the decision not to pay these women according to their abilities—dictated (in 98% of the cases) by men—is usually sealed at the time of employment. However, if any man had to maintain even one-half of the work duties that are

438

expected of a woman secretary, for a sustained minimal salary, he would never survive. Worst of all, a man, in the same company, using the same skills, with 20 years of experience, will typically have increased his earnings by at least $30,000. It's horrifying to suddenly look back over the past 20 years and realize that you are nowhere careerwise or financially.

Are you beginning to catch on? Let me paint a scenario that I assure you is all too familiar to many secretaries I know: After having worked as a secretary to the president of a company for two years—my 10 years of past experience have, I am told, nothing to do with the business he's in—my boss decides to hire a computer programmer at an executive salary. We'll call him Jack, and he has brought five years of experience to the firm. My boss tells me that Jack's years of experience will be a great asset.

I have been given the extra duties of taking over Jack's secretarial needs, even with my present responsibilities. I do not complain. After all, I am expected to be a "super secretary."

Jack, as a new employee, is unsure of himself. John, my boss, gives Jack his undivided attention during the first three months of his employment—shows him the ropes—and then leaves him on his own. Of course, Jack spends much time trying to know the boss through his secretary. I am bombarded with questions such as, "what do you think John's decision would be on this particular problem?" Six months down the road, Jack comes to me elated with his salary hike and promotion to computer analyst. That's amazing! I had to learn how to use the computer and word processor on my own, both of which I have used for several years. Neither has entitled me to a promotion or a pay hike.

I think you get the picture. I had that "necessary information" that Jack needs about how my boss ticks, and I am also now Jack's secretary with a constantly growing workload. I am expected to know everything that is going on in the company. I am also expected, at times, to make executive decisions. Am I paid for it? Absolutely not, and those are only minor examples of what I really am, what I really do, and what really goes on. Yet the position of secretary has not lost its stigma with men. Such is the corporate hierarchy.

Perhaps you are thinking I should be grateful for making enough money to be able to meet my monthly obligations. Well, I'm not. I'm damned angry. Think about it. At age 65, if I remain a secretary, I will be indigent; no one will hire me, because I will be too old. My income has never been big enough to allow me to put money away for a nest egg. And the Social Security system will probably be broke by then, because I am part of the "baby boomer" generation. Unless I take action to change my career now, the results will be devastating.

My advice to women contemplating secretarial careers is that if they have any big plans, they shouldn't even "think secretary." Chances are, they will eventually come to the same realization that I have, and it's frightening! It is unlikely they will ever be promoted, and their salaries will seldom be based on experience and abilities, simply because no one wants to admit the great range of responsibilities a secretary must carry out.

I predict that secretaries will be in great demand in the not-so-distant future because there is a growing undercurrent of unrest in companies among secretaries. They are expressing dissatisfaction not only because of their salaries, but because the position itself lacks respect and there is a continuing rejection of their demonstrated business acumen and capabilities.

Several years ago, many women were trying very hard to change this situation in firms for which they worked. As a result, many lost their jobs and were replaced by unsympathetic and unsuspecting females who had not yet experienced what I have touched on here. Women muffled their voices because employers took the "no care" position. The general attitude among those employers was (and still is) that "if you don't like it, walk, because there is always someone else waiting in line for your job." Now, women again seem to be aware of the problem and are voicing their complaints more openly. However, the risk associated with "talking back" is still strong enough to require anonymous letters, such as this one.

Speaking for myself (and many other secretary friends), my training, skills, experience, organizational abilities, talent for handling crisis situations and details, and the ability to make transitions make me an essential and integral part of the company for which I work. You, my boss, are the needle and I am the thread, and together we help this organization to grow. But when the knot is tied at the end of the thread, the growth of the company has ceased.

Sincerely,
Secretary X

Elizabeth Neeld Comments:

✦ *This essay appeared in the Manager's Journal column of the* Wall Street Journal. *In the essay the writer, Jane Tiffany, speaks out loudly and clearly. She is discussing the circumstances under which she and thousands of other secretaries work. And she does so with gusto, vividness, and clarity.* ✦ *There is energy fueling this essay. You can hear it in "I ask you to forgo the usual floral arrangement in exchange for hearing me out." You can hear it in "I'm fed up with what goes on." You can hear it in "it's about time you tried to understand." The commitment of the writer to make her point is strong!* ✦ *Tiffany next relates the general state of affairs for women like herself across the country: they receive a minimum salary sealed at time of employment, receive next to no increase in earnings after twenty years of employment, and yet also receive the pressure to be highly qualified professional women.* ✦ *Then to make her point very clear, she draws a picture for her boss. Here's the scenario, she says. And she tells us the story of Jack, the executive assistant. She's now a secretary who works for two men, not one. This scene helps the writer make a powerful point.* ✦ *A large number of specific details helps the writer deliver her message. In addition to the story of Jack, there are the details of turning sixty-five, the Social Security system, women losing their jobs in the past, the current attitude of "if you don't like it, walk," the risk of "talking back." We get details of her daily responsibilities—handling crises, making executive decisions at times, teaching the executive assistant, learning the computer and word processor on her own. All these specifics contribute to her writing being vivid and clear.* ✦ *The language the writer uses also makes the writing vivid: "I'm damned angry." "I will be indigent." "Women muffled their voices." The imagery is strong: "You, my boss, are the needle and I am the thread, and together we help this organization to grow. But when the knot is tied at the end of the thread, the growth of the company has ceased." In this metaphor we get what she means.* ✦

CARL Q. CHRISTOL

Space Law: Justice for the New Frontier

Cosmos 954 was a doomed satellite. The first signs of erratic behavior came within weeks after launch, and on January 24, 1978, after only four months in orbit, its glowing fragments fell to Earth over northwestern Canada. Satellites reenter the atmosphere all the time, but Cosmos 954 was not like most other Soviet spacecraft. This one was nuclear powered, and an international outcry ensued over its space-age fallout. With the help of American specialists, the Canadian government ultimately spent $14 million that winter tracking down the radioactive debris under bleak, inhospitable conditions.

It wasn't until 1981 that the Soviet Union agreed to repay Canada for its efforts, and then the amount was only $3 million. Yet, had it not been for a pair of international agreements negotiated earlier by the United Nations, the Soviet reluctance to settle the claim might have been more pronounced. In fact, these same legal principles and rules would have applied if damage or harm had resulted during the fall of Skylab 1 over Australia in 1979.

The two documents are titled "Agreement on the Rescue of Astronauts, the Return of Astronauts, and the Return of Objects Launched into Outer Space" (1968) and "Convention on International Liability for Damage Caused by Space Objects" (1972). In the case of Cosmos 954, these required the Canadians to recover the debris and return it to the U.S.S.R., for which they were reimbursed. Canada could also have requested Soviet assistance during the recovery operation but opted not to.

This episode highlights just one example of how the reach of our legal system is extending into space. Note, however, that the most important extraterrestrial treaties were signed when space flight was still in its infancy and the realm above our atmosphere a lonely frontier. By contrast, today "outer space" is an increasingly crowded settlement of scientific, commercial, and military enterprises. Unresolved issues of law and diplomacy are becoming more pressing, and how they are settled will influence the character of space activities far into the future.

The U.N. Role

Since 1959 the United Nations has been the principal forum for the development of international space law. Through its actions have come a total of five major agreements. . . . Taken together, they constitute a functional set of "do's" and "don't's" for space activities.

The last of the documents, the controversial "Moon Treaty," has been ratified by only five countries; it entered into force in July, 1984. An examination of this agreement's political and technical issues, and how they were raised and resolved, can provide some insight into the lawmaking processes that affect space exploration.

The Moon Treaty had its origin in the U.N.'s Committee on the Peaceful Uses of Outer Space, or COPUOS, where it was under consideration from 1972 until 1979. So many years were required because the committee does not settle issues by vote but must instead reach unanimous consensus on the terms of a proposed agreement. This means that any single member nation can prevent a measure from ever reaching the General Assembly. In this case the long-sought consensus was achieved in 1979, and the assembly soon voted unanimously in favor of the treaty.

The CHM Controversy

Countries must next ratify a measure separately before they can be bound by its provisions. But the Moon agreement has become controversial because it contains a challenging new principle of international law, originally proposed by Argentina. It calls for the Moon and its natural resources to be the "common heritage of mankind" (or CHM). The committee's delegations, including one from the U. S., were not content to leave this principle worded only as an abstract hope. They mandated, for example, that it will become effective when the exploitation of the Moon's resources is imminent.

They also set forth the main objective to be accomplished through application of the CHM principle: (1) the orderly and safe development of lunar resources; (2) their rational management; (3) the expansion of opportunities for their use; and (4) an equitable sharing of the benefits so derived by all the treaty's adherents. The last point carries the additional requirement that the interests and needs of developing countries be given special consideration, whether or not those nations have contributed to lunar exploration. And it is this provision that has spawned so much debate over both the Moon Treaty and the similarly worded Law of the Sea Convention, adopted in 1982.

The United States consistently supported the CHM principle throughout the COPUOS negotiations and was instrumental in securing the Moon Treaty's final approval at the U.N. However, the U.S. has also taken the position that, pending the *large-scale* development of lunar resources, no moratorium on exploiting the Moon's mineral wealth should exist. Furthermore, it contends that any future international body established to distribute the benefits should strike a balance that is equitable—but not necessarily equal.

101 Space Morals

Beyond the American stance lie other factors that have interrupted the smooth, if slow, progress toward establishing a pragmatic legal framework for outer-space development. Specifically, there is an increasing rumble of discordant voices making privileged claims to space-based resources. Countries lacking satellite capability have consistently advanced the premise of a "world fairness revolution." In their eyes, the more fortunate nations have a moral duty to see that the Earth's common resources and material goods are shared with the less-fortunate ones. These voices sometimes mildly assert—but often stridently proclaim—such special entitlements.

Unfortunately, the controversy now swirling around the sharing of oceanic resources has spilled over (or out) into the arena of space, obscuring the Moon Treaty's positive elements. Of course, the souring of American-Soviet relations has not helped either. As a result, the Reagan administration has not yet sent the agreement to the Senate for approval, nor is it likely to do so in the near future.

Certainly, any legal regime of this breadth should be able to cope with opposing outlooks. In this case it should make clear the point that the freedom to explore, exploit, and benefit from extra-terrestrial resources is neither absolute nor unqualified. In light of differing national perspectives, the extension of international law to the space environment should be considered a major achievement.

Critical Provisions in the 1967 Treaty

Undoubtedly, the most important principle of space law is the proposition that certain unclaimed and perhaps uninhabitable portions of the universe constitute a common property or *res communis*. Best exemplified by the expression "freedom of the high seas," this ancient principle holds that no nation may exercise ultimate and exclusive control in certain areas.

Relying on the *res communis* doctrine, the 1967 Principles Treaty stipulates that the exploration and use of outer space be available to all without discrimination of any kind. It further establishes the right of unhindered access to space. Far from being restrictive, these precepts have allowed a wide range of activity to take place in the newfound "commons" beyond our atmosphere.

The 1967 agreement also provides that such activities be carried out "for the benefit and in the interests of all countries, irrespective of their degree of economic and scientific development, and shall be the province of all mankind." The point here is that the equality of nations has been defined in legal, but not practical terms; "equal access" to space does not mean a free ride, for example. However, as mentioned, less-developed nations have invoked the "mankind principle" with increasing frequency in their attempts to garner more of space exploration's benefits.

One interesting provision, borrowed from a 1959 treaty concerning Antarctica, calls for freedom to pursue scientific research and encourages the signatories to cooperate in such undertakings. Both civilian and military personnel can be involved, as long as peaceful activities are undertaken; the same applies to the use of military equipment. Astronauts are to be treated as envoys of humankind, given worldwide assistance if in distress, and returned safely and promptly to the country to which the spacecraft carrying them is registered. Parties to the agreement must publicize any discovery deemed potentially harmful to astronauts.

A country that has launched an object (or procured such service) is liable for damages the object causes on Earth, in the atmosphere, or in space. The treaty's participants can, by mutual agreement, observe one another's launches. With reasonable advance notice, expeditions from one nation can visit the space vehicles and installations belonging to another, but the owner retains jurisdiction over both its spacecraft and the visitors. Private launches, either by individuals or corporations, become the responsibility of the country where the launch occurs if it gave permission in advance. For international activities, such responsibility is shared by all the participants who are bound by the treaty.

The Militarization of Space

Although the United Nations has attempted to prevent military activity in space since the late 1950's, its efforts have been only partially successful. The 1967 Principles Treaty, for example, does not prohibit *all* weaponry in outer space, only those objects "carrying nuclear warheads or any other kinds of weapons of mass destruction." Thus, a loophole exists for "conventional" weaponry. Another of the treaty's provisions, which requires that the Moon and other celestial bodies be used exclusively for peaceful purposes, is similarly flawed, for it neglected to preclude the presence of mass-destruction weapons in open space.

Even the definition of "peaceful" has been open to interpretation. By analogy to peacetime military maneuvers at sea, analysts have made a good case for reconnaissance and communications satellites. These spacecraft can be viewed as defensive in nature, designed to prevent aggressive conduct. Such thinking assumes that "defense" is separate from "offense," making defensive or "peaceful" military activity legally permissible.

Still, the problem remained that many different kinds of space armaments were allowable under international law. Then, in August, 1981, the Soviet Union submitted a draft U.N. treaty that prohibited the permanent stationing of any weapon in space. It asked its signatories "not to destroy, damage, or disturb the normal functioning or change the flight trajectory of space objects" belonging to other treaty members. However, the Soviet proposal singled out NASA's Space Shuttle for special treatment by also prohibiting the temporary orbiting of weapons on "reusable manned vehicles of an existing type or of other types which States Parties may develop in the future."

Soviet Suggested Bans

Ironically, one type of space-based device banned by the Soviet Union's proposal would be its own antisatellite weapons (commonly called ASAT's). The Soviet version is launched on an intercontinental missile and reaches its target in space after orbiting the Earth twice. It can reach only low-altitude targets and, in testing to date, has failed about half the time. Perhaps the Soviets felt they would benefit by banning all such weapons before the United States could surpass this capability. However, the American ASAT system, currently under development, is launched from an Air Force jet and is thus allowable under the 1981 proposal because it is not actually stationed in space.

To close this loophole, on August 21, 1983, the Soviet Union countered with a more sweeping document that called for the prohibition of the use of force by—and against—any object in space. Moreover, three days earlier the late Yuri Andropov proposed a moratorium on Soviet ASAT testing, provided that other nations refrain from similar tests. At the time a delegation of U.S. senators was visiting Moscow, and he expressed to them a willingness to negotiate a ban on both existing and future ASAT systems.

Developments in this particular arena are occurring very rapidly. As of late August, Congress was headed toward a compromise bill that would impose a six-month moratorium on testing the U.S. system against actual targets. Furthermore, it would require President Reagan to make serious efforts toward negotiating "the strictest possible limitations" on such weapons "consistent with . . . national security." A similar action last year sought an outright ban on ASAT's, but the president has since stated that the difficulties in verifying compliance make a total ban impossible.

U.N. activity on space weapons has not ground to a halt, though no real progress can be made until the Americans and Soviets come to terms. An international symposium last March, which included the U.S. and U.S.S.R., examined governmental positions and private proposals for limiting the trend toward space-based armaments. Also, the Soviet proposals made in 1981 and 1983 are still under consideration.

A Summation

The space laws in place today, especially as set forth in the 1967 Principles Treaty, call for free and equal exploration of the realms beyond our atmosphere. They offer substantial benefits to those nations having the capability to get there, but they do not automatically allow the fruits of exploitation to be shared among all countries and peoples. In response, less-developed nations have endeavored to protect their current and future interests.

Even more serious is the looming danger of space warfare, a possibility that international agreements have failed to anticipate fully. When nations first considered the need to govern outer space in a formal way, it was assumed that activity there would be principally scientific and technological in character. Only later did the extraordinary military and commercial potential of space become apparent.

Over time, a political-legal confrontation has emerged. The "have's" are being asked to share with the "have-not's." Although much progress has been made, there remain a number of problems requiring fairly early answers. These problems are not wholly insoluble, for even protracted negotiations can be predicted and accommodated. Political decisions should emerge, and these will become the new principles of space law.

Elizabeth Neeld Comments:

✦ *When the shuttle Challenger blew up, killing the seven astronauts aboard, liability in matters of space travel became front-page news overnight. What went wrong? Who was responsible? Where was the error made and who was accountable for it? But long before the Challenger tragedy, the subject of space law was being seriously discussed around the world.* ✦ *In this essay, which appeared in* Sky and Telescope *in 1984, Carl Christol, a professor at the University of Southern California, talks about a very complex subject with enormous clarity. He discusses complicated space law in a way that an average reader can understand. How does he do it?* ✦ *Christol begins with a real-life example of the kind of happening that results in the need for space law. In 1978, the Soviet nuclear-powered satellite Cosmos 954 fell after only four months in orbit. It hit the earth in northwestern Canada. The Canadian government spent fourteen million dollars to gather the debris. In 1981 the Soviet Union agreed to repay Canada, but the amount of repayment was only three million dollars. Had it not been for some international agreements about space law, however, the situation might not have turned out even that well. By giving us this concrete, clear example of the need for space law, the writer engages us. He now has a audience ready to hear what he has to say.* ✦ *But Christol still has a difficult job ahead of him.*

He must talk about international agreements with names like "Agreement on the Rescue of Astronauts, the Return of Astronauts, and the Return of Objects Launched into Outer Space," and "Convention on International Liability for Damage Caused by Space Objects" in a way that the non-professional in legal matters can understand. One of the ways he does this is to state his subject in the form of a problem: "Unresolved issues of law and diplomacy are becoming more pressing, and how they are settled will influence the character of space activities far into the future." We are not talking merely about a problem now, but about one that can get much more serious in the future. The pull of this problem helps the writer keep the reader engaged. ✦ *When he talks about a complicated concept like CHM, the "common heritage of mankind," and whether or not the moon is such a thing, Christol makes the matter clear for us by listing the objectives that could be accomplished through the application of the CHM principles: (1) the orderly and safe development of lunar resources; (2) their rational management . . . and on through objective number (4). This listing helps produce clarity.* ✦ *Another way this writer illuminates a complex subject is by comparison. When he is talking about unclaimed and perhaps uninhabitable portions of the universe, he compares this to the ancient principle of "freedom of the high seas." He uses terms like "equal access" to help us understand problems in space. He talks about astronauts being treated as "envoys of humankind" who are to be given "worldwide assistance if in distress, and returned safely and promptly to the country to which the spacecraft carrying them is registered." We can understand this principle because it has been explained in terms of diplomatic law which we already understand.* ✦ *The conclusion of the essay does not contain a solution to the problem, but the problem is made vivid and clear for the reader: "Even more serious is the looming danger of space warfare." "The 'have's' are being asked to share with the 'have-not's.'" "Although much progress has been made, there remain a number of problems requiring fairly early answers." Even we readers for whom this is our first brush with a discussion of space law can understand, after reading Christol's essay, the truth of that!* ✦

PART THREE

Reading to See the Whole Picture

RALPH WALDO EMERSON

Seven men went through a field, one after
    another.
One was a farmer, he saw only the grass;
the next was an astronomer, he saw the
    horizon & the stars;
the physician noticed the standing water &
    suspected miasma;
he was followed by a soldier, who glanced
    over the ground, found it easy to hold,
    & saw in a moment how the troops
    could be disposed;
then came the geologist, who noticed the
    boulders & the sandy loam;
after him came the real estate broker, who
    bethought him how the line of the house-
    lots should run, where would be the
    driveway, & the stables.
The poet admired the shadows cast by
    some trees, & still more the music of
    some thrushes & a meadow lark.

Introduction

Have you ever tried to make a recipe that you got from a friend (or your mother), and no matter how closely you followed the instructions, your version just did not taste the same as the original? That's because there are so many factors in addition to the recipe that determine the outcome: the accuracy of the temperature of an oven, the humidity, the kinds of cooking utensils used, the length of time spent stirring, the angle of the slice of the vegetables, the quality of the ingredients, the size of a pinch of this and a dash of that, even your own mood. If the secret were in the recipe alone, everybody would be a fantastic cook, and everybody's dishes would taste just alike.

The same is true about writing.

If the whole secret to good writing were in the instructions that can be given about how to write, then we would all perform alike and turn out similar products. Thank goodness, however, that is not the case. So many factors in addition to rules about writing enter into determining what and how we write: how we personally and individually see the world, what shows up for us when we look at or think about a subject, what interests us, who we want to read our writing, and what our purpose is for writing. And then there are other factors: our habits of thought, our individual style, our habits and practices in how we work, the due date, the requirements of the place of publication or of the assignment, the amount of time we have to give the project, our emotional and physical health, the degree of clarity we have on the subject when we begin writing. The list could go on and on.

It is the configuration of all these factors that makes every piece of authentic writing different. (Inauthentic writing—writing that is parroted to sound just like something you have already read or that is made to conform to a set of dead formulas—will all be alike. And nobody will read it.) It is the configuration—the design— that all these factors make each time we write that allows each of us to express our *own* thoughts and world view and voice through our writing. When each of us writes authentically about a subject, it's like turning a kaleidoscope. You get a different—and beautiful— design every time.

In this section of the text we are going to *read to see the whole picture*. Every essay in this section is on the same subject. (And a luscious subject at that.) Chocolate. But every essay is unique even though it is about the same subject. Each essay is different because each writer:

> sees the world in an individual way
> is interested in certain aspects of the subject and not others
> has a particular purpose in mind when she or he writes
> is writing for a specific audience
> puts words and sentences together differently
> has a different time line to follow to complete the assignment
> is writing for a different publication
> has a set of experiences unlike anyone else
> organizes and combines ideas in her or his own style

And this list could also go on.

It is fascinating—maybe even amazing—to see what seven authors do when they write about the same subject. We see their own personalities reflected in the approaches they choose. We see their expertise and interests reflected in what aspects of the subject they choose to observe and discuss. We hear their individual voices. We become aware of their purposes in writing. We observe their thinking patterns and writing styles by looking at what shows up on the page. We take notice of how they see the world. We see what each one has paid attention to. The particular aspect of the subject covered in the essay is what mattered to each writer.

"All About Chocolate," by Patricia Connell was published in *Bon Appetit*, a magazine devoted, as it says in its masthead, to "America's Food and Entertaining." Are there any clues in the content of "All About Chocolate" that it was written for a cooking magazine? How are the order in which the author gives the facts, the clarity with which the writer explains, the inclusion and exclusion of certain details of the subject, the presence of a personal voice related to the place this essay was published? Patricia Connell writes about chocolate from a particular perspective—interest in the subject itself—and for a particular audience—people who read cooking magazines.

The next essay could have been written only by someone whose way of looking at a subject is from the perspective of "Is it healthy?" "The Temptation of Chocolate" tries to answer the question: how good is chocolate for you? Dick Robinson is president of the American Medical Writers Association in Florida. He writes frequently for *Health* magazine, in which "The Temptation of Chocolate" was published. Since Robinson is a medical writer, he approaches every subject from the standpoint of health. He looks at the world that way, through *his* interest, through his area of expertise. So it is likely that Dick Robinson could think and write about chocolate for a long time before he would choose to write about the geography of chocolate or the kinds of cooking chocolate—if he ever did. When this man looks at chocolate, what shows up for him are questions about health. And that, then, is what he writes.

Francesca Lunzer writes for *Forbes* magazine. Since *Forbes* is a business magazine, she is naturally going to look at a subject from the financial or economic point of view. In "Bittersweet Times in the Chocolate Industry," we read about bankruptcies, the cost of raw materials, government regulations, political instability affecting availability of raw materials, costs, and marketing problems. We can assume some kind of compatibility between the interests of Lunzer and the emphasis of *Forbes* magazine. If that compatibility weren't there, surely Lunzer would be writing some other kind of article, looking at chocolate from some other angle. In this piece, even though it is short, you can distinctly hear the voice of the writer. You get something of her sense of humor, her personality. By the time you finish, if you've been reading carefully, you know something about *her* in addition to knowing quite a bit about the current economics of chocolate.

What happens when a scientist thinks about the subject of chocolate? Well, he sees free-growing cocoa butter crystals, triglycerides, feather crystals, and chemical composition, just to name a few sides of the subject that show up for him. J. A. Miller reports in "Visions of Chocolate: Cocoa Crystals and Candy Quality" about the research of scientists at Pennsylvania State University who are doing microscopy studies on chocolate. This article, which appeared in *Science Digest*, illustrates again those important factors—personal interest and expertise—that determine what a writer pays attention to when he or she looks at a particular subject. Instead of seeing dollar signs, scientists looking at chocolate see questions such as, how are the crystals in this chocolate related to how glossy it is, how much does it snaps? Because they see the world from their own perspective, we learn something about chocolate that we would not know otherwise. We are enriched by the expertise made available to us when scientists write.

"Chocolate: The Jekyll and Hyde of Sweet Treats," is written for athletes, specifically bicyclists. Patricia Lynch writes for *Bicycling* magazine, and this short article looks at chocolate from the standpoint of how good it is for an athlete, yet another angle from which to discuss this subject. The angle is determined by the purpose of the writer, the place of publication, the audience, and the interests and expertise of the writer. There's one focus in this piece of writing. There's one purpose. She is writing for athletes, and she's writing to give them immediately useful information. This directly affects how the writer thinks about her subject.

The next two essays, "Chocolate's Oh-So-Sweet Seductions," and "A Visit to a Chocolate Factory," are written for general audiences and are meant to have mass reading appeal. The first one, by Jack Denton Scott, appeared in *Reader's Digest*; and the second, by John Bowers, appeared in *Cosmopolitan* magazine, a periodical written specifically for trendy women. Reading these two essays, we can see how writers look at a subject when they need to entertain, amuse, and interest their readers. These writers give a popular slant to the subject of chocolate. Their primary purpose is to engage the reader in the subject. You will find many of the same facts in these two essays that you saw in the earlier piece by Patricia Connell. This is a great opportunity to see how the purpose of the writer, the place of publication, the audience, and the personal style of the writer make a new configuration out of the same facts.

Reading to see the whole picture allows us to tell the truth about good writing. Good writing is not just the result of knowing "how to write." It is also a result of being willing to sound like a person when you write, of being appropriate to your audience and place of publication when you write, of looking at a subject from the angle of your particular interest and expertise, of how much time you have to write, of how extensively you've been asked to cover the subject when you write—and a dozen other things. The configuration, the design, of all these factors makes each piece of writing an original. Because good writing is a configuration of new factors each time, every writer's approach to a subject will be different. This makes for well-rounded coverage of the subject. It also makes for variety. And individuality.

It's the same principle of mother's peach cobbler tasting like nobody else's. Not even yours, even when you follow the same recipe.

PATRICIA CONNELL

All About Chocolate

Candy consumption has been down in the last few years, with one big exception: chocolate. And it seems the more luxurious the product (and the price tag), the better. Americans are spending $4 billion a year on their favorite confection—even though, person for person, we eat less than half the 22 pounds consumed annually by the Swiss, and we lag behind the rest of Western Europe, too.

Most American chocolate is made by one of 21 major manufacturers, who in turn supply bakers, confectioners and retailers. Don't believe it for a minute if a local candymaker claims to manufacture his own chocolate. He may combine several to form a special blend, but you can be sure he does not start from the bean. Chocolate making nowadays is big business.

From Blossom to Bean

The tropical "cacao belt," where it all begins, extends around the globe just north and south of the equator. Chief among cacao producers are the Ivory Coast, Brazil, Ghana and Nigeria, but there are plantations in Asia, Africa, Latin America and the West Indies.

The thousands of blossoms appearing yearly on a typical cacao tree will set only abut 20 to 30 fertilized pods, ultimately producing two to three pounds of beans. (Although it is not practical to improve the tree's productiveness with hand-pollinating techniques, which are prohibitively expensive, researchers are hard at work on ways to encourage benign insects to pollinate cacao more efficiently.) The tree flowers and fruits virtually all year long, undergoing one spring harvest and another one in the autumn.

Though there are many intermediate hybrids, most cacao trees belong to one of two general types, known as Forastero and Criollo. The thick-skinned, violet Forastero, grown principally in Brazil and West Africa, is the "base" bean, constituting 90 percent of the world crop. Easier to cultivate than Criollo but more bitter and pungent in flavor, Forastero-type beans are the basic component of all chocolate. The soft, thin-skinned and cream-colored Criollo, grown mainly in its native Ecuador and Venezuela, is the premier "flavor" bean, lending floral and nutty nuances to the chocolate into which it is blended. Expensive, high-quality chocolates tend to start with a higher portion of Criollo beans—up to 50 percent, compared to 10 percent for cheaper products.

Rows of the beans are embedded in white pulp within the four- to twelve-inch-long pods, which resemble elongated melons. The harvesters who cut the pods from the trees are followed by teams of gatherers who collect the pods in heaps and break them open with a blow from a machete or club. The beans are removed from the pulp and may be dredged in sawdust so they can be separated more easily.

Once extracted from their pods, the cacao beans—which exposure to air has changed from their light ivory or lavender color to a pronounced purple—are piled in boxes or baskets for several days to ferment. Temperatures of 125°F or more are generated during fermentation, and the process accomplishes several things: The raw, bitter taste of the bean is mellowed, enzymes that start to develop the characteristic chocolate flavor are activated and the germ of the bean is killed so that sprouting cannot occur. When fermentation is complete the beans have turned brown to the center—their first step toward becoming recognizable as the source of chocolate.

The fermented beans are now ready for drying, either in the sun (if weather permits) or indoors with hot air. Over the course of several days, during which the beans will lose half their weight through moisture loss, they are turned frequently and picked over. Only when dried, and so no longer subject to rapid molding and spoilage, are the beans shipped from the cacao plantation to manufacturers.

Processing and Roasting

Though the last few years have seen a trend toward further processing right in the producing countries, most cacao is still exported to European and American chocolate manufacturers. In this country the chief ports of entry are Norfolk, Virginia, and Philadelphia—not surprising, given that Pennsylvania, with three major plants, makes more chocolate than any other state in the union. At the factory the beans are stored in climate-controlled silos until they are needed.

First comes a preliminary cleaning to remove any foreign matter that may still be present—bits of pod, pulp, jute sacking. After the beans are sorted by size, they are roasted, at 230°F to 280°F, in rotating drums or on a moving belt for anywhere from 30 minutes to two hours. As with coffee beans, roasting is critical to the development of cacao's flavor and aroma; during this time bitterness is further reduced, the true chocolate fragrance is developed, and the beans turn a rich brown. The extract time and temperature depend on numerous variables, such as bean variety (Criollos demand a "low roast," Forasteros a fuller and darker one), type of finished product (beans destined for cocoa will be more heavily roasted than those for chocolate), and the processor's style (most Europeans prefer a darker, Americans a lighter roast). The process must also be tailored to the individual beans, since one batch will vary from another in origin, age, degree of fermentation, moisture content and so on.

After roasting, the beans are quick-cooled and transported to the winnowing machine, or "cracker and fanner," where they are completely cracked and the now-brittle shells are blown away. What is left is the meat of the cacao bean, in the form of its natural segments or "nibs." At this point the nibs from various batches are blended according to zealously guarded proprietary formulas.

The nibs, which average 53 percent to 54 percent cocoa butter, are now milled between steel discs. The process generates enough frictional heat to liquefy the cocoa butter, which is solid at room temperature, and convert the mass to a thick paste known as chocolate liquor. It is this liquor that constitutes the base of all chocolate and cocoa products. Unsweetened baking chocolate—the simplest form of chocolate available—is nothing more than the pure liquor molded into blocks.

Cocoa Powder or Chocolate Bar?

From here on the process goes in one of two directions, depending on whether the end result will be cocoa or chocolate. The essential difference between these two products is that cocoa is chocolate liquor with much of its cocoa butter removed (for if present, it simply floats as an unattractive oily layer on the surface of a cup of hot cocoa), while eating chocolate is the liquor with additional cocoa butter mixed in for rich smoothness.

To make cocoa powder, the liquor is pumped into enormous hydraulic presses in which most of the cocoa butter is squeezed out. It drains away as a light yellow liquid that is reserved for chocolate making (and for other uses, particularly in cosmetics). What remains is a hard brown "press cake" which, when finely pulverized, is cocoa. How it will be labeled is determined by federal standards: "Breakfast cocoa" retains at least 22 percent cocoa butter (van Houten, for example, has about 25 percent), plain "cocoa" (which includes Hershey's) has anywhere from 10 percent to 22 percent, and the "low fat" version has a cocoa butter content of under 10 percent.

An optional final step in cocoa manufacture is "dutching," which, like the defatting procedure, was introduced in Holland in the late 1820s. Dutch-process cocoa, usually intended for drinking rather than cooking or baking, has been treated with an alkali such as potassium carbonate. The result is a mellower flavor (from neutralization of the cocoa's bitter acids), darkened color and improved dispersibility in water. Manufacturers often call this improved "solubility," though the term is erroneous; cocoa powder does not dissolve in water.

Whether or not dutching enhances the flavor of cocoa is a matter of taste. Some people like the gentler taste of the dutched version, while others find it too mild. You may want to compare one of the imported dutched products (such as van Houten, Droste or Poulain) to Hershey's cocoa, which is not dutched, to see which you prefer. Dutch-process cocoa is easy to recognize: It must state on the label that it has been "processed with alkali."

If it is to turn out as chocolate rather than cocoa, the liquor travels another, more complex route. First it is blended with additional cocoa butter and sugar, and with dried or condensed milk in the case of milk chocolate. The paste is then refined by being passed through pairs of heavy rollers. With each passage the mixture becomes smoother as the tiny chocolate and sugar particles are ground still finer.

The Last Refinement

Most sweetened chocolate undergoes yet one more refining step, know as "conching." The mixture is turned into large open steel troughs, the "conches" that give the process its name, where it is heated to anywhere from 130°F to 200°F and stirred with metal rods or rollers for widely varying periods of time. Sweetened cooking chocolate goes through a relatively brief conching, perhaps a few hours, as does that used for making inexpensive candies. Fine-quality chocolate, however, will be conched for many hours, after which it emerges smooth, velvety and mellow in flavor. Some Swiss *chocolatiers* are renowned for conching their products for up to 72 hours—a luxury made possible at the birth of the industry over 100 years ago by the country's plentiful hydroelectricity.

The exact time and temperature of conching are critical factors in the production of high-quality chocolate, and, like cacao bean blends, are kept closely guarded secrets by manufacturers. The chief purpose of conching is to develop the chocolate's flavor by aerating the mix and driving off moisture and volatile acids. This is particularly important for milk chocolate; while the dark varieties can and should be further mellowed by aging, milk chocolate will become stale if aged long enough for its acids to dissipate. The temperature maintained in the conches must be high enough to assist the volatilization process, and (if the manufacturer so designs it) may caramelize the sugar slightly.

The conching process also breaks up any clumps of sugar or cocoa particles, rounds off the rough edges of the sugar crystals (though it does not appreciably reduce particle size any further), and evenly distributes the cocoa butter. During conching, flavorings such as vanilla are blended in, as are additives like lecithin, commonly used to keep the cocoa butter fully emulsified with the other ingredients. For high-quality chocolate, more cocoa butter may be added during the conching.

Finally, to temper the chocolate before it is molded, the still-liquid mixture is agitated in water-cooled kettles until the temperature is lowered to 85°F or 90°F. The tempering step thickens the chocolate to give it the proper flow for molding, but more important, it causes the fat to crystallize into a regular structure that promotes improved keeping qualities: Correct temper helps keep the cocoa butter from migrating to the surface of the chocolate and forming a grayish "bloom." After tempering, the chocolate is ready for molding into bars or blocks, or for pumping into storage tanks to await its eventual shipment to commercial confectioners.

A World of Chocolate Types

The exact constituents of this final product are subject to infinite variation. A large manufacturer may produce dozens or even hundreds of basic chocolate types to meet wholesale customers' specifications. The products' proportions of cocoa butter, chocolate liquor and sugar will vary, as will bean roast and flavorings; for example, top-of-the-line chocolate may be distinguished by its use of pure vanilla instead of synthetic vanillin. The situation is further complicated by the terms "extra-bittersweet," "bittersweet," "semisweet" and "sweet,"none of which has a standard meaning. Broadly speaking, they are in ascending order of sweetness, and a given company's bittersweet will have a lower sugar content than, say, its sweet chocolate. But there is no guarantee of consistency among different firms; one manufacturer's bittersweet may in fact be sweeter than another company's semisweet, and so on.

What is standardized is the proportion of chocolate liquor in the various chocolate types. Bitter chocolate must consist of pure chocolate liquor (of which 50 percent to 58 percent is cocoa butter), with optional flavoring such as vanilla. Bittersweet and semisweet, considered synonymous by the FDA, must contain at least 35 percent chocolate liquor, and sweet, 15 percent. Milk chocolate can include as little as 10 percent chocolate liquor, but must have 12 percent milk solids; because the actual chocolate content is small, manufacturers generally use the most strongly flavored beans for milk chocolate. In each case the remainder of the product is virtually all sugar.

Some European chocolates state their percentage of "cocoa solids" on the wrapper. This term usually refers collectively to chocolate liquor and added cocoa butter. It is misleading, however, because in lumping the two together the actual chocolate liquor content is disguised, and it is the percentage of liquor in

relation to other ingredients that determines the intensity of chocolate flavor. Bittersweet, semisweet and sweet types can all be
used more or less interchangeably in cooking, but the sweeter kind
will pack a slightly less potent chocolate taste.

Specialty Chocolates

In addition to these basic varieties there are also specialty chocolate products with particular uses for cooks and confectioners.
Because of their relatively low cocoa butter content, chocolate
morsels and chips retain their shape well at high temperatures,
but lack the rich smoothness of block chocolates containing more
fat. Conversely, the candymaker's *couverture* chocolate has a high
percentage of cocoa butter. This makes it particularly fluid when
heated, so that candy centers can be given an even coating.

The so-called "compound" chocolates, constituting a whole
separate class, are used principally as coatings for candy bars, ice
cream, cookies and other products in which the chocolate's role is
secondary. To make compound chocolate the manufacturer re-
places cocoa butter and part or all of the chocolate liquor with a
less expensive mixture of cocoa and vegetable fats. For candy and
baked goods the fat, often hydrogenated coconut or palm kernel
oil, has a higher melting point than cocoa butter, making the coating harder; for ice cream the fat has a lower melting point, so that
it can be applied in a thin layer and is flexible rather than flaky at
low temperatures. Compounds are also used to make "imitation"
chocolate chips, premelted "chocolate flavor" packets, and so on.
These products are labeled this way because they do not contain
enough chocolate liquor to meet the federal minimums for chocolate.

"White chocolate" is another compound product, and the term
is a misnomer: Since it contains no chocolate liquor, white chocolate really is not (again by federal standards) chocolate at all. For
this reason it is often referred to as "confectioners coating" or the
like. High-quality versions, usually imported, are made with cocoa
butter, sugar, milk solids and flavorings; cheaper ones substitute
other fats for the cocoa butter.

The main difference between them—indeed, between all compound chocolates and the real thing—is that other vegetable fats
lack the unique melting properties of cocoa butter. While cocoa
butter has little if any actual taste, it is the best possible vehicle for
"delivering" the taste of chocolate. Because it melts at a few de-

grees below body temperature, it dissolves gradually in the mouth, allowing the taste of the chocolate to develop slowly and linger a long time. The fats used in compound have a "mouth feel" that is waxy or oily in comparison to cocoa butter, so they do not have the luxurious richness of the genuine article.

European Versus American

In practice the difference between real and compound chocolate may barely be noticeable, depending on the use to which the product is put; the opulent texture of a fine chocolate would be lost in a granola bar coating. European confectioners have traditionally concentrated on the chocolate, using high-quality coatings around fairly simple centers and fillings, while American candymakers tend to put more emphasis on the centers. This at least partly explains the different looks of European and American filled chocolate candies. The European type is generally "shell molded"—the top and bottom halves of each piece are molded separately, filled and joined—while American chocolates are more often "enrobed," meaning that rows of centers are squirted with chocolate as they progress along a moving belt. The coating on an enrobed chocolate can be quite thin, but the molding process requires a thick, sturdy shell that will necessarily wind up as the most important component of the finished candy.

Whatever the shape in which you prefer your chocolate, there are standard criteria for judging its quality. It should look glossy, not dull or dry, which may indicate too low a cocoa butter content. A gray surface bloom does not prove inferiority, but does show that the chocolate has been subjected to temperature variations that caused the cocoa butter to migrate to the surface and reharden there. The aroma of good chocolate should be of chocolate, not cocoa; this will seem a meaningless distinction only to those who have never compared them. The bar should snap cleanly, not crumble when broken, for if crumbly it is probably stale. A fine quality chocolate should feel buttery, not sticky or gritty, as it melts on the tongue, and needless to say it should have no off-flavors or disagreeable aftertaste.

As most of us know only too well, any chocolate that meets these criteria (and, let's face it, many that do not) more than amply explains the botanical name of the cacao tree: *Theobroma*, or "the food of the gods."

DICK ROBINSON

The Temptation of Chocolate

Americans love chocolate. We give gold-wrapped boxes of the stuff on every possible occasion: Valentine's Day, Mother's Day, Christmas Day, Groundhog Day . . . If we *don't* have a good excuse for giving a box of chocolates, we resort to treating ourselves to chocolate croissants for breakfast, hot chocolate with lunch, double chocolate chip ice cream after dinner. Americans love chocolate so much that we spend nearly $4 billion a year on 2 billion pounds of it (10 pounds per person)!

But chocolate has an aftertaste: Most of us suffer from what can only be called "chocolate-covered guilt." We worry about getting fat, developing cavities, breaking out in ugly pimples. Well, relax. Having investigated chocolate, we've come up with a surprising conclusion: In reasonable quantities it isn't so bad for you after all.

The Calorie Count

Three chocolate kisses, one medium-size apple and one small banana all contain about 80 calories. Problem is, you *can* eat just one banana, but who can eat just three kisses? Real chocoholics, therefore, may skip meals to save calories for chocolate (*not* wise). Here, in the belief that knowledge is the key to self-control, are the vital statistics for some of the most popular chocolates in this country (ounces given are for standard-size packages):

BRAND	CALORIES
6 Hershey's Kisses	150
Hershey's milk chocolate bar (plain, 1.45 oz.)	220
Hershey's milk chocolate bar with almonds (1.45 oz.)	230
M & M's (plain, 1.69 oz.)	240
M & M's (peanut, 1.67 oz.)	240
Reese's peanut butter cups (1.69 oz.)	240
Mr. Goodbar (1.65 oz.)	250
Mars bar (1.87 oz.)	260
Milky Way bar (2 oz.)	260
Snickers bar (2 oz.)	270
3 Musketeers bar (2.28 oz.)	280

A Damper on Your Diet

Remember when you mother warned you not to eat chocolate before dinner because it would spoil your appetite? She was right— all the fat and sugar in chocolate *does* tend to kill hunger. If you're on a diet, it's O.K. to allow yourself an *occasional* chocolate goodie to help fill you up before dinner as long as it doesn't throw off your calorie count. (Of course, if you are a chocoholic who can't stop with one, forget it.)

Inside Info

What's in a piece of chocolate? It depends on who made it. Some chocolates have more than 300 ingredients in their secret formulas—leaving little room for chocolate. Usually only 12 to 15 percent of an assembly-line milk chocolate bar is "raw" chocolate, according to the Chocolate Manufacturers Association. The rest is sugar (45 to 55 percent), powdered whole milk (15 to 17 percent), extra cocoa butter (a vegetable fat found in pure chocolate), lecithin (which keeps ingredients from separating), artificial flavorings such as vanilla and, often, preservatives.

Expensive, exotic chocolates generally include more chocolate, depending on the type used. A sweet (or dark) chocolate typically contains 20 to 25 percent pure chocolate. Bittersweet (semisweet) chocolate contains at least 35 percent chocolate, and baking (bitter) chocolate is 100 percent chocolate.

Expensive gourmet milk chocolates are made with cocoa beans, sugar, fresh cream, real butter, cocoa butter and natural flavorings (no preservatives). They are blended for up to three days, whereas run-of-the-mill chocolates are usually refined for only eight hours or so.

A Chocolate a Day . . .

"Milk chocolate is in some ways more nutritious than a wholesome apple," says Richard T. O'Connell, president of the Chocolate Manufacturers Association of the U.S.A. That's a suspect statement from someone who makes a living from chocolate, so HEALTH investigated his claim and found there's truth in it.

Our analysis of figures from the chocolate industry of the U.S. Department of Agriculture shows that compared to a medium-size apple (five ounces), a typical plain milk chocolate bar (1.5 ounces) has 11 times more protein, 10 times more calcium, seven times more phosphorus, five times more riboflavin (vitamin B_2) and 8 percent more potassium, all of which are essential nutrients.

On the other hand, the chocolate bar has three times as many calories as the apple, 17 times more fat and 40 times more sodium.

Caffeine? Cholestrerol?

Pure chocolate contains no cholesterol. The fat in chocolate's cocoa butter is saturated, but studies have shown that unlike other saturated fats, cocoa butter seems to have no effect on blood cholesterol. (No one knows why.) Chocolate mixed with butter or milk, however, contains cholesterol.

Worried about the caffeine in chocolate? Rest easy—a chocolate bar contains less than one-tenth the caffeine of a cup of brewed coffee.

Eat It Today, Wear It Tomorrow?

Some good news: According to a study done at the University of Pennsylvania, chocolate does *not* cause or even aggravate acne. What's more, a study out of the National Institute for Dental Research in Bethesda, Maryland concluded that chocolate may be less damaging to teeth than many other snacks because the cocoa butter in it coats the teeth, preventing sugar from reaching the bacteria that produce cavity-causing acids. Of course, if the chocolate is combined with caramel or other sticky candy, it's not going to do your teeth much good.

Anatomy of a Chocolate Bar

A typical 1.5-oz. (41 grams) milk chocolate bar contains:

220 calories
9 mg. caffeine
40 mg. sodium

Minerals:	% of RDA
Calcium	8
Iron	4

Vitamins:	% of RDA
Riboflavin (B_2)	6
Thiamine (B_1)	2
Niacin (B_3)	*
A	*
C	*

*Less than 2%

Nutrients:	% by weight	grams
Carbohydrates	56	23
Sugar	54	22
Fat	32	13
Protein	7	3

Ingredients: Milk chocolate, sugar, milk, cocoa butter, chocolate, soya lecithin (an emulsifier), vanillin (artificial vanilla flavoring).

RDA—Recommended Daily Allowance
mg.—milligrams

The Food of Love

Before entering his harem, Aztec ruler Montezuma reportedly used to drink a large goblet of pure bitter chocolate because he considered it an aphrodisiac. He also served chocolate to the maidens brought to him as offerings.

Though few people still regard chocolate as an aphrodisiac, it does have other magical "powers." When you're infatuated or in love, your brain produces a substance that gives you a natural high, *phenylethylamine*. Chocolate packs loads of the same substance.

So in the unfortunate event that you fall out of love, don't be surprised if you find yourself craving chocolate; what you really need is to replenish your supply of phenylethylamine.

FRANCESCA LUNZER

Bittersweet Times in the Chocolate Industry

You can't say that Americans don't have their priorities straight. Last year they spent $4 billion on chocolate, which is a bit more than the amount spent on personal computer hardware and software put together.

Despite that kind of spending, the industry is going through a bittersweet period. Small sign of the times: Krön Chocolatier, among the first of the chocolate boutiques (hand-dipped fresh fruit, even large chocolate tennis rackets), filed for protection from its creditors under Chapter 11 of the Bankruptcy Act last October. Larger sign of the times: Hershey Foods, the $1.7 billion (sales) chocolate giant, is diversifying like mad out of solid chocolate products and into lighter snacks, in response to the new health- and fitness-conscious consumer. Hershey has entered the $250 million granola bar market, a market that has grown rapidly in recent years.

Is America losing its sweet tooth? Not really. Chocolate consumption is a healthy 2.2 billion pounds per year, up 13.6% since 1980. The real problem is economic: Good chocolate is expensive, getting more so, and, despite the example of "designer" chocolates like Michel Guerard's, at $36 for 1½ pounds, there is a limit to how much you can charge before consumers decide to spend their money elsewhere.

Keeping that limit from being reached, says Leonard Teitelbaum, a food analyst for Merrill Lynch, depends entirely on adroit marketing. "At $25 per pound," says Teitelbaum, "there's no way you can [make giving expensive chocolate a] normal occasion. The recipient of the gift therefore has to know that he is getting something expensive. It's the cachet that sells."

Developing the right cachet for a brand of expensive chocolate is itself not an inexpensive proposition. While marketers such as Krön are wrestling with that problem, they also have to confront a rising raw material cost structure.

The best bittersweet chocolates and chocolate coatings use what the industry calls flavor beans, rather than the common filler beans used in making cocoa powder and cheaper chocolates. The trouble is that flavor beans make up only 7% of all beans now produced. On top of that, the Food & Drug Administration requires that chocolate liquor, which is the basis for all chocolate products, must have a 50% to 58% cocoa butter content. Additional cocoa butter, a by-product of the chocolate manufacturing process, is mostly purchased separately by chocolate manufacturing companies because their own chocolate production does not yield enough cocoa butter to satisfy either taste or FDA rules. As a result, says Barry Zoumas, Hershey's vice president for science and technology, "You can't really reduce chocolate cost except by making the processing itself more efficient."

To add to these problems there is the general volatility of the bean market: Flavor beans come from a tight band of equatorial countries, most notably Ghana. Constant changes in government and general instability have played havoc with supplies.

All that makes the competition at the upscale end bitter, and likely to bring in the biggest players. Krön's major competition is Godiva, a division of Campbell Soup Co. since 1969, which sells through its own stores and in many department stores. Godiva chocolates, unlike Krön's handformed products, are machine-made. Nevertheless, Andrew Carduner, managing director of the partnership that took over Krön after it went into bankruptcy, may have to concede some portion of the luxury market to Godiva, just because Krön does not have the marketing clout of a large company behind it. Instead of Godiva, Carduner sees his competition as small importers, the kind who may have one small shop in New York and another in Los Angeles and thrive on favorable word-of-mouth rather than expensive promotion.

While the heirs to Krön cope with that problem, the high-end chocolate market has already caused the larger companies to upgrade some of their products. And, after all, if what you really want is a great bar of chocolate after lunch instead of a solid chocolate telephone, it is now easier and less expensive to come by. The best example is Nestlé. It reformulated its basic bar in 1983, using lessons learned from its coatings division, which makes up half its chocolate business and whose chocolate-buying customers include among others, Krön Chocolatier.

J. A. MILLER

Visions of Chocolate: Cocoa Crystals and Candy Quality

The gloss, grittiness and snap, the look, taste and texture of chocolate candy are a matter of bow ties and feathers, according to microscopy studies of cocoa butter crystals. These ties, feathers and other crystalline forms determine characteristics important to the confectionery industry and to consumers in the United States, who eat an average of 8 pounds of chocolate goodies every year.

A surprisingly large number of crystal forms and some striking relationships among them have been revealed by a new method of characterizing free-growing cocoa butter crystals. "The crystal forms are usually defined by melting point, which has been confusing," says Paul S. Dimick of The Pennsylvania State University, in University Park. "We are actually looking at the crystals, and we see more than the six forms reported in the literature. We see about 12 different types." In addition, he has observed one crystal form, called a bow tie, evolve into another, called a feather.

Dimick and Douglas M. Manning have applied two sophisticated microscopy techniques to cocoa crystals. Polarized light microscopy reveals a cross-sectional view of the internal structure of the crystal. Scanning electron microscopy shows the surface.

The crystalline structure of cocoa butter depends on its composition. Cocoa butter is primarily made up of molecules called triglycerides, each of which has three fatty acids attached to a molecule of glycerol. The crystalline structure depends on how the triglycerides are positioned into a rigid pattern.

The formation of a feather crystal at 86°F was observed step-by-step by Manning and Dimick. The first crystallization produced a form with a constriction in the center. This bow tie form enlarged primarily on the outer surfaces while the central area remained constricted. Then the crystals spread and eventually assumed a circular shape. The bow tie form has a high concentration of certain triglycerides that are the first to crystallize at this temperature, and then they promote stable crystallization of others, Dimick says.

The chemical composition of the cocoa butter, and thus its crystalline form, depends on the variety of cocoa bean from which it is pressed as well as such environmental factors as the amount of rainfall where the bean was grown. So far Dimick and Manning have been using a pure cocoa butter from the Ivory Coast. But eventually Dimick hopes, with crystal microscopy, to define parameters of cocoa butters from different countries, and even develop methods to determine if chocolate products have been adulterated with cocoa butter substitutes.

PATRICIA LYNCH

Chocolate: The Jekyll and Hyde of Sweet Treats

You can find chocolate almost anywhere, from a vending machine to a posh New York City restaurant. People who can't resist it in any form call themselves chocoholics.

As an athlete, you may be wondering whether this treat is a legitimate source of quick energy of just a junk food. The answer seems to lie somewhere between the two extremes.

Chocolate's advantages have to do with its make-up: It is nearly 50 percent sugar. Road racers and tourists who do not meet their energy requirements through a balanced diet often find chocolate's sugar content useful as a supplement, as Manfred Krager, a professor of nutrition at the Pennsylvania State University, points out. Even Olympic athletes indulge, and with good reason. Elite cyclists and runners can burn between 3,000 and 4,000 calories in a workout, and candy bars and cake make up the deficit.

The best time to indulge in chocolate, which contains the energizer caffeine besides sugar, is while in training. You might want to eat small finger-sized bars during a century or other distance events or indulge afterwards.

But don't eat chocolate right before you compete! As a concentrate source of sugar, it initially raises your blood sugar and stimulates the pancreas to produce insulin. Insulin combats high levels of blood sugar, and the rapid drop can leave you feeling weak and dizzy.

Once you begin exercising, however, you can eat chocolate without any fears at all—exercise inhibits the production of insulin. To be on the safe side, Elsworth Buskirk, Director of the Laboratory for Human Research at the Pennsylvania State University, suggests not eating chocolate an hour or more before an event.

It's also important not to gorge on too much chocolate, because the empty calories found in chocolate may cause you to gain weight if there's an imbalance between intake and expenditure.

So, the key is moderation.

Chocolate isn't the wonder snack it is often thought to be, but a candy bar eaten an hour or more before a race can't hurt—and it can help provide needed calories and the "up" you may need during a long event.

JACK DENTON SCOTT

Chocolate's Oh-So-Sweet Seductions

In 1980, two employees of the famous Swiss chocolate industry were nabbed trying to sell to China and Russia some of their tiny nation's most closely guarded secrets: 40 recipes for making chocolate. In Switzerland this was considered as serious as military espionage, for the Swiss make money, not war, including over $75 million a year by exporting their incomparable confections.

Actually, the Swiss "traitors" had precedent for their sneaky actions. In 1519, conquistador Hernando Cortés introduced chocolate to the world by bringing the original recipe out of Mexico's royal Aztec court to Spain. Less cautious than the Swiss, Aztec ruler Montezuma II toasted Cortés in *chocolatl*, and permitted him to watch it being made. Montezuma was known for tossing back 50 golden goblets of the dark, bitter liquid a day, and always drank a big beaker before entering his harem, believing that *chocolatl* not only gave him strength and energy but also was an aphrodisiac.

At least in the strength and energy areas, nutritionists have since proved Montezuma right. Besides having carbohydrates and fat, the average 1.5-ounce milk-chocolate bar contains four percent of the U.S. Recommended Daily Allowance of protein, two percent of thiamine, four percent of riboflavin, six percent of calcium and two percent of iron.

Napoleon was a believer in the quick-energy benefits of chocolate, and always carried it with him on campaigns. Chocolate has also been part of the ration of U.S. frontline soldiers. It has gone aboard American and Soviet space flights, and Sir Edmund Hillary took chocolate with him when he conquered Mount Everest.

Does Not Cause Acne

More good news: scientific tests prove that chocolate usually neither causes nor aggravates acne. And a study by the Eastman Dental Center in Rochester, N.Y., found that milk chocolate and chocolate-chip cookies, with their high content of protein, calcium, phosphate and other minerals, are less damaging to tooth enamel than other snack foods.

At first, the bitter drink Cortés brought back wasn't well received in Spain. But when sugar was stirred in, chocolate began to take off. The Spanish tried to keep the techniques of its cultivation and manufacture secret, but a Florentine was finally able to break the monopoly in 1606 by bringing the recipe to Italy. Once there, nothing prevented chocolate's spread to other countries—except, perhaps, its exorbitant price.

By 1763 chocolate was so popular in England—where milk was first added to the beverage—that beer and ale makers reportedly called for legislation restricting its manufacture. In 1765, John Hannon, a chocolate maker from England, with financial backing from Dr. James Baker, established the first U.S. chocolate factory in Dorchester, Mass. Baker's remains the oldest chocolate trademark in the country.

The Chocolate Tree

The magic that is chocolate begins with a tree. Aptly named *Theobroma* (food of the gods) *cacao*, it flourishes within 20 degrees of the equator in such countries as the Ivory Coast, Ghana, Nigeria, Brazil and Mexico. Capable of growing to 60 feet, but in plantations usually pruned to 20 feet, the cacao tree blooms continuously and can produce up to 100,000 yellow-white or pink-white blossoms a year in a never-ending explosion of color. What the chocolate makers want from the tree, however, are its seed pods, which are harvested two times a year for up to 40 years. Inside the hard pod shell, which changes color from green to yellow to red or purple as it ripens, are 20 to 60 almond-shaped, bitter-tasting cocoa beans. It takes 400 of them to make a pound of chocolate, and a single tree yields only 20 to 30 pods a year. Such is the demand that the world's annual output of about 1.6 million metric tons of unprocessed beans is worth more than $3 billion.

After fermenting and drying, the beans are shipped to chocolate manufacturers, who select the kind they need for making their secret blends. (Like tea and coffee, blending is what makes chocolate distinctive.) The beans are then cleaned, roasted, and cracked into pieces called nibs, which contain just over 50-percent cocoa butter (a pure vegetable fat) and are the basis of all chocolate and cocoa products.

Tempering and Enrobing

Grinding liquefies the cocoa butter, and the result is chocolate "liquor." If the liquor is poured into molds and allowed to harden, it becomes bitter, or baking, chocolate. If not, chocolate makers follow their own recipes for the next step, which is to sweeten the liquor by adding varying amounts of sugar and cocoa butter, plus milk for milk chocolate. The resulting grainy mix is ground fine, and stirred and kneaded for hours or even days—a process called conching—until it is velvety smooth.

Tempering comes next, which is a method of varying the texture even further through the use of different temperatures. Now the chocolate is ready for creativity to flower as it is transformed into tasty candy. While it is still warm, nuts, fruits and other fillings are dipped in it—or "enrobed" in a faster method that pours chocolate over the various fillings. It may be molded into myriad forms—ranging from a model of the Empire State Building to a San Francisco cable car, from a moose head to a unicorn or a Rolls-Royce—or even a magnum of champagne. To Melbourne, Australia, goes the honor of concocting the world's largest chocolate sculpture, a 4484-pound, ten-foot-tall Easter egg.

Money No Object

Money is apparently no object to the chocolate addict. One fancy brand of chocolates, Godiva, can be bought in U.S. stores packed in an ornate, lacquered Russian box—for about $350 a pound. For a time, Godiva's makers offered delivery of its chocolates by a woman on horseback, in a flesh-colored body stocking and accompanied by minstrels. Price: just under $3000.

Some people devote their lives to chocolate—Milton Zelman, for instance, publisher of the chocolate-scented, New York-based bimonthly *Chocolate News*. A walking chocolate encyclopedia, Zelman estimates that Americans eat more than 1.8 billion pounds of chocolate a year, worth about $3 billion. Over 800 million pounds of this consumption is in the form of chocolate bars, with M & M/Mars' Snickers bar probably the most popular.

Although Zelman believes that the Swiss and Belgians make the best chocolate, for my part I have found certain American chocolates equal or superior to all expensive foreign brands. The hand-dipped truffles and Celestial Miniatures of the Casanova Chocolate Company, of Milford, Conn., take a lot to beat. So do the Gianduja Pralines of New York City's master chocolate maker Heinz Robert Goldschneider, who practices his art at Le Chocolatier. His Brionis, milk-chocolate creams, are so smooth they almost melt before they get to the mouth.

But for my money and taste, Manhattan's Krön Chocolatier makes the best chocolate in the United States. Tom Krön sells over five million of his original hand-dipped-in-dark-chocolate fresh strawberries a year. And he is also fast becoming famous for his custom chocolate making—a perfect, life-size female leg and greeting-cards-to-read-and-eat are just a few examples.

And who could forget chocolate's most distinctive contribution to its multitude of harmonious marriages—its scrumptious union with almonds? Milton Snavely Hershey began mass production of this combination in 1894. Today, the Hershey Chocolate Company is one of the world's largest producers of chocolate and cocoa products.

How are we to explain the worldwide appeal of this most magical of sweets, won from the paradoxically bitter seed of the *chocolatl* tree? Maybe Montezuma knew more even than nutritionists give him credit for. According to a theory put forth by Drs. Donald F. Klein and Michael R. Liebowitz of the N.Y. State Psychiatric Institute, the brain of a person "in love" is awash with a substance called phenylethylamine, which brings a rosy high similar to that induced by amphetamines. Chocolate, it so happens, is loaded with phenylethylamine. Which may explain why those who have loved and lost often go on chocolate binges—in effect, self-medicating themselves to bring back the highs of love.

And can it be only coincidence that two famous lovers of history, Casanova and Madame du Barry, were chocolate freaks? Maybe, as some fans claim, chocolate is the food not only of the gods but also of love.

JOHN BOWERS

A Visit to a Chocolate Factory

Traffic races along Interstate 81—trailer trucks spewing diesel fumes, panel trucks rattling, and private cars going ten miles over the limit, their drivers staring glassy-eyed ahead. Signs herald Allentown, Bethlehem, and Harrisburg, but I could be anywhere—although as farms flash by I do occasionally spot a grazing heifer and notice a Pennsylvania Dutch "hex" sign on a red barn. At exit 28, I cut down a narrow blacktop road for a few miles, and suddenly I haven't the slightest doubt about where I am. Street lamps are in the shape of candy Kisses, two intersecting avenues are named Cocoa and Chocolate, and on a grassy slope beside a huge factory, brown hedges have been trimmed to spell HERSHEY COCOA. My nose is in heaven. I am in Hershey, Pennsylvania.

"This place is really Brigadoon," says Cindy Roof, director of publicity, advertising, and promotion at Hershey Park. "I grew up here and once tried to leave. Got as far as Philadelphia and became totally disoriented. I had to come back."

There are no jails in Hershey, not one poor person anyone knows about. In this child's paradise you can eat all the chocolate you want—mountains and mountains of it. (Hershey workers get it free.) In seventy-six acre Hershey Park, the 330-foot Kissing Tower is topped with a rotating chocolate-colored cabin whose Kiss-shaped windows provide a view of Hershey's gentle green slopes. Down in a valley looms the chocolate plant. Twenty-four silos hold a total of ninety million pounds of cocoa beans—enough for five and a half billion Hershey bars. Out on the horizon is the curving sweep of the Milton S. Hershey Medical Center, with its white-domed Founder's Hall, larger than the Jefferson Memorial in Washington—a tribute to Milton Snavely Hershey and his wife, Catherine. Inhale anywhere within five miles and you will, except on the stillest day, breath the distinct aroma of chocolate. This is, after all, the home town of the largest chocolate factory on earth.

Liberace Buys $300 Worth Every Year

Like some one and a half million visitors a year, I am taking a tour—in tunnel-of-love fashion—through Chocolate World. A remote-controlled chair glides me down dim corridors, past illuminated exhibits that show how cocoa grows in the tropics, around simulated roasting ovens and replicas of the candy-making machines in the real Hershey plant across town. We learn that the Aztecs taught Spanish conquerors about cocoa, and Spain introduced it to the rest of Europe a century later. In Switzerland, a man named Daniel Peter invented milk chocolate—a product composed principally of concentrated milk, sugar, cocoa powder, and cocoa butter. By this time my mouth is watering in anticipation, and it doesn't help that a shameless management is pumping chocolate scent through the air vents.

At last, I am dropped off in a skylighted area where piles of sweets are waiting to be grabbed.

Until 1973, visitors were given a guided tour of the plant itself, but this practice ended when crowds became too large and work suffered. "It went to some of our employees' heads," an executive tells me. "They began acting like Clark Gables."

In the gift shop of Chocolate World hands reach in a slow, dreamy way toward hills of wrapped candy bars. Some of these items aren't seen in the corner candy store—a ten-pound Hershey bars sells for forty dollars. Liberace comes to Hershey every year and buys $300 worth of chocolate, mostly cases of Golden Almond bars, almost unbearably rich, thickly studded with whole fresh almonds, and wrapped in gold foil.

Now that there is a Chocolate World, the plant itself has few visitors. As I enter, a portrait of Milton Snavely Hershey greets me sternly. The receptionist's desk holds the requisite assortment of miniature chocolate bars. I nibble on a Kit Kat while inserting soft plugs in my ears and placing a hair net over my beard. Kim Payne, community-relations coordinator wearing a hard hat, is about to show me around. Even with the ear plugs the machine-gun rattle of wrapping machines is deafening.

One flight up are the vast holding tanks that store chocolate paste at 110°F. Down through a series of pipes this paste flows to depositor machines where it cools to 82°F., then pours into metal molds that take it through a cooling tunnel. The molds are jiggled to remove air bubbles from the chocolate. During this trip the paste turns into a solid at between 45° and 60°F., and just before the molded bars disappear into wrapping machines a woman in a surgically clean white smock looks for flaws—any bar with a crack in it, an air bubble, a misshapen edge. Finding one, she plucks it out and slings it into a scrap bin, which resembles a large brown bathtub. This mountain of rejected chocolate will be melted again and recycled. My hand automatically goes toward an inviting hunk when a look from Kim Payne stops me. "We don't eat from the bins," he says.

All the familiar bars one remembers from trips to the movies and neighborhood candy counters emerge from the wrapping machines. Workers pack Mr. Goodbars and Hershey bars in boxes with a flick of the wrist. They look one way and their hands go another. I stand with Kim Payne before a giant Hershey Kiss wrapping machine whose steady jackhammer beat is sending thousands of the tinseled nuggets along a conveyor belt. Two women, as intense as scientists at the microscope, run their hands caressingly over the silver deluge, searching for imperfections. I finally notice that Kim Payne has been trying for some time to make himself heard over the din. "These women get 1,200 Kisses a minute," he yells. (Humor of this nature is heard quite frequently in Hershey.) The precise process of wrapping Kisses is a well-guarded secret as is the exact formula for making Hershey chocolate.

Next I visit the test kitchen. Surprisingly, it has ordinary stoves and refrigerators, like those in private homes, and bright light streams in the windows. Here, home economists spend whole days testing recipes for cookies and other confections, which include a Hershey ingredient.

Taste-test panelists arrive, nibble, and look off into space. If they consider the product matchless, the recipe may land on the package of the Hershey ingredient—say, Reese's Peanut Butter Chips. (Package recipes change frequently.) Pasta recipes have also been coming out of the Hershey kitchen, ever since the company's acquisition of San Giorgio-Skinner Company. Now I am dazed by the mingled aromas of garlic and chocolate coming from the stoves. I touch the Kit Kat in my pocket for security.

An Emergency Might Arise

In the analytic laboratory Carolyn Houston Burnett, lab coordinator, tells me, "Someone is always on duty here, because you never know when an emergency might arise—for instance, if one batch of chocolate doesn't mold properly. You could have the same problem at home, when the fudge mysteriously won't harden. Maybe there was too much moisture in the chocolate or not enough butterfat. We're like detectives, and it's not unusual to be called out of bed at three in the morning and rushed to the plant to solve a mystery.

Burnett's lab is also charged with making sure the taste of Hershey chocolate keeps the product selling well. "We experiment with our formulas and give samples to a taste panel. Hershey bars do change. People in the 1930s might have liked one taste of chocolate, people of the 1980s another."

She herself didn't have a particular passion for chocolate when she came to work at Hershey eight years ago. "I became addicted after the first six months," she says, with a laugh. "It's available free at every coffee machine. But now I've lost some of my interest. Maybe seeing so much of it around. . . ."

I know I'll never see so much chocolate gathered in one spot again as in the "conching" room. Here the chocolate is mixed in huge vats—called "conches" because the old containers resembled a sea conch. The modern ones look more like swimming pools and hold anywhere from ten to ninety thousand pounds of chocolate paste. Sixteen granite rollers whoosh brown goo back and forth at a mesmerizing pace, and I am reminded of a novel by Anne Roiphe called *Long Division*. In it a little girl who is touring the factory falls into a vat and bobs up looking like a big M&M. A lifeguard immediately strips down to underwear with the Hershey insignia, dives in, and rescues her. This happens now and then, the tour guide says, and this is why lifeguards are posted by each tank. Pure fiction, of course, but there *is* an urge to tumble in. Kim Payne cautions, "Don't you touch! It's over a hundred degrees!"

One-third of the plant's two-million square feet is taken up with conching—or rubbing, as the steady rolling and smoothing is more technically known. Every batch is rubbed for at least three full days. Milton Snavely Hershey believed that the real secret of good chocolate was in this process.

"The milk that goes into chocolate can also affect its taste," Kim Payne says, "Milk for chocolate must come from closeby, so it's fresh."

Hershey's History

Hershey chose the dairy region of Pennsylvania for his plant because that's where the milk was. The plant today receives over one million gallons every day from about a thousand neighboring farms. He also chose the hamlet of Derry Township in 1902 because it had been his boyhood home. Hershey was born in 1857 to devout Mennonite parents. He quit school early and became apprenticed to a printer but failed at once when he dropped his cap between the rollers and ruined an entire press run. He was next apprenticed to a candy maker, learned the trade, but couldn't make a living in Philadelphia, Denver, Chicago, or New York.

To fund his various ventures, Hershey had borrowed money from his Mennonite relatives and lost it all. They were therefore not overjoyed when he returned home for one last business fling. He made caramels at first, quite successfully, then turned to milk chocolate—some say, because he realized he could mold his name more easily in chocolate than caramel.

At the age of forty-one, Hershey married Catherine Sweeney— shortly after meeting her in a candy store. He brought his bride to the home he shared with his mother; but the two women were immediate antagonists, so he moved mamma to another house. The marriage continued happily.

The childless Hersheys founded the Milton Hershey School for orphaned boys in 1909, and it plays an integral part in the Hershey saga to this day. In 1918, widower Hershey donated Hershey Foods Corporation—worth at that time about sixty million dollars—to the orphanage. He had lost interest in making money, preferring to spend his time running his other enterprises and traveling to Cuba to smoke Havana cigars and overlook a sugar refinery. The orphanage kept its 100-percent interest in the company until 1927, when 20 percent was sold to the public. Today Hershey Foods Corp. handles the candy business; HERCO, Inc., runs the amusement centers, hotels, zoo, golf courses, gardens; and the Hershey Trust Company oversees the Milton Hershey School.

Hershey might not have cared about money, but he was obsessed to the end of his days with the importance of work and frugality. He never went to Europe, which he adored, simply for pleasure but had to check out the almond crop in Italy before he could enjoy, say, the opera in Milan. When his mother learned that he was planning to build a magnificent playground (later Hershey Park) for the sheer enjoyment of his workers, she was furious. "It would be a luxury, son, and that is sinful." He wrestled with his conscience for some time before going ahead.

Hershey's character has influenced his candy's image and goes a long way in explaining the confection's success. It is plain and honest, not the fancy sweet one serves with the crème de menthe. No swain ever gave his true love a basket of Mr. Goodbars when Godiva chocolates were within reach. Yet a number of sophisticated women will confess that one of their great secret urges is to gorge themselves on Hershey bars. Nothing else will do.

The price and size of the standard bar keeps changing, confusing ascetics who may indulge in one only every year or so. Like the five-cent cup of coffee, the famed nickel bar is, of course, no more. Hershey Foods tried at first to hold the price steady, as the cost of cocoa beans kept rising, by reducing the bar's weight. In 1949, the nickel bar weighed one ounce, and in early 1969, its last year at that price, the weight was down to three quarters of an ounce. Today it costs thirty cents and weighs 1.45 ounces.

Hershey keeps expanding like a lush tropical plant and introducing new products, but it never forgets the old stand-bys. Hershey Kisses were born in 1907 and look the same today, wrapped in silver foil with a tiny white streamer sticking out— although recently pink and blue foil-wrapped Kisses are available, too. On a day in 1925, when the founder was hanging around the lab, a chemist handed him a sample and said, "This is a good bar," to which Hershey replied, "Let's call it Mr. Goodbar, then." The biggest seller is not the milk chocolate bar but Reese's Peanut Butter Cups. (The H.B. Reese Company, which was founded in Hershey in 1923, was acquired in 1963.)

In addition to a broad line of candies that includes, among others, Kit Kat, Krackel, and Special Dark, Hershey Foods has diversified recently into fields outside of chocolate, taking on San Giorgio-Skinner Company and the Friendly Ice Cream Corporation chain of New England. All purvey foods that are not exactly slenderizing—but Hershey can't help what it is. Times do change, though, even here. New housing developments and shopping malls are springing up—and the head of cash management for Hershey Foods Corp. who handles an annual flow of $2 billion, is a thirty-five-year old woman—the first in high-level management in the company's history. Carol Mickelsen, an assistant treasurer, is an attractive brunette who came to Hershey eight years ago from New York, where she was a bank employee. "You've heard of culture shock? It was spring when I got here, working hours were 8:00 A.M. to 4:30 P.M. I was home in ten minutes and then there were five hours of daylight left. As far as the eye could see people were swimming or playing tennis or jogging. . . . Hershey is a wonderful place to be single in."

Set in the Past

No matter what the winds of change bring, much of Hershey will remain irrevocably set in the past. The corporate headquarters, where top executives mull over multimillion-dollar takeovers, is located in the former mansion of the founder at Highpoint Hill. In 1930, when Hershey had given away nearly everything else, he gave his home to the Hershey Country Club, asking only for a room on the second floor to sleep in—it was sinful to keep a whole mansion to yourself. The Country Club used it until 1970, it was unoccupied until 1977, then the Hershey executives decided that *that* was sinful and had the mansion restored. The octagonal dining room on the first floor—Hershey's favorite spot—has the original Oriental rug, purple plush chairs, and mirror-polished mahogany table. Fine strong light from the stained glass ceiling warms the modestly sized room even on a cloudy day. Through the windows you can look down the hill, past a green wedge of golf course, to the huge Hershey plant with its twin smoke stacks inscribed in white letters: HERSHEY.

One yearns after a while to find a single place in town where the Hershey name is not. This is difficult. It's said that toward the end of his days Hershey could be seen wandering through town all alone, picking up litter but leaving every discarded Hershey candy wrapper with his name right side up. In Cuba he built a clean, orderly town around his sugar refinery (which was sold in the 1940s), and guess what he called it? Not Havana. Armchair analysts might say that, having no heirs, a man with his ego needed to make sure his name lived on after him. Shortly before his death in 1945, he was bombarded by letters from strangers, all claiming to be relatives. Hershey didn't answer a single one, for he knew he was the last of his line. "In the end, the Hershey School was the only family he had," an executive told me.

The orphanage was started in 1909 with four boys, housed a thousand by the time Hershey died, and takes care of 1,250 today. (Girls were admitted in 1976.) Students are either orphans or have one parent unable to care for them. They live in regular homes, not dormitories, with house-parent couples who solve disputes and assign chores. Eighty-five of these homes are dotted in various locations over Hershey's ten thousand acres.

Hershey had one inviolate rule for the orphans: They had to have Thanksgiving turkey all together. All they could eat. Plenty of chocolate milk. When business got him down, Hershey liked to be driven to the school in his limousine. He would josh good-humoredly with the boys for an hour, then leave as suddenly as he had arrived. William E. Dearden, sixty, now the chief executive of Hershey Foods Corp., is a former "home" boy who used to think the mysterious man must have a drinking fountain and toilet in his big black car. He had everything else. Dearden came to the Hershey School in 1935 in knickers. He went on to college, a tour in the navy, and after a brief flirtation with a career away from chocolate, came back to Hershey, to eventually run the company.

Top executive offices of the Hershey company are on the second floor of the mansion. I stroll down the carpeted hall with Kim Payne in late afternoon while the executives are at a meeting. The offices resemble cozy sitting rooms more than traditional business chambers. Most look out on glorious gardens. All—no exceptions—

have trays of miniatures, Rolos and Kit Kats predominating. The trays are positioned near where a visitor might sit, not within striking range of the executive's desk chair.

I Can Turpentine These Boys

As the executives return from the meeting they wear large smiles and jostle each other more like schoolboys than men with million-dollar chocolate futures on their minds. One detaches himself to calmly board a red motorcycle in the parking lot, his briefcase attached. He wears a white helmet and a subdued pin-striped suit. All of these men's clothing look interchangeable with Hershey's attire in his official portraits: dark suits and rich ties. Their eyes quickly take in my beard and jeans.

Bill Dearden stands six feet five inches and weighs 215 pounds. With his no-nonsense gun-metal-framed glasses, wavy gray pompadour, and country boy's look, he could just as easily be the head deacon of the First Baptist Church, arriving early for prayer meeting. Yet somewhere within is the strain of toughness that gets one's will imposed. I catch a glimmer of that other side of the good-natured former "home" boy when I say, in parting, "Well, everyone at Hershey seems to operate in a relaxed style. Not like New York."

"Oh," says Dearden, a tiny glint lighting his eyes, "I know how to put the turpentine to these boys if things get lax. I know *that*."

Everyone is cordial in Hershey. All seem to carry candy bars to seal a transaction or adjourn a meeting. Say hello and Hershey chocolate crosses your palm. Eat at the Inn at Hershey and you receive an assortment of miniatures free at the end of your meal. Check in at the Hershey hotel and the desk clerk hands you a chocolate bar along with your key.

Hershey built the hotel during the Depression, to keep local residents employed at a time when not quite enough work was available at the plant. For decades he had wanted his hotel, but his mother thought the idea wantonly extravagant. He defended himself hotly: "Other men have yachts to play with, mamma. The hotel is my yacht!"

His building ended up as a pastiche of every place Hershey had enjoyed visiting. He started an architect working on the project by handing him a picture post card of a thirty-room Mediterranean inn he and his wife had enjoyed staying in. He also wanted a Spanish patio with tiled floors and a Spanish balcony—in celebration of his love affair with Cuba.

Sitting on the sweeping veranda late at night, with the town of Hershey spread out below, one seems far removed in time. No sirens, no soot, no raucous, pulsating music. The air is literally sweet, and the fiery red glow from the Hershey plant smoke stack is somehow comforting. One's troubles slide away, leaving only a swelling stomach, the lingering taste of a Golden Almond bar— and, alas, the premonition that leaving Hershey may be just as disorienting as driving in. This proves to be correct.

I pull over at a truck stop on Route 22, nine miles from Hershey, the next afternoon. A waitress slings a hamburger onto the counter in front of me. The man on the next stool is comatose over a mug of coffee. Pinball machines zing. A steady roar from the highway rattles plates. But I really know I've bid Hershey *adieu* when I stand at the cashier's counter, with its rows of chewing gum, breath mints, and candy. Hershey products once again take up only their modest, allotted space. What I suddenly miss in a rush is the sight of tubs of Golden Almond and no shame to the thought of diving in.

PART FOUR

The Way a Writer Reads: Essays for Further Study

RALPH WALDO EMERSON

*Select & collect all those words & sentences
that in all your reading have been to you
like the blast of trumpet.*

Introduction

You now know how a writer reads. A writer reads to enjoy. To see the world the way another person sees it. To participate vicariously in events that the writer has experienced personally. A writer reads for pleasure.

A writer also reads to learn how to write. A writer reads *constructively*, to determine how someone has *built* a piece of writing. To learn new ways to put thoughts together. To discover new forms. To see options and variety in the *craft* of writing.

Finally, a writer reads to see the whole picture. The writer takes notice of the unique and awesome configuration every piece of writing represents: this author's individual interests, specific way of looking at the world, and particular commitment interplay with writing about x subject at x time for x purpose for x audience. When writers read to see the whole picture, they are struck by the original configuration every piece of writing is, and they learn from and honor that. Being able to see the whole picture is what makes *any* piece of writing interesting because each time there is a new configuration.

The essays which follow are excellent pieces of writing to *read the way a writer reads*: first, just to enjoy; second, to learn from; and third, to see the whole picture. Each of these writers is a master. Each has been recognized world over as a writer *par excellence*, the best at what he or she does. Each has a strong individual stance as a human being in the world. You will learn from them as human beings, and you will learn from them as writers.

E. B. White writes in "The Sea and the Wind That Blows" about the lure of sailing and the sea. Jorge Luis Borges, who until his death in 1986 was the grand old patriarch of South American writers, writes in "Burning Books" about his reverence and love for books. Beryl Markham, the spunky aviator who lived and flew in Africa in the early 1900s, writes in "He Was a Good Lion" about her experience of being attacked by a lion as a child. "A Wolf in the Heart" is Barry Lopez's depiction of the close and enviable relationship Indians have always had with wolves. Joan Didion does honor to the great painter in her essay "Georgia O'Keefe" at the same time that she tells us something about herself and her daughter. In "The Boy's Desire," Richard Rodriguez shares an intimate event from his childhood that also carries with it a suggestion that "the order of the universe [does] not tremble" when societal customs do not hold sway. Donald Hall writes in "Ping-Pong:

Rootcellar Fiveball" about the place playing Ping-Pong has had in his life.

Reading and discussing these essays will allow you to consolidate all you have learned. You will see what rich rewards you have gained by the work you have done. It's time to congratulate yourself. You have learned to read *the way a writer reads*.

E. B. WHITE

The Sea and the Wind That Blows

Waking or sleeping, I dream of boats—usually of rather small boats under a slight press of sail. When I think how great a part of my life has been spent dreaming the hours away and how much of this total dream life has concerned small craft, I wonder about the state of my health, for I am told that it is not a good sign to be always voyaging into unreality, driven by imaginary breezes.

I have noticed that most men, when they enter a barber shop and must wait their turn, drop into a chair and pick up a magazine. I simply sit down and pick up the thread of my sea wandering, which began more than fifty years ago and is not quite ended. There is hardly a waiting room in the East that has not served as my cockpit, whether I was waiting to board a train or to see a dentist. And I am usually still trimming sheets when the train starts or the drill begins to whine.

If a man must be obsessed by something, I suppose a boat is as good as anything, perhaps a bit better than most. A small sailing craft is not only beautiful, it is seductive and full of strange promise and the hint of trouble. If it happens to be an auxiliary cruising boat, it is without question the most compact and ingenious arrangement for living ever devised by the restless mind of man—a home that is stable without being stationary, shaped less like a box than like a fish or a bird or a girl, and in which the homeowner can remove his daily affairs as far from shore as he has the nerve to take them, close-hauled or running free—parlor, bedroom, and bath, suspended and alive.

Men who ache all over for tidiness and compactness in their lives often find relief for their pain in the cabin of a thirty-foot sailboat at anchor in a sheltered cove. Here the sprawling panoply of The Home is compressed in orderly miniature and liquid delirium, suspended between the bottom of the sea and the top of the sky, ready to move on in the morning by the miracle of canvas and the witchcraft of rope. It is small wonder that men hold boats in the secret place of their mind, almost from the cradle to the grave.

Along with my dream of boats has gone the ownership of boats, a long succession of them upon the surface of the sea, many of them makeshift and crank. Since childhood I have managed to have some sort of sailing craft and to raise a sail in fear. Now, in my seventies, I still own a boat, still raise my sail in fear in answer to the summons of the unforgiving sea. Why does the sea attract me in the way it does? Whence comes this compulsion to hoist a sail, actually or in dream? My first encounter with the sea was a case of hate at first sight. I was taken, at the age of four, to a bathing beach in New Rochelle. Everything about the experience frightened and repelled me: the taste of salt in my mouth, the foul chill of the wooden bathhouse, the littered sand, the stench of the tide flats. I came away hating and fearing the sea. Later, I found that what I had feared and hated, I now feared and loved.

I returned to the sea of necessity, because it would support a boat; and although I knew little of boats, I could not get them out of my thoughts. I became a pelagic boy. The sea became my unspoken challenge: the wind, the tide, the fog, the ledge, the bell, the gull that cried help, the never-ending threat and bluff of weather. Once having permitted the wind to enter the belly of my sail, I was not able to quit the helm; it was as though I had seized hold of a high-tension wire and could not let go.

I liked to sail alone. The sea was the same as a girl to me—I did not want anyone else along. Lacking instruction, I invented ways of getting things done, and usually ended by doing them in a rather queer fashion, and so did not learn to sail properly, and still cannot sail well, although I have been at it all my life. I was twenty before I discovered that charts existed; all my navigating up to that time was done with the wariness and the ignorance of the early explorers. I was thirty before I learned to hang a coiled halyard on its cleat as it should be done. Until then I simply coiled it down on deck and dumped the coil. I was always in trouble and always returned, seeking more trouble. Sailing became a compulsion: there lay the boat, swinging to her mooring, there blew the wind; I had no choice but to go. My earliest boats were so small that when the wind failed, or when I failed, I could switch to manual control— I could paddle or row home. But then I graduated to boats that only the wind was strong enough to move. When I first dropped off my mooring in such a boat, I was an hour getting up the nerve to cast off the pennant. Even now, with a thousand little voyages notched in my belt, I still feel a memorial chill on casting off, as the gulls jeer and the empty mainsail claps.

Of late years, I have noticed that my sailing has increasingly become a compulsive activity rather than a simple source of plea- sure. There lies the boat, there blows the morning breeze—it is a point of honor, now, to go. I am like an alcoholic who cannot put his bottle out of his life. With me, I cannot not sail. Yet I know well enough that I have lost touch with the wind and, in fact, do not like the wind anymore. It jiggles me up, the wind does, and what I really love are windless days, when all is peace. There is a great question in my mind whether a man who is against wind should longer try to sail a boat. But this is an intellectual response—the old yearn- ing is still in me, belonging to the past, to youth, and so I am torn between past and present, a common disease of later life.

When does a man quit the sea? How dizzy, how bumbling must he be? Does he quit while he's ahead, or wait till he makes some major mistake, like falling overboard or being flattened by an acci- dental jibe? This past winter I spent hours arguing the question with myself. Finally, deciding that I had come to the end of the road, I wrote a note to the boatyard, putting my boat up for sale. I said I was "coming off the water." But as I typed the sentence, I doubted that I meant a word of it.

If no buyer turns up, I know what will happen: I will instruct the yard to put her in again—"just till somebody comes along." And then there will be the old uneasiness, the old uncertainty, as the mild southeast breeze ruffles the cove, a gentle, steady, morning breeze, bringing the taint of the distant wet world, the smell that takes a man back to the very beginning of time, linking him to all that has gone before. There will lie the sloop, there will blow the wind, once more I will get under way. And as I reach across to the red nun off the Torry Islands, dodging the trap buoys and toggles, the shags gathered on the ledge will note my passage. "There goes the old boy again," they will say. "One more rounding of his little Horn, one more conquest of his Roaring Forties." And with the tiller in my hand, I'll feel again the wind imparting life to a boat, will smell again the old menace, the one that imparts life to me: the cruel beauty of the salt world, the barnacle's tiny knives, the sharp spine of the urchin, the stinger of the sun jelly, the claw of the crab.

JORGE LUIS BORGES

Burning Books

Last night I had a very strange dream. I dreamed a great library was on fire. I believe it was the famous library at Alexandria with its infinite number of volumes being ravaged by the flames. This is an obsessive dream of mine, repeated with some frequency. "Does this have some special significance?" I ask myself. Might it not be that I owe my readers a book on the history of books?

It would be marvelous to write the history of books. I don't believe I am sufficiently qualified to meet the challenge of an enterprise of such scope. Although, on the other hand, I do think I could carry it out from a point of view that did not involve the physical history of books. The physical aspects of books don't really interest me very much, particularly those books by bibliophiles which generally have a tendency to be unreasonably long. I am interested in the various ways in which books have been valued throughout history. But now that I think of it, Spengler has beaten me to it with some excellent pages devoted to the history of books in his own *The Decline of the West* ("Western Decadence").

I, too, have written some pages about books. In *Other Inquisitions* there is an essay called "About the Cult of Books" in which I synthesize some of my thoughts on the topic. Also, I wrote a poem I titled "Alexandria" in which I refer specifically to the great library of Alexandria, and to Omar the Caliph, who caused its burning. . . .

Yes. In this poem it occurred to me to have Omar the Caliph speak and say something he undoubtedly had never said because he was a Caliph and Caliphs never say anything of the sort. Omar thought of the library as the world's memory. The huge library of Alexandria contained all there was to know in the world. He then gives the order to burn the library but thinks the act will prove unimportant. And Omar says in part of my poem:

> If, of all these books
> Not one were left, every
> Page and every line, each
> Work and each of Hercules' loves,
> Every lesson and every manuscript
> Would return to be created again.

That is to say, if all of the past is contained in the library then all of the past has sprung from man's imagination. I believe that beyond its rhetorical virtue, if it has any, the poem seeks to establish that each generation, in fact, rewrites the books of previous generations with slight differences; differences in intonation, differences of syntax; but we are always re-creating the same fables, rediscovering the same metaphors. That is why to some extent I am in agreement with Omar the Caliph—not the historical Omar but the one I created in my poem.

I remember my father, a great reader, standing me in front of his library telling me to read whatever I wanted, but that he would recommend no single book to me. That's how I started reading, somewhat at random, discovering, in the process, my favorite books of all time.

I once said the main event in my life was my father's library. And that, unlike Alonso Quijano, that adventurer Don Quixote, I have never left that library. There, during the first decade of this century, I undertook my first readings; readings which, with the passage of time, have always remained the same. When I returned from Europe in 1925, I managed to recover a copy of the same edition of the *Quixote* I had read as a child. It is the Garnier edition with steel etchings which I still save as a most treasured possession. It has a red cover with gold letters. As time has gone by I have gone along retrieving books from my childhood. In our time we profess a reverence for books which the ancients never had. To what can we attribute the fact the ancients professed no reverence for books, I wonder?

I think there are two reasons: the first is that all of mankind's great masters, curiously, have been oral teachers; the second is that the ancients viewed books as substitutes for the spoken word. That oft-quoted phrase *scripta manet verba volat*—the written word remains while the spoken word flies—does not mean the spoken word is ephemeral but rather that the written word, while long lasting, is also lifeless. It occurs to me now that the spoken word has a winged, light quality, "swift and sacred," as Plato said, referring to poetry.

But let us take another example, that of Pythagoras, who never wrote because he did not want to tie himself down to the rigidity of the written word. He did this deliberately, perhaps having in mind the concept "the letter kills but the spirit revives." Pythagoras undoubtedly felt this way and decided not to bind his spirit in this way. Aristotle never speaks of Pythagoras but rather of Pythagoreans. Pythagoras wanted his disciples to keep the body of his thoughts alive after his corporal body had died. That is where the frequently quoted Latin phrase *Magister Dixi*—"The Teacher said it"—comes from. It does not mean the teacher imposes his opinion on his disciples; it means the disciples continue to think on their own but, should someone oppose them, they say "The teacher said it." That phrase is a species of formula in which to find refuge and continue to profess the living thoughts of the teacher. When Aristotle speaks of Pythagoreans, he tells us they professed a belief in the dogma of eternal return (the repetition of history) which Nietzsche was to belatedly discover.

Of course, the theory of eternal return of cyclical time was refuted by Saint Augustine in "The City of God." But was it not a theory which was also touched upon by other great thinkers?

Yes. Among them Hume, Bianchi, and the materialists. Saint Augustine, with a beautiful metaphor, also says in "The City of

God" that "The Cross of Christ saves us from the circular labyrinth of the stoics." But, returning to the great oral masters, were not Buddha, Christ, and Mohammed the most important?

Undoubtedly! Moreover, Mohammed was illiterate! In the case of Christ there is only one report that he ever wrote anything and there has been much dispute over it. When they are about to stone the adulteress, he writes something in the sand which no one sees. He immediately erases it. Some hold he wrote: "He that is without sin, let him cast the first stone." But there are others who say God could write nothing but his own name. Schopenhauer, in his *History of Philosophy*, suggests an explanation which I share: He says Christ writes the law in the sand—the one which says all adulteresses must be stoned—then he erases it. The mystery is still alive but I tend towards this last deduction because if Christ wrote it, erased it, then said, "He who is without sin let him cast the first stone," undoubtedly what he erased was the law calling for such merciless punishment. Buddha was another oral master who left us a legacy of admirable teachings and phrases. Socrates, too, was a great oral teacher. I have always believed that Plato, in order to correct the stubborn silence of books, invented the so-called Platonic dialogues. That is to say, Plato recreated himself in the form of many personalities: Socrates, Gorgias, and the rest. When he says books are like effigies one believes to be alive but when asked a question they do not answer, he refers to the muteness of books. I believe in that way his famous dialogues were born. We can also believe that Plato did it as a way of consoling himself over the death of Socrates. Whenever a problem was posed to him, he would respond with, "Socrates would have said such and such," or "What would Socrates have said about this?" Thus, in one way, he forged an immortality for Socrates who was a great teacher who left no written record.

I now recall that they once asked Bernard Shaw if he believed the Holy Spirit had written the Bible, and he answered "Any book worth rereading was written by the Spirit."

I share completely in that belief. A book should go beyond the original intent of the author. For example, *Don Quixote* is more than just a simple book about chivalry or a satire of the genre. It is an absolute textbook in which chance or random thought plays no part. The truth of the matter being that the author's intent is a poor, human creation and therefore fallible. It is necessary that a book contains something more in all cases; it is a mysterious "something." When one reads an ancient book, it is as if we are reading about all of the time which has passed from the day it was written as well as our own. A book may be full of errors, we can reject the author's opinions, disagree with him about everything, but the book always retains a sacred quality, something immortal, something divine which makes us happy. This beauty is something common which can be found in all things; for example, I know nothing of Yugoslavian literature but that does not preclude my suddenly finding in some book by a Yugoslavian writer a phrase which dazzles me by its brilliance. That is why it is convenient to perpetuate a reverence for books which I believe is still the best formula for finding wisdom. A book grows with the passage of time. *Hamlet* today is not exactly the same book conceived by Shakespeare at the beginning of the seventeenth century. *Hamlet* is also the *Hamlet* of Goethe, Coleridge, and Bradley. The same is true of *El Quixote* or *Martin Fierro*. Their readers have enriched them.

Why do I continue to profess a reverence for books? Perhaps because I continue to play at not being blind.

And this is in the nature of a confession. I continue to buy books and continue to fill my house with books. I feel the friendly pull of books. I don't know; it seems to me that books offer one of the possibilities of great happiness to mankind. A few months ago they made me a present of a fabulous edition of the Brockhaus Encyclopedia. The presence of these more than twenty volumes, with handsome maps and etchings, and what surely must be no less than Gothic lettering, which I cannot read, filled me with joy. Those books, which to me are almost sacred, are there; I feel their pleasing presence. Perhaps this might seem a bit pathetic but it is not like that at all; it is something authentic, something real.

There are those who speak of the eventual disappearance of books; they assure us that modern means of communication will bury books in favor of something more dynamic which will require less of a man's time than what is taken up by reading. Do you want to know what I think of that?

I believe books will never disappear. It is impossible for it to happen. Of all of mankind's diverse tools, undoubtedly the most astonishing are his books. All the others are extensions of the body. The telephone is an extension of his voice; the telescope and microscope extensions of his sight; the sword and the plow are extensions of his arms. In *Caesar and Cleopatra*, when Bernard Shaw refers to the Library of Alexandria, he says it is mankind's memory.

I would add it is also mankind's imagination. Humanity's vigils have generated infinite pages of infinite books. Mankind owes all that we are to the written word. Why? What is our past but a succession of dreams? What difference is there between dreaming and remembering? Between remembering dreams and recalling the past? Books are the great memory of the centuries. Consequently their function is irreplaceable. If books were to disappear, history would disappear. So would men.

BERYL MARKHAM

He Was a Good Lion

When I was a child, I spent all my days with the Nandi Murani, hunting barefooted, in the Rongai Valley, or in the cedar forests of the Mau Escarpment.

At first I was not permitted to carry a spear, but the Murani depended on nothing else.

You cannot hunt an animal with such a weapon unless you know the way of his life. You must know the things he loves, the things he fears, the paths he will follow. You must be sure of the quality of his speed and the measure of his courage. He will know as much about you, and at times make better use of it.

But my Murani friends were patient with me.

'Amin yut!' one would say, 'what but a dik-dik will run like that? Your eyes are filled with clouds today, Lakweit!'

That day my eyes were filled with clouds, but they were young enough eyes and they soon cleared. There were other days and other dik-dik. There were so many things.

There were dik-dik and leopard, kongoni and warthog, buffalo, lion, and the 'hare that jumps.' There were many thousands of the hare that jumps.

And there were wildebeest and antelope. There was the snake that crawls and the snake that climbs. There were birds, and young men like whips of leather, like rainshafts in the sun, like spears before a singiri.

'Amin yut!' the young men would say, 'that is no buffalo spoor, Lakweit. Here! Bend down and look. Bend down and look at this mark. See how this leaf is crushed. Feel the wetness of this dung. Bend down and look so that you may learn!'

And so, in time, I learned. But some things I learned alone.

There was a place called Elkington's Farm by Kabete Station. It was near Nairobi on the edge of the Kikuyu Reserve, and my father and I used to ride there from town on horses or in a buggy, and along the way my father would tell me things about Africa.

Sometimes he would tell me stories about the tribal wars—wars between the Masai and the Kikuyu (which the Masai always won), or between the Masai and the Nandi (which neither of them ever won), and about their great leaders and their wild way of life which, to me, seemed much greater fun than our own. He would tell me of Lenana, the brilliant Masai ol-oiboni, who prophesied the coming of the White Man, and of Lenana's tricks and stratagems and victories, and about how his people were unconquerable and unconquered—until, in retaliation against the refusal of the Masai warriors to join the King's African Rifles, the British marched upon the Native villages; how, inadvertently, a Masai woman was killed, and how two Hindu shopkeepers were murdered in reprisal by the Murani. And thus, why it was that the thin, red line of Empire had grown slightly redder.

He would tell me old legends sometimes about Mount Kenya, or about the Menegai Crater, called the Mountain of God, or about Kilimanjaro. He would tell me these things and I would ride alongside and ask endless questions, or we would sit together in the jolting buggy and just think about what he had said.

One day, when we were riding to Elkington's, my father spoke about lions.

'Lions are more intelligent than some men,' he said, ' and more courageous than most. A lion will fight for what he has and for what he needs; he is contemptuous of cowards and wary of his equals. But he is not afraid. You can always trust a lion to be exactly what he is—and never anything else.'

'Except,' he added, looking more paternally concerned than usual, 'that damned lion of Elkington's!'

The Elkington lion was famous within a radius of twelve miles in all directions from the farm, because, if you happened to be anywhere inside the circle, you could hear him roar when he was hungry, when he was sad, or when he just felt like roaring. If, in the night, you lay sleepless on your bed and listened to an intermittent sound that began like the bellow of a banshee trapped in the bowels of Kilimanjaro and ended like the sound of that same banshee suddenly at large and arrived at the foot of your bed, you knew (because you had been told) that this was the song of Paddy.

Two or three of the settlers in East Africa at that time had caught lion cubs and raised them in cages. But Paddy, the Elkington lion, had never seen a cage.

He had grown to full size, tawny, black-maned and muscular, without a worry or a care. He lived on fresh meat, not of his own killing. He spent his waking hours (which coincided with everybody else's sleeping hours) wandering through Elkington's fields and pastures like an affable, if apostrophic, emperor, a-stroll in the gardens of his court.

He thrived in solitude. He had no mate, but pretended indifference and walked alone, not toying too much with imaginings of the unattainable. There were no physical barriers to his freedom, but the lions of the plains do not accept into their respected fraternity an individual bearing in his coat the smell of men. So Paddy ate, slept, and roared, and perhaps he sometimes dreamed, but he never left Elkington's. He was a tame lion, Paddy was. He was deaf to the call of the wild.

'I'm always careful of that lion,' I told my father, 'but he's really harmless. I have seen Mrs. Elkington stroke him.'

'Which proves nothing,' said my father. 'A domesticated lion is only an unnatural lion—and whatever is unnatural is untrustworthy.'

Whenever my father made an observation as deeply philosophical as that one, and as inclusive, I knew there was nothing more to be said.

I nudged my horse and we broke into a canter covering the remaining distance to Elkington's.

It wasn't a big farm as farms went in Africa before the First World War, but it had a very nice house with a large veranda on which my father, Jim Elkington, Mrs. Elkington, and one or two other settlers sat and talked with what to my mind was always unreasonable solemnity.

There were drinks, but beyond that there was a tea-table lavishly spread, as only the English can spread them. I have sometimes thought since of the Elkington's tea-table—round, capacious, and white, standing with sturdy legs against the green vines of the garden, a thousand miles of Africa receding from its edge.

It was a mark of sanity, I suppose, less than of luxury. It was evidence of the double debt England still owes to ancient China for her two gifts that made expansion possible—tea and gunpowder.

But cakes and muffins were no fit bribery for me. I had pleasures of my own then, or constant expectations. I made what niggardly salutations I could bring forth from a disinterested memory and left the house at a gait rather faster than a trot.

As I scampered past the square hay shed a hundred yards or so behind the Elkington house, I caught sight of Bishon Singh whom my father had sent ahead to tend our horses.

I think the Sikh must have been less than forty years old then, but his face was never any indication of his age. On some days he looked thirty and on others he looked fifty, depending on the weather, the time of day, his mood, or the tilt of his turban. If he had ever disengaged his beard from his hair and shaved the one and clipped the other, he might have astonished us all by looking like one of Kipling's elephant boys, but he never did either, and so, to me at least, he remained a man of mystery, without age or youth, but burdened with experience, like the wandering Jew.

He raised his arm and greeted me in Swahili as I ran through the Elkington farmyard and out toward the open country.

Why I ran at all or with what purpose in mind is beyond my answering, but when I had no specific destination I always ran as fast as I could in the hope of finding one—and I always found it.

I was within twenty yards of the Elkington lion before I saw him. He lay sprawled in the morning sun, huge, black-maned, and gleaming with life. His tail moved slowly, stroking the rough grass like a knotted rope end. His body was sleek and easy, making a mould where he lay, a cool mould, that would be there when he had gone. He was not asleep; he was only idle. He was rusty-red, and soft, like a strokable cat.

I stopped and he lifted his head with magnificent ease and stared at me out of yellow eyes.

I stood there staring back, scuffling by bare toes in the dust, pursing my lips to make a noiseless whistle—a very small girl who knew about lions.

Paddy raised himself then, emitting a little sigh, and began to contemplate me with a kind of quiet premeditation, like that of a slow-witted man fondling an unaccustomed thought.

I cannot say that there was any menace in his eyes, because there wasn't, or that his 'frightful jowls' were drooling, because they were handsome jowls and very tidy. He did sniff the air, though, with what impressed me as being close to audible satisfaction. And he did not lie down again.

I remembered the rules that one remembers. I did not run. I walked very slowly, and I began to sing a defiant song.

'Kali coma Simba sisi,' I sang, 'Asikari yoti ni udari!—Fierce like the lion are we, Askari all are brave!'

I went in a straight line past Paddy when I sang it, seeing his eyes shine in the thick grass, watching his tail beat time to the metre of my ditty.

'Twendi, twendi—ku pigana—piga aduoi—piga sana!—Let us go, let us go—to fight—beat down the enemy! Beat hard, beat hard!'

What lion would be unimpressed with the marching song of the King's African Rifles?

Singing it still, I took up my trot toward the rim of the low hill which might, if I were lucky, have Cape gooseberry bushes on its slopes.

The country was grey-green and dry, and the sun lay on it closely, making the ground hot under my bare feet. There was no sound and no wind.

Even Paddy made no sound, coming swiftly behind me.

What I remember most clearly of the moment that followed are three things—a scream that was barely a whisper, a blow that struck me to the ground, and, as I buried my face in my arms and felt Paddy's teeth close on the flesh of my leg, a fantastically bobbing turban, that was Bishon Singh's turban, appear over the edge of the hill.

I remained conscious, but I closed by eyes and tried not to be. It was not so much the pain as it was the sound.

The sound of Paddy's roar in my ears will only be duplicated, I think, when the doors of hell slip their wobbly hinges, one day, and give voice and authenticity to the whole panorama of Dante's poetic nightmares. It was an immense roar that encompassed the world and dissolved me in it.

I shut my eyes very tight and lay still under the weight of Paddy's paws.

Bishon Singh said afterward that he did nothing. He said he had remained by the hay shed for a few minutes after I ran past him, and then, for no explainable reason, had begun to follow me. He admitted, though, that, a little while before, he had seen Paddy go in the direction I had taken.

The Sikh called for help, of course, when he saw the lion meant to attack, and a half-dozen of Elkington's syces had come running from the house. Along with them had come Jim Elkington with a rawhide whip.

Jim Elkington, even without a rawhide whip, was very impressive. He was one of those enormous men whose girths alone seem to preclude any possibility of normal movement, much less speed. But Jim had speed—not to be loosely compared with lightning, but rather like the speed of something spherical and smooth and relatively irresistable, like the cannon balls of the Napoleonic Wars. Jim was, without question, a man of considerable courage, but in the case of my Rescue From the Lion, it was, I am told, his momentum rather than his bravery for which I must forever be grateful.

It happened like this—as Bishon Singh told it;

'I am resting against the walls of the place where hay is kept and first the large lion and then you, Beru, pass me going toward the open field, and a thought comes to me that a lion and a young girl are strange company, so I follow. I follow to the place where the hill that goes up becomes the hill that goes down, and where it goes down deepest I see that you are running without much thought in your head and the lion is running behind you with many thoughts in his head, and I scream for everybody to come very fast.

'Everybody comes very fast, but the large lion is faster than anybody, and he jumps on your back and I see you scream but I hear no scream. I only hear the lion, and I begin to run with everybody, and this includes Bwana Elkington, who is saying a great many words I do not know and is carrying a long kiboko which he holds in his hand and is meant for beating the large lion.

'Bwana Elkington goes past me the way a man with lighter legs and fewer inches around his stomach might go past me, and he is waving the long kiboko so that is whistles over all of our heads like a very sharp wind, but when we get close to the lion it comes to my mind that that lion is not of the mood to accept a kiboko.

'He is standing with the front of himself on your back, Beru, and you are bleeding in three or five places, and he is roaring. I do not believe Bwana Elkington could have thought that that lion at that moment would consent to being beaten, because the lion was not looking the way he had ever looked before when it was necessary for him to be beaten. He was looking as if he did not wish to be disturbed by a kiboko, or the Bwana, or the syces, or Bishon Singh, and he was saying so in a very large voice.

'I believe that Bwana Elkington understood this voice when he was still more than several feet from the lion, and I believe the Bwana considered in his mind that it would be the best thing not to beat the lion just then, but the Bwana when he runs very fast is like the trunk of a great baobob tree rolling down a slope, and it seems that because of this it was not possible for him to explain the thought of his mind to the soles of his feet in a sufficient quickness of time to prevent him from rushing much closer to the lion than in his heart he wished to be.

'And it was this circumstance, as I am telling it,' said Bishon Singh, 'which in my considered opinion made it possible for you to be alive, Beru.'

'Bwana Elkington rushed at the lion then, Bishon Singh?'

'The lion, as of the contrary, rushed at Bwana Elkington,' said Bishon Singh. 'The lion deserted you for the Bwana, Beru. The lion was of the opinion that his master was not in any honest way deserving of a portion of what he, the lion, had accomplished in the matter of fresh meat through no effort by anybody except himself.'

Bishon Singh offered this extremely reasonable interpretation with impressive gravity, as if he were expounding the Case For the Lion to a chosen jury of Paddy's peers.

'Fresh meat' . . . I repeated dreamily, and crossed my fingers.

'So then what happened . . . ?'

The Sikh lifted his shoulders and let them drop again 'What could happen, Beru? The lion rushed for Bwana Elkington, who in his turn rushed from the lion, and in so rushing did not keep in his hand the long kiboko, but allowed it to fall upon the ground, and in accomplishing this the Bwana was free to ascend a very fortunate tree, which he did.'

'And you picked me up, Bishon Singh?'

He made a little dip with his massive turban, 'I was happy with the duty of carrying you back to this very bed, Beru, and of advising your father, who had gone to observe some of Bwana Elkington's horses, that you had been moderately eaten by the large lion. Your father returned very fast, and Bwana Elkington some time later returned very fast, but the large lion has not returned at all.'

The large lion had not returned at all. That night he killed a horse, and the next night he killed a yearling bullock, and after that a cow fresh for milking.

In the end he was caught and finally caged, but brought to no rendezvous with the firing squad at sunrise. He remained for years in his cage, which, had he managed to live in freedom with his inhibitions, he might never have seen at all.

It seems characteristic of the mind of man that the repression of what is natural to humans must be abhorred, but that what is natural to an infinitely more natural animal must be confined within the bounds of reason peculiar only to men—more peculiar sometimes than seems reasonable at all.

Paddy lived, people stared at him and he stared back, and this went on until he was an old, old lion. Jim Elkington died, and Mrs. Elkington, who really loved Paddy, was forced, because of circumstances beyond her control or Paddy's, to have him shot by Boy Long, the manager of Lord Delamere's estates.

This choice of executioners was, in itself, a tribute to Paddy, for no one loved animals more or understood them better, or could shoot more cleanly than Boy Long.

But the result was the same to Paddy. He had lived and died in ways not of his choosing. He was a good lion. He had done what he could about being a tame lion. Who thinks it just to be judged by a single error?

I still have the scars of his teeth and claws, but they are very small now and almost forgotten, and I cannot begrudge him his moment.

BARRY LOPEZ

A Wolf in the Heart

One of the problems that comes with trying to take a wider view of animals is that most of us have cut ourselves off from them conceptually. We do not think of ourselves as part of the animal kingdom. Indians did. They thought of themselves as The People (that is the translation from the native tongue of most tribal names) and of animals as The Wolves, The Bears, The Mice, and so forth. From here on in this chapter, the line between Indians and wolves may fade, not because Indians did not perceive the differences but because they were preoccupied with the similarities. They were inclined to compare and contrast their way of living with, say, the weasel's way or the eagle's way. They would say, "We are like wolves in that we . . ." They were anthropomorphic—and animistic. Highly so. We aren't talking, really, about our wolf anymore. We are talking about their wolf. We are, in a sense, in a foreign country.

The question the old Nunamiut man answered was an eminently sensible one in his view. The caribou-hunting tactics of wolves in the Brooks Range and those of the Nunamiut *were* similar. And similarity in hunting technique in the same geographical area was found elsewhere. Wolves and Cree Indians in Alberta maneuvered buffalo out onto lake ice, where the big animals lost their footing and were more easily killed. Pueblo Indians and wolves in Arizona ran deer to exhaustion, though it might have taken the Pueblos a day to do it. Wolf and Shoshoni Indian lay flat on the prairie grass of Wyoming and slowly waved—the one its tail, the other a strip of hide—to attract curious but elusive antelope close enough to kill. And if we have made the right assumptions at Paleolithic sites in North America such as Folsom, early man killed mammoths in the same mobbing way wolves did, because men did not yet have extensions of themselves like the bow and arrow. They had to get in close with a spear and stab the animal to death.

The correspondence in life-styles, however, goes deeper than this. Wolves ate grass, possibly as a scour against intestinal parasites; Indians ate wild plants for medicinal reasons. Both held and used hunting territories. Both were strongly familial and social in organization. To some extent both went to specific areas to hunt certain types of game. (Two or three wolf packs today come to hunt sheep at a place called Okokmilaga on the North Slope of Alaska's Brooks Range. Various tribes, Ponca and Sioux among them, traveled to the same leks in South Dakota to hunt sage grouse.) Both wolf and Indian had a sign language. The tribe, like the pack, broke up at certain times of the year, and joined together later to hunt more efficiently. In times of scarcity, Indian hunters ate first; this also seems to be the case with wolves.

Highly intriguing is the fact that white-tailed deer in Minnesota sought security from Indian hunters by moving into the border area between warring tribes, where hunters were least likely to show up, and the fact that deer do the same with respect to wolves—seek security along the border zones between wolf territories, where wolves spend the least time hunting.

The most interesting correspondence between wolf and Indian, however, may be that involving the perception of territory.

When Indians left their own country and entered that of another tribe—a group of young Assiniboin warriors, for example, sneaking off on foot into the country of the Gros Ventre to steal horses—they moved like wolves: in small packs; at night and during the crepuscular hours; taking advantage of ground contours to observe but remain hidden; moving in and out of the foreign territory quickly. Often on foot and in unfamiliar surroundings, they had to remain invisible to the inhabitants. Elusiveness, therefore, was a quality Indians cultivated and admired. It served them as well as it served the wolf who, in a hard winter, trespasses into neighboring packs' territories to look for food, to make a kill, and to go home before anyone knows he's been there.

The definition and defense of home range was as important to the Indian as it seems to be to the wolf. The defense was mostly of food resources in general and of the physical area adjacent to the village in particular; under certain circumstances trespassers were killed. If a party of Flathead warriors was surprised in northern Idaho by a party of resident Kutenai, the Flatheads might be attacked and killed to a man. If it was bitter cold and storming, they might signal each other that it was too cold to fight (wolves probably wouldn't). If the Flathead party was reduced to one man who fought bravely and was thought, therefore, to have strong medicine, he might be let go. Fatal encounters and nonfatal encounters between trespassing and resident wolves bear a striking similarity. In Minnesota, for example, in 1975, a small pack of wolves moving through the territory of a much larger pack was suddenly surprised by the larger pack. One animal in the small pack was killed, two ran off, and the fourth, a female, held ten or eleven wolves to a standoff in a river before they all withdrew and left her.

Some tribes were stricter about boundaries and more bellicose about trespassing incidents than others, as are some wolf packs. The boundaries of most Indian territories, like those of wolves, were fluid; they changed with the movement of the game herds, the size of the tribe, the evolution of tribal divisions, and the time of year. For both wolf and Indian, where the principal game animal was nonmigratory, as deer and moose are, territorial boundaries were more important than they were in areas where principal game species were migratory, like caribou. There are instances where neighboring wolf packs have fought each other and then joined territories, just as some tribes established alliances—the five nations of the Iroquois, for example. And I mentioned earlier that the Pawnee and Omaha, traditional enemies, had an agreement whereby each could enter the other's territory to hunt buffalo.

The Indian practice of passing family hunting territories on to succeeding generations throws even more light on this interesting correspondence of territorial spacing, hunting rights, and trespassing. Family hunting territories were most important, again, where food could be found in the same place all the time. The salmon-eating tribes on the northwest coast and the Algonkian deer eaters in the northeastern woodlands both had appropriate family and clan hunting territories that were passed from one generation to the next. Among the Tlingit, a northwest coast tribe, each family had its own place on the rivers where it fished and an area where it gathered berries. No one else would fish or berry there unless invited to do so. In the eastern woodlands, especially in northeastern Minnesota, resident wolves seem to have a strong sense of territory as defined by the major food source (white-tailed deer), at least as strong as the family hunting territories that existed in that same country when the Chippewa lived there.

Which leads to another thought, more abstract, about trespassing. It was often assumed that Plains Indians went out intending to kill their rivals. This was not true. They went out to deliberately face rivals in a very dangerous game. The danger itself, the threat of death, was the thrill, not killing; and to engage in it repeatedly was recognized as a way to prove strength of character. Analogously, it might be valuable to consider the encounters of rival wolves as a similar kind of deadly recreation. Just as intriguing is the idea that some game animals assent to a chase-without-death with wolves. Caribou and yearling wolves, for example, are often seen in harmless chases getting a taste of death. Building spirit. Training. Wolf *and* caribou.

That wolves and Neolithic hunting people in North America resembled each other as predators was not the result of conscious imitation. It was convergent evolution, the most successful way for meat eaters to live. Conscious *identification* with the wolf, on the other hand, especially among Indians on the Great Plains, was a mystical experience based on a penetrating perception of the wolf's lifeway, its gestalt. And it could, on occasion, become conscious imitation.

Native American perceptions of the wolf varied largely according to whether or not a tribe was agricultural. It was naturally among the hunting tribes that the wolf played the greater mythic-religious role because the wolf himself was a great hunter, not a

great farmer. He was retained for a while in the mythology of agricultural tribes and regarded by them as an animal of great power
and mystery, but his place there was slowly eclipsed by anthropomorphic gods of the harvest.

In the native American cosmology, insofar as it can be regarded as the same from tribe to tribe, the universe was perceived
in six directions: the space above; that below; and the four cardinal divisions of world horizon. Frequently on the plains the bear
represented the west, the mountain lion the north, the wolf the
east, and the wildcat the south. They were regarded as the creatures with the greatest power and influence in the spirit world.

It should be understood, however, that the Indian did not rank-
order animals. Each creature, from deer mouse to meadowlark,
was respected for the qualities it best seemed to epitomize; when
those particular qualities were desired by someone, that animal
was approached as one who knew much about that thing. The
animals assigned the greatest cosmological significance—the
bear, lion, wolf, cat, and eagle—were not regarded as the "best"
animals. They were chosen primarily because they were the great
hunters. The stealth of the cats, the endurance of the wolf, the
strength of the bear, the vision of the eagle—these were the qualities held in high esteem by human hunters.

The Pawnee of present-day Nebraska and Kansas differed from
most other tribes in that they divided their world horizon into four
semicardinal points, assigning the wolf to the southeast. In the
Pawnee cosmogony the wolf was also set in the sky as a star, along
with the bear and the two cats, to guard the primal female presence, the Evening Star. The Wolf Star was red—the color associated with the wolf by virtually every tribe (red did not signify blood;
it was simply an esteemed color).

In time, the wolf became associated among the four seasons
with summer, among the trees on the plains with the willow,
among the great natural forces with clouds (the others being wind,
thunder, and lightning).

Like the Nunamiut, most Indians respected the wolf's prowess
as a hunter, especially his ability to always secure game, his stamina, the way he moved smoothly and silently across the landscape.
They were moved by his howling, which they sometimes regarded
as talking with the spirit world. The wolf appears in many of their
legends as a messenger in fact, a great long-distance traveler, a
guide for anyone seeking the spirit world. Blind Bull, for example, a

Cheyenne shaman, was highly respected among his people before his death in 1885 as one who had learned about things from the comings and goings of wolves, from listening to their howls. The wolves, for their part, took Blind Bull's messages to various places in the real and spiritual world. The wolf as oracle, as interlocutor with the dead, is an old idea.

The wolf was also held in high regard because, though he was a fiercely loyal familial animal, he was also one who took the role of provider for the larger community (for carrion eaters like the fox and raven). This was something that tribal Indians understood very well, for in difficult times a man had the dual responsibility of feeding his own family as well as others. An Hidatsa man named Bear in the Flat acknowledged this lifeway of the wolf when he took as one of his sacred medicine songs the "Invitation Song" of the wolf—the howl the wolf used to call coyotes, foxes, and magpies to the remains of his kill. (The situation is neatly imitated among Bella Coola hunters, who sing a song to call the wolf to one of *their* kills—a bear. They would take a bear's hide but believed bears did not wish to be eaten by humans.)

The interrelationships between one's allegiance to self and household on the one hand and one's duty to the larger community on the other cannot be overemphasized; it was a primal, efficient system of survival that held both man and wolf in a similar mesh.

Consider again the Indian's perception.

Each of the animals—mosquitoes, elk, mice—belonged to a separate tribe. Each had special powers, but each was dependent on the others for certain services. When, for example, the Indian left his buffalo kill, he called out to the magpies and others to come and eat. The dead buffalo nourished the grasses; the grasses in turn fed the elk and provided the mouse with straw for a nest; the mouse, for his part, instructed the Indian in magic; and the Indian called on his magic to kill buffalo.

With such a strong sense of the interdependence among all creatures and an acute awareness of the ways in which his own life resembled the wolf's (hunting for himself, hunting for his family, defending his tribe against enemy attack as the wolf protected the den against the grizzly), the Indian naturally turned to the wolf as a paradigm—a mirror reflection. He wished directly for that power ("Hear me, Great Spirit! I wish to be like the wolf"); and he imitated him homeopathically by wearing his skin. He wished always to be as well integrated in his environment as he could *see* the wolf was in the universe. Imagine him saying: "Help me to fit, to be valuable in the world, like the wolf."

To fit into the universe, the Indian had to do two things simultaneously; be strong as an individual, and submerge his personal feelings for the good of the tribe. In the eyes of many native Americans, no other animal did this as well as the wolf.

The wolf fulfilled two roles for the Indian: he was a powerful and mysterious animal, and so perceived by most tribes; and he was a medicine animal, identified with a particular individual, tribe, or clan. In the first role he was simply an object of interest, for reasons already given. He might be marginally so in the eyes of some (most California tribes, where there were no wolves, thought little of the wolf) or of major importance to others (Cheyenne, Sioux, Pawnee).

At a *tribal* level, the attraction to the wolf was strong because the wolf lived in a way that made the tribe strong: he provided food that all, even the sick and old, could eat; he saw to the education of his children; he defended his territory against other wolves. At a *personal* level, those for whom the wolf was a medicine animal or personal totem understood the qualities that made the wolf stand out as an individual; for example, his stamina and ability to track well and go without food for long periods.

That each perception contributed to and reinforced the other— as the individual grows stronger, the tribe grows stronger, and vice versa—is what made the wolf such a significant animal in the eyes of hunting peoples. The inclination of white men to regard individual and social motivations in themselves as separate led them to misunderstand the Indian. The Indian was so well integrated in his environment that his motivation was almost hidden; his lifeway was as mysterious to white men as the wolf's.

This is obviously a complex thought, but in the light of it, the Indian's preoccupation with wolves becomes more than quaint. The wolf was the one animal that, again, did two things at once year after year: remained distinct and exemplary as an individual, yet served the tribe. There are no stories among Indians of lone wolves.

Though the wolf was respected, he had his uses, too. Wolf fur was good for a parka ruff. A wolf pelt was powerful medicine, a good item in trade. Wolves sometimes preyed on an Indian's fish traps or meat caches or got after his horses. Indians rarely killed wolves, but when they did it was for these reasons.

The common methods for capturing and killing wolves before steel traps were available were the pit fall and the deadfall. The pit fall consisted of a deep hole, wider at the bottom to keep the wolf from running up the walls, covered over with grass and brush, and baited with meat. Some tribes put sharpened stakes at the bottom to kill the wolf when it fell in.

Deadfalls of rock, ice, and slabs of snow were more common in the north where pits were hard to dig. Pulling on a piece of bait, the wolf would trip a balanced weight that crushed or pinned him.

Rawhide snares that caught the animal around the neck were also in use. Some Eskimos coiled sharpened willow sticks or strips of baleen in frozen tallow balls, which were then left out for the wolves to eat.

Two sorts of knife trap were also used. A wolf knife consisted of a sharp blade encased in fat and frozen upright in a block of ice. The wolf licked the fat until he cut his tongue badly enough to bleed to death. The other knife trap was a baited torsion spring that stabbed the wolf in the head when triggered.

But it never was easy.

Among the Cherokee there was a belief that to kill a wolf was to invite retribution from other wolves. Many tribes felt that killing a wolf would cause game to disappear. And there was widespread belief that a weapon that had killed a wolf would never work right again. It either had to be given away, usually to a child to be used in future as a toy, or taken to a shaman to be cleansed. A Cherokee cure for a gun that had killed a wolf was to unscrew the barrel, insert small sourwood (Oxydendrum arboreum) sticks ritually treated in a fire, and lay it in a running stream till morning.

When the Kwakiutl of coastal British Columbia killed a wolf, they would lay the carcass out on a blanket. Small strips of meat would be cut off and each person who had participated in the killing would eat four of them, expressing his regret at the wolf's death and calling him a good friend. The remains of the carcass were wrapped in the blanket and carefully buried.

The Ahtena Indians of southern Alaska brought a wolf they'd killed into camp on their shoulders, chanting: "This is the chief, he is coming." The dead wolf was taken inside a hut, where he was propped up in a sitting position and a banquet meal was set before him by a shaman. Each family in the village contributed something. When it was felt the wolf had eaten all he wanted, the men ate what was left. No women were permitted inside.

When certain Eskimos killed a wolf, they would bring it to the edge of the village and leave it out for four days. The man who had done the killing would walk around his house four times, expressing his feelings of regret for the wolf, and abstain from relations with his wife for four days.

Because there was such risk involved, a common practice of those who needed a wolf skin was to hire someone who knew the rites of atonement to kill the wolf. This person then might explain to the dead wolf that he had been hired by some *other* village so the wolf would take out any revenge at the wrong place. The Chukchi Eskimo of northeastern Siberia routinely told any wolf they killed that they were Russians, not Eskimos.

The pelt was normally all that was taken from a wolf, though teeth, claws, and internal organs were needed for decorative or religious purposes. The pelt was used by shamans in curing ceremonies like the one Bird Shirt performed; to wrap sacred, usually commemorative, articles to make a "wolf bundle"; and as totemic representation of the wolf's presence. Kills in the Night, a Crow medicine woman, for example, used a wolf pelt to escape a Lakota war party that was chasing her and her daughter, Pretty Shield. After dusting their horse tracks with it, Kills in the Night put the wolf skin over their heads and singing a medicine song led her daughter away. The Lakota became confused in a sudden thundershower and lost the woman's trail.

The most widespread use of the wolf pelt on the plains, however, was among scouts, who used it in initiative disguise.

The Skidi Pawnee were plains scouts *extraordinaire*. The hand sign in plains sign language for *Pawnee* was the same as that for *wolf*; index and middle finger of the right hand were raised in a V next to the right ear, then brought forward. Waving the sign from side to side signified the verb *to scout*. Dressed in their wolf skin cloaks, known as the Wolf People because the wolf figured so strongly in their foundation myth, there were no others like them. The Cheyenne, Comanche, and Wichita called the Pawnee wolves because "they prowl like wolves . . . they have the endurance of wolves, and can travel all day, and dance all night, and can make long journeys, living on carcasses they find on their way, or on no food at all."

The Pawnee conceptualization of the wolf was that he was an animal who moved like liquid across the plains: silent, without effort, but with purpose. He was alert to the smallest changes in his world. He could see very far—"two looks away," they said. His hearing was so sharp he could even hear a cloud as it passed overhead. When a man went into the enemy's territory he wished to move exactly like this, to sense things like the wolf, to be Wolf.

The sense of being Wolf that came over a Pawnee scout was not the automatic result of putting on a wolf skin. The wolf skin was an accouterment, an outward sign to the man himself and others who might see him that he was calling on his wolf power. It is hard for the Western mind to grasp this and to take seriously the notion that an Indian at times could *be* Wolf, could actually participate in the animals's spirit, but this is what happened. It wasn't being *like* a wolf; it was having the mind set: Wolf.

White historians wrote off the superior tracking abilities of the Pawnee, Arikara, and Crow scouts that the army used to "native intelligence" and a "hocus-pocus" with wolf skins. What was actually present was an intimacy with the environment, a magic "going in and out," so that the line of distinction between a person and his animal helper was not always clear. The white, for the most part, was afraid of, separated from, the environment. He spent his time flailing at it and denouncing it, trying to ignore that in it which confused or intimidated him.

Pawnees wore their wolf pelts like capes during exploration of an enemy territory, the flat pelt falling across the shoulders and the wolf's head coming up over the man's head so the wolf's ears stood up erect. (Hidatsa scouts slit the pelt vertically and wore it over the shoulders, with the wolf's head lying against the chest.) A Sioux named Ghost Head wore a wolf skin tied tightly around his waist whenever he went against his enemies. In the evening he would make a small fire, smoke the skin in sweet grass (*Hierochloe odorata*), and seek to align himself with the wolf spirit represented therein, asking that the presence of his enemies be revealed to him by the (real) wolves around him, whom he considered his helpers.

It was customary for scouts returning to camp or signaling to each other to howl like wolves.

I would like to encourage some reflection on all these ideas by mentioning several ways in which the wolf was associated with the more or less mundane among various tribes. The number of examples is remarkable.

The wolf showed up as a child's carved, wooden toy among the Nehalem Tillamook on the Oregon coast and three thousand miles away, among the Naskapi of Labrador, in a game of lots called wolf sticks, in which the wolf stick was the long stick among several shorter ones. On the plains, children played a game of tag called wolf chase with a "rabbit" who was "it." In the north, Eskimos made an object (known to anthropologists as a bull-roarer) that made a noise when whirled overhead on the end of a tether, which they called a wolf scarer.

The Sioux called the December moon The Moon When the Wolves Run Together. The Cheyenne believed a wolf's being caught asleep at sunrise was a sign of its imminent death. In a story the Crow told, the pin-tailed grouse was created with a wolf claw for a beak. So-called wolf berries (*Sympboricarpus occidentalis*) that grew in the upper Missouri country were used in solution as a wash for inflamed eyes. And wolf moss (*Everina vulpina*) was boiled to produce a yellow dye by several tribes.

We who have largely lost contact with wild animals, have indeed gone to lengths to distinguish ourselves from them, can easily miss the significance of such a view of the human world in which the natural world is so deeply reflected. The view is fully integrated. It produces, often, an utter calm, a sense of belonging.

It is this need, I think, that people most wish to articulate when they speak of "a return to the earth."

JOAN DIDION

Georgia O'Keeffe

"Where I was born and where and how I have lived is unimportant," Georgia O'Keeffe told us in the book of paintings and words published in her ninetieth year on earth. She seemed to be advising us to forget the beautiful face in the Stieglitz photographs. She appeared to be dismissing the rather condescending romance that had attached to her by then, the romance of extreme good looks and advanced age and deliberate isolation. "It is what I have done with where I have been that should be of interest." I recall an August afternoon in Chicago in 1973 when I took my daughter, then seven, to see what Georgia O'Keeffe had done with where she had been. One of the vast O'Keeffe "Sky Above Clouds" canvases floated over the back stairs in the Chicago Art Institute that day, dominating what seemed to be several stories of empty light, and my daughter looked at it once, ran to the landing, and kept on looking. "Who drew it," she whispered after a while. I told her. "I need to talk to her," she said finally.

My daughter was making, that day in Chicago, an entirely unconscious but quite basic assumption about people and the work they do. She was assuming that the glory she saw in the work reflected a glory in its maker, that the painting was the painter as the poem is the poet, that every choice one made alone—every word chosen or rejected, every brush stroke laid or not laid down—betrayed one's character. *Style is character*. It seemed to me that afternoon that I had rarely seen so instinctive an application of this familiar principle, and I recall being pleased not only that my daughter responded to style as character but that it was Georgia O'Keeffe's particular style to which she responded: this was a hard woman who had imposed her 192 square feet of clouds on Chicago.

"Hardness" has not been in our century a quality much admired in women, nor in the past twenty years has it even been in official favor for men. When hardness surfaces in the very old we tend to transform it into "crustiness" or eccentricity, some tonic pepperiness to be indulged at a distance. On the evidence of her work and what she has said about it, Georgia O'Keeffe is neither "crusty" nor eccentric. She is simply hard, a straight shooter, a woman clean of received wisdom and open to what she sees. This is a woman who could early on dismiss most of her contemporaries as "dreamy," and would later single out one she liked as "a very poor painter." (And then add, apparently by way of softening the judgment: "I guess he wasn't a painter at all. He had no courage and I believe that to create one's own world in any of the arts takes courage.") This is a woman who in 1939 could advise her admirers that they were missing her point, that their appreciation of her famous flowers was merely sentimental. "When I paint a red hill," she observed coolly in the catalogue for an exhibition that year, "you say it is too bad that I don't always paint flowers. A flower touches almost everyone's heart. A red hill doesn't touch everyone's heart." This is a woman who could describe the genesis of one of her most well-known paintings—the "Cow's Skull: Red, White and Blue" owned by the Metropolitan—as an act of quite deliberate and derisive orneriness. "I thought of the city men I had been seeing in the East," she wrote. "They talked so often of writing the Great American Novel—the Great American Play—the Great American Poetry. . . . So as I was painting my cow's head on blue I thought to myself, 'I'll make it an American painting. They will not think it great with the red stripes down the sides—Red, White and Blue—but they will notice it.' "

The city men. The men. They. The words crop up again and again as this astonishingly aggressive woman tells us what was on her mind when she was making her astonishingly aggressive paintings. It was those city men who stood accused of sentimentalizing her flowers: "I made you take time to look at what I saw and when you took time to really notice my flower you hung all your associations with flowers on my flower and you write about my flower as if I think and see what you think and see—and I don't." *And I don't.* Imagine those words spoken, and the sound you hear is *don't tread on me.* "The men" believed it impossible to paint New York, so Georgia O'Keeffe painted New York. "The men" didn't think much of her bright color, so she made it brighter. The men yearned toward Europe so she went to Texas, and then New Mexico. The men talked about Cézanne, "long involved remarks about the 'plastic quality' of his form and color," and took one another's long involved remarks, in the view of this angelic rattlesnake in their midst, altogether too seriously. "I can paint one of those dismal-colored paintings like the men," the woman who regarded herself always as an outsider remembers thinking one day in 1922, and she did: a painting of a shed "all low-toned and dreary with the tree beside the door." She called this act of rancor "The Shanty" and hung it in her next show. "The men seemed to approve of it," she reported fifty-four years later, her contempt undimmed. "They seemed to think that maybe I was beginning to paint. That was my only low-toned dismal-colored painting."

Some women fight and others do not. Like so many successful guerrillas in the war between the sexes, Georgia O'Keeffe seems to have been equipped early with an immutable sense of who she was and a fairly clear understanding that she would be required to prove it. On the surface her upbringing was conventional. She was a child on the Wisconsin prairie who played with china dolls and painted watercolors with cloudy skies because sunlight was too hard to paint and, with her brother and sisters, listened every night to her mother read stories of the Wild West, of Texas, of Kit Carson and Billy the Kid. She told adults that she wanted to be an artist and was embarrassed when they asked what kind of artist she wanted to be: she had no idea "what kind." She had no idea what artists did. She had never seen a picture that interested her, other than a pen-and-ink Maid of Athens in one of her mother's books, some Mother Goose illustrations printed on cloth, a tablet cover that showed a little girl with pink roses, and the painting of Arabs on horseback that hung in her grandmother's parlor. At thirteen, in a Dominican convent, she was mortified when the sister corrected her drawing. At Chatham Episcopal Institute in Virginia she painted lilacs and sneaked time alone to walk out to where she could see the line of the Blue Ridge Mountains on the horizon. At the Art Institute in Chicago she was shocked by the presence of live models and wanted to abandon anatomy lessons. At the Art Students League in New York one of her fellow students advised her that, since he would be a great painter and she would end up teaching painting in a girls' school, any work of hers was less important than modeling for him. Another painted over her work to show her how the Impressionists did trees. She had not before heard how the Impressionists did trees and she did not much care.

At twenty-four she left all those opinions behind and went for the first time to live in Texas, where there were no trees to paint and no one to tell her how not to paint them. In Texas there was only the horizon she craved. In Texas she had her sister Claudia with her for a while, and in the late afternoons they would walk away from town and toward the horizon and watch the evening star come out. "That evening star fascinated me," she wrote. "It was in some way very exciting to me. My sister had a gun, and as we walked she would throw bottles into the air and shoot as many as she could before they hit the ground. I had nothing but to walk into nowhere and the wide sunset space with the star. Ten watercolors were made from that star." In a way one's interest is compelled as much by the sister Claudia with the gun as by the painter Georgia with the star, but only the painter left us this shining record. Ten watercolors were made from that star.

RICHARD RODRIGUEZ

The Boy's Desire

The fog comes to mind. It never rained on Christmas. It was never sharp blue and windy. When I remember Christmas in Sacramento, it is in gray: The valley fog would lift by late morning, the sun boiled haze for a few hours, then the tule fog would rise again when it was time to go into the house.

The haze through which memory must wander is thickened by that fog. The rooms of the house on 39th Street are still and dark in late afternoon, and I open the closet to search for old toys. One year there was a secondhand bike. I do not remember a color. Perhaps it had no color even then. Another year there were boxes of games that rattled their parts—dice and pegs and spinning dials. Or perhaps the rattle is of a jigsaw puzzle that compressed into an image . . . of what? of Paris? a litter of kittens? I cannot remember. Only one memory holds color and size and shape: brown hair, blue eyes, the sweet smell of styrene.

That Christmas I announced I wanted a bride doll. I must have been seven or eight—wise enough to know not to tell anyone at school, but young enough to whine out my petition from early November.

My father's reaction was unhampered by psychology. A shrug—"*Una muñeca?*"—a doll, why not? Because I knew it was my mother who would choose all the presents, it was she I badgered. I wanted a bride doll! "Is there something else you want?" she wondered. No! I'd make clear with my voice that nothing else would appease me, "We'll see," she'd say, and she never wrote it down on her list.

By early December, wrapped boxes started piling up in my parents' bedroom closet, above my father's important papers and the family album. When no one else was home, I'd drag a chair over and climb up to see . . . Looking for the *one*. About a week before Christmas, it was there. I was so certain it was mine that I punched my thumb through the wrapping paper and the cellophane window on the box and felt inside—lace, two tiny, thin legs.

I got other presents that year, but it was the doll I kept by me. I remember my mother saying I'd have "to share her" with my younger sister—but Helen was four years old, oblivious. The doll was mine. My arms would hold her. She would sleep on my pillow.

And the sky did not fall. The order of the universe did not tremble. In fact, it was right for a change. My family accommodated itself to my request. My brother and sisters played round me with their own toys. I paraded my doll by the hands across the floor.

The other day, when I asked my brother and sisters about the doll, no one remembered. My mother remembers. "Yes," she smiled. "One year there was a doll."

The closet door closes. (The house on 39th Street has been razed for a hospital parking lot.) The fog rises. Distance tempts me to mock the boy and his desire. The fact remains: One Christmas in Sacramento I wanted a bride doll, and I got one.

DONALD HALL

Ping Pong:
Rootcellar Fiveball

In one million basements, the
green table with white lines and chipped edges, making for unfair
bounces, wedges between the former coal bin and the tidy blue
gas furnace. As I grew up, our cellar was like the other cellars, and I
played my father when he came home from work, inviting him by
snapping my fingers and flipping my wrist back and forth. Even
when he came home tired and depressed from the office, which
was much of the time, he played ping pong with me. At the beginning he always won, except when he threw me a game once a week
or so. But I practiced. Between school and the time he came home,
I wedged one half of the table top—the plywood had been sawed
in half to get it down the bulkhead—against the ceiling beams and
practiced against this backboard. By the time I was twelve, I was
beating him most of the time. By the time I was fifteen and he was

forty, I was beating him all the time, as he stood weary and hopeless by the blue gas furnace, his eyes failing and his head shaking. I
threw him no games. He died of lung cancer just after his fifty-
second birthday.

All the years of growing up—while I was a pushover in football,
errant in baseball, earthbound in basketball, unankled in hockey—
my wrist snapped a blue pebbled paddle against a light white ball
and increasingly made the ball hit corners, drop over nets, spin
unpredictably, scoot, bounce backwards. Long afternoons I practiced my weak backhand against the backboard until it was
stronger than my forehand; then I built up my forehand again. I
learned the footwork that shifts itself into the best place for the
opponent's return. I learned not to slam but to change pace. I
learned to vary placement, to spin up, spin down, spin left, spin
right. I learned to slow the ball down, the way in any sport you
achieve slow motion by long practice. Now if someone else's shot
hit the table's edge, I could catch it on my paddle before it hit the
floor and arc it up over the table end and over the net, so that it
landed spinning the wrong way.

Other people in our suburb had ping-pong tables in their cellars, and I played other adolescents from time to time. Mostly I
won, even against better athletes, because I practiced more and
because they did not take ping pong seriously. At camp, at prep
school, in college I played ping pong, winning a low-key tournament once or twice. On the *Liberté* going to Europe, on the *Mauri-
tania* coming back, going and coming across the Atlantic half a
dozen times, I rose in tourist-class tournaments to the top, only to
lose to some ringer who carried his own paddle with him.

In Ann Arbor, Michigan, where I settled down, I had no cellar
big enough for a table. Therefore I played wearing leather-soled
shoes in other people's cellars during cocktail parties, my necktie
interfering with my backhand. Because I played seldom, I usually
lost, at the start, a game or two . . . seldom did I lose three games.
The serve would come back first, then top spin, backhand under-
cut, forehand that would spin first one way and then another, and
finally base-line placements. By the third game, I had learned the
local handicaps that characterize gas-furnace pong: the forehand
shortened by a two-by-four, the water-pipe hazard to a loop shot,
the light that gets in your eyes when you go down for a low backhand, and the particular nicks of a particular table.

We would come upstairs sweaty, shirts out, sobered up, hair
messed and faces flushed like teenagers returning from the drive-

in; we would march to the bar for a drink, and my masculine superiority would swell to fill the mild suburban room. Ping pong was my twelve-point buck, my trophy case, my narwhal's tusk, my Saracen's skull from the Crusades.

One time a poet came to visit, from a wing of poetry different from my own; our factions had only recently declared truce after years of combat. We sat in my living room to talk politely but circumspectly. Conversation turned to sports. I learned that my guest had grown up a competitive tennis player, seeded in the South. Doubtless I must have introduced the subject of ping pong, and at once we became less circumspect. I supposed that I could handle him; he demurred with a gentle vehemence; I begged permission to disagree with polite but insuperable confidence; he found my confidence amusing if not touching in light of his own undeniable superiority; I found his conceit brash but delightful, humorous but pathetic, in view of my own eminence . . . In short we played brag-ball with tireless, tiresome resourcefulness, but there was no table in my cellar at which to prove the point. We must have top-spun our boasting for twenty minutes before a bored observer finally suggested that we take our male validation down to the Michigan Union and rent a ping pong table.

Doubtless I would not be telling this story if it had ended otherwise: we played twenty-odd games; the visitor won the first nine by decreasing margins, and then I won thirteen or fourteen. A year or so later I read a poetry chronicle in which small but respectful attention was paid a book of mine—but, the author said, *can Hall play ping pong!* . . . So I began to believe. My conquests in gas-furnace pong were monotonous. When I had not been beaten for a number of years, I decided it was time to emerge from the cellar. In the *Ann Arbor News* I read notices of the AATTA—table tennis, they called it in the association—and solicitations to sign up for league play in the gymnasium of Forsythe Junior High School. I telephoned the number and was asked if I would enter the league at the beginning or the intermediate level. I wanted to blush for them. Modesty forbade inquiry about the advanced, and, as I hesitated, the voice on the telephone suggested that, in case of doubt, beginning was recommended. I gave my name and agreed to show up on Monday night next, expecting to leap like the prodigy from first grade to graduate school.

PART FIVE

Study Section

RALPH WALDO EMERSON

'Tis the good reader that makes the good book.

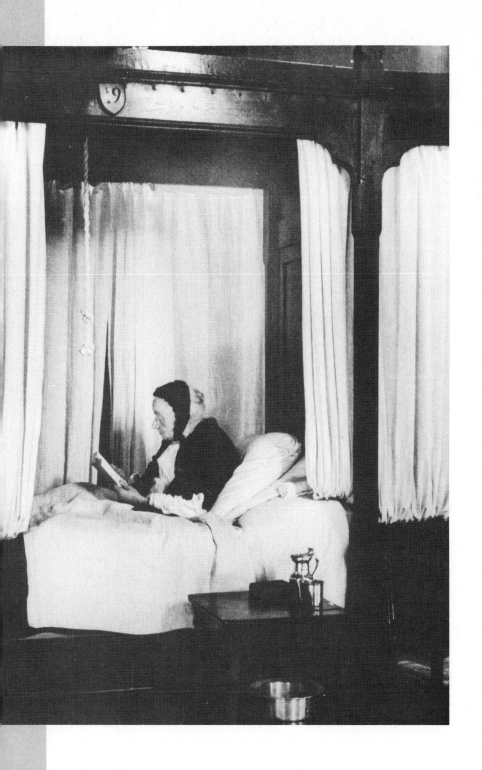

PART ONE

READING

to Enjoy

The purpose of the Reading to Enjoy section of your text is to allow you to become involved in, and share with writers, their interests, their commitments, their joys, and their sorrows. Some of the pieces will expand your horizons with new facts and new information. Some will make you aware of problems that concern people enough that they want to write about them. You also can just revel in other writers' pleasures, their wins, their joys—and their disappointments, sadnesses, and pain.

The way to study this section is to be sure you have given the writers their due. Have you read the pieces with a commitment to sharing and participating with the writers? Have you read the pieces uncritically and with a light touch? Have you allowed yourself to *enjoy* the way other people see the world and what other people are interested in and have done? The pieces in this section illustrate that writing is an act of generosity.

This section of your text can broaden your horizons; it shows you how many things can be written about in many different ways. You are able to see the many ways that words serve people as they live *life*. Writing is truly *useful* to people, important, and in many cases essential.

As you study this section of the text, you will come to *appreciate* the fact that people write. And you will be inspired to write more yourself.

535

READING

to Enjoy
Information

In essays that give information, the writer's purpose is to *tell* you something—preferably something that you don't already know. This means that the writer will not be the center of attention. You don't read *writing that tells*—writing that gives *information*—to learn more about the personality of the writer or to explore the life or the vision of the writer. It is true that if the writing is effective, the writer is present; it *is* the *person* who has marshalled the facts, selected the information, arranged the parts, shifted, organized, and focused. But the writer's intention in writing to give *information* is that the content of the writing be the focus.

A person might think that *writing to tell*—to give *information*—would be boring, or at best dependable and drab—like a workhorse pulling the plow instead of the thoroughbred winning the race.

But these essays that give *information* are spritely. They bounce with energy. They have spark. They illustrate what is possible when writers are *excited* about their subject and really *care* about sharing their enthusiasm with their readers.

QUESTIONS

1. What was the most *fascinating* information you learned from reading each of these essays? What makes something *interesting* to you? What writing traits do these authors have that cause you to be *drawn in* by what they have to say?
2. What additional appreciation for the Swiss Army Knife did you have after you read the essay about it?
3. Were you surprised at how much you enjoyed reading about something as mundane as pistachio nuts? What approach did this writer take that turned an ordinary subject into writing that has imagination and spark?

4. Although Bob Young's essay is about being a successful business executive, his "secret" is one that everyone can use at any time in her or his life. How can you apply the "secret" of this essay to your life now?
5. "Charles & Diana Get Married" is great gossip. How would you define gossip? Are you expected to believe gossip? What titillated you in this piece?
6. In what way would you say each of these essays illustrates the statement that writing is an act of generosity?
7. What are some of the ways that you have found writers use to make you enjoy information?

READING

*to Enjoy
Persuasion and
Argument*

For thousands of years, human beings have been aware of the power of the written word to change people, their situations, and what they know. Moses brought down the Ten Commandments, written in stone, to change the behavior of the Israelites in the wilderness. The founding fathers of this country wrote the Declaration of Independence to change their relationship with England and to change what the colonists thought of themselves. Albert Einstein made assertions that changed what we know about our universe.

So writing intended to *persuade and argue—writing to change—*implies a belief and a trust on the writer's part that words have power, that words create action, that words produce change. When writers write to *persuade and argue*, they intend to cause action, movement, alteration of some sort. The writers want you to take a position or a stand that you didn't have before, so that you will argue for something you didn't argue for before, so that you will assert what you did not assert before, so that you will act as you perhaps have not acted before.

QUESTIONS

1. In a one-sentence summary—one sentence for each essay—state the writer's argument.

2. What two or three points do you find most persuasive in "Physicians for Nuclear Disarmament"? What has the writer done or said that makes these particular points persuasive to you?

3. "The Passing of Route 66" requires a bit of nostalgia to appreciate the argument of the essay. Did the writer manage to evoke enough nostalgia in you as you read to have you care about what he cares about—preserving at least the signs of the old Route 66? If so, how did he manage to do this in his writing? If not, what could he have done that would have made you care more about this situation than you did?

4. Do you see any solution to the problem that Juthica Stangl talks about in "India: A Widow's Devastating Choice"? Does she see a solution? What would you say the author wants us, the readers, to think or do after we read this essay? Why is the essay worth reading and thinking about, even if you cannot think of much that an individual in America can do?

5. What are Martin Luther King, Jr.'s main arguments in "A Christmas Sermon on Peace"? How is his powerful pulpit voice present in this printed essay?

READING

to Enjoy
A Personal Voice

How do we know people? By things they say and do. In reading to enjoy a *personal voice*, we discover what a writer is like as a person. This kind of writing—*writing to express*—reveals, explains, states writers' thoughts, gives voice to writers' feelings and imagination.

When writers write *to express*—to speak in their personal voices—they say, "Here I am. This is what I have done. This is what I have thought. This is what I have felt. This reveals something about *me*."

And the risk, of course, is that we, the readers, may not appreciate what the writers wrote. But that is a risk they have to take. And that they are willing to take. They stand and speak in their *personal voice.*

In addition to having the privilege of enjoying a writer's personal voice in this section of your text, you also have an opportunity to see in how *many* ways writing shows up in life. From our experiences in the classroom, we may make the mistake of thinking that writing consists of essays, themes, exams, and reports. But writing is far more vast in scope, as this section shows: obituaries, good-bye letters, recipes, memoirs, personal accounts, contracts, announcements, invitations, poetry, prayers, and many others. You will find that you will have many opportunities to use writing in similar ways. This section can inspire you to *see* writing in its many forms and to *use* writing in its many forms yourself.

QUESTIONS

1. In one sentence for each piece in this section, encapsulate your sense of the person who wrote it. What did you learn about the author by reading the piece? What did the writer reveal about her or his way of living in the world? What do you know or what can you say about the writer that you did not know or could not say before you read these pieces? By limiting yourself to one sentence for each author, you will be able to get at the heart of what the *personal voices* sounded like.
2. Which of these pieces would you guess required the greatest risk for the writers?

3. Each piece of writing that expresses a *personal voice* touches some emotion in us—joy, sadness, loneliness, exuberance and excitement, fear, melancholy, pleasure, pain, amusement, anger, confidence. List each piece in this section and then write the emotion or emotions it elicited in you.

4. After reading this section of your text, how would you answer someone who said, "I don't need to take freshman English. I'm not going to write when I get out of school!"?

YOUR OWN WRITING POSSIBILITIES

1. Write an essay to give *information, to tell* your readers something you assume they do not know. The only requirements for your subject are that it be something you are *truly excited* about and that you know something about. You should *want* to share this with your readers.

   Decide who your audience will be for this essay—perhaps your classmates and professor, or perhaps a general audience.

2. Consider some issue you feel strongly about—costs of higher education, parents' behavior, children being difficult, nuclear energy, ending hunger or ending war, the role of women (or men), society's attitude toward divorced people, etc.

   Choose an issue and write persuasively about it. You may write an essay, a letter, a sermon, a speak-out column piece, an editorial to be delivered on television, an editorial for a newspaper or newsletter, or some other form that appeals to you.

   Decide who your audience will be before you begin writing. And decide what you want this audience to *do* or how you expect them to *change* after they have read your piece.

3. What does the section on Reading to Enjoy a Personal Voice stimulate you to want to write? Perhaps a letter you've been putting off, a tribute to someone who died, a poem, a song, a personal memoir about a special day in your life, a description of what it is like to do something you know how to do (like Shirley MacLaine talking about dancing), a contract, a memo, a prayer, an invitation or announcement?

   Choose one of these forms and write a piece with the purpose of *expressing your personal voice.* Share this piece of writing with the appropriate person or persons. If it is acceptable to you, share the piece with your classmates and your professor.

READING

to Learn to Write

Originality

The Culinary Alchemy of Eggs, page 112

PARTICIPATORY READING

Questions on What the Writer Said

(*Content, Purpose, Viewpoint*)

1. The author of this essay is a professor of chemistry. The essay was published in a prestigious scientific journal. The subject of this essay is boiling eggs.

   What is original (and maybe even a little odd, strange, or unlikely) about this essay when you consider all three of these facts?
2. What can you learn about the author's outside interests and past experiences by reading this essay? Where are the clues that reveal this information?
3. What valuable information that you can use in the kitchen did you learn from this essay?
4. Why is the Originality section an appropriate place for this essay?

CONSTRUCTIVE READING

Questions on How the Writer Wrote

(*Choices, Strategies, Style*)

1. The writer begins this essay by talking about his mother's cooking when he was a little boy. Why is this kind of opening good strategy on the writer's part?

2. What does the writer do to sound like an individual with a personal voice? How might you expect a chemistry professor to sound when he or she writes an essay for a scientific journal?
3. How did Grosser use humor to end the essay? How does the ending relate to the beginning?
4. If you were to "chunk" Grosser's essay, how many major sections would there be? (Chunking means you divide the essay into parts: from here to here is the beginning; from this sentence to that sentence is the writer's first point; here is the transition to the next point; from here to here is the second point, etc,; from this sentence to that one is the ending.) Discuss reasons that might explain the particular order the writer chose for these sections. How does Professor Grosser get from one section to another without abrupt breaks in thought?

INQUIRY READING

Questions on What the Writer Meant

(*Language, Concepts, Distinctions*)

1. What do words like *carom, frenzied and chaotic collisions,* and *molecular demolition derby* add to this essay?
2. Look at these two sentences from the essay:

   > Only now do we find the real reason for the protein's solitary behavior. It coiled itself up not from narcissism, but as a defensive maneuver, for when it opens out into a streamer, it exposes a soft underbelly of richly seductive targets for chemical attack and bonding.

   What is unusual about using this kind of language to discuss an object like a protein? What would you miss if you did not know the meaning of *narcissism*? To what is the writer indirectly comparing a protein when he uses this language?
3. In discussing how to determine if an egg has been boiled or not, the author uses an analogy of a figure skater. How does this help him make his point?
4. Early in the essay, Grosser writes, "My mind started to boggle." From this sentence alone, what can you predict about the tone and voice present in this essay?
5. What is alchemy? How is alchemy related to the cooking of eggs? What does the title of this essay add to its impact?

THE LARGER PICTURE

Questions to Consider

1. This essay was adapted from Grosser's book *The Cookbook Decoder, or Culinary Alchemy Explained*. Who might be the audience for this book? What is the relationship between the audience for the book and the audience for this essay?
2. This essay was published in *American Scientist*, the journal of The Scientific Research Society, which has been, since 1886, the honor society of scientists. What made an essay on boiling eggs appropriate for this journal's audience?

YOUR OWN WRITING POSSIBILITIES

1. Go to the library and find out the explanation for some common phenomena such as these (or a subject of your own choosing):

    rainbows: Why do rainbows always repeat the same color sequence in the same way?
    What are the circumstances under which they appear?

    sinkholes: What causes them?
    Where can they be found?

    bread rising: What is the explanation?
    What can go wrong?

    Write an essay on the subject. Use your classmates as your audience. Write so that they will learn from and be interested in what you have to say.

2. Write a companion essay or a spin-off essay based on "The Culinary Alchemy of Eggs." Perhaps it will be about the time you did not boil an egg correctly. Or it might focus on your secret for making delicious deviled eggs. It might be a parody explaining why chicken fries the way it does or what happens when ice cream freezes—make up all details if you want to. Again, choose your classmates as your audience and be committed to their getting pleasure out of reading the essay.
3. Choose a subject that you know quite a bit about (or can learn quite a bit about by reviewing and reading your textbook) from another course you are now taking: biology, chemistry, mathematics, physical education, physics, etc. Write an essay for your classmates in which you make the subject clear and stimulating.
4. After you read this essay, do some thinking-on-paper writing such as *double-entry writing*. Double-entry writing works like this: you draw a line down the middle of the page (or mentally divide the word processor screen). On the left you copy a paragraph, sentence, phrase, or word

from the essay. On the right you write the thoughts you have when you read what you have copied on the left. (The right-hand entry will always be longer than the left.) After you have written everything you want to say about the left-hand entry, copy another paragraph, sentence, phrase, or word from the essay. Again, write whatever thoughts you have when you read that entry. Continue until you have completed at least five entries.

5. Write an essay on the subject of what makes "The Culinary Alchemy of Eggs" an original piece of work. Reread the introduction to the Originality chapter in your text and reread the commentary accompanying the essay before you begin your own writing. Keep your professor in mind as your audience, and remember that he or she—like everyone else—gets bored, likes to be stimulated, wants to get value from taking the time to read, and wants to hear your voice in the essay, not the sound of a robot or an anonymous faceless figure in the crowd.

The Lie Detector, page 120

PARTICIPATORY READING

Questions on What the Writer Said

(*Content, Purpose, Viewpoint*)

1. Why is it good news to Lewis Thomas that we human beings cannot lie without producing stress?
2. Thomas says that animals and insects lie, too. Why do they?
3. At the conclusion of the essay, as he thinks about a broad application of his idea, Thomas has a humorous suggestion. What is it? What makes this an effective ending?
4. Biologically speaking, why is it good for human beings to restrain from lying to each other?
5. Why is the Originality section an appropriate place for this essay?

CONSTRUCTIVE READING

Questions on How the Writer Wrote

(*Choices, Strategies, Style*)

1. The introduction of this essay is about discouragement and ways to alleviate it. What does Thomas gain by beginning the essay this way? How does he tie his introduction into lie detectors?
2. The conclusion of this essay is a bit tongue-in-cheek and strikes a lighter tone. Why do you suppose Lewis Thomas chose to end the essay this way?

3. What is the thesis (or main message) of this essay? Where does it appear? How is it stated?
4. The writer uses the pronoun "I" many times in this essay, yet the essay is not about a personal experience. What tone does Thomas develop by using "I"? What keeps the essay from being *about* Lewis Thomas, even though he refers to himself often?

INQUIRY READING

Questions on What the Writer Meant

(*Language, Concepts, Distinctions*)

1. What would readers miss if they did not know the meaning of the word *placebo*?
2. Which of the following words or phrases do readers not need to know in order to understand this essay? Get in a group with two or three of your classmates and first locate each of these words in the essay. Then determine among yourselves if readers need to know the meanings of the words or phrases in order to understand the writer's message. Decide what determines which of these words readers need to know the meaning of and which they could get by without knowing.

> lobule
> neurohormones   nubile insects
> etiologic agent   nucleated cell
> sociobiological   peripheral vascular system

THE LARGER PICTURE

Questions to Consider

1. John Updike has called Lewis Thomas' essays "perky and compact," and says they "usually end on the upbeat." Does "The Lie Detector" fit this description?
2. Thomas says in this essay that he wouldn't want us to go as far as science could probably go in detecting lying. What would be the end result if every lie were immediately detectable? What would change in the world? Why does Thomas think such changes would be undesirable? Do you think they would be desirable or undesirable?
3. In the essay commentary Thomas' vision is referred to: "There is a tendency for living things to join up, establish linkages, live inside each other, return to earlier arrangements, get along whenever possible." How does "The Lie Detector" fit this vision?

YOUR OWN WRITING POSSIBILITIES

1. Lewis Thomas has said:

   A framework for meaning is somehow built into our minds at birth. Write an essay in which you describe how this assertion relates to the essay you've just read, "The Lie Detector." You have several options in choosing the form for your writing. Here are just three possibilities. Choose from these or add one of your own:

   a. A monologue in which you pose the question to yourself and then answer it. You are the audience for your writing, although you may wish to share with any interested party whom the question might intrigue.

   b. An expository essay in which you make an assertion in your thesis about the relationship you see between the statement above and "The Lie Detector," and in which you "prove" this thesis by examples, evidence, or illustrations. Your professor would likely be the audience for this writing.

   c. A dialogue or conversation in which two voices explore the relationship between the statement and the essay. You and others interested in this subject would be the audience.

2. There are many ways to "think on paper" about something you have just read. One of these ways is called *track switching*. Using this technique, you make five different assertions about your subject, one at a time. (A sample off-the-top-of-the-head assertion about "The Lie Detector" might be: "Lie detectors could make angels of everyone." The assertion doesn't have to be "true." It merely has to be some statement you're willing to make—if ever so tentatively—about the subject.)

   After making each assertion, you write for five minutes on that assertion. At the end of the first five minutes, make up a second assertion and write for five more minutes. You continue this until you have made five different assertions and have written for twenty-five minutes. What happens in this kind of "discovery" writing is that you generate new thoughts on the subject and make connections you hadn't made before.

   Do a track switching piece of writing on "The Lie Detector."

3. In "The Lie Detector" Lewis Thomas says, "Trust is a fundamental requirement for our kind of existence, and without it all our linkages would begin to snap loose."

   Write one of the following types of essays, using this statement as your subject.

   a. A personal experience essay in which you relate an event from your life that proves Thomas' statement right.

b. A persuasion essay in which you take the role of a politician or senior government official and write an essay suitable for the op-ed page of a major newspaper convincing Americans about the importance of trusting other countries and governments in the world.

c. A persuasion essay in which you play the same role and write for the same audience but take the opposite side of the question.

Who Was Karl Bodmer, Anyway? *page* 127

PARTICIPATORY READING

Questions on What the Writer Said

(*Content, Purpose, Viewpoint*)

1. What question puzzled the author of this essay, a question for which he never found an answer?
2. Why did the Indians want to have their pictures painted by Karl Bodmer?
3. Calvin Tomkins achieves at least two results with this essay. He lets the reader know about the paintings of the German artist, Karl Bodmer. What other result does he achieve?
4. By reading this essay thoughtfully, you can detect some of Tomkins' standards—the qualities he thinks make good art. What are some of these standards Tomkins reveals indirectly in the essay?

CONSTRUCTIVE READING

Questions on How the Writer Wrote

(*Choices, Strategies, Style*)

1. This essay covers three periods of time: Bodmer's lifetime in the 1800s, "one day last summer" when Tomkins went to the museum to see the Bodmer show; and "now," the moment during which Tomkins is writing the essay.

   Why do you suppose Tomkins begins the essay with "one day last summer"? What does he gain by doing this? Does he lose anything? How does Tomkins use "now" time in the essay?

2. How is Tomkins, the writer, present personally in the essay? What keeps the essay from being about him rather than about Bodmer? What does his presence in the essay allow him to accomplish?

3. What historical events did Tomkins insert into this essay? How is the essay improved by the inclusion of these details? How does Tomkins bridge from the present to the past back to the present?
4. What makes the ending of the essay effective?
5. What role did Tomkins' curiosity play in this essay?

INQUIRY READING

Questions on What the Writer Meant

(*Language, Concepts, Distinctions*)

1. What is a salon artist? Why do you need to know this to help you understand the essay?
2. Tomkins writes, "and then he went home to paint noble stags and sylvan glades." What is added to the reader's understanding by knowing what "noble stags and sylvan glades" look like and what a reference like this connotes?
3. One influence that may have affected Bodmer's work when he was in America was Alexander von Humboldt's ideas about landscape painting. Read this section of the essay again. What is added to your reading of the essay by understanding what von Humboldt meant in this discussion?
4. Find out about the Barbizon school of art in France. What does this information add to your reading of the essay? Is it necessary for you to know this? Is it useful?

THE LARGER PICTURE

Questions to Consider

1. Why do you think Bodmer never painted great art again?
2. Tomkins alludes to the fact that Bodmer painted the Indians right before many of the tribes were to be destroyed forever by conquest and disease. He says:

   I can't argue that Bodmer was alert to these historical currents. But in his best work he cut so close to the truth of appearances that I think he broke through it into something more profound: the extreme stillness at the moment of great change.

   What does this statement mean to you?
3. What kind of person would one need to be in order to "see" in the Bodmer exhibit what Calvin Tomkins saw when he was there?

YOUR OWN WRITING POSSIBILITIES

1. Taking the role of Karl Bodmer, write a letter from the artist to a friend or relative which explains why, after returning from America, he never painted with the same success again.
2. Taking the role of Prince Maximilian, write a letter to Karl Bodmer in which you attempt to inspire and stimulate the artist to do good work again.
3. Think of someone you know, or know of, who for one brief moment in life rose to greatness. (This "moment of greatness" does not have to be well known.) Write an essay in which you (a) discuss this moment or time of greatness, and (b) speculate why for that person the moment of greatness never came again. Write the essay with your classmates and professor as your audience.
4. Write an entry for an imaginary journal that Karl Bodmer might have kept the years he was painting the Indians and the West in America.
5. Visit an art exhibit featuring the work of one artist. Write a review of that exhibit in which you do more than discuss the paintings and the factual details about the artist. Attempt in your review to raise larger questions or provide broader insights. Choose as the audience for this essay your college newspaper or a popular magazine such as *Esquire*.

In the Jungle, page 136

PARTICIPATORY READING

Questions on What the Writer Said

(*Content, Purpose, Viewpoint*)

1. Make two lists side by side on your page: (a) a list of oddities, unusual objects, strange scenes that Annie Dillard saw in the jungle and (b) a list of ordinary, very "American" things she saw in the jungle. What can you say about what might have been Dillard's purpose in providing both viewpoints—the strange and the familiar—in this essay?
2. What makes this out-of-the-way place—the Napo River in the Ecuadorian jungle—not out-of-the-way at all, according to Dillard?
3. Make a list of five facts that surprised you about these people living in the jungles of Ecuador. Why were these facts surprising?
4. In what ways is this essay informative? About what? What is the value of this information?

CONSTRUCTIVE READING

Questions on How the Writer Wrote

(*Choices, Strategies, Style*)

1. Annie Dillard reports a conversation she had with a free-lance reporter from Manhattan who was with her group in the jungle. What value does this conversation serve in helping Dillard make her point clear to the reader?
2. When she is talking about the Napo River, Dillard says, "The Napo River itself is wide (I mean wider than the Mississippi at Davenport) ...." Why was using this comparison good strategy on Dillard's part? How does the comparison help the reader?
3. What is the main point in this essay? Where do you find it in the text? What does Annie Dillard do to make her main point convincing?
4. Choose the five most vivid images in this essay. Why are vivid images essential in an essay on a subject like this?

INQUIRY READING

Questions on What the Writer Meant

(*Language, Concepts, Distinctions*)

1. Annie Dillard tells about the children in the jungle singing "Nearer My God to Thee" in the dialect Quechua. Dillard and her group sang "Old McDonald Had a Farm" in English for the children and included the sounds of the animals as they sang. She reports, "Of course, they thought we were out of our minds."

    Why would the children, hearing the song and the animal sounds, think the Americans were "out of their minds"?
2. If "poetic language" were defined as "impassioned feeling expressed in imaginative words," where in Dillard's essay would you find "poetic language"? (Example from the last paragraph of the essay: "catching sunlight the way a cup catches poured water.") Choose three other instances of "poetic language" from the essay. How is this "poetic language" appropriate to Dillard's purpose in the essay?
3. Here is a sentence from the essay: "Inside the jungle you are more likely to notice the snarl of climbers and creepers round the trees' boles, the flowering bromeliads and epiphytes in every bough's crook, and the fantastic silk-cotton tree trunks thirty or forty feet across." Are

there any meanings of words in the sentence which you do not know? Is it necessary to know the meaning of all the words in the sentence? Why?

THE LARGER PICTURE

Questions to Consider

1. Does this essay entice you to want to go to the Napo River in the Ecuadorian jungle? Why or why not?
2. Critics have asserted that some things we read can make us better people. How could reading Annie Dillard's "In the Jungle" conceivably make someone a better person?
3. When Dillard won the Pulitzer Prize for *Pilgrim at Tinker Creek*, one critic said that the book was aptly named since Dillard's literary life is a "pilgrimage, a journey of inquiry and speculation toward God." Could this essay be said to be consistent with the writer's journey of inquiry toward God? How?

YOUR OWN WRITING POSSIBILITIES

1. In the commentary on this essay, Annie Dillard's childhood was reported: at the age of ten she discovered the book *The Field Book of Ponds and Streams* in the library, and she read it every year after that. Reading and rereading this book, she said, made her aware of the great variety of life to be found in ponds and streams—"daphnia, planaria, water pennies, stonefly larvae, dragonfly nymphs . . . all of which one could carry home." When she was twelve, she began to study these creatures under the microscope.

   Write an essay in which you assert or argue that the roots of "In the Jungle" go all the way back to when Dillard was ten or twelve years old. Be generous with the proof for your assertion or argument. Write this essay with your classmates and your professor as your audience—and remember that they are the same kind of human being you are: they want to be able to be interested in what you have to say, and they want to gather value from what they read.

2. Someone once made up a "formula" for writing a poem:

   The poem has five lines.
   The first line is a single noun.
   The second line is two adjectives.
   The third line is three verbs.
   The fourth line is a phrase of five words.
   The fifth line is an adjective and a noun.

Here is an example of a "formula poem":

Cabin
Sheltered, snug
Endures, roughs it, rejuvenates
Always there by the lake.
Tennessee homeplace.

Write a "formula poem" using images, scenes, and words from Annie Dillard's essay.

3. Choose a place that you know about that most people would call out-of-the-way. Write an essay in which you make this place real for your readers and in which you convince them that the place is not that out-of-the-way after all.

   Imagine that you are writing this essay for a travel magazine with a name like *Adventure in Travel* which is read mainly by college students and young adults.

4. Write an essay about a place you know about. This may be a place familiar to your readers or unfamiliar to them. Your intention in this essay will be to focus on giving information about the place. Write to tell the readers all about this place. Make the place real to them. Make the readers feel as if they had been to this place by the time they finished reading the essay. Imagine that your essay will be printed in a publication sponsored by the Tourism Department of the state (or country) in which the place you are writing about is located.

The Education of an Engineer, page 143

PARTICIPATORY READING

Questions on What the Writer Said

(*Content, Purpose, Viewpoints*)

1. Samuel Florman tells about an incident that happened when he was in the Navy and stationed in the Caroline Islands. What was this incident and why was it important in Florman's life?
2. What was unusual about Florman's education as an engineer?
3. This essay is Florman's personal story, yet the essay has a purpose much broader than merely the relating of a man's personal story. What is the essay's larger persuasive purpose?
4. How are the ideas of Kafka, Goethe, and Samuel Johnson important to Florman in making his point in this essay?
5. What is original about this essay?

CONSTRUCTIVE READING

Questions on How the Writer Wrote

(*Choices, Strategies, Style*)

1. Look at the opening of this essay. What makes this beginning effective?
2. Look at the ending of the essay. What makes this ending effective? How does this ending relate directly to the beginning of Florman's essay?
3. Where in the essay does Florman articulate most clearly and most specifically the main point he is making? What does Florman gain by stating his point where he does in the essay?
4. This is a long essay. Defend its length. Why is all the information necessary? Now criticize its length. What could Florman have left out with no harm done to the essay?
5. What keeps this essay from being only a personal experience essay? How is Florman's assertion woven into the essay? Find specific locations where both themes—the personal story and the larger theme—are woven in together.

INQUIRY READING

Questions on What the Writer Meant

(*Language, Concepts, Distinctions*)

1. In this essay Florman contrasts engineering education and liberal arts education. What characteristics does an engineering education have? What characteristics does a liberal arts education have?
2. Why, according to Florman, would an engineer be a better engineer if he or she had both kinds of education? How do the two come together, complement each other, support each other?
3. What has his liberal arts education contributed to Florman's life? Be as specific in your answer as possible.
4. What chance does Florman think his ideas on how an engineer ought to be educated have for being accepted by the engineering community? Why is it hard—if not impossible—for a concept like liberal arts education to alter a prevailing concept like engineering education?

THE LARGER PICTURE

Questions to Consider

1. This essay appeared in a periodical for the general reading public, not an engineering magazine. In what way do you think the essay interests and gives value to a non-engineer?
2. What larger issues does this essay make you, personally, think of?

3. Why is it unnecessary to know the work of the writers Florman mentions in this essay—writers such as Kafka, Dickens, Faulkner—to get the point he is making? How is your reading of the essay enriched if you do know some of these writers' works?
4. One might say the conclusion in this essay is "guardedly optimistic." Do you agree? What direction do you think, after reading this essay, engineering education is likely to take in the future?

YOUR OWN WRITING POSSIBILITIES

1. Florman, in supporting his argument that engineering students should study the liberal arts, quotes Mark Van Doren. Van Doren said that if a person studied the liberal arts, he "could avoid the bewilderment of one who suspects he has missed the main thing. There is no happiness like this."

   What "main thing" might engineers miss if they do not study the liberal arts? Write an essay in which you define the "main thing" you think people miss who do not know the liberal arts. Write this essay for publication in an engineering society publication on your campus.
2. Take issue with Samuel Florman. Write an argumentative essay in which you dispute his point that engineering students should study the liberal arts. Imagine that this essay will be published in the same magazine in which Florman's essay appeared, a periodical for the general reading public.
3. Write a journal entry in which you discuss your own experiences in studying the liberal arts. What have you learned? What is your opinion about the importance of studying the liberal arts? What has your study of liberal arts courses added to your life? Share this journal entry with a friend, classmate, or your professor. You might also use the journal entry as the basis for your participation in class discussion.
4. The essay ends with a Samuel Johnson quote:

   > Life is not long, and too much of it must not pass in idle deliberation how it shall be spent.

   Write an essay in which you agree or disagree with this statement. Be generous in the number of examples you use to prove your point. Consider your classmates and your professor as your audience. Commit yourself to give more than just your opinion in this essay but to give value to the readers by giving them something provocative or stimulating to think about.

The Crash of Flight 90, page 162

PARTICIPATORY READING

Questions on What the Writer Said

(*Contents, Purpose, Viewpoints*)

1. According to this essay, who deceived himself the most in the crash of Flight 90?
2. How do the authors relate the study of biology to the study of human behavior?
3. The editors of *Science Digest* begin this article with a long introduction written by the editors: "The following article is unsettling. The editors believe that its disturbing thesis may help us understand why some disasters occur . . . ." Why is the essay potentially disturbing? What is its disturbing thesis? Why did the editors introduce the essay this way?
4. The authors of this essay include a long quotation from Dr. Aaron Waters. What is the point of this quotation?
5. How were the pilot's and copilot's actions self-deceptive, according to the authors?

CONSTRUCTIVE READING

Questions on How the Writers Wrote

(*Choices, Strategies, Style*)

1. Find in the text of the essay the "point of no return," the point after which the accident was certain to happen. Is this "point of no return" also the turning point of the essay itself? Explain your answer.
2. What do the writers gain, from the standpoint of proving the point of their essay, by including the quotation from Dr. Aaron Waters?
3. This essay makes use of much quoted dialogue. How do the authors incorporate this dialogue into the essay? How do they make transitions between the quoted dialogue and their own words? What gives the essay unity?
4. How do the authors incorporate technical information into the article? How do they make this technical information easy to understand?
5. Where in the essay do the authors articulate most specifically and clearly the point they are arguing? Why do you think they placed this statement where they did in the essay?

INQUIRY READING

Questions on What the Writers Meant

(*Language, Concepts, Distinctions*)

1. Discuss the self-deception theory in biology. How do the authors say this theory relates to human beings?
2. It is in the words—the language they used—the pilot and copilot spoke that the authors find their clues to the self-deception they assert the pilot and copilot fell victim to. Study the pilot's and copilot's words—their language. Are the authors' assertions about self-deception justified?

THE LARGER PICTURE

Questions to Consider

1. The authors conclude their essay with these words:

   > We conclude that the human element of self-deception is the main factor leading up to the disaster. This conclusion has implications for air safety . . . .

   How could this conclusion be related to the 1986 explosion of the *Challenger* in which seven astronauts died?
2. In what ways was the connecting of self-deception theory in biology to self-deception in human beings new to you? How plausible do you find this connection? How valuable and/or useful?
3. Do you agree with the authors' contention that the kind of discussion they have carried out in this essay has implications for air safety? Explain your answer.

YOUR OWN WRITING POSSIBILITIES

1. Extract from the essay the quoted conversation between the pilot and copilot. Rewrite this conversation so that the plane does not take off and the tragedy is averted. Read this new version of the pilot and copilot's conversation to your classmates.
2. Imagine that you had been a classmate of the pilot or copilot when he was in college. Write a letter to the editor of *Science Digest* in which you (a) express gratitude for the publication of this article, or (b) take issue with the magazine for publishing the article. Define either stand you decide to take.
3. Write an essay in which you agree or disagree with the magazine's decision to publish this essay. Consider your classmates and your professor as your audience.

4. Write an essay in which you assert that the pilot and copilot did engage in self-deception or that they did not. Substantiate your argument fully. Imagine that the essay is going to be published in the same magazine in which "The Crash of Flight 90" appeared.

Yaz, page 172

PARTICIPATORY READING

Questions on What the Writer Said

(*Content, Purpose, Viewpoint*)

1. Why did the author come all the way from Minnesota to Boston to watch the last games Yaz played?
2. This essay is about Carl Yastrzemski, but it is also about the author. What do we learn about David Wetmore? What makes that information interesting? Worth reading?
3. In what ways is this essay a tribute to Carl Yastrzemski?

CONSTRUCTIVE READING

Questions on How the Writer Wrote

(*Choices, Strategies, Style*)

1. This essay alternates among the present (now, when the author is writing and thinking about baseball), the recent past (the days Yastrzemski played his last games), and the distant past (the memories the author has about baseball.) How does David Wetmore combine the three different "times" in his writing? What keeps us from getting confused when he switches from one time to another? Why is it necessary for the writer to include each time in the essay?
2. By the second paragraph of the essay the author has us in the park watching Yaz's last games. In the last paragraph of the essay he has us back in the park watching Yaz's last games. Why is this an effective way for the writer to organize his essay?
3. What is the writer's main message—main point—in this essay? How do you know this is his main point? On what do you base your decision? Where do you find this main point in the essay?
4. Wetmore is a stranger to the reader. Why can he even pretend to himself that the reader will be interested in hearing about his life? What does make this stranger's experiences interesting to us when we read the essay?

INQUIRY READING

Questions on What the Writer Meant

(*Language, Concepts, Distinctions*)

1. The author writes, "For myself, I keep the fan's faith." What does this concept—the fan's faith—mean?
2. The author also writes, "Fans are famously fickle—and cruel." What does this mean? How is this statement a contradiction in terms with the statement in question 1? How is it not a contradiction?
3. The author says that baseball "enacts fantasy, drama, and tragedy on a wide stage, in a spectacle that lasts for more than six months every year, with ups and downs reversing and repeating themselves in daily episodes." What makes this comparison of baseball to literature (fantasy, drama, tragedy) appropriate?
4. The author makes a distinction between a game that is a team game and a game of individuals. He asserts that baseball is a game of individuals, not a team game. Do you agree or disagree?

THE LARGER PICTURE

Questions to Consider

1. What would make this essay interesting to someone who did not watch baseball games and had never heard of Carl Yastrzemski?
2. How is this an essay about mortality? How is it an essay about loss? What kinds of loss?

YOUR OWN WRITING POSSIBILITIES

1. Write an essay in which you share with your readers your love (or dislike) for baseball. Use personal experiences to illustrate your points. Keep in mind as you write this essay the commitment that every writer must have: to give value to his or her readers.
2. The author says that baseball is a parallel to life. He talks about the simplicity of the game's fundamental confrontations—throwing and hitting, catching and running. He talks about baseball as a game of skill and violence and control. A game of waiting and of checking unleashed energy. A game of individuals meeting tests. A game that repeats itself.

   Write an essay in which you compare baseball to life. Consider these options for your imagined audience: (a) a group of city officials who are unwilling to fund the building of a new ballpark for young people to play baseball in; (b) a speech to be delivered at a sports banquet following the completion of baseball season; (c) your professor.

3. Imagine that you are Carl Yastrzemski's wife, son, or daughter. Write a letter to the author of this essay. Give another side of the story.
4. Write an essay about a loss you have experienced. Put this loss in the larger context of growing up. Consider your classmates and your professor as your audience.
5. Write an essay in which you compare another sport or activity—dancing, football, learning to play the piano or another musical instrument, basketball, learning to cook—to life. Imagine that you are writing for the readers of a newsletter published by an association/company involved in the activity. (A newsletter put out by a cookbook club, an intramural football association, etc.)

QUESTIONS AND WRITING POSSIBILITIES

Originality as a Characteristic of Good Writing

1. Discuss how each essay in this section illustrates originality in writing.
2. What do the writers in this section all seem to have in common?
3. What are some of the secrets to being able to have an original viewpoint on any subject?
4. What did you learn about achieving originality in your own writing from studying this section?
5. The essays in this section illustrate originality in writing about (a) a process ("The Culinary Alchemy of Eggs"), (b) an object ("The Lie Detector"), (c) an activity ("Who Was Karl Bodmer, Anyway?"), (d) a place ("In the Jungle"), (e) a concept ("The Education of an Engineer"), (f) an event ("The Crash of Flight 90"), (g) a person ("Yaz").

   Applying the principles you have learned about being original when you write, write an essay in which you treat your subject with originality. Choose one of the seven possibilities listed above. Determine a real or imagined audience for your essay before you begin.

READING

To Learn to Write

Thesis

Political Parables for Today, page 186

Questions on What the Writer Said

(*Content, Purpose, Viewpoint*)

1. The theme of the first parable discussed, The Rot at the Top, comes from the American detective story. Explain the relationship between the theme of the parable and American detective stories.
2. What are some of the central experiences of American history in which the political parables are rooted? Why do you think these experiences resulted in stories which we tell and retell in our history?
3. What parable does Benjamin Franklin's life illustrate? How?
4. Robert Reich, the author of this essay, did more than just list and discuss the four parables. What was his larger purpose? What point did he make at the end of the essay?

CONSTRUCTIVE READING

Questions on How the Writer Wrote

(*Choices, Strategies, Style*)

1. The method of organization that Reich uses in this essay could be described like this:

   Introduction: Discussion of coming campaign season
   Main Point: We have national parables
   Identification and discussion of the four parables, using examples the reader can recognize
   Main point: The parables can be linked together in different ways
   Discussion and illustration of main point
   Conclusion: The way the parables are connected will change again

How is this an appropriate arrangement for this essay? How would you state the thesis of this essay in one sentence?

2. The amount of space taken up by the identification of the four parables is much less than the amount of space taken up by the discussion of how the parables get linked together and show up in politics as specific programs. How is this allocation of space related to the author's thesis and purpose for writing?

3. Reich uses examples that range from early American history to current times in discussing the four parables. How is the point he is making in the essay strengthened by this wide range of examples? Why should he need to use such a wide range of examples to support his assertion?

4. Does the writer in any way reveal his own political leanings? What evidence can you give for your answer?

5. *Serpico*, *Chinatown*, *Rocky*, *Dirty Harry*, *Death Wish*, and *Rambo* are some of the movies referred to in this essay. What makes movies an excellent choice to use as the source for the examples in this essay?

INQUIRY READING

Questions on What the Writer Meant

(*Language, Concepts, Distinctions*)

1. What is a parable? What other parables do you know? What is the purpose of parables?

2. What does a reader miss if she or he does not know references such as these?

> muckrakers like Upton Sinclair and Ida Tarbell
> Aaron Copland's music
> Frank Capra's films
> Keynesian management of the economy

3. How was Lyndon Johnson's War on Poverty related to the concept of the Benign Community?

4. Look at a current edition of your local newspaper. What stories can you find there that embody the concepts of the four parables in this essay? What is the "version" of the parable that these local stories tell?

THE LARGER PICTURE

Questions to Consider

1. If you were asked to talk about the author of this essay, based only on having read the essay, what would you say about him?

2. Does any member of your family tell stories about daily life which are similar to the four parables discussed in this essay? What purpose do

these stories serve? Do you always know the "end of the story" almost as soon as the person begins? Do the stories *ever* change? Do they link up in new ways over the years the way Reich describes the political parables linking up in new ways as time passes?

YOUR OWN WRITING POSSIBILITIES

1. Think of a relative or a friend who has a set of stories he or she is always telling. The characters may change, but the stories stay the same. (Example: Story—I'm the persecuted one. Characters change over the years—my parents persecuted me; my teachers persecuted me; now my boss is persecuting me.) Write an essay in which you identify these stories told by your relative and show their importance. Discuss what value these stories have to the teller. What kind of clues about the relative's life do the stories contain? Imagine an audience for your essay similar to Robert Reich's: the general reading public.
2. Write a fantasy in which you describe the version of the four parables that the American public will be telling in the year 2050. Imagine that your audience are readers of a popular science fiction magazine or a magazine like *Omni*.
3. From the movies that Robert Reich mentions in this essay, choose one you have seen. (See question 5 under Constructive Reading.) Write an essay in which you discuss how the movie illustrates the parable. How does the story in the movie relate to life? Imagine your professor as the audience for this essay. Remember that the professor shares the same background as you in one respect—he or she has read the same essay. Remember also that the professor wants to be stimulated and informed by what you have to say.

Talk to the Animals, page 193

PARTICIPATORY READING

Questions on What the Writer Said

(*Content, Purpose, Viewpoint*)

1. What is the author's viewpoint on the possibility of dolphins and human beings communicating? How is that viewpoint revealed?
2. What does the closing paragraph of this essay reveal about Kevin Strehlo's viewpoint?
3. How is dolphin speech made?
4. What problems are still to be solved before communication between dolphins and human beings can be more advanced?

CONSTRUCTIVE READING

Questions on How the Writer Wrote

(*Choices, Strategies, Style*)

1. Kevin Strehlo reports on a particular experiment led by Dr. John Lilly—yet the essay is more than a report. How has the writer accomplished writing something more than a report? What has the writer done to provide a context or frame for the information about the Lilly work?
2. Is the author's choice of title appropriate for this essay? What does the title add to the essay? What else does the title make you think of?
3. Look at the opening and closing of this essay. They are not about the experiment itself. What is the "subject" of these opening and closing paragraphs? What does Strehlo gain by choosing to open and close the essay the way he does?
4. This essay first appeared in *Popular Computing* magazine, yet it is of interest to people who know nothing about computers. What did Strehlo do as a writer that resulted in the essay being appropriate for both the computer magazine and the non-computer-expert?
5. The thesis in this essay is a mild, gentle, and suggestive one, not a firm or strong assertion. How would you word Strehlo's thesis? What makes the author's decision to use a suggestive thesis rather than a firm thesis a good one?

INQUIRY READING

Questions on What the Writer Meant

(*Language, Concepts, Distinctions*)

1. Who in ancient times was Janus? For what reasons is Janus an appropriate name for the computer system being used in the Lilly experiment? What would readers miss if they didn't know who Janus was?
2. What is a vocoder?
3. What does Strehlo do to make complex scientific information clear in this essay? Give specific examples from the essay.
4. A report from the National Zoological Park's Symposium on Animal Intelligence said that dolphins do have interchanges that can be categorized as (1) aggressive (the dolphin claps its jaw and blows air explosively), (2) calling (the dolphin makes loud whistles), and (3) transition (the dolphin makes sounds while resting in the tank). The researcher said about these sounds: "Dolphin vocalizations are not random sounds, but do indeed add up to an interaction having specific patterns. But whether or not it's a language remains to be seen."

   What is the difference between interactions that have specific patterns and interactions that are language?

THE LARGER PICTURE

Questions to Consider

1. Were you convinced by this essay? What was the most convincing evidence for you?
2. What surprised you?
3. Dolphins have been revered as sacred animals since ancient times. What relationship between current research on dolphin communication and the ancient idea that dolphins are sacred animals can you see?
4. A few days after the seven astronauts were killed in the *Challenger* accident, NASA held a special memorial service. As part of this memorial service, one of the administrators went up in a plane and dropped a wreath of flowers out over the ocean a few hundred yards from land. The *New York Times* reported on the memorial service, and the report contained this intriguing information: at the exact time the wreath was dropped into the water a school of dolphin vaulted into the air in a single formation, arching up into the sky and entering the water below in unison. In light of this essay, what explanation might you offer for this unusual happening?

YOUR OWN WRITING POSSIBILITIES

1. Write a persuasive essay in which you attempt to convince a friend who does not believe in dolphin/human communication that such is possible.
2. Imagine that you have been hired as a writer for the television program, "Amazing Stories." Write the script for a story about dolphins and humans communicating in a time of crisis.
3. Imagine a dialogue between two dolphins after they return to their tank following one of the scientist's experiments. Write the conversation these dolphins might have.
4. Turn "Talk to the Animals" into a technical report. Using the facts and information in the essay, write a report on the Lilly experiment. Imagine that you work for an oceanographic research company, and you are writing this report for your boss.

How to be Creative in Modern Industry, page 201

PARTICIPATORY READING

Questions on What the Writer Said

(*Content, Purpose, Viewpoint*)

1. What makes teamwork central to creativity in industry today?
2. What does the availability of global communications contribute to creativity in industry today?
3. Why is the example of putting men on the moon a most appropriate one for Morita to use in this essay?
4. How does Morita say technology is related to creativity?

CONSTRUCTIVE READING

Questions on How the Writer Wrote

(*Choices, Strategies, Style*)

1. Akio Morita gives only one example from the experience of his own company, Sony, in this essay. What does he gain by limiting the examples he could have used from Sony? What does he lose?
2. What is the author's thesis? Where do you find it in the essay?
3. Although the "bones"—the structure—of this essay are easy to see, the essay is not a "cut and dried" piece of writing sounding as if it were written by formula. What produces for the reader the sense that a human being wrote this piece, not a robot?

INQUIRY READING

Questions on What the Writer Meant

(*Language, Concepts, Distinctions*)

1. What is the importance of setting goals as a way to increase creativity? Don't those two concepts seem to contradict themselves—goal setting and being creative? Isn't goal setting structured and creativity spontaneous? Explain what keeps the two concepts from contradicting themselves.
2. How does the author define creativity? Where do you find the definition(s) in the essay?
3. Discuss the relationship between the concept of goal setting as Morita uses it in the moon example and the concept of commitment. How are the two the same? How are they different?
4. The title of this essay suggests that the piece is a "how-to" essay. In one sense of the word, it is, and in another sense of the word, the essay does not show "how-to." Discuss these two uses of the term "how-to" essay.
5. Collaboration is a key concept in Morita's thinking. What is collaboration, in his sense of the term?

THE LARGER PICTURE

Questions to Consider

1. Why is Akio Morita an excellent choice to write an essay on creativity in modern industry?
2. Reread the commentary on this essay. How does Morita's own life exemplify creativity?

YOUR OWN WRITING POSSIBILITIES

1. Choose a company or a person you know who exemplifies the kind of creativity Morita talks about in this essay. Write an information essay about this company or person in which you explain how creativity shows up in the products of the company or the work of the person. Imagine as your audience readers similar to Morita's audience: people who buy and read *Omni* magazine.
2. Choose two people you know, one who is extremely creative and one who is not creative. Write an essay in which you compare these two people—compare things like their attitudes, their ways of working, their leisure activities, their choice of friends, their reading habits, and anything else you think relates to the presence or absence of creativity. Be certain the essay includes a thesis which is your own definition of what produces creativity. Write this essay for anyone who is interested in being more creative. Imagine that the essay is going to be published in a magazine like *Reader's Digest* or in a company newsletter.
3. Make as extensive a list as possible of the ways in which you are creative. Write this list in your journal, if you keep one. Follow the list with a short discussion of any insights you had about your own commitment to being creative as you read and studied Morita's essay.

Right and Wrong, page 206

PARTICIPATORY READING

Questions on What the Writer Said

(*Content, Purpose, Viewpoint*)

1. Science is often seen as being exact or precise, but K. C. Cole shows how the line between right and wrong is blurred in science. What does she say?
2. Why should all scientific tenets be accepted more tentatively than many people hold them?
3. According to Cole, Einstein proved Newton wrong only in what way?
4. What do Austrian railroad timetables have to do with the points made in this essay?

CONSTRUCTIVE READING

Questions on How the Writer Wrote

(*Choices, Strategies, Style*)

1. K. C. Cole has been praised for her ability to make scientific discussion clear to a nonexpert reader. Identify at least three things that she does in this essay that contribute to the information being accessible to everyone, nonscientific reader and scientific reader alike.
2. What is Cole's thesis? Where is the clearest articulation of this thesis in the essay? What does the author gain by locating her thesis where she does in the essay?
3. Several times in the essay Cole talks about her son. What might be her strategy in including these personal stories and references?
4. Cole is very "present" in this essay: not only does she talk about her son, but she also tells about being in a junior high school class talking to students and about being in an elementary school talking to the teacher. What keeps the essay from being *about* K. C. Cole, even though these personal references are included?
5. The student's question, "But what if Einstein was wrong?" sets up the entire essay. Why was using this question a brilliant choice on Cole's part?
6. Cole quotes many people in this essay. Reread several of these quotes and notice how she makes the transitions from her own voice to the quoted voices and how she integrates the quotes within her essay. Discuss the transitions and integration with your classmates.

INQUIRY READING

Questions on What the Writer Meant

(*Language, Concepts, Distinctions*)

1. K. C. Cole says, " 'Wrong' more nearly means 'limited.' " What is the customary definition of "wrong," and how does the author's definition differ?
2. How does the author redefine "right"? What makes this a redefinition?
3. Cole refers to Ernest Rutherford's idea that people "talk moonshine." What does "talk moonshine" mean?
4. How can something be "righter" than something else?
5. Cole says, "categorizing ideas as clearly right or wrong may not be scientifically useful, but *philosophically* it is immensely appealing. No one likes to be left in intellectual purgatory." What is the distinction she is making between science and philosophy?

6. Cole uses vivid imagery such as, "Einstein climbed the tower of Newton's scaffolding and saw things from a better perspective." Find other examples of vivid imagery and discuss how they contribute to the effectiveness of the essay.

THE LARGER PICTURE

Questions to Consider

1. How were your own definitions of right and wrong altered or expanded by reading K. C. Cole's essay?
2. How can science be so exact and so tentative at the same time?
3. Recently a scientist discovered that the number which has been used for decades as the accurate speed of sound was wrong. What effect will this new information have on scientists?

YOUR OWN WRITING POSSIBILITIES

1. Choose one of these quotations from Cole's essays:

   New ideas expand, generalize, refine, hone, and modify old ideas—but rarely do they throw them out the window.

   Laughing over other people's wrongs comes largely from taking what we know for granted.

   Some ideas are righter than others.

   Right ideas are seeds that flower into righter ideas, whereas wrong ideas are often sterile and do not bear fruit.

   Right ideas are stepping stones.

   Right ideas . . . do not imply 100 percent accuracy.

   In the end, the importance of being wrong is greater than one might think—because a well-thought-out wrong idea serves as a basis of comparison, a springing-off point, for right ideas.

   a. Spend fifteen to twenty minutes exploring what you think about the quotation you have chosen by using *focused writing*. (During this time you are not writing for anyone else; you are writing only to "think on paper" about the quotation for yourself.)
   b. After you have completed your focused writing on the quotation, write a short personal perspective/personal opinion essay in which you give your opinion on the quotation. Imagine that your essay will appear on the editorial page of your local newspaper, in your company's newsletter, in a column such as "My Turn" in *Newsweek*—any place that is likely to publish a personal perspective/personal opinion essay.

2. Write about a time you were wrong but being wrong actually led you to being right. Share this personal experience with a classmate, a friend, or a member of your family.

3. Picture *the* person you know who would be most likely to refuse to accept anything K. C. Cole has had to say about the concepts of "right" and "wrong." Write a persuasion essay in which you attempt to convince this person that Cole's definitions and discussion of "right" and "wrong" are useful and valuable.

4. Write a letter of argument addressed to Cole. In this letter, take issue and disagree with what she had to say in the essay.

Making Money: Taking a Risk, page 220

PARTICIPATORY READING

Questions on What the Writer Said

(*Content, Purpose, Viewpoint*)

1. Most people probably do not share the same viewpoint about worry as this author does. What is the common attitude about worry and how does it differ from the attitude recommended in this essay?

2. How would you depict the writer's philosophy of life?

3. Do you know a Sober Sylvia or a Mad Mary? (The person might be male or female.) Discuss the attitudes and actions of these individuals with your classmates. What do you think is the explanation for the much larger number of Sober Sylvias in the world as contrasted to the number of Mad Marys?

CONSTRUCTIVE READING

Questions on How the Writer Wrote

(*Choices, Strategies, Style*)

1. Max Gunther uses personal anecdote to back up his assertion. What makes this technique effective? What are the weaknesses of personal anecdote as evidence to back up an assertion? Why was personal anecdote most likely the best kind of backup Gunther could have used in this writing situation?

2. What is Gunther's thesis? Where does it appear most clearly stated in the essay?

3. Discuss the effectiveness of the form of this essay—the statement of an axiom followed by discussion—in developing the point Gunther was making.

4. What does Gunther do in this essay to convince the reader to accept his statement that adventure is what makes life worth living?
5. Following the statement of the axiom that opens this essay, Gunther introduces Sober Sylvia and Mad Mary. He gives their personal stories for a few paragraphs and then inserts discussion. Following this discussion he returns to Mary and Sylvia. Then he closes the essay with a return to the axiom. What does he gain by the choice he made to "embed" his discussion in the context of the personal anecdote?

INQUIRY READING

Questions on What the Writer Meant

(*Language, Concepts, Distinctions*)

1. Gunther contrasts the ordinary attitude toward worry with the philosophy about worry behind the Zurich Axioms. How do these two concepts about worry differ? Does one appeal to you more than the other? What are the disadvantages of each? the advantages?
2. What is an axiom? How does it differ from an assertion?
3. *Adventure* and *risk-taking* are two other concepts Gunther discusses in this essay. What does he have to say about each?

THE LARGER PICTURE

Questions to Consider

1. Is anything missing in Gunther's argument? If so, what? If not, explain your answer.
2. Gunther uses the example of athletics to illustrate that worry is desirable. He says that sports is a case of carefully created risks and that people wouldn't attend sporting events if they did not get satisfaction out of worrying. How does the difference between being a participant in a sports event and being a spectator relate to Gunther's point?
3. The book from which this essay came, *The Zurich Axioms: Investment Secrets of the Swiss Bankers*, was excerpted when it first came out in *Inc* magazine, a publication for entrepreneurs and independent business owners. Why was that magazine a good place for the book's excerpts to appear?

YOUR OWN WRITING POSSIBILITIES

1. Argue for and argue against Gunther's thesis. Write for ten minutes taking the pro side of the argument, and then write for ten minutes taking the con side.

When you have completed this "thinking on paper," write a persuasive or argumentative essay in which you try to convince your readers that Gunther is right or that he is wrong (or both). As part of your essay, recognize and refute some of the assertions of the other side. Imagine that your audience is a classmate who holds exactly the opposite opinion from yours. Let some of your classmates read your essay and tell you how persuasive and convincing you are.

2. Write "another side of the story." Imagine that you are Sober Sylvia. Write a letter from Sober Sylvia to Max Gunther in which she tells him things he has never known about her life and her attitude toward money.

3. Choose one of these assertions from the essay:

> Worry . . . is the hot and tart sauce of life. Once you get used to it, you enjoy it.

> If your main goal in life is to escape worry, you are going to stay poor.

> Life ought to be an adventure, not a vegetation. An adventure may be defined as an episode in which you face some kind of jeopardy and try to overcome it.

> Worry is an integral part of life's grandest enjoyments.

Write an essay in which you agree with or disagree with the quotation. Imagine that the essay will be printed on the editorial page of your local newspaper.

4. Write a review of this chapter, as if you were a book reviewer for the local newspaper. Imagine that the review will be published on the "New Books" page in next Sunday's paper.

I Want to be Alone, page 229

PARTICIPATORY READING

Questions on What the Writer Said

(*Content, Purpose, Viewpoint*)

1. Identify statements the author made in this essay that you are surprised he was willing to let appear in print. What risks did the writer take to say what he did?
2. How would you describe Lawrence Wright's attitude toward the Women's Rights Movement?
3. What dilemma is at the heart of the situation this essay discusses?

CONSTRUCTIVE READING

Questions on How the Writer Wrote

(*Choices, Strategies, Style*)

1. You don't know Lawrence Wright. He has written a very personal essay. What has he done as a writer that allows this essay to be interesting to his readers who are strangers to him?
2. The author uses a form of chronological narrative as the structure for his essay. What makes this a wise choice? How does he vary this chronological narrative? What is the benefit of these variations when they appear?
3. How does Wright incorporate flashback into this essay?
4. Discuss the appropriateness of the title of this essay.
5. Where is Wright's thesis located in the essay?

INQUIRY READING

Questions on What the Writer Meant

(*Language, Concepts, Distinctions*)

1. To what is Wright referring when he says, "I began to feel like Hercules . . . it was a job I would like to hand back to Atlas"?
2. What do you need to know to understand this reference: "I look upon those days the way Englishmen must remember the British Empire"?
3. What do readers miss if they don't know what a Steig cartoon is?
4. Wright uses vivid imagery throughout the essay—such as, "it's like swimming with rocks in my pockets." Find at least four other examples of vivid imagery and discuss the contribution the imagery makes to the effectiveness of the essay.
5. "The stoicism of that gesture made me approach her respectfully." What does this line mean?
6. "That was a rueful discovery to make about myself." What is a *rueful* discovery? Why was this discovery rueful to Wright?

THE LARGER PICTURE

Questions to Consider

1. Although this is a personal experience essay, its theme is about much larger societal issues. What are these issues?
2. Could this essay have been written in any century earlier than the twentieth?
3. Is this essay particularly "American" in its dilemma and conflict?
4. In one sense this essay is about an age-old dilemma. In another sense, it's about a very modern dilemma. Discuss both of these dilemmas.

YOUR OWN WRITING POSSIBILITIES

1. Lawrence Wright quotes Francis Bacon:

> He that hath wife and children hath given hostages to fortune, for they are impediments to great enterprises, either of virtue or mischief.

   Write a personal viewpoint essay in which you discuss this quotation. Imagine that your audience will be the readers of E*squire* or M magazines. (M is a magazine with men as its targeted audience.)
2. Write a personal viewpoint essay on the above quotation, with the readers of M*s.* magazine as your audience.
3. Write a companion essay called "I Also Want to Be Alone." Let the voice in the essay be Lawrence Wright's wife, Roberta.
4. This essay appeared in *Texas Monthly* magazine. Imagine that you are one of Wright's children—either Gordon or Caroline—and you have been interviewed by a member of the magazine's editorial staff to give your opinion on what your father said in his essay. Write the response you would give the reporter.
5. Imagine that you are one of Wright's children—Gordon oCaroline. Write a letter to your father after reading his essay.

QUESTIONS AND WRITING POSSIBILITIES

Thesis as a Characteristic of Good Writing

1. What does a thesis provide for a piece of writing?
2. Is it ever possible for a thesis not to be present in a piece of writing but be "understood"? Discuss.
3. Someone has said that all good essays are more than the sum of their parts—they are more than just the thesis and its support. Discuss this statement.
4. Any writer who feels a sense of responsibility to her or his reader thinks about thesis before presenting the piece of writing as communication to others. How, then, is it an act of irresponsibility and thoughtlessness not to think about a thesis before you give your writing to others to read?
5. In the selections in this section, we have seen a thesis at the beginning of the essay, in the middle, and at the end. We have seen a thesis repeated in various places in the essay.

   Think about the usual way you write. Do you almost always place your thesis at the beginning of the essay? Write an essay in which you deliberately locate your thesis somewhere new. Experiment with a different form that results in the thesis appearing somewhere other than the place you usually put it.

READING

to Learn to Write

Form

Traditional Form
Narration/Description

A Snake in the Studio, page 244

A Snake in the Studio, page 244

PARTICIPATORY READING

Questions on What the Writer Said

(*Content, Purpose, Viewpoint*)

1. What is the writer's viewpoint toward snakes?
2. What is the writer's purpose in sharing this experience with readers?

CONSTRUCTIVE READING

Questions on How the Writer Wrote

(*Choices, Strategies, Style*)

1. The writer chooses to include in her essay a guess about where the snake came from. Since the predominate structure of the essay is a moment-by-moment account of the snake being in the studio, the choice to include the explanation about where the snake might have come from had to be deliberate. What is gained by including this explanation? Would such an explanation have been missed if it were not there? Does the explanation interfere with the flow of the narrative?
2. Part of the "story" in this essay is a description of an external fact—the snake; part of the "story" in the essay is a description/discussion of an internal situation—the writer's emotions. How does she integrate these two "stories"?
3. Among the many vivid images that heighten the senses when we read this essay is a reference to the Virginia Woolf books on the bookshelf. What is added to the essay by this image?
4. What do you suppose determined the details that the writer chose to

include? She includes, for instance, the red and white electrical cord, but she does not include a description of a window. How arbitrary are the choices a writer makes for what to include and what not to include? What would be one of the strongest determiners of what gets included and what doesn't?

5. The writer says at the end of the essay, "and the snake flowed steadily across the old wooden sill and out into the light and the shocking heat." Shocking to whom?

6. The writer sequences her details unusually; i e., she describes the color of the snake toward the end, while in most narrative/descriptive essays, this information would come first. What is the effect of her sequencing?

7. There are many "layers" of time in this essay. There is present time—when the snake is in the studio. There is past time—when the writer has been in an earthquake earlier, when the snake's home had been disturbed. There is even hypothetical time—"snakes could teach something to actors, I think." How does the writer incorporate all three uses of time without jolting the reader?

8. The writer not only uses her own voice, but she writes as if she knows the thoughts of the snake: "All is intact, the length of me is unhurt and alive." "Be still." She says of the snake: "It had clearly got over its original fright and deduced that it *could* get out, because it had got *in*."

    What does the writer achieve by speaking the snake's voice as well as her own? Does using this writing strategy turn the event into fiction?

INQUIRY READING

Questions on What the Writer Meant

(*Language, Concepts, Distinctions*)

1. What does the writer mean when she says, "the snake curved along the wall by the door with a movement like pouring—only a horizontal pouring, an asymmetrical, rapt progress."?

2. What is "minnowlike precision"?

3. Use your knowledge of the way a snake moves to explain these words: "many infinitely fine readjustments of aim, reversals, and slantwise investigations."

4. What is gained by the reader knowing the meaning of this phrase, "the snake . . . no longer [seemed] quite so surrealistically regal."

5. Choose six images and/or examples of vivid language that you would insist the essay could *not* do without. What is the rationale for your choices?

THE LARGER PICTURE

Questions to Consider

1. Is this essay nonfiction or fiction? Explain your answer.
2. If you were asked to describe this writer and you only knew about her because you had read this essay, what would you say about her?
3. This essay is about a personal experience. What makes it interesting (and valuable) to readers who do not know the writer?

YOUR OWN WRITING POSSIBILITIES

1. Choose an incident from your own life that contained surprise, fright, and resolution. Write an essay about this incident, modeled after "A Snake in the Studio." Remember that the key to powerful narrative/descriptive writing is vivid imagery. Be generous with words of the senses. Imagine a similar audience for your piece—the general reading public.
2. Imagine that you were the snake. Write the essay that the snake would have written about being in this studio.
3. Write a journal entry or thinking-on-paper piece of writing exploring what you would have done if you had been in the studio instead of this writer.

Traditional Form

Classification

Thirteen Ways of Looking at the Masters, page 249

PARTICIPATORY READING

Questions on What the Writer Said

(*Content, Purpose, Viewpoint*)

1. Even though this essay is about a "light subject," there are hints in the writing that John Updike is an intellectual man. Where are some of these clues?
2. Can you tell from reading this essay whether or not the author likes golf? Please substantiate your answer.
3. Make a list of ten new facts you learned about golf and/or the Masters by reading this essay.
4. Which of Updike's thirteen ways of looking at the Masters surprised you the most? Which interested you the most? Which stimulated your thinking the most?

5. Were you aware, after reading just the title, that this essay would be about golf? What other interpretations of the title are possible?

CONSTRUCTIVE READING

Questions on How the Writer Wrote

(*Choices, Strategies, Style*)

1. Imagine this scene: Updike is at the Masters with his wife. He takes notes during the tournament, perhaps after he has gone back to the house where he was staying, perhaps while he is on the course. He sits down to write an essay based on his notes.

   What makes the traditional form which he chose—classification—an excellent choice? What are the limitations of this form? What does this form enable him to do that other forms would not?
2. The thirteen categories contain some surprises. Which ones do you find unusual or unexpected?
3. What is the effect of Updike's choosing "As a Religious Experience" as the last category in the essay?
4. Could the thirteen categories be put in any other order and the essay be as effective? Explain your answer.
5. Updike chose thirteen categories. Are these the only thirteen possible categories with which the Masters could be described? Can you think of some others?

INQUIRY READING

Questions on What the Writer Meant

(*Language, Concepts, Distinctions*)

1. What does a reader gain by knowing what Updike meant by "unpainted dwellings out of illustrations to Joel Chandler Harris"?
2. What do you miss if you don't know the meaning of the French words in this phrase, "and barefoot *jeunes filles en fleurs*?
3. Talking about Arnold Palmer, Updike calls him "every inch an agonist." What does he mean?
4. If you had to make up one word to represent the sound of a golf ball hitting a person's head, what would that word be? What word does Updike use? How appropriate do you find that word?
5. To what is Updike referring when he says, "but the unified field, as Einstein discovered in a more general connection, is unapprehendable"?
6. What is the meaning of this sentence: "The other sad truth about golf spectatorship is that for today's pros it all comes down to the putting,

and that the difference between a putt that drops and one that rims the cup, though teleologically enormous, is intellectually negligible."

7. To what is Updike referring when he says, "Sneed's fate seemed sealed then: the eighteenth hole, a famous bogey-maker, waited for him as ineluctably as Romeo's missed appointment with Juliet"?

8. This essay has no introduction and no conclusion. Does it need them? Discuss.

THE LARGER PICTURE

Questions to Consider

1. This essay first appeared in *Golf* magazine. Updike has managed to write an essay that was appropriate for that periodical and which is also interesting to non-golfers. What is his secret?

2. At any time when you were reading the essay, did you want to be at the Masters? If so, at what point in the essay were you most enticed to want to attend?

YOUR OWN WRITING POSSIBILITIES

1. Make a list of thirteen (or six or ten or whatever number you choose) ways you could look at the Super Bowl, the Kentucky Derby, the Indy 500, Wimbledon, the World Series, or some other sporting event you have attended. If you have not attended a major sporting event such as these mentioned, choose a high school or college football game, track or swim meet, or even a high school senior prom.

   Write an essay about this event, using the ways of looking at it as the form for your essay. Imagine that your essay will be published in a magazine highlighting the particular event about which you are writing.

2. Make a list of thirteen ways you would look at your parents. Put this list in your journal.

3. Choose a problem with which you are currently grappling. Make a list of thirteen ways to look at this problem. Share the list with someone who knows about—or will care about—the problem's resolution.

4. Imagine that your hometown (state/country) is going to be featured in a travel magazine with circulation across the United States.

   Write a classification essay describing a number of ways to look at your hometown (state/country). Have as your purpose in writing to entice people to want to visit the place.

   You may use the Updike model for this essay, but please include an introduction and a conclusion in your essay, even though Updike does not. The introduction and conclusion are needed to pull your reader into the subject matter. You may not have an immediately receptive audience, such as Updike could reasonably expect of the readers of *Golf* magazine. Hence, you need the introduction and conclusion.

Traditional Form

Process

How to Bake on a Boat, page 261

PARTICIPATORY READING

Questions on What the Writer Said

(*Content, Purpose, Viewpoint*)

1. What makes this essay interesting to someone who has never even been on a boat?
2. What are some of the unusual instructions Sue Lucksted has to include in the recipe for yeast bread since the bread is going to be made on a boat?
3. What questions were you left with after you read this essay?

CONSTRUCTIVE READING

Questions on How the Writer Wrote

(*Choices, Strategies, Style*)

1. How does the author establish her relationship with you, the reader? How would you describe this relationship?
2. What do you know about the writer from reading this essay?
3. What do the recipes add to the article? Why do you suppose the author included them? What do the drawings add? Are they necessary?
4. What make the beginning and the ending of this essay effective?

INQUIRY READING

Questions on What the Writer Meant

(*Language, Concepts, Distinctions*)

1. What is the meaning of "O fair galley slave"? To what does this phrase allude?
2. What are flame tamers?
3. What does "your 'one burner'" refer to?

THE LARGER PICTURE

Questions to Consider

1. What other abilities or skills, in addition to cooking, would someone need to follow the writer's instructions in this essay?
2. What kind of person would think about baking on a boat?
3. Someone reading an early draft of this book said that he would buy the whole book just because of this one essay, "How to Bake on a Boat." What about the essay do you suppose made the reviewer feel the way he did?

YOUR OWN WRITING POSSIBILITIES

1. Choose a process with which you are very familiar, such as making bread, cooking chili, making and pouring cement, training a dog, or any other process that you know or can learn a lot about.

    First, make a list of the steps in this process.

    Then write an essay on this process. Provide a context for discussing the process that will capture the reader's interest.

    Consider your audience a friend, another student, your professor, or the general reading public. And remember that your readers are busy, so they will not continue to read something that does not give them value. Be certain that your intention is to make a contribution to your readers' understanding and knowledge with this essay.
2. On greeting cards you sometimes find directions for achieving an intangible result—such as sustaining family unity—which have been written as a process to be followed. For instance, the greeting card might read, "To Achieve Family Unity . . . Take two committed parents, add a respectful yet individual child, spice with outings to the beach and camping trips into the mountains. . . ."

    Using the traditional form of the process essay, write directions or instructions for accomplishing an intangible result—such as staying in love, earning an adult's respect, being promotable on the job, etc. Enjoy the "tension" between using a traditional form usually used for tangible results—explaining the steps in a process—for talking about intangible results.

    Consider your audience the general public who buys greeting cards.
3. Choose a scientific or technical process that would be unfamiliar to most readers and write an essay in which you explain how this process happens. Commit yourself to explaining this process clearly and to interesting your readers. Imagine your audience to be similar to the audience for "How to Bake on a Boat"—the general reading public.

A *New Definition of a Cowboy,* page 268

PARTICIPATORY READING

Questions on What the Writer Said

(*Content, Purpose, Viewpoint*)

1. What relationship did Gretel Ehrlich draw between southern gentle-men and cowboys in Wyoming?
2. What stimulated the writer to give a new definition of cowboys?
3. What are the circumstances under which cowboys work—the true circumstances as contrasted to the "movie" circumstances?
4. What explains the viewpoint Gretel Ehrlich takes toward cowboys?

CONSTRUCTIVE READING

Questions on How the Writer Wrote

(*Choices, Strategies, Style*)

1. Reread the essay's introduction. This introduction reveals several very important things that aid Gretel Ehrlich in achieving her overall purpose in the essay. What does the introduction reveal?
2. How is the writer present in the essay? How does the writer's presence contribute to the definition she is giving? How does it interfere?
3. This essay is an excellent example of mixing general statements with specific examples to back up the general statements. Find such a combination—general statement/specific example—and discuss with your classmates how the writer balances the general and the specific.
4. Ehrlich incorporates quotations sparingly but powerfully. Find a place in the essay where she has used a quotation. What does this quotation placed at this spot contribute to the effectiveness of the essay?
5. Often the purpose of a definition essay is to dispel common beliefs about someone or something. In what way does this essay challenge the common beliefs about cowboys?

INQUIRY READING

Questions on What the Writer Meant

(*Language, Concepts, Distinctions*)

1. Gretel Ehrlich uses this essay not only to redefine the cowboy but also to redefine many other common concepts that are related: "strong and silent," "rides off into the sunset," "being tough on the ranch," "man's

man." Discuss each of these concepts, first articulating the generally accepted meaning of the phrase and then giving the writer's reinterpretation of the phrase.

2. The writer says, "If he's gruff, handsome, and physically fit, he's androgynous at the core." What does *androgynous* mean?
3. Ehrlich refers to the "iconic myth." What is an iconic myth?
4. Describing a cowboy, the writer says, "Their lips pucker up, not with kisses but with immutability." What does this sentence mean?

THE LARGER PICTURE
Questions to Consider

1. How is this an essay about conceptions of men in general, not just cowboys?
2. How would one of the cowboys in Wyoming about whom the author writes respond to this essay?
3. Is this an essay likely to bring people together or divide them?
4. What other occupations have similar characteristics to the occupation of being a cowboy?
5. What does this quotation mean: "No one is as fragile as a woman but no one is as fragile as a man."

YOUR OWN WRITING POSSIBILITIES

1. Choose an occupation about which you think most people hold a stereotypical view but which you see another way. Perhaps it is the occupation of minister, teacher, doctor, parent, automobile mechanic, law enforcement officer, judge, lawyer, computer operator. . . .

   Write an essay in which you redefine this occupation, using your own experience as the background for what you have to say. Imagine that your audience is similar to the audience for "A New Definition of a Cowboy," the general reading public.
2. Write a personal viewpoint essay in which you explore the cost of stereotypical thinking to male and female relationships. Choose as your audience those people who read *Cosmopolitan* and *Esquire* magazines.
3. Write an essay in which you draw a character sketch of someone you know who is not a cowboy but who fits the definition of a cowboy that Gretel Ehrlich gives here.

   Choose as your audience your classmates and professor.
4. Choose one of the following quotations and write a "thinking-on-paper" piece of writing, exploring what this quotation means to you. You might want to put the "thinking-on-paper" piece in your journal or share it with a friend.

After you have thought on paper about the quotation, you can use the quotation as the basis for an essay with an audience similar to Ehrlich's, if you wish.

Cowboys are just like a pile of rocks—everything happens to them. They get climbed on, kicked, rained and snowed on, scuffed up by wind. Their job is to just "take it."

No one is as fragile as a woman but no one is as fragile as a man.

I feel as if I'd sprained my heart.

Traditional Form
Cause and Effect

The Thucydides Syndrome, page 273

PARTICIPATORY READING
Questions on What the Writer Said

(*Content, Purpose, Viewpoint*)

1. In some ways this article about a medical subject reminds the reader of a detective story. How?
2. On what specific evidence do the writers base their hypothesis that the plague in Athens is similar to modern toxic shock syndrome (most often associated with women's use of tampons)?
3. Why do these doctors think that the Thucydides syndrome may not be extinct?
4. What is the specific anatomical diagnosis the doctors make of the Thucydides syndrome?
5. What do the writers recommend in their final paragraph? Is there anything surprising to you about this recommendation?

CONSTRUCTIVE READING
Questions on How the Writer Wrote

(*Choices, Strategies, Style*)

1. The writers were required in this article to integrate world history, medical history, and current medical diagnosis and discussion. Choose one section of the essay that contains all three elements and discuss how the writers achieved the integration.
2. What makes the opening of the essay effective?
3. The conclusion of the essay is not about the Thucydides syndrome

itself. What are the writers attempting to do in this conclusion? Is it an appropriate conclusion? Why?

4. Where in the essay do the writers state most clearly their thesis?
5. What evidence do the writers give to support their thesis? Where does this appear in the essay?
6. The form of this essay is cause and effect. The essay begins with the effect and leads to the cause. Would the essay have been as effective if the writers had begun with the cause and led up to the effect? Could they have arranged the essay this way if they had wanted to?

INQUIRY READING

Questions on What the Writer Meant

(*Language, Concepts, Distinctions*)

1. Many medical words appear in this essay, like *gross lymphadenopathy, hemorrhagic diathesis, acute toxic gastroenteropathy, bullous impetigo, damaged respiratory mucosa, impetiginous skin lesions,* and so on.

   Discuss whether it is necessary to know the meanings of words like these to get the meaning of the essay.
2. The writers say: "This constellation of symptoms, findings, and clinical course is so vivid that we propose it be termed the Thucydides syndrome."

   What usefulness would such a new term serve for the medical profession? What would it take for the term to become part of the "language" of the medical profession?
3. Read the following sentence: "In the interest of economy of space, we condense . . . the most meaningful epidemiologic features of Thucydides' account."

   What will the readers miss if they do not know the meaning of "epidemiologic features"? What considerations determine whether or not readers need to know the meaning of an unfamiliar word?
4. In this sentence, "In seeking a specific pathogenesis for the Thucydides syndrome . . . ," what does *pathogenesis* mean?
5. In medical terms, what is a syndrome? What distinguishes it from a disease or a disorder?

THE LARGER PICTURE

Questions to Consider

1. What did you learn from reading this essay, in addition to the authors' hypothesis about the cause of the Athens plague?
2. There are five authors for this essay. Discuss with your classmates the challenges that must have been present for five people to collaborate on one piece of writing. How is having multiple authors valuable as well as challenging?

3. Even though it first appeared in a medical journal, this essay was reported on and summarized in the *New York Times*, which does not ordinarily report on medical articles. Why do you think the *Times* considered this news?

YOUR OWN WRITING POSSIBILITIES

1. The writers of this essay saw a problem in their profession that intrigued them and then studied it. While your "profession" may not be medicine, you do know about problems around you—and you very likely have some opinions (or evidence) of the cause of these problems or the effect of a problem.

   For instance, there is the problem of decline in church attendance. Do you have an informed opinion or information on the cause? Do you have strong feelings about the possible effect?

   Or consider the problem of parents and young people being at odds with each other. Do you know something about the cause? the effect?

   Perhaps racoons are attacking the wooden roofs of houses in your neighborhood and you know something about why racoons do that. You also know what the effect will be if the racoons are not stopped.

   And there are many other areas about which you know. Choose a problem and write a cause-and-effect essay in such a way that your local newspaper would consider it news and report on it.
2. Write a short paper on how this essay, "The Thycydides Syndrome," is useful as history. Consider your professor the audience for your essay.
3. A biblical prophet once said: "There is nothing new under the sun." Apply this quotation to the essay on Thucydides syndrome and do some "thinking-on-paper" about the implications of putting the quote and the essay together. Discuss your thinking with your classmates.

Traditional Form
Analogy

The Language of Clothes, page 284

PARTICIPATORY READING
Questions on What the Writer Said
(*Content, Purpose, Viewpoint*)

1. What viewpoint does Alison Lurie have toward the fashion industry?
2. The writer suggests that blue jeans, sneakers, and baseball caps are "slang words" in the language of clothes. Do you agree? Explain your answer.

3. Lurie says that people who choose their clothes because of comfort, durability, availability, and price are still using clothes as language. What message are they giving?
4. What is the equivalent in clothes to the incessant use of "you know" in speech?

CONSTRUCTIVE READING

Questions on How the Writer Wrote

(*Choices, Strategies, Style*)

1. One of the characteristics of "The Language of Clothes" is the presence of humor. In speaking about a person wearing a fancy Swiss watch, she says, "we know that its owner either bought it at home for three times the price of a good English or American watch, or else he or she spent even more money traveling to Switzerland." Find other sentences in this essay that you find humorous. What does this humor add to the essay?
2. Locate paragraph 8, which begins, "In *Taste and Fashion*, one of the best books ever written on costume . . . ." In the sentence beginning, "According to him . . . ." Alison Lurie uses an unusual sentence construction. Discuss the merits of this construction. Does it impede your reading or assist it? Does the sentence need a period at the end?
3. Lurie does not always attempt to connect the sections of her writing. For instance, when she finishes writing about clothes that are taboo and begins to write about foreign garments (indicated by the headnote "A Head Full of Half-Baked Western Ideas"), she makes no transition. Does she need one? Why or why not?
4. In other sections of the essay, the writer does include a transitional phrase or sentence to connect the next point to the previous point. When she begins the section called "Clothes That Are Taboo," she writes the transitional phrase, "Besides containing 'words' that are taboo, the language of clothes, like speech, also includes . . . ." What would be your explanation for what determines whether or not Lurie uses transitional phrases or sentences?
5. Read the ending of the essay. Does it conclude the entire essay or just the last section? Is this ending sufficient? Satisfying to you as the reader?

INQUIRY READING

Questions on What the Writer Meant

(*Language, Concepts, Distinctions*)

1. What does Alison Lurie mean when she says, "Today such buttons . . . are purely vestigial and have no useful function"?

2. What makes the language known as Basque "almost unique"?
3. What are "archaisms?"
4. What is a Savile Row suit?
5. What does the writer mean when she says, "In practice, of course, the sartorial resources of an individual may be very restricted"?
6. Lurie is attempting in this essay to bring forth a new understanding of the purpose of clothes. What is that understanding? What changes in your own thinking does reading about this new understanding result in?

THE LARGER PICTURE
Questions to Consider

1. What would you say is the predominate way people think about their clothes? What would be added to a person's life if she or he saw clothes the way the writer of this essay sees them?
2. Would it be necessary to be rich in order to deliberately use clothes as language in a full-fledged way?

YOUR OWN WRITING POSSIBILITIES

1. Choose three people you know. Write a short vignette on each person in which you describe the language that person's clothes speak. Consider your classmates and your professor as your audience.
2. Write an argumentative essay in which you defend or criticize Alison Lurie's approach to talking about clothes. Do you agree with her or disagree? Is she overdoing it or is she opening up new possibilities? Choose your classmates and your professor as the audience for your essay.
3. Describe in a journal entry or just for your pleasure your dream wardrobe.
4. Lurie has used *analogy* as the structure for her essay. Choose an analogy familiar to you and write an essay based on this analogy: "Life is like a mountain railroad . . . "; "Life as a journey . . . "; "There's a river that flows through the life of everyone . . . " (the great Roberta Flack song); "The free life is like kite flying . . . "; "Getting along with your parents (or children) is like taking a long hike in the mountains . . . "; etc.

   Choose the general reading public as your audience. Imagine that your essay will appear in the college newspaper.

Traditional Form

Examples

Mankind's Better Moments, page 293

PARTICIPATORY READING

Questions on What the Writer Said

(*Content, Purpose, Viewpoint*)

1. Barbara Tuchman is very clear in letting the readers know her purpose in writing this essay. What is her purpose?
2. Tuchman includes man's ability to play as one of humanity's "better moments." What explanation does she give for why play is so positive?
3. How does the writer accommodate the evil and ugliness of life in her discussion about our better moments?
4. In what way is Tuchman's last example—Izaak Walton—an encouraging example to the individual?

CONSTRUCTIVE READING

Questions on How the Writer Wrote

(*Choices, Strategies, Style*)

1. The use of examples provides the structure of this essay. The examples are not of the same nature: one is about a practical and necessary achievement of the Dutch; one is about an aesthetic, spiritual achievement—the building of cathedrals; one is about adventure and courage and risk in the lives of explorers; one is about man's ability to play; and one is about friendship.

    What does Barbara Tuchman achieve by using such a wide range of examples? What would have been lost, for instance, if she had used three different examples of explorers instead of one of explorers, one of the Zeider Zee, and one of Mardi Gras? When would it be appropriate and wise to use examples all of the same nature—say, all explorer examples?
2. Read the first sentence of each of the writer's examples. What makes these sentences excellent transitions for the reader, enabling the reader to shift to the author's next point?
3. In what way is the writer present in this essay?
4. Locate the paragraphs in this essay that provide the frame for the essay—that introduce it and conclude it. What do these paragraphs of context provide for the examples, which are, of course, the heart of the essay?

5. In talking about the Zeider Zee, Barbara Tuchman says, "Four polders, or areas rising from the shallows, would be lifted." What can you learn from this sentence about the writer's commitment to and consideration for her readers? Find other examples in the essay of this kind of thoughtfulness toward the reader.

INQUIRY READING

Questions on What the Writer Meant

(*Language, Concepts, Distinctions*)

1. What new distinctions about play can the reader learn from Barbara Tuchman's discussion of the Chinese?
    What does the phrase "like 'moving in a cup of jade,'" mean for you? What would enrich that meaning for you? What does Barbara Tuchman think we could learn from the extravaganza of play in 1660?
2. What possibility is more clear to you as a result of reading about Izaak Walton? What makes this example especially encouraging?
3. What are Barbara Tuchman's concepts of good and evil in human beings?
4. The title of this essay is "Mankind's Better Moments." Who is likely to take offense at the wording of this title? How do you think Barbara Tuchman would answer this criticism?
5. The author quotes from a eulogy given for Benjamin Franklin: "He pardoned the present for the sake of the future."
    What does this mean?

THE LARGER PICTURE

Questions to Consider

1. Barbara Tuchman has said, "I think that history *is* storytelling. Details about how people live and so on interest me very much, but I try to insert them without letting the reader know. I like to tell a story that carries the reader."
    Discuss this quote in relation to "Mankind's Better Moments."
2. Tuchman has characterized the current age as follows: "Our epoch . . . insists upon the flaws and corruptions, without belief in valor or virtue—or the possibility of happiness." Do you agree? Why? What is Barbara Tuchman's recommendation to alter this?
3. What can you guess about Tuchman's reading habits from reading this essay?

YOUR OWN WRITING POSSIBILITIES

1. Barbara Tuchman has said, "Our situation today is quite dangerous, since so many people spend so much time creating adversary situations. Everybody seems to be searching for the worse in everybody else . . . I have always believed that good will prevail. . . . It is not a matter of optimism, it's a matter of hope."

   Write an essay in which you discuss your own philosophy about the good and bad in human nature and how it is all going to turn out. Choose an audience for your essay similar to the audience Barbara Tuchman wrote for—educated readers.

2. Write a persuasive essay in which you attempt to convince your readers of the importance of play in their lives. Refer to Tuchman's essay if you so desire. Imagine an audience of readers who play very little, if at all, in their lives.

3. Pretend that you were asked to write an essay on the better moments in your own life. Do a "thinking-on-paper" piece of writing to discover what moments you would describe. What surprises you about the list that emerged? What insights did you gain by exploring this subject with yourself?

4. Write an essay using examples as the structure in which you honor your town's better moments, your country's better moments, your school's better moments, your family's better moments, or the better moments of an individual you know.

   Imagine your classmates and your professor—or an audience similar to Tuchman's—as your readers.

Traditional Form
Comparison/Contrast

Mexico's Two Seas, page 307

PARTICIPATORY READING

Questions on What the Writer Said

(*Content, Purpose, Viewpoint*)

1. What in Carlos Fuentes' background makes his viewpoint about vacation spots in Mexico worth considering?
2. This piece was written for a magazine titled *Sophisticated Traveler.* In light of this fact, what do you suppose was Fuentes' main purpose in writing the essay?

This travel essay also has some political overtones. Where are they? Do you find these political overtones intrusive? Explain your answer.

3. How much is Fuentes' choice of the Veracruz sea rooted in his own family history? How would this essay have been different if it had been written by a travel columnist who had never lived in Mexico?

4. How much of what Fuentes loves about Veracruz could he find *only* in that city?

5. Given the information Fuentes has provided, which sea would most American tourists choose?

CONSTRUCTIVE READING

Questions on How the Writer Wrote

(*Choices, Strategies, Style*)

1. Immediately—within the first three paragraphs of the essay—we are *located* in Fuentes' subject for his essay. With his economy of style, he gets right to the point. How does he locate us, the readers, exactly in the area that he is going to be talking about?

2. Make a list of the points Fuentes makes about Veracruz. How many of these are positive? How many are negative? Can you see any determining reasons for the order in which the points are placed in the essay?

3. Make a list of the points Fuentes makes about Ixtapa-Zihuatanejo. How many are positive? How many are negative? Can you see any determining reasons for the order in which the points are placed in the essay?

4. Fuentes uses no transition when he moves from discussing Veracruz to discussing Ixtapa. Does the essay need a transition at this point?

5. Do you find the essay's ending convincing?

6. In what way was this essay not about two seas? What could you suggest as an alternate title for the essay?

7. Comparison/contrast essays examine both the similarities (comparisons) and differences (contrasts) between subjects. How are Veracruz and Ixtapa-Zihuatanejo similar? How are they different?

INQUIRY READING

Questions on What the Writer Meant

(*Language, Concepts, Distinctions*)

1. Fuentes' grandfather had "Mephistophelean eyebrows." What does this mean?

2. What are Fuentes' political beliefs? How are these concepts related to his choice of vacation spot?

3. Mexico is a long way from the Mediterranean. What does Fuentes mean when he says, "Veracruz is the final beach of the Mediterranean"?

4. Where are Tyre, Sidon, Syracuse, and Cadiz? How important is it to know their location to understand Fuentes' reference when he is talking about Veracruz?

5. What does the phrase "which add their screeches to this Mexican Babel" mean?

6. Fuentes describes the Camino Real Hotel as looking like "an over-baked typewriter"? What do you think he means?

7. Explain the reference, "At one time, this must have looked like the land of the pharaohs."

8. What is a "strobe-lighted Luxor"?

9. Fuentes speaks of understanding "Mexico in the classical image of Janus, facing two ways, backward and forward." How do the two beaches represent the backward and forward of Mexico?

THE LARGER PICTURE

Questions for Consideration

1. Fuentes gives us some important information about the kind of family he grew up in. Summarize this information. In what way is this information related to Fuentes' concept of what makes a good vacation spot?

2. Would it have been possible, given who he is, for Fuentes to like Ixtapa?

3. Do you think Fuentes gave a fair comparison of the two seas?

YOUR OWN WRITING POSSIBILITIES

1. If you have been to either of the two places Fuentes describes, write your own travel essay about the location. Imagine that your audience, like Fuentes', are readers of *Sophisticated Traveler*.

2. Choose two places you have visited on vacation which could vie for being the best place to visit—Los Angeles vs. San Francisco; the city vs. the country; Florida vs. California, the beach vs. the mountains. Write a travel essay in which you compare and contrast these two places, ending with a recommendation of one or the other for your reader. Imagine that your readers will be friends who are planning a vacation and want your advice.

3. Choose two very different types of vacations which you have taken. Perhaps you went on a rafting trip one year and to New York City another year. Write a travel essay about these two vacations, exploring the pleasures and pains of each. Imagine an audience of readers of a travel magazine.

4. How do we choose our vacation spots? What do we expect our vacation spots to do for our lives? Explore this question in a journal entry or in a ''thinking-on-paper'' writing exercise. What insights did you gain from your writing?

Created Form

How to Visit a Museum, page 318

PARTICIPATORY READING

Questions on What the Writer Said

(*Content, Purpose, Viewpoint*)

1. We often associate talk of museums with stuffiness and highbrow intellectual conversation. How would you describe David Finn's viewpoint toward museums and toward talking about them?
2. List three of Finn's instructions that you found the most useful, and why.
3. What does Finn say about detail on art objects?
4. What does he say about time—the amount of time it takes to appreciate an art object?
5. What did Kenneth Clark use as a measurement for how long he could look at a piece of art?

CONSTRUCTIVE READING

Questions on How the Writer Wrote

(*Choices, Strategies, Style*)

1. Discuss the importance of the word *you* in this essay. What does David Finn gain by directly addressing the audience in this way? Does he lose anything?
2. What makes the opening of this essay effective?
3. How does the conclusion of the essay tie into its opening?
4. Identify the order in which Finn presents his recommendations and suggestions for going through a museum. What does he talk about first, second, etc.? Is this a good order in which to put the points? Why? Could the points have been put together in some other order and have worked equally well?
5. Finn makes use of specific examples to illustrate what he means. Find

the first time he uses a specific example. How does this example make his point clearer to you? How does it make the writing more interesting to you?

INQUIRY READING

Questions on What the Writer Meant

(*Language, Concepts, Distinctions*)

1. David Finn makes a distinction between looking and seeing. What is the difference?
2. What is meant by someone "fortifying himself with nips of information"?
3. What concepts about museums and about ourselves must we alter in order to enjoy visiting a museum?

THE LARGER PICTURE

Questions to Consider

1. What keeps many people from going to a museum? Why do many people have no desire to go to a museum?
2. David Finn is a business executive. In what way does this occupation make him a good person to write a book designed to help reluctant visitors enjoy museums more?

YOUR OWN WRITING POSSIBILITIES

1. Write an essay in which you recall a time you went to a museum and did not get very much satisfaction from the experience. Emphasize in your essay how that experience would have been different if you had already read David Finn's essay. What you will be doing in this essay is alternating or layering your own past experience with the information Finn has given. Consider your classmates and professor as the audience for your essay.
2. Write a letter to Finn in which you respond to his recommendations on how to visit a museum.
3. Is there something you like to do that most people don't? Something you have gotten the "key" to over the years and know how to make enjoyable? Write an essay similar to Finn's in which you give your readers insights into how they could make the experience enjoyable for themselves. Consider the general reading public as your audience.
4. Write a journal entry or "thinking-on-paper" exercise in which you record your feelings about museums. What difference has this essay made in how you think about museums? Explore this question also.

No More Blues, *page 326*
PARTICIPATORY READING

Questions on What the Writer Said

(*Content, Purpose, Viewpoint*)

1. How does the writer of this essay relate power and freedom? How is risk related to both power and freedom?
2. What is the writer's viewpoint on the way Black women singers were treated in the past? How is this viewpoint expressed?
3. How would you state Phyl Garland's purpose in writing this essay?
4. What surprising facts did you learn from reading this essay?

CONSTRUCTIVE READING

Questions on How the Writer Wrote

(*Choices, Strategies, Style*)

1. Phyl Garland begins this essay with a specific example. What makes the particular example that she uses an excellent strategy for beginning the essay?
2. How does the writer make a transition from the example with which she opens the essay to the discussion of Black women singers of the past?
3. What technique does Garland use to move from talking about Black women singers of the past to return to talking about Black women singers of the present?
4. How does the specific purpose of this writer determine the form she uses for her essay?
5. The writer concludes the essay with another specific example. What makes the example effective as a conclusion?
6. Garland uses vivid words such as "spatter": "The lore of Black music is spattered with such stories." Find other examples of the use of vivid language in the essay.
7. What makes "No More Blues" an effective title?

INQUIRY READING
Questions on What the Writer Meant

(*Language, Concepts, Distinctions*)

1. What does the writer mean when she says, "This lady is about taking care of business"?
2. Talking about the earlier Black female musician, Phyl Garland says, "she was a creature whose image was shaped by a history of hard times, raw deals, and short change." What does "short change" mean?
3. How is *power* defined in this essay?

THE LARGER PICTURE

Questions to Consider

1. How is the history of early Black women singers a part of the history of Black women in general? Of women in general?
2. What keeps this from being just a comparison/contrast essay? What is the author attempting to do, in addition to comparing earlier times to now?

YOUR OWN WRITING POSSIBILITIES

1. Think of a situation that has greatly changed your life. It may be a divorce in your family, entering college, finding out someone had not been truthful, not getting something you had worked very hard to achieve. Write an essay in which you describe the changes that this event or situation brought in your life. Describe the past—before the event occurred—and describe the present—after the event has oc-curred. Be sure to include in your essay what you have learned from this situation or event. Consider your classmates and your professor as your audience.
2. Do research on some subject such as salaries and working conditions of ball players in the past and today; opportunities for women golfers or tennis players in the past and in the present; work choices for women in the past and in the present; the change in attitude toward country singers in the past and in the present. After you have com-pleted your research, write an essay in which you inform your reader about these differences and make some point about the change. Con-sider your audience the same as Phyl Garland's—the general reading public.
3. Write a tribute to (a) Black women singers of the past, (2) someone you know who did not get what she/he deserved, (3) pioneer women. This tribute might be a poem, song lyrics, or a short piece for your journal.

Our Endangered Night Skies, page 337

PARTICIPATORY READING

Questions on What the Writer Said

(*Content, Purpose, Viewpoint*)

1. What sources of sky pollution were a surprise to you?
2. What is the danger caused by light pollution?
3. What harm has already been done?

4. Does the author suggest directly or implicitly what can be done about the problem?
5. What makes this problem provocative?

CONSTRUCTIVE READING

Questions on How the Writer Wrote

(*Choices, Strategies, Style*)

1. This essay was written by a professor and was published in *Sky and Telescope* magazine. What does Woodruff Sullivan do to make the subject interesting to all readers?
2. How does the author make technical information accessible to the general reader?
3. Make a list of the main points Sullivan makes in this essay. Now rearrange this list, keeping the essay coherent and clear. How many ways can his points be rearranged? What can you say about the way he chose to arrange what he had to say?
4. How does the writer set up the problem he is going to discuss?
5. What is missing from this essay?

INQUIRY READING

Questions on What the Writer Meant

(*Language, Concepts, Distinctions*)

1. The writer says, "When the fleets are out squidding . . . ." Would the sentence have had a different impact if the writer had said, "When the fleets are out fishing . . . ."? Discuss.
2. What is slash-and-burn agriculture?
3. Talking about the places where human activity results in light sources, Sullivan lists "in the African savanna." What is *savanna*?
4. What is the difference between an *optical astronomer* and a *radio astronomer*?
5. The writer says, "With most of its radio emissions clumped into narrow ranges of longitude, the spinning Earth sweeps over the heavens like an interstellar radio lighthouse." What does this mean?

THE LARGER PICTURE

Questions to Consider

1. The author concludes the essay with this sentence: "At a time when our species desperately needs a continual nightly vision, we have instead wrapped the Earth in an electromagnetic fog." Why does our species desperately need a continual nightly vision? And why especially now?
2. Are you alarmed by this problem? Discuss.

YOUR OWN WRITING POSSIBILITIES

1. Write a personal experience essay in which you tell about a time when the night sky was very important in your life—perhaps it was a night when you fell in love; maybe it was a night when you were camped in the woods; perhaps it was a night when you were standing by the ocean. Place this personal experience in the context of the problem Woodruff Sullivan has discussed in "Our Endangered Night Skies." How would your life have been different if you have not been able to see the lights in the sky?

   Writing this essay will allow you to "bring home" the implications and the impact of the problem Professor Sullivan discusses. Imagine the *Sky and Telescope* readers are your audience and that your essay will be printed as a follow-up to Sullivan's.

2. Think about a problem in an area in which you have expertise or "inside knowledge"—perhaps something related to the subject you are majoring in or that you know firsthand from work experience. Write an essay alerting people to this problem. Assume this will be their first exposure to the problem. Consider the general reading public your audience.

3. Write a fantasy or science-fiction scenario about life after the skies are so polluted that you cannot see the stars, the planets, or other heavenly bodies.

HIROSHIMA REMEMBERED: THE U.S. WAS WRONG; THE U.S. WAS RIGHT, *pages 343 and 347*

PARTICIPATORY READING

Questions on What the Writer Said

(*Content, Purpose, Viewpoint*)

1. One writer concentrates on American politics in his argument and the other concentrates on Japanese actions in his. How do their points of view reflect their own previous experiences?
2. What new facts did you learn from each essay?

CONSTRUCTIVE READING

Questions on How the Writer Wrote

(*Choices, Strategies, Style*)

1. Where does Gar Alperovitz's thesis appear in his essay? Where does the thesis in John Connor's essay appear? How is the placement of each thesis appropriate to the author's purpose?

2. Look at the opening of John Connor's essay. How does the type of opening he uses foreshadow the approach he is going to take in his essay?
3. Reread each essay and make separate lists of the points each man makes. Write these points as sentences in your list. What can you see about the writers' strategies by looking at lists of points they made?
4. How did each man's purpose determine the form he chose for his essay?
5. Do you find the conclusion of Alperovitz's essay effective? Discuss.

INQUIRY READING

Questions on What the Writers Meant

(*Language, Concepts, Distinctions*)

1. Gar Alperovitz talks about the "master card" of diplomacy. What does "master card" mean? To what is the term an allusion?
2. John Connor uses language such as "parents bashed their babies' brains out." Why was this choice of vivid language appropriate to the writer's overall purpose in the essay?
3. Discuss the emotional overtones of Connor's essay. How do these overtones serve him in accomplishing his purpose as a writer?
4. What makes emotional overtones irrelevant to Alperovitz's writing?

THE LARGER PICTURE

Questions to Consider

1. Which writer was more convincing? Discuss.
2. How could Gar Alperovitz have made his essay more emotional? Would this have added to its effectiveness?
3. How could John Connor have made his essay less emotional? Would this have added to its effectiveness?
4. What do these essays, written forty years after the fact, reveal about how long it takes to know all the facts about an incident? Do you suppose we know all the facts now about the Hiroshima bombing?

YOUR OWN WRITING POSSIBILITIES

1. Write an argumentative or persuasive essay in which you defend the position taken by one of these writers and criticize the position taken by the other. (Another option would be to defend both or criticize both.) Consider the readers of the *New York Times'* op ed page as your audience.
2. Write a letter to one of these authors, expressing your opinion about what he had to say.

3. Write a letter to the *New York Times*, expressing your appreciation for and/or displeasure at the publishing of these essays.
4. Write a journal entry in which you explore your own feelings about the dropping of the bombs in Japan. Share your writing with a friend or a classmate.

How to Get the Women's Movement Moving Again, *page 353*

PARTICIPATORY READING

Questions on What the Writer Said

(*Content, Purpose, Viewpoint*)

1. Discuss how Betty Friedan's visit to Kenya developed her awareness of the needs of the women's movement.
2. Why would Friedan say that her essay was addressed to "quite a few men," rather than to all men?
3. What is Friedan's viewpoint about the health of the women's movement?
4. What does Friedan think are the *real* issues the women's movement should be facing? What issues is the women's movement centering on, instead, according to Friedan?
5. What specific insights did Friedan get when she was attending the Nairobi conference? What particular observations of hers sparked these insights?
6. Rank Betty Friedan's ten steps for getting the women's movement moving again in the order you think would most quickly produce the greatest results.

CONSTRUCTIVE READING

Questions on How the Writer Wrote

(*Choices, Strategies, Style*)

1. What does Betty Friedan do at the very beginning of the essay to engage the reader?
2. How does Friedan make the transition from the introduction of the essay to the discussion of her trip to Nairobi? What makes this transition work?
3. What larger context does the writer set up to contain the ten points that are at the heart of her essay? How does this context give life to the ten points?
4. What determines the order of Friedan's ten points?

5. How does the writer conclude the essay? What makes this ending effective?
6. This essay is based on personal experience and personal viewpoint, yet it is not a writer-centered essay. Discuss what keeps the essay from being writer-centered.

INQUIRY READING

Questions on What the Writer Meant

(*Language, Concepts, Distinctions*)

1. What is the distinction Betty Friedan makes between "any woman who has ever said 'we' about the women's movement" and the women who have said, "I'm not a feminist, but . . . ." How are these two groups different?
2. To what famous poem does Friedan's line, "I was too passionately involved . . . to acquiesce quietly to its going gently so soon into the night," refer?
3. Friedan refers to "the black-veiled Iranian women, in their chadors and their armed male guards." What is a "chador"?
4. What does the phrase "obscenity of poverty" mean?
5. What does "the feminization of poverty" mean?
6. When Friedan says, "Women may have to think beyond 'women's issues' to join their energies with men to redeem our democratic tradition," what does "women's issues" mean?
7. What is the contrast Friedan makes between the American women's movement and the global women's movement?

THE LARGER PICTURE

Questions to Consider

1. How does Betty Friedan's essay reveal the global nature of the women's movement?
2. Discuss with your classmates whether or not you agree with the assertions Friedan makes.

YOUR OWN WRITING POSSIBILITIES

1. Write an essay in which you agree or disagree with Betty Friedan's position on the women's movement. Consider the general reading public your audience.
2. Write a personal viewpoint essay in which you give your own opinion about the women's movement. Imagine that your audience will be the readers of the editorial page of your local newspaper or the readers of a women's magazine.

3. Make a list of the pluses of the women's movement—what has been positive about its aims and its achievements. Now make a list of the minuses of the women's movement—what negative outcomes have resulted. Put these lists in your journal.
4. Write an essay (or letter) about what women and men in your community could do together that would benefit women. (Option: write about what women and men in your community could do together that would benefit men.) Consider your local newspaper the place of publication for your essay or letter.

I *Still See Him Everywhere,* page 365

PARTICIPATORY READING

Questions on What the Writer Said

(*Content, Purpose, Viewpoint*)

1. What was Richard Morsilli's purpose in giving the speech that is included in this essay?
2. Why did Richard Morsilli and Jo Coudert write the essay?
3. How is the essay more than a speech?
4. What surprising thing did you learn about a fox?

CONSTRUCTIVE READING

Questions on How the Writer Wrote

(*Choices, Strategies, Style*)

1. What is the purpose of the "second voice"—the voice in Richard Morsilli's head—in this essay?
2. What would be missing if this essay had just included the speech made to the teenage students? What is Morsilli able to say by using the "double voice" in his writing that he could not have said in the speech?
3. What determines the order of the points in the speech portion of this essay?
4. What determines the order of the points in the double-voice portion of the essay?
5. How do the authors of this double-voiced essay unify their work and make it cohere?
6. What makes the conclusion of the essay effective?
7. Discuss the appropriateness of the essay's title.

INQUIRY READING

Questions on What the Writer Meant

(*Language, Concepts, Distinctions*)

1. What determines the distinction Richard Morsilli makes between what he can or will tell the students and what he chooses to keep to himself?
2. Straightforward, unembellished language is used throughout the speech and comments. How does this contribute to the power of what is being said?
3. Is this essay argumentative? Is the thesis stated or implied? Does Morsilli need to state his thesis to make us realize the point he is making?

THE LARGER PICTURE

Questions to Consider

1. What role do you suppose Jo Coudert, Richard Morsilli's coauthor, played in writing the essay?
2. This essay appeared in *Reader's Digest* in 1984. According to the magazine, no piece in 1984 was more widely read. What would you say could explain the essay's enormous popularity?

YOUR OWN WRITING POSSIBILITIES

1. Write an essay using "double voice" created form. This essay could be (1) a combination of a letter to someone close to you plus the voice in your head as you write the letter; (2) a combination of a speech you are giving plus the voice in your head; (3) a combination of a story you are telling and your comments about that story. Imagine a suitable audience for your essay.
2. Write a persuasion essay urging tougher penalties for those people caught driving while drunk. Consider the general reading public as your audience.
3. Write a letter to Richard Morsilli in which you respond to the message in his essay.
4. Write an essay about the death of someone you loved. Mail or give this essay to someone else who also knew this person.

A Writer's Notebook from the Far East, page 373

PARTICIPATORY READING

Questions on What the Writer Said

(*Content, Purpose, Viewpoint*)

1. What was the writer's purpose for taking a trip to the Far East?
2. What was the writer's purpose in sharing her notes from this trip with readers?
3. What is Maxine Hong Kingston's viewpoint about the future of stories, dancing, painting, etc., around the world?
4. Of the incidents, conversations, and events on which Maxine Hong Kingston reports, which remain most vivid for you?
5. What was the author's message in this essay?

CONSTRUCTIVE READING

Questions on How the Writer Wrote

(*Choices, Strategies, Style*)

1. Even though the form of this essay is a list of notes made on a trip, there is more to the essay than just notes. How did the author structure the notes to make them become an essay and not just random thoughts taken from her notebook?
2. Where in the essay can you find Maxine Hong Kingston's thesis? Is its placement effective?
3. What did using notes as the form for her essay allow the writer to do? What did the form allow her to avoid doing? What did the form not allow her to do?
4. The first paragraph and the last three paragraphs of the essay are not notes. What is the function of these paragraphs?
5. Kingston has said: "My writing is an ongoing function, like breathing or eating. I started writing as a child. I'd write down anything and [my] books are just part of the things I wrote. I have this habit of writing things down. Anything. And then some of it falls into place, as in these two books."

    Discuss this approach to writing.

INQUIRY READING

Questions on What the Writer Meant

(*Language, Concepts, Distinctions*)

1. Make two columns on your paper. Label one column *Note* and label the other column *Concept*. In the left-hand column put a very brief summary

of what the note says. In the right-hand column write a statement of the concept this note illustrates or refers to or is concerned with.

Example:

Note	Concept
1. The first note is about a man who would not translate the words "free speech" during the author's speech.	The concept this incident illustrates is the absence of free speech or of a commitment to free speech around the world.
2. The second note reports a conversation about people going to jail for speaking up.	The concept this note illuminates is. . . .

2. Maxine Hong Kingston says that "our planet is as rich and complex as a Balinese painting." Find out what a Balinese painting looks like, if you do not already know. What makes this a good analogy—to refer to a Balinese painting in describing the planet Earth?

THE LARGER PICTURE

Questions to Consider

1. What do you know about each of the countries Maxine Hong Kingston visited?
2. What contribution can this essay make to readers?
3. In order to enjoy and benefit from this essay, what does the reader have to be willing to do?
4. Kingston is recognized as a writer about Chinese-American culture and family. Are her nationality or previous subjects reflected in this essay? Discuss.
5. This essay appeared in Ms. magazine. Is it an essay for women only? Explain.

YOUR OWN WRITING POSSIBILITIES

1. Imagine that instead of living where you do that you are visiting there. For two or three days take notes on what you see and hear. Then write an essay using a form like "A Writer's Notebook from the Far East," in which you order your notes, add an introduction and a conclusion— all to make some point you feel important and interesting enough for your readers to enjoy and benefit from. Imagine the general reading public as your audience.
2. In a poem called "To the Not Impossible Him," Edna St. Vincent Millay wrote:

> The fabric of my faithful love
>   No power shall dim or ravel

> Whilst I stay here,—but oh, my dear,
>   If I should ever travel!

Write a response to this poem. What does it make you think of? What dreams does it ignite?

3. We have all heard the old adage that travel broadens us. It is clear in reading Maxine Hong Kingston's essay that travel can teach a person a lot, and show a person much that she did not know firsthand before traveling.

   Write an essay in which you advocate traveling in order to broaden oneself. Use one or more of your own trips as examples in the essay. Imagine your audience to be readers of your hometown newspaper.

4. For two or three days take notes on your life. As Kingston has said about how she writes, write everything down. Anything. Then look back over your notes after you are finished and see what falls into place. Write about this experience in your journal or use it as the basis for writing an essay.

Chatterbox: *Homage to Saint Catherine of Siena*, *page 378*

PARTICIPATORY READING

Questions on What the Writer Said

(*Contents, Purpose, Viewpoint*)

1. What was Catherine Goodhouse's obsession? How did Richard Selzer, the author of this essay and Catherine Goodhouse's doctor, "treat" this problem?
2. Describe the incident in which Catherine Goodhouse got her "healing." How would you explain this incident?
3. What do you know about Selzer's viewpoint on medicine by reading this essay?
4. What do you think was Selzer's purpose in writing this essay?

CONSTRUCTIVE READING

Questions on How the Writer Wrote

(*Choices, Strategies, Style*)

1. The form of this essay is most unusual. There is some discussion by the author, setting up the essay, and then the entire remainder of the essay is a letter supposedly written by one of the author's patients to her brother. Selzer says the letter was in her diary which was sent to her brother after her death and that the brother sent the diary to

Selzer. Even though the letter/diary makes up most of the essay, what makes Richard Selzer and not Catherine Goodhouse the ''author'' of the essay?
2. What is the thesis of this essay? Where does it appear?
3. What is the purpose of the first eight paragraphs of the essay? How does the author connect these paragraphs with what follows?
4. The essay opens with a two-sentence paragraph. What makes this effective?
5. Selzer provides no conclusion of his own to the essay. Does it need one? Why?
6. What makes the title effective? What is the importance of having a subtitle for the essay?

INQUIRY READING

Questions on What the Writer Meant

(*Language, Concepts, Distinctions*)

1. Explain the essay's subtitle: ''Homage to Saint Catherine of Siena.''
2. In her story, Catherine Goodhouse uses the analogy of a bird in a cage from an incident during her school days to explain how she felt when the old man put his hands up to her throat. Explain the relationship between these two events.
3. Catherine Goodhouse uses very poetic language in her letter. For instance, she says, ''He was like a stub of a white candle melted, run over, but with the flame undiminished.''

    Find at least three examples of this poetic language and discuss its effectiveness.
4. A reviewer has said that Richard Selzer's words change medical lessons into timeless maxims. Discuss this assertion in relation to the essay you have just read by Selzer.

THE LARGER PICTURE

Questions to Consider

1. What do you think happened that day in the nursing home when the old man put his hands around Catherine Goodhouse's throat?
2. The jacket for the book from which this essay came reads:
   Letters to a Young Doctor is a visionary, lyric collection of autobiographical reflections, parables, fictions, and case histories which taps a stream of knowledge that has been flowing since the dawn of mankind. Discuss this statement in relation to ''Chatterbox: Homage to Saint Catherine of Siena.''
3. Would it make any difference to you if you discovered that the author had made up the letter he supposedly received from his patient? Would the impact and the message of the essay be altered?

YOUR OWN WRITING POSSIBILITIES

1. Using a letter, diary or journal entry, poem, passages from the Bible, or excerpts from something you have read, write an essay using the form illustrated by "Chatterbox: Homage to Saint Catherine of Siena." Set up the essay by writing an introduction and a context for what you are then going to quote, and let the quoted material be the heart of your essay. You may or may not need to write your own conclusion to the essay.

   In order to be able to write this essay, you will need to "see" something in the piece you are going to quote. It is this thing that you "see" that will be the thesis of your essay.

   Consider the general reading public as your audience.

2. Write an essay about a time when you were helped or healed or taught in a most unusual way. Consider the general reading public as your audience. Or imagine that the essay will appear in a magazine that focuses on well-being and health.

3. Write the letter you think the old gentleman who put his hands on Catherine Goodhouse's throat might have written about the incident. Imagine that the letter was written to one of the gentleman's relatives, perhaps his daughter.

4. Write a journal entry about things that make people well but are not connected to traditional medical treatment.

QUESTIONS AND WRITING POSSIBILITIES

Form as a Characteristic of Good Writing

1. What insights or new awarenesses about form did you get by studying this section of your text?

2. What can you say about the importance of the writer's voice in the essay? How does the author's voice being present bring even traditional forms of writing alive?

3. What is likely to be the outcome when someone approaches a writing assignment this way: "I have to write a comparison/contrast essay"?

4. The approach in question 3 puts the cart before the horse. What should always precede any decision about the *form* your writing is going to take?

5. Which do you find easier to write—pieces in traditional form or pieces in created form? Discuss.

6. Pick out at least two essays in this section to use as illustrations of how the writer's purpose and the form of the writing are interwoven. Discuss the implications of this for your own writing.

7. Review the essays in the Created Form section of this section. Choose one of these forms—which you have never used before—and experiment by writing an essay in this form. This will be an "artificial" exer-

cise in that you are concentrating on the form first, which you never do in authentic writing. But for the purposes of experimenting with form, you can work to find a subject that will fit the form, rather than the other way around. This will allow you to "try out" a form unfamiliar to you.

Be sure you decide who the audience is for your essay before you begin to write.

Let your classmates and professor know how you liked using the form with which you experimented.

READING

To Learn to Write

Gusto, Vividness, and Clarity

The Curse of the Little Round Cans, page 389

PARTICIPATORY READING

Questions on What the Writer Said

(*Content, Purpose, Viewpoint*)

1. What is the author's viewpoint about the attention owners pay to pets?
2. What do you think was Penny Moser's purpose in writing this essay?
3. What is the thesis of this essay? Where is it located in the essay? What makes its location effective?
4. What were four facts you found absolutely astounding in this essay?

CONSTRUCTIVE READING

Questions on How the Writer Wrote

(*Choices, Strategies, Style*)

1. What does the author do to make the opening of this essay effective?
2. Do you believe the author actually became interested in this subject as a result of feeding her own cats? If this did not really happen, how was it an excellent strategy on Moser's part to pretend that it did?

3. What does the author do to make facts and figures interesting to the reader? How do these facts and figures add clarity to the essay? Choose two or three examples from the essay to back up your answer.
4. What technique does Moser use to make the ending of the essay effective?
5. Identify at least three different aspects of the cat food industry that Moser discusses in this essay. Can you see any reason for the particular order in which she discusses these aspects—any reason why she discusses one aspect first, another aspect second, another aspect third? What can you say about the order or structure of the main topics in the essay?
6. Locate five examples of vivid language in this essay. Discuss what this vividness contributes to your enjoyment as a reader.
7. How does the writer's inclusion of information about her own life add to the essay? How does she keep this information from interfering with the central content of the essay? How does the personal information complement the central contents?
8. The writer says, "My little darlings have something called Special Dinners Farm Style [hah!] Dinner for breakfast." Discuss the presence of the "hah!" in that sentence.

INQUIRY READING

Questions on What the Writer Meant

(*Language, Concepts, Distinctions*)

1. What does "mouth feel" refer to?
2. What is the "plop factor"?
3. The writer says, "Both my cats . . . struck their preprandial frenzy pose." What does this mean?
4. What do the words "feline palatability" mean?
5. When the writer says that "in the manufacture of digest, meat is enzymatically broken down," what does she mean?

THE LARGER PICTURE

Questions to Consider

1. Here are some 1986 facts about cats in America, taken from the *New York Times*:

   From 1972 to 1983, the number of cats in households increased by 104 percent—from 25.5 million to 52.1 million.

   Two-thirds of all pets are eventually abandoned.

   New York City annually loses more than $1 million caring for unwanted pets in the city.

More than ten million pets are being killed each year by city pounds and humane societies.

The American pet food industry brings in $5 billion each year.

A tax on pet foods and supplies would provide a much more equitable source of funding for animal shelters and spay and neuter clinics.

In light of these facts, what would you say about (a) having pets, (b) the pet food industry, (c) solutions to the problem?

2. This essay first appeared in *Discover* magazine. The editor of this magazine said, "Our conviction was that every branch of science, no matter how complex, could be made intelligible and interesting to the public."

First of all, what is the justification for this essay on cat food to appear in a science magazine written for educated lay persons?

How does Penny Ward Moser make a complex subject intelligible and interesting to the public?

YOUR OWN WRITING POSSIBILITIES

1. Reread the facts in question 1 under The Larger Picture. Write an essay in which you defend the keeping of pets and suggest what might be done about the related pet problem. Imagine that your essay will be printed in a magazine read by the general public.
2. One critic has said that the $5 billion dollar a year American pet food industry, for obvious reasons, encourages pet breeding and pet marketing.

   Write an essay in which you (a) take to task, or (b) defend the pet food industry.

   Consider the general reading public your audience.
3. Write about your own experiences in owning a pet or knowing someone who owned a pet. This might be a humorous, entertaining essay, or it might be an essay concentrating on emotional attachments and benefits of having pets. Consider the general reading public your audience.
4. Do a "thinking-on-paper" exercise in which you first argue in favor of having pets and then argue against having them. Conclude this exercise by writing about the insights you gained during the writing. Share this writing with a friend or classmate. You can also use it as a way to think about your subject before you begin writing an essay.

Adult Education, page 398

PARTICIPATORY READING

Questions on What the Writer Said

(*Content, Purpose, Viewpoint*)

1. How would you summarize this essay in one sentence?
2. Without looking back at the essay or the commentary, make a list of words you remember from the essay. What can you say about this list of words?
3. If the writer of this essay, Milton Kaplan, were an actor in a television drama, what would he look like? Who would you suggest play him? What would his character on the show be like?
4. What is the "question" around which the essay is centered?

CONSTRUCTIVE READING

Questions on How the Writer Wrote

(*Choices, Strategies, Style*)

1. This is a very personal story, yet it is interesting to and benefits the reader. What has the writer done that makes this the case?
2. What gives this essay drama?
3. Choose the four or five vivid images that most appeal to you. Why are these appealing?
4. Discuss the appropriateness of the title of the essay.

INQUIRY READING

Questions on What the Writer Meant

(*Language, Concepts, Distinctions*)

1. Milton Kaplan uses the phrase, "the blob of humanity." What does this mean? How does it counter the normal sentimental reaction to babies?
2. When the writer's grandson was born, he wasn't a "person" to Kaplan. What is the distinction between what the baby was and what he became? What brought about this change?

THE LARGER PICTURE

Questions to Consider

1. Is there anything surprising to you about a *man* writing this essay? Would it have been more "natural" to have had a woman writing about her grandson in this way? Discuss.
2. Kaplan talks about "seeing the world once again through a baby's eyes." How does a baby see the world differently than we do?

YOUR OWN WRITING POSSIBILITIES

1. Write an essay about the birth and growth of a child in your life—your own child, a brother or sister, a relative, or a friend. What did you learn? What did you realize that you had not realized before? Use vivid, specific examples in telling your story. Imagine that your audience are the readers of a column in a magazine such as the column in the *New York Times Magazine* in which Milton Kaplan's essay appeared.
2. Write a letter to a child in your life. Use the letter as an opportunity to let the child know her or his importance in your life. If the child can read, give him or her the letter. If not, read the letter to the child.
3. Write an essay about your own childhood. What were the joys of discovery for you? What did you lose when you were no longer a child? Use vivid language so that your story is alive for the reader. Consider the general reading public your audience for this essay.
4. Go on your own "journey of exploration" to a familiar place (a mall, a park, your home, school or church) and try to see it again as if you were seeing it for the first time. *Really* notice specific things that have become very familiar to you over time. Write about your experience using vivid and clear images. Imagine your classmates as your audience, or write about your experience in a journal entry.

Miss Pilger's English Class, page 403

PARTICIPATORY READING

Questions on What the Writer Said

(*Content, Purpose, Viewpoint*)

1. What keeps this essay from becoming too sentimental? How would you describe the writer's viewpoint on classes in English for foreign speakers?
2. What was Maureen Dowd's purpose in writing this essay?
3. What was the most surprising thing you learned from reading the essay?

CONSTRUCTIVE READING

Questions on How the Writer Wrote

(*Choices, Strategies, Style*)

1. What makes this essay work for you?
2. This essay reads almost like a short story. What elements of "story writing" are present that give the essay life?
3. What makes the opening and the closing of the essay effective?
4. Choose a section from the essay to illustrate how Maureen Dowd weaves facts and statistics into her story about Miss Pilger's class.

5. What does the title do for this piece of writing?
6. What gives this essay gusto, vividness, and clarity?

INQUIRY READING

Questions on What the Writer Meant

(*Language, Concepts, Distinctions*)

1. This essay is about the power of language to open up possibilities in life. Discuss the interrelation of being able to speak and write a language with being able to accomplish one's goals.
2. What is Miss Pilger's concept of how to educate and teach people?

THE LARGER PICTURE

Questions to Consider

1. The Department of Education estimates that 13 percent of adults in America cannot read English. There is a 9 percent illiteracy rate for adults whose native language is English and a 48 percent illiteracy rate for adults whose native language is not English.

   In light of these statistics, what can you say about the need for classes that teach English to people who can't speak, read, and write the language.
2. Discuss the value of humor in an essay on a subject of this sort.
3. Teaching English to foreign speakers is a controversial subject— especially teaching children to be bilingual. Do you see any difference in teaching children English and providing classes for adults who cannot speak English? What areas of controversy do you see in both situations?

YOUR OWN WRITING POSSIBILITIES

1. Write an essay in which you argue for (or against) the offering of classes in English for foreign speakers at public expense. Consider some specific newspaper's op ed page as the imagined place of publication for your essay.
2. Write a letter to Miss Pilger as if you were one of her adult students. Share this letter with a friend or classmate.
3. Write an essay on the subject of what makes a good teacher, using Miss Pilger as one of your models. Add other good teachers from your own experience. Assume your audience will be readers of a magazine for teachers or student teachers.
4. Write a journal entry about the emotions that were elicited as you read "Miss Pilger's English Class." Did you feel sadness? Apathy? Sympathy? Empathy? Joy? Happiness? Anger? Share your journal entry with a friend or classmate.

Talking Cost, page 415

PARTICIPATORY READING

Questions on What the Writer Said

(*Content, Purpose, Viewpoint*)

1. The content of this essay focuses on a way to make a subject that is usually not very popular clear and enticing. What explains the speaker's ability in the essay to achieve this clarity and interest?
2. Tom Richman is the writer of this essay. Bob Popaditch is the speaker in the essay. How is Richman's purpose in writing the essay different from Popaditch's purpose in speaking to his employees?
3. What is the thesis of this essay? How is it related to the writer's purpose?
4. Are there any holes that you can find in Popaditch's breakdown of what it will take to increase sales?

CONSTRUCTIVE READING

Questions on How the Writer Wrote

(*Choices, Strategies, Style*)

1. What keeps this essay from being a report? What is the difference between an essay and a report?
2. What does Richman achieve with his introduction to the essay?
3. How did an example from Richman's youth clarify the ending he chose to give the essay?
4. Which do you think more important to the impact of this essay—the opening or the closing?
5. How does Richman insert himself into the retelling of Popaditch's conversation with his employees? Why is it important that the author's presence be felt now and then during this discussion?

INQUIRY READING

Questions on What the Writer Meant

(*Language, Concepts, Distinctions*)

1. Summarize in one sentence the principle Bob Popaditch follows to make complex, uncomfortable information engaging and clear.
2. What is Tom Richman's point about language at the end of the essay? How does it relate to Popaditch's principle?

YOUR OWN WRITING POSSIBILITIES

1. Take a subject many people would find confusing, and write an essay in which you use the Popaditch approach to make the subject clear. (Possible subjects: the principle behind daylight saving time; the rules in professional football; taking out a mortgage or a car loan; how a bill becomes a law; how a video cassette recorder works; how spending money can save money; how satellites work; etc.)

   Write this essay as a speech to a particular group of people or as an essay to be published in an appropriate periodical.

2. Imagine that you have been invited to a fifth grade class to explain some process about which you know—how photosynthesis works, what makes a motor go, how to weave, how to knead bread, how to make pie crust, how to fly-fish, how to play soccer, etc.

   Write the speech you will give to these fifth graders making this process clear to them.

3. Write a journal entry that one of Bob Popaditch's employees might have written when she or he got home that night after hearing the talk about cutting costs. Share this journal entry with a friend or a classmate.

Avalanche! page 421

PARTICIPATORY READING

Questions on What the Writer Said

(*Content, Purpose, Viewpoint*)

1. What specifically did you learn from this essay?
2. What startled you in this essay?
3. What percentage of this essay would you estimate to be facts and statistics and what percentage to be story/narrative?

CONSTRUCTIVE READING

Questions on How the Writer Wrote

(*Choices, Strategies, Style*)

1. Jonathan Beard combines interviews, researched information, and narrative in this essay. Find sections of the essay that illustrate how he blended these writing strategies to produce a unified essay.
2. What makes the opening of the essay effective?
3. How did Beard make the conclusion of the essay vivid for his readers?

4. What does the writer gain by embedding the factual information about avalanches in stories and interviews?
5. Why do you suppose the author put an exclamation mark after the title of the essay?

INQUIRY READING

Questions on What the Writer Meant

(*Language, Concepts, Distinctions*)

1. What does "return period" mean?
2. What are the differences among soft slab, hard slab, and wet slab?
3. What is "temperature gradient metamorphism"?
4. What is "ski checking"?
5. What is "avalanche zoning"?
6. How is "swimming" related to being caught in an avalanche?

THE LARGER PICTURE

Questions to Consider

1. What contributes to this essay having gusto, vividness, and clarity?
2. In addition to avalanches, consider some of nature's other shows of power—tornadoes, hurricanes, volcanoes, earthquakes. What can you say about human beings' ability to cope, handle, or manage these natural phenomena?

YOUR OWN WRITING POSSIBILITIES

1. Choose a subject which you would truly *enjoy* finding out about. Go to the library and do some quick research on this subject. Then write an essay, using "Avalanche!" as your model, that informs your reader about the subject and interests your reader. Design a specific audience before you begin writing.
2. If you have ever been involved in an avalanche, tornado, hurricane, or other natural phenomenon, write an essay about this event. Consider your classmates and professor the audience for your essay.
3. Write a journal entry in which you explore the implications of what you have read in this essay on your own wintertime activities. Share this journal entry with a friend or a classmate.
4. Interview someone who is an expert in something you know little about. Write up this interview as a magazine article.
5. Write a narrative essay that someone who had been in an avalanche might write. Share this essay with your classmates and professor.

Dressed to Kill, page 430

PARTICIPATORY READING

Questions on What the Writer Said

(*Content, Purpose, Viewpoint*)

1. Make a list of the six most surprising facts you learned from reading this essay. Discuss this list with your classmates.
2. Can you detect a "position" on the subject of football from the author? Is he pro? Con? Somewhere in between? Explain your answer.
3. This essay was written to give information, not to stir an emotional response in the reader. Yet most readers have an emotional response to the essay. What was your emotional response? What produces that response, since it is not actual content in the essay but, instead, what we as readers *think* about the content we read in the essay?

CONSTRUCTIVE READING

Questions on How the Writer Wrote

(*Choices, Strategies, Style*)

1. This essay contains many of the same elements that newspaper articles contain. What are some of the elements? What makes this an essay, however, not just a newspaper article?
2. Where is the writer's thesis in the essay?
3. "Dressed to kill" normally means something very different from its use in this essay. How is the use of this familiar phrase an effective title for this essay?
4. Discuss the effectiveness of the ending of the essay.

INQUIRY READING

Questions on What the Writer Meant

(*Language, Concepts, Distinctions*)

1. How do the analogy of a bullfighter and the metaphor of armor fit in this essay?
2. What are Canadian broomball shoes?
3. How does the writer use "panty" as a spot of humor in the essay?
4. What does the writer mean by this phrase, "The football armor *piece de resistance* is the helmet"?

THE LARGER PICTURE

Questions to Consider

1. What made this essay appropriate for publication in *Popular Mechanics*?
2. How does Dennis Eskow achieve gusto, vividness, and clarity in this essay?

3. What questions does this essay leave you with? Discuss them with your classmates.

YOUR OWN WRITING POSSIBILITIES

1. Write an essay about the equipment used in a sport other than football. (Examples: dancing, polo, swimming in competition, ice hockey, lacrosse, baseball, basketball.) Explain what this equipment is, how it is used/worn, why it is necessary, etc. Write this essay for an audience interested in the sport but unknowledgeable about the equipment and paraphernalia needed when playing the game or performing the sport.
2. Write an imaginary conversation a professional football player carries on with himself as he is getting dressed. Share this conversation with a friend or a classmate.
3. Write a letter a professional football player's mother might write to him after reading this essay.
4. Write an essay defending or criticizing the sport of football. If your essay is one of defense, be sure that you account for the danger in the game. If your essay is one of criticism, be sure your essay accounts for the fun of the game for players and spectators alike. Choose an appropriate audience for the essay before you begin.

Stepping out from Behind the Phone and Word Processor, page 438

PARTICIPATORY READING

Questions on What the Writer Said

(*Content, Purpose, Viewpoint*)

1. What would you say are the two or three strongest points the writer makes in this letter?
2. What is the writer's viewpoint about the likelihood of a change in the situation?
3. What is the writer's purpose?

CONSTRUCTIVE READING

Questions on How the Writer Wrote

(*Choices, Strategies, Style*)

1. Why is a letter a most appropriate form for this piece of writing?
2. Why was the use of Jack, the assistant, excellent strategy on the writer's part?
3. What makes the opening of the letter effective?
4. How would you describe the tone of this letter? How is this displayed in the writing?
5. Is the letter appropriately titled? Who most likely gave the piece its title?

INQUIRY READING

Questions on What the Writer Said
(*Language, Concepts, Distinctions*)

1. Discuss the writer's use of the metaphor of needle and thread.
2. What words carry the writer's energy and anger right into the writing?
3. Choose at least three examples of vivid imagery in this letter and discuss their effectiveness in the piece of writing.

THE LARGER PICTURE

1. In what way does this letter reflect a problem in our society? What is the solution to this problem?
2. This piece appeared in a regular column in the *Wall Street Journal* called "Manager's Journal." Discuss the appropriateness of the letter for this column.

YOUR OWN WRITING POSSIBILITIES

1. Write the letter Secretary X's boss might have returned to her.
2. Write a letter for the "Letters to the Editor" column of the *Wall Street Journal* in which you respond to Secretary X's letter.
3. Write an argumentative or persuasive essay in which you provide a solution to Secretary X's problem or in which you take issue with Secretary X's viewpoint. Assume your audience is the general reading public.
4. If you have seen the movie *Nine to Five*, write about the viewpoint of that movie related to this letter. Consider the general reading public to be your audience.

Space Law: Justice for the New Frontier, page 442

PARTICIPATORY READING

Questions on What the Writer Said
(*Content, Purpose, Viewpoint*)

1. What did you learn from reading this essay?
2. What way of thinking about the world did you gain by reading this essay?
3. The writer of this essay is not merely giving information that he finds interesting. He has a particular purpose, intention, and aim in writing this essay. What is it?
4. Was any of the content of this essay confusing? Discuss with your classmates.

CONSTRUCTIVE READING

Questions on How the Writer Wrote

(*Choices, Strategies, Style*)

1. What does the writer do to lead us into his subject? What makes this writing strategy work?
2. Choose a section of the essay to illustrate how the writer made complicated information clearly understood. What did he do as a writer to accomplish this clarity?
3. What does the title of this essay "tell" you?
4. Do you find the ending of the essay effective? Discuss.

INQUIRY READING

Questions on What the Writer Meant

(*Language, Concepts, Distinctions*)

1. Discuss the distinction between "space law" and "earth law." What makes it different? Complex in special ways? Hard to legislate? Critical to the future?
2. What is the "CHM principle"?
3. What does the writer mean by a "world fairness revolution"?
4. What is the most important principle of space law?
5. What are the meanings of "have's" and "have-not's"?

THE LARGER PICTURE

Questions to Consider

1. What do you think is the likelihood for cooperation worldwide on space law?
2. What optimism is warranted by the past laws that have been worked out and agreed upon? What is there to make us pessimistic about the possibility of worldwide cooperation on space law?
3. What makes space law an increasingly important subject?

YOUR OWN WRITING POSSIBILITIES

1. Write an essay in which you discuss the likelihood of new, necessary space law being established and being effective. Use specific references or concrete examples to back up your point of view. Write this essay for a general reading audience.
2. Write a scenario which could occur at the United Nations upon the advent of a catastrophe in space. Share this scenario with a classmate or friend.

3. Write an essay in which you discuss the impact of the information in this essay on your own thinking. Consider your classmates and professor as your audience.

4. In light of the Chernobyl nuclear accident and the Challenger accident, what can you say about the efficacy of law to prevent disasters? Do a "thinking-on-paper" writing exercise on this subject. Use this "thinking-on-paper" as a basis for class discussion or for an essay you will write. If you choose to write an essay on the subject, imagine that it will be printed as a response essay in the same magazine that "Space Law: Justice for the New Frontier" was printed (*Sky and Telescope*).

QUESTIONS AND WRITING POSSIBILITIES

Gusto, Vividness, and Clarity as a Characteristic of Good Writing

1. Discuss how each of the essays in this section demonstrate *gusto, vividness, and clarity.*

2. What would you say is the secret to having *gusto, vividness, and clarity* in your own writing?

3. Which essay's subject would you think to be the most difficult to write about with *gusto, vividness, and clarity*? How do you account for the writer's being able to achieve these qualities with this unlikely subject?

4. In the introduction to this section, it was suggested that there is no such thing as a boring subject—only subjects about which the writer has not yet discovered the excitement and interest the subject contains. Which of the essays in this section best illustrates the truth of this assertion?

5. What connection can you see between the presence of the author's strong and personal voice in the essay and a sense of *gusto, vividness, and clarity* in the writing?

6. Choose a subject about which you think most people would never expect anything written with *gusto*. Write an essay on this subject in which you surprise the reader by having the piece of writing show your "hearty and keen enjoyment and liking for" the subject. (This, of course, is the secret of writing with *gusto*.)

READING

*to See the Whole
Picture*

QUESTIONS

1. What would make it very unlikely that the author of a particular piece in this section would have written any other piece in this section?
2. Which essays could you imagine being written by another author represented in the section? Identify the essays and the other authors you could imagine writing them. Explain your answers.
3. Which of the pieces in this section do you think were written specifically for the audience who eventually read them?

    Which could have been written for the general reading public and then found their home in some magazine to which the piece was submitted after it was written?

    Which pieces do you think were written as they were first and foremost because the author wanted to express a particular viewpoint, *not* because the essays were being aimed at a particular audience? This would mean that the viewpoint/occupation/purpose of the writer dic-

623

tated the kind of piece she or he would write; and then an appropriate audience/place of publication would have to be found to fit the piece after it was written.

4. After studying this group of essays and articles, what can you say about what it takes to "see" or "know" a particular subject in one of its multi-aspects?

5. What can you say after reading the pieces about the purpose of Reading to See the Whole Picture?

6. John Poppy, formerly Senior Editor at *Look* magazine and Managing Editor at *Saturday Review*, has said:

> There's one view of the universe at a time embodied in each of us and that's the precious commodity that the writer has. So, the writer's task is to somehow get yourself into a state in which you can listen clearly to yourself, informed by all the other people you listen to and read and whatnot. But they're not who's speaking. You're who's speaking.

Apply this quotation to the essays and articles in this section of your text.

YOUR OWN WRITING POSSIBILITIES

Choose a subject that you already know something about or are interested enough in to do some quick research in the library.

Write an essay on this subject from the viewpoint most interesting to you, most "like" you, showing how you as an individual look at this subject.

Then write a second essay on this same subject deliberately attempting to alter your viewpoint. Write as a scientist (if you're not a scientist) or a humorist or a medical writer or an economist—someone you are *not*. Notice how the appropriate audience often comes in tandem with the approach you are going to take to the subject. If an audience doesn't "come along" with the approach you are taking, decide who your audience will be before you begin to write.

Discuss with your classmates the experience of shifting to write as another person would write. What did you have to do to be able to accomplish this shift? What did you learn about your subject by making this shift?

THE WAY A WRITER READS

Essays for Further Study

QUESTIONS

1. The writer in each of these essays is *present* as an individual in the essay; yet each essay is about something much more than just the *writer*. How would you summarize what each of the essays is "about" beyond the personal experience or position of the writer? Discuss with your classmates the paradox of a writer's ability to be present in an essay yet have the essay be about something other than himself or herself.

2. The subjects of these essays range from boats and books to dolls, wolves, art, lions, the land, and Ping Pong. Sometimes new writers think there have to be "fit" subjects about which to write, subjects worthy of being written about—serious enough, deep enough, important enough. What can you say after reading these essays about what it takes to make any subject appropriate as the subject of an essay?

3. Think about these essays in light of what you learned from studying Part 4, Reading to See the Whole Picture, in your text. How does each writer's *perspective on* the world determine what he or she writes?
4. What would you say about the audiences the writers wrote for in these essays?

YOUR OWN WRITING POSSIBILITIES

1. E. B. White once wrote a correspondent:

   As long as there is one upright man, as long as there is one compassionate woman, the contagion may spread and the scene is not desolate. Hope is the thing that is left to us, in a bad time. I shall get up Sunday morning and wind the clock, as a contribution to order and steadfastness.

   Write an essay in which you reflect on this quotation and the essay you have just read by E. B. White.
2. Jorge Luis Borges once said:

   If I were asked to name the chief event in my life, I should say my father's library.

   Write an essay about the importance of books in your own life. (Or unimportance, if that is the case.)
3. Beryl Markham said about the book from which "He Was a Good Lion" comes:

   I just wanted to bring back a good life in a good country so I could look at them both again.

   Write an essay in which you attempt to do the same: write about a good time in your life in a good place so that you can experience this time once again.
4. Georgia O'Keeffe wrote once:

   I have picked flowers where I found them—have picked up sea shells and rocks and pieces of wood . . . When I found the beautiful white bones on the desert I picked them up and took them home too. I have used these things to say what is to me the wildness and wonder of the world as I live in it.

   Write an essay in which you use things you have noticed, picked up, loved, that represent the wonder of the world as you live in it.
5. Barry Lopez says about the wolf that perhaps we should think of it neither as a rapacious animal nor as a wholly benevolent creature but as a mammal, which, like a home-loving human, enjoys family life but is also subject to frailties, crotchets, hunger pangs, and illnesses that sometimes cause him to act strangely and destructively.

   Write an essay in which you explore this view of animals, using your own experience with an animal to substantiate the thesis of your essay.

ACKNOWLEDGMENTS

PART TWO

READING TO LEARN TO WRITE

Originality

Thesis

Form: Traditional

Penguin, Inc and The Liz Darhansoff Literary Agency.

"The Thucydides Syndrome" by Langmuir et al. from *The New England Journal of Medicine* October 17, 1985. Reprinted by permission of The New England Journal of Medicine and the author.

"Clothing as a Sign System" from *The Language of Clothes* by Alison Lurie. Copyright © 1981 by Alison Lurie. Reprinted by permission of Random House, Inc. and William Heinemann Limited.

From "Mankind's Better Moments" by Barbara Tuchman from *American Scholar*, Autumn 1980. Copyright © 1980 by Alma Tuchman, Lucy T. Eisenberg and Jessica Tuchman Matthews. Reprinted by permission of Russell & Volkening, Inc. as agents for the author.

"Mexico's Two Seas" by Carlos Fuentes, first published in *New York Times Magazine*. Copyright © 1984 by Carlos Fuentes. Reprinted by permission of Brandt & Brandt Literary Agents, Inc.

Form: Created

From "How to Visit a Museum," reprinted from the book *How to Visit a Museum* by David Finn, published by Harry N. Abrams, Inc., 1985. All rights reserved.

"No More Blues" by Phyl Garland from *Essence*, May 1985. Reprinted by permission of the author.

"Our Endangered Night Skies" by Woodruff T. Sullivan III from *Sky & Telescope*, May 1984. Reprinted by permission.

"The U.S. Was Wrong" by Gar Alperovitz, "The U.S. Was Right" by John Connor, *New York Times*, August 4, 1985. Copyright © 1985 by The New York Times Company. Reprinted by permission.

Excerpts from "How to Get the Women's Movement Moving Again" by Betty Friedan from *The Second Stage*. Copyright © 1981 by Betty Friedan. Reprinted by permission of Summit Books, a division of Simon & Schuster, Inc. and Sphere Books Ltd.

"I Still See Him Everywhere" by Richard Morsilli, with Jo Coudert, *Reader's Digest*, July 1984. Reprinted by permission of Jo Coudert.

"A Writer's Notebook from the Far East" by Maxine Hong Kingston. Copyright © 1983 by Maxine Hong Kingston. Reprinted by permission of John Schaffner Associates.

"Chatterbox" from *Letters to a Young Doctor* by Richard Selzer. Copyright © 1982 by David Goldman and Janet Selzer, Trustees. Reprinted by permission of Simon & Schuster, Inc.

Gusto, Vividness, and Clarity

"The Curse of the Little Round Cans" by Penny Ward Moser from *Discover*, September 1985. Copyright © 1985 by Time, Inc. Reprinted by permission.

"Adult Education" by Milton Kaplan, *New York Times Magazine*, December 29, 1985. Copyright © 1985 by The New York Times Company. Reprinted by permission.

"Miss Pilger's English Class," by Maureen Dowd from *The New York Times*, November 3, 1985. Copyright © 1985 by The New York Times Company. Reprinted by permission.

"Avalanche!" by Jonathan Beard from *Science Digest*, March 1984. Reprinted by permission of the author.

"Dressed to Kill" by Dennis Eskow. Reprinted from *Popular Mechanics*, October 1983. © Copyright The Hearst Corporation. All Rights Reserved.

"Stepping Out From Behind the Phone and Word Processor" by Jane E. Tiffany from *The Wall Street Journal* April 21, 1986. Reprinted by permission.

"Space Law: Justice for the New Frontier" by Carl Q. Christol from *Sky & Telescope*, November 1984. Reprinted by permission.

PART THREE

READING TO SEE THE WHOLE PICTURE

"All About Chocolate" by Patricia Connell from *Bon Appetit*, February 1985. Copyright © 1985 by Bon Appetit Publishing Corp.

"The Temptation of Chocolate" by Dick Robinson. Reprinted from *Health*, February 1984 by special permission. Copyright © 1984 by Family Media, Inc. All rights reserved.

PART FOUR

THE WAY A WRITER READS: ESSAYS FOR FURTHER STUDY

PART FIVE

STUDY SECTION